CONTEMPORARY ECONOMIC THINKING

SELECTED READINGS

Gordon F. Boreham

HOLT, RINEHART AND WINSTON OF CANADA, LIMITED
TORONTO   MONTREAL

Printed in Canada

1 2 3 4 5   75 74 73 72 71

To my family, Marilyn, Mark, Susan, and Lisa and all my students, past, present, and those to come.

PREFACE

This book is a collection of readings on contemporary economic issues and policies. Its purpose is to provide fundamental insights into the operation of our economic system by presenting, in readily accessible form, authoritative statements of prominent and eminent persons, past and present, economist and noneconomist, Canadian and non-Canadian, as well as raising the appropriate questions concerning our milieu and its social institutions. By reading about the development of economic analysis, about the happenings of current importance, as well as some of the visions of a good society, the beginning student can, if he wishes, go beyond the necessarily limited world of the introductory textbook and gain a glimpse of the wider perspective of the scope and setting of economics and the place which it occupies in the intellectual community.

This book is designed to supplement *Economic Thinking in a Canadian Context* which I wrote in collaboration with Richard H. Leftwich of Oklahoma State University. The order of presentation, is, therefore, closely integrated with the chapter outline of the basic text. Given the broad spectrum of readings, however, this book could just as easily be used with any one of the standard "principles of economics" texts on the market. Given the communicability of the selections, moreover, it could be profitably read by the interested layman who has not benefited from formal course work in economics.

The book is divided into five parts. Each part is in turn divided into sections averaging about three readings apiece. Each part has its own introduction; so do the sections. Most important, each reading is long enough to convey the "substance and feel" of the position being stated by the writer, and is preceded by a brief editorial comment that pinpoints the basic theme or conclusions. In addition, a biographical sketch of each writer is included to give the student an idea of the writer's professional qualifications. While I have made no effort to include readings on all of the issues raised within a standard text, I believe that I have touched upon most of the salient matters that do arise in any elementary course in economics.

There are a number of major respects in which my choice of readings differs from that of other comparable readers. The scope is cosmopolitan. Articles are not restricted to any one country or its inhabitants. In addition, many selections may properly be classed as "interdisciplinary" for they range into those aspects of economics which also fall within the sphere of government and politics, sociology, business management, history, philosophy, ecology, and so forth. Moreover, a general spirit of social criticism characterizes many of the selections in this book. In many cases opposite positions on the outstanding public policy issues of today are presented in consecutive readings. In order to illuminate and clarify the theoretical material, I have included a few case studies.

This book also includes readings of a kind that are not often brought to the attention of a person commencing the study of economics. These readings relate to the following subjects: the teaching of economics; economic writing and research; Canadian contributions to the discipline of economics; the main sources of disagreement among economists; the relevance of economics to the central issues of our time. These readings are intended to help students feel economics, like economics, and live economics.

I wish to express my appreciation to the authors and publishers who have generously permitted the reprinting of their works in this volume. Specific acknowledgement is given with each selection. Out of consideration for the limitations of space and the avoidance of repetition, I have edited and abridged some selections; tables and diagrams have been renumbered; footnotes that were not essential to an understanding of the piece have been omitted, and others have been renumbered. In all instances, however, I have been careful to avoid distortion in order to preserve the character and original meaning of each selection.

University of Ottawa   Gordon F. Boreham
May, 1971

Gordon F. Boreham is Professor of Economics at the University of Ottawa. He obtained BCom and MA degrees from the University of Ottawa and a PhD degree from Columbia University in the City of New York. In addition to contributing many articles to scholarly journals, Professor Boreham has co-authored two previous books: *Money and Banking: Analysis and Policy in a Canadian Context* and *Economic Thinking in a Canadian Context*. He has been awarded research fellowships by the Canada Council and the Italian Ministry of Foreign Affairs, and has travelled and lectured widely throughout the world.

In addition to his teaching duties, Professor Boreham serves as a consultant to several corporations. He was a member of the research staff of the Royal Commission on Taxation in 1963 and the Royal Commission on Health Services in 1964.

CONTENTS

I. FOUNDATIONS OF ECONOMIC SCIENCE

It is increasingly being recognized that ideas are ultimately more powerful than physical force. Indeed, as the late John Maynard Keynes, the greatest economist of our age, has observed:

> The ideas of economists, both when they are right and when they are wrong, are more powerful than is commonly understood. Indeed, the world is ruled by little else. Practical men, who believe themselves to be quite exempt from any intellectual influences, are usually the slaves of some defunct economist. Madmen in authority, who hear voices in the air, are distilling their frenzy from some academic scribbler of a few years back . . . . Soon or late, it is ideas, not vested interests, which are dangerous for good or evil.

At any rate, relatively few Canadians have been exposed to any kind of formal learning about economic issues. As a result, if ignorance paid dividends, most people could make themselves millionaires several times over through their economic illiteracy. One hundred years ago such incomprehension might have been excusable. Today it is intolerable. The world of economics is all about us, affecting much that we do, and think, and are. Thus, from a purely selfish point of view, it pays people to understand how their economy works. Moreover, the affairs of government, in large and increasing measure, are economic in substance or in effect. Hence, in a democracy, it is extremely desirable that economic knowledge should be widely diffused. In truth, the case for economics is made of the same stuff as the case for human freedom itself. Unfortunately, however, not everyone realizes this.

The purpose of Part One, then, is to introduce the student to economics and to provide him with a background for further study. The four sections which it contains deal with the substance and methodology of economics, the distinction between economic analysis and economic policy making, trends in economic teaching and writing, and the development of economics as a discipline in Canada.

A. THE NATURE AND METHOD OF ECONOMICS

In a general way, we all know what economics is about. It is concerned with the production, exchange, and consumption of goods and services. Yet when we attempt to provide a working definition of economics we find that it covers such a wide field of human activities that no short definition can be entirely adequate.

Adam Smith, the founder of modern economics, said economics is "an inquiry into the nature and causes of the wealth of nations." Alfred Marshall defined economics as "the study of mankind in the ordinary business of life," covering the acquisition and use "of the material requisites of well being." Lionel Robbins said economics "is the science which studies human behaviour as a relationship between ends and scarce means which have alternative uses." None of these definitions is particularly precise. This is as it should be because the scope of economics is itself not precise, for the activities devoted to the satisfaction of man's material needs and desires cannot be precisely separated from his other activities. The following selections deal with what economists do — when they choose to call it economics.

It is generally recognized that Adam Smith's esteemed work on the *Wealth of Nations* is one of the world's truly great books, and a rich mine of wisdom on a very wide range of subjects — economic; psychological, sociological, and historical; moral and political. Smith wrote before the Industrial Revolution was well launched and some of his theories were voided by its development. But as an analyst of institutions and an influence on later economists, he has never been surpassed. Reading 1 provides us with an unusual basis for studying Smith's great economic treatise. By focussing on Smith's attitude toward members of different classes and of their relation to the good of society as a whole, this selection gives us a glimpse of his entire outlook, which is not only interesting in itself, but is also illuminating in the study of his main work.

Scarcity is the most important concept in economics. It is the one pervasive, inescapable, inevitable fact. Since there is economic scarcity in the world, all societies have one thing in common: they must provide a framework within which four basic types of economic decisions can be made. These four decisions are the concern of Reading 2. To understand this selection is to know the nature of economics and the basic functions of economic systems.

So much for what economics is about and what economists claim to do. How should economics be studied? Is it a science in the same sense that the natural sciences are? Must it be a "positive" science? Does the usefulness of economics rest on its ability to predict with accuracy actual economic behaviour? Why study economics? What is the fundamental difference between economics and business management? Reading 3 deals with such questions. In doing so, it also helps us see more clearly the subject matter of economics.

Reading 4 serves as an excellent warning to students who consider economic analysis to be similar to historical description. Economic models — representations of major "cause and effect" relationships in an economy — are explained and their use is described. Such mathematical models are relatively new; they have only recently been developed and are now constantly being refined.

1. PUZZLES OF THE "WEALTH OF NATIONS"*

Arthur H. Cole

Every well-bred economist knows that a man named Adam Smith was born at Kirkcaldy in 1723, published a somewhat notable book in 1759 entitled *The Theory of Moral Sentiments,* and in 1776, when he was fifty-three years old, produced an extraordinary pair of volumes called *An Inquiry into the Nature and Causes of the Wealth of Nations.* Most young economists nowadays, I fear, do not read either work of the great Scotsman as we all once did[1] — in the days when one could still take time to enjoy also the leisurely pace of Thackeray and Dickens, even Scott. Students who just skim the *Wealth of Nations,* or parts of it, would surely miss what has attracted my attention; and even scholars interested in Smith's economic principles would hardly perceive what I have in mind, namely, that he was noteworthy for his "unbounded benevolence," as one near-contemporary described him, and that he was "slow to think evil" as a recent biographer alleges.[2]

Apparently it was out of this abounding good nature that Smith alluded to "the avarice and injustice of princes and sovereign states, abusing the confidence of their subjects"; that he took opportunity to mention "the conveyances of a verbose attorney"; and that, with a more sweeping serenity, he recorded an observation of "the overweening conceit which the greater part of men have of their own abilities."

Biographers of Smith have been led to state that perhaps he was not as obviously religious as some of his contemporaries. He was perhaps a deist, even if he was a philosopher and a friend of Hume. John Rae reported that Smith's "opening prayers" at Glasgow were thought to "savour strongly of natural religion," and occasioned no little shaking of heads.[3] Perhaps, then,

---

*Reprinted from Arthur H. Cole, "Puzzles of the 'Wealth of Nations'," *The Canadian Journal of Economics,* February, 1958, pp. 1-8, by permission of the editor and author.
Dr. Cole, who is now retired, was Professor of Economics, Harvard University, Boston.

[1] Apparently the practice of reading Smith from cover to cover began to fade some time ago. J.S. Nicholson, in his introduction to an 1884 edition of the *Wealth of Nations,* spoke of the item as "one of those books which are much talked of and little read."

[2] Alexander Carlyle, quoted by William R. Scott, *Adam Smith as Student and Professor* (Glasgow, 1937), p. 76; and Scott himself, *ibid.,* p. 100.

[3] John Rae, *Life of Adam Smith* (London, 1895), p. 60.

one might expect Smith to have been somewhat less charitable toward wearers of the cloth than he was toward other groups.

To be sure, the author did grant to the clergy courage or religious obstinacy under persecution, at least if the victims enjoyed public support. He called upon "the experience of all ages" to testify to the fact that, relative to "no order of men" was it "so dangerous, or rather so perfectly ruinous, [for governments] to employ force and violence, as upon the respected clergy of any established church." But there was hardly any subdivision of the aggregate of "established" or "nonestablished" religious groups that gained Smith's approbation. Thus, "candour and moderation" were, it seemed to him, "seldom to be found among the teachers of those great sects . . . supported by the civil magistrate"; clergy of "ancient and established systems . . . reposing themselves upon their benefices" were liable to attack from "teachers of new religions" because they "had neglected to keep up the fervour of faith and devotion in the great body of the people"; "the proud dignitaries of opulent and well-endowed churches" were likely to display "contemptuous and arrogant airs"; clergy with small benefices were prone to appear "ridiculous" by reason of the "vices of levity and vanity"; while the exponents of the "little sects" did not escape criticism: their morals were frequently "rather disagreeably rigorous and unsocial."

Smith's attitude toward members of the Catholic persuasion was somewhat ambivalent. He went out of his way a bit once or twice to praise individual representatives, such as "the Jesuit Gumila" and "Father Charlevoix," although in the latter case for the rather modest virtue of reporting nothing in his accounts of Canada "less considerable than it really was." Also Smith quite understandably seemed almost to commend the arrangement by which "the inferior clergy" in the church of Rome were "kept more alive by the powerful motive of self-interest than perhaps in any established protestant church."

However, he did not approve of the "numerous race of mendicant friars, whose beggary" was "not only licensed, but consecrated by religion," and whom he compared in another place to "the hussars and light infantry of some armies; no plunder, no pay." And despite some Catholic writers such as Father Charlevoix aforesaid, he seems to have been considerably annoyed by other writers connected with that church. These latter were quite surely in his mind, when, in deriding certain accounts of the public works of China, he spoke of their having "generally been drawn up by weak and wondering travellers; frequently by stupid and lying missionaries."[4]

It appears highly probable that Smith had reference particularly to the men whose materials Father Jean-Baptiste du Halde drew upon for his *Description of China*. To be sure, du Halde's volumes did not exist in the Scotsman's library. However, there were features about them that could well have drawn Smith's displeasure. The author had never been to China; he relied on the memoirs of some two dozen missionaries; and the book abounds in such extravagant statements as that "the industrious Chinese"

---

[4] It was this passage that started me on the inquiry of which this essay is the product. It was quoted to me by the late Professor Thomas Sanders of the Harvard Business School. He was English born and bred; he had studied the *Wealth of Nations*; later in life he had in Japan married the daughter of a missionary; and apparently he could not reconcile Smith's characterization of the missionaries with what he knew from personal observation. Professor Sanders asked me, in the course of our first casual conversation together, whether I could explain Smith's attitude. I could not, and I doubt if I can do so yet.

cut "numberless Canals through all their Lands"; the Chinese are very "careful in making the Roads smooth and level, which are often pav'd"; and that "in some Provinces the High Roads are like so many great Walks between two great Rows of high Trees." Still the book, which appeared in French in 1735, was favoured with English editions of 1736, 1738, and 1741, with a German translation in 1747-56, and even a Russian one in 1774-77. It seems quite probable that Smith had in mind Father du Halde's twenty-seven authorities when he mentioned both the "weak and wondering travellers" and the "stupid and lying missionaries."

Perhaps it was the presence of shafts such as the one just quoted that led Professor Nicholson to remark that the argument in the *Wealth of Nations* was "often relieved by quiet touches of humour and occasionally by good-natured satire." Admittedly quite a few varieties of men provoked Smith to reactions of one sort or another. One must view him as indulging in a private chuckle when he wrote that people could not reckon "soldiers the most industrious set" of citizens, or that Scottish banks had "never distinguished themselves by their extreme imprudence." The more frequent reaction was sharper. A man might often regain health in spite "of the absurd prescriptions of the doctor"; one could observe "the usual idleness of apprentices"; and Cicero was presumably right in thinking that there was "nothing so absurd . . . which has not sometimes been asserted by some philosophers."

Politicians and statesmen aroused rather more extreme emotions. Smith had a good word for the local French "parliaments" by reason of their incorruptibility, which condition he attributed to the mode of compensation of their members — not fixed salaries, but fees dependent on their diligence. Otherwise he found such things as officers of government "being generally disposed to reward both themselves and their immediate dependents rather more than enough"; that the English government, in matters of public expenditure, had achieved the worst of both monarchy and democracy: in time of peace conducting itself "with the slothful and negligent profusion that is perhaps natural" to the former, and in times of war acting "with all the thoughtless extravagance that democracies are apt to fall into."

Smith's most forthright appraisal of the whole genus came when he referred to "that insidious and crafty animal, vulgarly called a statesman or politician"; his severest chastisement of political life when he alleged "attacks which these leading men" were "continually making upon the importance of one another, and in the defence of their own" to constitute "the whole play of domestic faction and ambition"; and his most incisive castigation of higher government officials in the resounding charge: "The statesman, who should attempt to direct private people in what manner they ought to employ their capitals, would not only load himself with a most unnecessary attention, but assume an authority which could safely be trusted, not only to no single person, but to no council or senate whatever, and which would nowhere be so dangerous as in the hands of a man who had folly and presumption enough to fancy himself fit to exercise it."

Curiously enough the businessman fared scarcely better at Smith's hands. I say "curiously enough" because it would seem that anyone who held self-interest to be generally so beneficent a force, and who admitted that businessmen were motivated by that sort of interest, would have been more charitable toward some of the manifestations or excesses of that driving energizer. Smith does give reluctant commendation to the promoter or the innovating entrepreneur. In his *Theory of Moral Sentiments* he alleged that a tradesman would be thought "a poor-spirited fellow among his neighbours," who did not "bestir himself to get what they call an extraordinary job, or some uncommon advantage." In the *Wealth of Nations,* an idle man is alleged to be in danger of being despised among men of business; the merchant is apparently praised as "commonly a bold undertaker" of improvements on agricultural property that he may acquire, in contrast to the country gentleman who is a "timid" one; and the "projector" is credited with having "golden dreams," with "splendid," if somewhat "visionary ideas."

In his *Lectures* Smith had seemingly presented a sophisticated argument on the point that merchants were undeservedly denigrated. In primitive societies it was considered generous and noble to do or give something without expectation of reward or return; but to indulge in barter was mean; and the low social status of the merchant continued to some extent to persist even in "a refined society" such as England. Smith goes on to philosophize that "this mean and despicable idea" of earlier days regarding the merchant "greatly obstructed the progress of commerce."

In the *Wealth of Nations,* however, this generous attitude and this lesson seem to have been forgotten. To be sure, now the "manufacturer" is often bracketed with the "merchant" for proper opprobrium, but the former was probably — in 1776 — most likely to have been the man who "put out" materials to be worked up in country labourers' homes — at least still half a merchant. At all events, the two are beaten almost unmercifully and in many relationships: "the avidity of our great manufacturers"; "the sophistry of merchants and manufacturers"; "the clamour and sophistry of merchants and manufacturers"; "the mean rapacity, the monopolizing spirit of merchants and manufacturers"; or "the sneaking arts of underling tradesmen."

Merchants pursue "their own pedlar principle of turning a penny wherever a penny was to be got"; merchants speak "with all the passionate confidence of interested falsehood"; and "the capricious ambition of kings and ministers [had not during the seventeenth and eighteenth centuries] been more fatal to the repose of Europe, than the impertinent jealousy of merchants and manufacturers."

The pursuit of monopoly was a frequent charge against such businessmen. A conversation among people in the same trade was likely to end in "a conspiracy against the public"; monopoly was "a great enemy to good management"; "the highest eulogy" that could "ever justly be bestowed upon a regulated company" was that it was "merely useless"; while Smith saw "fraud and abuse" as "inseparable from the management . . . of so great a company" as the East India.

To be successful was surely no source of forgiveness by the great Scotsman. The rich were not highly regarded. They were accused of "indolence and vanity"; "great wealth" was "frequently [to] be admitted as an apology for great folly"; while "disorders" were believed "generally [to] prevail in the economy of the rich." And wealth was corrupting of natural powers: landowners by their indolence, "which is the natural effect of the ease and security of their situation," were too often rendered "not only ignorant, but incapable of that application of mind which is necessary in order to foresee and understand the consequences of any public regulation"; while "luxury in the fair sex" had the very unhappy result, it seems, "always to weaken, and frequently to destroy altogether, the powers of generation." "A pampered fine lady is often incapable of bearing any [children], and is generally exhausted by two or three."

Ostentatious display was perhaps the social sin that provoked Adam Smith most easily. In his *Theory of Moral Sentiments* he had spoken already of the "hypocrites of wealth and greatness." In his later book he became more specific: "the chief enjoyment of riches consists in the parade of riches"; "the rich not being able to distinguish themselves by the expence of any one dress, will naturally endeavour to do so by the multitude and variety of their dresses"; while the quantity of plate will tend to increase "from vanity and ostentation." The idea of "conspicuous consumption" was not new with Thorstein Veblen.

One is driven to wonder why the great Scotsman was led to take so unpleasant a view of merchants, of the rich, and especially of the exhibitionism of the latter. To be sure — despite what Nicholson, Rae, Scott, and others have said about his being "friendly and generous" or "slow to think evil" — Smith gives much evidence of a pretty low opinion of mankind in general. Man is full of all sorts of frailties. "In every profession, the exertion of the greater part of those who exercise it, is always in proportion to the necessity they are under of making that exertion"; "the pride of man makes him love to domineer, and nothing mortifies him so much as to be obliged to condescend to persuade his inferiors"; and "it is the interest of every man to live as much at his ease as he can." But even those who seek better things do not necessarily please the learned doctor; they are accused of possessing "the undiscerning eye of giddy ambition."

However, there was a specific case close to Smith's hand which might have influenced his opinion — unconsciously perhaps — in a number of the foregoing matters. I have in mind the "tobacco lords" of Glasgow. As far as I know, they are not mentioned even by inference in the *Wealth of Nations,* although the London merchants are described as generally not "such magnificent" creatures as those of Cadiz or Lisbon, nor, on the other hand, "such attentive and parsimonious burghers as those of Amsterdam." The "tobacco lords" are not mentioned, but, if accounts of their behaviour are to be believed, Smith must have found them hard to bear.

The Glasgow merchants dealing in tobacco were exceedingly successful in the first three-quarters of the eighteenth century. The trade was launched only with the union of England and Scotland in 1707; by 1742 Glasgow had passed Bristol, Liverpool, and Whitehaven in volume of this trade; and, before the American Revolution ruined all this commerce, a dozen or fifteen fine new houses for successful merchants had been erected. These businessmen seem to have deserved the good fortune that was theirs; they could have been commended by Smith in his *Moral Sentiments* for bestirring themselves "to get an extraordinary job, or some uncommon advantage." They displayed a greater willingness to bear risks than did many of their London competitors; and they introduced innovations in the trade.

However, there were unfavourable features of the business. In the earliest years it was charged that the success of the Scots was due to the venality of the North British customs officers, and to their ignorance and sloth that made fraud easy without corruption. New legislation attempted to correct matters. Possibly these accusations stemmed wholly from the jealousy of English tobacco merchants; and it is true that the volume of Glasgow's tobacco trade continued to grow through the investigations and after the new statutes. Still there was the aroma of unscrupulous merchants — "clamour and sophistry," "sneaking arts," and "mean rapacity."

Their effort at "ostentation" in architecture tended to set them apart — houses with "entablatures, urns, and balustraded roofs." And then what a peculiar sort of behaviour these merchants adopted! John Strang, writing as early as 1857, told of their decking themselves out in scarlet cloaks, curled wigs, cocked hats, and gold-headed canes. "They were the princes of Plainstanes [the central market area of the city], and strutted about there all day as the rulers of the destinies of Glasgow." And, wholly congruent with such parading, they exhibited a "hauteur and bearing . . . assuming the air and deportment of persons immeasurably superior to all around them."[5] With the almost inevitable narrowness of interests of such men, it is not to be wondered at that Smith gained a rather poor impression of how merchants achieved success, and what success did to them.

Lord Brougham is quoted as finding the *Wealth of Nations* "one of the most entertaining of books," while Professor E.R.A. Seligman, in the introduction to the Everyman's Library edition of the treatise, speaks of finding it "full of imperturbable good humour." Accordingly, perhaps we ought to try to see just what Smith did like.

The largest class upon whom he smiled was the farming group. To be sure, the landlord himself is accused of "conceit of his own superior knowledge [of farming] (a conceit in most cases very ill founded)"; he "seldom means to leave" the tenant any more than the smallest share; while "the elegance of his dress, of his equipage, of his house, and household furniture, are objects" of his anxious thought. Still "country gentlemen and farmers are, to their great honour, of all people, the least subject to the wretched spirit of monopoly"; the tenants are "sober and industrious"; their "understanding [of their technology] is generally much superior" to that of the mechanic; and the "planter who cultivates his own land, and derives his necessary subsistence from the labour of his own family, is really a master, and independent of all the world." In at least some agricultural callings, man might demonstrate social values and even perhaps find contentment.

Of banking and most bankers, Smith seemed to approve in general. "Judicious operations of banking" appeared to him to provide a "sort of waggon way through the air," by which commerce may be speedily moved; "the stability of the bank of England is equal to that of the British government"; and, even if "the conduct of all" the Scottish banking companies "has not been unexceptionable," still they too escape serious criticism.

The principle of honour, if not among thieves, at least among individuals with whom Smith had little in common was illustrated with a distinct show of approval in three different areas. "In the race for wealth, and honours, and preferments," he wrote in his *Moral Sentiments,* the egotist "may run as hard as he can, and strain every nerve and every muscle, in order to outstrip all his competitors. But if he should justle [*sic*], or throw down any of them, the indulgence of the spectators is entirely at an end. It is a violation of fair play, which they cannot admit of."

Again, in the case of employers' combinations against their workmen, Smith in his later book seems to commend steadfastness among the participants. "To violate this [type of] combination is every where a most unpopular action, and a sort of reproach to a master among his neighbours and equals."

---

[5] John Strang, *Glasgow and Its Clubs* (Glasgow, 1857), pp. 35–7. See also Jacob M. Price, "The Rise of Glasgow in the Chesapeake Tobacco Trade, 1707–1775," *William and Mary Quarterly* No. 3 (1954), pp. 179–200; and George Eyre-Todd, *History of Glasgow* (Glasgow, 1934), Vol. 3, pp. 237–38, 247. Professor Herbert Heaton tells me that Strang was repeating in 1857 what had been common for half a century in the accounts of eighteenth-century Glasgow.

Thirdly, there was the matter of receiving smuggled goods. Smith disliked import duties, and tended to blame such laws for the acts of the smuggler. Then he went on to argue: "To pretend to have any scruple about buying smuggled goods, though a manifest encouragement to the violation of the revenue laws, and to the perjury which almost always attends it, would in most countries be regarded as one of those pedantic pieces of hypocrisy which, instead of gaining credit with any body, serve only to expose the person who affects to practise them, to the suspicion of being a greater knave than most of his neighbours." Yet in 1778 Smith was to become commissioner of customs!

Drinking, at least in moderation, came in for commendation. Smith is reported in his *Lectures* to have stated that "man is an anxious animal and must have his care swept off by something that can exhilarate the spirits." In the *Wealth of Nations*, he commented on "the wholesome and invigorating liquors of beer and ale"; while also asserting that "great labour . . . requires to be relieved by some indulgence, sometimes of ease only, but sometimes too of dissipation and diversion." The Scot was broadminded.

Then there is a miscellany of well-regarded items. The training which "naturally forms a merchant" leaves him with habits of "order, economy, and attention." The "delightful art [of gardening] is practised by so many rich people for amusement" that Smith is perhaps inclined on this score to be a little kindly toward them. "The poorest family can often maintain a cat or a dog," and this is apparently a good thing. "The strongest men" are "the chairmen, porters, and coal heavers in London," and "the most beautiful women perhaps in the British dominions" are "those unfortunate women who live by prostitution." (These two groups had two features in common: they stemmed from "the lowest rank of people in Ireland," and consequently they lived on potatoes.)

Surely it is a strange medley of callings and actions — and a rather meagre list — to be set against the many features of the economic and social system with which Smith found wide-ranging fault.

There may be deep-plunging morals to be drawn from the foregoing demonstration: that one should not remain single; or, living to the age of fifty-three, he should not write a book; that a great man's biographers are not to be believed in all particulars; or that books in political economy should be dull. Perhaps a psychoanalyst should be brought in to complete the study. I would not know.

One lesson seems sufficient: when some specially vigorous judgment is quoted from the great Scotsman — that a politician is an "insidious and crafty animal," or tradesmen are capable of "sneaking arts" — it will be appropriate to reflect that this thorn came from a bouquet full of rather thorny roses. Whether Adam Smith deliberately put such prickly blossoms there — for literary effect — or in his premature cantankerousness did not realize that such barbs were being placed all through the book — this question each admirer of the Scotsman may answer for himself.

And, in a way of speaking, this conclusion bespeaks failure of my research. I had hoped by assembling what I thought to be a few unguarded phrases of praise or criticism — for example, "stupid and lying missionaries" — to discover what unconscious biases the author really possessed. The "few" became too numerous. And even the reverse question, that is, of what did Smith unconsciously approve, seems in the end to lead us nowhere: probably bankers and smugglers, fair play, "something that can exhilarate the spirits," gardening, and — for the sake of argument — "the most beautiful women perhaps in the British dominions"! — hardly a significant garland of thornless blooms.

At all events the *Wealth of Nations* is obviously worth examination. David Hume, on first reading the book, is alleged to have remarked that its curious facts would help it to gain the public ear; and Professor C.R. Fay states in his recent appraisal of the book: "The *Wealth of Nations* was a great period piece, and on that account it is a jewel for all time." I would be inclined to add that its curious psychological revelations and its dazzling turns of phrase should help to preserve it from complete oblivion among scholars, even hurried present-day scholars, interested in the evolution of economic thought.

2. UNDERSTANDING THE ECONOMIC PROBLEM*

Ben W. Lewis

. . . Democracy — and this we have on the very highest authority — means *government by the people.* But the affairs of government, in large and increasing measure, are *economic* affairs. To be sure, they have political and other overtones, but no one who casts his glance even casually over the range of matters with which modern governments have to deal will doubt that these matters are economic in substance or in effect. Look for a moment: money, credit, commerce, corporations, tariffs, quotas, foreign aid, development, monopoly, fair trade, farm support, small business, oil prorates, highways, rails, communications, private power, public power, inflation, employment, management-labour relations, distribution of income, education, health, public debt — and taxes.

The simple business of living in our age calls increasingly upon men to participate actively with other men, in the gigantic undertaking of collective governmental decision making on a vast array of complex economic problems and issues. It is demanded of these men that they have economic understanding. The stakes, to put the matter bluntly, are the survival of democracy and human freedom. Freedom will not remain if democracy expires, and democracy will not last beyond the day when it fails to discharge the political-economic tasks which we ask it to perform. Remember, democracy is government of and by the people, and the capacity of the people to perform will set the level of performance which it is possible for democracy to attain.

Freedom and democracy are abstract concepts, but the matter of their preservation is concrete and immediate. This is our democracy, and we are "the people" on whose economic understanding and economic sense the outcome of our epic adventure in self-government rests.

. . . I have resisted the temptation to speak of the need of each individual in our highly specialized and interdependent economy for knowledge and skills which will help him to operate more effectively as a buyer and seller of

*Reprinted from Ben W. Lewis, "Economic Understanding: Why and What," *The American Economic Review*, May, 1957, pp. 653—70, abridged, by permission of the editor and author.
Dr. Lewis was Professor of Economics at Oberlin College, Kansas, from 1925 to 1967. He has been with the Ford Foundation since 1967.

goods and services. Men need to know about credit facilities and practices, instalment buying, insurance, tax forms, social security provisions, and a host of other matters, in order to move intelligently in making and enjoying their living. But information about these matters is not to be accepted as economics, or in lieu of economics. Such information may come to the student as a by-product of his study of economics, and it is often both possible and productive to employ topics of this kind as a vehicle for developing economic understanding. It may be that many of these things should be taught for their own sake. . . . But the call for more and better economics in the schools does not derive from the need for formal instruction in whether to buy or rent a home, or the conditions under which term-insurance is to be preferred to an annuity. A man may be very shrewd in his personal dealings in these matters and still be sadly deficient in economic understanding.

. . . Economic understanding does not consist in the accumulation of a stock of economic information or of an array of useful economic facts. It does not consist of the possession of a "Do-it-yourself" kit of answers to public economic problems or of a package of rules of sound thinking for solving these problems. Nor does it consist of skills or precepts to be employed in the conduct of economic transactions. Economics makes use of all these things, but we are talking here about economic *understanding,* and "understanding" means *understanding.* Understanding is concerned with "why"; its interest in "what" is strictly ancillary to its interest in "why."

I will venture the proposition that to have economic understanding is to have a genuine sense of "what it's all about" as far as the economic phases of our lives together are concerned — a "feel" for economic issues — a rather clear impression of "having been here before" in the presence of economic situations calling for policy judgments, and hence a sense of direction and a workmanlike touch.

I believe economic understanding is to be gained through an understanding of the central core of economics that dominates all economic situations and issues — *the economic problem* faced by all societies of men who live and make their living together. We have economic systems or economies because we are confronted by *the economic problem*; economies, all economies irrespective of characteristics or qualities, are fashioned, moulded, and maintained solely because this problem exists. To understand the economic problem is to know the purpose and functions of economic systems, and thus to have a clear unmistakable point of reference, a firm home base, from which to proceed in considering any and all questions of economic public policy. I do not claim eternal and universal economic salvation as the reward for such understanding, but I do not hesitate to say that, in its absence, only confusion can prevail.

The economic problem, let us be reminded, is simply "What disposition shall society make of its *limited human and natural resources* in light of the *unlimited needs and desires* which these resources can be used to satisfy?"

Let me labour this thesis, lightly. But, first, another precautionary negative before I am accused of treating you solely to a bill of thawed-out economic ideas chipped out of our nineteenth-century deepfreeze and of ignoring the shattering impact upon our thinking of today's dynamic flows, growth modelling, and equation splitting. The economic problem is not confined to static division; it does not reflect an assumption that product is fixed in amount and that economic alternatives relate only to kinds and direction. The problem is "What *use* shall be made of our resources?", and I offer "use" to you as a *dynamic* concept which confronts us with choices bearing on fullness and growth as well as with choices of kind — with questions of "how much" and "how quickly," as well as with questions of "what?"

The economic problem emerges from two basic, interrelated conditions — (1) man's unlimited desires for goods *in the aggregate* and (2) the limited human and natural resources available to society for the production of goods in the aggregate.

Mankind has unlimited desires for goods in the aggregate. Each one of us wants at least a minimum of material goods and services to satisfy his basic needs — such things, for example, as food, shelter, household furnishings, clothing, medical services, and so forth. But each of us desires much more than this basic minimum of essentials. Each would like more, and more varieties, of all these things and many things in addition. The fact is that if each of us did not have to restrain himself by some notion of what he could afford, his individual desires or wants would run on endlessly. In the aggregate, such limitless desires, multiplied in volume by the number of individuals who inhabit the world, go far beyond anything that society can ever dream of actually satisfying from its limited resources.

Society's human and natural resources available for the production of goods in the aggregate are limited. The goods and services with which we satisfy our desires do not grow in limitless quantities upon limitless trees; they do not appear out of nowhere when we rub a magic lamp or utter a secret word. Goods must be *produced* (even those few that do "grow on trees" have to be picked — or picked up — and prepared for use). Production requires the use of *human resources* (labour) and *natural resources* (land, water, ores, minerals, fuels, and so forth), together with techniques and methods for organizing and combining and processing these resources. And we know that basically, these resources are *scarce relative to human needs and desires.* Despite our marvelous advances in technology and despite the fact that our standard of material living has on the average risen markedly over the centuries, we can never produce such an abundance of goods that everyone in the world can have all he wants of everything, with lots left over.

Let there be no confusion on this point. Occasionally in our society we are confronted by so-called surpluses of *particular* products (the "butter surplus," the "potato surplus," for example, or the "surplus of used automobiles"). These represent supplies of particular goods in excess of the amounts which buyers with purchasing power at a particular time and place are willing to buy at prevailing prices. In an economic sense they represent particular overproduction in relation to effective demand for particular goods — misproduction or malproduction, or a use or allocation of society's resources of which society, by its market calculus, indicates it does not approve. In the world as we know it, "too many" potatoes means "too few" of other things; it can never mean "too much of everything." And even in the case of a particular surplus at a particular time and place, it does not necessarily follow that human desires for the particular goods are not going unsatisfied somewhere else in society at the very same time. Breakdowns in society's institutional arrangements for bringing goods and desires together are not to be interpreted as evidence of society's power to produce without limit. By the same token, we must not be misled by terms and phrases which suggest contradictions where none exist. Specifically, there is no contradiction between an "economy of scarcity" and an "economy of plenty," where "scarcity" is understood as a *condition* of economizing, and "plenty" is understood as its *goal*.

It behooves us, thus, to take care in the use we make of our resources — to be concerned about their use, to manage them, to "economize" them. The reason we bother to manage or "economize" our resources is simply that, since they are limited in supply relative to the uses to which we would like to put them — that is, since in an economic sense they are "scarce" — *it makes a difference* to us how they are used. The degree and manner and direction of their use and the disposition of the product resulting from their use have, of sheer necessity, been primary, basic concerns of all societies through the ages. This is what the study of "economizing," or *economics as a social science,* is about — it is *all* that economics is about.

Presumably any society will want its scarce resources to be "fully" employed (particularly its labour resources), and so used that their power to produce is great and expanding and that the "right" goods are produced in the "right" amounts and, in each case, by using the "best" combinations of resources. Any society will be concerned, too, that the goods which are produced from its scarce resources are divided fairly among its members.

But the use of such terms as "fully," "right," "best," "fairly," and so forth, in defining the disposition to be made of resources suggests that alternative uses are possible and that society is faced with the never-ending problem of making millions of continuous and simultaneous decisions in the management or "economizing" of its resources. Surely we want our resources to be used fully and in the right and best way, but how "full" is "fully"? Exactly which ways are "right" and "best" and "fair"? We must remember, too, that society's answers to some of the questions may condition and set limits on its answers to other questions: a decision to promote technological advance *may* make employment less stable, a decision to divide the aggregate product more evenly among everyone *may* have an adverse effect upon the total amount produced, and public policies designed to bring about full employment *may* also promote productive inefficiency and aggravated inequities as an undesired consequence. Nonetheless, answers *must be* provided by society to the economic problem faced by men who want to live in harmony and well-being in a world where not everyone *can* have all he wants of the goods and services that make up his material living, and where, hence, the use made of our limited, valuable economic resources is a matter of concern to every living person.

Thus it is that all societies of men who make their living together must inevitably establish and maintain (or acquiesce in) an *economic system* or *economy* — a set of man-made arrangements to provide answers to the all-important *economic* questions which make up the overall economic problem:

a. How fully shall our limited resources be used?
b. How shall our resources be organized and combined?
c. Who shall produce how much of what?
d. To whom and in what amounts shall the resulting product be divided among the members of society?

It is the job of the economic system (*any* economic system) to make the decisions and turn out the answers *that society wants,* whatever they may be, to these questions; and economics as a discipline is a study of the economic problem in all its parts, and of the institutional arrangements which men have devised to grind out the necessary answers to the questions which it poses.

The data and materials, the concepts and the "principles" with which the study of economics is concerned and the problems to which it attends all stem from and bear on this central problem — how *do* we and how *might* we dispose of the resources upon which the level and quality of our material life depend? This is *the economic problem*; all other economic problems and issues — for example, the farm problem, the labour-management problem, the problem of taxation, the inflation problem, the problem of full employment, the antitrust problem — are simply partial manifestations of it in particular quarters and under particular conditions, and can be dealt with effectively only in conscious relation to the central problem — the *core* of economics. This should be the starting point of our economics teaching, and its destination. Between the starting point and the terminus, students should become familiar with the significant features of our own mid-twentieth century economy with its ever-changing combinations of individual markets and collective governmental economic activities and processes. They should become aware of its rationale and of how it has come to be what it now is, and of how it contrasts with earlier and other economic systems. They need to know something of the structure and operations of our major economic institutions, and the mechanics of income determination, resource guidance, and income distribution. They should experience the centring of issues and the marshalling and weighing of considerations involved in the determination of policy in one or two areas of public economic policy. But all this — systems, processes, institutions, mechanics, policy problems — I repeat, all this should be tied constantly to the core of economics — the economic problem — and related at every turn to the purposes for which men build economic systems because that problem exists.

. . . Our story can be told and it can be understood. To what purpose?

A person who possesses economic understanding will relate his consideration of public economic issues, easily and purposively, to the central core — to the starting point, to home base. He will have a sense of the interrelationship of economic phenomena and problems — the "oneness" of the economy — the tie-in between each sector of the economy and the whole, and between the economy and himself.

He will know his "way around" and his "way home" in the economy. He will face such choices as those between alternative satisfactions, between present and future goods, between alternative methods of production, between production and leisure, between stability and security and innovation and progress, and between economizing by the market and economizing by government, under whatever conditions and guises these choices may appear, with awareness and a balanced sense of consequences.

He will know that products come from production, and will have an appreciation of the contribution made by diverse groups to the totality of production.

Familiarity with the mechanics of economics will not blind him to the reality that the operating forces in any political economy are human. He will know that economic life involves, essentially, the rational living together of human beings — a constant adjustment and readjustment in economic matters comparable to, indeed a part of, the constant adjustment and readjustment that characterize the total business of living together. He will realize that these adjustments frequently bring discomfort, even pain, to those established (vested) interests that are required to adjust, but that failure of one group to adjust may mean privation for other groups and stagnation for the economy as a whole. And he will relate this to situations in which his own interest lies in resistance to change (tariff, price supports, "fair trade," "featherbedding") as well as to those in which his own interest would be served by the adjustment of others.

He will distinguish between areas where "scientific" economic answers are possible, areas where such answers are impossible because necessary information or data are absent, and areas where only value judgments are called for and possible. He will realize that it is not the function of economics to provide answers to ethical or value problems, but, rather, to help to define and identify such problems and to place them in sharper focus.

Finally, his realization that, in the very nature of the case, economic problems permit of very few "right" answers will be one measure of the depth of his economic understanding — and the realization will fill him with a sense not of futility but of purpose. It will point up for him his personal role in the political economy in which he lives.

3. THE SCOPE AND METHOD OF ECONOMICS*

Frederick St. Leger Daly

. . . Fifty years ago John Neville Keynes wrote the *Scope and Method of Political Economy* and since that time only one full book in English, that I know of, has been published on this topic — Lionel Robbins's *The Nature and Significance of Economic Science.*

The first thing that should be stressed about the economic method is that it should be economic method, not methods. It would be bad to think of method as deductive or inductive, for the interrelation is too close. For an economist, the division is fatal. Put them in different stalls and there is no offspring.

Deductive is the often criticized *a priori* reasoning. If demand is constant and elastic, what happens to total revenue when price is cut? Answer: total revenue increases.

Under *inductive* are grouped, perhaps unhappily grouped, those approaches to economic problems which seem to deal first with facts: the mere collection of data such as figures on bank deposits or on output. . . .

If I mention next *institutional* studies, you will sense immediately the difficulty of separating these from the foregoing types of research . . . . They are different only in that the structure of certain institutions, such as commercial banks and corporations, come to the foreground more obviously as being of importance.

A fourth type — *historical* — most obviously overlaps these three, the main difference being that the facts lie in the more distant past, the periods that may be studied are of longer duration, the change present in the institutions of greater magnitude, and, unfortunately, the desired statistics often less available. . . .

. . . The four types of studies mentioned — deductive, inductive, institutional, historical — overlap and interrelate to form an essential unity of method.

---

*Reprinted from F. St. Leger Daly, "The Scope and Method of Economics," *The Canadian Journal of Economics*, May, 1945, pp. 165–76, by permission of the editor.
Mr. Daly was Assistant Professor of Economics at Tufts College, Boston, from 1936 until he took a leave of absence in 1940 to offer his services to the Canadian Government, first as an economist and then as a soldier. He died in 1944.

Some defenders of the deductive method have glorified it, as did Lionel Robbins, as *the* economic method and have gone to some trouble to claim for it the title of science — an entirely useless waste of effort. The most successful analogies have been to mathematical or chemical formulae. Let us take a familiar example. The demand for the product of a firm in monopolistic competition increases. How will the firm alter its output and the price of its product? Now if we know or if we assume for our problem the cost conditions of the firm and the demand; if we further assume the firm also knows these things and is motivated by a desire to maximize its profits, then we can state definitely what the new price and output will be. The answer is exact and definite, both as to the direction of change and as to the quantity of change. That the answer is as exact as the solution of a series of mathematical equations is not surprising, for everything in the problem . . . may be expressed in terms of mathematical equations. That this is so is important enough to be noted, but it has been to the misfortune of economics that some earlier writers upon methodology, enchanted by the exactness here exhibited, have overemphasized this one aspect of economic method. More recently Professor Robbins, desirous of claiming equal status for economics with the natural sciences, calls these exact deductive inevitabilities "the laws of economics" and phrases his treatment in such a manner that the mutual interrelationship of deductive and inductive methods can only be kept in mind by a firmly predetermined reader.

In certain fundamental respects, at least, this mutual interrelationship is the same in economics as it is in any of the natural sciences. Greater knowledge of facts checks past tentative conclusions obtained from reasoning about them, and stimulates further reasoning by suggesting new channels of thought.

It is clear, then, that I feel that Lionel Robbins's discussion of method is one-sided, to say the least. It is wrong in its interpretation of what economic method is. Despite the fact that later in his book he points out the necessity for, and some of the functions of, factual, institutional studies, the emphasis upon the abstract approach is exceedingly one-sided. It is dangerous in the incorrect picture of economic method it gives to an outsider coming to this source for his knowledge of economics. It is bad in that any influence he might have upon economists is all in one direction only. There is need for better deductive tools of analysis but the need for inductive work is, at the present state, greater.

Before attacking Professor Robbins further, it should be said in his defence that he has been considerably misinterpreted, a misinterpretation that should not have been made by anyone at all familiar with the literature on methodology. When he states that the economist is not concerned with ends, for example, that he does not care whether the state strives for self-sufficiency or for greater international trade, he most obviously does not mean that he is not interested in this, nor that he should not bring what influence he can to help achieve the end he desires. For a glance at his writings shows he hates government regulation of international trade and will fight it to his last breath. All he meant was that in deciding for or against freedom in international trade, there are other issues at stake than the economic results of the policy chosen. If we fight as economists over these noneconomic issues, he argues, we hamper the possibility of calm study and agreement upon the economic results of any policy. As economists we study and agree upon the economic causes and results of the inequality of wealth and income distribution. Here we should agree. Then we doff our caps and gowns and fight for the policy we want, for here we may disagree about the economic results we desire and about the psychological and sociological aspects of the problem. Of the desirability of keeping one's study and analysis as uninfluenced by personal desires, as objective as possible, there can be no doubt. Of the effectiveness of Professor Robbins's split-personality policy, there seems to me to be great doubt. To have an economist, advocating a policy designed to increase employment, constantly saying "I am not an economist when I do this," is a verbal quibble that is quite useless. When writers of elementary texts pick up this fiction and state in Chapter I that the economist is not interested in ends, it becomes positively harmful. What are we interested in? It is precisely the ends we are interested in: more employment, bigger incomes, etc.

What I think economics is should be fairly evident by now. Professor Robbins's definition is: "Economics is the science which studies behaviour as a relationship between ends and scarce means which have alternate uses." A definition should explain. That definition gives you a picture of an economist as nine-tenths amateur psychologist. An economist may understand it. To a noneconomist, it sounds, as one economist has expressed it, as if we slipped into corner grocery stores and watched the wriggling and contortions of a child spending three cents on candy.

I can see little need for a concise definition of economics. . . . I can see real harm, for a brief statement never conveys the right meaning. The economist should, of course, be aware of the content of his field and especially of the limitations of his own equipment, but that awareness is not achieved by definition. Further, the fact that in specific problems the content merges with that of other fields, makes a clear-cut delimitation impossible. If you agree that the utility or monopoly problem is part of economics, you must admit at once that the economist, the student of government and law must work in co-operation in its solution. That clearly has implications for method. . . . There is no edge to the field where the knife slices down — to this point, economics; beyond, another field. If you do not agree, try to separate the economic from the noneconomic aspects of unemployment or, as has been suggested, try as an economist alone to measure the net cost to the government of a slum-clearance program.

Nor, it seems to me, can we meet the desire for exactness by saying that every problem has its economic and noneconomic aspects. In a broad sense, such a division is fundamental and important. It is a division all of us make constantly. In evaluating tariffs, for instance, military as well as economic considerations are involved. But this realization that economics and military science are two different fields does not make the dividing line between economics and all other fields exact. That the presence of pellagra in the southern states, or a suggestion of some socialization of medical service, are both economic and medical problems, leads no one to the conclusion that economics and medicine are the same thing.

In summary, economics is a special field because there are certain problems which are dominantly economic and because in certain other problems there are some aspects that are dominantly economic, so that the economist needs to study these problems as an economist himself, and in conjunction with other specialists. But economics is a field that cannot be exactly demarcated from others because the fields merge and overlap.

It might have been a successful method of describing economics to have listed some of the major economic problems facing society today (1939) and merely to have stated that economics was the study of these with the goal an understanding of them, so that improvement in these conditions might be brought about, if possible: one-third of the railroad mileage now in liquidation, ten million men unemployed, the national income still far below the level of ten years ago, business losses during 1938, the steel industry working at about half capacity, one-third of the families of the United States with incomes of less than $800 per year.

Despite this list, which could be readily expanded, certain people have the feeling that we have little need for economics today. This attitude may be held by individuals with otherwise very different points of view and for a combination of reasons that may differ widely. We may consider three broad groups and in doing so, discuss, as we should, the major criticisms brought against economics.

There are those who, like Lancelot Hogben of *Science for the Citizen*, want a planned socialism and do not see the economic problem involved; some who are sympathetic to Professor Hogben's ideas minus the planned socialism, but do not sense the necessity of attacking the economic problems as such; and those who state that the economic problems of today are vitally important but that economics has nothing to offer for the solution of them. We shall discuss these in turn.

If I may interpret Professor Hogben's scientific humanism: it is humanism, for the goal is the betterment of mankind; it is scientific, because it involves a scientific study of the resources we have, . . . and so a scientific plan can be drawn up by scientists, technicians, and specialists for the best possible fulfillment of scientifically determined needs.

He says, "As a biologist, I am in favour of planned production based on biotechnology because I cannot conceive how planned consumption is possible without planned production, and I cannot conceive of any rational basis for human society, unless it implies planned consumption to ensure the maintenance of population." Now, I ask you, put this man in the same room with Professors Hayek and Robbins at the London School of Economics and what is going to happen? Hayek and Robbins will insist that Hogben overlooks the problem of allocation of resources in a centrally planned economy while Hogben reiterates that he can find the needs, that he knows the resources and that he can bring the two together. Whereupon Hayek and Robbins will try to make Hogben see that this bringing together of needs and resources *is* the economic problem.

Turning to the second group mentioned above, we find this same scientific humanistic outlook held by some who would object strongly to socialism and would, in fact, prefer rather less than we now have of government planning or regulation. For the scientific study of needs and of resources, and for the scientific training of specialists and technicians, we can have nothing but the highest approval. But this is only part of the solution. We also need individuals with broad sympathies, with idealism, with a social point of view. . . . We need individuals who are in a position to understand the social results that follow from their actions as individuals, as businessmen, trade-union members, and the results that follow from the action of government.

Consider the inequality of the distribution of income. It may be that inequality does not make people unhappy. Certainly the economist is not the most authoritative person to speak regarding this. It may be that inequality makes life happier, that it is needed as a driving force, that it adds zest. But, inductively, we know that the well-to-do, getting a large percent of the income, do a large percent of the saving. Is there not an economic problem quite unassociated with questions of justice. . . ? To argue that there is no problem because money saved is invested and used to put men to work, or that the nineteenth-century or pre-1929 experience shows that a desire to save leads to progress, is to fall back on personal abstract deduction of a most inadequate type and to present a pseudo-inductive argument that a scientific mind should reject immediately. There is nothing in the training of a businessman which equips him to understand such a problem. For no single firm is faced with the . . . economy as a whole. . . . The businessman must step beyond the limitations of his viewpoint and begin to make himself an economist. . . . The training for such a step is part of the reason for the teaching of economics in college. Beyond that is the fact that such economic problems exist and require exact, intensive study.

Does the utility of economics rest upon its ability to predict with accuracy future events in the business world? We do not expect a doctor to predict the state of one's health nine months from today. We do value somewhat a statement that, barring unforeseen developments, one's health may reasonably be predicted. But mostly we value a doctor because he can give advice to help cure specific troubles, if they can be·cured, and how to live to be healthy. It is upon the ability to give similar advice for the health of the economy that economists should be judged.

If we debate the issue on just those grounds, what should and can be said? It is felt by some, that economists have not given the right advice, otherwise we would not still be in partial depression; that their advice conflicts, one saying one thing, one another; that it conflicts because economics is deductive, *a priori*; that it never can be otherwise because the forces to be studied are too many and too complicated. Conclusion: economics is useless.

Just as the economist does not feel so self-important as to think he caused the depression starting in 1929, so he knows that it is not he that has stopped recovery short of full recovery. Businessmen put men to work and expand output when they foresee profits. They would do so now if they expected it to be profitable. The economist has not taken away and hidden these profits. But in the face of the criticism that economists have not spoken with one clear, forceful voice as to what ought to be done, the economist should be and must be humble. Why are some economists uncertain? Why do some differ? Why are there "bad" economists? The economist should feel that situation more keenly than any outside critic, for it touches him more closely.

Part of this confusion comes from the seeming willingness of the public to accept as an economist anyone who speaks upon economic matters. One got tired in the early days of the New Deal of pointing out that most of the members of the "brain trust" were not economists and never had been. But the tendency to accept anyone speaking on economic matters as an economist remains.

Actually, economists agree much more than they disagree. Naturally their disagreements attract more attention, for these are the points that are debated. Although they agree substantially upon most of the phases and factors in the business cycle, they disagree . . . about some aspects of policy. As this problem — the restoring of profits to businessmen, of employment to workers, of income to the people — most interests the public, and rightly so, it is to be expected that disagreement among economists here should be most commented upon and most condemned.

Economic life constantly presents choice — choice of policy. It is present every time a municipality or governmental body considers a tax program; every time a regulatory body considers railroad or utility rates; every time a union considers wage or working-condition demands; every time a trade association considers price, output, new capacity, limitation of competitive methods. These decisions cannot be avoided. They will be made either on the . . . best possible economic advice, or they will be . . . made with the use of crude, abstract reasoning fallaciously supported by an inadequate display of facts.

If economics is to develop further, or save itself from deteriorating into loose, abstract reasoning and guesswork, it must be studied and taught in college. If there are to be economic specialists to satisfy the growing demand by government and industry, they must be trained just as any other specialist must be trained. But the question is much broader than this. Economics takes its place, and I think a very important place, on the curriculum for the nonspecialist as well as for the specialist.

There is as much mental training and mental discipline in the mastery of economic writing . . . as in any other college subject. The opinion that good economic writing is vague and loose could only be held by someone whose knowledge of economics is vague and loose. An error by the student in reasoning about economics, or an error in his knowledge of the facts that are relevant to the problem, is as much an error here as in any other field of knowledge and as clearly wrong. A student in economics would be astonished to be told that . . . in the grading of his paper there is no right or wrong, but only a matter of judgment.

Nor do these remarks conflict with the fact that in certain problems the student must learn to weigh and pass judgment upon the importance of, and emphasis to be given to, certain factors. Many problems in his life are going to call for just that ability — the ability to pass such judgments in as objective and unprejudiced a manner as possible — that too is part of the contribution economics makes to his education.

If we mean by culture, breadth of knowledge and understanding, . . . then surely economics stands at the forefront of cultural subjects. For it is a study of those institutions and forces that will be present in everyday living, that concern jobs, taxes, strikes, the unemployed, the self-made man, government regulation, the rich, the poor — those things we have with us always.

And these things need to be understood both with sympathy and objectivity. Objectivity, sympathy, a sense of social responsibility, and an awareness of the social implications of conduct are essential to the successful functioning of democracy. A college should develop the character and intellectual outlook of its students, should set a pattern of response that is as free from prejudice as possible, that emphasizes the social responsibility of the individual. There is no better training ground for this than the current economic problems that form the students' immediate environment.

Economic problems will be faced and, we hope, faced successfully by our graduates and their contemporaries. . . . The cure for cancer will come from doctors and the responsibility will rest mostly with medical science, but the cure for idle factories will come from the ordinary citizen. Decisions regarding economic policies will be taken by the individual, partly in his role in industry, partly in his role in government as voter. The economist can give advice, but the businessman, the union leader, the Congressman, the voter, will make the final decision. This puts much of the responsibility upon our colleges.

It should be clear that the economics I have been discussing is much more than the training received in a vocational business school. There is room for both in a college and to a considerable extent they overlap, but they are not the same thing though both may be called economics. The vocational course, as given in American colleges, deals primarily with the efficient and profitable management of a firm. The place of the firm in the economy as a whole, the effects of the firm's actions upon the economy as a whole, are to a large extent left outside the scope of the course. It is this which is the fundamental difference between the two types of courses, and it does not make one pragmatic, inductive, and factual — the other, theoretical and abstract. One is narrower in scope; the other broader, and the broader treatment calls for a different emphasis. One emphasizes, in some schools almost exclusively, the methods of running a firm that will bring profits. The other goes beyond the firm in much fuller fashion to study the general economic forces that cause the firm to act as it does, and the effects of its action upon business in general and the economy.

It is my opinion, if the choice must be made, economics is the more important training for a future businessman to have. Though professional courses may aid, . . . the future businessman obtains his training through practical experience and, while future advance can indeed be made particularly in the guidance and management of personnel and in employer-employee relationships (for which a course in labour is essential), it still remains true that in the field of the internal running of a business the American businessman's record is one of at least relative efficiency. It is in the broader aspects of the relationship of firm to industry, of firm to government, of firm to the general economy that the need for advance is most obvious; and the training for an understanding of these problems is either obtained in college or, for most men, not at all.

4. MODELS AS ECONOMIC TOOLS*

Federal Reserve Bank of Chicago

Presentation of the 1969 Nobel Prize in Economics — the first ever awarded in this field — to Ragnar Frisch and Jan Tinbergen emphasized the wide-spread use of large-scale mathematical models in current economic research. Frisch and Tinbergen were honoured for their pioneering efforts in this area of economics during the 1930s. Specifically, the award was made to the two economists "for having developed and applied dynamic models for the analysis of economic processes." Today, models based on the ideas of these and other men are popular tools of economic research, and the use of large-scale mathematical models continues to grow.

A model as a physical representation, such as a model airplane, is familiar to everyone. To be useful in research, however, a model must provide some representation of the interrelationships among measurable magnitudes. Thus, the model airplane is put in a windtunnel to exhibit the relationship between aspects of aircraft design and velocity with respect to aerodynamic per-formance. The researcher varies aircraft design and wind velocity to observe such measures as air flow turbulence and structural integrity.

Mathematical models are also useful research tools. Like a physical model, a mathematical model's usefulness depends on its ability to predict the change in some measurable magnitude that will occur with changes in some other measurable magnitude.

For economists, a model is usually a mathematical representation of an economic phenomenon. Models are old tools in economics — any demand curve is a representation of the interrelationship of price and quantity desired in a particular market. The type of model Frisch and Tinbergen pioneered is the multiequation representation of a relatively complex economic structure, such as the national economy.

Today there are models of national economies for a number of countries — both developed and developing. These models may involve anywhere from a half dozen to 200 or 300 equations. In general, an increase in the number of magnitudes the researcher wishes to examine increases the number of

*Reprinted from Federal Reserve Bank of Chicago, *Business Conditions*, November, 1970, pp. 9–15, by permission.

equations in the model. Agencies such as the Federal Reserve Board and the Council of Economic Advisers have developed models of the US economy. Others have been built by the Office of Business Economics of the US Department of Commerce, the Brookings Institution, and academic groups at MIT and the Universities of Michigan and Pennsylvania.

Building a Model

To demonstrate how an economic model works and how it may be used, a simplified model of the national economy is helpful. An economic model usually begins with a general conception of the relationships involved. A general conception of the national economy, for example, might be expressed by three relationships.

The first would state that consumption expenditures depend upon (are a function of) the level of income. The relationship may be written as $C=f(Y)$, where C stands for consumption expenditures and Y for current income. The expression $f(\ )$ simply denotes that some form of relationship exists. The second relationship would state that investment expenditures are a function of the change in income between this period and the last period. The equation here may be written as $I=g(Y_{-}Y_{-1})$, with I standing for investment expenditures, Y again for the current period's income, Y_{-1} for income last period, and $g(\ )$ for a functional relationship. A period may be any length of time for which one has data on the magnitudes. Usually, a period is a quarter, occasionally a year. The last relationship would be an identity and would simply state the requirement that, by definition, income must be equal to consumption expenditures plus investment expenditures plus government expenditures. Symbolically, $Y=C + I + G$, with G used for government expenditures.

This first step — that of postulating a set of relationships between the magnitudes (variables) the model builder wishes to explain and those variables that immediately affect them — involves some simplification. For example, the first relationship posits that the level of consumption expenditures in the national economy is determined solely by the level of income. This obviously ignores the effects of any causal influences other than income. But the advantages of simplification are evident in light of an alternative postulating that consumption expenditures depend upon all other economic magnitudes. This would be cumbersome and of little value in formulating the explanatory relationships that are the goal of all sciences.

The next step in developing a model is to give these general relationships more specific form. Often this is done in nonquantitative terms, as in the statement that consumption will be greater the higher the level of income. More precision is obtained, however, when the relationships are stated mathematically in an equation. There are a number of equations which can represent any general relationship. Following are examples of equations that satisfy the postulated relationship between consumption (C) and income (Y), namely that consumption is a function of income:

$$C=aY$$
$$C=b + dY$$
$$C=\frac{e}{Y}$$

The first equation states that consumption is some proportion or fraction (a) of income; the second equation that consumption is proportional to income plus some base level (b) of consumption; and the third that consumption is inversely related to income.

The choice of the particular equation form is at the discretion of the model builder. He may experiment with a number of different forms to determine which he feels best describes or fits the relationship, given the data available for the magnitudes involved.

Determining the exact values of the fixed numbers — the lower case letters in the example — for the general form of the equation is referred to as the estimation of the model. This is usually accomplished by the use of statistical techniques, such as regression analysis, which, given the general form of the equation, determine the numerical equation that provides the best explanation of the available data according to certain explicit criteria. When the fixed numbers in a mathematical model are determined by statistical techniques, the model is termed an econometric model.

Taken together, these equations form the model. A hypothetical model made up of the relationships described above might look like this:

$$C = 30. + .60Y$$
$$I = 140. + 1.2 \, (Y - Y_{-1})$$
$$Y = C + I + G$$

This is a model with three equations and four unknown economic variables (C standing for consumption expenditures, I for investment expenditures, G for government expenditures, and Y for income). The values of the numbers in the equations (i.e., 30., .60, 140., and 1.2) are called coefficients. Coefficients are fixed numbers that provide the best explanations of the relationships between the values of the variables in the equations. The first of the above equations, $C = 30. + .60Y$, expresses the relationship $C = f(Y)$ where the specific form of the functional relationship is the second of the three possibilites shown earlier, that is, $C = b + dY$, with b now replaced by the number 30., and d by the number .60.

Each of the equations represents a relationship among economic variables. When values have been determined for each economic variable in the model so that all the equations are satisfied simultaneously, it is said that a solution has been found. In obtaining a solution, each equation is used to determine the value of one economic variable. Thus, the values of as many variables as there are equations may be obtained mathematically from the set of equations that constitute the model.

The variables whose solution values are obtained from the model's equations are called endogenous variables. The total number of variables appearing in the model, however, is greater than the number of equations. Consequently the model maker must assign values to all nonendogenous variables before he can obtain values for the endogenous variables. Variables whose values are assigned by the model maker are called exogenous variables, and the number of these is equal to the number of variables in the model minus the number of equations in the model. The choice of which variables are to be the exogenous variables and which the endogenous variables depends on the purposes of the model user.

Once the values of the exogenous variables have been inserted in the model, values for the endogenous variables then may be obtained from the equations themselves. The process of obtaining various solutions as the model maker varies the assigned values of the exogenous variables is referred to as running simulations on the model.

Since there are three equations and four unknowns in our example, the user of this model must insert the value of one exogenous variable (along with the value of income in the previous period) before he can obtain the values of the three endogenous variables. The values obtained for the endogenous variables will be those values consistent with the level of the exogenous variable inserted into the model. In our example, if one wishes to know the effects of a certain level of government expenditures, then government expenditures will be the exogenous variable inserted. If one wishes to know what level of government expenditures is required to achieve a certain level of national income, then national income will be the exogenous variable inserted.

A model has many advantages for the economic researcher. A model provides a precise way of expressing a conception of economic phenomena. When the model has been given specific mathematical form, it presents the interrelationships among variables and it states what changes in which variables would be produced by a change in one or more other variables in the model.

A multiequation model is invaluable in handling problems dealing with such complex economic phenomena as the national economy. Policy-making agencies require knowledge of the simultaneous effects of various policies across a broad spectrum of economic variables. Constructing a multiequation model allows one to examine the interrelationships among such goals as national output, unemployment, the balance of payments, interest rates, and housing construction. A multiequation model also permits the inclusion of accounting requirements for solutions. For example, the third equation in the model reflects the accounting identity that expenditures on consumption, investment, and government purchases must sum to national income. In a very detailed conception of the economy, there may be many of these accounting requirements. Their inclusion in a mathematical model automatically ensures that all will be satisfied.

Putting it to the Test

After a model has been constructed, it is usually tested, and the test of any model is how well it predicts. The importance of the quality of a model's predictions to the economic researcher cannot be overemphasized. The credence the researcher places in the implications of a model for various hypothetical situations depends on his belief that the model represents the way the economy behaves. This belief depends, in the final analysis, on the accuracy with which the model reproduces economic phenomena.

Accuracy may be tested by the model's predictions for future values of endogenous variables. This type of prediction into the future is referred to as *ex-ante* prediction.

To use the model for *ex-ante* prediction, it is necessary that the exogenous variables for the next period be forecast. Thus, an *ex-ante* prediction may prove to be incorrect for two reasons: the model user may have incorrectly forecast the exogenous variables, or the model may not reflect the actual interrelationships in the economy. In a large model the number of exogenous variables may be very large (perhaps more than 100), so that many variables must be forecast before an *ex-ante* prediction can be made. Model builders usually try to limit the number of exogenous variables, which are both difficult to forecast and important to the solution. But even with the difficulties involved, a model allows a systematic approach to prediction. Various alternative levels of key exogenous variables may be assumed and the corresponding implications for each of these assumptions derived. For example, if predictions were made for four or five plausible levels of government expenditures in the next period, model users would be able to pick what each considered to be the most realistic estimate of government expenditures in that period and thereby observe the implications of the model, given that level of government expenditures.

A model may be used to predict more than a single time period into the future. This requires forecasting the exogenous variables for as many future periods as one wishes the model to predict. The solution for the first period in the future would provide the values the model predicts for the endogenous variables for this first period. The solution for the second period in the future would be obtained by using the forecast levels of exogenous variables for the second period. Values for endogenous variables (if the model's solution requires that past levels of endogenous variables be specified) would be obtained from solutions provided by the model for the previous period. In our example, this means that solution values for income would be used after the first period as the value of income the previous period. In this manner, a model may produce a sequence of solutions extending over a period of time. This process is called dynamic simulation.

"Predicting" the Past

The validity of models may be tested by reproducing economic events of the past as well as by predicting the future. These "predictions of the past," called *ex-post* predictions, are much more important to economic researchers as guides to a model's accuracy than predictions of the future. As noted earlier, *ex-ante* predictions are subject to error from two sources; mistakes or "misspecifications" made in building the model itself, and errors made in forecasting the exogenous variables. When a model is used to represent the past behaviour of the economy, the values of the exogenous variables are known. All effects of forecast errors are eliminated. The model's accuracy — or lack of it — is tested directly. Any errors in "prediction" are attributable to the model alone.

There are other important reasons why economists test how well a model "predicts" the past. The investigator is able to evaluate a model's *ex-ante* predictions only with the slow unfolding of events. In a year's time, the investigator would obtain only one new observation if the period in the model were a year, and only four new observations if the period were a quarter. In the study of a subject such as the national economy, the economist is not able to run experiments at will. It is imperative, therefore, that in testing the validity of the model he bring to bear all his knowledge of broad relationships between economic variables based on past observation. As an example, most present day economists believe that, other things being equal, unemployment rises as output falls, and that interest rates are higher in extended periods of peak output than in extended periods of low output. A model whose predictions violated these relationships would be viewed sceptically by most economists. *Ex-post* simulations allow researchers to test a model and its underlying theory against past data, or interrelationships among various economic magnitudes based on past observation.

The accuracy of the *ex-post* predictions of a model over the past period whose data were used to specify the exact form of the model may not necessarily be indicative of the model's ability to predict. Since the period used for testing is the same as that used to estimate general relationships, the model's performance would be expected to be better over that period than over other periods. Thus, the performance of the model over this "fitting" period may be more a reflection of the ingenuity and perseverance of the investigator than the intrinsic value of the theory underlying the model. Also, a model's accuracy may be affected by changes that occurred in the periods outside the "fitting" period. For example, if the equation determining investment was fitted over a period where the investment tax credit was one rate and then used for predictions in a period when the tax credit was a different rate, it may be that the relationship between investment (**I**) and income (**Y**) is substantially different for the two periods.

It should be emphasized that the building of a model need not predispose an investigator toward any particular theory. Different models may be constructed embodying widely different conceptions of behaviour for the same phenomena. The general relationships that the model builder posits and the specific forms he chooses for these relationships are critically important in determining the final model. If a model predicts poorly — assuming, of course, that it is based on accurate data and correct methods of estimation — the error lies with the theory on which the model is based — or at least the specific form of the theory that the investigator has embodied in the model.

Real World Applications

The application of a model to real world problems and decisions involves a subjective decision by the potential model user. Much depends on the regard that the user has for the accuracy of the interrelationships between variables embodied in the model and the accuracy of the alternative methods available in predicting what he wishes to forecast. If a model that initially appeared to be based on theory inconsistent with prior beliefs nevertheless predicted well (i.e., better than the alternatives) time after time, those previously held beliefs, or at least those inconsistent with the model, would come under serious scrutiny.

A mathematical model is also useful for drawing out the implications of hypothetical situations that may never have existed. For example, different hypothetical past levels of exogenous variables may be entered into the model and the results compared with each other, or with the results when actual levels of past exogenous variables are used. This type of investigation is useful in establishing which exogenous variables have been major determinants of economic movements and which have played only ancillary roles.

In addition, a model may be used to draw out policy prescriptions. Suppose an agency has discretionary control over the level of some economic variable (the policy variable) and has determined the path that it wishes another economic variable (the target variable) to follow in the future. By inserting the desired levels of the target variable into the model as one of the exogenous variables, the solutions would give the levels of the policy variable consistent with the desired levels of the target variable. The levels of government expenditures necessary to achieve a desired path for national income may be determined in this way. An extension of such model use to examine policy rules also is possible, as in running simulations in which government expenditures are made to grow at a certain annual rate. These results could be compared with the results of other policy rules, or the results given by the actual level of government expenditures in *ex-post* simulations. The information from this type of use of the model would be particularly valuable for an agency able to control any of the variables.

Room to Grow

The advantages of models as tools for the efficient investigation of complex economic phenomena are clear. The reason for the greatly expanded use of models in recent years, however, lies not with the advantages of models as economic tools, which have long been evident, but rather with recent developments that have rendered the use of large models practical.

A prerequisite for the use of very large-scale models has been the availability of adequate data. A model made up of 100 equations may require for its operation 200 or more data series, and an even greater number of data series for use in construction of the equations. Data of this type on a quarterly basis have been greatly expanded in the postwar years. The development of this data base — in quality, sophistication, and detail — has been the result of continuing improvements in statistical collection.

More recently, there has been a dramatic breakthrough underlying the use of mathematical models. This has been the development and refinement of electronic computers. The computer not only can perform a great number of computations in a very short time, but it does so with great accuracy, an important consideration when so many computations are interrelated.

The estimation of a mathematical model involves not only the exact specification of the particular form of each equation but often a great deal of experimentation with various forms for each relationship. Without a computer, experimentation with alternative forms of the relationship would be sharply curtailed, and the specification of the particular form would be vastly more expensive in terms of resources consumed.

Depending upon the form in which a model is estimated, its solution may be obtained either by analytical methods that give the exact solution or by sequential approximations that produce a solution at some predetermined level of accuracy. If the model is of even relatively moderate size, either of these methods involves extensive computational work which makes access to a computer a necessity in order to obtain solutions.

Future growth in the use of economic models will be influenced primarily by developments in the analytical tools used to construct and utilize the models. New developments in computers promise to play an important role in the expanding use of models to analyse economic phenomena.

B. ECONOMIC THEORY AND ECONOMIC POLICY

Economic theory is "positive" or "nonnormative." It tells us what was and what is, and it may cast some light on what will be. But it cannot tell us, *by itself*, what *ought* to be. Nevertheless, economic theory, or economic analysis as it is often called, is an essential tool for public policy. Economists always have been, and must be, profoundly concerned with contemporary economic issues. How can economic theory aid in public policy decisions if it cannot prescribe what should be done? To answer this we must recognize that a public policy problem ordinarily raises two types of questions. First, what will be the consequences of the proposed policy? This is a question of facts and the relationships between them, hypothetical or otherwise, for which the economist, as social scientist, may offer expert opinions. Secondly, given the results, are the effects of the policy good or bad, desirable or undersirable? This is a matter of subjective judgment for which the economist, as scientist, can offer no unequivocal answer.

If the two questions could be kept distinct, few difficulties would arise. Reasonable and intelligent men can usually agree on matters of fact and principle, but the same men are likely to differ widely as to what is good or bad or as to what policy the nation should follow in a particular situation. Actually, what frequently happens is that ethical judgments are concealed rather than revealed. It is largely for this reason that competent economists may often differ among themselves.

Of course to argue that it is important to keep in mind the distinction between economic analysis and economic policy making is most emphatically not to bar the economist as a scientist from reaching ethical judgments or from seeking the means of social improvement. Indeed, economics would be considered a most barren subject if it never led to any gains in terms of social welfare. The point is simply this: economic analysis requires no ethical judgments; in dealing with policy it is difficult to escape them. Since value judgments cannot — and should not — be banned, they must be properly labelled. All that the scientific study of economics requires is a careful distinction between objective knowledge and value judgments.

In actual practice, economists have been very much concerned with matters of economic policy. Economics is much too serious a thing to be left to amateurs. Be that as it may, Reading 5 concludes that the influence of economic theory upon economic policy has been relatively slight. Conversely, other selections in this book contend that the ideas of economists have had a vast and increasing influence on public affairs. The popular notions that "economists never agree on anything" or that "if economists of this world were laid end to end they wouldn't reach a conclusion" (G.B. Shaw) are very far from the truth. In Reading 6, a leading US economist explains why economists disagree.

5. RELATIONS BETWEEN ECONOMIC THEORY AND ECONOMIC POLICY*

Clair Wilcox

How has economic theory affected public policy? Such is the assignment. To fulfill it would require a lifetime of research, the results set forth in several volumes. Something less than that will be attempted here.

At the outset we must dismiss the view that economics cannot concern itself with policy. Policy, it has been said, depends upon value judgments and value judgments are unscientific. The economist can tell the policy maker how best to get wherever he wants to go. But he cannot comment on the destination, be it paradise or perdition.

Economists, in the field of microeconomics, once felt that they had found a scientific means of judging policy. Action could be appraised by its effect on welfare; welfare could be measured by utility. Policy could be commended if it increased utility, condemned if it reduced utility. But the value of maximum utility had not been scientifically established; it had simply been assumed.

Utilities were found, in time, to be incommensurable. The economics of welfare lost its scientific tool. Employing new devices, the economist was again enabled to judge efficiency in allocation. But he was powerless, without indulging in value judgments, to appraise equity in distribution. And so it was argued that economics should ignore the ends of policy and confine itself to the means.

With the development of macroeconomics, however, the economist had been freed of his dependence on the utility calculus. Now he could appraise action by its effect upon employment. Policy that added to employment could be commended, policy that subtracted from employment condemned. Here, again, the economic scientist was in business. Making no value judgments, he stood on solid ground. But did he? The value of full employment had not been scientifically established; it had been taken for granted.

Value judgments, in fact, are not to be avoided. They govern the choice of

*Reprinted from Clair Wilcox, "Relations Between Economic Theory and Economic Policy," *American Economic Review*, May, 1960. pp. 27—35, by permission of the publisher and the author's wife.

Dr. Wilcox was Professor of Political Economy at Swarthmore College, Pennsylvania, from 1927 to 1968. He died on December 31, 1970.

problems for study. They provide the standards by which action is appraised. The best that can be done is to make them explicit. The requirement of objectivity will thus be satisfied.

Rightly or wrongly, economists have always dealt with policy. From Adam Smith to J.M. Keynes, each of the masters has addressed himself to the issues of his time. Political economy has been as much political as economic. Today, the profession continues faithful to its tradition. Economists, in books and articles and letters to the editor, tirelessly urge this policy or that. Economists draft campaign documents and give advice to pressure groups. Whole platoons of economists are paraded before committees of Congress. Economists advise the White House, the Treasury, and the central bank. They testify in trials before the courts. They arbitrate labour disputes, participate in negotiations with foreign governments, advise international organizations, shape programs for the development of countries all around the globe. Last — and we trust not least — they instruct the youth. With what effect?

Politicians, in their recurring effort to save the nation by exterminating wrong thinkers and eradicating wrong thoughts, have paid economists the compliment of assuming that their teachings strongly influence the course of events. Scholars have sometimes taken a similar view. The ideas of economists, wrote Keynes on the last page of the *General Theory*, "are more powerful than is commonly understood. Indeed the world is ruled by little else. Practical men, who believe themselves to be quite exempt from any intellectual influences, are usually the slaves of some defunct economist. Madmen in authority, who hear voices in the air, are distilling their frenzy from some academic scribbler of a few years back." The contribution of the great economists, says Robert L. Heilbroner in his preface to the *Worldly Philosophers*, "was more decisive for history than many acts of statesmen who basked in brighter glory, often more profoundly disturbing than the shuttling of armies back and forth across frontiers, more powerful for good and bad than the edicts of kings and legislatures. . . . They left in their train shattered empires and exploded continents, they buttressed and undermined political regimes, they set class against class and even nation against nation — not because they plotted mischief, but because of the extraordinary power of their ideas."

Such appraisals, if they were taken to be true, might well inflate the economist's self-esteem. But they find scant support in an examination of the facts. Whether one starts with theory and seeks its consequence in policy or starts with policy and seeks its origin in theory, direct and clear causation is seldom to be found. By this test, at least, the role of the economist in history has been a modest one.

There is an outstanding case, to be sure, in which a number of governments insist that their policies are based upon the teachings of an economic theorist. The theorist, of course, is Karl Marx. But the policies of Communist countries, in fact, bear as little relation to the theories of Marx as do the policies of Christian countries to the ethics of Christ. For light on our problem, we turn from the mythology of communism to economic theory and public policy in the United States.

First, there are important areas of theory where little or no effect on policy is to be found. This is true, for instance, of the theory of distribution. The theory of wages has had but little influence on the provisions of minimum wage laws, the content of collective bargains, the decisions of arbitrators, or the principles adopted by wage stabilization authorities in time of war. The concept of interest is useful, to be sure, in determining investment policy, and the theory of interest finds an application in the field of monetary policy. But the theory of rent has done no more than bolster propaganda for the single tax, and the theory of profit is without perceptible effect. So, too, with the theory of population. In India and Japan, national policy reveals an awareness of demography. In the United States, however, the only population policies are those embodied in laws designed to hinder birth control at home, and in the government's refusal, just announced, to consider requests for aid in financing birth control abroad. And these are a testimony, it would seem, not to the teachings of the Rev. Thomas Robert Malthus, but to the political power of the Catholic Church.

Second, there are economic policies for which no origin is to be found in economic theory. The policy of conservation is the work of foresters, agronomists, and engineers; natural resources have seldom attracted the attention of economists. Free public education can easily be justified on economic grounds; the considerations that led to its adoption were social and political. Credit for the restriction of immigration must go not to economic theorists but to the American Federation of Labor. Social insurance is largely an achievement of economists, but not of economics. Its failure to cover sickness is due not to any difference in principle but to the political power of the American Medical Association. In the regulation of railroad rates, recognition is now given to elasticity of demand, but this is to be attributed, not to familiarity with economic theory, but to the competition of the trucks. In the regulation of public utility rates, the concept of elasticity is unknown. The price and rationing controls of World War II were fabricated by economists, but these were products of pure invention in which economic theory played but little part. Pay-as-you-go collection of the income tax is hailed by economists as an automatic stabilizer; it was adopted to facilitate administration. Lend-lease, the Marshall Plan, the extension of aid for mutual defence and for the development of underdeveloped countries — all of the programs of foreign aid had their origin in military and political necessity. The current demand for promotion of economic growth is a consequence, certainly, not of theory but of anxiety caused by the rapid growth of the Soviet Union.

Third, there are policies for which theory, though needed, is lacking, and policies whose proper implementation requires of theory a guidance that it does not give. Development and growth, it is agreed, depend on innovation; yet we have no theory of innovation, no way to determine what share of a nation's resources should be devoted to research. In fixing the size of its budget, government should have a means of determining the optimum level of public expenditures; in levying taxes, it should have a means of determining the limits beyond which incentives would be impaired; but economics affords no rules whereby these determinations may be made. To maintain stability, the stabilizers ought to know how the level of wages affects the volume of employment and whether rigidity of prices is prejudicial or conducive to stability; they ought to know how to achieve the optimum combination of stabilizers, how to ensure their proper timing and their proper size. All of these are matters on which theory sheds a feeble light. In maintaining competition, the enforcement agencies and the courts need to know how monopoly can be identified, products defined, markets measured, and the structure of markets appraised, how far efficiency and innovation depend on scale, what terms in a decree will make an industry competitive — all of them matters on which economists have been of little help.

Fourth, there are fields where policy cannot grow out of theory because the theorists do not agree. One line of action is indicated by the theorists who believe that a stable level of prices is consistent with growth, another by those who believe that the level must be permitted gradually to rise if growth is to occur; one line by the theorists who attribute inflation to excessive demand, another by those who attribute it to rising costs; one line by the theorists who hold that spending responds to changes in the rate of interest, another by those who hold that it does not; one line by the theorists who argue that taxes reduce demand, another by those who argue that they raise prices; one line by the theorists who think that unions can raise wages, another by those who think that they cannot.

Fifth, there are policies that defy the rules of economics. It is possible to mention but a few: the mandatory support of agricultural prices at arbitrary percentages of fifty-year-old parity, the maintenance of resale prices for branded goods, the persisting limitation of urban rents, the tying of loans to other governments, the imposition of quotas on imports of sugar and petroleum, the payment of excessive prices for silver to be dug up in the West and reburied in the East, the irrigation of land at public expense to add to the surplus that the government will buy. In these and other instances, in the United States, the allocation of resources is distorted at the behest of pressure groups. The underdeveloped countries, too, though the recipients, in recent years, of high-powered instruction in the art of rational economic calculation, still foolishly persist in allocating their resources with no more rationality than do the countries whence advice has come.

There are a few cases — a very few — in which it seems that policy can be traced almost directly to the views of economic theorists. Here, we may include: (1) the attempt made by the New Deal in its early days, for better or for worse, to induce recovery by manipulating the value of money, (2) the initiation of the reciprocal trade agreements program and its expansion under the General Agreement on Tariffs and Trade, (3) the emphasis placed on grants rather than loans in the lend-lease program and in postwar foreign aid, (4) the construction of a new system of international exchanges under the International Monetary Fund, (5) the adoption of the Employment Act of 1946 and the creation of the Council of Economic Advisers, and (6) the accord reached by the Treasury and the Federal Reserve authorities in 1951. Diligent research might well disclose another case or two.

In almost every instance where economic theory and public policy coincide, however, one finds a combination of theoretical views and political pressures. At times, the theory leads the pressure. At times, the two go hand in hand. At times, the theory follows the pressure and gives it rational support. In some cases, policy acknowledges a debt to theory but pays it only in part. In others, policy remains the same when theory has changed. In still others, policy changes when theory has remained the same. Always it is difficult to determine what is cause and what effect.

The policy of maintaining competition, embodied in the Sherman Act, was clearly consistent with classical theory which held that the optimum allocation of resources was to be effected through competitive markets. But enactment of the law was a concession to politically powerful groups who felt themselves to be at a disadvantage and demanded equality of opportunity. Interpretation of the antitrust laws in the basing point cases was derived from the analysis of delivered pricing made by Frank A. Fetter a quarter-century before. But the government's campaign against basing point systems originated in the demand of communities in the South and West for the removal of an artificial obstacle to their development. During the years when theory assumed that competition could be perfect, the antitrust laws were indifferently enforced. No sooner did theorists discover that competition was necessarily imperfect than enforcement took a new lease on life. When supported by theory, antitrust was feeble; when deprived of this support, it grew in strength.

The policy of free trade, in nineteenth-century Britain, found a solid basis in the theory of comparative advantage. But the repeal of the Corn Laws is to be attributed as much to the rise of industry and labour as to the teachings of Ricardo. Protectionism has had its theoretical defenders in the United States, but tariff policy from the Civil War to the Great Depression ran counter to generally accepted doctrine. In the thirties and the forties, under the trade agreements program, policy turned toward greater freedom. But in the fifties, though the authority to negotiate agreements was retained in form, it was rendered impotent in fact. Trade theory had not changed; political resistance had gained strength.

Progression in tax rates, when first adopted, was supported by the theory of marginal utility. Today, progression is retained though its psychological basis in marginal utility has long since been denied. Progression had its real foundation, clearly, not in economic theory, but in the popular sense of justice. This sense of justice now is served, of course, by keeping progression in form while political pressures are satisfied by opening escapes for which scant economic logic can be found.

Economists have recognized the necessity for direct controls to check inflation in time of war. Congress has voted the controls. But under pressure from agriculture, business, and labour, it has written provisions into the laws that have seriously handicapped their enforcement. Decontrol at the end of World War II was speeded, not by a belief that the general interest would be better served by freedom of markets, but by the demands of those who saw in spiralling prices an opportunity for quick profits.

Use of the powers of the central bank to stabilize the economy has been urged by economists since the early twenties. Yet the Federal Reserve Board moved tardily to restrain speculation in the twenties and to promote recovery in the thirties; it acquiesced in the inflation of the forties to facilitate financing by the Treasury. It was not until 1951 that the views of economic theorists were given recognition in the Treasury-Reserve accord. Today, economic opinion is virtually unanimous in opposing retention of the statutory ceiling on interest on long-term bonds, but congressmen, fearing a higher charge for loans to their constituents, refuse to change the law.

Unionization and collective bargaining were first accepted by public policy — and, indeed, endorsed by most economists — at a time when economic theory argued against monopolization of the labour supply. They were legitimatized by theory when economists embraced the view that labour markets cannot be competitive and when they came to hold that wage reduction is the wrong way to increase employment. Unions thus were granted respectability; they would have survived if it had been denied. Of late, the dangers of labour monopoly have been rediscovered by economists; the same discovery has been made by congressmen. Here, as elsewhere, it would be difficult to argue that theory was the chicken and policy the egg.

We take up last the case that first comes into mind. Keynes taught that government could counter depression by spending more and taxing less. The New Deal, at the same time, ran a deficit. It is widely believed that the relationship here was one of cause and effect. The New Dealers, it is said, embraced Keynesian theory and applied Keynesian policy. But the evidence does not support this view. Keynes, himself, was critical of the congeries of measures that was improvised in Roosevelt's early years. Roosevelt, on the other hand, was not impressed by Keynes. Nor were the brain trusters Keynesians. Had they been so, they would have bet more money on deficit spending and less on NRA. Until 1938, the deficits were unintentional. They first appeared, in fact, under Herbert Hoover, whom nobody has accused of being a Keynesian. They were increased by measures designed to give relief to the unemployed and to homeowners, farmers, and businessmen. They would have been incurred if Keynes had confined his writings to the theory of probability. In 1938, however, the lesson had been learned. As a consequence of the contraction of demand that followed the imposition of wage and payroll taxes, the use of deficits to stimulate employment was deliberately planned.

Today, economists differ in detail from Keynesian theory, and businessmen and politicians still denounce the policies proposed by Keynes as communistic. But Keynesian analysis, in its fundamentals, is generally accepted, and Keynesian policy is embraced by Republicans as well as Democrats. No administration that wants to stay in office will ever again permit the number of unemployed to rise above a moderate figure. No administration will seek to solve the problem of depression by cutting wages and prices and putting business through the wringer. Instead, government will spend more and tax less. This may be due to the fact that Keynes has permeated our thinking. It is also due to the fact that the consequence of each course of action has been learned through experience; that inflation is known to carry no political penalty, while deflation is known to spell political suicide.

The influence of theory on policy is difficult to weigh. Policy is a product of many causes: environmental factors, political pressures, the ideas in men's minds. The demands of the environment are obvious; the pressures of politics clamorous. Ideas take a subtler form. Though not consciously acknowledged, though even repudiated, they may still affect the processes of thought. Though not susceptible to measurement, their influence may nonetheless be real. There is power, certainly, in the ideas, now widely held, that government has the duty and the power to maintain employment, that wages are never to fall, that all the gains from productivity are to go to labour, that social welfare and national security can be measured by real income per capita, that growth can be measured by the rate at which this income may rise.

According to Keynes, however, the theory that is brought to bear on policy is usually that of an earlier day. The world is ruled by little else than the ideas of economists, but these ideas, unhappily, are likely to be out of date. Practical men are the slaves of an economist, but a defunct economist. Madmen in authority distil their frenzy from an academic scribbler, but from a scribbler of a few years back. Theory takes on power when it has lost relevance. But here, Lord Keynes accords to his profession something less than is its due.

The economist, at the very least, is constantly aiding policy makers in their task by equipping them with new and sharper tools of analysis. Through national income accounting and through projections of economic trends, he has enabled them to deal more effectively with problems of economic stability and growth. Through input-output analysis, he is showing them how to ensure consistency in planning the combination of resources. Through operations research, linear programming, and activity analysis, he is enabling them to select the one, among alternative combinations, where values can be maximized or costs minimized. By undertaking to perfect cost-benefit analysis, he seeks to provide them with a means of establishing priorities for public investment. By attempting to construct a theory of bargaining, he seeks to throw light on the problems of negotiation.

Better analysis, however, need not result in better policy. Government, under political pressure, may still follow a course that renders lower benefits at higher costs. But there will be a difference. By their very existence, careful analyses of alternatives will affect the choices that are made. They will make it easier for government to resist the demands of pressure groups. They will strengthen the hands of groups exerting counter pressures. They will cause unsound proposals to be modified and their terms improved. They will ensure that wrong decisions, where they must be made, are made in full awareness of their cost. Sound economic analysis may be disregarded; it is not to be ignored.

There is no reason to assume, however, that theory and policy need always go hand in hand. Though problems whose solution is attempted by the theorist are usually those requiring decisions as to policy, they need not always be so. In economics, as in physics, there should be room for pure research. The policy maker, on the other hand, will frequently face problems with which the theorist has never dealt. He will be forced to make decisions by the pressure of events. He cannot wait until the theorist catches up. All this is as it should be. We need not bemoan the fact that the theorist theorizes, that the policy maker makes policy.

Even where their problem is the same, the theorist may speak a language that the man of action does not understand. The higher his level of abstraction, the more elaborate his models, the more remote may seem his contact with reality. But here, interpretation may be all that is required. Theory, however recondite, may find an application in the sphere of policy.

Theory is doubtless more influential in some areas than in others. It may be decisive in fields where the issues presented for decision are technical in character and where conflicts of interest are not existent, not realized, or not organized, or where conflicting pressures are in balance. It may be effective where it is moving with the current, enjoying majority support. Theory will seldom be influential where it runs counter to a political interest that is clearly realized and effectively organized.

Philosophers of history have differed regarding the influence of ideas on the course of events. There is no agreement, certainly, that ideas are controlling. If this is true of ideas in general, it must be even more so of academic theories in particular. Here, theory in economics differs little from theory in other fields. Since the economist deals with matters where conflicts of interest are involved, it is probable that he exerts less influence than does the natural scientist. Since he deals with practical affairs, it is probable that he exerts more influence than does the theologian or the philosopher. One may also suggest that he does as much as the political scientist to affect the processes of politics, as much as the historian to determine the course of history. If his theories are less than decisive in shaping policy, the economist finds himself in a goodly company.

6. WHY ECONOMISTS DISAGREE*

Milton Friedman

Introduction

Let three economists gather and there are bound to be at least four opinions about desirable economic policy — so runs the standard cliché, naturally followed by: if doctors disagree, how can patients prescribe?

Like most clichés, these are half-truths. The appearance of disagreement among economists is grossly exaggerated. In talking with one another, economists naturally spend little time repeating what all accept. They discuss their disagreements. When they present their views in public, the same pressures that impel a businessman to differentiate his product from his competitors' impel an economist to present his views in a form that makes them appear distinctive and individual. Parrots are not much imitated — at least deliberately.

Even more important, economists who present their views to the public temper their strictly economic judgments with considerations of political acceptability and feasibility, and do so to very different degrees. A classical example was John Maynard Keynes' advocacy of a tariff for Britain in 1931. Qua economist, he favoured devaluation of the pound as the best remedy for Britain's economic ills. But he concluded that devaluation was not politically feasible. Hence he came out for a tariff as a way, albeit an unsatisfactory way, to achieve the equivalent of a concealed devaluation. Within six months of Keynes' advocacy of a tariff, Britain devalued. Keynes, of course, with his unusual flexibility, immediately reversed himself and no longer supported a tariff — but, as he notes in a footnote added subsequently when one of his pieces urging a tariff was reprinted, not all of those whom he had converted were equally adaptable.[1]

---

*Reprinted from Milton Friedman, *Dollars and Deficits*, Englewood Cliffs, New Jersey: Prentice-Hall, Inc., 1968, pp. 1—16, with permission of Prentice-Hall Inc.

Dr. Friedman is Professor of Economics at the University of Chicago, past president of the American Economics Association, and recipient of the John Bates Clark Medal in 1951.

[1] John Maynard Keynes, *Essays in Persuasion*, (New York, 1932), p. 286.

A current example — in an area not dealt with here — is the minimum wage rate. It would be hard to find a reputable economist — of whatever political persuasion — who does not agree that legal minimum wage rates increase unemployment among the unskilled. It would be almost as hard to find one who regards other consequences of legal minimum wage rates as sufficiently favourable to outweigh the adverse effects on employment. Yet most economists are deterred from advocating elimination of legal minimum wage rates because they recognize that this would be widely regarded as "reactionary" and "hard-hearted." They choose instead to remain silent on the issue.

Another example concerns the price of gold and of the dollar. Probably the great majority of economists who specialize in money and international trade favours abandoning any fixed price for gold and permitting greater flexibility in the price of the dollar (i.e. in exchange rates). Yet many an economist has hesitated to recommend such policies because he knew that officials in Washington were strongly opposed to them and even more to public discussion of them. Instead, he has proffered second-best solutions for our balance of payments problem.

This example illustrates also a different relation between economic and political considerations. The present arrangements for gold and exchange rates involve agreements among countries implemented partly by an international agency, the International Monetary Fund. The adoption of different arrangements would have implications for the political relations among countries. Some economists, who might favour a free price for gold and floating exchange rates if they considered only the economic effects of such a policy, believe that the political consequences would be adverse, and so adverse as to more than counterbalance the economic gains. As concerned citizens, they properly feel impelled in their public pronouncements to take into account all the effects of proposed changes in policy and not only the economic effects.

As some of these examples suggest, economists have not turned out to be good forecasters about what is politically feasible. That is one reason why I have been inclined myself to give little weight to political feasibility — in the sense of the prospect that any proposal will be quickly or readily enacted. (Of course, weight must be given to political feasibility in a very different sense, namely, how any measure would work once enacted — given the political system within which it operates.) I am a professional economist, an amateur political scientist. Is it reasonable — and in the public interest — for me to let my amateur political judgment override my professional economic judgment?

In any event, the tendency to mix economic with political judgments is a major reason why public expressions of opinion give an exaggerated impression of the disagreements among economists on economic matters proper.

By contrast with this appearance of disagreement, experience over many years has impressed me with a very different phenomenon. Time and again, I have attended discussion sessions among economists and noneconomists. Regardless of the topic, and regardless of how widely separated the reputed political positions of the professional economists present, the economists soon coalesce into a single group vis-à-vis the remaining participants. Their training gives them a common approach in attacking problems; the widely accepted common core of economic theory leads them rapidly to reach the same conclusions from common premises. It is the old story of the quarrelsome family ganging up on the outsiders.

But a half-truth is half true. Though much exaggerated, disagreement there is among economists on the causes and cures for our economic ills. No doubt I have not been immune to the temptation to differentiate my product. But even if full allowance is made for my sins in this respect, my views on desirable policy have not coincided and do not now coincide with the views of many other economists, though, in fairness both to myself and my professional colleagues, I must add that I have far more company now than I did when many of the items in my book, *Dollars and Deficits*, were first written — much less because of my persuasiveness than because of the persuasiveness of economic events.

How can there be such disagreements? How can it be that, after nearly two centuries of the scientific study of economics (which began seriously with Adam Smith's *Wealth of Nations* published in 1776), after numerous and elaborate studies of empirical evidence, after prolonged internal professional discussion, economists can disagree on such apparently simple matters as whether a tax increase will reduce inflationary pressure and, if so, by how much, whether a given monetary policy action will raise or lower interest rates, whether a higher or a lower price of gold would improve the balance of payments — let alone whether one or another of these measures should be adopted. And if economists do disagree on such questions, how can the citizen prescribe? Why should you give any special credence to my views in preference to the views of other reputable economists?

These are hard questions that admit of no easy answer — or at least none that I know of — and about which I have myself very mixed feelings. On one level, the task of the professional economist is surely first to persuade his fellow economists — and only when something of a professional consensus has been established, to tender advice to the public at large. If I cannot persuade my fellow economists, how can I have enough confidence in my nostrums to peddle them to the public? And how can I expect the public to accept mine rather than the other fellows'?

On another level, it is unwise to refrain from appealing to the public until a professional consensus emerges. A profession no less than a person develops accepted patterns of thought that are highly resistant to change.[2] This has its merits, but let there be no appeal outside the profession, and resistance to change will be carried too far. The history of science and of invention shows that, time and again, it is the maverick, the outsider, the person attacking vested intellectual or economic interests, who produces the new insight, the new invention, the fresh direction, the correction of long accepted error.

This argument is buttressed by the strictly practical consideration that the public must often choose — the sick patient cannot wait until full agreement has been reached among medical researchers about the nature, the cause, and the cure of his malady. Where there is a professional consensus, fine, but where there is not, better that the public know how wide is the range of considered opinions than that it be lulled by contrived unanimity among experts.

---

[2] For a fascinating example in another field, see Robert Ardrey, *African Genesis* (New York, Atheneum, 1961), which describes the conditioned reflex of the anthropology profession to the findings and theories of anthropologists, mostly from South Africa, that contradicted what were regarded as settled conclusions in the profession about the origin of man. I was particularly fascinated by the story because it so closely paralleled the fight in economics by some of us against entrenched Keynesianism.

The dilemma is real and admits of no simple solution. We shall have to muddle along, choosing our physicians and our economists as best we can, by relying on whatever indirect clues and leads establish our confidence in one opinion rather than another or whatever evidence of past success we can get to guide us for the future.

While I cannot therefore offer the reader any easy way to choose his economists, it may help him in making his choice if I indicate what seem to me the main sources of disagreement — real disagreement not expressed disagreement dominated by political considerations — among economists about the three areas of economic policy discussed in my book, *Dollars and Deficits*: inflation, monetary policy, and the balance of payments.

Disagreement about policy utimately arises from a difference of opinion about either the *consequences* of the policy proposed — a difference in scientific judgment — or the *desirability* of those consequences — a difference in value judgment.

I have long argued that policy differences among economists in the United States derive primarily from differences in scientific rather than in value judgments. This is particularly true for the issues discussed in my book. There is widespread agreement among economists on the desirability of relatively stable prices, high and stable levels of employment, and maximum freedom of international trade. This agreement is widely shared by the public at large for prices and employment but not for international trade. (This is one topic on which the technical body of economic analysis has produced a wide consensus among economists that differs from the naive bias toward "protection" in the body politic.) The agreement on these broad goals is greater than on the harder question of how much of each one to sacrifice if they prove incompatible — yet even here the main disagreement is on the scientific question of how much one goal can in fact be promoted by sacrificing another.

Differences in value judgments doubtless play a larger role for other economic policies — in particular, those connected more directly with the distribution of income. But even for such policies, much of the difference is scientific. I oppose, for example, our present highly graduated personal income tax not because I prefer inequality of income to equality but because I believe that our present tax is a fraud and a delusion which treats people in the same economic position differently, widens rather than narrows differences in income, and produces a great waste of human talent and ingenuity. And many economists who place equality of realized income far higher in their scale of values than I do agree with this evaluation.

Though I remain persuaded that differences in scientific judgment are far more important than differences in value judgment, a number of qualifications to this general proposition have increasingly impressed themselves on me — qualifications that arise mostly from the interaction between scientific and value judgments. Any scientific judgment necessarily involves elements of uncertainty. Economics deals with phenomena that are complex, varied, and interdependent. An economic change may affect hundreds of millions of people and numerous economic, political, and social phenomena. What happens in one place on the globe or in one segment of the economy may have its main effects not in that place or in that segment, but in very different ones. To take a clear and striking example: the perfecting of the cyanide process for extracting gold from low grade ore around 1890 had major effects on the gold industry in South Africa and on the whole development of South Africa — but it also produced twenty years of worldwide price inflation, and, among other far reaching effects, destroyed William Jennings Bryan as a serious contender for the presidency of the United States.[3]

A scholar's basic values undoubtedly affect the way he resolves the inevitable uncertainties in his scientific judgments when he comes to recommend policies — and it is proper that they should. A person like myself who regards freedom as the major objective in relations among individuals and who believes (itself a scientific not a value judgment) that the preservation of freedom requires limiting narrowly the role of government and placing primary reliance on private property, free markets, and voluntary arrangements — such a person will resolve his doubts about the precise effects of any measure in favour of policies relying on the market. By contrast, a person who regards welfare or security as the major objective in social relations and who believes (again a scientific not a value judgment) that this objective can best be attained by governmental measures controlling and regulating private activity — such a person will resolve his doubts in favour of policies relying on government. Each will place the burden of proof differently — one on the proponent of governmental intervention, the other, on the proponent of laissez faire.[4]

A second way that basic values enter into policy choices is through differences in time perspective. Given the same scientific judgments, the choice among policies will often depend on the importance attached to the short-term vs. the long-term consequences of the policies.

Interestingly, there tends to be a close connection between beliefs about the role of government and time perspective. The liberal in the original sense — the person who gives primacy to freedom and believes in limited government — tends to take the long view, to put major emphasis on the ultimate and permanent consequences of policies rather than on the immediate and possible transitory consequences. The modern liberal — the person who gives primacy to welfare and believes in greater governmental control — tends to take the short view, to put primary emphasis on the immediate effects of policy measures.

This connection is one of reciprocal cause and effect. The man who has a short time perspective will be impatient with the slow workings of voluntary arrangements in producing changes in institutions. He will want to achieve changes at once, which requires centralized authority that can override objections. Hence he will be disposed to favour a greater role for government. But conversely, the man who favours a greater role for government will thereby be disposed to have a shorter time perspective. Partly, he will be so disposed because centralized government can achieve changes of some kinds rapidly; hence he will feel that if the longer-term consequences are adverse, he — through the government — can introduce new measures that will counter them, that he can have his cake and eat it. Partly, he will have a short time perspective because the political process demands it. In the market, an entrepreneur can experiment with a new innovation without first persuading the public. He need only have confidence that after he has made

---

[3] Milton Friedman and Anna J. Schwartz, *Monetary History of the United States, 1867—1960* (Princeton University Press for the National Bureau of Economic Research, 1963), p. 8.
[4] See my *Capitalism and Freedom* (University of Chicago Press, 1962), esp. Ch. 1, for my own value position.

his innovation enough of the public will buy his product to make it pay. He can afford to wait until they do. Hence, he can have a long time perspective. In the political process, an entrepreneur must first get elected in order to be in a position to innovate. To get elected, he must persuade the public in advance. Hence he must look at immediate results that he can offer the public. He may not be able to take a very long time perspective and still hope to be in power.[5]

My own policy position has undoubtedly been affected by these inter-connections between value judgments and scientific judgments. Certainly, the monetary policy I have come to favour — a steady rate of growth in the quantity of money — is highly congenial to my preference for limited government and, where government is essential, for limiting government so far as possible by clearly specified rules rather than granting wide discretion to government officials. Certainly the policy I have long favoured for adjusting international financial transactions — a system of freely floating exchange rates determined in private markets without governmental inter-vention — fits in with my preference for the maximum use of the market and for the avoidance of government interference. And both of these, providing for institutional change and the avoidance of day-to-day government tinkering, reflect my tendency to take a long view rather than a short.

These connections are spelled out explicitly in several of the items in my book. Yet they explain only in part — and perhaps in minor part — the specific policy positions I have adopted. Many economists with whom I agree most fully about basic values — men like Ludwig von Mises, Jacques Rueff, Friedrich Hayek, Henry Simons, Lionel Robbins — do not agree with my policy positions in this area. They favour achieving automaticity and limitations on government by using a gold or other commodity standard and fixed exchange rates, or by an "independent" central bank, or by some alternative monetary rule, rather than by a steady growth in the quantity of money plus floating exchange rates. On the other side, many economists who would classify themselves as modern liberals — men like Harry Johnson, James Meade, and James Tobin — share my views about balance of payment policy though not about monetary policy.

To look at the matter from a different angle, no value judgments can explain why I have been led to the conclusion that is the central theme of the first part of this book — that inflation is primarily a monetary pheno-menon. There is nothing about that conclusion that is more congenial to my values than, for example, the view — held by many businessmen — that inflation is a result of strong labour unions and monopolistic producers, or the view — also widely held — that inflation is a result of government deficits. Indeed, in some ways these latter two explanations would be more congenial to my political and social values.

Again, no value judgment can explain why I regard the quantity of money rather than the rate of interest or "money market conditions" as the crucial variable for monetary policy. Or why I have been unable to find — so far — any more sensitive and satisfactory rule for monetary policy than a steady rate of growth. Or why I regard monetary policy as playing a more critical role than fiscal policy in promoting economic stability or producing economic instability.

---

[5] I am indebted for this point to a perceptive paper by W. Allen Wallis written for a "rational debate" under the auspices of the American Enterprise Institute for Public Policy Research. The paper will be published in a book containing the transcript of the debate.

And certainly, as already implied, my rejection of a gold standard as an appropriate mechanism under present conditions for imposing "discipline" on monetary and fiscal policy, and my advocacy of a free market price for both gold and the dollar cannot be explained by my value position.

So I am led to return to the proposition with which I started: the major reasons for differences of opinion among economists on inflation, monetary policy, and the balance of payments are not differences in values but differences in scientific judgments about both economic and noneconomic effects.

For these topics, differences in scientific judgments about economic effects centre primarily on the role of money in economic affairs.[6] This is an issue on which professional opinion has fluctuated widely. Before the Great Contraction of 1929-33, the dominant opinion attributed great importance to the quantity of money in determining the level of prices and the course of the business cycle. The Great Contraction produced a drastic change in this attitude. It was widely — though as I shall point out, erroneously — believed that monetary forces could explain neither the duration nor the intensity of that traumatic episode. Equally important — because you cannot beat a theory without a theory — Keynes, in his great work *The General Theory of Employment, Interest, and Money* (1936), offered an appealing alternative interpretation.

Said Keynes, the relation between nominal income and the quantity of money — what economists call the velocity of circulation of money — is highly unstable and undependable, particularly under conditions of unemployment. Under such conditions, he said, people are willing to vary the amount of money they hold within wide limits in response to small changes in rates of interest. Hence changes in the quantity of money would have little economic effect beyond producing small changes in interest rates. Alvin Hansen, and many of Keynes' other American followers, went further. Even if changes in the quantity of money did alter interest rates substantially, they said, the changes in the rate of interest in turn would have little effect on spending. Interest rates, they claimed, are a minor factor in determining how much businessmen want to invest in additional capital, and a negligible factor in determining what fraction of their income consumers want to spend.

What matters, said Keynes and his disciples, is not velocity — that is a will-o'-the-wisp — but the relation between investment and government spending, on the one hand, and income, on the other. People have a highly stable "propensity to consume," they contended, so that the amount they spend on consumption and the amount they save depends directly and dependably on the size of their incomes. If the amount that the public wants to save out of an income corresponding to full employment is greater than the amount that businessmen want to invest plus the amount that government is willing to spend in excess of its tax receipts, there will be a conflict that can only be resolved by a lower level of income in order to reduce

_____

[6] The next few pages draw on "The Role of Monetary Policy," *American Economic Review* (March, 1968), esp. pp. 1–3. Compare also "Postwar Trends in Monetary Theory and Policy," *National Banking Review* (September, 1964), pp. 1–9; and "The Monetary Theory and Policy of Henry Simons," *Journal of Law and Economics* (October, 1967), pp. 1–13. All three essays are reprinted in my *The Optimum Quantity of Money and other Essays* (Aldine Publishing Company, 1968).

saving to the amount that can be "absorbed" by "offsets to saving" (investment and government spending in excess of taxes, to speak loosely). This lower income will put downward pressure on prices but, in the modern world, this will show up mostly in output and employment. In any event, they argued, price declines would do little good, because they lower both costs and income.

On this view, the Great Contraction — and similar if milder episodes — reflected a collapse of investment spending, or a shortage of investment opportunities, or an excess of thriftiness on the part of the public. Monetary policy could do nothing to counter such a decline. Expanding the quantity of money would simply lead people to substitute money for other securities in their portfolios without any significant effect on spending. However, there was available an alternative — fiscal policy. Government spending could make up for insufficient private investment. Tax reduction could undermine stubborn thriftiness.

These views came to be widely accepted in the economics profession. For some decades, monetary policy was believed by all but a few reactionary souls to have been rendered obsolete. Money did not matter. What mattered was fiscal policy — government spending and taxing. That was the key instrument for controlling economic fluctuations, for achieving full employment, stable prices, and balance of payments equilibrium.

There is always a long lag before a change of opinion among the leaders of any profession is transmitted to the bulk of the profession. And there is an even longer lag before it is transmitted to public opinion in general. Only now is the Keynesian emphasis on fiscal policy becoming "conventional wisdom," to the intelligent layman; until only a few years ago, the elementary economics textbooks taught essentially the doctrine that I have just outlined, in about as stark and unqualified a form.

Yet the vanguard of professional opinion started to shift away from this unvarnished Keynesian position nearly two decades ago, and by now has swung very far indeed. Already by 1953, in a lecture I gave in Sweden, I was able to record the beginnings of a revival of belief in monetary policy.

Early postwar experience provided the immediate stimulus for a reaction away from the view that money doesn't matter. Many countries adopted "cheap money" policies under the influence of Keynesian ideas. Every country that did so was forced sooner or later to give up the pretence that it could indefinitely keep "the" rate of interest at a low level. In the United States, the public dénouement came with the Federal Reserve Treasury Accord in 1951. Inflation, stimulated by cheap money policies, not the widely heralded postwar depression, turned out to be the order of the day.

The revival of belief in the role of money and in monetary policy was strongly fostered also by developments in economic theory that pointed out a channel — namely, changes in wealth — whereby changes in the quantity of money can affect aggregate demand even if they do not alter interest rates. These developments undermined Keynes' key theoretical proposition, namely, that even in a world of flexible prices, a position of full employment might not exist. Henceforth, unemployment had again to be explained by rigidities or imperfections, not as the natural outcome of a fully operative process.

More important than any of these developments for my own personal views — perhaps also for the profession — was a reexamination of the evidence for the Great Contraction of 1929-33. Keynes and most other economists of the time believed that the Great Contraction in the U S from

1929 to 1933 occurred despite aggressive expansionary policies by the monetary authorities. Naturally, the monetary authorities proclaimed at the time that they were doing everything possible to stem the depression, that they were doing their best but that forces beyond their control meant that their best was not good enough. And many economists, Henry Simons and J.M. Keynes among them, accepted this apologia, at least in large part. It was this evidence, more than anything else, I believe, that led them to conclude that the Depression could not be explained in monetary terms. After all, Keynes himself had not only shared but helped develop and spread the earlier views that the quantity of money plays a critical role in inflation and economic fluctuations.[7] And it was the apparent impossibility of explaining the Great Contraction in monetary terms that, more than anything else, made the economics profession so receptive to Keynes' message.

Recent studies have demonstrated that the facts were very different from what they appeared to be to so many at the time.[8] The US monetary authorities followed highly deflationary policies, not expansionary ones. The quantity of money in the US fell by one-third in the course of the contraction. And it fell not because there were no willing borrowers. It fell because the Federal Reserve System forced or permitted a sharp reduction in the monetary base, because it failed to exercise the responsibilities assigned to it in the Federal Reserve Act to provide liquidity to the banking system. The Great Contraction is tragic testimony to the power of money — not as Keynes and so many of his contemporaries believed, evidence of its unimportance.

Facts are stubborn things. Sooner or later, they must be accommodated to. Had the facts for 1929-33 — and for other episodes — been as Keynes apparently assumed them to have been, I could not hold the views I do about the role of money. Had Keynes recognized that the facts were what they were, he would have had to modify his views.

But theories are stubborn things too. Nothing is harder than for men to face facts that threaten to undermine strongly held beliefs, to change views arrived at over a long period. And there are no such things as unambiguous facts. They are always subject to more than one interpretation. So it has been a slow process for the reevaluation of the monetary experience to alter received opinion.

This process has been hastened by another body of facts — the lack of success of the Keynesian approach in predicting the short-term course of the economy. The ratio of investment-type spending to income has proved far less stable and predictable than Keynes and his disciples thought that it would be. Some years ago, David Meiselman and I made extensive tests of the relative stability of the ratio (or its reciprocal, the Keynesian multiplier) and the velocity of circulation of money.[9] We concluded that velocity was considerably stabler than the Keynesian multiplier: indeed, that most of the evidence was consistent with the view that the multiplier is useless for predictive purposes except as a disguised reflection of monetary change. This paper produced a barrage of criticisms from other economists followed by

---

[7] Particularly in *Monetary Reform* (New York: Harcourt, Brace and Co., 1924).

[8] See Friedman and Schwartz, *op. cit.* Ch. 7.

[9] "The Relative Stability of Monetary Velocity and the Investment Multiplier in the United States, 1897-1958," in *Stabilization Policies,* Committee on Money and Credit (Englewood Cliffs, New Jersey: Prentice-Hall, 1963).

rejoinders by us, and re-rejoinders by them. The upshot, however, was a far cry from the original Keynesian, "money does not matter," position. Our critics all granted that the quantity of money played an important role in determining short-term fluctuations in income. But they interpreted the evidence as showing that the multiplier process also played an important role and berated us for overstating our case.

It was this experience that led me to tell a reporter for *Time* Magazine that "in one sense, we are all Keynesians now; in another, no one is a Keynesian any longer." We all use the Keynesian language and apparatus; none of us any longer accepts the initial Keynesian conclusions. (Unfortunately, *Time* only quoted the phrase "We are all Keynesians now" and thus gave a highly misleading impression of my opinion.)

Recent experience has produced another striking bit of evidence on the relative importance of monetary and fiscal forces that has had its impact on opinion. In 1966, there was a sharp reduction in the rate of monetary growth. At the same time, fiscal policy became decidedly more expansionary; the high employment budget showed a deficit — a rapidly growing deficit. The monetary change was deflationary, the fiscal change inflationary. The result — some six to nine months after the monetary change — was a slowdown in the economy in the first six months of 1967 — succeeded by an upturn some six months after a shift to an expansionary monetary policy. Monetary effects clearly dominated fiscal effects.

The cumulative effect of this evidence has produced such a change in professional opinion that I felt impelled in my 1967 presidential address to the American Economic Association, to warn that "the pendulum may well have swung too far, that . . . we are in danger of assigning to monetary policy a larger role than it can perform, in danger of asking it to accomplish tasks that it cannot achieve, and, as a result, in danger of preventing it from making the contribution that it is capable of making."[10]

The true test of a scientific theory — of a set of propositions about a class of observable phenomena — is whether it works, whether it correctly predicts the consequences of changes in conditions. But this is not an easy test to apply in any field and certainly not in economics. Controlled experiments permitting the near isolation of one or a few forces are virtually impossible. We must test our propositions by observing uncontrolled experience that involves a large number of people, numerous economic variables, frequent changes in other circumstances, and, at that, is imperfectly recorded. The interpretation of the experience is further complicated because the experience affects directly many of the observers, often giving them reasons, irrelevant from a scientific point of view, to prefer one rather than another interpretation of the complex and ever changing course of events.

Under these circumstances, little wonder that economists often disagree. The remarkable thing is rather the wide area of agreement, the common body of knowledge about how the economic system works.

---

[10] "The Role of Monetary Policy," *op. cit.*, p. 5.

C. ECONOMIC TEACHING AND WRITING

Economics is an interesting subject for most students for it deals with the constant struggle to "make ends meet." Yet many of those taking their first economics course find it "too theoretical," "impractical," "abstract," or in the updated version of the same complaint, "not relevant to the central issues of our times."

Reading 7 argues that teaching the economic principles course is the most important job an economist can do. It also describes the essential requirement for this course: "It must bear the bench mark of a concerned, deeply involved teacher, teaching at his level best." In addition, this selection contains an explicit plea for not overloading the introductory syllabus, nor allowing the tools of economic analysis to upstage the substance of the course. It concludes that, unless economists demonstrate that their discipline speaks to the condition of today, bright young students will desert economics in favour of any subject which promises to be more relevant.

Would economics serve the public more effectively if economists had more respect for words and their meanings? Reading 8 thinks so, and it indicates some of the pitfalls that should be avoided if an economist is to make his writing reasonably comprehensible. It is hoped that this selection will help make an end to clumsy or obscure writing in economics. Amen.

7. A RETROSPECTIVE LOOK AT UNDERGRADUATE ECONOMICS*

Ben W. Lewis

This occasion is something over which a man might well drool throughout a whole lifetime of anticipation. I am here by confirmed request to ramble through and reminisce about a lifetime; and, from the safe, secure vantage point of years of yesterdays, to recite to today's economists, for their benefit and redemption, their sins and shortcomings. "Tell us," you plead, "what it was like when the world and you were young. But more, tell us of our multiple re(trans)gressions and of what we ought to do that we are leaving undone. How have we strayed? How are we betraying our heritage?" This assignment, my friends, as you will someday appreciate if, like me, you are just luckier than hell, is the jackpot at the end of the rainbow.

True, there is a catch. I am invited to bask in my task — but only for twenty minutes. How much rich reminiscence and invaluable advice can be given wing in twenty minutes? This is not only to snatch back the Grail, it robs me of 60 percent of my fifty-minute birthright (quantitatively speaking). When the gavel strikes, my stage is to become a pumpkin, and I must be on my way wearing both slippers.

I am determined, however, to transmute this blight to bloom. If I am bereft of time, I am also relieved of obligation. No one can rightfully expect the accumulated insight of half a century to be both recounted and systematically supported in twenty minutes. I opt for recounting — stripped down. I shall recount and pronounce, and I renounce any obligation to defend my pronouncements. I shall offer no proof, no formulas, no hesitant, quavering hypotheses, and no ingratiating qualifications. Nothing but pronouncements in italics — sheer wisdom, topless truth! Let me add that nothing I shall say is confidential or restricted.

One moment while I lower the backdrop — the years I knew in my slender youth, the 1920s, the years of normalcy, the decade which ended in the Great Depression, the years 15—5BK.

---

*Reprinted from Ben W. Lewis, "A Retrospective Look at Undergraduate Economics," *American Economic Review,* May, 1970, pp. 370—78, by permission of the editor and author.
Dr. Lewis was Professor of Economics at Oberlin College, Kansas, from 1925 to 1967. He has been with the Ford Foundation since 1967.

Economics in the 1920s! The economy of which we taught was neat, clean-shaven, well-mannered, virile, self-disciplined, and rightfully confident. Its only markets were perfect markets (certainly perfect for us teachers), populated by single-minded, uncomplicated economic men, compelled automatically and unerringly by irresistible urges to economic choices which were demonstrably correct for each and for all — in the long run. Undisturbed by aphorisms yet unuttered, we lived and revelled "in the long run." *Ceteris paribus*, in substantial doses, was our anodyne and constant comfort.

Competition was razor-edged and all-pervasive — pure in mind and strong in body. We recognized only one degree of monopoly, and this we treated as an exception to be brushed off into a footnote located, in those golden days, at the bottom of the page, where footnotes belong.

Our forms of communication were, of course primitive. The language of our discourse was written and spoken English. We used words — the kinds of sounds I am uttering now — extended into full sentences, in professional conversation and address; and words and sentences were to be found in abundance in our textbooks and journals. Their use was not surreptitious; it was open and unashamed, calling neither for explanation nor apology. The few graphs we employed were gentle and unobtrusive and had as their purpose to explain and illuminate the text — by today's practice, of course, an amusing transposition of horse and carriage. Economic models were unheard of; any models in which we may have had an interest were not permitted in the classroom.

Ours was an economy of principles, law, and order. The "law of self-interest" and the "law of supply and demand" governed our microconcerns, and our macroconcerns were few and slight. Say's law insured us against anything more troublesome than exceptional, transitional unemployment, and the Salvation Army was in the wings to alleviate any undeserved individual hardship. The role of taxes was to raise public revenues required to protect us against disorder and aggression; the role of money was to serve as a medium of exchange; the money was kept in order by Gresham's law. No one dreamed of questioning the constitutionality of our laws, and their enforcement was not a problem; they were self-enforcing.

The 1920s went out with a resounding thud. The Great Depression was a shaker. It shattered both the real world and our world. It had its redeeming features: it increased enrolments in economics courses and it produced the first mass demand for college economists in business and government. Moonlighting was prestigious, not routine. Today's economists will never know how much their discipline owes to the New Deal for requiring dozens of their forebears, propelled into operational situations, to face up, "yes" or "no" to policy issues which they had been accustomed, at most, only to mull.

The Depression opened the door to Keynes — another shaker, and a real mover. But, no one thought to close and bolt the door, and (I have steeled myself not to say "unfortunately") through the open portal came a couple of mathematicians. They stayed to dinner. They, too, were movers — they moved in. They multiplied (what else?); order appeared again — but this time it was numerical order; my old world was gone; economics began its frantic scrambling for recognition as an exact science. Economics without mathematics was no longer economics. The body of texts and tracts took on the appearance of appendices — ruptured.

I must make myself believe that my world was well lost. I cannot but admire an array of elegant skills, first joined to and then engulfing economics, that can measure the immeasurable, quantify that which cannot be quantified, replace dull words and vague discussions with fascinating symbols, strange devices, and instant answers to unanswerable problems — which knows no error, only deviations — and even these to be scooped up and run through again and again until, exhausted, they become absorbed.

I must make myself believe in mathematical economics, even though I will never understand it. It has made a real home for itself within the spacious reaches of our discipline — a towering, imposing, and ingeniously functional home with all of the charm of an oversize filing cabinet. But, brooding in my tiny, windowless room in the basement, I could wish that the structure didn't crowd the property line quite so closely on all four sides.

You will have gathered that I am less than completely charmed by today's economics, and that I indulge myself in an occasional flash of doubt about some of its manifestations. At my age, my attitude is to be expected; if it had not crept upon me along the way, I should have felt compelled to acquire it by forced feeding. And it is, of course, of no moment.

But, I do have a grievance which I believe is of moment. The real burden of the unhappiness which I propose to unload here has to do with what we are doing and not doing with economics — and to economics — in the undergraduate classroom, particularly in the introductory course. I shall state my central proposition in terms it deserves: duty and sin. Economists engage in a variety of professional activities. Categorically, the most important of these, so overwhelmingly important that we cannot regard it as less than our greatest duty with no runner-up in sight is (a) to teach (b) the introductory course (c) as it should be taught to reflect fully our responsibility as a profession. Our greatest sin lies in our failure generally to accept and discharge this duty in the spirit and measure demanded by its urgency and consequence.

I shall not bother to argue here whether our posture toward the introductory course reflects cold calculation or aggravated indifference. Our apathy could not be deeper if it were, indeed, studied; it could scarcely be more widespread among us if we had taken a blood oath to effect and sustain it. The simple fact is that by and large, across and throughout our profession, the teaching of the introductory course, apart from the logistical problems it poses, is the very least of our concerns. We teach this course with our left hand in our pocket. Exceptions are sporadic and short-lived. I am happy to except from this characterization the heroic efforts represented by this session's papers and other exercises promoted by the AEA and the Joint Council. These reflect the birth pains of a systematic attack. In all honesty, however, any rift in the clouds that has yet appeared admits little light and no more than a teasing waft of warmth. It is far from clear that the pains augur more than a stillbirth.

Let me translate my evangelical message into native dialect. Economics is the study of the processes and criteria by which man selects the uses to which his limited resources are to be put. We accept as elementary that a use of higher importance or value is always to be preferred to uses of a lower order. Yet, in an area where we might be expected to be particularly sensitive — the allocation of our own valuable resources among competing professional activities — we do conspicuous violence to our own prime precept. It isn't that man-hours, apparatus and textbooks, and bluebooks aren't poured into the introductory course. But what of their volume in relation to the job to be done, and what of their quality and the depth of the purpose which they represent? Thousands of us have taken our turn in teaching the course as part of our initiation into the mysteries of our profession while we were working off our doctoral requirements, but at what cost in sacrifice of living students! Who among us has really had his heart in this enterprise, and for how long? How many choose it as a significant component of a career?

The case for giving top priority to the teaching of introductory economics is simple and forthright. You believe it or you don't. I do. It runs like this: our discipline is important; an understanding of economics by all who participate is vital to the functioning and preservation of a self-governing society. Increasingly the character and quality of our society is being determined by collective economic decision making. The sheer fact is that the public understanding of economics demanded by this condition has never been realized and is today conspicuously in short supply. I cite the quality of the current national discourse on tax reform and inflation as a striking example. Certainly, not everyone in our society needs to be a computer-card-carrying economist; but I insist that it is of great importance to every adult member of our society that he and every other member shall have an elementary, systematic understanding of the economic underpinning of our lives together — the nature of an economy (all economies), and of the processes and institutions by which economizing takes place. My plea is not for fine-spun sophistication; it is for awareness and simple, basic economic understanding — for everyone. Provision of the means to ensure such understanding fits — and bulges — all of the specifications of a public good.

Introductory economics in the colleges holds the key. It is only from this course that any hope is to be had for widespread, effective teaching of economics in the schools; and any significant extension of economic understanding in our society depends upon the further and deeper involvement of the schools. And it is only in the introductory course in the colleges that the great bulk of those who are to become college graduates have an opportunity for systematic exposure to economics, economies, and economizing.

Unfortunately, indeed tragically, far too few college students avail themselves of this alluring opportunity, and a major reason for this is that a large number (a "statistically significant" number) of those who have been conned into the course, or who have dropped in because they were cold or tired, have emerged disillusioned, still tired and noticeably cool. And bad news travels fast.

The news is bad for the introductory course, for our profession, and for our society. Because I have a stake in all three, I want my profession to give more of its positive concern and its active, professional attention to the business of teaching introductory economics, and I mean business, not talk and not time serving; I mean coats-off, rolled-up-sleeves, dirty-hands, driving business. The introductory course is worth all the concerned attention we can give it, for what it can contribute to the rational, enlightened conduct of our society's economic affairs. It is worth everything we can give it to make it an attractive option for every student in the entire college community. I am quite shameless about this. We have something to sell that everyone ought to buy. We owe it to them and to ourselves to constitute and package, and everlastingly to reconstitute and repackage our product so that everyone, in fact, will buy.

I know the stock reaction; we all know it. What do you mean, we have too few students? We have more now than we can properly admit, brand, bed down, grade, certify, and ship. We're overworked, we have no time for research and writing, we are mightily put upon. I admit all of this — and deny its alleged import. We may be pressing against the attention and the facilities which we are presently disposed to allocate to this task; undoubtedly we are annoyed by this yapping nuisance because the overwhelming bulk of our interest lies elsewhere, but we are not devoting anything approaching an optimum proportion of our energies and resources to the introductory course. I have spoken of this earlier, and I shall return to it; let me content myself here with the observation that it would be exhilarating to be confronted with logistical problems growing from an overwhelming surge of voluntary enrolments in introductory economics courses which were believed to be too good to be missed.

I have no chart or flight plan for the construction and conduct of *THE-introductory-course-too-good-to-be-missed*. I have some ideas — all good, but none unchallengeable — about such courses. There is no single course suited to all times and all places; there is none suited to all times in any place, or to all times for any teacher. But, everywhere and eternally there is one irreducible minimum requirement for even a decent course: it must bear the bench mark of a concerned, deeply involved teacher, teaching at his level best.

Any course, superior, decent, or indifferent, is personal. It cannot be packaged and peddled as a proprietary product. Each of us must write his own prescription for his own course, and sign it. Your course is your course, just as my course is mine. There is no escape; there should be none. This is far from saying that we cannot learn from each other, or that a man's course is a walled, bastioned castle, built for his protection. It is not his haven. None of us, if he is in the business, will find anything in his course but sweat, tears, and, hopefully, excitement — never comfort, and never more than scattered spots of satisfaction. If he finds refuge in his course, he may be on the staff and in the catalogue, but he is out of business. But, arena or refuge, it is his course; it can never be other than what he makes it and is willing to live with.

The essence of the experience is experimentation — constant experimentation, constant rethinking and constant trial and, of course, much error. This, I repeat, is the essence. The format of the course, its material and its emphases should be shaken up and repatterned year after year without cease — to shake up and rethread the mind of the shaker, and to demonstrate to students that learning is for everyone, not least a restless teacher. There is, of course, the off chance that experimentation might, just possibly, lay a pearl. But if it does, the end of the road is still over the hill. Today's pearl is tomorrow's egg.

Parenthetically, I should like to record the judgment that the great promise of the present program of the AEA Committee on Economic Education to improve teaching lies not in specification, but in what it may contribute to restlessness and experimentation.

In stating why the introductory course is our highest priority responsibility I have, necessarily, tipped my hand as to its orientation. I shall restate but not belabour my thesis. The introductory course should be policy-oriented, it should be called with deep conviction, "Introduction to Political Economy," and its conduct and thrust should redeem the promise of its title. The student — our student — should be lured into, instructed, informed, and involved intimately in, and made, as completely as may be, a

58

living part of the total evolving political economy in which he, whoever he is, will live the rest of his life.

I am aware that the public policy problems which press upon us are not exclusively economic in content, and I trust I am quite clear that economics, either alone or in combination with other disciplines, holds out no promise of single right answers to our problems as distinct from all other answers which are wrong. But, there is certainly no major public issue, and no minor one comes to mind, which is not shot through with economic considerations; and economics does hold the promise of answers arrived at with a realization of costs and consequences. I am firm in my conviction that if the economic policy choices we are driven to make are not supported broadly and firmly by the economic understanding of our people, the life we know will disintegrate. We will deserve to lose it.

Economies do not happen; they result from active and passive choice; workable economies are those that are made to work by combinations of individual and collective decisions. Running an economy — living and making a living together — in this crowded, complicated, confused century is proving to be a tough assignment. It has still to be demonstrated that we are up to the job. And time is wasting. Time is wasting, too, for the introductory course. It should be policy-oriented; it should be planned, packed, and pickled in economic public policy. Government, in its collective economizing role, should be woven into the presentation as an integral part of the economy. It is important for students to realize before they leave our loving care that collective economizing, exercised through the processes of their government, is no less "economic" than economizing by the market.

For the purposes which I believe should control, I would (to no one's surprise) build my course around the framework of "The Economic Problem." I would start with, return frequently to, and end on the strong notes of what, how, and for whom. The scheme and processes of economizing (both individual and collective, and the nature and essential tasks of an economy — all economies) would be laid out and nailed down. The great recurrent theme — the message — would be opportunity cost.

The scene would be "our economy," as it has been, as it is, and as it might be. The sets would be selected from the dozens of sectors and problems readily at hand, and I would mix them up and revise the selection frequently. I have seen too many popular areas and problems rise, flourish, gain ascendance, and then disappear without a trace to expect any of them to be here tomorrow. Fads are fun, but they are not for marrying. My problems would be drawn from markets of varying configurations and complexions and from the expanding field of government economic policy and action, and they would be recognizable by any practising economist as both micro and macro in character.

Let me digress briefly here to give vent to what even I must accept as an idiosyncrasy. I would use the concept of opportunity cost quite consciously to bridge the chasm which we have insisted on excavating between micro- and macroeconomics. I understand that micro is not macro, that individual choice is not collective choice, and that control of individuals by the market is not on all fours with control of the market (and its individuals) by government. So what? Are these distinctions imperatives? Precisely what is their economizing significance? I suggest that whether we are talking about individual investment in a canning factory or tax policy to control inflation or encourage growth, we are talking about choice in the use of scarce, valuable resources to accomplish what society finds acceptable, at the cost of other goods or ends foregone.

And while I am on this kick, let me air another, not unrelated, foible: a pox on flows! Money, capital, labour, trade do not flow. Individuals scent the air or feel its movement against an upraised moistened finger; their nostrils quiver; they decide; they act. They do not flow: even as aggregates they do not flow. We economists may be architects and, sometimes, carpenters of a sort, but the mysteries of cosmic plumbing still elude us. The point is scarcely earth shaking, but neither is it inconsequential. It would be just as well if it were made quite clear to our students that even macroeconomizing involves considered actions by individuals — that economies are not to be turned on and off by fingering a faucet.

The introductory course — "Introduction to Political Economy" — as I conceive it, is the introductory course for all students, for all seasons — for the once-only or terminal student, for pre-majors (committed or still-to-be-seduced), for pre-engineer, pre-law, pre-business, pre-education students, and for casual shoppers — for all college students except for those who can establish by examination that they have already been introduced. It should be taught as though it were the students' terminal course in economics, and (here I am probing, but on the basis of some revealing experience) as though all its students were prospective teachers. Try it sometime, and take your students with you.

The almost irresistible temptation to overload the table should be resisted. I suggest that the overall dimensions of the effort should be gauged by the needs of the terminal student, tempered by our best judgment of what he will take without gagging. This will provide quite adequately, as well, for those who are destined to take further work in economics — and it will leave enough undone to provide a rationalization for a light battery of advanced, undergraduate courses. And, might we dare to hope that somewhere in the intricate processes of the introductory course we might, just once chance upon the elusive secret of imparting transferability, so that at least the most discerning of our students might be enabled to confront new problems with a working sense of "having been there before"?

Now, a comment about tools as a preoccupation of the introductory course. Regularly, almost dutifully, we recite the proposition that a major thrust of the introductory course should be to equip students with the tools of economic analysis. If this means leading students to approach economic problems as economists approach them and to think as economists think, the proposition is unexceptionable (at least if the prototype economist is, himself, unexceptionable!). But if, as I have reason to believe is too often the case, emphasis upon tools means how to construct and operate apparatus and appliances, the proposition is not persuasive. If we proceed on the assumption that students are crying, "Give us the tools and we will finish the job," we will find that the students and the course rather than the job are finished. Tools rarely invite or involve students not already preoccupied with mechanics, and there is little point in trying to equip students who aren't there. It is worth recalling that the preferred perch for Mark Hopkins was one end of a log, not a logarithm.

For most terminal students in the introductory course, elaborate tools will be costly excess baggage if they bother to pick them up, and a costly nuisance if they don't. Prospective majors can be tooled up as required in later courses. Since none of us wants to push students from the introductory course into the cold world of economic and political-economic affairs to make his way with nothing in his hands, I suggest that we might strike a sensible balance if we ask ourselves two questions: tools for what, and, is this tool necessary?

The usefulness of any tool for the basic purpose of the course should be clear and compelling. Before tools are exposed as tools they should be wrapped in economic problems that are intrinsically worth attending to, and they should emerge unobtrusively from satisfying analysis of those problems. Students should come out of any exercise in mechanics with a sense of the meaning, not just the accuracy, of their calculations. Tools as such should never be given top billing, nor permitted to upstage the substance of the course.

I am informed that students now entering college are no longer frightened by tools, particularly by math, and that even before their beards are dry they are eager to employ their newly acquired manipulative skills. I have no reason to deny or deprecate this, just as I recognize and welcome the better preparation many of them have received in, say, foreign languages and other disciplines — including English and economics. Some of these students, to be identified by examination, might be given a license and placed under observation in a special section; others might be kept in during recess or after class. In all cases without exception, however, I should still ask: tools for what, and, is this tool necessary? There is so very much, beyond tools, to be imparted and absorbed.

I am quite aware that the dichotomy I am posing is overstated, but my plea is for understanding as distinct from skills — understanding that finds its way through the irrelevant and the misleading to the heart of issues, and then captures the relevant and marshalls it economically and convincingly into the service of rational, purposive discourse and decision. I want students to feel economics, to like economics, and to live economics.

There is one demised tool, wielded by the teacher, which in its own unique, old-fashioned way, used to make a powerful contribution to economic understanding. I speak, in sorrow, of the passing of the essay examination. Its place can never be approached even remotely by true-false and multiple-choice examinations which, at best, are much more a test of the composer than of the student. We must not grieve, I know, over that which cannot be restored to us, but I must record what some of us feel deeply in our hearts. We and economic understanding have lost, not only a friend, but a staunch and resourceful ally. And I must shed one tear for the students of today and tomorrow, who, in their brave new world of slides, television, earphones, transmitters, push buttons, X's and checkmarks, will be forever denied the exquisite thrill of composing and committing to paper a complete, coherent sentence.

I have been pretty prodigal here with my prejudices and precepts. I suppose that what I am really asking for is commitment — individual commitment. Every one of us is aware, perfectly aware, that there is an important job that must be done. With rare exception, every one of us avoids it. We all have our anesthetizing rationalizations, our convenient whipping boys; we are already overburdened with work of the only sort that carries professional recognition and advancement; the establishment, the board, the dean, the head are not interested; it's something no individual can do anything about; it's a job for the profession. Let me speak directly to these points.

Teaching economics is a great calling; it gets and will continue to get the recognition of a great calling in every instance where it is practised as a great calling. No one else is responsible; we are not pawns or prisoners of any establishment, nor can we hide within the billowing folds of our profession. We — you and I — are our profession. And, for God's sake, who else can do the job? This is for us — us as individuals. Nothing happens in this world unless individuals make it happen. Remember? No flows! Any of us, alone, can affect the total outcome; and any of us, alone, can pick up company. But, of greater moment, individual outcomes in their own right can be of transcendent importance. Every one of us can look back upon one teacher who for him made all the difference. Well, all the difference is all I ask.

8. WRITING AND READING IN ECONOMICS*

Walter S. Salant

In the past several months I have spent much time reading manuscripts written by my professional colleagues. Although this activity has taught me some economics, as one might expect, it has not been an unmixed pleasure. At some times, to be frank, it has been rather trying.

What has made it trying is that too much of the writing I have read is clumsy or worse: nearly incomprehensible. Crimes of violence are committed daily against the English language and the helpless reader is too often frustrated in his effort to understand the message. Frustration is what has goaded me into expressing my thoughts on this subject to you. The relief of self-expression is my purpose. If any manuscript benefits, that result will be welcome, but I don't expect it.

I fully recognize, as all economists must, that even the clearest expression of some of our thoughts cannot make them easy to understand. In economics, we deal increasingly with ideas and relationships that are complex and inherently difficult to grasp. For example, we must often use technical words to denote objects or concepts for which no other words exist. When a writer has good reason to use a technical word, however, he does have the duty of explaining its meaning when he first uses it, if he wants to be understood by a nonprofessional reader.

I do not quarrel with the use of technical words when their use is necessary. Indeed, I see no objection to using them even when, although not necessary, they are convenient and when the author can reasonably assume that his readers will understand them because he and his readers speak the same language. If somebody for whom an article is not intended objects that he cannot understand such words, his objection has no more merit than that of the proverbial English traveller in France who objects that Frenchmen do not speak English.

As far as we economists are concerned, however, when we want to be

*Reprinted from Walter S. Salant, "Writing and Reading in Economics," *Journal of Political Economy*, July–August, 1969, pp. 545–58, by permission of the editor and author.
Dr. Salant is Senior Fellow, Economic Studies Program, The Brookings Institution, Washington, D.C. He was senior staff member of the US Council of Economic Advisers, Washington, D.C., from 1946 to 1952.

understood by people who are not specialists, the gain in convenience must be very great to justify our using technical words and we should take a good deal of trouble to avoid them. We should accept that burden rather than place upon the reader the burden of understanding the unfamiliar.

Let me also say that I am not criticizing the use of mathematics when it is necessary. The answer to the complaint of the proverbial Englishman in France also applies to complaints about the necessary use of math. In fact, such use of it is merely a special case of the use of technical language. Muriel Rukeyser, in her biography of Willard Gibbs, the great Yale mathematician, physicist, and chemist, tells us that this reticent man, in all his thirty-two years on the faculty of Yale University, is remembered to have spoken only once at a faculty meeting. The faculty was engaged in a long debate on elective and required courses, including the relative emphasis to be placed on mathematics and languages. Gibbs rose and said, "Mathematics *is* a language," and sat down. That profound observation is, I think, now generally recognized to be true. What is significant for my present purpose is that mathematical language permits saying some things that, even if they could be said otherwise, could be said only at such great length and inconvenience that it is really not sensible to say them in words. When that is the case, people who cannot understand mathematical language are just out of luck.

But please notice that many things that can be, and often are, said in mathematical language could equally well be said in English. Until a great many more people speak and read mathematics as well as they speak English, there is no excuse for using mathematical symbols where words will do. Later I shall cite examples of mathematical statements that could have been made in English, not only equally well but much better and more concisely.

My main target is obscure or clumsy writing. It results from poor thinking or a feeble grasp of the principles of clear expression. Of course, the first requirement of clear writing is that the writer must know what he wants to say and say it in logical order. I would have assumed that this elementary fact did not need to be stressed if I had not seen evidence that it does. I have read manuscripts in which important points are in footnotes and unimportant ones are in the text. If your thoughts do not proceed in a logical sequence, no elegance or grace of language will make your writing clear. I might say, parenthetically, that while skilful manipulation of words cannot make clear what is unclear, a sufficiently skilled writer unfortunately can make the unclear or meaningless appear clear. But I do not believe that our profession includes many writers who combine that much skill in writing with that much muddleheadedness. Our problem is that many people cannot formulate clearly what they want to say and how to say it until they get something on paper. For them the unbreakable rule is: never impose your first draft on anyone else.

I think it should be taken for granted that before one begins to write, he should have in mind — and most of us need to have on paper — an outline of what he is going to say. That will enable him to see his article or book as a whole and to see if the points he wants to make are relevant to his message and are stated in logical order. If, while writing, the author becomes aware that he has deviated much from his outline, he should make an outline of what he actually has written and see if it, although different, is equally logical.

I do not seek to instruct anyone else about the details of style that make for excellence in writing. I am not capable of doing that, and even if I were, many books have been published on that subject already. Most of these books do not try to make literary artists. They state what is necessary to make writing merely clear and forceful — but that is not so "mere." Some of these books, such as *The Elements of Style* by Strunk and White, illustrate well the principles they set forth and the advice they offer. My purpose, apart from voicing sorely felt grievances, is more modest. It is merely to point out some of the pitfalls that should be avoided if one is to make his writing reasonably comprehensible. In doing so, I shall concentrate on sins that are peculiar to technicians, and especially to those who have fallen into the ways of the bureaucrat. That, I may say, includes some people who have never been bureaucrats themselves. While I shall concentrate on those sins, I shall also take the opportunity to indulge a few pet peeves.

Words and Their Meanings

I begin with the basic unit of language, the individual word. The English language has a number of words that mean similar but not precisely the same things. Writers with respect for the language preserve the distinction between such meanings. People who pride themselves, as most economists do, on their analytical power ought to be able to see these differences of meaning. They should also be able to see how much better it is to have different words for different thoughts or concepts, however slight the difference, than it is to use one word that does not say precisely what is meant when another one that does is available. As such misuse of words comes to be widely accepted, we lose a way of saying precisely what the misused word originally meant and gain merely a second word to say what we were already able to say otherwise, which is no gain at all. That is a waste — in the language of our trade, a cost without a benefit, a misallocation of scarce verbal resources. Economists above all should be eager to avoid it.

My favourite illustration of the distinction between meanings takes the form of a story — undoubtedly apocryphal — about Noah Webster, the lexicographer. It is said that Mrs. Webster returned home one day to find her husband embracing the maid. She said, "Noah, I am surprised." Webster, without relaxing his grip, looked up and said, "No, my dear, *I* am surprised. *You* are astounded."

Perhaps the distinction is too refined, or now obsolete. But it challenges you to think about what words really mean.

One example of a distinction almost universally ignored by economists is the use of "anticipate" as though it were a synonym for "expect." The *Survey of Current Business* gives official sanction to this misuse when it reports businessmen's expectations about sales. To anticipate something is not merely to expect it but to do something as a result of that expectation. Thus, if one says a businessman anticipates a rise in the prices of his raw materials, one does not, or should not, mean merely that he expects their prices to rise but that he buys larger supplies now than he otherwise would, or does something else as a result of the expectation. It is correct to describe that as "anticipatory" inventory accumulation, however lacking in grace that expression is.

Another example, perhaps also a refinement, is like the one I have just mentioned in not impeding understanding but in wasting a word. It is the confusion between "typical of" and "characteristic of." The expression "typical of," as its derivation from the word "type" suggests, means an attribute that is representative of a class, while "characteristic of" refers to something representative of the attributes of an individual member of a class.

Again, the word "hopefully" is not a synonym for "I hope." It means "full of hope" and refers to the state of mind of the person referred to by the noun it stands next to. Thus, if I were to say, "Hopefully you are listening to what I am saying," my meaning should not be that *I* hope you are listening — although I do — but that *you* have hope while you are listening. That statement may be false but that interpretation is correct. If I want to say *I* hope you are listening, I should say just that. In the light of the correct use, you can see how absurd it is to say, "Hopefully, the equation will give us a good forecast." The econometricians can do much with an equation, but they have not yet endowed it with the capacity to hope.

Another distortion of meaning is the confusion between "imply" and "infer." The difference between the meanings of these two words may be made clear by an explanation I devised for my children when they were very young ham-radio fans. The relation of "imply" to "infer" is the same as the relation of "transmit" to "receive" in broadcasting. The sender of the unstated message *implies* it. The receiver, who thinks he gets the message, or who deduces one does the *inferring*. If you do not know the difference between transmitting and receiving, you should turn in your license.

And "disinterested" does not mean not caring. It means not having a personal interest in the outcome or, more generally now, just being impartial.

Words have other attributes besides meaning. For example, they are parts of speech. I hope it is not news to anyone here that there really *are* different parts of speech — nouns, verbs, adjectives, and so on. Unfortunately, these differences are often overlooked. One confusion is between adjectives and adverbs. Confusion between their roles is not common, but in the past few years the word "otherwise" has been increasingly abused. Apparently its correct use became Top Secret sometime during the 1950s, along with many other things that need not have been classified. But I authorize myself to declassify it and say out loud that it is an adverb, not an adjective, trusting that you all know the difference. For example, it is just plain ungrammatical to say, "Most countries have barriers to imports, whether tariffs, quotas, or otherwise," although it would be correct to say that most of them impede imports by tariffs, quotas, or other methods.

A more common confusion between parts of speech — and one that can make prose very clumsy — is the confusion between nouns and adjectives. In general, nouns should be modified by adjectives. One would hardly guess that this is the rule from reading some of the manuscripts I have read recently. The authors seem to think that a noun should be modified by another noun.

The rule is general rather than universal, because some nouns have been used to modify other nouns for so long that such a use is imbedded in the language. It would be absurdly pedantic to object to that use now. For example, it would be absurd to insist that one should say "telephonic conversation." Similarly, it is shorter and acceptable to refer to an "input matrix," although the general rule suggests "matrix of inputs." But I would suggest one rule, lenient in substance but to be scrupulously observed. If you must use a noun to modify a noun, do not use more than one or, at most, two.

I have been reading manuscripts that assaulted the reader with three, four, and even five nouns placed consecutively. All but the last were intended as adjectives or parts of an adjectival phrase. For example, in one manuscript, I found within a few pages of each other all of the following: "high risk flood plain lands," which presumably means plain lands in which the risk of floods is high; "aircraft speed class sequencing," which uses three nouns to modify a word that might be a noun if it existed but does not really exist; and then, to top it off, "terminal traffic control program category," which contains five consecutive nouns. I leave it to you to figure out which of these words modifies which. There is no reason to obscure thought by using such elephantine language. "High risk flood plain lands" does have one adjective, namely, "high." Which word is it supposed to modify? Is it the lands that are high? One might even imagine that the floods are high. Only because "risk" standing by itself would make little sense can we tell that it is the risks that are high, not the floods or the lands or the plain lands. The reader must study the sentence to know what the author means. He is put to that trouble only because the author did not take the trouble to use the few necessary extra words.

If you must use a collection of nouns or a compound noun to modify another noun, at least put the reader on notice by putting hyphens between the nouns or phrases that you use as adjectives, for example, "balance-of-payments discipline" or "balance-of-payments considerations." But hyphenation is less important than sticking to the rule against using more than two nouns to modify another noun, and preferably using no more than one.

A third abuse of English words extends also to phrases. The abuse lies not in the use of words or phrases in a sense different from their correct meaning, but in their use in no clear or precise sense at all, so that they tell the reader nothing, except that the writer was either too fuzzy or too lazy to say precisely what he meant. One word that is now — I dare you to catch me saying "presently" — used increasingly but has no clear meaning at all, as far as I can tell, is "fund" when it is used as a verb referring to a program of expenditure. I know the word has something to do with money, but Lord knows, there is nothing special about *that*. The dictionary gives four definitions of it as a verb. One, familiar to those who know financial history, is "to convert into a more or less permanent debt bearing regular interest; as to fund a floating debt." That is not what is intended in the use I have in mind. A second is "to provide a fund to pay interest." It does not mean that. A third meaning is "to place in a fund; to accumulate." It does not mean that either. The fourth meaning, "to finance," is labelled obsolete. That comes closest to its meaning in the usage I refer to. I do not object to reviving the obsolete, but this meaning is too vague. Financing something, especially in government, as Washingtonians know well, is a process that includes many steps — authorizing, appropriating, budgeting, obligating, and paying. As it is now used, the word does not distinguish between those steps. In Washington, a city which should know better than any other the differences between these steps, this vague use of the word should be more scrupulously avoided than anywhere. But in Washington it flourishes. At Brookings, where we have two former directors of the Budget and one assistant director, let us bury it. If we do so, the only thing we have to fear is that it will be replaced by another word that will be longer and sound worse, and will not mean more. I offer as a possible winner "authopropligate."

Another example is the use of the word "area" to mean any subclassification of any thing, whether the dimension of the classification is geographical space or anything else. Here is an example: "Devising programs which will accomplish a specified purpose is an area to which systems analysis should devote increasing attention." I protest; "devising programs" is not an "area." The author meant, of course, that systems analysts, when devising programs, should devote more attention to providing incentives for whatever the author was talking about.

Actually, the original sentence contained other sins; it also implied that systems analysis rather than systems analysts had the ability to "devote attention." The author thus attributed consciousness to systems analysis — a claim that far exceeds even those previously made for it. By doing so, he put it in a class with those equations that were forecasting so hopefully. Moreover, the subject of the sentence that yielded this sample is eighteen words long, which makes it something less than poetic. This combination of sins led, in fact, to the following sentence: "Devising programs which will provide incentives for decentralized decision makers to pursue overall program objectives effectively and efficiently is an area to which systems analysis should devote increasing attention."

I have an equal prejudice against the use of "overall," which I once thought was a form of apparel. But perhaps this prejudice is purely personal. While the word "total" or "aggregate" or some similar word will usually say what the writer means, I concede that in some uses a synonym in better standing is hard to find.

Another fuzzy phrase is "in terms of." Although here, too, one must sometimes work hard to find an alternative, the use of this phrase is, in most cases, unnecessary and a result of sloppy thinking, faulty sentence structure, or laziness.

The sentence I quoted with the eighteen-word subject combined a number of sins against gracefulness. But grace is not the only matter at stake when these sins are committed. Clarity is at stake, too. If one combines the use of fuzzy phrases, technical jargon, nouns as adjectives, and nonstop phrases, one can make obscure what could be perfectly clear. For example: "Procedural changes in handling aircraft arrivals and departures yield very high cost effectiveness results in terms of reduction in average delays." Why, I ask myself, do those procedural changes have to "yield very high cost effectiveness results in terms of reductions in average delays"? Why cannot they just greatly reduce average delays?

I might add, incidentally, that the writer of this sentence suggested one procedural change that would speed things up. His suggestion would help — if you could tell what it was. He suggested a change in "priority procedures for arrivals relative to departures, using aircraft speed class sequencing." The use of "aircraft speed class sequencing" may reduce the delays of people who fly, but it greatly increases the delay of people who read.

As long as I am talking about the nuts and bolts of writing, let me say a single word about punctuation. Commas are helpful when correctly used. They tell the reader when to pause. But sometimes they are not merely helpful but indispensable. For example, it sometimes makes a big difference whether the clause introduced by "which" is preceded by a comma.

The Sunday book review section of the *New York Times* of June 30 contained a letter that brought out the importance of commas very effectively. I quote it in full:

> To the Editor:
> I write in reference to the intriguing first sentence of Wilson McWilliam's review of Gladwin Hill's book "Dancing Bear": "Gladwin Hill knows that there

is more to California than the mask of the bizarre behind which the state hides." I would appreciate your asking Mr. McWilliams just what makes him think that California is hiding a mask of the bizarre behind. I thought, that, on the contrary, they had sent it to Washington for display in the US senate but if he has other information I would appreciate his sharing it with me.

Ernst Pawel
Great Neck, New York

If that does not make sufficiently clear the power of the comma, consider the classified ad that was intended to say, "Secretary, about to be married, urgently needs a two-room apartment." As the ad was printed, it said, "Secretary, about to be married urgently, needs a two-room apartment."

Carelessness is not confined to punctuation, and neither is the misunderstanding that carelessness can cause. Indeed, carelessness is probably even more common and its results equally serious in the misuse of pronouns. Sometimes they appear with no antecedents at all. More commonly the antecedent exists, but instead of being a single word, it appears to be a whole preceding idea. A writer may develop a thought or a series of thoughts in a whole paragraph and then begin the next paragraph by saying, "This is incorrect," leaving the reader with no precise idea of what is incorrect. It is a good principle to avoid using "this" and "that" as pronouns. If you use them only as adjectives, the nouns they modify will make your meaning clear.

While the absence of an identifiable antecedent may lead to no understanding at all, either correct or incorrect, use of a pronoun that can refer to two or more possible antecedents may lead to positive misunderstanding. My former colleague, Roderick Riley, once said of another colleague who sinned in this way that he was a man of dubious antecedents. The misunderstanding that can result from dubious antecedents can even be fatal. You must have heard about the steelworker who was teaching an apprentice how to rivet. "I'll hold the rivet," he said, "and when I nod my head, you hit it with the sledge hammer." The apprentice did. His instructor left a widow and three children.

Another source of confusion is the dangling participle. The participle implies a subject. That implied subject should be the same as the subject of the clause to which the phrase is attached. The phrase is said to "dangle" when the two subjects are different. Here is an example taken from a discussion of the US program to control capital outflows: "By instituting the voluntary foreign credit restraint program, foreigners found access to trade finance more difficult." Of course the writer of the sentence knew perfectly well that the voluntary credit restraint program was not instituted by foreigners. Fowler, both in his *Dictionary of Modern English Usage* and in the book he wrote with his brother, *The King's English,* gives many illustrations of the dangling participle.

Mathematical Language

I now come to the problem which I consider most serious in manuscripts prepared by modern economists. It is generally referred to as the use of mathematics in the exposition, but the word "use" in that description is rather loose. Very often the mathematics is not really being used; all that is being used is mathematical notation. In other cases the mathematics is being used, but there is the question of whether its use is justified. Both abuses raise serious problems of communication. For one thing, if the abuses survive the editorial process and appear in what is finally published, they limit the writer's audience and alienate some of those who remain in it. Second, they are more likely to survive the editorial process than are other abuses; few, if any, staff editors are able to judge when the use of mathematical notation is necessary, and few have the confidence even to press the author to eliminate or substantially reduce it. Finally, the problem is serious because the practice, or the malpractice, is growing rapidly.

Let us first consider the use of mathematical symbols when no mathematical operations are being performed. The crudest use of such symbols is their use as substitutes for words in a prose sentence, as shorthand because the writer wants to avoid the trouble of writing the word for which the symbol stands. Such uses of symbols will ordinarily not get by editors. Their vigilance protects readers of the published work. But the writer who indulges in this practice is still victimizing his colleagues who read the manuscript before the editors have had an opportunity to do their work. You might suppose that the use of symbols as shorthand would not burden those who are asked to read the draft, because they are experts. But if the author uses more than a dozen symbols and uses them in a way that is not standardized and therefore familiar to experts, the reader must remember the author's definitions or, if he cannot, he must find them. If, in addition, these definitions are scattered throughout the preceding pages, the reader is like a man using a dictionary in which the words, instead of being arranged alphabetically, are in random order. Of course, there is no excuse whatever for using symbols without defining them at all. We are not writing *only* for mind readers. But it is necessary to say that there is very little excuse for using symbols at all merely as shorthand. If mathematics is not used, mathematical expressions are generally unnecessary and the problem of defining symbols need not arise. If symbols are used, all the definitions should generally be placed together or, if the symbol was last used a long time before, its definition can be repeated.

A more common practice than using symbols as shorthand within prose sentences is to use equations as shorthand for whole sentences that could be said equally well in words. This practice presents no obstacles to some readers but it does to others, and it contributes nothing. The reason some writers indulge in this practice is probably not that they are lazy but that they have been thinking in mathematical terms and that the use of symbols and nonverbal equations is more natural to them. Although the writer who does this is perhaps not being lazy, he is being inconsiderate. The costs of this practice may be low, but the benefits are nil. I can think of only one situation that justifies this practice, and I think it occurs rarely. Casting a statement in mathematical terms is justified if the verbal statement of the equation or the inequality would be more complicated or as unfamiliar to the reader as the mathematical statement. In that case, nothing is lost by using mathematical notation and something may be gained.

I now come to the use of mathematical operations, as distinguished from mere notation. Whether this use of mathematical language is justified is a less clear-cut question, and the answer involves judgments. But a few flat statements appear justifiable to me.

Mathematical operations are sometimes performed to derive propositions that would be obvious to anyone interested and intelligent enough to care about what the author has written. In such cases, the use of mathematics does not clarify the proposition. Indeed, it may even obscure it, because the reader, making the reasonable assumption that something not banal is about to be demonstrated, looks for it in vain. Here is an example:

> In this section we shall present the results for the level and changes in the value of direct investments based on the simplest of foreign funds models: $\Delta F_i = f_i \Delta A_i + u$. To derive an expression for the change in the value of direct investments, we use the above equation for foreign funds and the accounting identity (7) to obtain: $\Delta V_i = (1 - f_i)\Delta A_i - u$.

In this passage, the author uses the first equation and his accounting identity (7), which one has to look for in an unidentified preceding page, to derive the second equation. The reader might reasonably suppose that the second equation is not an obvious corollary of the first one but can be inferred from it only by use of mathematics. In fact, the author was saying merely that if the non-American proportion of the total funds that foreign subsidaries use to finance acquisition of assets is constant, then the proportion they finance with American funds is also constant.

I can see only two possible reasons why a writer should take his readers through such exercises to derive such propositions. One is that he thinks a proposition that appears obvious by intuition may not be precisely correct and wishes to demonstrate either that it really is or that the necessary and sufficient conditions for its validity differ from what the reader is likely to have thought. To those who, thinking they must prove absolutely everything, go to extremes of accuracy and rigour and force their readers to go with them, I can only tell a story about Mark Twain. When he was a young reporter, his editor instructed him never to state as a fact anything that he had not personally verified. Upon being sent to cover an important social event soon afterward, he wrote the following: "A woman giving the name of Mrs. James Jones, who is reported to be one of the society leaders of this city, is said to have given what purported to be a party yesterday to a number of alleged ladies. The hostess claims to be the wife of a reputed attorney."

The other possible reason for going to extremes in proving things that do not need proof is to show one's own ability to use one of the tools of the trade. Whether consciously or not, the producer of such a manuscript is serving himself rather than the reader, and he is doing so at some expense to the reader. Such pride in tool using for its own sake and such eagerness to demonstrate one's ability to use the tool at the expense of the people one is supposed to serve remind me of a charwoman in a large New York bank who was proud of her proficiency as a polisher of floors. She said, "When I started to work here the floors was in bad condition. But since I've been doing them three ladies has fell down."

Of course there are times when mathematical operations really have to be used to reach a conclusion. In such cases, the decision about using mathematics in the text should depend on the nature of the intended audience. But it is certainly a good rule for all publications that are not intended only for a professional audience to say in words both the conclusion and whatever can be said about the reasoning, and to confine the mathematics to an appendix. This principle can be followed without much strain. The author who follows it will still have the opportunity, if he wants it, to tell the mathematical reader how he reached his conclusions, and he will gain a wider audience.

Let no one think that application of this principle is beneath his professional dignity. Some very good economists who can handle mathematics have demonstrated that they can state complex propositions in clear English. The Irving Fisher Lecture by James Tobin, "Economic Growth as an Objective of Government Policy," is an example, and there are many others. Some leading economists — for example, Fritz Machlup and Tibor Scitovsky — pay a great deal of attention to how they say things.

Apparently words can express not only propositions of economic theory that are derived mathematically but, according to the late Stefan Valavanis, those of econometrics, too. In the Preface of his textbook *Econometrics*, he expresses this opinion in one sentence: "If anything in Econometrics (or in any other field) makes sense one ought to be able to put it into words." Copies of this statement suitable for framing should be made freely available to all members of our profession.

Grace and Force

So far, my remarks have dealt with rather elementary requirements of clarity, which is an essential requirement of all writing. Still, I cannot refrain from saying a word or two about grace and force in writing and from reporting the result of a bit of statistical research bearing on one element of style. Even if clarity should be our first aspiration, why not aspire to more — for example, to conciseness, force, and even vividness?

Merely to achieve clarity one need not pay much attention to how easily prose reads, although the two qualities are related. Still, ease of reading does help the reader retain his presumed original interest in a manuscript. You can take a long step toward making your manuscript not only clear but easy to read if you avoid using strings of nouns like those I mentioned early in my remarks, such as "aircraft speed class sequencing," and if you avoid fuzzy phrases such as "in the area of" and "in terms of." If, further, you pay attention to how the words sound, you may even make the reading of your manuscript enjoyable. At a conference in Bellagio, someone asked Fritz Machlup why he had used one word in a draft rather than another, longer one that the questioner thought more appropriate. Machlup said, "Because it is more euphonious." On being asked if he really paid much attention to that criterion when he wrote, he said, "Absolutely. I ask myself, 'Does it sing?' "

Some habits that are not serious vices help keep writing from being "clean." I shall cite only one, and I shall commit the misdemeanour in the course of describing it. There are many people who use the locution "there is (or are) . . . who (or which). . . ." I should have said, "Many people use the locution. . . ." The use of "there is (or are) . . . who (or which) . . ." is usually useless, heavy-handed, and windy. In one of the manuscripts I read recently, that construction was used three or four times on one page.

Another simple way of avoiding clumsiness is to prefer the short word to the long one and to avoid the unfamiliar word if a familiar one can be found that is equally correct, specific, and concrete. (Incidentally, the two qualities of being specific and being concrete are not the same. For an explanation of the difference, see *Fundamentals of Good Writing* [London: Dobson, 1952] by Cleanth Brooks and Robert Penn Warren, pages 338–42.) Length, unfamiliarity, abstractness, and generality are brought together in the phrase "maximizing the additivity" of something. The sad truth is that the writer who used those words combined them with "in terms of"; he really did say "in terms of maximizing the additivity." And he is not a fuzzy thinker. He knows what he wants to say. He just did not, in the draft I read, take the time to find a better way to say it. There must be a better way.

That the length of words affects the cleanness and force of writing is not news. The powerful effect of short words hits one most forcibly in Ernest Hemingway's prose. His sentences strike like bullets. All are clear-cut and forceful. It is remarkable how many are built entirely of words of one syllable. Indeed, I found nearly a whole page of his writing that contained hardly a word of more than one syllable. Recalling this finding, it occurred to me to measure the length of words used by a few economists, using the number of syllables as a measure of length. Of course one should allow for the more technical nature of most economic writing. Still, I daresay that some of us could describe a bullfight in a way that would make it as difficult to understand as an econometric model of the American economy. In order to avoid loading the dice against the writing that has goaded me into making these observations, I have compared one of these writings not only with Hemingway's but with those of two of the better writers among economists. To get a reasonable sample of each man's writing I have counted the words used in a few paragraphs of each manuscript or published book, one or two from portions that do not deal with technical matters, and one or two from portions that do. I do not claim that the sample was chosen scientifically. The results, for whatever they are worth, are summarized in Table 1.

The difference among the economists is perhaps not very great, although if one remembers that the minimum possible number of syllables per 100 words is 100, the difference between 175 and 163 is not negligible. The difference in ease of reading of Economist No. 1 and the other two economists exceeds what the difference in their syllable counts suggests. That fact shows that such a count has only a limited value. But it is striking that the Hemingway samples have only 122 syllables per 100 words and that only 4 percent of his words contain three or more syllables.

TABLE 1

Percentage of Words Having

Writer	One Syllable	One or Two Syllables	Three Syllables	Four or more Syllables	Number of Syllables Per 100 Words
Economist No. 1	57	76	18	6	175
Economist No. 2	52	81	14	5	173
Economist No. 3	64	81	13	6	163
Ernest Hemingway*	83	96	4	0	122

*From Ernest Hemingway's, *A Moveable Feast*.

When words are not only long but general and abstract, the combination is deadly. The difference between such words and short, specific, and concrete ones is strikingly brought out by George Orwell in his essay "Politics and the English Language," to which Herbert Morton, for many years the director of publications at Brookings, called my attention.[1] Orwell quotes a passage from the Bible and then paraphrases it in what he calls "modern English of

---

[1] George Orwell, *Collection of Essays* (New York: Doubleday, 1954).

the worst sort." I shall reverse that order and give you his version first. You will probably not find it notable in any way because it is written in the style we read every day. Here it is in modern English:

> Objective consideration of contemporary phenomena compels the conclusion that success or failure in competitive activities exhibits no tendency to be commensurate with innate capacity, but that a considerable element of the unpredictable must invariably be taken into account.

Now here, with a few introductory words omitted, is how the same idea is expressed in Ecclesiastes:

> The race is not to the swift, nor the battle to the strong, neither yet bread to the wise, nor yet riches to men of understanding, nor yet favour to men of skill; but time and chance happeneth to them all.

Apart from the "neither yet," the "nor yets," and "happeneth," which give this version its touch of the archaic, this *could* be written by a good modern writer on poverty. But you will all know how to bet on which version will be more closely approached by those who are now writing on the subject.

If we all aspired to be Hemingways, we should have to work at least as hard on our writing as he did. In *A Moveable Feast* Hemingway said it sometimes took him a whole morning to write a paragraph. When you read that book you will see why. Although it would be a poor use of resources for economists to spend that much time in polishing, it is obvious that many of us should spend a good deal more time in revising our drafts than we do now. None of us has a right, even at the stage of drafting, to impose on others writing that does not meet the requirement of clarity. He who does so not only irritates the colleagues who must read what he writes, and wastes their time, but also forgoes the larger audience that might otherwise read what he has to say. He thereby forgoes the influence his work might have.

D. ECONOMICS IN A CANADIAN SETTING

Economics first appeared in a Canadian university curriculum more than ninety years ago; thirty years later several universities were offering groups of courses in economics that could qualify a student for the equivalent of an honours degree in economics; but it is only in the past forty-five years that a continuous and expanding flow of professional writing in economics by Canadians has developed. Reading 9 reviews briefly Canadian contributions to the discipline of economics since 1945. It focusses on Canadian economic writings of a universal character. It indicates that Canadian economists have a recognized place in international scholarship. And it implies that we are now in a position to produce good Canadian textbooks at the university level.

9. CANADIAN CONTRIBUTIONS TO THE DISCIPLINE OF ECONOMICS SINCE 1945[*]

Harry G. Johnson

My task is to discuss Canadian contributions to the discipline of economics since 1945.[1] In approaching it, I shall interpret the concept of "a contribution to the discipline of economics" fairly narrowly, to mean a piece of work of general interest to the international profession of economists, one that can be said to have contributed something to the general advance of our subject. The adoption of this standard implies, I should emphasize, the exclusion of a great deal of worthy economic writing and research, since work that does not advance the discipline may nevertheless be important in its own right, either because it increases our knowledge of the working of the Canadian economy or because it applies known tools and concepts to an important problem. This consideration is particularly important in relation to Canadian economics in the postwar period, since so much economic research has been sponsored by federal or provincial governments and oriented toward the clarification and illumination of problems of economic policy. Further, it should be remarked that the assessment of its contributions to the discipline is only one measure of the performance of a national profession. Another, and from the social point of view probably much more important, test is the quality of undergraduate instruction that the profession provides. This consideration is also highly relevant to Canadian economics in the postwar period, since until well into the 1950s Canadian economists were primarily concerned with undergraduate teaching rather than with research, and in most institutions of higher learning in the country this is still their chief responsibility. By that test, I think it is fair to say that Canadian economics stands high in the international league table, in the sense that, according to my own observation, Canadian university teachers of economics devote a great deal of their time to keeping the content of their

*Reprinted from Harry G. Johnson, "Canadian Contributions to the Discipline of Economics since 1945," *Canadian Journal of Economics,* February, 1968, pp. 129–46, by permission of the editor and author.
Dr. Johnson is Professor of Economics at the University of Chicago, and the London School of Economics, London, England. He is a former president of the Canadian Economics Association.

[1] For an earlier assessment covering a longer historical period, see K.W. Taylor, "Economic Scholarship in Canada," *Canadian Journal of Economics and Political Science,* 26, No. 1 (February, 1960), pp. 6–18; V.W. Bladen, "A Journal is Born: 1935," *ibid.,* pp. 1–5, is also relevant.

courses up to date and in touch with the moving frontier of the subject, thereby ensuring a high-quality, internationally competitive output of graduates.

This fact, indeed, poses a problem in defining the scope of this paper, since a significant proportion of Canadian graduates in economics have chosen to make their professional careers in other countries — mainly the United States and the United Kingdom — and it is a subtle problem in nationalism whether their contributions should be classed as Canadian or not. To do so might appear as excessive presumption of national pride; not to do so however, would be to ignore what is perhaps the most important channel of Canadian contribution to the international discipline of economics. A parallel problem, of increasing importance in the postwar period owing to the increasing international mobility of the profession, is how to treat economists born and trained elsewhere who have migrated to Canada to work here either permanently or for a period of years.[2]

I have decided to resolve these issues by restricting the concept of "Canadian contribution" to contributions by Canadian resident economists, including in the latter non-Canadians working in Canadian universities; the only serious difficulty this raises is the possibility of outraging Australian national pride by the inclusion of Murray C. Kemp as a Canadian contributor. I shall, however, modify this definition at certain points, to avoid too narrowly nationalistic an approach, in three ways: first, I shall mention briefly some contributions by Canadians resident abroad; second, I shall mention some contributions by nonresidents that have been prompted by Canadian problems or experience; and third, since the publication of a good professional journal is itself a contribution to the progress of a subject, I shall mention some contributions that have been published in the now defunct *Canadian Journal of Economics and Political Science.*

Before the war, Canadian economics was noted almost exclusively for the so-called "Toronto School" of economic history, dominated by the towering genius of Harold A. Innis, which school was considered distinctive enough to merit a review article in *Economic History.*[3] The approach of the Toronto economic historians of that generation has been carried forward in the work of the present generation of Canadian economic historians, notably of W.T. Easterbrook, K. H. Buckley, and J. H. Dales, while the social philosophizing into which Innis' meditation on the cultural implications of newsprint led him has flowered in the contemporary phenomenon of McLuhanism. The central historiographical concept of the Toronto School, the developmental role of staple production, has influenced the work of the American economic historian, Douglass C. North, and has also penetrated into the theory of international trade as a rival to the "vent for surplus" model of development through trade.[4] Aside from economic history, however, Canadian economics was extremely weak in publications: there were no introductory Canadian texts until Logan and Inman's *A Social Approach to*

---

[2] John Rae, in a much earlier period, is the outstanding example. See Craufurd D.W. Goodwin's *Canadian Economic Thought: The Political Economy of a Developing Nation, 1814–1914* (Durham: Duke University Press, 1961).

[3] C.R. Fay, "The Toronto School of Economic History," *Economic History* (Supplement to *Economic Journal*) 3, (January, 1934), pp. 168–71.

[4] R.E. Caves, " 'Vent for Surplus' Models of Trade and Growth," in R.E. Baldwin, ed., *Trade, Growth, and the Balance of Payments: Essays in Honor of Gottfried Haberler* (Chicago: Rand McNally, 1965).

Economics (Toronto: University of Toronto Press, 1939) and V.W. Bladen's *An Introduction to Political Economy* (Toronto: University of Toronto Press, 1941). A.F.W. Plumptre's *Central Banking in the British Dominions* (Toronto: University of Toronto Press, 1940) was the only research publication that could be classified as a significant Canadian contribution to the literature of economics. During the war, however, two books were published that established a Canadian claim to competence in the realm of pure theory. The first was Mabel F. Timlin's *Keynesian Economics* (Toronto: University of Toronto Press, 1942), a remarkable personal achievement which extended the Keynesian model by replacing the long-term interest rate by an analysis of the structure of interest rates and its role in the general equilibrium of the system. The second was Burton S. Keirstead's *Essentials of Price Theory* (Toronto: University of Toronto Press, 1942), which can be regarded as the first real Canadian textbook in formal economic theory. In the war and early postwar period, Timlin and Keirstead were for practical purposes the Canadian economic theorists — though Benjamin Higgins should be mentioned for his work on the theory of secular stagnation and subsequently on growth models, and one should not overlook the contribution of G.A. Elliott in training a generation of graduate students at Toronto up to Chicago standards in value and distribution theory. Timlin subsequently became interested in Canadian monetary policy and in the economics of migration, the subject of her Presidential Address to this Association.[5] Keirstead early became concerned with a problem that has increasingly occupied the attention of the leading economic theorists of the world, the theory of economic growth and related problems in distribution theory. His major publications — *The Theory of Economic Change* (Toronto: University of Toronto Press, 1948), *An Essay in the Theory of Profits and Income Distribution* (Oxford: Oxford University Press, 1953) and *Capital, Interest, and Profit* (Oxford: Oxford University Press, 1959) — were presented as work in progress, and range so diffusely over philosophical, political, and economic issues as to fail to appeal to logically minded theorists. But they contain interesting ideas and approaches, especially in relation to institutional influences on growth and distribution and the analysis of dynamic processes, and the *Essay on the Theory of Profits and Income Distribution* in particular attracted the interest of Joan Robinson and G.L.S. Shackle in England and of François Perroux and his colleagues in the Institut de Science Economique Appliquée in Paris.

Since the war, the number of active Canadian economists has grown rapidly, and their range of interests has broadened to include virtually all aspects of economics. In the remainder of this paper, I shall be concerned with assessing their contributions to the subject. What I propose to do is to discuss the main areas in which I consider that scientifically significant work has been and is being done. This is necessarily an exercise in personal judgment, dependent on personal knowledge, with the results of which others may well disagree. Consequently, as a preliminary, I shall present the results of two methods of calculation that are, I believe, reasonably impersonal, in that they are based on the judgments of others than myself.

The first method makes use of the series of surveys of economic theory sponsored by the Rockefeller Foundation and published in the *Economic*

---

[5]Mabel F. Timlin, "Canada's Immigration Policy, 1896–1910," *Canadian Journal of Economics and Political Science,* 26, No. 4 (November, 1960), pp. 517–32.

Journal and the *American Economic Review* in recent years.[6] Twelve of these surveys include a bibliography, the items in which may be presumed to represent contributions to the advance of the science. I have worked through these bibliographies in search of Canadian contributions under three heads: contributions by resident Canadian authors, contributions by nonresident Canadian authors, and contributions published in the *Canadian Journal*. The results are shown in the accompanying Table 1; for brevity, nonresident Canadian contributors are entered by name only, with number of contributions mentioned in parentheses. I should point out that the method is not entirely reliable, and specifically is biased toward underrepresentation of Canadian work because some of the authors of the *Surveys* apparently relied primarily on their own national journals to trace the development of their subjects and because some of the surveys were written several years ago, and hence miss more recent contributions by the growing number of young Canadian economists. In addition, of course, the definitions of the subjects of the surveys themselves confine the results to only a part of economics, though this may strengthen the test because the surveys were intended to cover the more rapidly developing fields of professional interest.

Out of the twelve surveys, only four — monetary theory and policy, inflation theory, welfare economics, and international trade — refer to articles published in the *Canadian Journal*; and in only two fields are these articles written by Canadian authors. Again, out of the twelve surveys, only four — welfare economics, growth theory, international trade theory, and cost-benefit analysis — refer to works by resident Canadian authors, though eleven of the twelve mention works by nonresident Canadians. Two points stand out from the table. The first, not surprisingly, is the small number of Canadian resident economists listed: thirteen names, of which four are co-authors of one book, with one author (Murray C. Kemp) accounting for nearly half of the entries. This paucity of authors is not surprising because the habit of writing for professional publication is hard to acquire and easy to break. The second, somewhat more surprising, is that in spite of the early loss of Keirstead and Higgins, McGill continued to be the dominant centre for the production of economic theory in Canada, at least on this measure. A third point worth noting, however, is that in the new postwar field of cost-benefit analysis, Canadian economics is represented by two books, written by economists primarily associated with the western universities.

The second impersonal method makes use of the records of contributions to and participation in the annual round tables sponsored by the International Economic Association, an association of national associations of which this Association was a founding member. This again is a source rather biased against representation of the Canadian profession, since the control of the Association has naturally been dominated by the two most important national associations, the Royal Economic Society and the American Economic Association, and participation in its round tables has equally naturally been governed with an eye to fairness of national representation, with the smaller national professions like the Canadian probably being underrepresented by comparison with the numerically larger — but not necessarily professionally stronger — national professions of the continental

[6] American Economic Association and Royal Economic Society, *Surveys of Economic Theory,* Vol. 1–3 (London: Macmillan; New York: St. Martin's; 1965 and 1966).

TABLE 1
THE SURVEYS OF ECONOMIC THEORY

Resident Canadian Authors	Nonresident Canadian Authors	Canadian Journal of Economics and Political Science
Monetary Theory and Policy by Harry G. Johnson, *Economic Journal*, 1962	J.K. Galbraith, H.G. Johnson, R.G. Lipsey, R.A. Mundell, H.M. Somers	R.E. Kuenne, "Keynes's Identity, Ricardian Virtue, and the Partial Dichotomy," 1961
		E. Miller, "Monetary Policies in the United States since 1950: Some Implications of the Retreat to Orthodoxy," 1961
Survey of Inflation Theory by M. Bronfenbrenner and F.D. Holzman, *AER*, 1963		
None	J.K. Galbraith, H.G. Johnson, R.G. Lipsey (2), Lloyd G. Reynolds (3), Thomas A. Wilson	M.W. Reder, "The Theoretical Problems of a National Wage-Price Policy," 1948
Recent Theories Concerning the Nature and Role of Interest by G.L.S. Shackle, *Economic Journal*, 1961		
None	H.G. Johnson, H.M. Somers (3)	
A Survey of Welfare Economics 1939–59 by E.J. Mishan, *Economic Journal*, 1960	G.F. Break (2), S.G. Checkland, H.G. Johnson (3), R.G. Lipsey (4) J. Viner	J.A. Crutchfield, "Common Property Resources and Factor Allocation," 1956
R. Dehem, "Welfare Losses," *Econometrica*, 1950 (abstracts)		H.S. Ellis, "Competition and Welfare," 1945
M.C. Kemp, "Arrow's General Possibility Theorem," *Rev. Econ. Stat.*, 1954; "Welfare Economics: A Stocktaking," *Economic Record*, 1954; "The Efficiency of Competition as an Allocator of Resources," 2 parts, *CJEPS*, 1955; "Psychological Change, the Terms of Trade and Welfare," *Economic Journal*, 1955		M.C. Kemp, "The Efficiency of Competition as an Allocator of Resources," 2 parts, 1955

TABLE 1 Cont'd

Resident Canadian Authors	Nonresident Canadian Authors	Canadian Journal of Economics and Political Science
M.C. Kemp and A. Asimakopulos, "A Note on Social Welfare Functions and Cardinal Utility," CJEPS, 1952		M.C. Kemp and A. Asimakopulos, "A Note on Social Welfare Functions and Cardinal Utility," 1952
K.W. Klawe, Review of A.J. Macfie, Economic Efficiency and Social Welfare, CJEPS, 1946		K.W. Klawe, review of A.J. Macfie, Economic Efficiency and Social Welfare, 1946
		A.Y.C. Koo, "Welfare and Direct Taxation," 1955
M.F. Timlin, Review article on A.P. Lerner, The Economics of Control, CJEPS, 1945; review article on H. Myint, Theories of Welfare Economics, CJEPS, 1949		M.F. Timlin, Review article on A.P. Lerner, The Economics of Control, 1945; review article on H. Myint. Theories of Welfare Economics, 1949
J.C. Weldon, "On the Problem of Social Welfare Functions," CJEPS, 1952		J.C. Weldon, "On the Problem of Social Welfare Functions," 1952
The Theory of Economic Growth: A Survey by F.H. Hahn and R.C.O. Matthews, Economic Journal, 1964		None
A. Asimakopulos, "The Definition of D.F. Gordon Neutral Inventions," Economic Journal, 1963		
A. Asimakopulos and J.C. Weldon, "The Classification of Technical Progress in Models of Economic Growth," Economica, 1963.		
H.A.J. Green, "Growth Models, Capital and Stability," Economic Journal, 1960		
Comparative Advantage and Development Policy by Hollis B. Chenery, AER, 1961	B. Higgins, J. Viner	
None		None

TABLE 1 Cont'd

Resident Canadian Authors	Nonresident Canadian Authors	*Canadian Journal of Economics and Political Science*
The Pure Theory of International Trade: A Survey by Jagdish Bhagwati, *Economic Journal,* 1964		
A. Asimakopulos, "A Note on Productivity Changes and the Terms of Trade," *Oxford Economic Papers,* 1957 M.C. Kemp, "The Relation between Changes in International Demand and the Terms of Trade," *Econometrica* 1956; "Technological Change, the Terms of Trade and Welfare," *Economic Journal,* 1955; (with R. Jones) "Variable Labour Supply and the Theory of International Trade," *Journal of Political Economy,* 1962; "The Gain from International Trade," *Economic Journal,* 1962; *The Pure Theory of International Trade,* 1964. R. Wonnacott, *Canadian-American Dependence,* 1961	H. Grubert, H.G. Johnson (14), R.G. Lipsey (2), R.A. Mundell (3), R. Robinson (2), J. Viner, D.F. Wohl	D.F. Wohl, "Capital and Labour Requirements for Canada's Foreign Trade," 1961
Regional Economics: A Survey by John R. Meyer, *AER,* 1963	J.S. Chipman	None
None		
Theories of Decision Making in Economics and Behavioural Science by H.A. Somers, *AER,* 1959	J.K. Galbraith	None
None		
Operations Research by Robert Dorfman, *AER,* 1960	None	None
None		

TABLE 1 Concluded

Resident Canadian Authors	Nonresident Canadian Authors	Canadian Journal of Economics and Political Science
Research on Household Behaviour by Robert Ferber, *AER* 1962 None	Jean M. Due, M.G. Reid (5)	None
Cost-Benefit Analysis: A Survey by A.R. Prest and R. Turvey, *Economic Journal*, 1965 W.R.D. Sewell, J. Davis, A.D. Scott, and D.W. Ross, *Guide to Benefit-Cost Analysis*, 1962; D.M. Winch, *The Economics of Highway Planning*, 1963	Tillo E. Kuhn	None

European countries and more recently of India, Brazil, and Russia. Nevertheless, the round tables have *sought* to bring together the leading experts on a selected subject of major international professional interest, from the member national professions, so that the invitation to contribute a paper to a round table, and to a lesser extent — given the severe constraint on total numbers of participants — the invitation to participate in the discussion, may fairly be accepted as an indicator of past or present contribution to economics as an international discipline.

I have tabulated Canadian participation in the proceedings of the International Economic Association — including conferences, regional conferences, and joint conferences as well as round tables — under three classifications: resident Canadian economists contributing papers, resident Canadian economists participating in the discussion, and nonresident Canadian economists contributing or participating. The results are presented in Table 2.

The general results are scarcely flattering. Canadians appear — though when they do they appear in force in pairs — as contributors of papers to only four of the twenty-odd conferences that have been held since the first one in 1950. In the first three cases, those who appear may without disrespect be termed members of the prewar generation of Canadian economists — quite naturally, given the dates and the character of the International Economic Association at that time — and their contributions dealt with traditional policy problems of the Canadian economy — international trade, combines control, and immigration. The exception from this generalization is the paper by Keyfitz, which reflects the fact that Canada's leading expert on demography happened to have been assigned to the assistance of an underdeveloped country. Only in the fourth case, the joint *FAO-IEA* conference on fisheries, is the postwar generation represented — by A.D. Scott and by H. Scott Gordon. Their papers exemplify work in an area to which Canadian economists can justly claim to have made a significant contribution in the postwar period, the economics of natural resources and conservation.

The chief basis for this claim is A.D. Scott's *Natural Resources: The Economics of Conservation* (Toronto: University of Toronto Press, 1955), which became a standard reference on the subject despite the signs of its being a published PhD thesis. But there is enough other published work by Canadian economists — notably H. Scott Gordon[7] — in this area to justify a claim to broader contribution to a developing field of research.

It will be noted from the table that the latest appearance of a Canadian resident economist as a contributor of a paper to an International Economic Association conference was in 1956. This is a rather surprising fact, given both that some of the conference subjects are subjects on which good Canadian economists have been working intensively, and that the conferences have occasionally included quite junior economists from other Commonwealth countries, two conferences having indeed been specifically designed

---

[7] See especially H.S. Gordon, "The Economic Theory of a Common-Property Resource: The Fishery," *Journal of Political Economy,* 62, No. 2 (April, 1954), pp. 124–42. Since the availability of the American Economic Association's *Index of Economic Journals* makes it an easy matter to look up the contributions of any economist — with the possibly important exception of foreign-language contributions and contributions to symposia and conference proceedings published in book form — this paper will not attempt a full documentation of the scholarly contributions of the various authors mentioned.

TABLE 2

INTERNATIONAL ECONOMIC ASSOCIATION CONFERENCES

Year	Conference Topic	Resident Canadian Authors	Resident Canadian Participants	Nonresident Canadian Authors or Participants
1950	The Problem of Long-Term International Balance	G.A. Elliot, "Notes on the Canadian Position in International Trade" B.S. Keirstead, "the Conditions of Multilateral Trade"	V. Fowke	None
1951	Monopoly and Competition and Their Regulation	V.W. Bladen, "Canada" F.A. McGregor, "Preventing Monopoly — Canadian Techniques"	None	None
1952	The Business Cycle in the Postwar World	None	None	None
1953	Economic Progress	None	R. Dehem	None
1954	The Theory of Wage Determination	None	None	H.G. Johnson L.G. Reynolds
1955	The Economics of International Migration	M.F. Timlin, "Immigration Countries: Canada" N. Keyfitz: "Migration and the Economy of Indonesia"	None	None
1956	The Economics of Fisheries (joint with FAO)	A.D. Scott, "Optimal Utilization and the Control of Fisheries" H.S. Gordon, "Obstacles to Agreement on Control in the Fishing Industry"	None	None
1956	Stability and Progress in the World Economy (Congress)	None	Unknown	J. Viner
1957	The Economic Consequences of the Size of Nations	None	None	L. Tarshis
1957	Economic Development for Latin American (Regional Conference)	None	None	None
1958	The Theory of Capital	None	None	None
1959	Inflation	None	G. Britnell	None

TABLE 2 Concluded

Year Conference Topic	Resident Canadian Authors	Resident Canadian Participants	Nonresident Canadian Authors or Participants
1960 The Economics of Take-Off into Sustained Growth	None	None	None
1960 Economic Development with Special Reference to East Asia (Regional Conference)	None	None	None
1961 International Trade Theory in a Developing World	None	None	H.G. Johnson
1961 Economic Development for Africa South of the Sahara (Regional Conference)	None	None	S. Enke S. Hymer
1962 Economic Development (Congress)	None	H.C. Eastman (perhaps others)	L.G. Reynolds
1962 The Theory of Interest Rates (Younger Economists)	None	None	None
1963 Activity Analysis in the Theory of Growth and Planning (Younger Economists)	None	None	None
1963 The Economics of Education	None	A.D. Scott	B.F. Haley
1964 Price Formation in Various Economies	None	None	None
1964 The Distribution of National Income	None	None	B.F. Haley
1965 International Capital Movements (with World Bank)	None	None	R.A. Mundell
1965 Agriculture in Industrial Societies and Repercussions in Developing Countries	None	H.C. Eastman	B.F. Haley
1965 The Economic Problems of Housing	None	None	None
1966 Public Economics: Analysis of Public Production and Consumption and Their Relations to Private Sectors (with Centre National de la Recherche Scientifique)	None	None	None

for "younger economists." I would attribute it to three factors. One was the tendency of the International Economic Association to assume that to be recognized as a good Commonwealth economist one must have been up at Cambridge. Another was the growing concern of the Association with the economic development of the less developed countries — and more recently with bringing economists from Eastern Europe together with Western economists — along with the growth of the number of countries having respectable national professional associations. The third was the increasingly anomalous status of the Canadian Political Science Association, which was not so organized as to represent the interests of and maintain contact with the growing numbers of professional economists in Canadian universities. In this respect, the CPSA contrasted sharply with both the professionalism of the American Economic Association, and the ambitiousness of the national associations in various developing countries.

So much for the two impersonal methods of assessing the contributions of Canadian economists to the discipline of economics since the war. I think that the results grossly understate the significant work that has been done by the postwar generation of Canadian economists, especially in recent years. In the remainder of this paper I shall present the reasons for this judgment.

In my own *personal* assessment of Canadian contributions to the discipline of economics since the war, I shall begin with a listing of books by Canadian resident economists that have, according to my own knowledge, had a significant international impact, and then go on to discuss the main fields of economic research to which Canadian economists have made significant contributions.

With respect to books, I have already mentioned B.S. Keirstead's *Essay in the Theory of Profits and Income Distribution,* and A.D. Scott's *Natural Resources*. A book which has attained a classic status in its field is Gideon Rosenbluth's *Concentration in Canadian Manufacturing Industries* (Princeton: Princeton University Press, 1957), which is distinguished by its having made a contribution to statistical research method in the study of industrial organization — a connoisseur's test of a scientific contribution to our discipline in the modern age. Two of the staff studies for the Royal Commission on Canada's Economic Prospects deserve mention in this context: J. H. Young's *Canadian Commercial Policy* (Ottawa: Queen's Printer, 1957), though unnecessarily simple in its theoretical conception, presented an aggregate measurement of the cost of protection to the Canadian economy comparable to the Australian *Brigden Report* of thirty years earlier, and, besides being quoted for its estimate, helped to stimulate a theoretical discussion of the proper method of measuring the cost of protection that has been particularly active in the pages of the *Economic Record*. The study of *Output, Labour, and Capital in the Canadian Economy* (Ottawa: Queen's Printer, 1957), by William C. Hood and A.D. Scott was distinguished partly by its effort to tie its statistical work to the newly emerging concern with models of economic growth, but more by the high professional quality of the statistical work itself.[8] The decision not to give formal publication to the staff studies of the Royal Commission on Banking and Finance may have deprived other Canadian economists of similar international acclaim; at least,

---

[8] In connection with the *Royal Commission on Canada's Economic Prospects,* mention should be made of an important analysis of the Canadian economy written by two American economists, R.E. Caves and R.H. Holton, *The Canadian Economy: Prospect and Retrospect* (Cambridge: Harvard University Press, 1959).

however, it can fairly be said that the *Report* of the Commission[9] is in many ways a superior document to the *Reports* of the Radcliffe Committee and the Commission on Money and Credit. It is too early to appraise the staff studies of the Carter Commission, but it is already apparent that the *Report* of that Commission is a document of international significance.[10]

Finally, one should mention two textbooks by Canadian resident authors, the superior quality of which has led to their being widely used in other countries — Donald Bailey Marsh's *World Trade and Investment* (New York: Harcourt, Brace, 1951) and E.F. Beach's *Economic Models: An Exposition* (New York: Wiley, 1957). If one wished to identify Murray C. Kemp as a Canadian economist on the basis of his long stay at McGill, one would add his *The Pure Theory of International Trade* (Englewood Cliffs: Prentice Hall, 1964).

To turn from books published to fields of active research, there are four broadly defined areas in which I think Canadian economists have made or are making significant contributions to the scientific discipline of economics. These are the economics of natural resources, monetary economics, public finance and especially the theory of federal finance, and international economics. The contributions to the economics of natural resources have been documented previously; the others I shall discuss shortly. All four fields of research obviously reflect a concern with policy problems important to the management of the Canadian economy, a concern that has been stimulated (and financed) by federal and provincial governments. H. A. Innis would have discerned in this fact cause for the deepest alarm, and I myself expressed some doubts about the dominating influence of government-sponsored policy research on Canadian work in economics in my Presidential Address last year.[11] But the classic tradition of our discipline has been for general principles to emerge from the study of particular policy problems; and many, though not all, of the significant contributions owe nothing to policy-oriented sponsorship. To complete the picture, I should mention that in my judgment Canadian economists have made contributions in the fields of welfare economics and demand theory (R. Dehem, J.C. Weldon, A. Asimakopulos, H.A.J. Green, D.M. Winch), growth theory (B. H. Higgins, A. Asimakopulos, J.C. Weldon), and econometrics (G. Rosenbluth, S.F. Kaliski, T.M. Brown, Wm. C. Hood).

My assessment of a significant contribution to monetary economics is the hardest to document, since competence and contribution in this field are almost invariably allied with specialized knowledge of the national monetary institutions and acknowledged by respect rather than by wide quotation of and reference to the products of scholarship. The quality of Canadian scholarship in this field is attested by a number of textbooks and monographic studies, such as E.P. Neufeld's *Bank of Canada Operations, 1935-54* (Toronto: University of Toronto Press, 1955), R. Craig McIvor's *Canadian Monetary. Banking and Fiscal Development* (Toronto: Macmillan, 1958), and J.A. Galbraith's *The Economics of Banking Operations* (Montreal: McGill University Press, 1963), together with the *Report* of the Porter Commission.

[9] *Report of the Royal Commission on Banking and Finance* (Ottawa: Queen's Printer, 1964).
[10] *Report of the Royal Commission on Taxation* (Ottawa: Queen's Printer, 1967).
[11] "The Social Sciences in the Age of Opulence," *Canadian Journal of Economics and Political Science*, 32, No. 4 (November, 1966), pp. 423—42. See also the Presidential Address of A.D. Scott, "The Recruitment and Migration of Canadian Social Scientists," *ibid.*, 33, No. 4 (November, 1967), pp. 495—508, and J.H. Dales, "Canadian Scholarship in Economics: Achievement and Outlook" (an address to the Royal Society of Canada, 7 June, 1967), for similar misgivings.

Contributions to the international literature of the subject, however, consist mainly of studies of the Phillips curve in Canada, earlier by S.F. Kaliski [12] and more recently by G.L. Reuber and associated scholars, first for the Porter Commission and now for the Economic Council of Canada. [13]

In his work for the Porter Commission, Reuber significantly advanced the "trade-off" analysis employed in various studies sponsored by the Commission on Money and Credit in two ways. First, in place of the conception of the community as "trading-off" rates of inflation against rates of unemployment according to some social utility function defined over these disparate variables, he defined comparable economic costs for inflation and unemployment and was thus able to quantify the least-social-cost position on to the Phillips curve. Unfortunately, as recent theoretical work by E.S. Phelps [14] has shown, the conception of the Phillips curve is too naïve to be used in this way: if the Phillips curve notion is to be used as a basis for policy, it is necessary to incorporate the influence of experienced inflation on the wage and price formation process, and when this is done the trade-off problem appears as one of an intertemporal comparison requiring the discounting of increasing future losses from inflation against decreasing future gains from lower unemployment. Second, Reuber introduced a concept new in policy analysis, the reaction function of the central bank, relating its policy actions statistically to lagged values of variables representing its policy objectives, the function being capable of interpretation as expressing either the preferences of the central bank among its objectives or the bank's view of the objective trade-off function confronting it. This concept has subsequently been applied by various American economists to the analysis of Federal Reserve policy. [15]

Reuber's contribution of the central bank reaction function parallels one aspect of significant Canadian work in the field of public finance — Albert Breton's contributions to the development of a theory of government as a rational economic decision-unit exchanging policies for votes, in place of the essentially Fabian conception of government as society's omniscient regulator that prevails in the English tradition of economic theory. While this general idea originated in the American literature, Breton has greatly extended it by integrating with it the public finance concept of a "public good," conceiving of nationalism as a public good, and applying the analysis to the traditional problems of public finance in a federal state and to new problems, notably the purchasing policies of governments. Breton is, of course, a relatively recent arrival among Canadian contributors to the field of public finance; I mention him first only to bring out the parallelism of

---

[12] "The Relation between Unemployment and the Rate of Change of Money Wages in Canada," *International Economic Review*, 5, No. 1 (January, 1964), pp. 1–33.

[13] G.L. Reuber, "The Objectives of Canadian Monetary Policy, 1949–61: Empirical 'Trade-Offs' and the Reaction Function of the Authorities," *Journal of Political Economy*, 72 (April, 1964), pp. 109–32; *The Objectives of Monetary Policy*, working paper prepared for the Royal Commission on Banking and Finance (Ottawa: Queen's Printer, 1962); R.G. Bodkin, E.P. Bond, G.L. Reuber, and T.R. Robinson, *Price Stability and High Employment: The Options for Canadian Economic Policy*, special study prepared for the Economic Council of Canada (Ottawa: Queen's Printer, forthcoming). The last of these is concerned with the unemployment-wage-price relationship only, and not with the trade-off function.

[14] E.S. Phelps, "Phillips Curves, Expectations of Inflation and Optimal Unemployment Over Time," *Economica*, 34, No. 135 (August, 1967), pp. 254–81.

[15] W. Dewald and H.G. Johnson, "An Objective Analysis of the Objectives of American Monetary Policy, 1953–61," in Deane Carson, ed., *Banking and Monetary Studies* (Homewood, Ill.: Richard D. Irwin, 1963).

concept with Reuber's work on monetary policy, since I believe that this kind of approach to government policy opens a fruitful frontier for further significant work in several areas of economics. The federal structure of Canadian government, and the complexity and political importance of federal-provincial transfers, have always given Canadian economists a special interest in federal finance. What distinguishes postwar Canadian work on this problem — which started with A.D. Scott's "A Note on Grants in Federal Countries" (*Economica*, 1950) and has continued with contributions by Scott, J.F. Graham, A. Breton, and others to the academic literature and less readily recognizable contributions embedded in the literary underbrush of tax commissions and federal-provincial conferences — is the effort to ground the principles of federal-provincial fiscal relations in the fundamental theory of welfare economics. This is extremely difficult logical territory, and the debate continues, but progress in understanding the issues has definitely been made through the efforts of Canadian theorists.

I come, finally, to my own field of special interest, international economics. If one ignores the distinction drawn earlier between resident and nonresident Canadian economists, it would not be an exaggeration to claim that in the postwar period Canadians have virtually dominated the field, due allowance being made for James Meade's two monumental volumes on *The Theory of International Economic Policy* (London: Oxford University Press, 1951 and 1955), and the numerous important articles of P.A. Samuelson. Canadian contributors to the development of international economic theory since the war include A. Asimakopulos, C. Barber, J.H. Dales, J.S. Chipman, H.C. Eastman, S. Enke, S. Hymer, H.G. Johnson, S.F. Kaliski, M.C. Kemp, R.I. McKinnon, R.A. Mundell, R.G. Lipsey, R.G. Penner, S. Stykolt, L. Tarshis, J. Viner, Ronald and Paul Wonnacott, and J. H. Young. On the narrower definition of work by resident economists (or work by nonresidents stimulated by Canadian problems), there is still an impressive list of contributions, especially in recent years.

The main work I have in mind has been stimulated by two major debates about Canadian policy — the debate over the mismanagement of the floating exchange rate and the debate over tariff policy. In both cases, the results have been of general interest to the international profession. Before I discuss them, however, I should like to mention some contributions that lie somewhat outside the mainstream of Canadian work in international economics but have stimulated further work by other scholars. One was a passage in a paper on Canadian tariff policy by Clarence Barber,[16] which outlined the concept of the effective rate of protection (rate of protection of value added); this concept has been the subject in recent years of a rapidly growing theoretical and empirical literature, which has revolutionized contemporary ideas on the nature and importance of tariff protection policies.[17] The others comprise the Bladen Report on the automotive industries, my review of it (which owed a great deal to discussions with J.H. Dales), and subsequent articles by Paul Wonnacott and myself on Canadian tariff policy in

---

[16] "Canadian Tariff Policy," *Canadian Journal of Economics and Political Science,* 21, No. 4 (March, 1955), pp. 513–30, especially p. 523 ff.

[17] See, in particular, Harry G. Johnson, "The Theory of Tariff Structure, with Special Reference to World Trade and Development," in H.G. Johnson and P.B. Kenen, *Trade and Development* (Geneva: Librairie Droz, 1965), pp. 9–29; and W.M. Corden, "The Structure of a Tariff System and the Effective Protection Rate," *Journal of Political Economy,* 74, No. 3 (June, 1966), pp. 221–37.

the automotive industries.[18] These explorations, which drew to some extent on Barber's concept, have clarified the theory of a type of tariff policy — the system of content protection — that turns out to be widely employed in the more or less underdeveloped countries, generally at the cost of substantial waste of resources.

Turning to the major areas of Canadian research interest in international economic policy questions, theorizing and research on the mismanagement of the floating rate has had the effect of clarifying the understanding of the influence of the mobility of capital on the problems of managing an economy on a floating exchange rate,[19] and has contributed to the literature the concept of the optimum currency area as a new approach to the formulation of the classic debate over fixed versus floating exchange rates,[20] as well as the concept of the assignment problem — which objective of policy should govern the use of which instrument — and the theory of the fiscal-monetary policy mix.[21] Most of the formal analysis of this range of problems has been written by nonresident Canadian economists; but it was very much "in the air" of domestic policy discussions, and also incorporated in more literary, less formally mathematical writings by resident Canadian economists.

While this body of literature constitutes a related series of important contributions to the theory of international economic policy,[22] Canadian contributions to the theory and measurement of the effects of tariffs on industrial structure, and the related problem of the economics of foreign direct investment, to my mind are of a far greater general scientific significance — and these contributions are almost exclusively the work of resident Canadian economists.

It is not possible to list all these contributions or to document the cumulation of research results. The magnitude of the overall contribution may best be indicated by the fact that no fewer than four monographic studies have been or will be published this year — an ironic date for their publication, since their findings challenge the conventional wisdom of Canadian economic policy. These are J.H. Dales's *The Protective Tariff in Canada's Development* (Toronto: University of Toronto Press), A.E. Safarian's *Foreign Ownership of Canadian Industry* (Toronto: McGraw-Hill), H.C. Eastman and S. Stykolt's *The Tariff and Competition in Canada* (Toronto: Macmillan), and Ronald and Paul Wonnacott's *Free Trade between the*

---

[18] Report of the Royal Commission on the Automotive Industry (Ottawa: Queens' Printer, 1961); H.G. Johnson, "The Bladen Plan for Increased Protection of the Canadian Automotive Industry," *Canadian Journal of Economics and Political Science*, 29, No. 2 (May, 1963), pp. 212–35; H. G. Johnson, "The New Tariff Policies for the Automotive Industries," *Business Quarterly*, 19, No. 5 (March, 1964), pp. 43–57; P. Wonnacott, "Canadian Automotive Protection: Content Provisions, the Bladen Plan, and Recent Tariff Changes," *Canadian Journal of Economics and Political Science*, 31, No. 1 (February, 1965), pp. 98–116.

[19] For example, R.A. Mundell, "Capital Mobility and Stabilization Policy under Fixed and Flexible Exchange Rates," *Canadian Journal of Economics and Political Science*, 29, No. 4 (November, 1963), pp. 475–85; R.R. Rhomberg, "A Model of the Canadian Economy under Fixed and Fluctuating Exchange Rates," *Journal of Political Economy*, 72, No. 1 (February, 1964), pp. 1–31.

[20] R.A. Mundell, "A Theory of Optimum Currency Areas," *American Economic Review*, 51, No. 4 (September, 1961), pp. 657–65; R.I. McKinnon, "Optimum Currency Areas," *American Economic Review*, 53, No. 4 (September, 1963), pp. 717–25.

[21] The assignment problem is the unique contribution, and the theory of the fiscal-monetary policy mix to an important extent the contribution, of R.A. Mundell.

[22] The contemporary position of this theory, as represented by the contributions to a conference on international monetary problems organized by R.A. Mundell and held in Chicago in September, 1966, is summarized in Harry G. Johnson, "Theoretical Problems of the International Monetary System," *Pakistan Development Review*, 7, No. 1 (spring, 1967), pp. 1–28.

United States and Canada: The Potential Economic Effects (Cambridge, Mass.: Harvard University Press). These works are of international significance because the problems on which they shed light are urgent problems throughout the world economy. Direct foreign investment in a country, especially by American corporations, is generally opposed on emotional grounds, in less developed countries and developed countries alike. Safarian demonstrates exhaustively that for Canada the case against foreign investment is unproven; his book ranks with the only two other studies of the kind that have been undertaken, by Dunning for the United Kingdom and Brash for Australia.[23] The other three studies, all of which are concerned with the tariff, are important in two international contexts: first, in relation to the worldwide objective of promoting the development of less developed countries; and second, in relation to the general movement toward the freeing of trade in industrial products among the developed countries. In the first context, they serve to document with references to Canada a proposition that is just emerging from experience in planning the economic development of the less developed countries, namely that the attempt to promote development through the tariff and other protective policies results in a high-cost, inefficiently small-scale industrial sector dependent for its continued existence on continued protection. In the second context, they verify the faith that underlies the movement toward industrial free trade, that specialization in a large market is the efficient route to prosperity and economic growth.

It is an interesting fact that none of these books adopts the approach of traditional international trade theory. Dales's book deliberately sets itself against such theory — and I find it unnecessarily irritating on that account, as well as for the excessive self-consciousness of its use of a comparative historical methodology. The Wonnacotts' book mixes trade theory with a strong dose of location theory, and I wish it had given more attention to the requirements of general equilibrium. The Stykolt-Eastman study draws its impressively powerful methodology from the Bain tradition in the study of industrial organization. Safarian's study employs the questionnaire method of study of industrial organization and I think it suffers from the lack of a rigorous theoretical foundation. Nevertheless, problems are more important than proprieties, and each work is in its own way a significant contribution to scientific understanding of the facts of economic experience. The publication of these four books, together with the *Report* of the Carter Commission, will make 1967 a vintage year for Canadian contributions to economics.

In conclusion, let me emphasize that in this paper I have attempted to assess Canadian contributions to the discipline of economics since 1945 from a particular point of view, that of significant contributions to economics as an *international* science. Had I adopted a different standard, the progress of knowledge about and understanding of the Canadian economy and its problems, the content and balance of this paper — and especially the names of economists singled out for special mention — would have been very

---

[23] J.H. Dunning, *American Investment in British Manufacturing Industry* (London: Allen & Unwin, 1958); D.T. Brash, *American Investment in Australian Industry* (Canberra: Australian National University Press; Cambridge, Mass.: Harvard University Press, 1966).

different. I hope that at some future date someone will tackle the subject from that point of view: but it would probably take a book and not a paper to do it justice.[24]

[24] Any account from this perspective of the evolution of Canadian economics since 1945 would have to include (a partial list only) the contribution to the maintenance of scholarly standards and the stimulus to research provided by G.A. Elliott and J.H. Dales as successive editors of the *Canadian Journal of Economics and Political Science;* the stimulus and support to individual scholarly research provided by the Queen's University Summer Institute of Economic Research, and especially the help given to younger scholars by Professor M.C. Urquhart; the services in organizing and directing the research of various royal commissions and more recently the Economic Council of Canada of such economists as William C. Hood, Douglas Hartle, and D.J. Daly; the similar services of H.E. English in organizing and directing the research of the Canadian-American Trade Committee; the maintenance of interest and a high standard of instruction in economic theory at McGill University by J.C. Weldon and Murray C. Kemp; the enlivening influence on Canadian economics generally of the combination of wit, scholarship, and command of English style that characterizes H.S. Gordon, together with the courage displayed by Gordon and others in persuading a group of Canadian economists to speak out collectively against the disastrous monetary mismanagement of Governor James Coyne of the Bank of Canada; and the entrepreneurial skill of such economists as G.L. Reuber and R. Craig McIvor in rebuilding moribund departments into active and promising ones, and of others in building viable departments of economics in newly established universities.

On the strictly scholarly side, the monumental compilation of the *Historical Statistics of Canada* (Cambridge: Cambridge University Press; Toronto: Macmillan; 1965), edited by M.C. Urquhart and K.H. Buckley, must be regarded as an impressive contribution to the available research materials.

II. MICROECONOMICS: MARKETS FOR GOODS, SERVICES, AND RESOURCES

There are two essentially different levels of analysis at which the economist may derive laws concerning economic behaviour. The level of *macroeconomics* is concerned with obtaining an overview, or general outline, of the structure of the economic system and the relationships between the major aggregates which comprise the economy. *Microeconomics* is concerned with *specific* economic units and a *detailed* consideration of the behaviour of these individual units. More specifically, microeconomics deals with output of a specific product rather than total output; the number of workers employed by a single firm rather than total employment; the revenue or income of a particular firm or household rather than national income; the expenditures of a given firm or family rather than aggregate expenditures; the price of a particular product rather than the general price level, and so forth. In company, microeconomics and macroeconomics provide a rounded picture of the operation of a free enterprise economy.

The objective in Part II is to shed light on the mechanisms in a capitalist or private enterprise economy that determine what is to be produced and that organize production. We shall be concerned with the economic analysis of how it works and with economic policy measures enacted by the government, presumably to make it work better. For convenience, the readings in this part of the book are divided into eight groups: sections dealing with the operation of a market economy, consumer behaviour, the theory of the firm, the monopoly problem, resource allocation, the distribution of income and the problem of poverty, economic implications of labour unions, and with the new directions that microeconomics has been taking.

A. THE MARKET MECHANISM

As already mentioned, every economic system must determine (1) the kinds of goods to be produced, (2) how much of each good is to be produced and what resources are to be allocated to its output, and (3) the ultimate division of the goods among those who are to enjoy them. While every economy must perform these functions, economies of different types may perform them in different ways and achieve very different results.

In well-established traditional societies, custom, habit, and tradition determine how the basic economic decisions will be made. Such economies exist today in parts of Asia and Africa. In socialistic societies of the authoritarian type such as Soviet Russia, some central authority representing the interests of the nation dictates the basic decisions. In practice, this authority would almost certainly be the government's central planning board, which generates the well-publicized periodic five-year or seven-year plans. In free-enterprise economies the basic decisions are freely made by consumers and firms who are subject only to the pressures and restraints of competitive market forces. That is to say, decisions are determined by supply and demand operating through the market-and-pricing mechanism. In a sense, a free-enterprise economy is an unplanned economy. There is no perfect example of this type of system today, although the Canadian and American economies come as close as any.

A free-enterprise system, then, depends largely on the forces of the market to control and co-ordinate economic activities. Reading 10 provides an unusual picture of the emergence of a market economy and shows, in microcosm, the workings of basic economic forces: fluctuations of individual prices; the development of a standard of value and a medium of exchange (cigarettes); inflationary and deflationary movements in prices; the difficulties of price fixing; the price system as a mechanism for communicating information. Also deserving mention is the fact that this selection has become a minor classic in economics.

10. THE ECONOMIC ORGANIZATION OF A PRISONER OF WAR CAMP*

Richard A. Radford

Introduction

After allowance has been made for abnormal circumstances, the social institutions, ideas, and habits of groups in the outside world are to be found reflected in a Prisoner of War Camp. It is an unusual but a vital society. Camp organization and politics are matters of real concern to the inmates, as affecting their present and perhaps their future existences. Nor does this indicate any loss of proportion. No one pretends that camp matters are of any but local importance or of more than transient interest, but their importance there is great. . . .

One aspect of social organization is to be found in economic activity, and this, along with other manifestations of a group existence, is to be found in any POW camp. True, a prisoner is not dependent on his exertions for the provision of the necessaries, or even the luxuries of life, but through his economic activity, the exchange of goods and services, his standard of material comfort is considerably enhanced. And this is a serious matter to the prisoner: he is not "playing at shops" even though the small scale of the transactions and the simple expression of comfort and wants in terms of cigarettes and jam, razor blades and writing paper, make the urgency of those needs difficult to appreciate, even by an ex-prisoner of some three months' standing.

Nevertheless, it cannot be too strongly emphasized that economic activities do not bulk so large in prison society as they do in the larger world. There can be little production; as has been said, the prisoner is independent of his exertions for the provision of the necessities and luxuries of life; the emphasis lies in exchange and the media of exchange. A prison camp is not to be compared with the seething crowd of hagglers in a street market, any more than it is to be compared with the economic inertia of a family dinner table.

---

*Reprinted from Richard A. Radford, "The Economic Organization of a POW Camp," *Economica*, November, 1945, pp. 189–201, by permission of the editor.
Mr. Radford was an economist with the International Monetary Fund, Washington, D.C.

Naturally then, entertainment, academic and literary interests, and games and discussions of the "other world" bulk larger in everyday life than they do in the life of more normal societies. But it would be wrong to underestimate the importance of economic activity. Everyone receives a roughly equal share of essentials; it is by trade that individual preferences are given expression and comfort is increased. All at some time, and most people regularly, make exchanges of one sort or another.

Although a POW camp provides a living example of a simple economy which might be used as an alternative to the Robinson Crusoe economy beloved by the textbooks, and its simplicity renders the demonstration of certain economic hypotheses both amusing and instructive, it is suggested that the principal significance is sociological. True, there is interest in observing the growth of economic institutions and customs in a brand new society, small and simple enough to prevent detail from obscuring the basic pattern and disequilibrium from obscuring the working of the system. But the essential interest lies in the universality and the spontaneity of this economic life; it came into existence not by conscious imitation but as a response to the immediate needs and circumstances. Any similarity between prison organization and outside organization arises from similar stimuli evoking similar responses.

The following is as brief an account of the essential data as may render the narrative intelligible. The camps of which the writer had experience were Oflags and consequently the economy was not complicated by payments for work by the detaining power. They consisted normally of between 1,200 and 2,500 people, housed in a number of separate but intercommunicating bungalows, one company of 200 or so to a building. Each company formed a group within the main organization and inside the company, the room and the messing syndicate, a voluntary and spontaneous group who fed together, formed the constituent units.

Between individuals there was active trading in all consumer goods and in some services. Most trading was for food against cigarettes or other foodstuffs, but cigarettes rose from the status of a normal commodity to that of currency. RMks existed but had no circulation save for gambling debts, as few articles could be purchased with them from the canteen.

Our supplies consisted of rations provided by the detaining power and (principally) the contents of Red Cross food parcels — tinned milk, jam, butter, biscuits, bully, chocolate, sugar, etc., and cigarettes. So far the supplies to each person were equal and regular. Private parcels of clothing, toilet requisites, and cigarettes were also received, and here equality ceased owing to the different numbers despatched and the vagaries of the post. All these articles were the subject of trade and exchange.

The Development and Organization of the Market

Very soon after capture, people realized that it was both undesirable and unnecessary, in view of the limited size and the equality of supplies, to give away or to accept gifts of cigarettes or food. "Goodwill" developed into trading as a more equitable means of maximizing individual satisfaction.

We reached a transit camp in Italy about a fortnight after capture and received quarter of a Red Cross food parcel each a week later. At once, exchanges already established, multiplied in volume. Starting with simple direct barter, such as a nonsmoker giving a smoker friend his cigarette issue in exchange for a chocolate ration, more complex exchanges soon became an accepted custom. Stories circulated of a padre who started off round the camp with a tin of cheese and five cigarettes and returned to his bed with a complete parcel in addition to his original cheese and cigarettes; the market was not yet perfect. Within a week or two, as the volume of trade grew, rough scales of exchange values came into existence. Sikhs, who had at first exchanged tinned beef for practically any other foodstuff, began to insist on jam and margarine. It was realized that a tin of jam was worth half a pound of margarine plus something else; that a cigarette issue was worth several chocolates issues, and a tin of diced carrots was worth practically nothing.

In this camp we did not visit other bungalows very much and prices varied from place to place; hence the germ of truth in the story of the itinerant priest. By the end of a month, when we reached our permanent camp, there was a lively trade in all commodities and their relative values were well known, and expressed not in terms of one another — one didn't quote bully in terms of sugar — but in terms of cigarettes. The cigarette became the standard of value. In the permanent camp people started by wandering through the bungalows calling their offers — "cheese for seven" (cigarettes) — and the hours after parcel issue were bedlam. The inconveniences of this system soon led to its replacement by an Exchange and Mart notice board in every bungalow, where under the headings "name," "room number," "wanted," and "offered" sales and wants were advertised. When a deal went through, it was crossed off the board. The public and semipermanent records of transactions led to cigarette prices being well known and thus tending to equality throughout the camp, although there were always opportunities for an astute trader to make a profit from arbitrage. With this development, everyone, including nonsmokers, was willing to sell for cigarettes, using them to buy at another time and place. Cigarettes became the normal currency, though of course, barter was never extinguished.

The unity of the market and the prevalence of a single price varied directly with the general level of organization and comfort in the camp. A transit camp was always chaotic and uncomfortable: people were over-crowded, no one knew where anyone else was living, and few took the trouble to find out. Organization was too slender to include an Exchange and Mart board, and private advertisements were the most that appeared. Consequently, a transit camp was not one market but many. The price of a tin of salmon is known to have varied by two cigarettes in twenty between one end of a hut and the other. Despite a high level of organization in Italy, the market was morcellated in this manner at the first transit camp we reached after our removal to Germany in the autumn of 1943. In this camp — Stalag VIIA at Moosburg in Bavaria — there were up to 50,000 prisoners of all nationalities. French, Russians, Italians, Jugoslavs, were free to move about within the camp; British and Americans were confined to their com-pounds, although a few cigarettes given to a sentry would always procure permission for one or two men to visit other compounds. The people who first visited the highly organized French trading centre with its stalls and known prices found coffee extract — relatively cheap among the tea-drinking English — commanding a fancy price in biscuits or cigarettes, and some enterprising people made small fortunes that way. (Incidentally, we found out later that much of the coffee went "over the wire" and sold for pheno-menal prices at black market cafés in Munich: some of the French prisoners were said to have made substantial sums in RMk's. This was one of the few occasions on which our normally closed economy came into contact with other economic worlds.)

Eventually, public opinion grew hostile to these monopoly profits — not everyone could make contact with the French — and trading with them was put on a regulated basis. Each group of beds was given a quota of articles to offer and the transaction was carried out by accredited representatives from the British compound, with monopoly rights. The same method was used for trading with sentries elsewhere, as in this trade secrecy and reasonable prices had a peculiar importance, but as is ever the case with regulated companies, the interloper proved too strong.

The permanent camps in Germany saw the highest level of commercial organization. In addition to the Exchange and Mart notice boards, a shop was organized as a public utility, controlled by representatives of the Senior British Officer, on a nonprofit basis. People left their surplus clothing, toilet requisites, and food there until they were sold at a fixed price in cigarettes. Only sales in cigarettes were accepted — there was no barter — and there was no haggling. For food at least there were standard prices: clothing is less homogeneous and the price was decided around a norm by the seller and the shop manager in agreement; shirts would average say 80, ranging from 60 to 120 according to quality and age. Of food, the shop carried small stocks for convenience; the capital was provided by a loan from the bulk store of Red Cross cigarettes and repaid by a small commission taken on the first transactions. Thus, the cigarette attained its fullest currency status, and the market was almost completely unified.

It is thus to be seen that a market came into existence without labour or production. The BRCS may be considered as "Nature" of the textbook, and the articles of trade — food, clothing, and cigarettes — as free gifts — land of manna. Despite this, and despite a roughly equal distribution of resources, a market came into spontaneous operation, and prices were fixed by the operation of supply and demand. It is difficult to reconcile this fact with the labour theory of value.

Actually there was an embryo labour market. Even when cigarettes were not scarce, there was usually some unlucky person willing to perform services for them. Laundrymen advertised at two cigarettes a garment. Battledress was scrubbed and pressed and a pair of trousers lent for the interim period for twelve. A good pastel portrait cost thirty or a tin of "Kam." Odd tailoring and other jobs similarly had their prices.

There were also entrepreneurial services. There was a coffee stall owner who sold tea, coffee, or cocoa at two cigarettes a cup, buying his raw materials at market prices and hiring labour to gather fuel and to stoke; he actually enjoyed the services of a chartered accountant at one stage. After a period of great prosperity he overreached himself and failed disastrously for several hundred cigarettes. Such large-scale private enterprise was rare but several middlemen or professional traders existed. The padre in Italy, or the men at Moosburg who opened trading relations with the French, are examples: the more subdivided the market, the less perfect the advertisement of prices; and the less stable the prices, the greater was the scope for these operators. One man capitalized his knowledge of Urdu by buying meat from the Sikhs and selling butter and jam in return: as his operations became better known, more and more people entered this trade, prices in the Indian Wing approximated more nearly to those elsewhere, though to the end a "contact" among the Indians was valuable, as linguistic difficulties prevented the trade from being quite free. Some were specialists in the Indian trade, the food, clothing, or even the watch trade. Middlemen traded on their own account or on commission. Price rings and agreements were suspected and the traders certainly co-operated. Nor did they welcome newcomers. Unfortunately, the writer knows little of the workings of these people: public opinion was hostile and the professionals were usually of a retiring disposition.

One trader in food and cigarettes, operating in a period of dearth, enjoyed a high reputation. His capital, carefully saved, was originally about 50 cigarettes, with which he bought rations on issue days and held them until the price rose just before the next issue. He also picked up a little by arbitrage; several times a day he visited every Exchange or Mart notice board and took advantage of every discrepancy between prices of goods offered and wanted. His knowledge of prices, markets, and names of those who had received cigarette parcels was phenomenal. By these means he kept himself smoking steadily — his profits — while his capital remained intact.

Sugar was issued on Saturday. About Tuesday, two of us used to visit Sam and make a deal; as old customers, he would advance as much of the price as he could spare us, and entered the transaction in a book. On Saturday morning he left cocoa tins on our beds for the ration, and picked them up on Saturday afternoon. We were hoping for a calendar at Christmas, but Sam failed too. He was left holding a big black treacle issue when the price fell, and in this weakened state was unable to withstand an unexpected arrival of parcels and the consequent price fluctuations. He paid in full, but from his capital. The next Tuesday, when I paid my usual visit, he was out of business.

Credit entered into many (perhaps into most) transactions in one form or another. Sam paid in advance as a rule for his purchases of future deliveries of sugar, but many buyers asked for credit, whether the commodity was sold spot or future. Naturally, prices varied according to the terms of sale. A treacle ration might be advertised for four cigarettes now or five next week. And in the future market "bread now" was a vastly different thing from "bread Thursday." Bread was issued on Thursday and Monday, four and three days' rations respectively, and by Wednesday and Sunday night it had risen at least one cigarette per ration, from seven to eight, by supper time. One man always saved a ration to sell then at the peak price: his offer of "bread now" stood out on the board among a number of "bread Monday's" fetching one or two less, or not selling at all — and he always smoked on Sunday night.

The Cigarette Currency

Although cigarettes as currency exhibited certain peculiarities, they performed all the functions of a metallic currency as a unit of account, as a measure of value, and as a store of value, and shared most of its characteristics. They were homogeneous, reasonably durable, and of convenient size for the smallest or, in packets, for the largest transactions. Incidentally, they could be clipped or sweated by rolling them between the fingers so that tobacco fell out.

Cigarettes were also subject to the working of Gresham's Law. Certain brands were more popular than others as smokes, but for currency purposes a cigarette was a cigarette. Consequently, buyers used the poorer qualities and the Shop rarely saw the more popular brands: cigarettes such as Churchman's No. 1 were rarely used for trading. At one time, cigarettes hand-rolled from pipe tobacco began to circulate. Pipe tobacco was issued in lieu of cigarettes by the Red Cross at a rate of 25 cigarettes to the ounce and this rate was standard in exchanges, but an ounce would produce 30 homemade cigarettes. Naturally, people with machine-made cigarettes broke them down and rerolled the tobacco, and the real cigarette virtually disappeared from the market. Hand-rolled cigarettes were not homogeneous and prices could no longer be quoted in them with safety: each cigarette was examined before it was accepted and thin ones were rejected, or extra demanded as a make-weight. For a time, we suffered all the inconveniences of a debased currency.

Machine-made cigarettes were always universally acceptable, both for what they would buy and for themselves. It was this intrinsic value which gave rise to their principal disadvantage as currency, a disadvantage which exists, but to a far smaller extent in the case of metallic currency; that is, a strong demand for nonmonetary purposes. Consequently our economy was repeatedly subject to deflation and to periods of monetary stringency. While the Red Cross issue of 50 or 25 cigarettes per man per week came in regularly, and while there were fair stocks held, the cigarette currency suited its purpose admirably. But when the issue was interrupted, stocks soon ran out, prices fell, trading declined in volume and became increasingly a matter of barter. This deflationary tendency was periodically offset by the sudden injection of new currency. Private cigarette parcels arrived in a trickle throughout the year, but the big numbers came in quarterly when the Red Cross received its allocation of transport. Several hundred thousand cigarettes might arrive in the space of a fortnight. Prices soared, and then began to fall, slowly at first but with increasing rapidity as stocks ran out, until the next big delivery. Most of our economic troubles could be attributed to this fundamental instability.

Price Movements

Many factors affected prices, the strongest and most noticeable being the periodical currency inflation and deflation described in the last paragraphs. The periodicity of this price cycle depended on cigarette and, to a far lesser extent, on food deliveries. At one time in the early days, before any private parcels had arrived and when there were no individual stocks, the weekly issue of cigarettes and food parcels occurred on a Monday. The nonmonetary demand for cigarettes was great, and less elastic than the demand for food: consequently prices fluctuated weekly, falling toward Sunday night and rising sharply on Monday morning. Later, when many people held reserves, the weekly issue had no such effect, being too small a portion of the total available. Credit allowed people with no reserves to meet their nonmonetary demand over the weekend.

The general price level was affected by other factors. An influx of new prisoners, proverbially hungry, raised it. Heavy air raids in the vicinity of the camp probably increased the nonmonetary demand for cigarettes and accentuated deflation. Good and bad war news certainly had its effect, and the general waves of optimism and pessimism which swept the camp were reflected in prices. Before breakfast one morning in March of this year, a rumour of the arrival of parcels and cigarettes was circulated. Within ten minutes I sold a treacle ration for four cigarettes (hitherto offered in vain for three), and many similar deals went through. By ten o'clock the rumour was denied, and treacle that day found no more buyers even at two cigarettes.

More interesting than changes in the general price level were changes in the price structure. Changes in the supply of a commodity, in the German ration scale, or in the makeup of Red Cross parcels, would raise the price of one commodity relative to others. Tins of oatmeal, once a rare and much sought after luxury in the parcels, became a commonplace in 1943, and the price fell. In hot weather the demand for cocoa fell, and that for soap rose. A new recipe would be reflected in the price level: the discovery that raisins and sugar could be turned into an alcoholic liquor of remarkable potency reacted permanently on the dried fruit market. The invention of electric immersion heaters run off the power points made tea, a drag on the market in Italy, a certain seller in Germany.

In August, 1944, the supplies of parcels and cigarettes were both halved. Since both sides of the equation were changed in the same degree, changes in prices were not anticipated. But this was not the case: the nonmonetary demand for cigarettes was less elastic than the demand for food, and food prices fell a little. More important however were the changes in the price structure. German margarine and jam, hitherto valueless owing to adequate supplies of Canadian butter and marmalade, acquired a new value. Chocolate, popular and a certain seller, and sugar fell. Bread rose; several standing contracts of bread for cigarettes were broken, especially when the bread ration was reduced a few weeks later.

In February, 1945, the German soldier who drove the ration wagon was found to be willing to exchange loaves of bread at the rate of one loaf for a bar of chocolate. Those in the know began selling bread and buying chocolate, by then almost unsaleable in a period of serious deflation. Bread, at about 40, fell slightly; chocolate rose from 15; the supply of bread was not enough for the two commodities to reach parity, but the tendency was unmistakable.

The substitution of German margarine for Canadian butter when parcels were halved, naturally affected their relative values — margarine appreciating at the expense of butter. Similarly, two brands of dried milk, hitherto differing in quality and therefore in price by five cigarettes a tin, came together in price as the wider substitution of the cheaper raised its relative value.

Enough has been cited to show that any change in conditions affected both the general price level and the price structure. It was this latter phenomenon which wrecked our planned economy.

Paper Currency — Bully Marks

Around D-Day, food and cigarettes were plentiful, business was brisk, and the camp in an optimistic mood. Consequently the Entertainments Committee felt the moment opportune to launch a restaurant, where food and hot drinks were sold while a band and variety turns performed. Earlier experiments, both public and private, had pointed the way, and the scheme was a great success. Food was bought at market prices to provide the meals, and the small profits were devoted to a reserve fund and used to bribe Germans to provide grease paints and other necessities for the camp theatre.

Originally, meals were sold for cigarettes but this meant that the whole scheme was vulnerable to the periodic deflationary waves, and furthermore, heavy smokers were unlikely to attend much. The whole success of the scheme depended on an adequate amount of food being offered for sale in the normal manner.

To increase and facilitate trade, and to stimulate supplies and customers therefore, and secondarily to avoid the worst effects of deflation when it should come, a paper currency was organized by the Restaurant and the Shop. The Shop bought food on behalf of the Restaurant with paper notes and the paper was accepted equally with the cigarettes in the Restaurant or Shop, and passed back to the Shop to purchase more food. The Shop acted as a bank of issue. The paper money was backed 100 percent by food; hence its name, the Bully Mark. The BMk was backed 100 percent by food: there could be no overissues, as is permissible with a normal bank of issue, since the eventual dispersal of the camp and consequent redemption of all BMks was anticipated in the near future.

Originally one BMk was worth one cigarette and for a short time both circulated freely inside and outside the Restaurant. Prices were quoted in BMks and cigarettes with equal freedom — and for a short time the BMk showed signs of replacing the cigarette as currency. The BMk was tied to food, but not to cigarettes: as it was issued against food, say 45 for a tin of milk and so on, any reduction in the BMk prices of food would have meant that there were unbacked BMks in circulation. But the price of both food and BMks could and did fluctuate with the supply of cigarettes.

While the Restaurant flourished, the scheme was a success: the Restaurant bought heavily, all foods were saleable and prices were stable.

In August, parcels and cigarettes were halved and the Camp was bombed. The Restaurant closed for a short while and sales of food became difficult. Even when the Restaurant reopened, the food and cigarette shortage became increasingly acute and people were unwilling to convert such valuable goods into paper and to hold them for luxuries like snacks and tea. Less of the right kinds of food for the Restaurant were sold, and the Shop became glutted with dried fruit, chocolate, sugar, etc., which the Restaurant could not buy. The price level and the price structure changed. The BMk fell to four-fifths of a cigarette and eventually farther still, and it became unacceptable save in the Restaurant. There was a flight from the BMk, no longer convertible into cigarettes or popular foods. The cigarette reestablished itself.

But the BMk was sound! The Restaurant closed in the New Year with a progressive food shortage and the long evenings without lights due to intensified Allied air raids, and the BMks could only be spent in the Coffee Bar — relic of the Restaurant — or on the few unpopular foods in the Shop, the owners of which were prepared to accept them. In the end, all holders of BMks were paid in full, in cups of coffee or in prunes. People who had bought BMks for cigarettes, or valuable jam, or biscuits in their heyday were aggrieved that they should have stood the loss involved in their restricted choice, but they suffered no actual loss of market value.

Price Fixing

Along with this scheme came a determined attempt at a planned economy, at price fixing. The Medical Officer had long been anxious to control food sales, for fear of some people selling too much, to the detriment of their health. The deflationary waves and their effects on prices were inconvenient to all and would be dangerous to the Restaurant which had to carry stocks. Furthermore, unless the BMk was convertible into cigarettes at about par, it had little chance of gaining confidence and of succeeding as a currency. As has been explained, the BMk was tied to food but could not be tied to cigarettes, which fluctuated in value. Hence, while BMk prices of food were fixed for all time, cigarette prices of food and BMks varied.

The Shop, backed by the Senior British Officer, was now in a position to enforce price control both inside and outside its walls. Hitherto a standard price had been fixed for food left for sale in the Shop, and prices outside were roughly in conformity with this scale, which was recommended as a "guide" to sellers, but fluctuated a good deal around it. Sales in the Shop at recommended prices were apt to be slow though a good price might be obtained: sales outside could be made more quickly at lower prices. (If sales outside were to be at higher prices, goods were withdrawn from the Shop until the recommended price rose: but the recommended price was sluggish and could not follow the market closely by reason of its very purpose, which was stability.) The Exchange and Mart notice boards came under the control of the Shop: advertisements which exceeded a 5 percent departure from the recommended scale were liable to be crossed out by authority: unauthorized sales were discouraged by authority and also by public opinion, strongly in favour of a just and stable price. (Recommended prices were fixed partly from market data, partly on the advice of the MO.)

At first the recommended scale was a success: the Restaurant, a big buyer, kept prices stable around this level: opinion and the 5 percent tolerance helped. But when the price level fell with the August cuts and the price structure changed, the recommended scale was too rigid. Unchanged at first, as no deflation was expected, the scale was tardily lowered, but the prices of goods on the new scale remained in the same relation to one another, owing to the BMk, while on the market the price structure had changed. And the modifying influence of the Restaurant had gone. The scale was moved up and down several times, slowly following the inflationary and deflationary waves, but it was rarely adjusted to changes in the price structure. More and more advertisements were crossed off the board, and black market sales at unauthorized prices increased: eventually, public opinion turned against the recommended scale and authority gave up the struggle. In the last few weeks, with unparalleled deflation, prices fell with alarming rapidity, no scales existed, and supply and demand, alone and unmellowed, determined prices.

Public Opinion

Public opinion on the subject of trading was vocal if confused and change-able, and generalizations as to its direction are difficult and dangerous. A tiny minority held that all trading was undesirable as it engendered an unsavoury atmosphere; occasional frauds and sharp practices were cited as proof. Certain forms of trading were more generally condemned; trade with the Germans was criticized by many. Red Cross toilet articles, which were in short supply and only issued in cases of actual need, were excluded from trade by law and opinion working in unshakable harmony. At one time, when there had been several cases of malnutrition reported among the more devoted smokers, no trade in German rations was permitted, as the victims became an additional burden on the depleted food reserves of the Hospital. But while certain activities were condemned as antisocial, trade itself was practised, and its utility appreciated, by almost everyone in the camp.

More interesting was opinion on middlemen and prices. Taken as a whole, opinion was hostile to the middleman. His function and his hard work in bringing buyer and seller together were ignored; profits were not regarded as a reward for labour, but as the result of sharp practices. Despite the fact that his very existence was proof to the contrary, the middleman was held to be redundant in view of the existence of an official Shop and the Exchange and Mart. Appreciation only came his way when he was willing to advance the price of a sugar ration, or to buy goods spot and carry them against a future sale. In these cases the element of risk was obvious to all, and the convenience of the service was felt to merit some reward. Particularly unpopular was the middleman with an element of monopoly, the man who contacted the ration wagon driver, or the man who utilized his knowledge of Urdu. And middlemen as a group were blamed for reducing prices. Opinion notwithstanding, most people dealt with a middleman, whether consciously or unconsciously, at some time or another.

There was a strong feeling that everything had its "just price" in cigarettes. While the assessment of the just price, which incidentally varied between camps, was impossible of explanation, this price was nevertheless pretty closely known. It can best be defined as the price usually fetched by an article in good times when cigarettes were plentiful. The "just price" changed slowly; it was unaffected by short-term variations in supply, and while opinion might be resigned to departures from the "just price," a strong feeling of resentment persisted. A more satisfactory definition of the "just price" is impossible. Everyone knew what it was, though no one could explain why it should be so.

As soon as prices began to fall with a cigarette shortage, a clamour arose, particularly against those who held reserves and who bought at reduced prices. Sellers at cut prices were criticized and their activities referred to as the black market. In every period of dearth the explosive question of "should nonsmokers receive a cigarette ration?" was discussed to profitless length. Unfortunately, it was the nonsmoker, or the light smoker with his reserves, along with the hated middleman, who weathered the storm most easily.

The popularity of the price-fixing scheme, and such success as it enjoyed, were undoubtedly the result of this body of opinion. On several occasions the fall of prices was delayed by the general support given to the recommended scale. The onset of deflation was marked by a period of sluggish trade; prices stayed up but no one bought. Then prices fell on the black market, and the volume of trade revived in that quarter. Even when the recommended scale was revised, the volume of trade in the Shop would remain low. Opinion was always overruled by the hard facts of the market.

Curious arguments were advanced to justify price fixing. The recommended prices were in some way related to the calorific values of the foods offered: hence some were overvalued and never sold at these prices. One argument ran as follows: not everyone has private cigarette parcels: thus, when prices were high and trade good in the summer of 1944, only the lucky rich could buy. This was unfair to the man with few cigarettes. When prices fell in the following winter, prices should be pegged high so that the rich, who had enjoyed life in the summer, should put many cigarettes into circulation. The fact that those who sold to the rich in the summer had also enjoyed life then, and the fact that in the winter there was always someone willing to sell at low prices were ignored. Such arguments were hotly debated each night after the approach of Allied aircraft extinguished all lights at 8 p.m. But prices moved with the supply of cigarettes, and refused to stay fixed in accordance with a theory of ethics.

Conclusion

The economic organization described was both elaborate and smoothworking in the summer of 1944. Then came the August cuts and deflation. Prices fell, rallied with deliveries of cigarette parcels in September and December, and fell again. In January, 1945, supplies of Red Cross cigarettes ran out: and prices slumped still further: in February the supplies of food parcels were exhausted and the depression became a blizzard. Food, itself scarce, was almost given away in order to meet the nonmonetary demand for cigarettes. Laundries ceased to operate, or worked for £s or RMks: food and cigarettes sold for fancy prices in £s, hitherto unheard of. The Restaurant was a memory and the BMk a joke. The Shop was empty and the Exchange and Mart notices were full of unaccepted offers for cigarettes. Barter increased in volume, becoming a larger proportion of a smaller volume of trade. This, the first serious and prolonged food shortage in the writer's experience, caused the price structure to change again, partly because German rations were not easily divisible. A margarine ration gradually sank in value until it exchanged directly for a treacle ration. Sugar slumped sadly. Only bread retained its value. Several thousand cigarettes, the capital of the Shop, were distributed without any noticeable effect. A few fractional parcel and cigarette issues, such as one-sixth of a parcel and twelve cigarettes each, led to monetary price recoveries and feverish trade, especially when they coincided with good news from the Western Front. But the general position remained unaltered.

By April, 1945, chaos had replaced order in the economic sphere: sales were difficult, prices lacked stability. Economics has been defined as the science of distributing limited means among unlimited and competing ends. On 12th April, with the arrival of elements of the 30th US Infantry Division, the ushering in of an age of plenty demonstrated the hypothesis that with infinite means economic organization and activity would be redundant, as every want could be satisfied without effort.

B. HOUSEHOLDS AS CONSUMING UNITS

Consumer expenditures constitute the largest single category of spending in the Canadian economy. Consumers buy goods and services for personal consumption, and their ability to purchase and thereby satisfy economic wants is largely determined by the amount of income at their disposal. There are other factors determining consumption expenditures, however, and over a period of time, changes in these other elements will cause shifts in the level of consumption. Empirical studies of consumer expenditures indicate that consumers have rising aspirations, learn from others, and are often less than fully rational. From this it would seem to follow that the consumption desires of individuals have both a biological and a sociological foundation. In other words, both are important determinants of consumer expenditures.

The relation between consumption expenditures and income, generally termed the consumption function, can be applied to the individual consumer, to groups of consumers, or to the economy as a whole. Reading 11 examines the relevance of consumer attitudes and intentions, places them in a theoretical framework, and derives subtle and challenging conclusions regarding the extent to which a household in an affluent society has the power actually to control the size of its income.

11. AN ADAPTIVE THEORY OF CONSUMER BEHAVIOUR*

George Katona

Major propositions of what may be called an adaptive theory of consumer behaviour are supported in this paper by empirical data collected in surveys conducted over several years. . . . Fluctuations in consumers' discretionary expenditures and saturation with durable goods or its absence will be discussed in order to demonstrate the explanatory power of the theory.

The principal features of the traditional theory of consumer behaviour may be summarized, briefly and incompletely, by propositions about rationality and the dependence of expenditures on income: (1) the consumer chooses the best alternative among the conceivable courses of action open to him, and (2) the primary determinant of consumer expenditures, aside from tastes, is income (absolute or relative) or, according to more recent formulations, the normal or permanent income of the household.

In the proposed theory of consumer behaviour the assumption is abandoned that consumer behaviour is based on fully rational decision making. A genuine decision reached after careful weighing of alternative courses of action is an exception rather than the rule, in view of the great frequency of habitual behaviour as well as the influence of long-established stereotypes. Yet consumer behaviour is not capricious and is not incomprehensible, and in this sense is not conceived as irrational. This was found to be true in spite of the occasional occurrence of impulsive behaviour and frequent deviations of individual behaviour from the behaviour of large groups of consumers with which the theory is concerned.

Furthermore, change in tastes will not necessarily be considered an exogenous variable that is not studied in economics. A dynamic theory that concentrates on the understanding of change in behaviour must incorporate changes in tastes, preferences, and attitudes which result from the acquisition of similar information or experience by very many consumers.

---

*Reprinted from George Katona, "Consumer Behaviour: Theory and Findings on Expectations and Aspirations," *American Economic Review,* May, 1968, pp. 19–30, by permission of the author and publisher.
George Katona is Professor of Economics and Psychology at the University of Michigan, Ann Arbor Michigan, and Director of the Economic Behavior Program of the Survey Research Center.

Instead of postulating that consumers maximize the value of the future stream of satisfactions or that they always do what they think is best at the time, the crucial question to be raised is: Why is it that the best alternative may be different today from what it was yesterday? Similarly, the permanent income hypothesis disregards the following question: Why is it that the estimation of the sum of expected income streams may be different today from what it was yesterday?

The proposition that the household's normal or permanent income is the primary determinant of consumer expenditures implies the rejection of the determining role of current income (usually defined as the annual income in the year in which spending and saving are measured). We concur with this aspect of the proposition because the time horizon of people is longer than a single year and extends backward as well as forward. Normal or permanent income may represent a meaningful and appropriate concept for the understanding of consumer behaviour in certain cultures and at certain times. In a nonfluid society, in which the status of most people is determined by birth and class, people may have some idea of what is normal for them. The assumption that they disregard occasional deviations from the normal may then represent a useful starting point. But this approach is hardly applicable to a dynamic society. It is not applicable to present-day America, where far reaching changes occur during the lifetime of many people and where generally people believe that it is in their power to induce changes in their environment.

When environmental changes due to outside influence as well as personal influence are common, purposiveness is best defined in terms of adaptation. The theoretical model of consumer behaviour here proposed assumes purposive adaptation to changing circumstances, in contrast to the assumption that specific rules of behaviour are set up and followed in a rigid manner over long periods of time. The model must consider change in behaviour as well as the absence of change; that is, continuing with habitual behaviour. The theory of adaptive consumer behaviour is based on four principles.

Principles of Adaptive Behaviour

1. Human response is a function both of changes in the environment (stimuli) and the "person." Stimuli do not determine the response, but elicit it according to the motives and attitudes of the person responding. Motives, attitudes, and expectations are intervening variables that mediate between stimuli and responses and are acquired through past experience. They influence the perception of changes in the environment and the response to them. They are relevant for the understanding of economic behaviour when they are systematic and do not cancel out: that is, when similar intervening variables arise under similar conditions and when similar intervening variables arise among very many people at approximately the same time.

2. Individuals (and families) function as parts of broader groups. The groups to which people feel they belong, with which they identify themselves and share a common fate, may be constituted by face-to-face groups (friends, neighbours, colleagues), by the firm or corporation for which they work, as well as by such broad groups as all those in similar occupations, or the community, or the entire country. The intervening variables tend to

differ from group to group, but to be similar among members of the same group. Not only what happens to oneself, but also the perception of general economic trends, and of political trends as well, influence behaviour and even the appraisal of one's financial prospects. Favourable or adverse news on general trends, even if it is not expected to alter the personal financial situation, has an affective connotation which may influence aspirations and promote or impede the gratification of wants.

3. Wants are not static. Levels of aspiration are not given once for all time. They are raised with success and lowered with failure. Success and failure are subjective concepts indicating the individual's perception of his accomplishments as well as disappointments. They are group-determined by being viewed in relation to the success or failure of others in one's group. Usually aspirations are reality-oriented and are slightly higher or slightly lower rather than substantially higher or lower than the level of accomplishment.

When people feel that they are making progress and when they are optimistic regarding their own and the economy's prospects, new wants arise. These wants become pressing after the gratification of other wants. Contrariwise, when a person is uncertain about the future or is disappointed because he is unable to accomplish what he wishes, the process of adaptation consists of scaling down his aspirations. Perceived inability to improve one's situation may result in a feeling of saturation with goods. The extreme case consists of resignation and the stifling of wants. But the feeling of saturation may be temporary, at least in the absence of repeated severe shocks. Similarly, adaptation through raising aspirations is often interrupted by plateaus and reverses.

4. Frequently neither success nor failure is experienced. In the absence of major personal financial stimuli or of significant information about general economic trends, habitual behaviour prevails. Careful weighing of alternatives and choosing what appears most appropriate among the perceived alternatives is not an everyday occurrence. Because of inertia, the felt inability to cope with the manifold changes in the environment, and the effort required for decision making, genuine decisions are made under the impact of strong stimuli. Stimuli must be strong if they are to make people aware of a problem which calls for a new decision. In the absence of such stimuli, people continue to do what they have done before under similar circumstances; then habits determine behaviour.

Social learning, that is the acquisition of new opinions and attitudes by very many people, is slow and gradual, except under the influence of major events which call for a reorganization of the cognitive map and which occur rarely (for example, outbreak of war, revolution, runaway inflation). Group belonging influences the salience of information received as well as the learning process (social facilitation). Satisfaction and success serve as reinforcing factors and promote learning. Specific rewards, seen as attainable, constitute the strongest stimulus to effort.

The principles of adaptive consumer behaviour have been developed on the basis of empirical research. The work began by testing relatively simple hypotheses and continued by gradually revising and broadening the hypotheses. Two major parts of the empirical studies relating to discretionary expenditures will be summarized here in order to support the theory and illustrate the range of significant problems to which deductions from the theory are applicable.

It is postulated that consumers' discretionary expenditures are a function both of ability to buy and willingness to buy. Ability to buy is represented primarily by the income received in the period in which discretionary expenditures are made (usually a year) and also by the possessions of the consumer (the available financial assets, etc.) as well as by access to credit. Willingness to buy, the subjective component or the contribution of the "person," depends primarily on attitudes and expectations about personal finances and the economy as a whole.

Ability and willingness to buy interact. Each factor may change independently of the other. There is no one-to-one correlation between changes in the subjective evaluation of income trends or of economic trends, and the actual income changes or the actual economic developments. At certain times change in the ability to buy may be of paramount influence, while at other times willingness to buy may improve or deteriorate even when the changes in the environment are in the opposite direction.

In twenty years of studies intended to understand and predict the bunching of discretionary expenditures at certain times and their postponement at other times, the Survey Research Centre has taken into consideration various kinds of attitudes and expectations. A summary measure of some of these attitudes was constructed in the form of an Index of Consumer Sentiment. . . . [It was found that in 1952-66] aggregate consumer expenditures on durable goods and the extension of instalment debt [could be explained by] income (representing ability to buy) and the index (representing willingness to buy). . . .

The performance of the index at turning points is noteworthy. The sharp increase in automobile sales in 1955 was foreshadowed by a rise in the index of 1954; the 1958 recession was indicated by a decline in the index as early as the first half of 1957 (when incomes did not decline); the prolonged upswing in durable expenditures from 1961 to 1966 was reflected by an upward trend in the index as well as in incomes (the index reached its highest levels in August and November 1965); in 1966 the index declined sharply, again at a time when incomes did not decline.

The index, constructed in the same manner over several cycles, and in periods of upswing or downswing, may be viewed as reflecting attitudes which are of relevance for economic fluctuations in all postwar cycles. In addition, however, each business cycle is unique in many respects. Intervening variables indicating people's perception of unique developments and their attitudinal response to them have also been studied and proved useful in finding out why, at one time or another, consumer attitudes improved or deteriorated. Thus the high rate of spending in 1964-65 could be traced to confidence and optimism generated by such powerful stimuli as the tax cut of 1964, the frequent and sizeable gains in wages or salaries in 1964-65, information about declining unemployment and, in 1965, by the notion that the war in Vietnam would contribute to the growth of the domestic economy.

Beginning with early 1966 consumer sentiment deteriorated sharply. The decline indicated in advance the easing of automobile demand in the summer of 1966 and its sharp drop in the winter of 1966-67. Survey findings made it possible to attribute the decline in the index to experience with an expectation of price increases, awareness of rising interest rates, expectation of tax increases, and uncertainty and misgivings about the war in Vietnam.

The extent of the deterioration in consumer sentiment posed a threat of a substantial decline in consumers' discretionary expenditures and therefore of a recession in the consumer sector. Yet we skirted the recession, primarily because the incomes of very many consumers continued to advance and government expenditures increased greatly. Thus in 1966 the worsening in attitudes and expectations terminated earlier and at a higher level than the decline which ushered in the recession of 1958. Up to August, 1967, the improvement of attitudes was moderate rather than substantial.

These studies of the determinants of fluctuations in consumers' discretionary expenditures confirm that (1) both ability and willingness to buy are relevant, and (2) substantial changes in willingness to buy do occur among very many people at about the same time. Furthermore, these studies strongly support the notion that individuals see themselves as belonging to a larger whole and as sharing a common fate with it. Adaptation to business news occurs both when the news is favourable (as in 1965) and when it is unfavourable (as in 1966). . . .

The Impact of Personal Financial Progress

The model of income changes in two consecutive periods may make use of the Markov chain. A family that has experienced an income increase (+) may move along three paths. During the next period of time the family may have a further income increase, an income decrease, or stable income. Similarly, three moves are possible for a family with stable income (=), and three moves for a family with an income decrease (−).

The model applies not only to consecutive income changes, but also to sucessions of income changes and income expectations. Thereby a time perspective is considered which extends both backward and forward. The development in the first period stands for the experience of an income change, while the development in the second period is represented by income expectations that prevail at the end of the first period. Then we again distinguish nine moves; for instance, an income increase associated with the expectation of a further income increase (+ +), an income increase associated with the expectation of stable income (+ =), an income increase associated with the expectation of an income decline (+ −), etc.

Before considering past and expected trends together, we raise a question concerning the origin of expectations. The younger a person is, the more formal education he has, and the larger his income is, the more probable it is that he will entertain optimistic income expectations. In addition, past income change also influences the expectations. We find that many more of those respondents who had income gains in the past were optimistic than of those who had other forms of income changes, even after the effects of the demographic factors were parcelled out in multivariate studies. Past progress or success fosters optimistic income expectations.

Of greatest interest are the behavioural affects of "+ + trends"; that is, income increases associated with optimistic income expectations. Several measures of such trends have been collected in recent surveys; two of these measures will be discussed here: (1) personal financial situation at present better than a year ago and expected to be better next year; (2) income at present higher than four years ago and expected to be higher four years from now.

Subjective notions enter into both measures. This is true first of all of expectations which reflect people's aspirations. It is also true of the evaluation of the personal financial situation and even of reports about income changes over the past four years. In studying factors that influence consumer behaviour, the impact of subjective factors is of special interest.

Survey data were collected on various aspects of the discretionary behaviour of the same respondents for whom information on personal financial trends was available. The frequencies of all purchases of durable goods and of purchases on the instalment plan during the year prior to the determination of the expectations, as well as of plans to buy durables, were related to (1) cumulative gains (+ +), (2) gains that are not expected to continue (+ = or + −) or expected gains that do not follow past gains (= + or − +), and (3) the absence of past as well as expected gains. Since both the frequency of + + trends and of durable purchases increase with family income and decrease with the age of the family head, the relations must be studied after income and age effects are eliminated.

It appears that the relatively high rate of past durable purchases on the part of respondents with + + trends is due to income and age effects. But incurring new instalment debt and especially buying plans are associated with + + trends after the income and age effects are removed. There are indications that the failure to find an independent effect of the trends on past durable purchases is due to the inclusion of many relatively small or nondiscretionary transactions among the purchases of durables. The multivariate analysis shows that people with + + trends, in spite of frequent past purchases, express buying intentions more frequently than people with other trends. The largest differences appear when plans to buy new cars are considered. This was expected because the purchase of new cars is more often discretionary than is the purchase of household appliances or of expenditures on home repairs and improvements. Similarly, plans to make two major expenditures should involve the exercise of greater discretion than planning to make one such expenditure; the influence of + + trends is larger in the former than in the latter case.

The impact on behaviour of feeling and expecting to be better off is greater than that of experiencing and expecting rising income. Furthermore, expected income trends have a greater effect on buying plans than past trends. We conclude, therefore, that the subjective meaning of income changes does matter.

It is a central proposition of the adaptive theory of consumer behaviour that success makes for the arousal of new wants and an improvement in the standard of living. The finding that cumulative improvement in the personal financial situation is linked with an increased rate of instalment buying and of planning to purchase durable goods is in accord with that proposition.

Additional data were collected to shed light on the arousal of new wants after the gratification of other wants. The question of saturation may be studied by relating the various forms of personal financial trends to automobile turnover. Turnover rates were calculated from information on the times when members of a representative sample last bought a car and when they expected to buy their next car (within a year, within two or three years, etc.). It appeared that + + trends are associated with fairly short turnover rates (with definite plans to buy a car within two years after the last car had been purchased) and other trends with long turnover rates of the response, "We will not buy a car during the next three years" (which response implies a long rate). The association between + + trends and short turnover rates could not be explained by income and age alone.

The perception of progress or success stimulates fairly rapid "upgrading," while lack of progress results in failure to replace an old possession with a new one. This finding supplements earlier findings on the basis of which it was concluded that saturation depends primarily on lack of progress and pessimistic outlook rather than on the number and quality of goods possessed.[1] The older studies also provided justification for reversing the traditional assumption about consumption being a function of income. Income appeared to be a function of consumption needs and wants because the desire for more and better things induced many people to work harder, or to take up a second job, or for the wife to return to work.

Concluding Remarks

The price of affluence is not saturation and the lack of incentives. This conclusion contradicts the notion that saturation would eventually cause a collapse of the consumer economy. It has been frequently argued by social critics that prosperity must be its own gravedigger because after relatively short prosperous periods in which many people satisfy their wants, "people run out of things they can't do without."[2] Clearly, the transition from a need-economy to a wants- or aspirations- economy does not warrant such views.

We may recall the starting point of the author's studies of consumer behaviour: affluence makes for discretion of action by very many consumers. When not a few individuals, nor a thin upper class, but the majority of families have an income which suffices to cover more than subsistence needs, wants and aspirations are gratified which are discretionary and may be postponed or bunched. Then the frequency of genuine decisions increases and the study of consumer psychology becomes a necessary part of economic analysis.

J.K. Galbraith begins his 1967 book, *The New Industrial State*, with a similar assumption: "High production and income . . . remove a very large part of the population from the compulsions and pressures of physical want" (p. 4). He continues, however, in a vein different from this author: "In consequence their economic behavior becomes in some measure malleable. . . . Along with prices and costs, consumer demand becomes subject to management." Thus instead of my proposition that "affluence makes for discretion in action," Galbraith concludes that "affluence opens the way for control over the consumer."

---

[1] For instance, when asked to list things they would like to have or to spend money on, survey respondents mentioned many more desires in the early 1960s than in the early 1950s. It was not those who had bought many things in the recent past who expressed the fewest wants, but rather the old and the poor.

[2] It was also asserted that consumer demand had shifted from greatly needed and useful goods and services to the gratification of desires which were unimportant and were stimulated solely by advertising and the extension of credit. Galbraith, in *The Affluent Society,* used the expression "contrived wants," while Toynbee spoke of "bogus wants." Toynbee's statement may be repeated here: "An economy that depends for its survival on an artificial stimulation of material wants seems unlikely to survive for a long time." See also Thomas Balogh: "The resilience of the [American] economic system might be eventually sapped by the sheer satiety of the consumers" (*The Economics of Poverty,* New York: Macmillan, 1967, p. 161). This author has pointed out that all higher-order wants are learned and therefore do not originate with the individual alone; that changing and even influencing human beings is a difficult process which is usually incomplete; and that today's consumers, who are much better educated than their forefathers, are not puppets or pawns.

According to he traditional theory, Galbraith states, all power lies with the consumer: "the flow of instruction is in one direction — from the individual to the market to the producer" (p. 211). This "accepted sequence" must give way to the "revised sequence" in which "the producing firm reaches forward to control its markets and on beyond to . . . shape the social attitudes of those, ostensibly, that it serves" (p. 212).

Yet interaction characterizes communication and learning. Although we learn from experience with others — from the teacher, from information received by word of mouth and the printed page, or radio and television, and also from advertisements — it is we who learn. Conditioning and stamping-in are limiting cases of learning which are most applicable to a situation in which we are not involved (when the choice does not matter) and least applicable to changing social attitudes. The unidirectional form of the revised sequence represents an exception as does the accepted sequence. Both sequences negate consumers' discretion and contradict psychological principles of learning (except under circumstances of servitude or compulsion).

Success or failure of large producers in influencing their specific product's share in the market is of lesser importance than the management or regulation of aggregate demand. The latter has proved unsuccessful, even on the part of the largest mature corporations, as indicated by the substantial fluctuations in automobile demand which year after year surprise the car industry. Much of the effort of mature corporations goes into trying to swim with the current and to find out in what direction the consumer is moving and what is acceptable to him, in order to adjust production schedules accordingly.[3] No doubt, the consumer's choice is restricted by what is offered to him, and the two-way flow of the learning process involves some "management." But restricted choice is not equivalent to absence of choice. For, although the environment sets limits to human discretion, the consumers' margin of action is yet sufficient to influence the economy greatly.

The difference between the two positions — control by the "technostructure" versus importance of consumer psychology — can best be illustrated by quoting Galbraith further. He draws the conclusion that "it is to the nature and purposes of this management [by the mature corporation] . . . that the scholar must look if he is to have any adequate view of consumer behavior" (p. 214). This paper was written in the belief that an adequate view of consumer behaviour can be obtained only by considering principles of social learning and expectational dynamics, which indicate the influence of purposive adaptation to success and failure, as experienced in a personal as well as in a more general context.

The adaptive theory of consumer behaviour represents a low-level theory. To construct a more general theory, comparative studies of consumer behaviour in different societies may be utilized. Studies of consumer behaviour in other affluent societies in which social learning may be slower or faster than in the United States, as well as in less developed countries, may provide new insights into the nature of the adaptive process.

---

[3] Galbraith acknowledges that "the control of demand . . . is not perfect" (p. 30) and writes that the revised sequence has not replaced the accepted sequence, but that both still "exist side by side," the one in the segment of the economy ruled by large corporations and the other "outside the industrial system" (p. 213). Galbraith's failure to consider the psychology of the consumer is the more regrettable as he makes good use of entrepreneurial and group psychology in other parts of his book, in refuting theories about the power of impersonal market forces.

C. BUSINESS FIRMS

Most of the things produced in a free enterprise type of economic system are made and distributed through the market mechanism by productive units organized as private enterprises. These organizations serve the function of mobilizing economic resources for the creation of goods and services that satisfy consumer wants. Through them are made the decisions as to how human effort is employed, and how capital and other resources are used. Business firms are the basic producing and distributing units in a modern private enterprise economy.

When consumer goods are secured by the application of labour directly to land or natural resources, production is said to be direct. Production in which capital goods are used is called indirect or roundabout. Capital includes all types of durable equipment which are useful in the productive process and also semifinished goods which cannot be enjoyed by consumers until their production is completed. Since the indirect process is time consuming and produces relatively remote rather than immediate results, we must understand why it has so generally replaced direct production. Reading 12 goes to the heart of the issue and reveals clearly the benefits yielded by the use of capital.

The behaviour pattern of business firms is determined by a complex set of factors. It is generally assumed that the firm strives to maximize profits or minimize loss. Economists traditionally explain that either objective is achieved when marginal revenue and marginal costs are equal. On the other hand, it is often observed that business firms limit their activities to those whose returns equal average or "fully-allocated" costs. Accordingly, how useful is marginal analysis? Reading 13 takes up the question, and the author concludes that well-managed companies lean heavily on marginal analysis. Parenthetically, the marginal concept may be very useful in describing individual behaviour, even if nobody fashions his actual or potential behaviour in these precise terms. Although a mathematician may explain your behaviour when driving your car, for example, in terms of solving differential equations, you may remain forever unaware of this.

12. CAPITAL AND ROUNDABOUT PRODUCTION*

Eugen von Böhm-Bawerk

The end and aim of all production is the making of things with which to satisfy our wants; that is to say, the making of goods for immediate consumption, or "consumption goods." . . . We combine our own natural powers and natural powers of the external world in such a way that, under natural law, the desired material good must come into existence. But this is a very general description indeed of the matter, and looking at it closer there comes in sight an important distinction which we have not as yet considered. It has reference to the distance which lies between the expenditure of human labour in the combined production and the appearance of the desired good. We either put forth our labour just before the goal is reached, or we intentionally take a roundabout way. That is to say, we may put forth our labour in such a way that it at once completes the circle of conditions necessary for the emergence of the desired good, and thus the existence of the good immediately follows the expenditure of the labour; or we may associate our labour first with the more remote causes of the good, with the object of obtaining, not the desired good itself, but a proximate cause of the good; which cause, again, must be associated with other suitable materials and powers, till, finally — perhaps through a considerable number of intermediate members — the finished good, the instrument of human satisfaction, is obtained.

The nature and importance of this distinction will be best seen from a few examples. . . . A peasant requires drinking water. The spring is some distance from his house. There are various ways in which he may supply his daily wants. First, he may go to the spring each time he is thirsty, and drink out of his hollowed hand. This is the most direct way; satisfaction follows immediately on exertion. But it is an inconvenient way, for our peasant has to take his way to the well as often as he is thirsty. And it is an insufficient way, for he can never collect and store any great quantity such as he requires

*Reprinted from Eugen von Böhm-Bawerk, *The Positive Theory of Capital*, London: Macmillan, 1891, pp. 17–22.
Eugen von Böhm-Bawerk, who lived from 1851–1914, was one of the three outstanding economists of the Austrian school of economic thought. During his lifetime he was recognized as a great professor, and is best known for his study of the theories of capital and interest.

for various other purposes. Second, he may take a log of wood, hollow it out into a kind of pail, and carry his day's supply from the spring to his cottage. The advantage is obvious, but it necessitates a roundabout way of considerable length. The man must spend, perhaps, a day in cutting out the pail; before doing so he must have felled a tree in the forest; to do this, again, he must have made an axe, and so on. But there is still a third way: instead of felling one tree he fells a number of trees, splits and hollows them, lays them end to end, and so constructs a runnel or rhone which brings a full head of water to his cottage. Here, obviously, between the expenditure of the labour and the obtaining of the water we have a very roundabout way, but, then, the result is ever so much greater. Our peasant need no longer take his weary way from house to well with the heavy pail on his shoulder, and yet he has a constant and full supply of the freshest water at his very door.

Another example. I require stone for building a house. There is a rich vein of excellent sandstone in a neighbouring hill. How is it to be got out? First, I may work the loose stones back and forward with my bare fingers, and break off what can be broken off. This is the most direct, but also the least productive way. Second, I may take a piece of iron, make a hammer and chisel out of it, and use them on the hard stone — a roundabout way, which, of course, leads to a very much better result than the former. Third method — having a hammer and chisel I use them to drill a hole in the rock; next I turn my attention to procuring charcoal, sulphur, and nitre, and mixing them in a powder, then I pour the powder into the hole, and the explosion that follows splits the stone into convenient pieces — still more of a roundabout way, but one which, as experience shows, is as much superior to the second way in result as the second was to the first.

Yet another example. I am short-sighted, and wish to have a pair of spectacles. For this I require ground and polished glasses, and a steel framework. But all that nature offers toward that end is silicious earth and iron ore. How am I to transform these into spectacles? Work as I may, it is as impossible for me to make spectacles directly out of silicious earth as it would be to make the steel frames out of iron ore. Here there is no immediate or direct method of production. There is nothing for it but to take the roundabout way, and, indeed, a very roundabout way. I must take silicious earth and fuel, and build furnaces for smelting the glass from the silicious earth; the glass thus obtained has to be carefully purified, worked, and cooled by a series of processes; finally, the glass thus prepared — again by means of ingenious instruments carefully constructed beforehand — is ground and polished into the lens fit for short-sighted eyes. Similarly, I must smelt the ore in the blast furnace, change the raw iron into steel, and make the frame therefrom — processes which cannot be carried through without a long series of tools and buildings that, on their part again, require great amounts of previous labour. Thus, by an exceedingly roundabout way, the end is attained.

The lesson to be drawn from these examples is obvious. It is — that a greater result is obtained by producing goods in roundabout ways than by producing them directly. Where a good can be produced in either way, we have the fact that, by the indirect way, a greater product can be got with equal labour, or the same product with less labour. But, beyond this, the superiority of the indirect way manifests itself in being the only way in which certain goods can be obtained. . . .

That roundabout methods lead to greater results than direct methods is one of the most important and fundamental propositions in the whole theory of production. It must be emphatically stated that the only basis of this proposition is the experience of practical life. Economic theory does not and cannot show *a priori* that it must be so; but the unanimous experience of all the technique of production says that it is so. And this is sufficient; all the more that the facts of experience which tell us this are commonplace and familiar to everybody. But *why* is it so? The economist might quite well decline to answer this question. For the fact that a greater product is obtained by methods of production that begin far back is essentially a purely technical fact, and to explain questions of technique does not fall within the economist's sphere. For instance, that tropical lands are more fruitful than the polar zone; that the alloy of which coins is made stands more wear and tear than pure metal; that a railroad is better for transport than an ordinary turnpike road — all these are matters of fact with which the economist reckons, but which his science does not call on him to explain. . . .

In the last resort all our productive efforts amount to shiftings and combinations of matter. We must know how to bring together the right forms of matter at the right moment, in order that from those associated forces the desired result, the product wanted, may follow. But, as we saw, the natural forms of matter are often so infinitely large, often so infinitely fine, that human hands are too weak or too coarse to control them. We are as powerless to overcome the cohesion of the wall of rock when we want building stone as we are, from carbon, nitrogen, hydrogen, oxygen, phosphorus, potash, etc., to put together a single grain of wheat. But there are other powers which can easily do what is denied to us, and these are the powers of nature. There are natural powers which far exceed the possibilities of human power in greatness, and there are other natural powers in the microscopic world which can make combinations that put our clumsy fingers to shame. If we can succeed in making those forces our allies in the work of production, the limits of human possibility will be infinitely extended. And this we have done.

The condition of our success is, that we are able to control the materials on which the power that helps us depends, more easily than the materials which are to be transformed into the desired good. Happily this condition can be very often complied with. Our weak yielding hand cannot overcome the cohesion of the rock, but the hard wedge of iron can; the wedge and the hammer to drive it we can happily master with little trouble. We cannot gather the atoms of phosphorus and potash out of the ground, and the atoms of carbon and oxygen out of the atmospheric air, and put them together in the shape of the kernel of wheat; but the organic chemical powers of the seed can put this magical process in motion, while we on our part can very easily bury the seed in the place of its secret working, the bosom of the earth. Often, of course, we are not able directly to master the form of matter on which the friendly power depends, but in the same way as we would like it to help us, do we help ourselves against it; we try to secure the alliance of a second natural power which brings the form of matter that bears the first power under our control. We wish to bring the well water into the house. Wooden rhones would force it to obey our will, and take the path we prescribe, but our hands have not the power to make the forest trees into rhones. We have not far to look, however, for an expedient. We ask the help of a second ally in the axe and the gouge; their assistance gives us the rhones; then the rhones bring us the water. And what in this illustration is done through the mediation of two or three members may be done, with equal or greater result, through five, ten, or twenty members. Just as we control and guide the immediate matter of which the good is composed by one friendly power, and that power by a second, so can we control and guide the second by a third, the third by a fourth, this, again, by a fifth, and so on — always going back to more remote causes of the final result — till in the series we come at last to one cause which we can control conveniently by our own natural powers. This is the true importance which attaches to our entering on roundabout ways of production: every roundabout way means the enlisting in our service of a power which is stronger or more cunning than the human hand; every extension of the roundabout way means an addition to the powers which enter into the service of man, and the shifting of some portion of the burden of production from the scarce and costly labour of human beings to the prodigal powers of nature.

And now we may put into words an idea which has long waited for expression, and must certainly have occurred to the reader; the kind of production which works in these wise circuitous methods is nothing else than what economists call "capitalist production," as opposed to that production which goes directly at its object. . . . And capital is nothing but the complex of intermediate products which appear on the several stages of the roundabout journey.

13. MARGINAL POLICIES OF "EXCELLENTLY MANAGED" COMPANIES*

James S. Earley

In a recent article I presented evidence from management literature that leading cost accountants and management consultants are currently advocating principles of accounting analysis and decision making that are essentially "marginalist" in character and implication. The present article reports on a questionnaire survey designed to test empirically the acceptance and influence of these new principles among leading American manufacturing firms. It seeks to ascertain what relationships there are between organizational and accounting practices and the policies of the firms employing them. It seeks above all to test the validity of certain "nonmarginalist" propositions concerning business behaviour found in recent economics literature, and the "marginalist" hypotheses derived from the management literature.

The survey does not purport to cover a cross section of American business by size and type. It is deliberately restricted to a type of firm taken as "representative," in something akin to the Marshallian sense. These firms are leading firms, and are presumably in the vanguard in the use of the newer management techniques. Through diffusion, direct imitation, and the competitive pressures they create, they are likely to set the dominant patterns of *future* business practice. Inquiry is also directed especially toward multiproduct and multimarket companies, both because marginal accounting has most applicability in these cases and because such firms appear to be becoming increasingly representative of American business. It is confined to fairly large companies for similar reasons.

The basic list of companies to which the questionnaire was sent is that of the entire group of 217 manufacturing companies rated as "excellently managed" by the American Institute of Management; 110 usable replies were received.

More than most empirical studies of business policies, this one relies upon

---

*Reprinted from James S. Earley, "Marginal Policies of 'Excellently Managed' Companies," *The American Economic Review,* March, 1956, pp. 44—70, by permission of the editor and author.
Dr. Earley is Professor of Economics and Dean of the College of Social and Behavioral Sciences, University of California, Riverside.

inference from indirect evidence. Only a few direct questions concerning policies were asked. Most of the evidence refers to organizational structure, accounting practice, and certain oblique judgments of management, from which inferences as to behaviour are drawn. This strategy was deliberately chosen in the belief that it would yield more reliable evidence of wider theoretical value than more direct questioning. The inferential approach is fortified by two special features of the analysis — the search for *patterns* of responses, and *tests of consistency* of the patterns.

It is suggested by many recent theoretical and empirical studies in economics that the modern business firm behaves nonmarginally in at least two essential respects: in having predominantly a long-run and defensive viewpoint in its pricing, production, and investment policies (rather than an alert attitude toward its near-at-hand profit opportunities); and in using, in the main, a full-cost rather than incremental-cost calculus in its pricing, production, and investment decisions. These are the major nonmarginalist hypotheses tested in this survey.

The major hypotheses from the management literature, which run counter to those above, and in this respect and others are considered to be "marginalist" in their implications, are the following:

1. Among well-managed multiproduct companies there will be found a substantial amount of what I call marginal accounting. The essential characteristic of such accounting is systematic (1) segmentation and (2) differentiation of costs (and, where appropriate, also revenues). By segmentation is meant the separate calculation of the costs and revenues of each of the firm's operations and prospective actions (so-called "segments") — for example, each process, product or product group, market area, "function," division, plant, or contemplated action. Cost differentiation, which is as far as possible carried out for each segment, takes two forms: (1) the breaking apart of fixed and variable costs to obtain a variable cost function; and (2) differentiation between those fixed costs that can be specifically assigned to a segment and those that must be considered common to the enterprise as a whole.

Such accounting is "marginal" in two essential respects: first, it provides discrete data for considering each segment as an alternative field of management action; and second, in place of average cost information it provides data for estimating the *differences* in costs (and in revenues) that any action would entail.

2. In multiproduct, multiprocess enterprise, marginal accounting (and the basing of policies upon it) will be associated with, and facilitated by, an organizational structure differentiated, administratively and technically, along lines of major segments, such as product lines, functions, and market areas. This facilitates the above-mentioned segmentation and differentiation of costs and revenues and helps management focus upon each major sector of the enterprise as a profit-making entity.

3. Marginal accounting data will be found useful in a wide range of managerial problems, including (1) evaluation and control of operating efficiency; (2) minimizing costs (as by proper selection of processes and methods); (3) determination of the relative stress that should be placed among products and markets in selling; (4) pricing decisions, both short-range and long-range; (5) selecting, adding, or dropping products or market segments; and (6) product- and market-related investment (including disinvestment).

4. Marginal accounting analysis will lead firms to employ marginal techniques of planning and decision making (called by the National Association of Cost Accountants "cost-volume-profit analysis" and "marginal income analysis"), and to adopt marginalist viewpoints and policies. The basic principle of such marginalism being to concentrate upon the differences in costs, revenues, and profit that decisions involve and to neglect "inescapable" costs not affected by them, special attention will be given to ratios between price and variable costs ("marginal income ratios" in NACA terminology), and to differences between revenues and variable-plus-separable costs (so-called contribution margins). Overhead allocations and full-cost computations will tend to fall into disuse for decision-making purposes.

Specific policies likely to flow from marginal accounting analysis are: much reference to variable costs in short-range pricing decisions and in "selective selling"; attention to both variable and separable fixed costs in choices among markets and products and in product-related investment decisions; and differential pricing and other forms of "market segmentation" according to estimates of differing variable/fixed cost compositions, competitive pressures, and demand elasticities.

5. Such analyses and policies, especially if accompanied by budgeting and "profit planning," will be associated with a short-dated time horizon (at least as far as pricing and other product-related decisions are concerned), and a fairly keen and short-dated search for increased profit.

6. Pricing, product, and investment decisions will be made with a lively sense of impending innovation and obsolescence; hence the possible long-run reactions of rivals to the profits currently being made will not greatly influence these decisions. This is in contrast to full-cost theories in particular, which implicitly assume that firms make their decisions within the horizon of a given production function.

These are the major hypotheses to be tested. . . .

Company Organization

. . . Most of the companies show that their organization is conducive to cost and revenue differentiation by product groups and market areas (see Table 1). In these matters 78 percent of the respondents are aided either by having their plants mainly or wholly specialized by product lines, or by being organized administratively into product divisions. Selling activities are even more highly differentiated, and along both product and market area lines. Only one company does not organize its selling activities by either products or markets, and approximately two-thirds of them differentiate their selling activities in both these respects.

An index of the marginal or nonmarginal organizational characteristics of the respondents is presented in Table 1.

Variable/Fixed Cost Breakdowns and Their Transmission to Management

The practice of making variable/fixed (V/F) cost breakdowns and putting them into management's hands in connection with planning and decision making is overwhelmingly followed by these "excellently managed" companies, as Table 2 reveals. . . .

TABLE 1

SUITABILITY OF COMPANY ORGANIZATION TO MARGINAL ACCOUNTING ANALYSIS

	Component Index 1: Suitability of Organization*	Number of Companies	Percent of Total
(+ 2)	Strong marginalist evidence—product costs differentiable by either specialized plants or product divisions; selling costs by both products and market areas (A3 and B4)	59	56
(+ 1)	Substantial marginalism—product costs differentiable by either plants or divisions; and selling by *one* of products or markets	24	22
(− 2)	Strong nonmarginal evidence—product costs differentiable by neither specialized plants nor divisions; selling by neither products nor markets	1	1
(− 1)	Substantial nonmarginal evidence—product costs differentiable by neither plants nor divisions; selling by only *one* of products or markets	13	12
(0)	Ambiguous evidence—patterns other than those above	10	9

Average of component index: = + 1.2

*The figures to the left are the assigned positive and negative values of each category.

TABLE 2

AVAILABILITY OF VARIABLE FIXED COST BREAKDOWNS FOR MANAGEMENT PLANNING AND DECISION MAKING

Component Index 2: Availability of Product V/F Breakdowns	Number of Companies	Percent
Strong marginalist evidence: total (T), production (P), and selling (S) breakdowns all made available by products	83	79
Substantial marginalist evidence: *two* of T, P, or S product breakdowns made available	12	11
Strong nonmarginalist evidence: none of T, P, or S made available	4	4
Substantial nonmarginalist evidence: only *one* of T, P, or S made available	2	2
Ambiguous evidence: only two of three items answered and one of these made available	4	4

Average of component index: + 1.6

Uses of Variable/Fixed Cost Breakdowns

The responses strongly support the claim that variable cost functions are becomming a widely used multipurpose management tool. (See Table 3.)...

TABLE 3

USES OF VARIABLE COSTING: PERCENT OF RESPONDING COMPANIES CONSIDERING V/F COST BREAKDOWNS HELPFUL IN SPECIFIED PROBLEMS

Component Index 3: "Variable Costing"	Number of Companies	Percent
Strong marginalist evidence—V/F considered helpful in pricing (P), marketing (M), and product selection (S)	63	59
Substantial marginal evidence—V/F considered helpful in two of P, M, and S	31	29
Strong nonmarginalist evidence—V/F not considered helpful in any of P, M, or S	4	4
Mild or ambiguous evidence—V/F considered helpful in one of P, M, or S	9	8

Average of component index: + 1.5

Use of "Separable" Fixed Costing

Marginal accounting analysis can be brought to bear on many longer-range problems by combining V/F breakdowns with the identification of the separable fixed costs of segments or actions — here called S/C (separable/common) or separable costing. When combined with calculations or estimates of segment revenue, these combined operations lead to marginal accounting's measurement of long-range profitability — the segment or action's "contribution margin." This is a marginal (incremental) measurement in two respects: it shows the amount of fixed cost directly attributable to the segment or action independent of the common and average fixed costs of the enterprise, and it retains the variable cost function relating levels of production to differences in variable and hence in total costs.

While such measurements may be retrospective, they are especially useful in forward-looking decisions entailing additions or reductions in fixed

TABLE 4

USE OF SEPARABLE FIXED COSTS IN LONG-RANGE MANAGEMENT PROBLEMS

Component Index 4: Separable Costing	Number of Companies	Percent
Strong marginalist evidence: separable fixed costs used in dropping products (D), adding product capacity (I), and introducing new products (N)	57	56
Substantial marginal evidence: separable fixed costs used in two of D, I, or N	27	26
Strong nonmarginal evidence: separable fixed costs used in none of D, I, or N	10	10
Substantial nonmarginal evidence: separable fixed costs used in only one of D, I, or N	8	8

Average of component index: + 1.08

charges. Accordingly, [we] inquired whether, in contemplating a number of such actions, fixed cost calculations were made on an incremental or an allocation basis.

The incidence of S/C costing, while lower than that of V/F costing, is impressively high (see Table 4.). . .

Combined Use of V/F and S/C Costing

Table 5 tests the use of both (and neither) of these complementary types of cost differentiation. Even by this rigorous test, the marginal approach has a high incidence, ranging from 54 percent to 83 percent of the respondents except in distribution decisions. On the other hand, with this last exception the number using neither type of marginal costing is very small. An interesting measure of marginal vs. nonmarginal costing is provided by the ratios of companies using both V/F and S/C costing to those using neither, shown in the right-hand column. With the exception of the distribution facilities problem, these ratios are high.

TABLE 5

USE OF BOTH (AND NEITHER) V/F AND S/C
COSTING IN LONG-RANGE MANAGEMENT PROBLEMS

Questions 6 and 7	Number of Responding Companies	Number of Companies Using: Both	Neither	Ratio of Both to Neither
1. Adding production capacity for existing products				
(a) 7c, plus reference to variables in cost/volume analysis (6c)	101	83	2	42:1
(b) 7c, plus reference to variables in volume/price estimates (6d)	100	72	4	18:1
2. Dropping products or product groups: 7a, plus reference to variables in dropping products (6g)	100	65	8	8:1
3. Choosing new product types: 7d, plus reference to variables in choosing product types (6h)	100	54	16	3.4:1
4. Adding (and pricing) new products: 7e, plus reference to variables in cost/volume analysis (6c)	100	68	3	23:1
7e, plus reference to variables in price/volume estimates (6d)	99	59	6	10:1
5. Adding distribution facilities: 7f, plus reference to variables in volume/price estimates (6j)	99	35	33	1:1

Direct Evidence on Price Policy

Table 6 analyses the responses to four direct questions on pricing policy. Although of special significance when related to other portions of the questionnaire, these responses in themselves provide important evidence that most multiproduct companies do not base their prices on full costs, but instead differentiate cost-price ratios to reflect major factors recognized in the marginal analysis. The questions were phrased and ordered to try to secure evidence on the companies' normal policies, as distinct from what might be done in exigent circumstances, although this interpretation could not be relied upon independently of other evidence.

The first question (8) concerned the company's general pricing objective. A full-cost pricing philosophy could be expected to lead management to try at least to maintain more or less equal margins between prices and full costs on its various product and market segments. Yet almost three-quarters of the companies responded that this was not their policy. Most of these companies apparently either consciously pursue the advantages of price-cost differentiation or make so many exceptions to uniform full-cost-plus pricing that it has ceased to be recognized as an objective. . . .

TABLE 6

ADHERENCE TO MARGINAL AND FULL-COST PRICING POLICIES:
RESPONSES ON PRICING OF MULTIPLE PRODUCTS

Component Index 5: Pricing Policies	Number of Companies	Percent
Strong marginalist evidence—Do not try to maintain equal cost-price ratios (Q. 8), and modify prices for differing V/F compositions (Q. 9), buyer sensitivity to price (Q. 10 *or* 15), and expected competitive pressures (Q. 11)	34	33
Substantial marginalist evidence—differential pricing objective (Q. 8), modify price-cost ratios for either or both of V/F composition and buyer sensitivity to price	35	34
Strong nonmarginalist evidence—have equal cost-price objective and prices modified for none of above factors	1	1
Substantial nonmarginalist evidence—equal price-cost objective, and prices modified for one or two of above factors but not both V/F and buyer sensitivity	18	17
Ambiguous evidence—patterns other than above	16	15

Average of component index: + .81

Time Perspectives and Innovation Recognition

The latter portion of the questionnaire sought primarily to secure evidence regarding the time horizons of these companies, and the extent to which prospective innovative changes influence their pricing and product-related policies. A short horizon and keen innovation awareness is taken to be evidence of marginalist attitudes and behaviour, and an opposite posture indicative of nonmarginalism. The responses to the most relevant questions are summarized in Table 7.

The responses show a definite preponderance of short-range over long-range horizons, a preponderantly rapid pace of innovation, and prevailing sharp recognition of its implications. This is especially notable in the view, expressed by almost nine-tenths of the respondents, that staying abreast or out ahead in the innovative race is more important to their long-range business success than a "defensive" policy of basing prices closely on costs.

Composite Evidence: Interrelations Among Components

Judged either by responses to individual questions or the foregoing component indexes, the evidence of overall marginalism among these companies is very strong. The unweighted composite average of the six indexes is +1.23, or considerably above "substantial." When the plus and minus scores in each component are added algebraically, for each of the 88 companies ratable uniformly in this manner, not a single company presents nonmarginalist evidence on balance, and all but ten companies show more than negligible marginal characteristics. Approximately 60 percent of them show what can be considered from "substantial" to "very strong" marginalism.

TABLE 7

MANAGEMENT'S TIME PERSPECTIVE AND VIEWS REGARDING INNOVATION

Component Index 6: Time Perspective and Recognition of Innovation	Number of Companies	Percent
Strong marginalist evidence—give primary attention to short-range demand (Q. 15), cannot project costs more than two to three years ahead (Q. 17b), and speed of innovation considered more important than close cost-pricing (Q. 20)	45	44
Substantial marginalist evidence—two of above three responses	44	43
Strong nonmarginalist evidence—negation of above three responses	0	0
Substantial nonmarginalist evidence—only one of above responses	13	13

Average of component index: +1.2

Conclusions

A reasonable inference would seem to be that the use of marginal accounting techniques and a short time perspective and innovation sensitivity are each *independent* influences tending toward marginalist pricing. The kind of costing which is appropriate to something akin to conventional theory's short run is itself sufficient to incline companies toward pricing on essentially marginalist lines. The addition of other conditions that may lead management to take especially short views of their needs and opportunities simply increases this tendency.

When combined with other results of the survey, this conclusion has, it seems to the author, interesting theoretical and practical implications. The significant pattern of results can be summarized as follows: (1) short views, innovative sensitivity, marginal costing, and marginal pricing are all preponderant among the responding companies; (2) where considerable segmented variable cost data are brought to management's attention, the companies' short-range policies (inferred from the substantial attention given to variable cost functions in the various problems) are consistent with their long-range costing, pricing, and other product-related policies; (3) with such companies marginalism is apparently not dependent upon — though it is increased by — a short time perspective.

It appears reasonable to conclude from this pattern that the bulk of these excellently managed companies do not conceive of short-run *vs* long-run profitability as alternative and inconsistent goals, and that they seek to "maximize" their long-run welfare by alertly trying to maintain and increase their current profits within their practicable horizons. With regard to such companies, there arises a serious question whether it is valid to build our analytical models on theoretical time periods, short or long, as presently conceived. What seems to be typical of these companies is not "marginalism sitting," short or long run, but "marginalism-on-the-wing."

In any case the major messages seem to be fairly clear: (1) marginal accounting and costing principles have a strong hold among these companies, and the bulk of them also follow pricing, marketing, new product, and product-investment policies that are in essential respects marginalist. (2) Whether interested in short-run profits or long-run health, very few of these companies give any evidence of ignoring the opportunities and/or necessities of practising marginalism in the above range of problems.

Whether the same will be found true of most American firms only further study — and perhaps the passage of time — can tell. "In the long run," it is safe to say, the influence of firms such as these is bound to be substantial. At least as long as a reasonable amount of company autonomy and rapid innovation prevail, their influence is likely to be strongly in the direction of growing "marginalism" in American enterprise.

D. MARKET STRUCTURES

Market structures range from perfectly competitive situations to absolute monopolies. Between these two extremes lies an area in which market structures are imperfectly competitive. The purpose of this part of the book will be to define each of the various market structures and indicate their effects on the performance of the individual firm and of the industry as a whole in both the final product and resource markets. An analysis of the relation between market structure and the performance of the economic system is also provided.

Reading 14 is a brief excerpt from a classic on the free-enterprise system. It discusses the advantages of competition. It argues that rivalry among firms alone can be counted on to compel suppliers in a free economy to achieve results that will advance the common good.

Reading 15 is another of the classics in the development of economic thought. It argues that the basic force of economic progress is "the perennial gale of creative destruction," incessantly revolutionizing the economy from within. It also points out that some degree of monopoly and restrictive practice is necessary to minimize undesirable fluctuations in economic activity and provide the sort of environment in which invention and innovation could occur. On the other hand, however, it does not conclude that all government regulation of enterprise should be discontinued.

Often, microeconomic theory is presented in a vacuum, carefully cloistered from the practical realities of the business world. Reading 16, therefore, attempts to show that the operation of the National Hockey League can be explained by the application of basic microtheory based on a profit-maximizing hypothesis. It does so by constructing a theoretical model of the NHL and testing the implications of the model against its actual behaviour. After you have read it, what can you say about the implications of professional sport for current competition policy in Canada?

Canadian anticombines legislation, first introduced in 1889 and changed many times through the decades, seeks to eliminate certain practices in restraint of trade that serve to prevent the achievement of high levels of economic efficiency. Reading 17 presents a brief assessment of the effectiveness of Canadian competition policy since the 1950s and concludes that, while the impact of the combines legislation has been limited and uneven, it has become a more important factor in the minds of Canadian businessmen and hence in the operation of the economy.

14. THE CASE FOR COMPETITION*

John Maurice Clark

The chief agency on which defenders of the market economy have relied to keep self-interest within useful bounds and prevent it from becoming oppressive is the system of free competition. Without it free exchange between unequals could still be tyranny and its freedom a sham.

Competition is an outstanding example of an institution that nearly everyone approves, yet almost no one carries his approval through consistently. This is partly a case of the familiar double standard — competition for the other fellow, protection for me — but it is only partly that. It is partly because competition has two opposites which we may call monopoly and security, postponing for the moment the question of what these terms mean. Nearly everyone favours competition as against monopoly, and nearly everyone wants it limited in the interest of security. And hardly anyone pays much attention to the question where one leaves off and the other begins.

Competition is our main safeguard against exploitation. In our sophisticated civilization we dare not trust the terms of exchange to tribal custom and sense of honour, as some primitive peoples can. Under self-interest, people of our advanced stage of culture would naturally incline to give as little and get as much as possible; they would increase their gains by reducing their services, by producing less to sell for more. But competition works the simple miracle whereby each one increases his individual gains by increasing his services rather than reducing them: he makes more by producing more to sell for less.

The question how far this price-reducing pressure goes and how far it is safe and desirable to have to go, is one of the key questions in the nature and usefulness of competition. Put in other words, it is the question whether competition threatens security to an extent requiring some kind of protection. On this theme we might imagine a colloquy between prosecution and defence running somewhat in this fashion:

Prosecution: How can everybody get rich by selling for less? That is the way to make everybody poor.

*Reprinted from John Maurice Clark, *Alternative to Serfdom*. Copyright 1948, © 1960 by the Regents of the University of Michigan. Reprinted by permission of Alfred A. Knopf, Inc.
The late Dr. Clark was Professor of Economics, Columbia University, New York City, and one of the foremost figures in American economics.

Defence: You get rich by having other poeple sell to you for less. And if you sell for less yourself, you haven't lost as much as you have gained. The essential thing is that, in trying to gain by selling for less, people produce more, and that extra product remains and is not cancelled out. Some individuals may be ruined if they sell for too little — it's up to their common sense to stop short of that. But how can everybody get poor by all producing more?

Prosecution: When prices and wages all go down together in a slump, that seems to make the slump deeper, not lift us out of it. And in ordinary times millions of workers have injured their health and grown prematurely old, farmers have mined their soil and made dust-bowls, and irreplaceable treasures of coal and oil have been criminally wasted.

Defence: I grant you these abuses are serious; the level of competition needs to be protected to prevent that sort of thing. And it ought to be possible to mitigate slumps, so that wages and prices would not be driven down to destructive levels. But if you let people peg their own wages and prices, then you are back in the condition in which they are all trying to get rich by selling for more — which can't make them all rich — and producing less, which ends by making everybody poorer. We may have to set limits on competition, but we can't afford to abolish it. It stimulates production; and if it is reasonably equal and fair, it safeguards distribution against the building up of privileged classes.

Prosecution: The little man hasn't a fair chance against the big one; and the majority of business enterprises end in failure.

Defence: If the big man wins by efficiency, that is the customer's gain, meaning everybody's. If he wins in other ways, we should try to improve the rules so as to prevent it. If failures simply eliminate the inefficient, that is the price of progress.

This debate could go on for a long while, but perhaps the main points have been made. Returning to our key terms, "security," which has good associations, suggests safeguards for the essential needs of the little man, while "monopoly," which has bad associations, suggests swollen gains for the big man. The accepted view seems to favour the first and oppose the second. But the ends of security may be sought by the methods of monopoly; and the size of an interest is no sure index of whether it is seeking to protect the minimum needs of solvency or is out for all it can get.

What is Competition?

The first thing that seems to be needed is to supply a conception of competition that covers different degrees and is not limited to impossible perfection or destructive rigour. The question of desirable degree is a natural second step. Competition is rivalry for economic goods or gain: rivalry that centres in offering the other party a bargain good enough to induce him to deal with you in the face of his free option of dealing with others who are freely offering him the same kind of inducement for the same kind of return. The terms have to be worth your while — that is a bottom limit — and the top limit is set by the other party's freedom to go elsewhere if anyone else offers terms more attractive or more advantageous to him than yours are.

The rivalry may be in buying or selling or working for advancement. It merges into "substitution" where inducements of different kind or quality are offered. But the essential thing is that your gains are limited by the fact that you will lose business to your rivals if you let your offer become less attractive than theirs. Wherever this will happen, there is some competitive force at work. And the force and effectiveness of competition hinges, among other things, on how large and how speedy this transfer of business is, in response to a small inducement. The competitive check is not very effective unless, if your offerings get substantially inferior to your rivals', you will fairly soon lose all or most of your business.

1. The rivalry has certain general characteristics. Business competitors are under more pressure than monopolists to try to make the largest possible net return, because if they do not, they may not stay in business long. But there are high-cost and low-cost producers, and the low-cost concerns have some margin of discretion in this matter. The efficient production on which their superiority rests is precious, and they will do nothing to endanger it; but in other matters they are free to try experiments with long-run ideas of policy. They do not have to squeeze out the last dollar this year's market will afford. In some cases, where their superiority depends on having gained a lead in the race for improvement in which all are engaged, a 10 percent advantage in cost might be reckoned as equivalent to three or four years' normal progress in productivity, so that it might be lost if the low-cost concern should cease to progress for about that length of time; in other cases, where the superiority is due to location or some other enduring cause, this way of representing it might not be appropriate.

On the other hand, there is nearly always a quota of borderline producers who must better their current record or go out of business, and in some industries there is a fringe who can work only when demand is strong. They must make the most of every short-run possibility. The pressure of these concerns may affect their policies in selling, buying materials, or hiring labour. Competition of employers for labour sustains wages; but where a concern is under strong competitive pressure in the sale of its product, but is less competitive as a hirer of labour — a frequent situation — its competition may force it to squeeze wages down. This is one of the problems that union policy has to meet.

2. Under competition no one seller can control supply. If he withholds part of his own supply, incidentally to holding his price, others are free to fill the gap.

3. It is often said that under competition there can be no bargaining, but under the definition here adopted, bargaining is merely limited in scope.

4. Finally, one neglected feature of competition is the fact that, like most human matters, it is always evolving. The character and force of competitive tactics tend continually to change, as people learn what to expect of their rivals and try new ways of adjusting themselves to the rivalry. Therefore the character of competition seems to depend partly on how long a given type of competitive contact has been in operation. Competition may tend to settle down to a sort of stalemate unless fresh areas and types of competitive contact are continually being opened up; for example, by improved transportation bringing new producers into a market, or by the starting of new enterprises or the introduction of new processes or new products. Competition needs to be dynamic; if it gets to obeying fixed and rigid laws, it is already half dead.

Competition in price is sometimes contrasted with competition in quality. The distinction is real, but it would probably be more exact to speak of competition in price where quality is standardized, and competition of sellers offering different qualities, with price as a co-ordinate inducement. "Competition in quality" is real and powerful, and includes on the whole the healthiest forms of competition. If every seller is free to choose whether he will offer a quality close to his rivals' or markedly different, if the buyer is equally free to choose between them, and if this rivalry forces every seller to offer something that will attract free buyers, the rivalry is surely one of the most desirable sorts, and the mere difference in quality cannot in itself lead to monopoly profits.

It may, of course, get into a rut where differences in quality become stabilized, and price-differentials equally stabilized, so that a producer knows that any change in his price will be instantly followed by his rivals, just as may happen where quality is identical. It works best where there is a constant search for innovations that are substantial enough to lead to an alteration in the previous price-differentials.

One kind of innovation that seems particularly likely to be held back is one that greatly increases the durability of a product, all at once. This naturally tends to reduce total demand for the product; and where all the producers are virtually sure to adopt it if one takes the lead, even the leader may soon find his volume of business reduced instead of increased as a result. This is especially likely to happen if the number of producers is small. There might logically be cases in which an improvement of this sort would be more likely to be introduced if one concern held a patent on it than if all could freely copy it and promptly wipe out the first user's gains. This is perhaps the chief defect of quality-competition in practice; and it may be a cloud with a silver lining, as delaying a type of improvement that is especially likely to lead to "technological unemployment."

From this standpoint, the growing fertility of industrial chemistry in turning out an increasing variety of synthetic materials, and the resulting flow of different products, are among the healthiest features of the situation, starting fresh competitive contracts thay may serve as an antidote to the tendency of old ones to settle into a rut. Such innovations seem to be coming along so plentifully that we need not be afraid that technical progress will come to a standstill, even if shoemakers fail to adopt the most durable method of making waterproof heels. One of the costs of this progress is the burden of selection it imposes on the customer and the need for technical guidance to aid him in this increasingly difficult task.

15. AN ADAPTIVE THEORY OF COMPETITION*

Joseph A. Schumpeter

We have a considerable body of statistical data descriptive of a rate of "progress" (under capitalism) that has been admired even by very critical minds. On the other hand, we have a body of facts about the structure of the economic system and about the way it functioned. We wish to know whether that type of economy was favourable, irrelevant, or unfavourable to the performance we observe.

Profits Versus Welfare?

Unlike the class of feudal lords, the commercial and industrial bourgeoisie rose by business success. Bourgeois society has been cast in a purely economic mould. Prizes and penalties are measured in pecuniary terms. Going up and going down means making and losing money. This, of course, nobody can deny. But I wish to add that, within its own frame, that social arrangement is, or at all events was, singularly effective. The promises of wealth and the threats of destitution that it holds out, it redeems with ruthless promptitude. Wherever the bourgeois way of life asserts itself sufficiently to dim the beacons of other social worlds, these promises are strong enough to attract the large majority of supernormal brains and to identify success with business success. They are not proffered at random; yet there is a sufficiently enticing admixture of chance: the game is not like roulette, it is more like poker. Spectacular prizes much greater than would have been necessary to call forth the particular effort are thrown to a small minority of winners, thus propelling much more efficaciously than a more equal and more "just" distribution would, the activity of that large majority of businessmen who receive in return very modest compensation or nothing or less than nothing,

*"The Process of Creative Destruction" from *Capitalism, Socialism, and Democracy* by Joseph A. Schumpeter. Copyright, 1942, 1947, by Joseph A. Schumpeter. Copyright, 1950 by Harper & Row, Publishers, Inc. Reprinted by permission of the publishers.
The late Dr. Schumpeter was Professor of Economics, Harvard University, Cambridge, Massachusetts for about two decades, until his death in 1949. He had one of the greatest influences on modern American economics.

and yet do their utmost because they have the big prizes before their eyes and overrate their chances of doing equally well. Similarly, the threats are addressed to incompetence. But though the incompetent men and the obsolete methods are in fact eliminated, sometimes very promptly, sometimes with a lag, failure also threatens or actually overtakes many an able man, thus whipping up *everyone*, again much more efficaciously than a more equal and more "just" system of penalties would. Finally, both business success and business failure are ideally precise. Neither can be talked away.

In most cases the man who rises first *into* the business class and then *within* it is also an able businessman and he is likely to rise exactly as far as his ability goes. This fact, so often obscured by the autotherapeutic effort of the unsuccessful to deny it, is much more important than anything that can be gleaned from the pure theory of the capitalist machine.

But is not all that we might be tempted to infer from "maximum performance of an optimally selected group" invalidated by the further fact that it aims at maximizing profits instead of welfare? Outside of the bourgeois stratum, this has of course always been the popular opinion. Economists have sometimes fought and sometimes espoused it.

The so-called classical economists disliked many things about the social institutions of their epoch and about the way those institutions worked. They fought the landed interest and approved of social reforms — factory legislation in particular — that were not all on the lines of laissez faire. But they were quite convinced that within the institutional framework of capitalism, the manufacturer's and the trader's self-interest made for maximum performance in the interest of all. Confronted with the problem we are discussing, they would have had little hesitation in attributing the observed rate of increase in total output to relatively unfettered enterprise and the profit motive.

It is exceedingly difficult, at this hour of the day, to do justice to these views. They were of course the typical views of the English bourgeois class, and bourgeois blinkers are in evidence on almost every page the classical authors wrote. No less in evidence are blinkers of another kind: the classics reasoned in terms of a particular historical situation which they uncritically idealized and from which they uncritically generalized. Most of them, moreover, seem to have argued exclusively in terms of the English interests and problems of their time. This is the reason why, in other lands and at other times, people disliked their economics, frequently to the point of not even caring to understand it. But it will not do to dismiss their teaching on these grounds. A prejudiced man may yet be speaking the truth. Propositions developed from special cases may yet be generally valid. And the enemies and successors of the classics had and have only different but not fewer blinkers and preconceptions; they envisaged and envisage different but not less special cases.

From the standpoint of the economic analyst, the chief merit of the classics consists in their dispelling along with many other gross errors, the naïve idea that economic activity in capitalist society, because it turns on the profit motive, must by virtue of that fact alone necessarily run counter to the interests of consumers.

This later analysis we will take in two strides — as much of it, that is, as we need in order to clarify our problem. Historically, the first will carry us into the first decade of this century, the second will cover some of the postwar developments of scientific economics. Frankly I do not know how much good this will do the nonprofessional reader; like every other branch of our knowledge, economics, as its analytic engine improves, moves fatally away from that happy stage in which all problems, methods, and results could be made accessible to every educated person without special training. I will, however, do my best.

The Profit Motive Under Perfect Competition

The first stride may be associated with two great names revered to this day by numberless disciples — so far at least as the latter do not think it bad form to express reverence for anything or anybody, which many of them obviously do — Alfred Marshall and Knut Wicksell. Their theoretical structure has little in common with that of the classics, but it conserves the classic proposition that in the case of perfect competition the profit interest of the producer tends to maximize production. It even supplies almost satisfactory proof. It can be shown that firms which cannot by their own individual action exert any influence upon the price of their products or of the factors of production they employ will expand their output until they reach the point at which the additional cost that must be incurred in order to produce another small increment of product (marginal cost) just equals the price they can get for that increment. And this can be shown to be as much as it is in general "socially desirable" to produce. Where this is so, there exists a state of equilibrium in which all outputs are at their maximum and all factors fully employed. This case is usually referred to as perfect competition.

The Profit Motive Under Monopolistic Competition

Let us take the second stride. The classics recognized cases of "monopoly," and Adam Smith himself carefully noticed the prevalence of devices to restrict competition and all the differences in flexibility of prices resulting therefrom. But they looked upon those cases as exceptions and, moreover, as exceptions that could and would be done away with in time. If we look more closely at the conditions that must be fulfilled in order to produce perfect competition, we realize immediately that outside of agricultural mass production there cannot be many instances of it. A farmer supplies his cotton or wheat in fact under those conditions: from his standpoint the ruling prices of cotton or wheat are data, though very variable ones, and not being able to influence them by his individual action he simply adapts his output; since all farmers do the same, prices and quantities will in the end be adjusted as the theory of perfect competition requires. But this is not so even with many agricultural products — with ducks, sausages, vegetables, and many dairy products for instance. And as regards practically all the finished products and services of industry and trade, it is clear that every grocer, every filling station, every manufacturer of gloves or shaving cream or handsaws has a small and precarious market of his own which he tries to build up and to keep by price strategy, quality strategy, "product differentiation," and advertising. Thus we get a completely different pattern which there seems to be no reason to expect to yield the results of perfect competition. In these cases we speak of monopolistic competition. Their theory has been one of the major contributions to (recent) economics.

There remains a wide field of substantially homogeneous products such as steel ingots, cement, cotton gray goods, and the like — in which the conditions for the emergence of monopolistic competition do not seem to prevail. This is so. But in general, similar results follow for that field inasmuch as the greater part of it is covered by largest-scale firms which, either individually or in concert, are able to manipulate prices even without differentiating products — the case of oligopoly.

As soon as the prevalence of monopolistic competition or of oligopoly or of combinations of the two is recognized, many of the propositions which economists used to teach with the utmost confidence become either inapplicable or much more difficult to prove. The "beneficial" competition of the classic type seems likely to be replaced by "predatory" or "cut-throat" competition or simply by struggles for control in the financial sphere. These things are so many sources of social waste, and there are many others such as the costs of advertising campaigns, the suppression of new methods of production (buying up of patents in order not to use them), and so on. And most important of all: under the conditions envisaged, equilibrium no longer guarantees either full employment or maximum output in the sense of the theory of perfect competition. It *may* exist without full employment; it is *bound* to exist, so it seems, at a level of output below that maximum mark, because profit-conserving strategy, impossible in conditions of perfect competition, now not only becomes possible but imposes itself.

Well, does not this bear out what the man in the street (unless a businessman himself) always thought on the subject of private business? Has not modern analysis completely refuted the classical doctrine and justified the popular view? Is it not quite true after all, that there is little parallelism between producing for profit and producing for the consumer and that private enterprise is little more than a device to curtail production in order to extort profits which then are correctly described as tolls and ransoms?

These conclusions are in fact almost completely false. Yet they follow from observations that are almost completely true. But economists and popular writers have once more run away with some fragments of reality they happened to grasp. These fragments themselves were mostly seen correctly. But no conclusions about capitalist reality as a whole follow from such fragmentary analyses.

Most important of all, the modern standard of life of the masses evolved during the period of relatively unfettered "big business." If we list the items that enter the modern workman's budget and from 1899 on observe the course of their prices not in terms of money but in terms of the hours of labour that will buy them — that is, each year's money prices divided by each year's hourly wage rates — we cannot fail to be struck by the rate of the advance which, considering the spectacular improvement in qualities, seems to have been greater and not smaller than it ever was before. If we economists were given less to wishful thinking and more to the observation of facts, doubts would immediately arise as to the realistic virtues of a theory that would have led us to expect a very different result. Nor is this all. As soon as we go into details and inquire into the individual items in which progress was most conspicuous, the trail leads not to the doors of those firms that work under conditions of comparatively free competition but precisely to the doors of the large concerns — which, as in the case of agricultural machinery, also account for much of the progress in the competitive sector — and a shocking suspicion dawns upon us that big business may have had more to do with creating that standard of life than with keeping it down.

The essential point to grasp is that in dealing with capitalism we are dealing with an evolutionary process. It may seem strange that anyone can fail to see so obvious a fact which moreover was long ago emphasized by Karl Marx.

Capitalism is by nature a form or method of economic change and not only never is but never can be stationary. And this evolutionary character of the capitalist process is not merely due to the fact that economic life goes on in a social and natural environment which changes. Nor is this evolutionary character due to a quasi-automatic increase in population and capital or to the vagaries of monetary system. The fundamental impulse that sets and keeps the capitalist engine in motion comes from the new consumers' goods, the new methods of production or transportation, the new markets, the new forms of industrial organization that capitalist enterprise creates.

The contents of the labourer's budget, say from 1760 to 1940, did not simply grow on unchanging lines but they underwent a process of qualitative change. Similarly, the history of the productive apparatus of a typical farm, from the beginnings of the rationalization of crop rotation, ploughing, and fattening to the mechanized thing of today — linking up with elevators and railroads — is a history of revolutions. So is the history of the productive apparatus of the iron and steel industry from the charcoal furnace to our own type of furnace, or the history of the apparatus of power production from the overshot water wheel to the modern power plant, or the history of transportation from the mail-coach to the airplane. The opening up of new markets, foreign or domestic, and the organizational development from the craft shop and the factory to such concerns as US Steel illustrate the same process of industrial mutation — if I may use that biological term — that incessantly revolutionizes the econmic structure *from within,* incessantly destroying the old one, incessantly creating a new one. This process of creative destruction is the essential fact about capitalism. It is what capital-ism consists in and what every capitalist concern has got to live in.

Since we are dealing with a process whose every element takes consider-able time in revealing its true features and ultimate effect, there is no point in appraising the performance of the process as of a given point of time; we must judge its performance over time, as it unfolds through decades or centuries. A system that at *every point* of time fully utilizes its possibilities to the best advantage may yet in the long run be inferior to a system that does so at *no* given point of time, because the latter's failure to do so may be a condition for the level or speed of long-run performance.

Second, since we are dealing with an organic process, every piece of business strategy acquires its true significance only against the background of that process and within the situation created by it. It must be seen in its role in the perennial gale of creative destruction; it cannot be understood irre-spective of it or, in fact, on the hypothesis that there is a perennial lull.

But economists look at the behaviour of an oligopolist industry — an industry which consists of a few big firms — and observe the well-known moves and countermoves within it that seem to aim at nothing but high prices and restrictions of output. They accept the data of the momentary situation as if there were no past or future to it and think that they have understood what there is to understand if they interpret the behaviour of those firms by means of the principle of maximizing profits with reference to those data. In other words, the problem that is usually being visualized is how capitalism administers existing structures, whereas the relevant problem is how it creates and destroys them.

In capitalist reality as distinguished from its textbook picture, competition which counts is the competition from the new commodity, the new technology, the new source of supply, the new type of organization (the large-scale unit of control for instance) — competition which commands a decisive cost or quality advantage and which strikes not at the margins of the profits and the outputs of the existing firms but at their foundations and their very lives. This kind of competition is so much more important that it becomes a matter of comparative indifference whether competition in the ordinary sense functions more or less promptly; the powerful lever that in the long run expands output and brings down prices is in any case made of other stuff.

It is hardly necessary to point out that competition of the kind we now have in mind acts not only when in being but also when it is merely an ever-present threat. It disciplines before it attacks. The businessman feels himself to be in a competitive situation even if he is alone in his field. In many cases, though not in all, this will in the long run enforce behaviour very similar to the perfectly competitive pattern.

Many theorists take the opposite view which is best conveyed by an example. Let us assume that there is a certain number of retailers in a neighbourhood who try to improve their relative position by service and "atmosphere" but avoid price competition and stick as to methods to the local tradition — a picture of stagnating routine. As others drift into the trade that quasi-equilibrium is indeed upset, but in a manner that does not benefit their customers. The economic space around each of the shops having been narrowed, their owners will no longer be able to make a living and they will try to mend the case by raising prices in tacit agreement. This will further reduce their sales and so, by successive pyramiding, a situation will evolve in which increasing potential supply will be attended by increasing instead of decreasing prices and by decreasing instead of increasing sales.

Such cases do occur, and it is right and proper to work them out. But as the practical instances usually given show, they are fringe-end cases to be found mainly in the sectors furthest removed from all that is most characteristic of capitalist activity. Moreover, they are transient by nature. In the case of retail trade the competition that matters arises not from additional shops of the same type, but from the department store, the chain store, the mail-order house, and the supermarket which are bound to destroy those pyramids sooner or later. Now a theoretical construction which neglects this essential element of the case neglects all that is most typically capitalist about it; even if correct in logic as well as in fact, it is like *Hamlet* without the Danish prince.

Monopolistic Practices

Both as a fact and as a threat, the impact of new things considerably reduces the long-run scope and importance of practices that aim, through restricting output, at conserving established positions and at maximizing the profits accruing from them. We must now recognize the further fact that restrictive practices of this kind, as far as they are effective, acquire a new significance in the perennial gale of creative destruction, a significance which they would not have in a stationary state or in a state of slow and balanced growth. In either of these cases restrictive strategy would produce no result other than an increase in profits at the expense of buyers. But in the process of creative destruction, restrictive practices may do much to steady the ship and to alleviate temporary difficulties. This is in fact a very familiar argument which always turns up in times of depression and, as everyone knows, has become very popular with governments and their economic advisers — witness the NRA. While it has been so much misused and so faultily acted upon that most economists heartily despise it, those same advisers who are responsible for this invariably fail to see its much more general rationale.

Practically any investment entails, as a necessary complement of entrepreneurial action, certain safeguarding activities such as insuring or hedging. Long-range investing under rapidly changing conditions, especially under conditions that change or may change at any moment under the impact of new commodities and technologies, is like shooting at a target that is not only indistinct but moving — and moving jerkily at that. Hence it becomes necessary to resort to such protecting devices as patents or temporary secrecy of process. But these protecting devices which most economists accept as normal elements of rational management are only special cases of a larger class comprising many others which most economists condemn although they do not differ fundamentally from the recognized ones.

If for instance a war risk is insurable, nobody objects to a firm's collecting the cost of this insurance from the buyers of its products. But that risk is no less an element in long-run costs if there are no facilities for insuring against it, in which case a price strategy aiming at the same end will seem to involve unnecessary restriction and to be productive of excess profits. Similarly, if a patent cannot be secured or would not, if secured, effectively protect, other means may have to be used in order to justify the investment. Among them are a price policy that will make it possible to write off more quickly than would otherwise be rational. Again, means may have to be devised in order to tie prospective customers to the investing firm.

In analysing such business strategy as of a given point of time, the investigating economist or government agent sees price policies that seem to him predatory and restrictions of output that seem to him synonymous with loss of opportunities to produce. He does not see that restrictions of this type are, in the conditions of the perennial gale, incidents, often unavoidable incidents, of a long-run process of expansion which they protect rather than impede. There is no more of paradox in this than there is in saying that motorcars are travelling faster than they otherwise would *because* they are provided with brakes.

This stands out most clearly in the case of those sectors of the economy which at any time happen to embody the impact of new things and methods on the existing industrial structure. The best way of getting a vivid and realistic idea of industrial strategy is indeed to visualize the behaviour of new concerns or industries that introduce new commodities or processes (such as the aluminum industry) or else reorganize a part or the whole of an industry (such as, for instance, the old Standard Oil Company).

As we have seen, such concerns are aggressors by nature and wield the really effective weapon of competition. Their intrusion can only in the rarest of cases fail to improve total output in quantity or quality, both through the new method itself — even if at no time used to full advantage — and through the pressure it exerts on the preexisting firms. On the one hand, largest-scale plans could in many cases not materialize at all if it were not known from the outset that competition will be discouraged by heavy capital requirements or lack of experience. Even the securing of advantages that run counter to the public's sense of fair play — railroad rebates — move, as far as long-run effects on total output alone are envisaged, into a different light; they *may* be methods for removing obstacles that the institution of private property puts in the path of progress. In a socialist society that would be no less necessary. They would have to be secured by order of the central authority.

On the other hand, enterprise would in most cases be impossible if it were not known from the outset that exceptionally favourable situations are likely to arise which if exploited by price, quality and quantity manipulation will produce profits adequate to tide over exceptionally unfavourable situations. Again this requires strategy that in the short run is often restrictive. In the majority of cases, however, it is so successful as to yield profits far above what is necessary in order to induce the corresponding investment. These cases then provide the baits that lure capital on to untried trails. Their presence explains in part how it is possible for so large a section of the capitalist world to work for nothing: in the midst of the prosperous twenties just about half of the business corporations in the United States were run at a loss, at zero profits, or at profits which, if they had been forseen, would have been inadequate to call for the effort and expenditure involved.

All this is of course nothing but the tritest common sense. But it is being overlooked with a persistence so stubborn as sometimes to raise the question of sincerity. And it follows that, within the process of creative destruction, there is another side to industrial self-organization than that which these theorists are contemplating. "Restraints of trade" of the cartel type as well as those which merely consist in tacit understandings about price competition may be effective remedies under conditions of depression. As far as they are, they may in the end produce not only steadier but also greater expansion of total output than could be secured by an entirely uncontrolled onward rush that cannot fail to be studded with catastrophes.

Even as now extended, however, our argument does not cover all cases of restrictive or regulating strategy, many of which no doubt have that injurious effect on the long-run development of output which is uncritically attributed to all of them. And even in the cases our argument does cover, the net effect is a question of the way in which industry regulates itself in each individual case. It is certainly as conceivable that an all-pervading cartel system might sabotage all progress as it is that it might realize, with smaller social and private costs, all that perfect competition is supposed to realize. This is why our argument does not amount to a case against state regulation. It does show that there is no general case for indiscriminate "trust-busting" or for the prosecution of everything that qualified as a restraint of trade. Rational as distinguished from vindictive regulation by public authority turns out to be an extremely delicate problem which not every government agency, particularly when in full cry against big business, can be trusted to solve. But our argument, framed to refute a prevalent *theory* and the inferences drawn therefrom about the relation between modern capitalism and the development of total output, yields another outlook on facts and another principle by which to interpret them. For our purpose that is enough.

16. THE ECONOMICS OF THE NATIONAL HOCKEY LEAGUE*

J. C. H. Jones

Recently there have been attempts to bring the NHL under the Combines Act. These resulted from the NHLs failure to grant Vancouver and Quebec City franchises in the expanded league, and from the refusal to allow a former player to "retire" to join the Canadian National (amateur) Team. Consequently, on the assumption that such actions demonstrate that the NHL is a business like any other business and thus, presumably, should be treated like any other business, it must fall under the Act. Alternatively, it has long been argued by team owners that their prime interest is in "love of the game" and not in a purely business venture. It is the purpose of this paper to show that, given the unique features of professional sport, the conduct of the NHL can be explained without any behavioural assumption of "love," by the application of basic microtheory based on a profit-maximizing hypothesis. This is done by constructing a theoretical model of the NHL and testing the implications of the model against its actual conduct.

The Theoretical Framework

The unique feature of professional sport is that in the sporting production function no club[1] in and of itself produces a salable output (a game), only an input (the arena and/or the team). Therefore, each club must form a coalition with another club to produce a revenue-generating output. Total revenue is the product of number of games, number of seats sold, and average price per seat. Given that a coalition between at least two clubs is necessary, when the number of clubs exceeds two a super coalition of clubs (a formal organization, the league) is more effective and efficient in performing certain joint functions, for instance, distributing the group product

---

*Reprinted from J. C. H. Jones, "The Economics of the National Hockey League," *The Canadian Journal of Economics*, February, 1969, pp. 1-20, by permission of the editor and author.
Dr. Jones is Associate Professor of Economics, University of Victoria, British Columbia.

[1] Throughout this paper the following definitions hold: *Club*, an input made up of human and physical capital; that is, the team (a collection of players), the coach, and the management represent the human capital; the arena and equipment are the physical capital.

(scheduling), and dealing with the relationships between clubs and between the group and other groups.

Given mutual dependence, let us assume the following. First, the optimum goal of each club is to maximize profits. Second, the league desires to maximize the material welfare of its member clubs and therefore its optimum goal is that the clubs act so as to maximize joint profits. In an oligopoly situation neither optimum will be attained. Instead, because of the opposing forces which simultaneously move the clubs between the two optima, a qualified joint profit maximizing position will be achieved. In this case the position will be one which is compatible with maintaining the viability — that is, the survival — of the league. Given mutual dependence, a club cannot survive if all other clubs do not survive. Hence, the actions of each club must be constrained by the operational necessity of maintaining the league. Thus, the "equilibrium" position for the group is one in which the clubs are earning profits that are sufficient to keep them in the league and so preserve the viability of that organization.

Subject to the constraints that the league remain viable and that the institutional framework is given and does not change throughout the analysis,[2] let us assume that each club wishes to maximize profits. So, with output given, each club attempts to maximize revenue and minimize costs. In these circumstances we would expect the following.

On the revenue side, though the demand for the output is a function of the usual variables[3] (tastes, prices, incomes, quality, substitutes, etc.) the most interesting feature of the sporting demand function is competition between teams. Thus, other things being equal, the greater the degree of competition the larger the crowds and, hence, the greater the revenue. The degree of competition can be measured by the degree of uncertainty over the outcome of the game, so that the greater the uncertainty the larger the "gate." However, when uncertainty disappears and the result can be predicted with a high probability of success, attendance suffers. Consequently, mutual dependence is not confined solely to producing a game but also to producing a crowd, because the revenue of every club depends on the performance of both teams. Clear superiority or inferiority affects the gate of both teams because it reduces uncertainty. Therefore, for the league as a whole the greater the uncertainty of the outcome (the closer the teams are in rank standing, the "better balanced" the league), the greater the aggregate

---

[2]Given are: the number of teams, the number of games, arena seating capacity, the production function and the techniques specifying how the inputs should be combined (that is, game rules) including, number of players, size of ice surface, size of goal, etc. — in short, all factors considered in the Constitution, By-Laws, and Playing Rules of the NHL.

[3]Though no attempt is made here to specify all the factors which could affect attendance, the following are mentioned because they are more or less unique to hockey (although analagous factors are found in other sports): (1) the drawing power of a particular "superstar" (for example, Richard, Howe, Hull) or team irrespective of the projected outcome of the game. It is interesting to note that when exhibitions are staged between NHL and minor league clubs (when the outcome of the game is not important), very often the ability of a particular star on the NHL team is heavily stressed in pregame advertising; (2) the *style* of hockey played — defensive, offensive, the likelihood of fights, etc. Clarence Campbell, for instance, has said that offensive style hockey which increases scoring has a positive effect on attendance (see Paul Deacon, "Thinner Ice for Pro Hockey," *Financial Post,* April 19, 1952). Certainly over the years the rule changes have attempted to make hockey a faster, more wide-open game, for example, the forward pass, the red line, etc.; (3) the selling job that radio, TV, and newspaper sports writers do for hockey, sometimes called the "fourth estate benefit" (see W. C. Neale, "The Peculiar Economics of Professional Sport," *Quarterly Journal of Economics,* 78 (February, 1964), p. 3); (4) whether the game is played during the weekend or midweek; (5) parking and the weather; (6) in Toronto and Montreal "conspicuous consumption," and when Toronto plays Montreal — ethnic considerations.

attendance. Hence, the aim being to maximize revenue we would expect that, in contrast to most oligopolistic situations, the group wishes to promote competitive equality between clubs.

However, for each club to accept unequivocally joint profit maximization as furthering its own aim of profit maximization, it must be assumed that collusion is complete, and that no club has any incentive for winning continually. If these two latter requirements are not met, the desire to maximize uncertainty will no longer be paramount. If for instance the incentive to win exists, clubs will desire to increase the certainty of winning the game, rather than the uncertainty of its outcome.

This gives rise to two conflicts — first, between optimum group and club objectives and the means by which they may be achieved; and second, between clubs. If there are consistent winners and losers, the nonattainment of goals by losers will result in pressure to improve their positions. This interclub conflict could result in warfare which might destroy the league as a viable organization, so worsening the position of every club. Therefore we would expect a solution compatible with preserving the viability of the league. Although it will not be one which results either in joint profit maximization for the group or attempted profit maximization for each club, it will ensure group "equilibrium."

On the supply side, the single most important input is the human one — the players. This is the major element promoting uncertainty over the outcome of the game. Hence we would expect that most moves by the group to improve interclub competition would involve some means of redistributing or equalizing this element. In addition, the players distinguish NHL hockey on a quality basis from all other hockey. That is, NHL hockey is superior to all other hockey because its inputs are superior. Therefore, one would expect the NHL to attempt to obtain the best players available, vis-à-vis other competitive leagues. Finally, in the cause of minimizing the cost of this input we would expect the group to minimize interclub competition for factors.

Consequently, if the foregoing is correct we would expect that: (1) the league attempts to promote competitive equality between clubs primarily through the redistribution of players; (2) should collusion be incomplete then solutions other than (1) will be adopted in order to maintain group stability; (3) the group will attempt to employ the best players available so as to differentiate their product from other similar products; (4) they will attempt to accomplish (3) at minimum cost. In order to see if these predictions are borne out by the actual behaviour of the NHL the remainder of the paper is divided into: a brief outline of the pertinent organizational characteristics of the NHL and testing propositions (1) and (2); an examination of (3) and (4); and application of the theory to those 1966 issues which gave rise to the policy questions — the NHL expansion and the new professional-amateur hockey agreement.

Demand and Revenue

The organization of the NHL is defined by the following structural characteristics. The National Hockey League is made up of six clubs (in Canada, Toronto and Montreal, and in the United States, Boston, Chicago, Detroit, and New York), each of which holds a franchise which allows commercial exploitation of NHL hockey in a defined spatial area (the city in which the club is located plus a radius of fifty miles of the corporate limit). This monopoly right is marketable as the franchise may be sold and/or moved subject to the agreement of three-quarters of the remaining league clubs. Each club is selling a highly differentiated product (NHL hockey) and entry is completely blocked unless the group decides to admit new clubs. The league itself is governed by one representative from each club (Board of Governors) and a president who supervises its day-to-day operations. Its function, aside from providing a formal channel of communication, is chiefly administrative; the president is merely the agent of the owners, having nothing more than control over the "morals of the game." The intraleague relationships are explicitly defined by the league constitution and by-laws, although a considerable degree of latitude is allowed each club in its own spatial market area. For instance, each club is allowed to set its own admission prices, and negotiate TV and radio contracts; each team participates in seventy games, thirty-five at home and the same number "on the road"; the revenue from any game goes entirely to the home club and, assuming no TV receipts, depends on the number of paid admissions; and, any game is sold at a variety of different prices which, depending on one's view of the relationship between the seat and the view of the game, can be considered either product differentiation or price discrimination.

Proposition 1: Player Redistribution and Competitive Equality

The data necessary to test statistically the relationship between attendance and uncertainty as specified by the model are unfortunately unavailable.[4] However, it seems that, in order to attempt to ensure a degree of uncertainty the NHL clubs have adopted a system of what could be called co-operative "handicapping," the object of which is to try to ensure that individual clubs do not accumulate all the best players and so destroy interclub competition. The more obvious examples are as follows: (1) each club is allowed a maximum number of players under contract — a "reserve list" of thirty players plus three goalkeepers, and out of these thirty-three a NHL "protected list" of eighteen plus two goalkeepers. Any player not on a "protected list" but on a reserve list who is under contract to a NHL club can be "drafted" (claimed) by another NHL club for a fixed draft price of $30,000 (1967); (2) any NHL draft is based on the last club in the league having first pick of all nonprotected players. Then it is the turn of the fifth club and so on in inverse order of league standing; (3) during the course of a season a club may wish to assign a player to a club outside the NHL. This the club cannot do unless all clubs in the league agree, in effect "waiving" him through the league. If any other league club wants the player on waivers it may claim him at the predetermined waiver price. Again, the team ranked last in the league at the time waivers were asked has first choice.

Such handicapping is necessary because complete collusion does not exist. Although the clubs have solved many of the problems which disrupt typical oligopolistic arrangements — particularly, each club sets its own prices in its

---

[4] However, the case has been succinctly stated by Conn Smythe, "New York and Boston keep drawing because there are only six teams in the league . . . so you've always got an attraction coming in. But if you had two more teams that couldn't win games it would be different. If you had four rotten teams in the league you'd have a hell of a time getting people in the rink. They wouldn't buy season tickets for 35 games a year knowing that they had to take 15 or 20 lousy games." Quoted in Jack Olsen, "Private Game: No Admittance."

own monopolistic spatial area — collusion is still incomplete because playing talent is distributed unequally and there is incentive to win.

Proposition 2: Competitive Equality and Group Stability

If playing talent were not unequally distributed we would expect every game to end in a tie, or each team to win exactly half its games, or each club to win the league championship one-sixth of the time (preferably once every six years). None of these hypotheses is supported by the facts. For instance, in the twenty seasons from 1946-47 to 1965-66, Montreal finished first nine times and second seven; Detroit finished first nine times, second twice, and from 1948-49 to 1956-57 finished first every year except one, when they finished second. At the other end of the scale, during the same time span, Boston finished last five times, and fifth four times, the highest finish being second in 1948-49 and 1958-59; Chicago finished last nine times and fifth twice; New York finished last four times and fifth ten times; Toronto finished first twice, second five times, and last only once. Thus, given the unequal distribution of ability, maximum uncertainty cannot result.

At the same time there is an incentive to win. The first four ranked teams in the league compete for the Stanley Cup, a post-regular season finale which increases the revenue of these clubs. In addition, given the degree of uncertainty, a winning club draws larger crowds than a losing one. This latter point has been frequently noted and Chicago is often cited as the prime example. Despite the lack of data necessary to estimate accurately the demand function, there does appear to be a correlation between Chicago's performance (winning or losing) and attendance. This is shown in Table 1. Following the Second World War attendance was high but fell consistently as the club's record of futility continued (1946-47 to 1951-52). In 1952-53 the club made the "playoffs" and attendance rose but fell again as the club reverted to last place. In 1957-58 the team finally escaped last place and attendance increased. By 1958-59 they reached the play-offs and since then have never finished lower than third — a situation reflected in the club's attendance figures.

The upshot of incomplete collusion is conflict between optimum group goals and club goals, and between club goals. These conflicts could destroy the league so there must be some solution other than maximizing uncertainty. If we assume that the game results are not rigged in advance, two solutions (or some combination of the two) suggest themselves.

First, there should be a system of side payments whereby winners compensate losers. This could take the form either of profit redistribution or redistribution of that element which primarily promotes the uncertainty — the players. For instance, at the end of each season profits could be redistributed or the best players from the winning clubs could be transferred to the losing clubs. If a financial side payment were adopted the object would be to attempt to retain the club goal and achieve a form of joint profit maximization without maximizing uncertainty. Yet this would only ensure a more or less equal profit distribution because, unless it is assumed that the demand curve facing the individual club is quite inelastic, group revenue would fall as the degree of certainty increased. This, however, ignores all the difficulties which arise in practice when group revenue is shared. With player redistribution, the objective would be to maximize uncertainty by moving closer to the optimum group goal. In effect, this would completely subordinate club objectives to the group which, as long as there is any incentive to win at all, would be alien to the club. However, the draft and waiver system is a "human" side payment which goes partway toward solving the conflict problem by moving closer to the group goal of maximizing uncertainty. Nevertheless, it does not go all the way.[5]

TABLE 1

PAID ATTENDANCE AS A PERCENTAGE OF MAXIMUM SEATING
CAPACITY AND FINAL RANK IN LEAGUE FOR
CHICAGO BLACK HAWKS, 1946–47 TO 1966–67

Season	Final Rank in League	Paid Attendance as a Percentage of Maximum Seating Capacity*
1946–47	6	85
1947–48	6	84
1948–49	5	81
1949–50	6	67
1950–51	6	44
1951–52	6	26
1952–53	4	47
1953–54	6	24
1954–55	6	23
1955–56	6	26
1956–57	6	22
1957–58	5	35
1958–59	3	44
1959–60	3	49
1960–61	3	60
1961–62	3	70
1962–63	2	92
1963–64	2	99
1964–65	3	100
1965–66	2	105
1966–67	1	103

Source: Estimated from figures supplied by the NHL.
*Where the figures exceed 100 this means that all seats were sold and the
remainder of the crowd utilized standing room.

Second, the objectives of the clubs must undergo some reassessment because they are unattainable simultaneously, and joint profit maximization requires complete adherence to group objectives. Consequently, there must be recourse to a second-best solution which ensures group stability even though it represents a nonoptimum situation from the point of view of each club. To deny this is to ignore the implications of the fact that each club is mutually dependent on another club. Thus, although the best of all worlds for the club is the certainty of victory, because of mutual dependence such victory may be a Pyrrhic one at the gate. Hence for every club the minimum of all possible acceptable solutions is not to be a consistent loser; but the minimum of all possible maximum solutions is to qualify for the Stanley

---

[5] Interclub trades could be considered a form of side payment especially if they are motivated by the desire to strengthen weaker clubs. For instance, over the years there has been a noticeable tendency for winning teams to avoid trading with each other and to trade with losing teams.

Cup play-offs. In other words, in the NHL a "winning club" is one which makes the Stanley Cup play-offs which means finishing ranked in the first four in the league. From this point of view, the league championship is nothing more than a 210 game elimination contest to decide which clubs have the distinction of playing off the "The World's Hockey Championship."

The fact that there are *four* winners resolves much interclub conflict by increasing the chance that each club has of "winning." However, the clubs are not totally indifferent about their position in the first four rankings because the first- and second-place clubs play off against the third- and fourth-place clubs and have the home ice advantage for four out of the seven games. Thus, we have competition for "league standing." This tends to spread the degree of competition among more teams in the league.

At the same time, although the probability of winning the Stanley Cup is a positive function of league standing — since 1946-47 the league winner has won the trophy ten times, the runner-up six times, the third-place team three times, and the fourth, twice — the league winner has in fact only won it less than 50 percent of the time. Hence the degree of uncertainty over which is the superior team increases with the addition of the play-offs.

If this argument is correct one would expect to see the influence of striving to reach the play-offs reflected in attendance figures. Again, although total statistical information is imperfect, this would appear to be the case. For example, since 1948-49 Montreal has never played to less than 100 percent of seating capacity. But during that time it has never been out of the play-offs and has won eight Stanley Cups — five in a row. Since 1946-47 Toronto has never played to less than 100 percent of seating capacity. However, it has failed to make the play-offs only twice and has won seven Stanley Cups. Since 1946-47 Detroit has only missed the play-offs once and although it only reached 100 percent of seating capacity last year, attendance has been very stable, never falling below 72 percent of capacity.

When a club does not achieve its minimum objectives it will create pressure to change more fundamentally the rules of conduct which govern intraleague relationships. For instance, some clubs may not make the play-offs for a long period of time. Or again, the waiver rule may not fulfil its purpose because, as waivers can be withdrawn, they may be a search for market information as a prelude to trading. Then, if the league is to remain viable, more drastic changes will have to be made. The two most notable examples concern the introduction of: (1) the original intraleague draft in 1954 and (2) the universal amateur (Junior) draft in 1962.

1. In the late forties and early fifties there were in effect two divisions in the NHL: Detroit, Montreal, and Toronto — whose successes were reflected at the gate; and Boston, New York, and Chicago who had difficulty winning and drawing crowds. Chicago was about to drop out of the league. However, James D. Norris was "urged" to buy the club by the Board of Governors of the NHL even though he already has an interest in the New York Rangers (and holding an interest in more than one club was illegal under the NHL constitution). Norris agreed to buy the franchise, but the problem was the quality of the players. Norris attempted to buy players from the "have" clubs but their owners would not co-operate. The upshot was that in 1954 a draft rule was adopted by the NHL clubs over the protests of Montreal against whose highly productive farm system it was directed.

Under this system each club was only permitted to "protect" a maximum of eighteen players and two goalkeepers. Beyond this number a player under contract to any NHL club could be drafted for $15,000. This innovation assured the league as a whole of a pool of professional talent no matter how unproductive the individual farm systems might be, and went some way towards satisfying the weaker teams.

2. The introduction of the amateur draft arose out of the Shock incident. In the early sixties Boston was consistently last in the league. To try to rectify the situation Boston attempted to buy the best Junior prospect in Ontario and Quebec. This involved Boston in a price war with other NHL clubs over Ron Shock. Boston apparently won out with a bonus of $10,000 and signified their willingness to repeat the process with other juniors. Such financial competition was averted when the clubs agreed to establish the universal amateur draft whereby weaker teams could draft two players from their competitors' sponsored teams at a fixed price ($3,000). Once again, there was a pronounced shift in league policy to counteract the pressure placed on it by one club.

Both these examples illustrate two striking facts. First, both moves were in the direction of increasing the competitiveness of all clubs. Secondly, despite potential and actual conflict the interclub agreement is stable over time. Although most of the conditions for stable collusion are present — small numbers and a formal organization make policing easier, markets are spatially separated, there is no unilateral price policy, and there is group control over new innovations and entrants — the factor which distinguishes the professional sporting leagues from other oligopolistic coteries is mutual dependence. Once the implications of this are grasped the only factors that can destroy the group are: shifts in the demand for the product which forces withdrawal of the league or clubs; ignoring mutual dependence so that one or two teams become so superior as to reduce uncertainty to zero; the wish of members of the group to dissolve the league; or competition from some other group which sells a generically similar product.

Thus, on the revenue side the model appears to explain the activities of the NHL quite well.

Supply and Cost

On the supply side the model implied that the NHL would attempt to employ the best players available vis-à-vis other leagues so as to differentiate their product, and that they would do so at the minimum possible costs. The league largely succeeds in the former through its monopsonistic power in the labour market, the result being that NHL sells a superior product and simultaneously keeps out potential entrants. However, although interclub competition for players is reduced almost to zero, it is not certain that clubs maximize rents by forcing wages to opportunity costs because the lack of information allows only a highly speculative conclusion.

Proposition 3: Labour Market Control and Interclub Competition

The monopsonistic position of the NHL and its clubs is based on the standard player's contract and the protected list, on ownership of and affiliation agreements with, minor professional league clubs, and on the CAHA-NHL agreement which gives the NHL control of amateur hockey. The result is that the hockey labour market can be considered to be vertically integrated (see Figure 1). It may be roughly divided into three stages pyramidically: at the apex stands the NHL; one stage further back, the

FIGURE 1

VERTICAL INTEGRATION IN THE HOCKEY MARKET

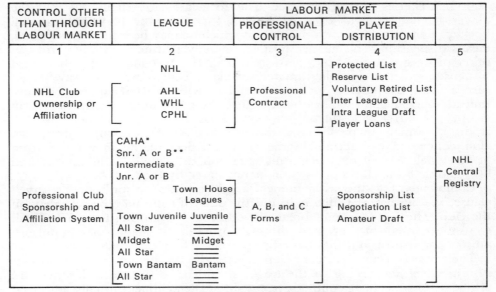

*The administrative breakdown into branches is shown in Table 3.
**The age limits for the competitive categories are Senior and Intermediate (no limit), Junior (under 20), Juvenile (under 18), Midget (under 16), Bantam (under 14), Pee Wee (not shown, under 12).

minor professional leagues; finally at the base the amateur leagues which are themselves vertically integrated on an age basis. Each of these stages may be thought of as adding quality to the input so that the NHL ultimately ends up with the superior player. Thus, in contrast to vertical integration in product markets, the NHL is not interested in the minor league outputs as inputs in the NHL, but only in the fact that by producing outputs the minor leagues add quality (seasoning) to their inputs which in turn become NHL inputs. Nevertheless, control over outputs does give the NHL clubs direct control over inputs.

Broadly, the vertical system works as follows: NHL clubs own and control clubs in the minor professional leagues and, through the "sponsorship" and "affiliation" system, amateur clubs (Figure 1, col. 1). At the amateur level, in order to play in Juvenile or Junior clubs, players have signed "option" agreements (col. 3), which gives the professional club ownership of amateur playing rights and the right to require the players to sign a professional contract when requested to do so. All professional players are tied to the NHL club by the contract (col. 3), and are distributed among teams and leagues according to distribution lists (col. 4). The whole distribution system is run by the NHL Central Registry (col. 5), an arm of the league charged with keeping track of and co-ordinating all changes in player distribution.

The major bases of monopsony power and their influence on interclub competition for players are as follows.

Standard Professional Contract: Although the club that signs a player has prior monopsonistic claim to his services (up to the limit imposed by the protected list), in effect he becomes part of the professional hockey player pool because he can be traded, drafted, or assigned to another club. The monopsonistic status of the club is determined by the "assignment," and "option" clauses of the contract. The former clearly spells out that the player has no control over where and for whom he plays professional hockey. Failure to report to the club to which he may be sold or transferred, means suspension. This in turn means, not only that he cannot play for any other professional club, but that, as the CAHA recognizes all professional suspensions, he cannot play amateur hockey. Thus there is no way he can earn a living by playing hockey other than with an NHL sponsored club. Indeed, once a contract has been signed there are only two ways he can escape the NHL and still play hockey. First, he may no longer have the ability to remain in professional hockey so that, after asking waivers, the club concerned can terminate the contract. Second, he may retire from professional hockey by placing his name on the club's "voluntary retired list" and with the club's permission be reinstated by the CAHA.

Complementing the assignment clauses is the "option" or "reserve" clause, the burden of which is to put the onus of contract renewal solely on the club. The player cannot break the contract by refusing to sign and still continue to play hockey, and although provision is made for compulsory arbitration, it turns out that the arbitrator is the league president.

The "reserve clause" in conjunction with the "protected list" produces a system which, according to the league president, is the most effective and efficient for producing competitive equality. The argument usually advanced to support this contention is that because the league is made up of rich and poor clubs, if the market were free, rich teams would bid away all the choice talent. The outcome would presumably be a diminution of the necessary uncertainty. However, this argument ignores the mutual dependence which must exist, the fact there has not been competitive equality in the NHL for the last twenty years, and that the cost of entry ensures that there are no rich and poor clubs. Moreover, the equality of competition can be brought about equally well by the free market. But the reserve rule makes it cheaper. Clearly, the reserve clause is an element of market control which stops the player from selling his services to the highest bidder. This is perfectly consistent with the club wishing to minimize cost.

The Minor Professional Leagues: In their organizational setup, distribution lists, and in the rules governing interclub conduct, the minors are almost exact replicas of the NHL. The single most pertinent fact is that they operate as a farm system for developing NHL players. They are dominated by the NHL either through direct NHL club ownership, affiliation agreements with NHL clubs, or the "joint affiliation agreement"[6] between the NHL and the minor leagues.

The degree of ownership integration varies with each NHL club — on the one hand, each owns a CPHL team, on the other, in 1966 only Toronto was fully integrated by ownership of Rochester, Victoria, and Tulsa.[7] But every NHL club either through ownership or affiliation is represented in each league (see Table 2). Broadly speaking "affiliation" defines a relationship between minor and major club whereby the NHL club loans players to the

---

[6] This agreement was drawn between the NHL, AHL, WHL, and the Quebec Hockey League. Since then the Quebec League has gone out of existence but available evidence suggests that things have not changed significantly with the addition of the CPHL, especially as all the clubs in this league are directly owned by NHL clubs.

[7] During the 1965-66 fiscal year Toronto sold its interest in Rochester, and at the end of the 1966-67 season the Victoria franchise was moved to Phoenix and sold to local interests.

TABLE 2

THE OWNERSHIP AND AFFILIATE RELATIONSHIP BETWEEN THE PROFESSIONAL LEAGUES AND CLUBS, AND THEIR JUNIOR SPONSORED CLUBS
(as of January 1967)

Professional and Junior Clubs

Leagues									
NHL JUNIOR*	Boston Estavan Niagara Falls	Chicago St. Catharines Dixie Beehive	Detroit Weyburn Hamilton	Montreal Montreal Peterboro	New York Kitchener Burlington	Toronto Marlboros Ottawa			
CPHL† JUNIOR*	Oklahoma Winnipeg Braves Winnipeg Warriors	St. Louis Sudbury Moose Jaw	Memphis Edmonton Oil Kings Edmonton Canadians	Houston Chatham Lachine Maroons	Omaha Brandon North Bay	Tulsa Markham London			
AHL‡ JUNIOR	Hershey Oshawa	Buffalo Sarnia	Pittsburgh Stratford (and minor assoc.) St. Jerome (and minor assoc.)	Quebec Regina Pats	Baltimore Kitchener Quebec	Rochester Cornwall Trois Rivières	Providence Nationale Maisonneuve	Cleveland Kirkland Verdun Maple Leafs	Springfield
WHL‡ JUNIOR	San Francisco Shawinigan Waterloo	Portland Flin Flon Fredericton (and whole assoc.)	Los Angeles Saskatoon	Seattle Ft. William Sorel Hawks Hull	Vancouver Winnipeg Rangers Kingston Frontenacs	Victoria Calgary Buffaloos Melville (Sask.)			

*Junior A and B
†Each club is owned by the NHL club vertically above it
‡The clubs in this league have working agreements with more than one NHL club.

minor club (or provides other financial assistance), and the minor clubs allow the NHL clubs to use spaces on their lists. From the point of view of control, the key element in the agreement is that, in contrast to NHL clubs, minor clubs can transfer players directly to the NHL without first obtaining waivers from clubs in their own league. In addition, should the farm system of a particular NHL club fail to produce sufficient talent, minor league players may be drafted (for interleague draft, see Figure 1, col. 4).

These relationships ensure that the distribution of professional playing talent is in the hands of the NHL and so automatically precludes the minor leagues from challenging the position of the NHL.

The Amateur Leagues: The main factors giving the NHL effective control of amateur hockey are the following three points from the CAHA-NHL agreement.

First, the CAHA recognizes the NHL as the sole and exclusive governing body and bargaining authority for professional hockey.

Second, the NHL obtains direct access to the labour market through the sponsorship system. Sponsorship means the exclusive right of *a professional* team to direct the affairs of any two amateur teams. However, due to ownership and affiliation at the minor professional level, the NHL club really directs eight or more amateur clubs. Taking Toronto as an example, this can be illustrated by Table 2. Toronto directly sponsors two Junior teams, the Marlboros and Ottawa. But in 1966 through its ownership of Tulsa, Rochester, and Victoria it sponsored Junior teams in Markham, London, Cornwall, Trois Rivières, Calgary, and Melville.

In addition to the NHL, two sponsored clubs rule, the CAHA definition of a *club* includes Senior, Intermediate, Junior or Juvenile, Midget, and Bantam teams, so that sponsorship can give rise to a chain of affiliates which increases the degree of vertical integration (Figure 1, col.2).

Table 3, in conjunction with Table 2, shows that there is geographical concentration of sponsorships in Ontario and Quebec, and in the large metropolitan centres throughout the country. This means that there has been considerable player mobility which has led to wholesale special exceptions to CAHA rules concerning inter- and intrabranch transfers.

Third, control of individual players is extended by use of "try out" ("A" form) and "option" ("B" and "C" forms) agreements, which attempt to bind amateurs to a particular professional club when they have reached sixteen years of age. While the A form merely gives negotiation rights, the B and C forms give the club an exclusive continuing option on the player's services both amateur and professional. Indeed, when a C form has been signed the player is a professional. As it is in the signing of amateurs that the greatest competition occurs between NHL clubs, the sponsorship list, the universal amateur draft, and the negotiation list attempt to circumscribe this. The former is analagous to the protected list and the latter makes for orderly negotiation.

Finally, a series of minor points reinforce NHL control. These include the CAHA's adoption (with minor changes) of NHL playing rules, acceptance of the voluntary retired list, and agreement that no amateur club can bind a player with a reserve clause. The total outcome is that the amateur-professional relationship is the same as exists between professional leagues — domination by the NHL.

TABLE 3

NUMBER OF SPONSORED JUNIOR TEAMS AND ALL JUNIOR TEAMS IN EACH CAHA BRANCH
(As of January 1967)

Branch	Number of Junior A Teams	Number of Other Junior Teams	Number of Sponsored Teams
British Columbia*	10	13	0
Alberta*	6	8	3
Saskatchewan*	6	6	6
Manitoba*	6	7	0
Thunder Bay†	8	0	1
Ontario Hockey Assoc.‡	13	111	11A + 9 B
Ottawa and District§	10	20	2
Quebec ‖	18	66	11
Maritimes#	12	0	1
Newfoundland*	7	0	0
Canada	96	231	50

*Branch covers the entire province.
†North-west Ontario, west of the 85th Meridian.
‡Ontario (excluding Thunder Bay, and Ottawa and District) plus the counties of Temiscamingue, Rouyn, Noranda, Abitibi East, and Abitibi West in Quebec.
§That part of Ontario east of and including the counties of Leeds, Lanark, and Renfrew, plus the counties of Pontiac, Hull, Gatineau, and Papineau in Quebec.
‖Quebec (excluding those parts of Quebec in Ontario Hockey Association and Ottawa and District).
#New Brunswick, Nova Scotia, and Prince Edward Island.

The total outcome is likely to be that, as the model forecasts, the NHL does employ the superior players vis-à-vis other competitive leagues.

Proposition 4: Monopsony Power and Player Costs

Given the monopsony power of the NHL and its clubs, is it exercised so that player costs are minimized? Because there is no information available on wages, what follows must be regarded as highly speculative.

In general there are two extreme views on the subject of wages of professional athletes and their opportunity costs. One suggests that given the monopsony power of most major league clubs in any sport — football, baseball, or basketball — there is no reason for wages to be above opportunity cost. The other view points out that the large sums paid to professional athletes are bound to be above their opportunity cost — where else could Willie Mays make $125,000 or Wilt Chamberlain $250,000 — which suggests that monopsony power is illusionary.

Hockey would appear to fall into the first category because there is no reason why wages should be above opportunity costs. With NHL control over entry, competition from any other league which could increase factor cost (as the American Football League did for the National Football League) is absent. Thus, the only way wages could rise above opportunity costs would be through interclub competition. But the option clause, protected list, and voluntary retired list severely limit such rivalry. Competition is a factor in signing amateurs (for example, the Shock incident) prior to option agreements, but again negotiation and sponsorship lists are confining factors.[8]

Nevertheless, the annual rash of prolonged barn painting and other assorted reasons for "holding out" suggests that the process of wage determination is more a matter of bilateral bargaining than the straight application of monopsony theory. The situation is indeed a bargaining one due to two factors. First, given that the demand for any input is wholly a derived demand, as the club desires to win, it is not completely indifferent over whether the player performs for the team or not. Thus if the club has to pay more for a winning team than a losing team it will do so. Second, if attendance is a function not only of the performance of the teams but also of individual stars (irrespective of the performance of the team) then once again the club would be willing to pay above opportunity cost. Of course both factors assume that the human inputs are heterogeneous and there is no possibility of substitution at a lower wage. The upshot is that monopsony power is not absolute. It is true that each club has the power to drive wages to opportunity costs and, coupled with the threat of suspension which automatically disbars a player from organized hockey, make this stick. But, given that winning is important and the "superstar" effect does exist, the player may be able to bargain his wage above pure opportunity cost.

The bargaining range is set by value product and opportunity cost. Where the wage actually falls within this range depends on the bargaining strength of the player and the extent to which the team is ready to enforce the rules and regulations. If the player is extremely valuable to the team in that there are no good substitutes, he may be able to bargain for a wage significantly above his opportunity cost. There is no doubt, for instance, that certain "superstars" make large salaries because of their ability to draw crowds, and therefore make important contributions to the gate. For example, although in the 1966-67 season Chicago finished first in the league for the first time ever, attendance was lower than in 1965-66 when the club finished second. Although we would have expected the reverse to be true, the statistics ignore one qualitative factor — in 1965-66 Bobby Hull broke the fifty-goal record. Similarly, in 1965-66 Boston finished fifth rather than last and, as expected, attendance increased. In 1966-67 they reverted to last, but attendance increased. One of the major reasons was the play of Bobby Orr. Yet it is doubtful if either of the above players received his value product.

However, what about the player whose ability is not unique and for whom there are reasonably good substitutes? His salary may be above his opportunity costs if there are substantial external benefits to winning or if there is group bargaining. In the first case, consider how much is a winning Montreal team worth to its owners, Molson Brewery? If the external benefits are strong then the club may give a player a substantial portion of his rent for a winning team.

In the second case, although group bargaining by players can be very effective because the game depends on the labour input, it requires that the players' group be sufficiently inclusive (the four professional leagues) so that

---

[8] Signing amateurs can be expensive as the following shows. "Detroit, Chicago, New York, Montreal, Toronto scrambled for Frank Mahovlich when he was a 14-year-old playing for Schumacher Lions. Leafs got him. They paid him $1,000 to sign a Junior B certificate; $1,300 a year for tuition, laundry money, and three trips home each of the 5 years he was at St. Michael's College; $1,000 to the scout who signed him to a 'C' form, $10,000 bonus to the 'Big M' to turn professional; $10,000 for his first year's salary." G. E. Mortimore, "What Happened to Hockey," *Globe & Mail,* (no date).

substitution is impossible. Under these circumstances the players' union was effective in raising both salaries and fringe benefits for all players during the fifties. The same is apparently true of the new association formed in 1967.

However, given the NHL view of what constitutes arbitration, and the monopsonistic power of the clubs, it would be very strange if the wages of all players were too far above their opportunity costs. While the club may not push salaries to their lowest levels — even on the basis of wishing to maintain player morale — there is certainly no reason to believe that the converse is true. Thus, although the clubs may fail to minimize player costs in line with their monopsony power, this is not due to any benevolent use of their power but rather to the fact that such power is not absolute. Consequently, if we take into account the need to win, the heterogeneity of inputs, strengths, and weaknesses in the bargaining process, the need to ensure player morale, etc., we could conclude that the clubs are minimizing player costs. However, it must be stressed that as we have no data this conclusion is highly conjectural.

Nevertheless, on balance we are probably justified in saying that on the supply side the implications of the model have been largely borne out.

Expansion and the New Agreement with the CAHA

The foregoing analysis dealt with the NHL as it existed prior to the 1967-68 season. In 1966 two events occurred which changed its character — the league expanded by granting franchises to Los Angeles, San Francisco, Philadelphia, Pittsburgh, Minneapolis, and St. Louis; and the NHL-CAHA agreement was rewritten. Do either of these changes invalidate the above analysis? The answer is no, and both changes can be explained by using the same hypothesis, that the clubs are interdependent profit maximizers.

Why did the league expand? The answer is primarily associated with the revenue which can be obtained from increasing the extent of the market through television.

Over the period 1960-61 to 1965-66, all NHL clubs were consistently playing at or moving toward capacity. By 1965-66, Chicago and Montreal were over 100 percent of seating capacity. Toronto had dropped below capacity for the first time in memory, while Detroit, New York, and Boston were playing at 96, 80, and 85 percent of seating capacity respectively. When full capacity attendance is achieved, revenue can be increased by boosting the size of the arena, increasing the number of games, and/or increasing ticket prices. However, if we make the reasonable assumption that there is a ceiling on arena size, number of games, and ticket prices, then there is a limit to the extent that the local market can be increased. This revenue ceiling can be removed by use of television at either a local or national level.

If there is positive excess demand in the local market it can be met either by closed circuit TV or local commercial stations. Commercial TV is probably the best way of attracting the marginal viewer, providing that the substitutability between "live" and TV hockey is relatively small. If it is not, the club runs the possibility of losing a large portion of its "live" audience, so that total net revenue may not increase. Indeed most clubs who have used TV to expand their local markets have gone to closed circuit television because it appears to offer less of the "substitutability" drawbacks associated with commercial TV.

On the other hand, when commercial TV is used the object is usually expansion in other than local markets. To reduce the danger for substitutability there are usually local blackouts when the local team plays at home. When there is no blackout, revenue may fall. For instance, in the 1956-57 season Boston had four out of ten games carried nationally by CBS, playing New York twice, Detroit once, and Montreal once. The average "live" gate from these four games was $14,892 compared with $24,910 per game "for nontelevised engagements against the same clubs." For these games the Bruins received $10,000 from CBS, therefore ending with a revenue loss of $1,018. Yet Montreal and Toronto have never suffered the same fate and consistently play to over 100 percent of seating capacity.

However, US national network TV does pay the most money for televising sport. Thus, if a team is playing to capacity crowds and is already utilizing closed circuit television, a national TV contract appears very profitable. But the prerequisite for a national contract is a national market. The expansion placed teams in the remaining major US television markets (excluding the south). The NHL did obtain a national TV contract from CBS.

Thus, solely on the basis of television it is possible to explain the distribution of new franchises and why Vancouver and Quebec City were omitted. The Canadian TV hockey market is already dominated by Montreal and Toronto. What advantages would accrue to Toronto and Montreal if expansion took place in Vancouver and Quebec City? As it was predictable that new teams would be inferior to Montreal and Toronto, it is doubtful if either the CBC or CTV could have been persuaded substantially to increase their price to accommodate two new teams. At the same time the addition of the Canadian cities was not necessary to get an American TV contract.[9]

Given the expansion, the basic model can also help explain in more detail the "stocking" of the new teams, and the formation of the new NHL division.

With the degree of control over players it was obvious that the new clubs would have to stock their teams from the rosters of the existing clubs.[10] If the maximum amount of competition was the league objective, this could only be promoted by a draft which allowed no protection of any player by any club. However, given the incentive to win, such a move would obviously not appeal to the existing clubs. Hence, no open draft.

In 1966, following pressure from various sources to take amateur hockey out of professional hands, the CAHA-NHL agreement was rewritten. However, although the new agreement appears to be more palatable, the NHL has in fact retained the same degree of monopsonistic control at possibly a cheaper price. The main provisions of the new agreement are as follows.

The NHL will terminate all sponsorship of amateur clubs. All amateurs will only be drafted when they reach twenty-one years of age and the "try out" and "option" agreements will be discontinued. The NHL will pay a set amount to the CAHA for each player drafted. Finally, a player development fund will be set up, financed by the NHL, to develop hockey players.

---

[9] However, Vancouver could have had a franchise if the city had sold to Stafford Smythe (principal owner of Toronto Maple Leafs) and associates a downtown block for $1. Smythe would then have provided a team and an arena. Whatever one thinks of the move and no matter how sympathetic one is to Vancouver's drive for major status, this proposal was a massive attempt at using full line forcing!

[10] This was also an an opportunity for the existing teams to reap a little extra reward. For $2 million per club the new teams were allowed to draft twenty players each, owned by the old clubs.

What advantages does this arrangement have from the point of view of the NHL? First, although it appears to give control of amateur hockey back to the CAHA and so dispel most of the public outcry over professional control, it really only makes this control more indirect. For instance, despite the loss of sponsorships and A, B, and C forms, etc., the NHL has the *exclusive* right to draft all amateurs who will still (according to the agreement) be playing under the NHL rules. The purpose of the option agreements, sponsorship lists, etc., was to reduce interclub competition for players; this purpose is *retained* by the new universal draft. In fact, it is probably retained at a cheaper price than would otherwise have had to be paid. With six new clubs entering the league there would have been extreme competition for players. This would have resulted in increased prices for players and increased costs of setting up amateur farm systems. With the new agreement all such cost disappears.

Second, financial control still rests with the NHL through control of the Joint Development Committee, which approves all payments to the CAHA leagues. As there is no information on how much it cost the NHL clubs to run their amateur farm systems, one cannot judge how adequate the amount of money invested by the NHL under this new arrangement is. However, it is doubtful that even by doubling the size of the NHL the funds going to amateur hockey will be doubled. Thus, there is again a potential cost saving to every club.

Third, ultimate control still resides with the NHL because if it is not satisfied with the number of or calibre of players developed, the CAHA has agreed to implement a program of accelerated player development.

Thus, in any weighing of costs and benefits it appears as if the NHL has increased its benefits at a lower cost.

Conclusion

Given the fact that the evidence appears to accord with what the model predicts we can justifiably say that the conduct of the NHL can be explained by the model. However, whether the model provides any indelible guides to public policy is another matter. The NHL clearly possesses monopoly and monopsony power, and if the possession of market power is enough to warrant application of the Combines Act then the NHL is liable. But as the Act presently stands there is some doubt as to whether any liability exists, because professional sport is considered a *service*, and *services* are immune from prosecution under the Act. Whether it is desirable that the NHL be placed under the Act (irrespective of its market power) is another matter. Perhaps there are wider questions of the public interest which are not represented by the Act. Nevertheless, what is clear is that a complete reappraisal of the Combines Act vis-à-vis professional sport should be undertaken.

17. ASSESSMENT OF CANADIAN COMPETITION POLICY*

Economic Council of Canada

Assessment of the Present Combines Investigation Act

There exists no neat, scientific method for assessing the economic impact of a piece of legislation such as the Combines Investigation Act. A simple count of the number of cases brought to court over a period and the percentage won or lost tells rather little; indeed, it may be misleading inasmuch as publicity and deterrence have traditionally been supposed to play an important role in Canadian competition policy. The perfect anticombines law, if such a thing could be imagined, would be known to all, and 100 percent effective in its deterrence, with the result that no cases whatever would occur! But the present law is far from perfect and its actual deterrent effect can only be assessed very impressionistically. Many people are understandably reluctant to discuss how their behaviour may have been influenced by criminal legislation, and the use of some such technique as a "deterrence survey" of Canadian businessmen would be unlikely to yield reliable results.

We have put forward in this Report the view that the encouragement of economic efficiency should be the objective of Canadian competition policy, and it is accordingly in relation to this objective that the present legislation should be assessed. This is a difficult task, however, inasmuch as the state of efficiency of the Canadian economy at any point in time and changes that may have occurred in its efficiency over time reflect the influence of a vast number of factors in addition to the Combines Investigation Act. Much the same thing may be said about the intensities and types of competition prevailing in the Canadian economy: they too are the product of many influences of which the Combines Investigation Act is but one.

Like most assessments of economic policy, therefore, that of Canada's present competition policy must be undertaken on a basis of imperfect knowledge. An initial point worth making is that over the postwar period, the scope of the legislation and the breadth and vigour of its enforcement have on balance increased.

---

* Reprinted from Economic Council of Canada, *Interim Report on Competition Policy*, July, 1969, pp. 63-72, by permission of Information Canada.

More research has been done; a greater number and a wider range of industrial situations have been investigated; and the legislation has become a more important factor in the minds of businessmen and hence in the operation of the economy. Partly because of this greater volume of activity, and partly also because of greater efforts to publicize the nature and objectives of the legislation, the Act has become better known to important elements of the public, and by virtue of this fact alone may well have increased somewhat in deterrent power.

It must immediately be added, however, that there appear to be few grounds for supposing that the total impact of the legislation on economic efficiency has been more than modest. Certainly, the impact has been uneven. The Act has mainly been effective in restraining only three kinds of business conduct deemed to be detrimental to the public: collusive price-fixing, resale price maintenance, and misleading price advertising. A fair number of instances of each type of practice have been struck down by the courts, and partly because of the examples thus provided, there has probably been an appreciable deterrent effect as well.

It is unlikely that the Act has done much to affect efficiency via changes in the structure of the Canadian economy. The main claim that might be advanced is that the banning of resale price maintenance has probably encouraged the entry into some sectors of price-cutting retailers. It is possible too that other prohibitions of conduct in the Act may have had some indirect effects on economic structure. But in respect of corporate mergers, which are one of the most important means by which changes in industrial concentration and other dimensions of economic structure take place, the Act has been all but inoperative. The only two cases brought to court under the merger provisions (the *Canadian Breweries* and *Western Sugar Refining* cases) were both lost by the Crown, and were not appealed. There may have been certain deterrent effects in this area (the Director's *Annual Reports* indicate that some prospective mergers have been abandoned following consultations under the "program of compliance" discussed below), but the Crown's lack of success in the courts has presumably limited the amount of deterrence achieved.

There have been no court cases in respect of the section of the Act dealing with price discrimination. As to whether this section has exerted any important deterrent effect, opinions differ. One qualified observer has made the following comment:

> Those who are called upon professionally to advise on problems relating to combines legislation are impressed by the importance attached to it by the business community. It is probably equally true to say that the prohibition against predatory pricing has at least eliminated grosser attempts by large organizations to pre-empt a market or to drive competitors out of business.

It should be carefully noted that the economic impact of the Combines Investigation Act is not solely a function of the terms of the law itself and the way in which it has been interpreted by the courts. The resources available for its enforcement, including notably resources consisting of persons skilled in economic analysis, have also been a very important factor. Had these resources been greater, so too would have been the economic effects of the legislation. Still another factor has been the size of fines imposed upon offenders. In general, these have not been such as to contribute greatly to the total deterrent effect of the Act.

Pursuing further the assessment of Canada's present competition policy, it is enlightening to look first at some of the points often raised by those who feel that the policy is not vigorous enough, then to turn to the views of those who feel on the whole that the policy is too vigorous. Some of these differing views are distilled from written submissions that we have received on the subject of combines, mergers, etc., while others are taken from other available literature. Many of the opposing positions in this field are of many years' standing, reflecting in some cases basic underlying dilemmas in the formulation and application of competition policy.

Those who would make Canadian competiton policy more vigorous put much of their emphasis on the uneven effectiveness and incomplete coverage of the Combines Investigation Act. It does not, for example, extend to most service industries. Then there is the question of whether, if it be granted that presently illegal price and other agreements tend to have adverse effects on consumers, these same effects may not come about in other ways that the Act does little or nothing to bar. May they not come about, for example, if instead of entering into an agreement, the firms involved simply merge? Even this may not be necessary: in cases where the number of firms in an industry is relatively small, there may exist a sufficient measure of tacit understanding among them that their economic behaviour is not greatly different from what it might be if they had either merged or formed a collusive agreement. The condition of oligopoly, with firms following a price leader or otherwise acting upon "recognition of mutual dependence," appears to be fairly common in the Canadian economy.

In addition to urging that more be done about mergers and oligopoly, some of those who favour a more vigorous competition policy have advocated the extension of the Act to cover a wider range of trade practices. The Act now covers refusal to sell only when used to enforce resale price maintenance. Other practices not now covered by the Act include the exclusive-dealing and tying arrangements described in the "TBA" Report of the Restrictive Trade Practices Commission.

But, while some observers have felt that Canadian competition policy is not vigorous enough, others (particularly businessmen) have criticized it in other ways. The business briefs that have been received by the Economic Council in connection with the government's Reference include most of the criticisms that Canadian businessmen have made of the Act over the last several years. Of criticisms that deal not with detailed procedures under the Act or with the repugnance to businessmen of its criminal law basis, but rather with its general character, philosophy, and approach, the following four would appear to be the most important:

1. Proceedings under the Act are often extremely drawn-out, leaving accused firms in a state of uncertainty for long periods of time.

2. Additional uncertainty is produced by failure to spell out offences clearly, with the result that businessmen often do not know whether their contemplated course of action will bring them into contravention of the Act.

3. Since the main underlying objectives of the Act are economic in nature, it is inappropriate that the courts, in deciding whether an offence has been committed, should not give more attention than they do to the probable economic effects of the business actions complained of. In other words, there should be less relative emphasis on industrial *conduct* and *structure,* and more on economic *performance.*

4. By the restraints that it exerts on agreements, mergers, and monopolies, the Act hampers the achievement of greater "rationalization" and specializa-

tion of Canadian industry, the promotion of exports, and the building up of large-scale, research-based enterprises.

It is worth pausing to consider a little further these four criticisms, for they help to illuminate some basic problems that all countries with competition policies have had to face in the formation and development of such policies.

To begin with, there is a certain incompatibility between criticisms (1) and (2), which call for greater speed and certainty in the application of competition policy, and criticism (3), which calls for more flexibility, discretion, and consideration of economic effects. Greater speed and certainty could be obtained by redrafting the entire Act as a series of relatively clear and unqualified *per se* offences; this would undoubtedly accelerate procedure and give businessmen a more precise idea of whether their proposed actions were likely to attract a prosecution. But the resulting Act, if it were reasonably free of loopholes and comprehensive in its coverage, would likely be found intolerably rigid.

Conversely, however, a move to have the courts give greater consideration to economic performance and probable economic effects would tend to lengthen procedures and increase uncertainty. As it is, many recent price-fixing cases have taken five years or more to complete from the opening of the initial investigation. How much longer would they have taken if the courts had had to consider, in addition to evidence bearing on whether or not a combine existed, a full range of evidence concerning the alleged economic effects (past, present, and future) of the combine? The difficulties that are involved in basing competition policy very largely on economic performance criteria and the analysis of probable economic effects were pointed out earlier.

Another dilemma is suggested by criticism (4) in the list above, concerning mergers, monopolies, rationalization, and specialization. The typical problem is that whereas a proposed merger or agreement regarding specialization, exports, or both may give some promise of bringing about longer production runs and lower unit costs, with possible favourable implications for international competitiveness, it may also create a monopoly or near-monopoly in the domestic market, with possible unfavourable implications for the domestic consumer. Much will, of course, depend on other circumstances, such as the extent to which the domestic market is protected from foreign competition by tariffs or transportation costs.

Returning to the matter of uncertainty, it is normally thought desirable for criminal law to be characterized by an especially high degree of certainty and fair warning. The Combines Investigation Act is notable for the use of a large number of qualifying words and phrases such as "unduly" (Section 32 on combinations), and "having the effect or tendency of substantially lessening competition or eliminating a competitor, or designed to have such effect" (Section 33A on price discrimination). On the face of things, these qualifications might seem likely to produce considerable uncertainty. Regard must be had, however, to the jurisprudence as well as to the letter of the Act. Where there has been little jurisprudence, as in the section on price discrimination, much uncertainty does exist; but where the courts have been more active, as in the section on combinations, the state of affairs under the Act has become clearer. Thus the word "unduly" ("to prevent, or lessen, unduly, competition in the production, manufacture, etc. . . . .") has acquired a specific quantitative significance. It has been interpreted in such a way that a price agreement covering the whole of the relevant market can now virtually be said to be illegal *per se,* while an agreement covering less than the whole but well over half of the market runs a substantial risk of being held illegal.

An important point about the jurisprudence in this area is that while the courts have been prepared to consider economic evidence relating directly or indirectly to the share of the market covered by agreements, they have steadfastly declined to consider evidence relating to the economic *effects* of agreements. This is well brought out in the decision of Mr. Justice Spence in the *Fine Paper* case:

> Surely the determination of whether or not an agreement to lessen competition was "undue" by a survey of one industry's profits against profits of industry generally, and a survey of the movement of the prices in that one industry against the movement of prices generally, would put the Court to the essentially non-judicial task of judging between conflicting theories. It would entail the Court being required to conjecture — and by a Court it would be nothing more than mere conjecture since a Court is not trained to act as an arbitrator of economics — whether better or worse results would have occurred to the public if free and untrammelled competition had been permitted to run its course.

The quantitative, share-of-market interpretation that the courts have placed on "undueness" has been such as to allow the striking down of a considerable number of price agreements. But in respect of mergers, where a similar piece of qualifying language prevails, the effects have been very different. In *Rex versus Canadian Breweris Limited,* the trial judge, Chief Justice McRuer, stated that it was not the motive but the effect of the merger that was important — "whether it has operated to the detriment or against the interest of the public, or is it likely to do so." Chief Justice McRuer asserted that these words, applied to mergers, had substantially the same meaning as "unduly," applied to combinations. It followed that if the effect of a merger was to virtually eliminate competition, an offence had been committed; otherwise not.

To demand that a price agreement, in order to be declared illegal, must embrace most of the relevant market leaves considerable room for successful prosecution by the Crown, since if an agreement had not this characteristic, its prospects of effectiveness would in most cases be too low to induce anyone to enter into it. But to apply a similar market standard to mergers all but rules out successful prosecution by the Crown since few mergers virtually eliminate competition even though some of them have considerable and long-lived effects on competition.

Establishing the share of the market covered by a price-fixing agreement is a relatively simple operation, since the area covered by the agreement itself is of considerable assistance in defining the market. However, the delineation of the relevant market in cases involving mergers and other restrictive practices confronts the Director of Investigation and Research, the Restrictive Trade Practices Commission, and the courts with a more difficult task. Sometimes the task is virtually synonymous with that of defining industry boundaries, an industry being thought of as a group of sellers who market a certain product or range of products. But in a world of product differentiation and product substitution, where should market lines be drawn? Should one think in terms of the market for a particular kind of steel product, of the market for all steel products, or of the market for steel, aluminum, plastics, and perhaps some other materials? The decision will turn on how readily market buyers can substitute one material or item for another. The geographic extent of markets, transport costs, and the relative costs of producing the substitute products will have to be taken into account. The result is very much a matter of judgment. For purposes of competition policy, market boundaries, if not always industry boundaries, should be drawn as narrowly as is required to ensure that no substantial group of buyers *within* the boundaries should be unable readily to substitute one product for another.

The present situation of Canadian competition policy with respect to mergers provides a good illustration of an area where it has proved impossible, within the confines of criminal court procedure, to provide the sort of examination of complex economic phenomena that would adequately satisfy the protection of the public interest. The MacQuarrie Committee was well aware of this kind of problem and attempted to devise a means of dealing with it while at the same time adhering to the assumption that the criminal law basis of Canadian combines legislation would have to be continued for the time being. In proposing the creation of a board very similar to what shortly thereafter emerged as the Restrictive Trade Practices Commission, the Committee was not only concerned to separate the functions of prosecutor and judge previously lodged with the Commissioner under the Combines Investigation Act; it also hoped to provide a means whereby significant economic issues in matters brought before the Commission could be thoroughly aired and reported on, and remedies other than (or in addition to) criminal prosecution could be proposed.

The task conceived for the Commission was an extremely difficult and challenging one, and if the expectations of the MacQuarrie Committee have not been wholly fulfilled in practice, this should not be taken as any reproach to the diligence and vigour with which members of the Commission have discharged their duties. The Commission has made some highly useful original contributions to the evolution of competition policy in Canada. Examples of such contributions would include the Commission's report on ocean shipping conferences and its active participation in certain general inquiries under Section 42 of the Combines Investigation Act. But it must be said also that, on the whole, the Commission itself has not been able to escape from the criminal law strait jacket to the degree hoped for by the MacQuarrie Committee. For reasons some of which are readily understandable, the Commission has paid close attention to the interpretation of the Combines Act by the courts and, to a considerable extent, has assimilated its role to that of the courts. It has not ventured into broader economic analysis to the extent that was anticipated and has not, by and large, provided an adequate solution to the problem of dealing with practices and situations that do not lend themselves well to treatment via the normal procedures of criminal courts.

Another means that has been utilized in an attempt to overcome some of the rigidities and other disadvantages of the present legislation has been the development of a "program of compliance" by the Director of Investigation and Research under the Combines Investigation Act. Under this program, businessmen have been encouraged to discuss with the Director *in advance* courses of conduct which they are contemplating, in order to determine whether the adoption of such courses would lead him to launch an inquiry under the Act.

Altogether, it is apparent that there are numerous causes for dissatisfaction with the present situation of Canadian competition policy. It cannot be expected that such a policy will ever please everyone. Remedies for undesirable situations must be provided, and those on the receiving end of these remedies will rarely if ever enjoy the experience. But it does appear to us that a point has been reached where competition policy can be restructured to meet, at least partly, some of the more serious and important criticisms that have been made of it, and where it can also be better related to national economic objectives. Thus altered, it should be able to command a wider measure of that public understanding and support that are essential to its successful operation.

E. RESOURCE PRICING AND EMPLOYMENT

Productive resources have prices, just as consumer goods do. Like commodity prices, they are largely determined by the interaction of supply and demand — the total supply of the specific resource and the aggregate demand for it. By now, of course, you know that the function of any price is to ration scarce goods (and resources) among competing buyers. Thus all we have to do is ascertain "proper" demand and supply functions. "Proper" is placed in quotation marks because the supply function for certain resources is rather difficult to discover. This is especially true of labour resources, where the desire for leisure and the action of trade unions must be considered.

The marginal productivity theory is the "orthodox" explanation of resource pricing. Reading 18 presents the marginal-productivity concept both in historical perspective (as the US economist John Bates Clark evolved it) and in a form that is consonant with contemporary thinking. This selection uses labour to illustrate the pricing and employment of resources. The multiple assumptions underlying the theory are examined, as well as Clark's interests and the necessity for general abstractions. The division between the "principle" and the "theory" is put forward and the component parts of each are summarized.

Although Canada is still primarily a market economy, government does influence many prices. We have noted that the agricultural sector of the Canadian economy represents an area in which there has been considerable government intervention in the operation of the price system. As a means of ensuring adequate living standards for workers, all provinces have enacted minimum wage legislation. This means that employers are required by law to pay a certain minimum wage. Are minimum wages justified? Reading 19 reviews the effects of a legal minimum wage on the allocation of resources, on aggregate employment, and on family income, and finds that minimum wages may not provide support for incomes where it is most needed — that is, among unorganized workers at the lowest sector of the wage scale.

18. MARGINAL PRODUCTIVITY*

Allan M. Cartter

Following Jevons (and unacquainted with his work at that time), J.B. Clark in the 1880s and 1890s developed his wealth-creation theory in a number of articles, and finally presented it in complete form in *The Distribution of Wealth* (1902). Since Clark's presentation made the greatest impact upon his fellow economists, it is perhaps best to begin with his presentation of the marginal productivity distribution theory.

One of the influences which interested Clark in distribution theory — we might say one of the major incitements — was the writing of Henry George. The impact of George on Clark, however, was just the opposite of the effect that Henry George had, for example, on George Bernard Shaw. In the latter case Shaw was converted by the evangelical land reformer. In Clark's case, the direction was reversed; having begun his career as a moderate Christian Socialist, the impact of George's writing was to carry Clark along a course of research which resulted finally in the book which some have referred to as a capitalist apologetic. As Clark stated in the preface to his *Distribution:*

> It was the claim advanced by Mr. Henry George, that wages are fixed by the product which a man can create by tilling rentless land, that first led me to seek a method by which the product of labor everywhere may be disentangled from the product of cooperating agents and separately identified; and it was this quest which led to the attainment of the law that is here presented, according to which the wages of all labor tend, under perfectly free competition, to equal the product that is separately attributable to labor.

In *Progress and Poverty*, first published in 1879, George had presented a universal "law of wages":

> Wages depend upon the margin of production, or upon the produce which labor can obtain at the highest point of natural productiveness open to it without the payment of rent. . . . Thus the wages which an employer must pay will be

---

*Reprinted with permission from Cartter's *Theory of Wages and Employment* (Homewood, Illinois: Richard D. Irwin, Inc., copyright 1959), pp. 12–19.
Dr. Cartter taught economics at Duke University, Durham, N.C., from 1952 to 1956 and was Dean of the Graduate School from 1956 to 1962. He has been Chancellor, New York University since 1966.

measured by the lowest point of natural productiveness to which production extends, and wages will rise or fall as this point rises or falls.

In other words, in real terms wages must equal the highest amount a typical labourer can produce on no-rent land, or equal the product of the last man whom it is profitable for an employer to hire at the margin of utilization of other factors. In an equilibrium situation these two products would be identical, equilibrium being brought about by the movement of labour between the agricultural and industrial sectors. In light of the later development of the marginal productivity theory, George would seem to deserve a more important place in the history of the development of economic theory than he has sometimes received, for certainly this intuitive insight was considerably ahead of most contemporary thinking on the subject. His weakness, however, and the point which stimulated Clark to contemplation of the problem, was that George always laid the stress upon the first of the two factors quoted above, that is, the productivity of labour on no-rent land. To George, brought up in the frontier economy of the mid-nineteenth century, the utilization of land at the margin was the impressive and determining factor; the industrial wage level seemed dependent upon the agricultural return. Clark, writing a generation later in a period of rapid industrialization, objected to what he termed George's "law of squatter's sovereignty," and was led to seek an analogous situation less distantly removed from the industrial scene. This he found in what he described as a "no-rent" margin or "zone of indifference" in the use of factors other than land. Clark argued that there is no need to look to agriculture to find no-return agents of production which were combined with labour.

> Everywhere, in indefinite variety and extent, are no-rent instruments; and, if labor uses them, it gets the entire product of the operation. Let the general rate of wages rise, and many of these instruments will be thrown out of use. Let the rate then fall, and the utilizing of them will be resumed. . . . The entire product that is created by utilizing the poorest instruments that are kept in action at all, goes to the men who work them. The amount of this product corresponds with and expresses the rate of general wages. . . . The men who use such instruments are a part of the final increment of labor, the market price of which regulates the price of all labor.

In presenting a summary of Clark's distribution theory, it is necessary to abstract from the real world, and imagine a completely static society, free from all the disturbances caused by progress.

> Reduce society to a stationary state, let industry go on with entire freedom, make labor and capital absolutely mobile — as free to move from employment to employment as they are supposed to be in the theoretical world that figures in Ricardo's studies — and you will have a regime of natural values. These are the values about which rates are forever fluctuating in the shops of commercial cities. You will also have a regime of natural wages and interest; and these are the standards about which the rates of pay for labor and capital are always hovering in actual mills, fields, mines, etc.

Here is a world of perfect markets, perfect information, perfect mobility, constant population, a constant amount of available capital, and an unchanging productive technology. By isolating from the process of economic change and development, Clark attempted to find the "natural values" of wages and other productive rewards, toward which all actual values in the real dynamic world around us tend at any moment of time.

Having imagined such conditions of a stationary state, we must further imagine a situation where the total stock of capital is not only constant, but where its form may be varied at will in the process of adapting physical instruments of production to varying quantities and abilities of available labour. Clark makes a distinction between "capital," which is a total stock or fund of formless instruments, and "capital goods," which are the specific instruments themselves. Thus a constant stock of capital does not mean that the form of these capital goods remains unchanged, but rather that the total fund remains constant while the forms this fund may take on at any moment are of an infinite variety. This is analogous to saying that an individual's accumulated wealth is $100,000, although this fund changes its form as the owner shifts from security holdings to real estate, or from cash to jewellery, etc. At first this seems to be a most unrealistic assumption, since mines and steel mills cannot be changed into soda fountains and atomic energy plants merely with the wave of a wand. Further reflection, however, suggests that if we allow sufficient passage of time, then capital goods do take on this kind of flexibility. When the New England cotton mill finally wears out, we do not have to replace it in the same locality, but can exhibit the mobility of capital by moving it to Georgia — or if we wish, we can now take the depreciation reserve and build not a new cotton mill but a chain of gas stations instead. Thus, in the long run, capital is extremely mobile, and almost completely adaptable.

Two more assumptions will be useful in investigating the mechanics of wage determination in this hypothetical world. We will assume, with Clark, that pure competition and perfect markets everywhere abound, and that we can treat labour as a homogeneous factor by speaking of a quantity of identical "labour units," rather than of a quantity of dissimilar labourers. Clark states that for the equivalent of this labour unit, "we may use the familiar term, unskilled labor, and treat the work performed by a man with no exceptional skill or endowment as constituting the unit of which we are speaking. A superior artisan, however, represents more than one such unit, and a successful business manager represents many of them." This simplification allows us to speak generally about the wage rate, rather than of a whole structure of wage rates for various degrees of skill.

In this hypothetical world, having assumed competition in labour markets, we will therefore expect that labour units, each knowing the demand conditions of the market and each seeking to maximize its income, will apportion themselves throughout the economy in such a manner that wages will be everywhere equal. If wages are higher in one firm than another, presumably workers will leave the lower paying establishment and seek employment in the high-wage firm, thus bidding wages down in the latter until both are again equal.

Employers, on the other hand, will attempt to utilize their available capital in such a way as to maximize their return, thus hiring as many labour units as can profitably be put to work with their existing capital. For the individual firm or industry, therefore, the addition of workers to a fixed quantity of capital will result in diminishing marginal returns, and the marginal product of labour units will decline as the number of these units applied to the existing capital fund increases. To reproduce Clark's graphic illustration, if the number of labour units is indicated on the horizontal axis, and the marginal product (or "specific product" in Clark's terminology) of these workers when applied to some given quantity of capital is represented on the vertical axis, then line BC shows the diminishing marginal product of labour. If the existing wage rate that the employer must pay to attract workers (that is, the competitive wage rate) is an amount equal to AE, then the employer's interest will be to employ additional workers as long as their addition to the total product is greater than the wage he must pay them. Thus, employment would be AD, and the equilibrium situation would be a wage precisely equal to the marginal product of labour. Notice in Figure 1 that we are diagramming marginal products, so that the total product produced is the whole area under the line BC. Thus with employment equal to AD, the area AECD will be the total product allocated to labour, and the triangular area EBC will be the product allocable to other factors of production. Thus it is easily seen that if the employer stopped short of employment AD, the total product left for other factors of production would be absolutely smaller than if he employed all of the AD units; similarly, continuing employment beyond AD would entail subtractions from the total reward left for factors other than labour, subtractions equal to the widening area between the wage line EC, and the still declining marginal product line BC. Just at the equilibrium level of employment, the marginal worker receives his full marginal product and there is no residue left for the return of other factors — that is, in Clark's phrasing, this is the "no-rent" margin where the payment to the worker just exactly exhausts the amount of extra product he adds to the total output. Since all labour units are identical and interchangeable and there is assumed to be equality of wage rates for all such units due to the pressure of competition, all units are paid just what the marginal unit is worth.

In the above illustration we have treated the wage-employment relationship as the variable which was determined, and the return to other factors as the residual product. To follow Clark's example, we can now turn our assumption around and assume for the moment that the quantity of labour units is constant, and the quantity of capital the variable factor. If this were indeed the case, and if we consider only these two factors of production, labour and capital (merely because this is simpler than working with three or four simultaneously), then our illustration would be as shown in Figure 2. In this case capital would be added in small doses to a fixed quantity of labour, and the curve would now be the marginal product of capital. The employment of capital at the given price (interest) of AE would profitably cease at AD amount, but this time the rectangular area AECD would be the determined reward for capital, and the residual triangle EBC the amount left for labour. Clark was insistent that the amount going to labour and the amount going to capital would be the same whether either was treated as the determined or residual factor — that is, that the EBC triangle in Figure 1 would be identical in area to the AECD rectangle in Figure 2, and vice versa for capital's share.

In the illustration above, we considered a firm or industry which was faced with a given rate of return for both labour and capital, determined by the competitive forces of the outside market. Although this is essentially the situation in which a firm or industry finds itself, it will be noted that in Figures 1 and 2 we determined the amount of each factor which would be employed under these given rates of return. This appeared, therefore, to be a theory of employment rather than a theory explaining the wage level or the return for capital. Let us turn, therefore, to the economy as a whole, where these rates of return are not given data. In this case what is fixed is

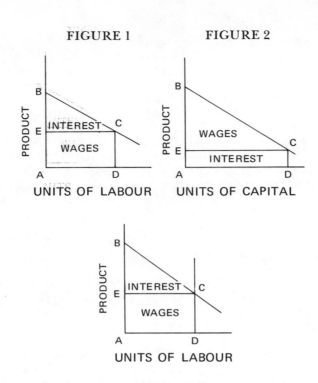

FIGURE 1 FIGURE 2

FIGURE 3

not the rate of return, but the available quantity of each factor. Thus, in Figure 3, which is merely a duplication of Figure 1, assume this represents the whole nation, and the available quantity of labour units is AD. If these units compete against one another for jobs, bidding the wage rate down if some units find themselves unemployed, and employers bidding the rate up if there are still profitable vacancies and no workers available, an equilibrium wage rate will finally be established at AE. In a sense, we can think of DCG as a supply curve of labour, and BC as a demand curve, each expressed in real terms. The only wage which will clear the market is obviously AE. Thus, in Clark's presentation, the marginal product of a given quantity of available labour determines its wage level when we consider the market as a whole; in the disaggregated picture, however, where a single employer finds the wage level determined by forces beyond his control, the marginal product of labour determines the level of employment. This point cannot be overemphasized, for it is often a source of misunderstanding. On the microlevel, the marginal productivity theory of Clark is an employment theory; on the macrolevel, it is a wage theory. In the parallel case of the demand for a product, we cannot meaningfully say price is determined by demand alone — all we can say is that the demand schedule for a product expresses a price-quantity relationship. Similarly, in the marginal productivity concept, the marginal product schedule defines a particular wage-employment relationship. Nothing meaningful can be said about the particular wage level which will exist in a specific case unless we have knowledge of both demand and supply conditions. In Clark's presentation, as indicated in the previous discussion, the supply of labour was assumed to be, in effect, perfectly inelastic. That is to say, Clark's assumption of a stationary state, including as it did the premise of a constant population with an unchanging level of education, skill, etc., is equivalent to assuming that the aggregate labour supply curve is of zero elasticity.

It may be useful in analysing Clark's marginal productivity theory to note that it comprises at least three component parts. First, there is the premise that the rational employer, in the attempt to maximize profits, will be guided by the marginal productivity of a factor in determining the relationship between the factor's return and its employment. This is essentially a dual assumption that the principle of diminishing returns is operative, and that employers are rational. We might name this premise the marginal productivity principle. Secondly, there is the premise of perfect competition, so that market forces tend to equalize rates of return for all factors over time. And thirdly, there is the premise of long-run general equilibrium in all markets. Given these three premises, we can then say that if there is a fixed (that is, inelastic) supply of labour in the market, the level of wages will be determined by the marginal product of labour.

Because of the criticisms which have been levelled at the marginal productivity theory . . . it is important to emphasize these three premises. It should be carefully noted that the first premise may be perfectly valid in a world in which the other two premises are not descriptively accurate. The marginal productivity principle (the first premise) would even be true in a world where some central agency determined wages in a completely arbitrary manner — in this case the rational employer would attempt to adjust his level of employment so that the marginal product of labour exactly equalled the arbitrary wage level. If this were the case, we could still say that the wage level in that firm or industry equalled the marginal product of labour; we could not, however, say that wages were determined by labour's marginal product. It might be clearer to restate the meaning of the first premise and say that the marginal productivity principle states that there is a direct functional relationship between the level of wages and the level of employment, and that a rational employer will attempt to adjust one or both of these variables so that the marginal product of labour is equal to the wages of labour. Only in a case where an employer had no control over the wage rate and the amount of employment would the marginal productivity principle be inapplicable. The Clarkian marginal productivity *theory*, however, requires, in addition to this premise, perfectly competitive markets and the conditions of long-run equilibrium to be fully descriptive of the wage determinants.

This dichotomy between what we have called the principle and the theory has been stressed largely because it is a source of considerable confusion and it is only by analysing the parts of the theory separately that we will be able to properly judge the merits of the whole.

19. MINIMUM WAGE LEGISLATION: AN ECONOMIC ANALYSIS*

George J. Stigler

The popular objective of minimum wage legislation — the elimination of extreme poverty — is not seriously debatable. The important questions are rather: (1) Does such legislation diminish poverty? (2) Are there efficient alternatives? The answers are, if I am not mistaken, unusually definite for questions of economic policy. If this is so, these answers should be given.

Some readers will probably know my answers already ("no" and "yes," respectively); it is distressing how often one can guess the answer given to an economic question merely by knowing who asks it. But my personal answers are unimportant; the arguments on which they rest, which are important, will be presented under four heads:
1. Effects of a legal minimum wage on the allocation of resources.
2. Effects on aggregate employment.
3. Effects on family income.
4. Alternative policies to combat poverty.

The Allocation of Resources

The effects of minimum wages may in principle differ between industries in which employers do and do not have control over the wage rates they pay for labour of given skill and application. The two possibilities will be discussed in turn.

Competitive Wage Determination

Each worker receives the value of his marginal product under competition. If a minimum wage is effective, it must therefore have one of two effects: first, workers whose services are worth less than the minimum wage are discharged (and thus forced into unregulated fields of employment, or into unemploy-

---

*Reprinted from George J. Stigler, "Economics of Minimum Wage Legislation," *American Economic Review,* June, 1946, pp. 358–65, by permission of the editor and author.
Dr. Stigler is Charles R. Walgreen Distinguished Service Professor of American Institutions, University of Chicago.

ment or retirement from the labour force); or, second, the productivity of low-efficiency workers is increased.

The former result, discharge of less efficient workers, will be larger the more the value of their services falls short of the legal minimum, the more elastic the demand for the product, and the greater the possibility of substituting other productive services (including efficient labour) for the inefficient workers' services. The discharged workers will, at best, move to unregulated jobs where they will secure lower returns. Unless inefficient workers' productivity rises, therefore, the minimum wage reduces aggregate output, perhaps raises the earnings of those previously a trifle below the minimum, and reduces the earnings of those substantially below the minimum. These are undoubtedly the main allocational effects of a minimum wage in a competitive industry.

The second and offsetting result, the increase of labour productivity, might come about in one of two ways: the labourers may work harder; or the entrepreneurs may use different production techniques. The threat of unemployment may force the inefficient labourers to work harder (the inducement of higher earnings had previously been available, and failed), but this is not very probable. These workers were already driven by the sharp spurs of poverty, and for many the intensity of effort must be increased beyond hope (up to 50 or more percent) to avoid discharge.

The introduction of new techniques by the entrepreneurs is the more common source of increased labour productivity. Here again there are two possibilities.

First, techniques which were previously unprofitable are now rendered profitable by the increased cost of labour. Costs of production rise because of the minimum wage, but they rise by less than they would if other resources could not be substituted for the labour. Employment will fall for two reasons: output falls; and a given output is secured with less labour. Commonly the new techniques require different (and hence superior) labour, so many inefficient workers are discharged. This process is only a spelling out of the main competitive effect.

Second, entrepreneurs may be shocked out of lethargy to adopt techniques which were previously profitable or to discover new techniques. This "shock" theory is at present lacking in empirical evidence but not in popularity.

There are several reasons for believing that the "shock" theory is particularly inappropriate to the industries paying low wages. All of the large manufacturing industry categories which in 1939 paid relatively low wages (measured by the payroll of wage earners divided by their average number) are listed in Table 1. A study of this table suggests two generalizations: (1) the low-wage industries are competitive, and (2) the ratio of wages to total-processing-cost-plus-profit is higher than in high-wage industries. The competitive nature of these industries argues that the entrepreneurs are not easy-going traditionalists: vigorous competition in national markets does not attract or tolerate such men. The relatively high labour costs reveal that inducements to wage economy are already strong. These considerations both work strongly against the shock theory in low-wage manufacturing industries in 1939. Since these industries were on the whole much less affected by the war than other manufacturing industries, they will probably be present in the postwar list of low-wage industries. The low-wage industries in trade and services display the same characteristics and support the same adverse conclusion with respect to the shock theory.

TABLE 1

EMPLOYMENT, AVERAGE ANNUAL EARNINGS OF FULL-TIME WAGE EARNERS, AND PERCENTAGE WAGES FORM OF VALUE-ADDED, IN LOW-WAGE MANUFACTURING INDUSTRIES, 1939

Industry	Employment	Average Earnings	Wages as Percent of Value Added
Men's and boys' furnishings	166,945	$632	52.2
Canned and preserved foods	134,471	660	28.0
Cigars	50,897	673	42.0
Cotton manufactures	409,317	715	51.1
Fertilizer	18,744	730	24.0
Wood containers	45,070	735	47.2
Women's accessories	58,952	740	41.3
Misc. fabricated textiles	49,242	746	36.2
Misc. apparel	38,288	769	45.5
Rayon and silk manufactures	119,821	779	54.4
Animal and vegetable oils	21,678	781	25.1
Costume jewellery, etc.	25,256	782	43.5
Sawmills, etc.	265,185	810	52.0
Leather products	280,411	847	50.9
All manufacturing		1,153	36.8

Source: *Census of Manufactures*, 1939.

Employer Wage Determination

If an employer has a significant degree of control over the wage rate he pays for a given quality of labour, a skillfully set minimum wage may increase his employment and wage rate and, because the wage is brought closer to the value of the marginal product, at the same time increase aggregate output. The effect may be elucidated with the hypothetical data in Table 2. If the entrepreneur is left alone, he will set a wage of $20 and employ fifty men; a minimum wage of $24 will increase employment to seventy men.

TABLE 2

HYPOTHETICAL DATA ILLUSTRATING EMPLOYER WAGE DETERMINATION

Number of Workers	Wage Rate	Marginal Cost of a Worker	Value of the Marginal Product*
10	$12		$36
20	14	$16	34
30	16	20	32
40	18	24	30
50	20	28	28
60	22	32	26
70	24	36	24

* Or marginal value product, if this is less.

This arithmetic is quite valid, but it is not very relevant to the question of a national minimum wage. The minimum wage which achieves these desirable ends has several requisites:

1. It must be chosen correctly: too high a wage (over $28 in our example) will decrease employment. The accounting records describe, very imperfectly, existing employment and wages; the optimum minimum wage can be set only if the demand and supply schedules are known over a considerable range. At present there is no tolerably accurate method of deriving these schedules, and one is entitled to doubt that a legislative mandate is all that is necessary to bring forth such a method.
2. The optimum wage varies with occupation (and, within an occupation, with the quality of worker).
3. The optimum wage varies among firms (and plants).
4. The optimum wage varies, often rapidly, through time.

A uniform national minimum wage, infrequently changed, is wholly unsuited to these diversities of conditions.

We may sum up: the legal minimum wage will reduce aggregate output, and it will decrease the earnings of workers who had previously been receiving materially less than the minimum.

Aggregate Employment

Although no precise estimate of the effects of a minimum wage upon aggregate employment is possible, we may nevertheless form some notion of the direction of these effects. The higher the minimum wage, the greater will be the number of covered workers who are discharged. The current proposals would probably affect a twentieth to a tenth of all covered workers, so possibly several hundred thousand workers would be discharged. Whatever the number (which no one knows), the direct unemployment is substantial and certain; and it fairly establishes the presumption that the net effects of the minimum wage on aggregate employment are adverse.

This presumption is strengthened by the existing state of aggregate money demand. There is no prospective inadequacy of money demand in the next year or two — indeed, the danger is that it is excessive. If the minimum wage were to increase the relative share of wage earners and, hence, the propensity to consume — which requires the uncertain assumption that the demand for inefficient labour is inelastic — the increment of consumer demand will be unnecessary, and perhaps unwelcome. (Conversely, the direct unemployment resulting from the wage law would diminish faster in a period of high employment.)

It is sufficient for the present argument that no large increase in employment will be induced by the legislation. Actually, there is a presumption that a minimum wage will have adverse effects upon aggregate employment.

Wage Rates and Family Income

The manipulation of individual prices is neither an efficient nor an equitable device for changing the distribution of personal income. This is a well-known dictum that has received much documentation in analyses of our agricultural programs. The relevance of the dictum to minimum wage legislation is easily demonstrated.

One cannot expect a close relationship between the level of hourly wage rates and the amount of family income. Yet family income and needs are the fundamental factors in the problem of poverty. The major sources of discrepancy may be catalogued.

First, the hourly rates are effective only for those who receive them, and it was shown in Section 1 that the least productive workers are forced into uncovered occupations or into unemployment.

Second, hourly earnings and annual earnings are not closely related. The seasonality of the industry, the extent of overtime, the amount of absenteeism, and the shift of workers among industries, are obvious examples of factors which reduce the correlation between hourly earnings and annual earnings.

Third, family earnings are the sum of earnings of all workers in the family, and the dispersion of number of workers is considerable. The summary in Table 3 for low income wage-earner families in Minnesota in 1939, shows that in the $250—$500 income class one-twentieth of the families had more than one earner and in the higher income classes the fraction rose to one-eighth.

TABLE 3

PERCENTAGE DISTRIBUTION OF WAGE-EARNER FAMILIES BY
NUMBER OF EARNERS: MINNESOTA, 1939

Family Income	One Earner	Two Earners	Three Earners	Four or More Earners
$250—$500	94.5	4.6	.7	.2
500— 750	92.4	7.1	.3	.2
750—1000	86.7	10.7	1.5	1.1
1000—1250	88.5	10.4	1.1	.1

Source: *Minnesota Incomes, 1938—39*, Vol. II (St. Paul, Minnesota Resources Commission, 1942), p. 152.

Fourth, although wages are, of course, the chief component of the income of low-wage families, they are by no means the only component. It is indicated in Table 4 that a tenth of the wage-earner families had cash investment income, a quarter had entrepreneural income, and a quarter owned their homes.

All of these steps lead us only to family income; the leap must still be made to family needs. It is argued in the next section that family composition is the best criterion of need, and whether this be accepted or not, it is clearly an important criterion. The great variation in family size among wage-earner families is strongly emphasized by the illustrative data in Table 5; an income adequate for one size is either too large or too small for at least half the families in that income class.

The connection between hourly wages and the standard of living of the family is thus remote and fuzzy. Unless the minimum wage varies with the amount of employment, number of earners, nonwage income, family size, and many other factors, it will be an inept device for combatting poverty even for those who succeed in retaining employment. And if the minimum wages varies with all of these factors, it will be an insane device.

TABLE 4

COMPOSITION OF INCOME OF WAGE-EARNER FAMILIES: MINNESOTA, 1939

Income Class	Total	Wages and Salaries	Income Entre-preneural Income	Room and Board	Investment Income Cash	Investment Income Total
Percentage of Families Receiving Income						
$250–$500		99.9	26.5	1.3	12.3	28.2
500– 750		100.0	25.2	1.7	10.1	24.2
750–1000		100.0	21.4	2.7	9.4	31.2
1000–1250		100.0	18.4	3.0	10.4	22.8
Average Amount						
250– 500	$ 387	$ 308		–$ 9	$64	
500– 750	631	560		62	82	
750–1000	865	766		53	82	
1000–1250	1124	1032		91	96	

Source: *Minnesota Incomes, 1938–39*, Vol. I (St. Paul, Minnesota Resources Commission, 1942), p. 42; Vol. II, p. 200.

The Problem of Poverty

Minimum wage legislation commonly has two stated objectives: the reduction of employer control of wages; and the abolition of poverty. The former and much lesser purpose may better be achieved by removing the condition of labour immobility which gives rise to employer control. Labour immobility would be reduced substantially by public provision of comprehensive information on employment conditions in various areas and industries. The immobility would be further reduced by supplying vocational training and

TABLE 5

PERCENTAGE DISTRIBUTION OF WAGE-EARNER FAMILIES BY NUMBER OF PERSONS: CHICAGO AND ATLANTA, 1936

Income Class	Number of Persons in Family 2	3 or 4	5 or 6	7 or more
Chicago				
$ 0–$250	39.6	43.6	14.9	2.0
250– 500	35.3	45.8	17.6	1.3
500– 750	31.8	53.7	13.0	1.6
750–1000	29.0	56.5	12.4	2.1
Atlanta				
0– 250	30.	55.	15.	0.
250– 500	20.1	48.1	16.5	5.3
500– 750	22.6	46.9	24.4	6.2
750–1000	21.6	48.1	23.5	6.7

Sources: *Family Income in Chicago, 1935–36* (Bureau of Lab. Stat. bulletin No. 642 [Washington, Supt. Docs., 1941]), 1, p. 117; *Family Income in the Southeastern Region* (Bureau of Lab. Stat., bulletin No. 647 [Washington, Supt. Docs., 1941]), 1, p. 148.

loans to cover moving costs. But employer wage control is not the important problem; let us turn to the elimination of poverty.

Incomes of the poor cannot be increased without impairing incentives. Skillful policies will, for a given increase in the incomes of the poor, impair incentives less than clumsy policies. But the more completely poverty is eliminated, given the level of intelligence with which this is done, the greater will be the impairment of incentives. This is a price we must pay, just as impairment of incentives is a price we have willingly paid to reduce the inequality of income by progressive income and estate taxes. Society must determine, through its legislators, what minimum income (or addition to income) should be guaranteed to each family. We shall assume that this difficult decision has been made.

One principle is fundamental in the amelioration of poverty: those who are equally in need should be helped equally. If this principle is to be achieved, there must be an objective criterion of need; equality can never be achieved when many cases are judged (by many people) "on their merits." We are driven almost inexorably to family size and composition as this criterion of need. It is obviously imperfect; the sickly require more medical care than the healthy. But it is vastly easier to accord special treatment to certain families for a few items like medical care than to accord special treatment to every family for the sum of all items of expenditure.

It is a corollary of this position that assistance should not be based upon occupation. The poor farmer, the poor shopkeeper, and the poor miner are on an equal footing. There may be administrative justification (although I doubt it) for treating the farmer separately from the urban dweller, but there is no defence in equity for helping the one and neglecting the other. To render the assistance by manipulating prices is in any case objectionable: we help the rich farmer more than the poor, and give widely differing amounts of help to the poor farmer from year to year.

The principle of equity thus involves the granting of assistance to the poor with regard to their need (measured by family composition) but without regard to their occupation. There is a possible choice between grants in kind and in money. The latter commends itself strongly: it gives full play to the enormous variety of tastes and it is administratively much simpler. Yet it raises a problem which will be noticed shortly.

Even if these general observations be accepted, the structure of administration is of grave importance, and I do not pretend to have explored this field. There is great attractiveness in the proposal that we extend the personal income tax to the lowest income brackets with negative rates in these brackets. Such a scheme could achieve equality of treatment with what appears to be a (large) minimum of administrative machinery. If the negative rates are appropriately graduated, we may still retain some measure of incentive for a family to increase its income. We should no doubt encounter many perplexing difficulties in carrying out this plan, but they are problems which could not be avoided, even though they might be ignored, by a less direct attack on poverty.

One final point: we seek to abolish poverty in good part because it leads to undernourishment. In this connection, dietary appraisals show that in any income class, no matter how low, a portion of the families secure adequate diets, and in any income class, as high as the studies go, a portion do not. The proportion of ill-fed, to be sure, declines substantially as income rises, but it does not disappear. We cannot possibly afford to abolish malnutrition, or malhousing, or maleducation, only by increasing incomes.

Either of two inferences may be drawn. The program of increasing income must be supplemented by a program of education — in diet, in housing, in education! Or the assistance to the poor should be given in kind, expertly chosen. The latter approach is administratively very complex, but quicker and in direct expenditure vastly more economical. These factors affect our choice, but a thought should be given also to the two societies to which they lead.

F. INCOME DISTRIBUTION AND POVERTY IN CANADA

The division of the fruits of economic activity among the resources that contribute to the productive process or among the people who control these resources is what economists call *distribution*. It may be viewed from different aspects. *Functional distribution* is the apportionment of the total income of society among the productive resources, regardless of who controls them. *Personal distribution* is the allocation of the economy's income among families and individuals.

As you have seen in the preceding section, marginal productivity theory provides the generally accepted explanation of income determination and income distribution. But this is all it does — explain. It does not justify any given income distribution, nor does it render inviolable a given distribution. In fact, our economic history is replete with efforts to alter the distribution system, largely in favour of greater income equality. Witness such measures as progressive income taxes, inheritance and gift taxes, minimum wage laws, unemployment insurance, old age security pensions, family allowances, fair employment practices enactments, and the like. All these reflect our concern with the low living levels of large numbers of our population and our determination to buttress the economic laws of the marketplace with legislation designed to ameliorate economic insecurity. Still, the problem of poverty remains very pertinent.

Reading 20 describes the dimensions of poverty in Canada. It identifies the problems in defining poverty, and the extent of low incomes in Canada. Some broad characteristics of low-income families are also examined, and a brief reference is made to the special characteristics of poverty among Canada's Indian and Eskimo populations.

Not surprisingly, poverty has been regarded primarily as a human and social problem. However, it is an economic problem to a much greater extent than most people have realized in the past. Reading 21, therefore, focusses on the economic costs of poverty and on the economic effects of poverty on the underprivileged. It also stresses the need for creating income-earning capacities and opportunities among the poor and the handicapped. The result would be to increase our production, with potential benefits not only for the poor themselves but for all Canadians.

One of the approaches to the reduction of poverty is the negative income tax. It is a proposal to supplement or replace government welfare programs by amending the income tax system to provide that families with incomes below certain levels automatically become eligible for direct transfers or subsidies from government. This solution was suggested some time ago by Professor George Stigler of the University of Chicago (see Reading 19), and has recently been popularized by several economists. The main features of the negative income tax scheme are sketched in Reading 22.

20. THE PROBLEM OF POVERTY*

Economic Council of Canada

Poverty in Canada is real. Its numbers are not in the thousands, but the millions. There is more of it than our society can tolerate, more than our economy can afford, and far more than existing measures and efforts can cope with. Its persistence, at a time when the bulk of Canadians enjoy one of the highest standards of living in the world, is a disgrace.

What is poverty in Canada? Those who have seen it, felt it, experienced it — whether as its victims or as those trying to do something about it — can supply some telling descriptions. But one of the notable characteristics of poverty in modern times is that it is so located in both city and country, and often so disguised (it does not, for example, invariably go about in rags), that it can pass largely unnoticed by those in happier circumstances. An occasional glimpse from a car window; a television show or Saturday supplement article — these may be the only manifestations of it which touch many a middle-class consciousness. Yet the figures — even the conservative, rather tentative estimates in this chapter — show indisputably that it is there, almost everywhere in Canada, on a larger scale than most Canadians probably suspect.

One reason for poverty's partial invisibility is that the poor tend to be collectively inarticulate. Many of them lack the education and the organization to make themselves heard. For example, most of them are outside the ambit of the trade union movement. They have few spokesmen and groups to represent them and give voice to their needs.

Another difficulty is that it is all too easy, in Canada, to file poverty away under the heading of certain other long-standing national problems, and in this way to lose sight of it as a major problem in its own right. Thus many Canadians may assume that the problem of poverty is close to identical with the problem of low average incomes in the Atlantic provinces and eastern Quebec (especially their rural areas) and among the Indian and Eskimo populations. But this is an inaccurate impression. The *incidence* of poverty — the chance of a given person being poor — is certainly higher in the areas and

---

*Reprinted from Economic Council of Canada, *Fifth Annual Review*, September, 1968, pp. 103-24, by permission of Information Canada.

among the groups just mentioned. But in terms of absolute numbers, between a third and a half of the total poverty in Canada is to be found among the white population of cities and towns west of Three Rivers. The resident of Montreal or Toronto need not travel far to see poverty first-hand; a subway fare will suffice. Much rural poverty, too, is to be found dispersed through areas where *average* income, by rural standards, is relatively high.[1]

There are two major problems in defining poverty. First, it is a *relative* concept. Second, while the availability of relevant statistics compels it to be discussed here largely in terms of low incomes, it means something more than simple income deficiency.

Let us deal first with the problem of relativity. It is of course true that generally agreed upon concepts of poverty alter through space and time. Thus, the situation of those Canadians whom the majority of their fellow citizens would deem to be suffering from poverty is hardly to be compared with that of the street sleepers of Calcutta. And if a typical 1968 "poverty line," defined in terms of real income, were extended back through time, most Canadians during the Depression of the 1930s, and perhaps even most Canadians of the 1920s, would be found to have been living below that line.

But neither of these facts makes poverty in Canada in 1968 any less real or painful. To feel poverty is, among other things, to feel oneself an unwilling outsider — a virtual nonparticipant in the society in which one lives. The problem of poverty in developed industrial societies is increasingly viewed not as a sheer lack of essentials to sustain life, but as an insufficient access to certain goods, services, and conditions of life which are available to everyone else and have come to be accepted as basic to a decent, minimum standard of living.

Poverty, thus defined, is not quite the same thing as low income. A statistician would say there is a very strong association between the two, to the extent that one can often be used as a rough-and-ready substitute for the other. They are not, however, identical. For example, the low-income population of Canada includes a small proportion of people such as the university student who gets by on $1,500 a year, but does not feel himself irrevocably poverty-stricken, first, because he has a family to fall back on if necessary, and second, because much better income prospects lie a short distance ahead of him. Much more serious and more widespread is the kind of low-income situation that carries with it a sense of entrapment and hopelessness. Even the best statistics can only hint at this. They cannot capture the sour atmosphere of poor health and bad housing — the accumulated defeat, alienation, and despair which often so tragically are inherited by the next and succeeding generations.

We believe that serious poverty should be eliminated in Canada, and that this should be designated as a major national goal. We believe this for two reasons. The first is that one of the wealthiest societies in world history, if it also aspires to be a just society, cannot avoid setting itself such a goal. Secondly, poverty is costly. Its most grievous costs are those felt directly by

---

[1] "The problem of low rural incomes can be associated to a degree with the problem of poor regions, but if this association is overemphasized, attention may be unduly diverted from the dispersed, but in absolute numbers still very substantial, poverty problem in prosperous regions. Although one-third of the 'poor' farms in Canada were located in areas where their proportion was so high that the areas themselves could be classified as poor, almost another third of the poor farms were located in areas where the opposite was true." Helen Buckley and Eva Tihanyi, *Canadian Policies for Rural Adjustment*. A study of the Economic Impact of ARDA, PFRA, and MMRA, Special Study No. 7, Economic Council of Canada (Ottawa, 1967).

the poor themselves, but it also imposes very large costs on the rest of society. These include the costs of crime, disease, and poor education. They include the costs of low productivity and lost output, of controlling the social tensions and unrest associated with gross inequality, and of that part of total welfare expenditure which is essentially a palliative made necessary by the failure to find more fundamental solutions. It has been estimated in the United States that one poor man can cost the public purse as much as $140,000 between the ages of seventeen and fifty-seven.

It should also be noted that in recent years there has been a burst of improvement in the available weaponry against poverty. Not only have new weapons been devised or proposed; but there has also been a development of techniques of evaluation by which the effectiveness of both old and new weapons can be assessed and enhanced. Much of this improvement has occurred since the US Government declared formal war on poverty with its Economic Opportunity Act of 1964. (The term "war on poverty" is appropriate in more than one sense, for, ironically enough, some of the techniques of policy planning and evaluation now being applied in the field of poverty originated within the military and defence planning establishments.) There have also been some extremely promising developments in Canada and some overseas countries. We would not wish to paint an overoptimistic picture, nor to suggest that much further experimentation and improvement are not required. But it is undoubtedly the case that the prospects for mounting a powerfully renewed offensive against poverty, with clear performance criteria and appropriate feedbacks of information on actual results obtained, and with a greater sense of involvement on the part of the poor themselves, are considerably better today than they would have been ten years ago.

The Extent of Low Incomes in Canada

In popular discussion of the problem of poverty, a traditional opening question has been: "Are the rich getting richer while the poor get poorer? " In other words, poverty has been viewed in terms of trends in the distribution of income through society as a whole. This is not a particularly useful way of coming to grips with poverty as it is defined here. Nevertheless, recent trends in the distribution of income are taken as a starting point in order to clear the ground for what we regard as a more fruitful approach.

As may be seen from Table 1, there has been relatively little change in the distribution of family income in Canada over the last fifteen years. In particular the share of total income received by the bottom fifth of families has altered only fractionally. Breaks in the statistics make it difficult to extend these comparisons further back in time, but it appears that there may have been a trend toward greater income equality between 1931 and 1951, with the share received by the bottom fifth showing an appreciable increase. Between 1951 and 1965, however — a period over which average family income increased very rapidly — little shift in percentage shares was apparent. (It should be noted that the distribution of family income in Table 1 is *before tax;* exactly corresponding figures of income *after tax* are not available, but Table 2 gives some idea of the effective rates of income tax applying to various income groups in 1961.)

The lower fifth, or lower third, or any other fraction of an income distribution, makes a poor statistical substitute for poverty as we have defined it. It bears no necessary relation to the needs of the poor — to their

TABLE 1

DISTRIBUTION OF NONFARM FAMILY INCOME
BEFORE TAX

	Distribution of Total Income			Average Income per Family
	1951	1961	1965	1965
	(Percentage)			(Dollars)
Lowest-income fifth of families	6.1	6.6	6.7	2,263
Second fifth	12.9	13.4	13.4	4,542
Third fifth	17.4	18.2	18.0	6,102
Fourth fifth	22.5	23.4	23.5	7,942
Top fifth	41.1	38.4	38.4	13,016
All families	100.0	100.0	100.0	6,669

Source: Based on data from Dominion Bureau of Statistics.

TABLE 2

CLASSIFICATION OF NONFARM FAMILIES AND
PERSONS NOT IN FAMILIES, BY INCOME GROUP, 1961

Income Group	Number of Families	Number of Persons Not Living in Families	Average Income Tax as a Percentage of Income*
	(000)	(000)	
Under $1,000	137	306	—
$1,000–$1,999	275	192	1.5
$2,000–$2,999	356	157	3.2
$3,000–$3,999	524	150	4.6
$4,000–$4,999	583	71	6.0
$5,000–$5,999	500	35	6.5
$6,000–$6,999	365	17	7.1
$7,000–$7,999	260	9	7.4
$8,000–$9,999	296	8	8.5
$10,000 and over	331	10	16.5
Total	3,627	955	8.1

*Applies to families and persons not living in families.
Source: Based on data from Dominion Bureau of Statistics.

degree of access to certain goods and services regarded as basic to a decent standard of life at any point in time. The proper object of an attack on poverty should be the careful identification and aiding of those whose circumstances do not permit them to achieve such a standard. Ultimately, the object should be the elimination of poverty.

In a later section of this chapter, we shall recommend thorough-going procedures for the setting of minimum living standards and the estimation of the amount of poverty in Canada.* Here, operating without the benefit of such procedures, we nevertheless feel it necessary to give the reader some general notion of the size and character of the poverty problem which proper estimates would be likely to reveal. The tentative and broadly illustrative character of the figures should be strongly emphasized. It would be most distressing to see them taken up as fixed, precise, and authoritative measures of poverty in Canada: rather, they should be superseded as soon as possible by better and more informative figures. To underline this point, two alternative estimates of "total poverty" are presented.

The two estimates are derived from a special study of the low-income population of Canada, carried out by the Dominion Bureau of Statistics on the basis of the 1961 Census.[2] Low-income families were defined as families with incomes insufficient to purchase much more than the basic essentials of food, clothing, and shelter. An examination of data on family expenditures, collected from a sample of about 2,000 families living in urban centres with populations of 15,000 or more, showed that, on average, families allocated about half of their income to these needs. It might therefore be concluded that where a family was using up a good deal more than half its income on essentials, that family was likely to be in straitened circumstances, having little money left over for such things as drugs, medical care, education of children, recreation, savings, etc.

For purposes of the first estimate, low-income families and individuals were defined as those using 70 percent or more of their incomes for food, clothing, and shelter. On this basis, low-income families and individuals would include single persons with incomes below $1,500, families of two with less than $2,500, and families of three, four, and five or more with incomes of less than $3,000, $3,500, and $4,000 respectively.

As of 1961, some 916,000 nonfarm families plus 416,000 individuals were living below these levels.[3] The total number of persons involved was about 4.2 million, including 1.7 million children under sixteen years of age. In all, they accounted for some 27 percent of the total nonfarm population of Canada.

There are a number of special difficulties in defining and estimating the incomes of farm families, and the figures in this area are not much more than educated guesses. It would appear that, in 1961, roughly 150,000 farm families,[4] comprising perhaps 550,000 persons, may have been living below the income levels set forth above. The addition of these people to the nonfarm group would have brought the low-income percentage for all of Canada, including farms, to just under 29 percent on the basis of the definition employed.

The Canadian economy has of course undergone a vigorous expansion since 1961, sufficient to lift the incomes of a good many families and individuals above the low-income lines we have specified. No comparative figures are available for farm families or for nonfarm individuals, but it would appear that by 1965 the percentage of nonfarm families living below

---

*Editor's note: these procedures are not reproduced here.
[2] J. R. Podoluk, *Incomes of Canadians,* Dominion Bureau of Statistics Census Monograph, 1968.
[3] Average incomes of low-income families in 1961 were:
Two persons in family $1,427
Three persons in family $1,851
Four persons in family $1,347
Five or more persons..$2,707
[4] The *total* number of families primarily dependent on farming for a livelihood in 1961 was in the order of 275,000. Thus more than half these families were below the income levels used here.

the specified levels (their incomes being expressed in 1961 dollars) had declined from 25 percent to 20 percent. This probably gives an exaggerated impression of the longer-term trend of improvement, inasmuch as in 1961 the economy was at a low point of the business cycle, with the ranks of the poor temporarily swollen by unusually large numbers of unemployed.

The above estimate is the more conservative of the two presented. Most readers who care to reflect on the income cut-offs with their own personal income situations, will agree that living standards at or just above the cut-offs are likely to be modest indeed.

In the second estimate, the cut-offs are raised somewhat by the device of assuming that the expenditures of 60 percent or more (instead of 70 percent or more) of income on food, clothing, and shelter by an individual or family indicates straitened circumstances. This brings the cut-offs up to $2,000 for a single person, $3,500 for a family of two, $4,000 for families of three and four, and $5,000 for families of five or more. Applied to the 1961 nonfarm population, these changes raise the low-income percentage from 27 percent to 41 percent.

At the beginning of this series of estimates, their "tentative and broadly illustrative character" was emphasized. They are not fully adequate measures of poverty. Such measures require among other things a thorough-going analysis of the needs and expenditure patterns of different types of families, and a consideration of assets, borrowing power, and income in kind as well as money income. It is useful also to distinguish between temporary and long-term poverty, and to allow for differences in living costs between different cities, towns, and rural areas.

But for all their shortcomings, the estimates presented here — particularly the first, more conservative set — suggest very strongly the existence of a major poverty problem in Canada. The statement that at least one Canadian in every five suffers from poverty does not appear to be a wild exaggeration. It is almost certainly close enough to the truth to be taken as one of the most serious challenges facing economic and social policy over the next few years.

Some Statistical Characteristics of Low-Income Families and Individuals

Statistics cannot adequately describe poverty. But used with care they are capable of furnishing important clues to types of policies likely to be effective against poverty. With this end in view, some further information is set forth here concerning the nonfarm low-income families and individuals included in the *first* of our estimates of the extent of poverty in Canada.

Two important warnings must be issued at the outset. Statistically, low-income families and individuals differ noticeably from the total Canadian population in respect of a number of things besides income. Certain characteristics of age, family size, place of residence, education, relationship to the labour force, and occupation are more commonly found among them than among the population at large. Put another way, where these characteristics are present, the chance of a family or individual having a low income (the *incidence* of low income) is high. These high rates of incidence are often significant as policy guides to particular kinds of poverty problems.

This can be demonstrated in terms of some of the characteristics covered in Table 3. It is evident from the incidence figures that income is more likely to be low when one or more of the following characteristics are present:

TABLE 3

SELECTED CHARACTERISTICS OF ALL NONFARM FAMILIES AND LOW-INCOME NONFARM FAMILIES, YEAR ENDING MAY 31, 1961

	(1)	(2)	(3)
	Number of Nonfarm Families		Incidence of Low Income
	All Families	Low-Income Families	(2) as a percentage of (1)
	(000)	(000)	
Nonfarm Families	3,627	916	25
Place of Residence:			
Metropolitan	1,901	314	17
Other Urban	959	250	26
Rural	767	352	46
Region			
Atlantic	349	158	45
Quebec	988	276	28
Ontario	1,363	254	19
Prairies	556	150	27
British Columbia	368	78	21
Sex of Head			
Male	3,344	795	24
Female	283	121	43
Age of Head			
Under 25	149	43	29
25—54	2,509	554	22
55—64	491	109	22
65 or over	478	210	44
Size of Family			
Two	960	280	29
Three	734	148	20
Four	758	157	21
Five or more	1,175	331	28
Number of Children under 16			
None	1,383	330	24
One	699	143	21
Two	679	156	23
Three or more	866	287	33
Nonfarm Families	3,627	916	25
Labour Force Status of Head			
In current labour force	2,996	573	19
Not in current labour force but worked during year	100	49	49
Did not work	531	294	55
Education of Head			
No schooling or elementary only	1,681	625	37
Secondary, 1—3 years	1,068	208	20
Secondary, 4—5 years	551	62	11
Some university	137	13	9
University degree	190	8	4

TABLE 3 Cont'd

	(1)	(2)	(3)
	Number of Nonfarm Families		Incidence of Low Income
	All Families	Low-Income Families	(2) as a percentage of (1)
	(000)	(000)	
Number of Earners in Family			
No earners	268	217	81
One earner	1,870	529	28
Two earners	1,114	142	13
Three or more earners	375	28	7
Major Source of Income			
Wages and salaries	2,909	533	18
Self-employment	306	76	25
Transfer payments	271	245	90
Investment income	75	26	35
Other income	55	25	45
No income*	11	11	100

*This relatively small group includes such people as recent immigrants and recently widowed women who had received no income in Canada over the period covered.
Source: Based on data from Dominion Bureau of Statistics.

1. the head of the family had no formal education beyond elementary school;
2. the family lives in a rural area;
3. the family lives in the Atlantic provinces;
4. the head of the family is not a member of the labour force;
5. no member of the family worked during the year;
6. the head of the family is sixty-five years of age or over; and
7. the head of the family is a woman.

From this list, it is all too easy to form a picture of poverty in Canada that consists of a relatively few stereotyped categories, most of them involving high dependence on government pensions and welfare payments. There are indeed many people in such situations, but a more balanced picture of the total low-income population of Canada is necessary. It is vital, in framing policy, not to be overinfluenced by rates of incidence, and in this way to form too simple and stereotyped a picture of poverty. Chart 1 points out the following facts:

1. 62 percent of low-income nonfarm families in 1961 lived in urban areas, and of this group more than half lived in metropolitan areas. (If the rough estimate of 150,000 low-income *farm* families in 1961 were included in the charts, the proportion of all low-income families living in urban areas would still have been more than 50 percent.)

2. 83 percent of low-income nonfarm families lived elsewhere than in the Atlantic provinces. 53 percent of them lived in Ontario and the western provinces.

3. 68 percent of the same group of families had heads who were in the labour force for at least part of the year.

CHART 1

PERCENTAGE DISTRIBUTION OF LOW INCOME
NONFARM FAMILIES, 1961

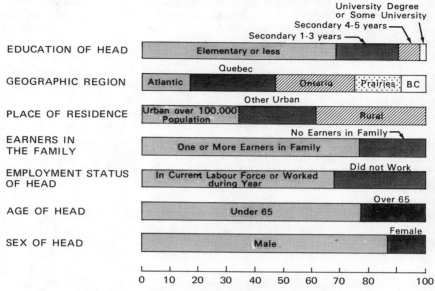

Source: Based on data from Dominion Bureau of Statistics.

4. 76 percent of the group had one or more earners in the family, and (see Table 3) 66 percent of families obtained most of their income from wage, salary, and self-employment earnings.

5. 77 percent of family heads in the group were under sixty-five years of age.

6. 87 percent of families in the group were headed by men.

It can thus be seen that a set of antipoverty policies directed toward major groups or geographical areas showing a very high *incidence* of low incomes would almost certainly fail to deal adequately with poverty. It would, for example, have a tendency to neglect unduly the very considerable group whose poverty problems are associated not with an absence of earnings, but with an insufficiency of earnings. It would tend to miss the many pockets of poverty that are scattered through relatively high-income regions — pockets which, in the aggregate, account for a large proportion of total poverty in Canada.

So much for the first warning concerning the interpretation of these statistics. The second warning is to avoid confusing characteristics with causes, and to bear in mind constantly how the total amount of poverty can be affected by broad, economy-wide forces such as the rate of economic growth in relation to potential. If the economy falls well below its potential, the incomes of many people will drop because they become unemployed. It is highly likely under these circumstances that unemployment will tend to strike hardest at those with least education; but to say simply that these persons' low incomes are *caused* by lack of education is not an adequate analysis of the situation.

With these two important cautions stated, we may now proceed to look at some further policy implications suggested by the low-income statistics.

197

Sources of Income

The principal source of income for most families, including low-income families, is earnings in the form of wages, salaries, and income from self-employment. Any factors that adversely affect the market value of labour services, or which prevent the services from being offered, may result in income falling below poverty lines. Among the more notable factors of this kind are lack of job skills (often associated with low levels of formal education), old age, disablement, ill health, and participation in low-paying occupations. The necessity of caring for young children may also prevent labour services from being offered. A small percentage of families are able to offset deficient labour income with returns from wealth holdings. But most must rely on some form of government transfer payment, such as pensions, unemployment insurance, or family allowances; hence the higher degree of reliance on such payments among low-income families, who, as a group, received 27 percent of their income from this source in 1961, compared with a figure of 8 percent for all families.

Where a low-income family is for one reason or another incapable of offering labour services, and is therefore largely dependent on government payments, the policy problem of how to aid that family is in one sense relatively simple: the major issue is the size of the income to be provided. But where there are earnings, but on an insufficient scale, or where there is an unexploited potential for earnings, the policy choices are less simple. Other things being equal, it is far better to help people to help themselves — to put them in a position to upgrade their earnings permanently through such measures as training and manpower mobility programs, and to exploit unused earnings potential (provided this does not involve a sacrifice of future to present earnings, as in the case of the youth who drops out of high school to augment family income). But self-help takes time, and meanwhile income support in the form of government payments may be needed. It seems a fair generalization that in the past Canadian social policy has tended to emphasize various forms of income maintenance, and has only recently moved strongly into the more difficult area of promoting self-help among low-income people.

Low-Income Occupations

Where the head of a family is in the labour force, his chances of having a low income are very much greater in certain occupations than in others. This statement is a well-worn commonplace, but the extent of the differences revealed in Table 4 is nevertheless striking. The incidence of low incomes in 1961 was more than twice the overall average in four occupational groups: farm workers; loggers and related workers; fishermen, trappers, and hunters; labourers.

Once again, it is necessary to draw a careful distinction between incidence and total numbers, and to note that the four occupations named accounted for only 22 percent of all the low-income family heads in the table. Nevertheless, it is worth remarking that the four occupations tend to be characterized by much seasonality and other irregularity of employment and earnings. This crosschecks with other information suggesting that, across the whole occupational spectrum, insufficiency of wage and salary earnings is often associated with intermittent and part-time work.

TABLE 4

OCCUPATIONAL DISTRIBUTION OF MALE NONFARM FAMILY HEADS, 1961

	(1)	(2)	(3)
	Number of Nonfarm Family Heads		Incidence of Low Income
	Total (000)	Low-Income Level (000)	(2) as a percentage of (1)
Managerial*	419	42	10
Professional and technical	256	12	5
Clerical	200	21	11
Sales	182	24	13
Service and recreation	246	50	20
Transport and communications	256	61	24
Farm workers**	34	19	56
Loggers and related workers	35	20	57
Fishermen, trappers, hunters	20	14	70
Miners, quarrymen, related workers	44	8	18
Craftsmen, production process and related workers	991	183	19
Labourers	149	60	40
Not stated	39	10	26
Total of male nonfarm family heads in current labour force	2,871	524	18

*Includes self-employed, as do other occupational classifications.
**Includes farm *workers* not living on farms.
Source: Based on data from Dominion Bureau of Statistics.

Education, Location, and Occupation

The association between low income and lack of education beyond the elementary level is particularly strong. Not only did families whose heads had less than secondary education show a high incidence of low income in 1961 (37 percent), they also accounted for more than two-thirds of all low-income families.

However, in addition to education there are other factors such as occupation, region, and place of residence (urban or rural).[5] In addition, there is some interaction between education and income, rather than a purely one-way causal connection. Thus the education levels of family heads were very likely influenced by the income and related circumstances of *their* parents; and their circumstances in turn are likely to influence the education levels achieved by their children.

In the cross-classifications of Charts 2, 3, and 4, low educational achievement continues to exhibit a strong association with low income, but does

---

[5] A regression analysis of the low-income data has suggested that many of the factors associated with a high incidence of low income tend to occur together. The explanatory variables used in the analysis were education, place of residence (urban or rural), age, region, and occupation. As a general rule, the partial effect of each variable was smaller than the corresponding incidences given in Table 3.

CHART 2
EDUCATION AND LOW INCOMES BY REGION, 1961

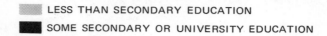

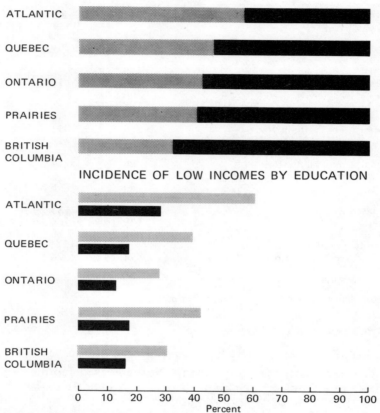

Source: Based on data from Dominion Bureau of Statistics and estimates by Economic Council of Canada.

not wipe out the influence of other factors. Thus, even where there is education beyond the elementary level, the incidence of low income continues to be notably higher in the Atlantic provinces than elsewhere, higher in rural than in urban areas, and considerably higher in some occupations than in others.

It seems clear that provision of adequate education generally, plus deliberate special efforts to help those whose family circumstances tend to discourage persistence in education, must form a highly important part of policy against poverty. As some of the other work of the Council has shown, the performance of the educational system has very long-range effects. To the extent that it fails to perform well in helping the children of low-income parents to break out of the poverty cycle, there are likely to be distressing social and economic costs for one and perhaps more generations.

CHART 3
EDUCATION AND LOW INCOMES BY PLACE OF RESIDENCE, 1961

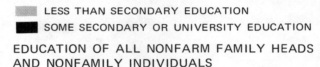

LESS THAN SECONDARY EDUCATION
SOME SECONDARY OR UNIVERSITY EDUCATION

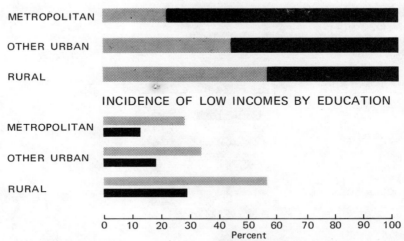

EDUCATION OF ALL NONFARM FAMILY HEADS
AND NONFAMILY INDIVIDUALS

METROPOLITAN

OTHER URBAN

RURAL

INCIDENCE OF LOW INCOMES BY EDUCATION

METROPOLITAN

OTHER URBAN

RURAL

0 10 20 30 40 50 60 70 80 90 100
Percent

Source: Based on data from Dominion Bureau of Statistics and estimates by
Economic Council of Canada.

It is also clear, however, that the upgrading of human resources involved in combatting poverty calls for a good deal more than strong improvement in the formal educational system. There must also be many other elements, such as adult retraining and manpower mobility programs, to help families and individuals escape from the low-income circumstances which entrap them.

Families Headed by Women

The high incidence of low income among families headed by most women is strongly related to the presence of dependent children. Most low-income families headed by women under sixty-five are families where there are two or more children under sixteen. For all such families, the incidence of low income is close to 50 percent.

The presence of dependent children often prevents a woman who is head of a family from entering the labour market, or restricts her to low-paid, part-time jobs. While transfer payments such as mothers' allowances will probably always play an important role in relieving this type of situation, it is evident that much improved day-care facilities for young children could also make a major contribution. Such facilities would also improve the situation of low-income families headed by men whose wives would be glad to seek paid work if given the opportunity.

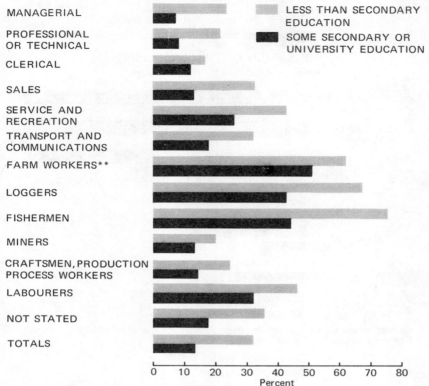

CHART 4
OCCUPATIONAL GROUPS AND INCIDENCE OF LOW INCOMES
BY EDUCATION, 1961*

MANAGERIAL   LESS THAN SECONDARY EDUCATION

PROFESSIONAL OR TECHNICAL   SOME SECONDARY OR UNIVERSITY EDUCATION

CLERICAL

SALES

SERVICE AND RECREATION

TRANSPORT AND COMMUNICATIONS

FARM WORKERS**

LOGGERS

FISHERMEN

MINERS

CRAFTSMEN, PRODUCTION PROCESS WORKERS

LABOURERS

NOT STATED

TOTALS

0   10   20   30   40   50   60   70   80
Percent

*Includes all nonfarm family heads and nonfamily individuals under 65 years of age.
**See notes to Table 4.
Source: Based on data from DBS and estimates by ECC.

Some Family Income Trends

The concept of low incomes changes with time. What may have been regarded in an earlier period as an adequate family income comes to be regarded later as inadequate, even after taking account of price changes. It is, nevertheless, useful to examine income trends to see what changes have taken place in the proportion of Canadian families in certian income brackets over a period of time. Consistent statistical data on family incomes go back to 1951. It is, therefore, possible to get some idea of how the distribution of family income evolved over the period from 1951 to 1965. With a substantial rise in the real income of the nation as a whole, it is only to be expected that there would have been a decline in the proportion of families in low-income brackets. For example, in 1951, nearly two-fifths of all nonfarm families received incomes of $3,000 or less. After making the necessary adjustments for changes in the value of the dollar, this proportion had dropped to slightly more than one-fifth in 1961, and by 1965 it had declined still further to less than one-fifth.

However, the growth in real incomes over this period was not shared equally by all family groups. The sharpest decline in the proportion of low-income families was among those whose major source of income was earnings. On the other hand, there was only a modest decline in the proportion of low-income families who were dependent upon income from sources other than earnings, or among families whose heads were not in the labour force.

Whether the head of the family was a man or a woman made a considerable difference in terms of income improvement over this fifteen-year period. The proportion of families with incomes under $3,000 and headed by women declined by only 24 percent. This contrasted with a drop of 58 percent in the case of families headed by men.

Another important characteristic associated with income improvements was age. The younger the age of the family head, the greater was the increase in income. For example, while average family income in real terms was 55 percent higher in 1965 than in 1951, families whose heads were under thirty-five had real incomes about 63 percent higher. On the other hand, the average family whose head was sixty-five and over had real income averaging only 34 percent higher. The obvious conclusion is that the young benefited more from economic growth over this period than the middle-aged and elderly.

Above-average increases in the incomes of families with younger heads probably reflect a number of factors. Younger age groups have higher levels of education and are thus generally more mobile, both occupationally and geographically. Their incomes are more likely to rise as a result of their own increasing productivity as well as productivity increases in the economy as a whole.

While family heads aged fifty-five to sixty-four are still employed, their earnings usually level off or start to decline relative to younger age groups. Furthermore, this age group is more vulnerable to unemployment than workers between the ages of twenty-five and fifty-four. The contraction of employment opportunities, especially for older workers with limited education and training, often results in a withdrawal from the labour force. Employment statistics show that on the average the less educated is the worker, the earlier is his departure from the labour force.

Age is also an important characteristic of low-income individuals who are not living in families. For example, 60 percent of such low-income individuals in 1961 were fifty-five or older, and nearly one-third of these were over the age of seventy. On the other hand, less than 25 percent of low-income individuals were between twenty-five and fifty-five. To a large extent older persons who are not part of a family are outside the labour force and thus primarily dependent upon government payments for income maintenance.

There is much further statistical material available concerning the characteristics of low-income Canadians.[6] Some of this material confirms tendencies already fairly well-known — for example, the poorer health of low-income people, and the crowded and otherwise substandard housing conditions which many of them face. No attempt is made here to give a well-filled-out picture of the low-income population; the object has been only to identify a limited number of characteristics which will begin to suggest the range of policies required to mount a truly comprehensive and effective attack on poverty.

---

[6]Much of this material is to be found in the series of 1961 *Census Monographs* being issued by the Dominion Bureau of Statistics. A useful general compendium of statistics relating to the low-income population is to be found in the document, *Profile of Poverty in Canada,* issued by the Special Planning Secretariat of the Privy Council, Ottawa.

No discussion of poverty in Canada can avoid making special reference to the Indian, Eskimo, and Métis members of our society.[7] A few simple statistics tell a brutal story. One is that the average life expectancy of an Indian woman in Canada is twenty-five years. Another is that the infant mortality rate among Eskimos is about 293 deaths per thousand live births, more than ten times the infant death rate for the population as a whole.

In Canada, partly because of constitutional practice and partly out of custom, Eskimos and Indians on reserves have been regarded as special groups of people requiring special policies. The Métis have tended, on the other hand, to be regarded as neither Indian nor white, and have therefore been largely excluded from both societies. For "registered" Indians and Eskimos, however, the applications of public policy have tended to make these peoples "wards of the state," or "citizens minus." To quote a recent study,[8] Indians, Eskimos, and Métis ought, as charter groups of Canadians, to be "citizens plus" rather than "citizens minus" as is now all too often the case.

The problems facing the Indian, Eskimo, and Métis peoples are very grave and are accentuated by a number of special factors: (1) rapid increase of population, in fact the most rapid of any ethnic group in Canada; (2) the rapidly declining opportunities for making a livelihood by the traditional occupations of hunting and trapping; (3) the low economic potential of Canada's 2,200 reserves, less than a third of which could possibly provide sufficient resources to support their present populations; and (4) the continuing difficulties faced by Indian, Eskimo, and Métis people in coping with, and adapting to, the problems of the major society, both because of present attitudes within the white community and because of strong cultural differences.

Such a listing is obviously incomplete, but there are additional limitations to any generalizations. The primary one is that we are referring to not one group, or even three, but to some hundreds of Indian bands, Eskimo settlements, and Métis communities scattered across the country. While all the Eskimos have a basically similar language, the Indians are fragmented both linguistically and culturally. The Métis, for their part, are the most forgotten people of the three.

Many excellent surveys, studies, and reports dealing with the circumstances and problems of Canada's "citizens minus" have recently appeared. While the competence of the Economic Council to appraise various findings in detail is obviously limited, we would like to stress some common conclusions.

1. Indians and Eskimos are treated too much as a special group in ways which exclude them from many of the ordinary provisions of public policy.

---

[7] In 1961, there were 192,000 Indians in Canada and 28,000 Eskimos. Métis were not separately identified in the 1961 Census, but if their rates of population increase over the preceding twenty years had been the same as those of the Indians and Eskimos, they might have numbered about 60,000 in 1961. By 1965, the total number of Indians was 218,000. A special survey by the Indian Affairs Branch in that year estimated that 78.5 percent of Indian households had incomes of less than $3,000 a year, 54.5 percent less than $2,000, and 28.2 percent less than $1,000.

[8] H. B. Hawthorn, ed., *A Survey of the Contemporary Indians of Canada,* (Ottawa, 1967). This Report is in two volumes, the second of which, dealing with education and with the internal organization of Reserves, is still in press.

This difficulty arises partly because Indians and Eskimos fall traditionally under federal jurisdiction, while many health and other public services as well as education are within provincial jurisdiction. The result has often been that Indians and Eskimos receive either inadequate services or special services which further segregate them from the larger society.

2. Particular efforts will be required to help those Indians, Eskimos, and Métis who are striving to integrate themselves into the larger society. Such integration does not mean the total assimilation and homogenization of these groups, but it does mean the increasing provision of opportunities for these peoples to take part in the main stream of Canadian life. The future economic life of most of these populations will undoubtedly lie within the larger industrial society.

3. A third major area of consensus is the need for a "community development" approach to the problems of education, individual development, adaptation to the larger environment, and community organization. In part, this work of community development has to do with the encouragement of new initiatives and economically viable enterprises within the band or settlement, and indigenous workers should be trained to work in the communities wherever feasible. In part also, the process will involve a better understanding between local groups seeking to develop local initiatives and the administrators of public policies, who tend to be too remote to be responsive to current needs. One promising development is the New Start Program currently being initiated by the Department of Manpower and Immigration in three northern areas of the Prairie Provinces. To the extent that the program proves successful in these test areas, it may generate techinques applicable in other communities with substantial Indian and Métis populations.

4. It is clear that however much can be done to develop economic activity on reservations and in other places where significant groups of native peoples live, a continuing substantial migration to urban areas must be expected, notably in western Canada. This process must be facilitated from both ends to a greater extent than hitherto. Those who move to the cities must be better prepared, educationally and in other ways, for a very different life. At the city end, more must be done to help these citizens to feel at home in their new environment, and to become responsible and contributing members of the community.

5. It would also appear useful to initiate an immediate study of federal and provincial legislation and administrative practices affecting native peoples. Two main objects of such a study would be to avoid allowing compelling needs to remain unmet because they fall between jurisdictions, and to identify instances where existing aid programs are not well adapted to meeting the particular problems of Indian reservations and similar areas.

21. THE ECONOMIC IMPLICATIONS OF POVERTY*

Economic Council of Canada

From now until at least the mid-1970s there are exciting possibilities for economic growth and development that could bring great benefits to most Canadians. But rapid growth in the national economy will not automatically assure either an adequate participation in the benefits of economic growth among *all* Canadians, or an adequate participation in the process of growth by all those who could play some part in it. Special attention therefore should be focussed on the need to achieve a *broad basis of participation* in the future economic development of our country. Among other things, this means that we must move to deal more effectively with the problem of poverty.

Our last Review described the seriousness of poverty in Canada — its large dimensions and its widespread prevalence in all parts of the country. We called for a national commitment to move toward the elimination of poverty. At the same time, we stressed the complex nature of the underlying factors involved in poverty, and hence the need to develop much better information and analysis as a basis for a really effective longer-term strategy for eliminating it. We also indicated that we intended to continue our work in this field; this chapter is a reflection of our continuing interest in this field.

The main purpose of this chapter is to persuade Canadians to think about poverty in a new way — a way which reflects its *economic* significance. Historically, the predominant view of poverty has been that it is primarily a human and social problem — a problem of how the fruits of the economic system should be shared and human misery alleviated. When poverty has manifested itself as a lack of income, the typical solution has been to transfer income to the poor. When it has manifested itself as a lack of access to particular services, the typical solution has been to provide access to certain services for the poor. This view of poverty appears to be predominant in the present complex of public and private efforts to minimize poverty in Canada, and has resulted in *social welfare* policies being the primary ap-

*Reprinted from Economic Council of Canada, *Sixth Annual Review*, September, 1969, pp. 107-22, by permission of Information Canada.

proach to alleviation. However, poverty is an economic problem to a much greater extent than most people have realized in the past. This is not to denigrate the human and social aspects of poverty. These are of vital importance. But there are also important economic aspects to poverty which have been generally overlooked, or at least underemphasized. We therefore attempt here to focus attention on the *economic costs of poverty*, on the *economic effects of poverty on the poor*, and on the *need for creating income-earning capacities and opportunities among the poor*.

Our approach starts from the premise that the greatest assets of a nation are its people and that the most important resources of an economy are its human resources. Our society and our economy are significantly weakened by the widespread poverty that exists in Canada today. To the degree that poverty contributes to the exclusion of individuals and families from the mainstream of society, it contributes to potential social tensions and unrest. To the degree that poverty places an economic burden on society, it acts as a brake on Canada's economic growth and detracts from the well-being of all Canadians.

The adult poor fall basically into two categories. In one group are those who cannot, or should not be expected to, earn incomes (for example, the aged and the chronically sick and disabled) and those who can and do work but whose income-earning capacity is essentially static (because they are near retirement, or for other reasons). On the other hand, there are those who are poor mainly because they have difficulties in finding or holding steady, rewarding jobs — difficulties arising from *remediable disadvantages*, such as lack of education or training, lack of information about job opportunities, inability to move to known job opportunities, poor work habits, and poor physical or mental health stemming from economic deprivation. These are also usually the first to suffer when unemployment rises.

If all the poor were in the first category, the solution to the problem of poverty might be simply to guarantee them a certain income. But only a minority of the adult poor are in this category. These should be ensured a decent minimum standard of living, without qualification; their incomes should be fully protected against inflation; and they should be assured of some participation in the rising average real standards of living which the growing productivity in our economy makes possible.

The majority of the poor in Canada, however, fall into the second category. They represent, in economic terms, unutilized or underutilized resources of human capital. Poverty in Canada can be reduced through measures designed to utilize more fully these resources by providing them with better access to job opportunities and through investments in human capital. The result would be to increase the output of the entire society, with potential benefits not only for the poor themselves, but for all Canadians. Policies that reduce poverty by creating new output, and therefore new incomes, are clearly preferable to policies that simply redistribute existing output and incomes. Poverty could be reduced, if not eliminated, by direct income *transfers* but as long as poverty reflects substantial unused manpower resources in the economy, redistributive schemes by themselves are likely to be second-best choices.

The Costs and Economic Implications of Poverty

The burden imposed by poverty on the Canadian economy is largely invisible in the usual aggregate economic measures. This partly explains the widespread lack of public appreciation of its existence. Yet the burden is real, and it takes two forms. These might be termed "lost output" and "diverted output."

Lost output is the additional production of goods and services that the poor would have created had their productive potential been better developed and effectively used. This additional production would, among other things, be reflected in higher personal incomes and purchasing power, and hence also in higher business sales volumes and government revenues. But these goods and services do not get produced and purchased. And such incomes do not get generated.

Diverted output, on the other hand, consists of the goods and services that are not produced because productive resources are diverted from other potential uses into activities made necessary by the failure to eliminate remediable poverty. For example, the existence of substantial poverty in Canada leads to the diversion of resources to deal with more sickness than would otherwise occur; it requires substantial resources to administer public welfare and assistance programs (including many hours of skilled manpower on a voluntary basis for fund raising); it requires larger expenditures for protecting persons and property and for administering justice; and in various respects, it places a heavier burden on our educational systems. In these and many other ways, it imposes additional costs on all Canadians in the sense that resources would otherwise have been available for other, more productive and more socially desirable uses.

There is no easy way to measure the total economic costs of lost and diverted output. Nevertheless, these costs are substantial.[1]

Before turning to a further consideration of some of the aspects of these costs and to possible means for reducing them, two popular misconceptions should be laid to rest.

First, the real costs of poverty to the economy as a whole do *not* refer to the large government transfer payments that are used to alleviate poverty, such as the transfers of income involved in family allowances, public assistance payments, old age security, unemployment insurance, payments under the Canada and Quebec Pension Plans, and tax exemptions.[2] These transfers are simply a substantial flow of funds passing through the government sector on the way from the "payers" to the recipients of the transfers (many of whom, on examination, turn out to be the same people, and most of whom are nonpoor). The government acts largely as a funnel; apart from the relatively small costs of administration, these flows do not reflect use by governments of the real resources of the economy. The distinction between transfer payments by governments and government programs that actually *consume* resources can be an important one, and one that tends to be obscured when government expenditures are lumped together and regarded as all of a kind. The costs of poverty related to lost and diverted output are

---

[1] *Lost output* estimates have been calculated under various assumptions by the Council staff and are available on request in the form of a technical mimeographed paper.

[2] It is perhaps not widely appreciated that tax exemptions constitute, in effect, a form of transfer payment. For example, for families with two young children who are in receipt of family allowances and have annual gross incomes of $2,700, $6,500, and $18,500, the exemptions in effect transfer to each $0, $114, and $270, respectively, in the form of tax savings. In other words, those whose incomes are too low to pay taxes gain nothing, and other families tend to gain in relation to their incomes. Of course, if tax exemptions were to be altered, any such change would have a significant effect on a relatively large number of lower-income families.

real costs to the economy, not simply transfer payments.[3] It is also relevant to note that to the extent that shifts in command over goods and services help to make the poor more productive and bring larger numbers of them into employment, they represent a form of investment, essentially similar to business investment, or to increased education and training, or other forms of expenditure yielding longer-term benefits for the whole economy.

The second misconception is an apparently widespread impression that the poor are somehow synonymous with those who don't work or don't want to work. This is simply incorrect. While there may be some voluntary poverty in Canada — for example, in the case of university students who temporarily forgo income in anticipation of later gains — the great bulk of the poor are clearly not voluntarily poor. The analysis of 1961 Census data in the *Fifth Annual Review* revealed that two-thirds of the heads of poor families (on the basis of fairly conservative estimates) were in the labour force and over three-quarters of poor families had *at least* one wage earner.

Lingering beliefs that the poor generally lack motivation are being undermined by a growing range of studies and evidence to the contrary. On the basis of careful investigations, it would appear that most of the poor are ready to seize appropriate job opportunities when these are available. The real sources of poverty among the potentially employable poor are generally to be found among such factors as a high incidence of inadequate skills and education, a lack of knowledge about how to seek out and exploit job opportunities, sickness, and a repeated thwarting of employment aspirations. Furthermore, some recent research suggests that the aspirations of the poor for economic opportunities and a middle-class style of life may be very strong, and that the desire to participate in a productive way in our society is more often frustrated than lacking.

To these aspects of labour force behaviour and aspirations, which give every evidence of embracing a very large fraction of the poor, must be added the relatively new and growing body of evidence about the development of human abilities. Until recently, it has been assumed that ability (such as reflected in IQ tests) was "given" at birth and that not much could be done to alter it. However, at the very least, environment has been found to play a significant role in the degree to which abilities are developed, and there is an emerging body of evidence supporting the proposition that even basic intelligence is modifiable. Thus the poor — apparently to a very substantial degree — may be no less able to participate in the economy than the nonpoor, and their poverty would appear most often to be a reflection of undeveloped abilities or inadequate job opportunities, rather than a lack of abilities.

If the unutilized or undeveloped human resources in Canada are potentially highly productive, why has our economic system failed to seek out and harness the potential of these resources? To some extent, this failure appears to be associated with institutional rigidities and attitudes — in the education system, in industry, in labour unions, in governments — which have become embedded in policies and practices that tend to make the economy function in a way that is pervasively discriminatory against the

---

[3]There may, of course, be some *real* cost to the economy if higher transfer payments to the poor from the nonpoor were to blunt incentives among the latter group. But there is little evidence to support the view that any such adverse effects on incentives would be very significant. Moreover, any such effects would perhaps tend to be offset by some accompanying favourable effects on the incentives of the poor.

poor. Such discrimination frequently prevents the poor from fully utilizing their skills in productive jobs and restricts their access to opportunities for improving their skills. Even some of the social welfare policies and programs operate, in some respects, with disincentives that make it difficult for the poor to pull themselves out of poverty. Both the removal of such discrimination — often entirely inadvertent discrimination — and better incentives for the poor to develop and use their income-earning abilities would contribute to higher potential output for the whole economy.

In the labour market, the poor are handicapped relative to the nonpoor. The poor tend to lack the resources to explore the best alternative opportunities. They make fewer informal contacts through social groups which might lead to jobs or information about job opportunities. Often the jobs they might fill are not advertised locally, or they are not advertised outside the area in which the job is located. Lack of resources may also handicap the poor when information is sold, as in newspapers or through other advertising media. Minority groups, in particular, as well as recent migrants, tend to have inadequate channels of information and communication.

The costs of transportation frequently put the poor at a disadvantage when they are looking for a job opening, or when they are required to appear in person before receiving a job offer. To the poor, the cost of moving their family to the location of a new job (or, alternatively, the additional expense and hardship of living away from home) is often prohibitive. The programs of the Department of Manpower and Immigration do not appear to be operating with a high degree of effectiveness in relation to the need for overcoming the barriers faced by the poor in this field. Much remains to be done to make the whole complex of these programs — from information and counselling services through the training and mobility-facilitating services — more adequate to meet the problems of those who are most in need of these services. Moreover, increased co-operation between the Canada Manpower Centres and the growing number of job placement services being developed by voluntary social agencies is needed.

Wage discrimination against the poor is also a problem, especially among women and certain minority groups who may be faced with unfair recruitment and employment practices. Discrimination may also be inherent in recruitment practices based on arbitrary educational qualifications not carefully related to the requirements of the job or which fail to take account of the skills and aptitudes of job applicants. Such practices, again, tend to work to the particular disadvantage of the poor. But they may also work to the disadvantage of employers. A reexamination of hiring practices and job specifications by governments and by business firms — in order to match skill levels of job applicants more closely to the whole spectrum of skill needs — would assist in reducing the economic costs of poverty. Such improved matching would also tend to keep costs and prices more stable. Recent US attempts to develop careers for the poor by redefining job specifications in a number of fields, such as health services, education, and social welfare, are particularly worthy of note in this context.

Other institutional arrangements tend similarly to discriminate — often unconsciously — against the poor in our society. Attitudes, policies, and decisions made by governments, businesses, labour unions, and farm and other private groups sometimes have the effect of deterring the more efficient use and development of human resources. For example, government subsidies (and perhaps some tax exemptions), along with some tariffs, may have the effect of locking individuals into low-income situations. Inadequate attention to the efficient use of both labour and capital in business firms may have similar effects. Some labour union rules and practices may discriminate against the entry of the poor into employment, and some forms of aid to farmers may, instead of promoting viable income growth and resolving other basic problems in agriculture, have instead the ultimate effect of preserving low-income agricultural activities. In both the government and the private sectors, more attention is needed to the implications of decisions that may adversely affect the poor, and to reducing the discriminatroy handicaps which they already suffer in seeking opportunities for more productive employment.

The poor are even more pervasively handicapped with respect to educational and training opportunities. The restricted personal resources of the poor deprive them of the chance of making the same investments in training and education that many of the nonpoor take for granted. The outcome is that the least investment is made by the very groups who need it most if poverty and its costs are to be eliminated. Within our public school systems, the low-income child frequently does not get the compensatory attention which he needs in order to be able to generate an adequate income in later life. Moreover, there is always a tendency for business firms and governments to undertake too little investment in human resources because they cannot be sure they will be able to retain human capital which they create. Workers migrate, and move from province to province or from firm to firm. Too little attention has been devoted to possible means of offsetting this tendency to underinvest and to developing more appropriate levels of investment in human resources, especially among the poor. It is important that this be done in ways that enhance rather than inhibit labour mobility, for in an age of accelerating technological and other change, our economic system will need increasing mobility if it is to function well.

Economic stabilization policies, too, have considerable relevance for the dimensions of poverty. The use of these policies to achieve sustained and balanced economic growth will tend to hold down and reduce the level of poverty over time. At the same time, serious or persistent inflationary pressures may require restriction of the growth of total demand through restraining fiscal and monetary policies in such a way that unemployment increases. In such a case, the poor may be caught in a situation of diminished employment opportunities, rising taxes (the overall tax system in Canada is regressive at low-income levels — that is, the poor are relatively overtaxed),[4] and diminished availability and increased cost of credit. All tend to fall more heavily upon this minority than upon the rest of society.

Having a more marginal attachment to the labour force, whether through their lower levels of skills, more checkered employment histories, higher incidence of sickness, or for whatever reasons (studies have revealed a whole cluster of variables that may be responsible), the poor feel the impact most heavily when unemployment rises and job opportunities become relatively scarce. Under such conditions, it is low-income families particularly who are faced with difficulties in finding jobs and obtaining credit. Some are compelled to seek welfare assistance, and growing welfare costs typically emerge in this situation. In short, the burden of maintaining price stability may tend

---

[4] "The schedule of effective tax incidence for the total tax structure is regressive up to an income level of at least $3,000 and possibly $5,000, and mildly progressive beyond." (Irwin Gillespie, *Studies for the Royal Commission on Taxation*, No. 2 (Ottawa, 1968), p. 72.)

to fall particularly heavily on the poor. In this context, a recent study in the United States has concluded that while some of the poor may be seriously hurt by inflation — notably the elderly poor — more of them are hurt by high unemployment.[5]

The Effects of Poverty on the Poor

How does poverty affect the poor? The answer could fill volumes. Some of the effects are quite visible and obvious. Poverty breeds ill health. It engenders a sense of hopelessness and frustration. It frequently means interrupted employment, unrewarding jobs, poor housing, and inadequate food. It prevents the poor from participating adequately in the life of the society.

Some indications about the ways in which the poor are deprived and about the degree of their deprivation can be gleaned from an analysis of the 1964 DBS Survey of Urban Family Expenditures. Chart 1 displays the relationship between the expenditures of the poor and the average expenditures of the nonpoor. In absolute dollar terms — the difference in the amounts spent — the poor are most deprived of sufficient food, clothing, shelter, and transportation. However, viewing the expenditures of the poor as a percentage of the expenditures of the nonpoor, those living in poverty are most deprived, in a relative sense, of transportation, of recreation, of furnishings and equipment, of reading material, of medical care, of personal care, of clothing, and of items to complement the formal education system.

One of the most important consequences of poverty is that it affects the ability of the poor to invest in themselves and thereby to lead more productive lives within the economy. This is illustrated by the lower relative expenditures on categories of goods and services which are particularly important as a basis for skilled and effective labour force participation, such as expenditures on education and reading.

A family's inability to invest in itself is likely to have particularly serious consequences on young children whose potential abilities are largely shaped in the years of early childhood. There is accumulating evidence to suggest that children of low-income families in Canada are most unlikely to have adequate access to needed resources in their early years. Even the possibility of significant child nutrition problems, seemingly so improbable in this country, must be taken seriously. A provincial minister of welfare recently stated publicly that some of the children in his province were too ill-clothed and ill-nourished to attend school. It is now well established that malnutrition in the early months of life will not only impair physical growth but may also damage mental development. From the infant born in 1969 to the school dropout of 1985 is the short span of years that may comprise a poverty generation, and improved understanding of the experience of poor children in Canada is urgently needed if poverty is to be effectively eliminated in Canada in our time.

In the past there has been much concern about the deeply indebted poor. Yet, it is important to keep in mind that ready access to credit for the poor may also be a vitally important factor at certain times to facilitate improved

---

[5] R. G. Hollister and J. L. Palmer, "The Impact of Inflation on the Poor," Discussion papers of the Institute for Research on Poverty, University of Wisconsin, 1969.

CHART 1
AVERAGE EXPENDITURES OF POOR FAMILIES
AS PERCENTAGE OF AVERAGE EXPENDITURES
OF NONPOOR FAMILIES

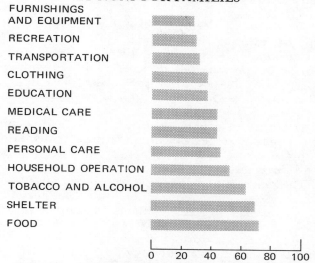

Note: Poor families are defined on the basis of the 1961 poverty lines set out in the *Fifth Annual Review*, updated to 1964.
Source: Based on data from the Dominion Bureau of Statistics.

income-earning capacity. For example, credit may be required for the purchase of a used car that may be needed to get to work — or for something as ordinary as the purchase of stockings or clothing for a woman seeking to return to work — and may make all the difference in a family's progress out of poverty.

The fact that the family is the most common economic unit in our society is often forgotten, and the importance to society of the family's economic viability is frequently not fully realized. A family operates in many ways like a business firm selling a product on the market. The inadequate incomes of families in poverty put such families in a position similar to that of managers of firms whose costs exceed revenues. Unable to increase production and sales for various reasons, and unable in the long run to continue even a level of maintenance costs that would permit continued sales, a firm may ultimately be forced out of business. From the viewpoint of the economy as a whole, this may be a desirable result, especially if it frees resources that have been relatively inefficiently used to flow to other, more productive uses. In the case of the family, however, the social and economic consequences for society are quite different. While a firm may go out of business and disappear, the family remains. If the potential abilities of members of the family remain undeveloped and unused, the family members may not only become virtual nonparticipants in the nation's social and economic life, but also a continuing burden on the society. If society is to benefit from the potential abilities rather than merely support the costs of poverty, the adults in the family must be enabled to participate in the labour force currently *and to prepare their children to do so in the future.* Thus *the concept of minimum standard of living must be based on a definition of the family not merely as a consuming unit, but also as a producing unit.* In our society, a substantial portion of the total investment in human capital is undertaken by family or individual initiatives. Public policies are needed to encourage this private investment process, and help to insulate it against the ravages of poverty.

We believe that one of the central tasks of antipoverty policies should be that of creating or restoring the economic viability of family units and of individuals not in families. This concern, if it is to be operationally effective, will require not only more carefully designed efforts to improve the income-generating capacities of the poor, but also substantially more cohesion and consistency than now exists in the provision of services and opportunities to the poor.

The overall structure of existing efforts in this field is currently one of extraordinary complexity, especially in operational terms, in our communities. Indeed, this structure essentially consists of largely unrelated efforts initiated by the three levels of government and by a great host of private organizations. The range of activities is so enormous that it is even difficult to collect information on their scope and nature. The federal government in 1967 issued an index to Human Resources Development Programs which listed over 200 different items. The New Brunswick Government's "Programs for People," listing close to 150 items, is an illustration of a similar effort to compile information about such programs at the provincial level. There are thus literally hundreds of items of legislation, thousands of regulations, and tens of thousands of administrative rules through which government efforts, by themselves, are carried out. To these must be added the vast array of private efforts of many different kinds.

In some communities, municipal or social planning agencies have attempted to compile directories about various forms of services and assistance available from public and private sources. And several cities, including Winnipeg and Ottawa, have attempted to go further, and to relate, at least in a preliminary way, the available services to local needs. But, in general, even reasonably comprehensive information is not readily available on the wide range of existing efforts in the social development field. In these circumstances, it is difficult to assess how well the present spectrum of antipoverty efforts is actually performing in bringing families out of poverty.

At the present time there are a great many undesirable and economically wasteful features associated with existing programs. Perhaps the most striking examples are to be found in the welfare programs. Welfare assistance is provided in a manner and amount that all too frequently undermines, rather than reinforces, the abilities and the aspirations of recipients to participate productively in the economic system. Taxes on incremental income at very high marginal rates, pervasively discriminated against by the economic system as discussed above, and singled out for public notice (a school principal in one Canadian city this year used the public address system to ask children of welfare recipients to stand up and come to his office for textbook vouchers), it is not surprising that recipients are alienated. The system often appears to provoke the very results it should be designed to avoid. In many cases, it discourages earnings, encourages school dropouts, and creates the paradox of people who would prefer to work being unable to afford to get off welfare. Moreover, it generally does not come into operation in a timely way, so that families may be virtually driven into poverty before help is available. In some provinces it virtually forces the heads of large families with inadequate incomes to stop work in order to get welfare. The entire system urgently needs to be examined with particular reference to its overall economic effects, and to the need for strengthening its preventive and rehabilitative capabilities.

Those poor in receipt of public welfare assistance are, however, a minority of the poor, under the rather conservative definition of poverty in our *Fifth Annual Review*. The majority of the poor contribute more to general tax revenues than they receive in the form of government welfare expenditures. Thus the overall incidence of the fiscal system for the "nonwelfare poor" is highly regressive. This system too should be examined for its overall economic effects on the poor.

In an attempt to obtain a better understanding, in a practical way, of the actual operation of antipoverty programs at the community level, the Economic Council undertook a limited survey of present activities in a number of Canadian cities early in 1969. From this survey, it is clear that the links between our welfare and manpower policies are greatly in need of review. There appears to be a widespread lack of co-ordination between welfare and manpower services; good co-ordination is needed here to help family units achieve economic viability. It is the poor who particularly need access to manpower programs, and this should be reflected both in the objectives and the operations of such programs in Canada.

Among some of the other results emerging from this survey are the following:

— a general concern that some of the poorest families, who may be the most backward in seeking needed assistance, are being missed by the existing programs, expecially in the case of poor farm families;

— encouraging progress in some communities toward bringing available services closer to those in need, especially through the establishment of neighbourhood centres in which a number of agencies, sometimes including government agencies, are co-operating;

— the inadequate information available to the poor, who often lack knowledge of the scope of welfare and other assistance, of what are their rights (under minimum wage legislation, for example), of eligibility criteria (for training programs, mobility grants, financial assistance through welfare offices), of rights of appeal from administrative decisions (with respect to welfare assistance, for example), of rights in law with respect to contracts (leases, door-to-door sales), of where to turn for advice and counsel (youth services, family planning, legal aid, nutritional consultants, and consumer information);

— the unfortunate existence of significant barriers to employment of secondary earners in the family (especially of mothers who wish to work), as a result of the lack of day-care nurseries and other ancillary services;

— the forward-looking separate and joint efforts of labour unions and co-operatives to develop self-help initiatives in the nonprofit housing field and to provide family budget counselling;

— the successful development of a number of community training workshops that are making special efforts to train disadvantaged poor persons in skills useful for gaining employment;

— attempts to reduce the difficulties facing especially vulnerable groups — such as single parents, the ethnic minorities in some communities, and the handicapped — in seeking out productive employment opportunities;

— constitutional difficulties that impair the effective operation of a number of important programs (such as manpower programs);

– growing encouragement and opportunities for the poor to participate in defining their needs as a basis for more effective antipoverty activities.

Canada's poverty problems are obviously different in a number of important respects from those of the United States. Nevertheless, as we observed last year, there is a great deal to be learned by Canadians from recent US experience — both the successful experience and, even more perhaps, the unsuccessful. The explicit national commitment to eliminate poverty, the setting up of an agency to discover what specific antipoverty measures will work (and when they work, to spin them off to agencies with operating responsibilities), the major effort to co-ordinate all federal human development programs (and beyond this, to move toward better co-ordination among federal government programs, those of the state and municipal governments, and those in the private sector), the focus in both the public and private sectors on the creation of job opportunities and increased training for the poor, and the special efforts directed toward enlarging opportunities for their children, are all very much in accord with the approaches recommended here. So too is the willingness to monitor and evaluate the effectiveness of specific programs.

Recent evaluations have in fact resulted in several changes in the structure of US antipoverty efforts:
— Head Start (a preschool program for disadvantaged children) and the Job Corps (a job-training program for disadvantaged youth) have both been spun off from the Office of Economic Opportunity and put under the aegis of government departments which have been given administrative and operational responsibility for these programs;
— the Office of Economic Opportunity has become a program development agency where new programs will be tested and passed to operating departments when they show clear signs of being effective;
— increasing numbers of on-the-job trainees are being financed under the Manpower Development and Training Act;
— Head Start evaluations which revealed that few if any tangible benefits from the program were discernible after a child had several months' experience in the regular school system have resulted in more extensive preschool programs, as well as adjustments within the educational system itself, and follow-up programs with the children;
— the business sector has been encouraged to co-operate in placing disadvantaged persons in jobs, and nearly 12,000 co-operating firms placed over 100,000 persons. In addition, certain labour unions in the model cities program have shortened required apprenticeship periods so that more of the disadvantaged workers in neighbourhoods affected by the program could participate.

The relevance of these and other similar programs for Canada should be explored and, if considered appropriate, should be effectively developed.

Concluding Observations

As we emphasized at the beginning of this chapter, its purpose has been to help to make Canadians think about poverty in a new perspective. The principal theme is that a very substantial proportion of the adult poor in Canada consists of those who either have, or could be provided with, income-earning potentials, and that there is a resulting high economic cost to our society in having failed to discover and implement more effective policies and programs to permit them to utilize these potentials. In other words, when we have such large numbers of poor in the working-force age groups, our economy is simply not producing as much as it could or should. Most of our existing policies and programs to assist the poor are not now predicated upon this point of view. We believe that this is a point of view that should have a larger influence on the development of effective anti-poverty programs in the future.

At this time, there is little information to guide the appropriate development of such programs. Considerable experimentation and testing may be needed to find out what programs could work well and efficiently in this field — in effect, a kind of "social engineering" akin to the industrial engineering long ago accepted as an essential basis for the development of complex new industrial products (such as new types of aircraft) or new industrial processes (such as new methods for processing raw materials). It is high time to begin to ask whether we can expect to design and develop highly effective and efficient major programs in the economic and social fields — programs that may involve the expenditure of hundreds of millions of dollars — unless we begin to move toward the use of far more professional man-hours on design and development of such programs.

This chapter has dealt with the large overall economic costs now imposed on our society by the existence of remediable poverty — or in more positive terms, the large economic benefits that would flow from its removal. We do not wish to leave the impression, however, that we have little or no concern for the overall human and social consequences that flow from the existence of poverty and that have such a direct and tragic impact upon the poor themselves. Rather, the removal of the economic costs of poverty must be recognized as a means rather than an end in itself — a means to social progress and increased human welfare. Greater emphasis on the economically oriented approaches to antipoverty measures is needed to ensure that the poor, and their children, are able to participate adequately in our society. The development of effective methods to help the poor generate adequate income, is, in our view, essential to ameliorating the direct human and social consequences of poverty, as well as to reducing its economic costs.

22. THE ALLEVIATION OF POVERTY: THE NEGATIVE INCOME TAX [*]

Milton Friedman

The extraordinary economic growth experienced by Western countries during the past two centuries and the wide distribution of the benefits of free enterprise have enormously reduced the extent of poverty in any absolute sense in the capitalistic countries of the West. But poverty is in part a relative matter, and even in these countries, there are clearly many people living under conditions that the rest of us label as poverty.

One recourse, and in many ways the most desirable, is private charity. It is noteworthy that the heyday of laissez faire, the middle and late nineteenth century in Britain and the United States, saw an extraordinary proliferation of private eleemosynary organizations and institutions. One of the major costs of the extension of governmental welfare activities has been the corresponding decline in private charitable activities.

It can be argued that private charity is insufficient because the benefits from it accrue to people other than those who make the gifts — again, a neighbourhood effect. I am distressed by the sight of poverty; I am benefited by its alleviation; but I am benefited equally whether I or someone else pays for its alleviation; the benefits of other people's charity therefore partly accrue to me. To put it differently, we might all of us be willing to contribute to the relief of poverty, *provided* everyone else did. We might not be willing to contribute the same amount without such assurance. In small communities, public pressure can suffice to realize the proviso even with private charity. In the large impersonal communities that are increasingly coming to dominate our society, it is much more difficult for it to do so.

Suppose one accepts, as I do, this line of reasoning as justifying governmental action to alleviate poverty; to set, as it were, a floor under the standard of life of every person in the community. There remain the questions, how much and how. I see no way of deciding "how much" except in terms of the amount of taxes we — by which I mean the great bulk of us — are willing to impose on ourselves for the purpose. The question, "how," affords more room for speculation.

[*]Reprinted from Milton Friedman, *Capitalism and Freedom,* Chicago, University of Chicago Press, 1962, pp. 190-95, by permission of the editor and author.
Dr. Friedman is Paul Snowden Russell Distinguished Service Professor of Economics, University of Chicago.

Two things seem clear. First, if the objective is to alleviate poverty, we should have a program directed at helping the poor. There is every reason to help the poor man who happens to be a farmer, not because he is a farmer but because he is poor. The program, that is, should be designed to help people as people, not as members of particular occupational groups or age groups or wage-rate groups or labour organizations or industries. This is a defect of farm programs, general old-age benefits, minimum-wage laws, pro-union legislation, tariffs, licensing provisions of crafts or professions, and so on in seemingly endless profusion. Second, so far as possible the program should, while operating through the market, not distort the market or impede its functioning. This is a defect of price supports, minimum-wage laws, tariffs, and the like.

The arrangement that recommends itself on purely mechanical grounds is a negative income tax. We now have an exemption of $600 per person under the federal income tax (plus a minimum 10 percent flat deduction). If an individual receives $100 taxable income, that is, an income of $100 in excess of the exemption and deductions, he pays tax. Under the proposal, if his taxable income is minus $100, [or] $100 less than the exemption plus deductions, he would pay a negative tax, that is, receive a subsidy. If the rate of subsidy were, say, 50 percent, he would receive $50. If he had no income at all, and, for simplicity, no deductions, and the rate were constant, he would receive $300. He might receive more than this if he had deductions, for example, for medical expenses, so that his income less deductions was negative even before subtracting the exemption. The rates of subsidy could, of course, be graduated just as the rates of tax above the exemption are. In this way, it would be possible to set a floor below which no man's net income (defined now to include the subsidy) could fall — in the simple example $300 per person. The precise floor set would depend on what the community could afford.

The advantages of this arrangement are clear. It is directed specifically at the problem of poverty. It gives help in the form most useful to the individual, namely, cash. It is general and could be substituted for the host of special measures now in effect. It makes explicit the cost borne by society. It operates outside the market. Like any other measures to alleviate poverty, it reduces the incentives of those helped to help themselves, but it does not eliminate that incentive entirely, as a system of supplementing incomes up to some fixed minimum would. An extra dollar earned always means more money available for expenditure.

No doubt there would be problems of administration, but these seem to me a minor disadvantage, if they be a disadvantage at all. The system would fit directly into our current income tax system and could be administered along with it. The present tax system covers the bulk of income recipients and the necessity of covering all would have the by-product of improving the operation of the present income tax. More important, if enacted as a substitute for the present ragbag of measures directed at the same end, the total adminstrative burden would surely be reduced.

A few brief calculations suggest also that this proposal could be far less costly in money, let alone in the degree of governmental intervention involved, than our present collection of welfare measures. Alternatively, these calculations can be regarded as showing how wasteful our present measures are, judged as measures for helping the poor.

In 1961, government spent something like $33 billion (federal, state, and local) on direct welfare payments and programs of all kinds: old-age assistance, social security benefit payments, aid to dependent children, general assistance, farm price support programs, public housing, and so forth.[1] I have excluded veterans' benefits in making this calculation. I have also made no allowance for the direct and indirect costs of such measures as minimum-wage laws, tariffs, licensing provisions, and so on, or for the costs of public health activities, state and local expenditures on hospitals, mental institutions, and the like.

There were then approximately fifty-seven million consumer units (unattached individuals and families) in the United States. The 1961 expenditures of $33 billion would have financed outright cash grants of nearly $6,000 per consumer unit to the 10 percent with the lowest incomes. Such grants would have raised their incomes above the average for all units in the United States. Alternatively, these expenditures would have financed grants of nearly $3,000 per consumer unit to the 20 percent with the lowest incomes. Even if one went so far as that one-third whom New Dealers were fond of calling ill-fed, ill-housed, and ill-clothed, 1961 expenditures would have financed grants of nearly $2,000 per consumer unit, roughly the sum which separated the lower one-third in the middle 1930s from the upper two-thirds. Today, fewer than one-eighth of consumer units have an income, adjusted for the change in the level of prices, as low as that of the lowest third in the middle 1930s.

Clearly, these are all far more extravagant programs than can be justified to "alleviate poverty" even by a rather generous interpretation of that term. A program which *supplemented* the incomes of the 20 percent of the consumer units with the lowest incomes so as to raise them to the lowest income of the rest would cost less than half of what we are now spending.

The major disadvantage of the proposed negative income tax is its political implications. It establishes a system under which taxes are imposed on some to pay subsidies to others. And presumably, these others have a vote. There is always the danger that instead of being an arrangement under which the great majority tax themselves willingly to help an unfortunate minority, it will be converted into one under which a majority imposes taxes for its own benefit on an unwilling minority. Because this proposal makes the process so explicit, the danger is perhaps greater than with other measures. I see no solution to this problem except to rely on the self-restraint and good will of the electorate.

Writing about a corresponding problem — British old-age pensions — in 1914, Dicey said, "Surely a sensible and a benevolent man may well ask himself whether England as a whole will gain by enacting that the receipt of poor relief, in the shape of a pension, shall be consistent with the pensioner's retaining the right to join in the election of a Member of Parliament."[2]

The verdict of experience in Britain on Dicey's question must as yet be regarded as mixed. England did move to universal suffrage without the disfranchisement of either pensioners or other recipients of state aid. And there has been an enormous expansion of taxation of some for the benefit of

---

[1] This figure is equal to government transfer payments ($31.1 billion) less veterans' benefits ($4.8 billion), both from the Department of Commerce national income accounts, plus federal expenditures on the agricultural program ($5.5 billion) plus federal expenditures on public housing and other aids to housing ($0.5 billion), both for year ending June 30, 1961, from Treasury accounts, plus a rough allowance of $0.7 billion to raise it to even billions and to allow for administrative costs of federal programs, omitted state and local programs, and miscellaneous items. My guess is that this figure is a substantial underestimate.

[2] A. V. Dicey, *Law and Public Opinion in England,* 2nd ed. (London, 1914), p. xxxv.

others, which must surely be regarded as having retarded Britain's growth, and so may not even have benefited most of those who regard themselves as on the receiving end. But these measures have not destroyed, at least as yet, Britain's liberties or its predominanatly capitalistic system. And, more important, there have been some signs of a turning of the tide and of the exercise of self-restraint on the part of the electorate.

Liberalism and Egalitarianism

The heart of the liberal philosophy is a belief in the dignity of the individual, in his freedom to make the most of his capacities and opportunities according to his own lights, subject only to the proviso that he not interfere with the freedom of other individuals to do the same. This implies a belief in the equality of men in one sense; in their inequality in another. Each man has an equal right to freedom. This is an important and fundamental right precisely because men are different, because one man will want to do different things with his freedom than another, and in the process can contribute more than another to the general culture of the society in which many men live.

The liberal will therefore distinguish sharply between equality of rights and equality of opportunity, on the one hand, and material equality or equality of outcome on the other. He may welcome the fact that a free society in fact tends toward greater material equality than any other yet tried. But he will regard this as a desirable by-product of a free society, not its major justification. He will welcome measures that promote both freedom and equality — such as measures to eliminate monopoly power and to improve the operation of the market. He will regard private charity directed at helping the less fortunate as an example of the proper use of freedom. And he may approve state action toward ameliorating poverty as a more effective way in which the great bulk of the community can achieve a common objective. He will do so with regret, however, at having to substitute compulsory for voluntary action.

The egalitarian will go this far, too. But he will want to go further. He will defend taking from some to give to others, not as a more effective means whereby the "some" can achieve an objective they want to achieve, but on grounds of "justice." At this point, equality comes sharply into conflict with freedom; one must choose. One cannot be both an egalitarian, in this sense, and a liberal.

G. LABOUR UNIONS

Labour unions occupy a powerful and permanent position on the Canadian scene. It is all the more remarkable that a mere thirty years ago their influence, at least nationally, was minor. Not until the Second World War did they begin to assume the stature that they enjoy today, for before that time they were skillfully and successfully opposed by industry. About one-third of the entire nonagricultural labour force is now unionized. If you subtract foremen, executives, professional people, and the self-employed, the proportion is much higher. Labour leaders negotiate between 12,000 and 15,000 collective agreements each year. These contracts cover their two million members and influence the wage rates, hours, and working conditions of another three million or so nonunion workers. Few large firms initiate changes in policy that affect their workers without checking with union representatives. It is standard practice for union officials to be asked to testify before parliamentary committees and provincial legislatures. And trade-union support generally spells the difference between success and failure for scores of candidates for public office across the country. It is thus clear that unions are intimately woven into much of our economic and political life.

The author of Reading 23 considers the major labour issue of the day as the problem of adapting the structure of the labour market to rapid technological change in the presence of some natural worker resistances and in the absence of completely rational management control. To him, collective bargaining serves as a stimulus to greater technological efficiency.

Mention of technological change leads us squarely to "featherbedding," a term applied to union regulations or practices designed to increase artificially the number of workers employed. It should be added that featherbedding is sometimes difficult to distinguish from legitimate rules concerning the conditions of work. But there are enough makework schemes to create a problem. Reading 24 provides a theoretical analysis of featherbedding; the conditions under which it appears, its impacts, and alternatives for dealing with the underlying problem of labour displacement.

23. LABOUR UNIONS ARE WORTH THE PRICE*

Max Ways

Comment by W. Maxey Jarman

"We have no ultimate ends. We are going on from day to day. We are fighting only for immediate objects. . . ." Adolph Strasser, head of the Cigar Makers' Union, to a US Senate committee in 1873.

Right now and in the years ahead American labour leaders are sure to need all their resilience and their inventive resource. For a mighty wave of denunciation is rolling in upon the unions. Indignation over strikes rose in vehemence through 1962 and especially in early 1963, when a longshoremen's strike posed a major economic threat, and a strike and lockout of New York newspapers exasperated nerve centres of US opinion.

After these disputes were settled, few people noticed that an extraordinary degree of labour peace prevailed, however insecurely, throughout the nation. Instead, there was an acute awareness of other strike dangers ahead. Americans seemed convinced that the burden of strikes was increasing, although the standard statistical indicators suggested the contrary. In 1962 time lost in strikes was only one-sixth of one percent of time worked, doubtless less than the cost of the common cold or the common hangover. (See Figure 1.) But merely correcting the statistical picture was not going to assuage the indignation; the public (or significant parts of it) had lowered its boiling point on strikes. Therein lay grave danger to the unions — and to others.

The widespread demand that strikes be replaced, at least in essential industries, by "some better way" shies away from the question: *what* better way? Representatives of management and labour avoid strikes in hundreds of contracts signed every month, but unless the strike remains as a possibility no genuine collective bargaining can occur. When George Meany says, "Strikes are part of the American way of life," he is not exulting in labour's power to disrupt, but rather expressing awareness that there are no known alternatives to collective bargaining that would not do far more damage to

---

*Reprinted from *Fortune Magazine* May, 1963, by special permission; copyright 1963 Time Inc. Comment is reprinted by permission of the writer.
Mr. Ways is a member of *Fortune Magazine's* Board of Editors.
Mr. Jarman is Chairman of the Finance Committee, Genesco Apparel, Nashville, Tennessee.

the American system. All the foreseeable substitutes involve, directly or indirectly, massive extension of government power to fix wages and other conditions of labour. Although collective bargaining as it is now practised in the US does involve many serious departures from an ideal market system, it is a lot closer and more responsive to markets than any system of government intervention could be.

Yet today's labour leaders are haunted men; what haunts them is not some ghost from the past but the uncertainties of the US industrial prospect. "Automation" is the centre of their daily practical problems. Their attitudes toward the present period of rapid technological and organizational change

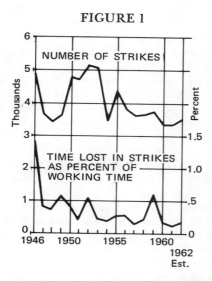

FIGURE 1

NUMBER OF STRIKES

TIME LOST IN STRIKES AS PERCENT OF WORKING TIME

in 1920, representing nearly 18 percent of all nonagricultural workers, a proportion that was not exceeded until 1937. The onset of the Depression sent membership all the way down to 2,700,000, or 11.5 percent of its potential, in 1933. In 1945 the unions had 14,300,000 members, over 35 percent of potential; the 1960 figures were 17 million and 31.5 percent.

Damage done by strikes is difficult to measure. In these two standard indicators, the bottom curve counts time lost only in companies actually struck, but in many strikes additional losses are suffered by suppliers or customers of the struck plants. On the other hand, "time lost in strikes" often overstates the damage; a short strike in the steel industry, for example, may not reduce annual production because extra production before and after strikes compensates for the loss. It is often said that as the economy becomes more interdependent, the indirect effects of strikes become more serious. But some economists doubt this on the ground that in a more highly developed economy there are more alternative sources for the goods or services withheld by strikes.

The unions' failure in the postwar period to organize a larger part of their potential membership is not necessarily a symptom of weak leadership. Historically, union growth has come in spurts. An impressive percentage gain came between 1897 and 1904 when union membership rose from 450,000 to over two million. In the World War I period, the 2,700,000 members of 1914 almost doubled to five million

are formed within a profound ambivalence they share with the men and women they represent and with Americans generally. All demand the fruits of progress and at the same time resist such painful changes as the breaking up of work patterns, the discarding of skills, the shifting of relative wage rates, and the loss, however temporary, of jobs.

The top leaders of American unions are too smart to oversimplify the problem as one lesser labour leader does: "Look. You can't stop progress in this country. I tell the bosses that and I tell the men that. You can't stop progress. *You can only slow it down*." The vast majority of American labour leaders say — and honestly believe — that technological advance should move faster. Few of them think they know "the" answer to the problem of how to speed progress and at the same time cushion the painful impact of change. Just now, their public answer is a shorter work week to reduce unemployment, but this is less a practical goal than a symbolic way of calling attention to the insecurity that dogs the men they represent. The unions' more practical and less visible answer is an infinitely complex edifice of arrangements, worked out industry by industry, company by company, and craft by craft, by which they seek — sometimes clumsily and outrageously but sometimes with brilliant ingenuity — to adjust the economic facts of a progressive technology to the social and psychological fact of man's profound resistance to being changed by forces outside himself, or pushed around, or treated as a thing.

Teeming With Innovation

The effort toward giving union members a sense of participation in the control of their working life is and always has been at the heart of American unionism. Accelerated technological change increases the pressure from below on the leaders to provide the protection workers want; at the same time it increases the danger that the steps the unions take to fulfill their function will exact too great a price from the US economy.

This dilemma — and not the cost of strikes — is today's and tomorrow's real "labour problem," and much union energy in recent years, has been directed toward dealing with the difficulties posed by the pressures of rapid industrial change. To handle this task unions themselves have had to change, to improvise new devices in dealing with employers, with one another, and with their own members. Although accused of stagnation, the unions are, in fact, teeming with innovation and efforts toward internal improvement.

The Steelworkers, for example, is not a model union; some of its old friends complain that the fire and enthusiasm of its early years have been frozen into a bureaucracy. But bureaucracy can be another name for competent, functionalized administration, and this union has constructed working channels of two-way communication running from the plant floor to the top of a vast (900,000 member) structure. It does much of its bargaining on a national basis, yet it is able to handle effectively the host of individual grievances that arise in their plants. This is no small achievement. Many British unions that bargain nationally have lost touch with the shop stewards, who often disrupt production by acting independently of the national body; on the Continent national unions have, in general, even less top-to-bottom structure than in Britain. In consequence, workers' specific grievances, instead of being resolved within a contractual framework, melt into an ugly lump of politicized class grievance against the bosses and the system.

The Steelworkers and management are now trying to remove a wide range of issues from the pressures of deadline negotiations. The Human Relations Committee is a year-round joint study group investigating such questions as seniority and work rules. These matters can be of immense importance to individual workers, but, unless the rules are knowledgeably and carefully written, they can impose inefficiencies that cost much more than the benefits are worth. It's too early to say whether steel's Human Relations Committee will do any real good, but at least a sane and novel approach has been made. More interesting is the recent agreement worked out between the Steelworkers and Kaiser Steel Corp. Groups of Kaiser workers now receiving incentive pay may vote to give this up (each getting a substantial lump-sum payment for a transitional period); these workers and all others will receive a third of cost savings Kaiser makes by automation or in any other way; to minimize the displacement of workers that may result from cost cutting, workers will be protected by new, job-security provisions and strengthened seniority rules. None of the authors of this plan hails it as "the" answer for industry in general or even for the whole steel industry. It is to be a four-year experiment in one company where management and workers, apparently, are acutely aware of the need for cutting costs in the face of competition, while giving the workers as much protection as possible.

Walter Reuther's United Automobile Workers is another union that can hardly be accused of stagnation either in collective bargaining or in efforts to improve the quality of its internal organization. For years the UAW has vainly proposed to the automobile companies that joint study groups be set up in advance of negotiations. In 1963 for the first time the automobile companies seem interested in exploring the plan. Meanwhile, in the way it runs its own affairs, the UAW has made a novel approach to the protection of individual members aggrieved by union decisions. Such cases are bound to occur where unions are large, their contracts and procedures complex, their staffs expert, and their officers possessed of the self-confidence that comes with experience in which the rank and file cannot share. Reuther, than whom there is no more self-confident man, is proud these days of having established in the UAW a "supreme court" of seven eminent men, not members of the union, who can decide appeals by aggrieved members against UAW organs or officers, including Reuther. This "court" has heard 122 cases, and its existence is said to have had a substantial effect in making UAW leaders at all levels more careful of the rights of dissidents.

When the Plumbers Go Starry-Eyed

The four biggest unions in the US — the outcast Teamsters, the Steelworkers, the UAW and the Machinists — account for a highly significant quarter of all organized workers, and these four are all exceedingly lively unions. But the vigour and change reach further down. Even the unions of the building trades, usually the prime example of reactionary, restrictive "business unionism," show signs of effort toward internal improvement. In recent years they have reduced the damage done by interunion conflict over job jurisdiction.

The plumbers' union, not in the past a progress-minded group, has responded to the challenge of changing technology by operating one of the best training programs of any union. Purdue University helped to train instructors. Scores of locals have set up their own classrooms. Journeymen as well as apprentices are the students. Not long ago the union's president, Peter T. Schoemann, presented diplomas to a group of trainees whose average age was sixty. "What are you old birds going to school for?" asked Schoemann, who is sixty-nine. He was told, "We got tired of holding the pipe while the young men made the weld. Now we've learned to make the weld and they can hold the pipe." Strictly "selfish," of course — but the kind of motivation that built a great nation.

Heart of the training program is lavishly illustrated textbooks that cost several hundred thousand dollars to develop. Union leaders hold out the pipe fitters' manual, inviting the awe and admiration usually reserved for the *Book of Kells*. When the plumbers go all starry-eyed about a training book, it is certain that not all sense of progress has disappeared from the American labour movement.

Why Unions aren't Growing

Management will be deluded if it accepts the widespread opinion that the unions' failure to increase their proportion of the total work force is a sign of weakness. Membership figures must be read against the background of union history and in the framework of present US employment trends.

In the first place, the labour movement — unlike the telephone business and the diaper-wash industry — is not comfortably pinned to the population curve. Membership in American unions has always advanced in sprints and these sprints are connected more with broad changes in US life than with the quality or energy of labour leadership. The biggest numerical gains, in fact, have been associated with wartime or postwar labour shortages. In terms of percentage of the labour force, the unions have done better at holding their World War II gains than they did in the years after 1920. American unionism since 1945 has passed through searing vicissitudes — struggles in some unions over communism, the effects of the Taft-Hartley law, the McClellan investigation — without any substantial exodus of members.

Moreover, US unions have been working against a tide: production workers, among whom unionism has always been strongest, have been declining in proportion to the total work force. Some liberal intellectuals, in their present antiunion mood, will not accept this excuse for union "stagnation"; they demand that unions make more strenuous efforts to break out of their old strongholds and organize the unskilled and the growing number of white-collar workers. But in both categories the obstacles to union progress are too deep-seated to be overcome by mere improvement of union leadership or a surge of union organizing "energy."

Before the mid-thirties unskilled industrial workers were mainly white — and unions made little headway in organizing them. Many unskilled production workers — along with skilled and semiskilled — were enrolled during the rapid progress of industrial unionism from 1936 to 1945. But this still left outside of unions many unskilled workers in the service trades, which are now expanding, and in numerous pockets of employment not accessible to industrial unionism. These unskilled workers today have a high proportion of Negroes, Puerto Ricans, and Mexicans, but race is not among the main reasons why more are not organized. Unskilled workers are so easy to replace that they have little inherent bargaining power — the stuff unionism can mobilize and make more effective, but which it cannot create. Moreover, service workers, rarely concentrated in large groups, tend to be harder to organize than factory workers.

In some quarters the idea seems to be that the 1,750,000 Negroes now in unions could be multiplied if labour leaders took a much stronger stand in championing Negro rights and aspirations. In fact, union leadership has a good recent record of antidiscrimination — a record that has undeniably hurt union organizing drives among southern white workers. Whatever may be the ethical merits of the case for even stronger union policies favouring underprivileged groups, there is little chance that adoption of such policies would result in a big net gain in union membership. Those at the bottom of the social escalator may "need" unionism most, but unionism has been most effective within a middle band of workers who have substantial preunion bargaining power.

Why the White-Collars are Unorganized

Above the middle band lies the unions' other area of frustration, the white-collar workers, of whom less than 15 percent are unionized. Market demand for white-collar workers has been stronger than for production workers. Just before, during, and just after World War II, however, production workers apparently were closing the pay-and-working-condition gap between themselves and the white-collars. This overtaking movement has ceased, and the white-collars may be drawing away again.

Many of the fringe benefits (for example, sick pay, vacations) on which blue-collar unions are now concentrating have for years been standard in much white-collar employment. The main white-collar advantage — and the one that makes this group hard to unionize — is continuity of job, "the annual wage." Hourly paid production workers, subject to layoff at management discretion, are less reluctant than white-collar workers to interrupt their pay by striking. Where a very high proportion of a white-collar group has been organized (for example, actors) there is often a background of discontinuous employment. The upper levels of white-collar workers have one other pertinent advantage over production workers: a measure of built-in control over the pace and pattern of their own work. Managers usually don't need a union to tell them that "overbossing" of technicians results in lost efficiency.

The majority of white-collar workers are not likely to be organized unless there are major shifts in the terms of their employment. Such shifts may appear. Years ago, when white-collars were a small minority in most businesses, it was easy to provide them with continuous employment; today the growing proportion of white-collar workers represents in many companies a cost rigidity that is hard to take when business is slack. If management tries to meet this difficulty with white-collar layoffs, or if office automation is too rapid, or if white-collar jobs become overbossed, there may be huge union gains among this group. But in the absence of such changes it is hard to believe that a mere stepping up of union "energy" is going to organize millions of workers who have, without unions, an increasing market power already superior to that of unionized production workers.

In sum, the odds are that in the near future total union membership will not increase or decline sharply.

What Does Unionism Cost?

The present wave of antiunion feeling raises again the question of what effect unions have on the economy. In such an appraisal there are some bear traps for the unwary. The two groups that sound off most loudly about the effect of unions are labour leaders and labour baiters; they tend to agree with each other in rating the impact of unionism very high. The labour leader gives unions credit for a generation of rapid gains by workers, and the labour baiter says almost the same thing when he fixes upon unions the chief blame for rising costs and prices. The truth seems to be that the economic impact of unions is not so great as either group asserts.

In a remarkably clear, concise, and balanced new book, *The Economics of Trade Unions,* Albert Rees of the University of Chicago, working from a number of detailed studies, has arrived at some sophisticated opinions about the cost of unions. One way of getting at the wage effect is to compare the wage rates of union members with those of unorganized employees doing comparable tasks. Rees' educated guess is that the overall difference at any point in time amounts to between 10 and 15 percent. In some industries that are almost completely organized, unions reach periods when they are unable to raise the relative wages of workers at all. An example is the Amalgamated Clothing Workers, once one of the most effective unions. Since the war it has been stymied, and the usual cries have been raised of tired, old leadership. But the Amalgamated had excellent leadership in depth, and it is hardly plausible that the sudden lowering in the union's effectiveness is traceable mainly to leadership. The explanation, according to Rees, is that market factors heavily condition union effectiveness. In the men's clothing field, the postwar market has been soft and many employers are in trouble. In such a situation, even the strongest union must choose between scaling down its wage demands or accepting greater unemployment among its members.

Following the late Henry C. Simons and others, Rees believes that union action in raising wages tends to decrease employment opportunities. (Even where the number of jobs increases, the expansion of employment is slower than it would have been if wage rates had not been pressed upward by union action.) Usually, unemployment in an industry acts as a brake on wage demands. The great exception to this for years has been the United Mine Workers, which forced up wage rates while making no effort to slow the mechanization that was spurred by rising labour costs. The number of coal miners declined from about 450,000 in 1947 to 119,000, while hourly earnings almost doubled.

Rees says that it cannot be proved that unions measurably increase "the workers' share" of total income at the expense of the owners of capital. Union gains are probably paid for by other workers or consumers. On the other hand, Rees defends unions against the charge that they are solely or mainly responsible for "cost-push inflation." Unions can aggravate inflationary dangers arising from monetary or other causes, but their "push" on costs becomes inflationary only when wrong policies are pursued elsewhere in the economy.

The chief cost of unions is not strike losses or cost-push, but the distortions and rigidities that unionism introduces into the market system. Rees says: "If the union is viewed solely in terms of its effect on the economy, it must in my opinion be considered an obstacle to the optimum performance of our economic system."

He has, however, more to say. Although he is an economist, Rees knows that life is not an exercise in economics. American unions rose not in response to an economic theory, but as a complex institutional form of expressing the complex reactions of workers to the pressures of industrial society. "By giving workers protection against arbitrary treatment by employers, by acting as their representative in politics, and by reinforcing their hope of continuous future gain, unions have helped to assure that the basic values of our society are widely diffused and that our disagreements on political and economic issues take place within a broad framework of agreement." He notes that American manual workers are committed to the preservation of a political democracy and a free-enterprise economy and that they are not, "as in many other democracies, constantly . . . attempting to replace it with something radically different." Rees concludes: "The economic losses imposed by unions are not too high a price to pay" for the psychological, social, and political benefits.

What About the "Right to Manage"?

Even if this judgment is true about the past and present, what are the prospects? Are the future costs imposed by unions on the economy likely to become "too high"?

In recent years direct union pressure on wage rates has slowed down a bit. But a great deal of present labour activity and conflict is on fronts other than wages; most of these issues are connected with adjustments to technological change; many of them involve the possibility of high economic loss by union infringement on management's "right to manage."

While this danger is real, the actual picture is more complex and more balanced than is generally supposed. In the first place, unions in many industries have had the effect of speeding up the pace of technological improvements. One railroad executive put it this way: "If it wasn't for those damn unions, we'd be using as many man hours to do every job as we did twenty years ago. Every time they get an increase, we have to get off our duffs and find a cheaper way to do things."

This quote represents an important hidden truth about "the right to manage." If it is assumed that complete managerial control exists prior to any union infringement on management power, then every concession to unions in the form of work rules and other limitations represents a diminution of management power. Examination of the masses of these limitations that have been written in the last fifty years — and are still being written — might lead to the conclusion that management is gradually being pushed into a corner where it has less and less control of the enterprises for which it is legally responsible. But anybody who observes the American business scene knows that picture to be false; management has, in fact, a greater degree of control than it had fifty years ago, and its control increases year by year.

The explanation lies in the falsity of the original assumption that "complete management" preceded union interference. Complete management, the total subjection of action to rational control, never exists. Whether confusion be attributed to original sin or to the undomesticated Freudian id, the truth is that in human affairs, individual or group, the segment of unmanaged activity exceeds the segment of managed activity. (Saints and the Bell Telephone System may be exceptions to this rule.) Masters never exercise complete rational control over slaves, nor parents over children, nor any man over himself, nor managers over a work process.

For example, the imposition by unions of seniority rules in layoffs seems to be an encroachment on the right to manage. But before the unions interfered, the selection of the particular individuals to lay off was often not really a management decision (that is, it was not worked out rationally in terms of the interest of the enterprise). Foremen and supervisors, unguided by policy from above, selected by favouritism or at random the workers to be retained or laid off. Nobody in his right mind would argue that seniority was the most efficient or economically rational way of selecting workers for continuous employment or for promotion. But in many cases what seniority rules replaced was not rational management but merely power exercised in a way that seemed unfair and arbitrary to workers. It seemed so because that's what it was.

The struggle over the control of labour is not simply management vs. unions. The older struggle is that of management vs. chaos, or unmanagement. Unions make it a three-cornered fight. Nobody can promise that union encroachments upon "the right to manage" will not advance faster than management's ability to win from chaos new frontiers of rational control. In industries where that has happened the costs of unionism may be disastrous. But the general record of a hundred years of unionism indicates that — so far — union power and management effectiveness have *both* advanced together.

Featherbeds for Sale

When they encroach upon the right to manage, American unions are not trying to take over enterprises; they are trying to restrict or cushion change or to give the workers a sense that some power over the job is in their hands. Since American unions are themselves immersed in market psychology, every union encroachment has a price at which it may be traded for some other potential union advantage.

A most remarkable example of this occurred on the west coast in 1961. For thirty years Harry Bridges had built up a fantastically restrictive set of work rules. Unneeded men were required for all sorts of specific jobs around the docks. When Bridges was asked what these supernumeraries should be called, his cynical humour answered: "Witnesses." The burden was becoming so intolerable to employers that they "bought" all the restrictive work rules in a single package in return for large employer payments into a special fund that will make possible earlier retirement and larger pensions for longshoremen. The agreement endangered some hundreds of dock-worker jobs, but these were held by "B-men" without voting rights in Bridges' union. The employers have obtained, at a price, a free hand to improve productivity on the west coast wharves.

What Bridges did in a wholesale deal, other unions do all the time on a retail basis. Much has been heard lately about the printers' insistence on "setting bogus" or "dead horse." But it is less widely known that "dead horse" is often stored up, unset, on the spike and then traded off at the end of a contract term for small additions to wage or other concessions. After the east coast longshoremen's strike was settled in February, there was a sudden flareup on a Manhattan pier, where an employer had introduced an unusual distribution of the work gang between the pier, the deck, and the hold. The workers considered this a violation of an agreement to maintain local work patterns unchanged; apparently they had it in mind that the right to change the pattern could be "sold" in some future negotiation. Union officals had to tell them that on this particular pier the right had already been conceded to the shipowner.

The proliferation of specific work rules in American union contracts is not paralleled in other industrial countries — but the actual situation in other countries is not necessarily better from management's point of view. British managers are conscious of worker resistance to automation and change even though that resistance has not been embodied in specific contractual provisions. One result is that the hidden worker resistance in Britain is used by managers to reinforce their own inertia, with the consequence that the pace of industrial change in Britain is slower than in the US. One rogue whale of a shipowner in New York holds that the slowness of technological change on the waterfront there is attributable mainly to the inertia of shipowners, who for decades were dealing with a weak and racket-ridden union. Now that the east coast longshoremen are somewhat stronger they may make wage and other bargaining gains; squeezed, the shipowners may be forced into cost-cutting improvements.

The US practice of writing specific rules into contracts at least exposes the featherbedding to view where it can be argued about, bargained about, and sometimes traded off. It is somewhat more difficult for management to deal with the deep-seated worker resistance, which surfaces only in unofficial slowdowns and general foot-dragging.

Exegesis on the Famous Word "More"

The extreme untidiness, the messiness, of collective bargaining in the US is apparent on all sides. One union is deciding to stress wages while another decides to deemphasize wages and stress security; or the same union reverses its emphasis from one year to another. But these shifting decisions do not express mere whim; they are responses to changing conditions in various industries, and changing fears and desires of particular groups of workers. So untidy, so shifting, so relative is the American labour scene that it *must* be deeply involved in the most untidy, shifting, and relative of all human institutions, the market.

This involvement is no accident but the development of the character that Samuel Gompers imprinted on American unions as boldly as his signature which adorns the charters that hang in Washington union offices. For Gompers' great invention was the word "more" as a description of what the unions wanted. Usually this word is recalled as an example of the unions' unappeasable voracity; but in its original context and its long-range effect its significance is different. On New York's East Side when Gompers was young, a hundred ideologies of labour competed with one another. His predecessor as head of the Cigar Makers, Adolph Strasser, rebelled against the belief that unions should be considered instruments for gaining utopian goals. In 1873, testifying before a US Senate committee, Strasser was asked, "What are your ultimate ends?" And he answered: "We have no ultimate ends. We are going on from day to day. We are fighting only for immediate objects — objects that can be realized in a few years." Gompers, accepting the thought, boiled it down to "more, now."

Thereby the US labour movement committed itself to the US market system. Again and again ideologues, many of them Marxists, have tried vainly to turn American unions from their "purposeless" pursuit, their concentration on responding to immediate pressures and on improvement within a short perspective of a few years. Gompers' "more" was a nonutopian acceptance of limits rather than an arrogant demand. He didn't want to get to an ideal society; where he wanted the workers to go was merely ahead.

Anybody who wants to understand the labour movement had better start

with the object itself in all its historical complexity and the multiple contradictions and defects of its present position. He had better not start with a
preconceived notion of what a labour movement, considered as an instrument for attaining the ideal society, ought to be. An example of the latter
approach is the complaint of a liberal intellectual, disillusioned with unions,
who declared that government intervention must increase because "collective
bargaining has failed to solve the labour problem." Indeed, it has failed —
and in a free society there can never be any "solution" to the labour
problem, the price problem, the investment problem, or the woman
problem.

Why Government Should Stay Out

Accepting unions and collective bargaining with their inherent and ineradicable defects does not imply accepting all present union practices or pressures. Such acceptance does not preclude further legislation cutting back the
degree to which government influence is thrown on the side of unions. To
say that unions in general "are worth the price" is not to say that the union
shop is inviolable or that the restrictive practices of the stagehands' union are
worth what they cost. The future of collective bargaining, moreover,
depends as much upon employer resistance to excessive union demands as it
depends upon employer concessions to reasonable demands. What is "excessive" and what is "reasonable" can be determined only company by company, and year by year. The terms on which labour is performed — in their
impermanence, complexity, particularity, and susceptibility to market pressures — are *prices*. Terms of this sort are not appropriate subjects for government action, because the basic mode of government action is law, which is
supposed to be stable, uniform, and general.

When raw wage rates were the main subject of collective bargaining, it was
hard enough to imagine how a government in peacetime might set wages. But
it is infinitely harder now that the emphasis in bargaining has shifted to the
more complex and particular field of arrangements for cushioning the social
impact of rapid technological change. If a government imposed, say, the
Kaiser plan on one company, it might be tempted to impose it on others
where specific conditions were different. Or else government would abandon
its appropriate mode of action — legality — and would decide each labour
case on its particular circumstances; that way lies the corruption of constitutional government, a more serious matter than the inefficiencies of collective
bargaining. Even assuming — and this is quite a large assumption — that any
given administration would be even-handed in its treatment of management
and labour, the more fundamental objection to government intervention
remains: the difficulty of determining labour prices by legal machinery.

The Devil We Know

The Kennedy Administration certainly does not *want* to take over the role
now performed by collective bargaining. But an impatient public opinion,
goaded by the Administration's own activism, could come to consider as
"inevitable" massive government intervention in labour disputes. In fact,
such a trend is probable unless the President resolves to hold intervention to

an absolute minimum. Reflecting on his own experience and not speaking in criticism of his successors, former Secretary of Labour James Mitchell has said that it is always easier for a government official to intervene than not to intervene in major labour disputes. When those telegrams from governors begin to arrive in Washington, when the congressional delegations troop to the Labour Department and the White House, when the editorials scream that the government must "do something" to end a strike — it's hard not to say, "We'll look into it and see what we can do." Looking leads to judgment, and judgment to government pressure for specific terms of settlement. Soon no real bargaining occurs anywhere because one side or the other thinks it will get a better break in Washington than in a test of bargaining strength.

The American labour movement today is certainly no worse than it ever was, and a strong case can be made that it is getting better. Unions and techniques of collective bargaining may not improve fast enough to meet the challenge of the years ahead. The same doubt can be cast on management — and on government. Unions are not only the devil we know, but they are also institutions that fit this society far better than would government regulation of the terms of labour.

The above article drew the following letter to the editor from a corporation executive:

> To the Editors:
>
> I am shocked at "Labour Unions are Worth the Price."
>
> For a supposedly responsible business publication to whitewash the union situation at a time that it seemed we might be getting some sentiment for reform is almost inconceivable.
>
> To point out how ridiculous some points are is almost an impossible job, because so many are so obviously biased from a labour union viewpoint. To quote George Meany as saying that "strikes are a part of the American way of life" and therefore good is ridiculous. By the same token, thirty years ago we could have said that bank runs are a part of the American way of life and actually they only affect a small percentage of the total number of banks and therefore why bother about them.
>
> To say that "management has a greater degree of control of business than it had fifty years ago" makes no sense whatsoever.
>
> To say that "no better way than strikes has been suggested for settling labour disputes" is also ridiculous. Responsible people throughout the country have made many suggestions. Other countries have adopted systems that have certainly been an improvement over what we have in this country. To give labour unions the unbridled power, exempting them from all kinds of laws, and put them in the position they now have, and then come out and say that this is a good thing is certainly too much to swallow. To let labour unions be in the position where they can disregard the welfare of the public and hold up the entire country, as the Teamsters Union could do now, is almost unthinkable. To permit the disregard of common law and justice that goes on with union activity, and intimidation of individual workers, is certainly not the mark of an enlightened society.
>
> To try to paint a picture that the cost of labour unions is a very small cost makes no sense. The cost of labour unions in intangible ways, in the stint system, in the restraint of progress, in the backward kind of political power that they have used, add up to an enormous cost.
>
> W. MAXEY JARMAN
> Genesco Corporation

Nashville, Tennessee

24. THE FEATHERBEDDING PROBLEM*

Paul A. Weinstein

A growing number of disputes appear to involve the problem of feather-bedding. At the heart of these conflicts is the question of who should bear the cost of technological change. While there are a number of theoretical alternatives to technological displacement, featherbedding is the most satis-factory from the position of both the union and the potentially displaced workers. There has been increasing pressure on unions not to resort to featherbedding demands, but external pressure, even when directed by the President, has not proved effective. Some collective bargaining agreements have offered alternatives to featherbedding when there is a structural change, but the advice to follow the lead of constructive agreements that propose to end constraints on firms and effect a better utilization of our manpower resources has gone unheeded. The failure to settle featherbedding issues has cast doubt upon collective bargaining and the market as an appropriate institution.

This paper will treat the following topics: first, the necessary and sufficient conditions for the emergence and continuance of featherbedding; second, the impact of the featherbedding rules on decision making in both the short and long run; third, alternatives to featherbedding for meeting structural unemployment.

Conditions for Featherbedding

Employment insecurity gives rise to featherbedding under special circum-stances. The following generalizations are significant in understanding the acceptance or rejection of this particular response to the problem of in-security.

Featherbedding occurs in industries that are characterized by noncom-

*Reprinted from Paul A. Weinstein, "The Featherbedding Problem," *The American Economic Review,* May, 1964, pp. 145–52, by permission of the editor and author.
Dr. Weinstein is Associate Professor of Economics, University of Maryland, and Director of Research, Maryland Department of Economic and Community Development.

petitive operation prior to formalization of the rules. The economic environment for featherbedding is very similar to that required for racketeering. In both cases the firms must have some expropriatable surplus, or else the working rule or extortion leads to downward instability. In the main, the distinction between these two phenomena is in the utility functions of the maximizing institution and the division of the rewards. Therefore, it is inappropriate to examine the impact of the rules on the assumption that they disturb an optimal competitive position.

For example: the industries protesting most about these rules — and where in fact they are found in abundance — are the transportation industries and the building trades. Both are noncompetitive in character. The railroads, for example, are under extreme control in nearly every activity, from quality of product to price, while the building trades continue to be a hotbed of localized monopoly in which the government has a role through licensure and demand. Given this state of affairs, some might suggest we dismiss the problem merely as one of internal allocation of quasi-rents. Featherbedding ties up manpower in unproductive activities, and to dismiss the problem as one internal to the firm leaves the larger manpower problem unresolved. It is better to have a higher utilization of human resources even if there is monopoly, though quite obviously it is best to free both labour and product markets.

The spread of these practices, which increase costs, to competing industries reduces one of the constraints on the union imposing them. The rationale is identical to the explanation of the failure of featherbedding in pure competition. The market restraints on unions are diluted when competitive industries work under similar circumstances. For example, it is clearly advantageous to the railroads to have airlines face the problem of manning requirements on jet services, as well as the problem of restrictions on abandonment by public authorities. A great comfort to the Brotherhood of Locomotive Firemen and Helpers should be the increase in the crew consist on some commercial airlines resulting from the joint demands of flight engineers and the Airline Pilots Association.

The unions involved in featherbedding are narrowly organized along craft lines. There is almost a total absence of these rules in industrial or multicraft unions. The economics of this is important in understanding the role of the market in eliminating restrictive practices and restricting their introduction. The advantages of featherbedding accrue to a specific group, and this serves as a restraint upon gains to other workers in the firm. In an industrial union small groups rarely elicit the support of the entire organization for their own narrow ends, because the larger group has nothing to gain.

Union rivalry also leads to featherbedding as a defensive strategy. Featherbedding is found when there is a cluster of craft unions in an industry. These unions abide with each other under unstable conditions for a number of reasons. The organizations are competitive, pursuing individual goals with little regard for the impact of their policies on nonmember employees.

A current dispute in the airline industry concerns the manning of the third seat in the cockpit. Should it be a member of the Flight Engineers with some pilot training or a pilot with an engineer's license? One result of course has been the three pilot-one engineer crew on some lines. The Emergency Boards examining this dispute have pointed to the need for union merger as a necessary condition for the settlement of the problem.

While employment goals of unions are not frequently dominating, much of the literature on trade union utility functions implies that this is an aberration. These older models of trade unions, like those of Fellner, Ross, and Dunlop, were influenced by the flush labour markets of the 1940s. Such a position can hardly be accepted in the light of recent labour experience. While an interest in employment has long been noted in craft unions, one notes the growing interest of industrial unions in employment security. More and more we observe union leaders placing increased emphasis on employment factors rather than on wages. The type of activity pursued by unions with employment interests varies markedly from featherbedding at one extreme to the program recently effected by Kaiser, the *ILA-PMA* and Armour. It would appear that there is a series of alternative trade union utility functions and that there is a need for a systematic analysis of why a trade union chooses one alternative rather than another.

The technological requirements for featherbedding are at least as important as the industry and union structure. An almost universal characteristic is the gradual substitution of one form of technology for another. The displacement is evolutionary, wiping out the wage-rent differential of skilled groups. This type of change establishes the conditions for the imposition of the rules, as well as pointing the way toward their elimination. Thus, the type of rule we are concerned with arises shortly after the commercial introduction of a technology that is likely to affect adversely a relatively small and usually skilled group in the work force. Quite frequently featherbedding emerges from the carrying forward of a set of practices appropriate for one technology to another where it is alien.

The specific labour groups engaged in featherbedding do not allow employers to modify the job assignments of the workers. This fact along with analysis of broader categories of inputs implies that the elasticity of substitution for specific groups in a firm is zero or close to it. To analyse the effects of featherbedding with the aid of a Cobb-Douglas function having a positive and constant elasticity of substitution for other factors appears most inappropriate. The results using that model imply that the marginal productivity of capital increases as a result of featherbedding — a conclusion that evaporates when a more realistic production function is employed. However, this is an empirical problem, and one that needs examination before a definitive answer to the impact of featherbedding can be provided.

The Impact of Restrictive Rules

There are two avenues of analysis open: static analysis, which is fairly well developed, and dynamics, which is largely in an embryonic state. Some conclusions about featherbedding under static conditions are summarized, while some interesting dynamic questions are posed.

Theoretically a featherbedding rule could require a fixed amount of labour to be hired for a specified economic period. Under this procedure labour would be a semivariable cost and thus be analogous to any other lumpy factor.

However, the rules considered under the rubric of featherbedding do not specify that a fixed amount of labour be hired. On the contrary, they usually call for the retention of an existing labour-output ratio. Examples are the "bogus" role, double heading, and standby. In each case the amount of redundant work to be performed by the firm is a function of output, thus affecting the height and slope of variable costs and, given the structure of the industry, reduced output. Consequently, we can say that the rules do reduce output and raise costs and prices in a short run.

The first dynamic question concerns the impact of featherbedding on supply. Does the existence of featherbedding affect the labour supply function? Unfortunately this is not easily answered, but let me point out the implications under either of two sets of conditions. First, if we assume that there is some onus connected with a job that is reputed to involve featherbedding, then the supply to the industry would shift to the left and in the extreme would possibly disappear; that is, would be perfectly inelastic at zero offerings over the relevant wage range. In the long run, the problem might then be self-correcting from the supply side. An alternative would be for the wage rate to be adjusted upward to compensate for the disutility of being in an undesirable occupation. Thus, a consequence of featherbedding would be an upward pressure on wages that cannot be stopped in a short run. If the rule does not adversely affect supply, then the problem can never be self-adjusting from the supply side. This obviously opens the question to some other type of policy.

A second dynamic problem concerns the impact of the rules on the rate of technological change and investment. It is commonly assumed that these restrictive rules retard progress. Clearly the intent of the rules is to lower the marginal efficiency of investment on labour-saving changes. The employer is not free to reap the full cost-reducing advantages of the change and unless the demand for the final product is perfectly inelastic some of the increase in cost must be shifted to ownership or other factors. The meagre work on this problem is inconclusive, but indicates that the rules have some, though marginal, negative effect. I would argue that it is theoretically possible for the rules to stimulate change under certain conditions.

Let us assume that there is a new technology that allows the production of a product without the use of a factor used in the old technology. Assume further that there is a rule requiring a fixed labour-output ratio for one of the factors. Then the level of the featherbedding cost as measured by the slack variable depends on the mix of the two techniques. In the early stages of the substitution of the technologies there is little of the new and much of the old. Therefore the cost of the rule is minor. However, the more the new technology is substituted for the old, the higher is the relevant featherbedding cost. The maximum cost is obtained prior to the complete substitution of the new technology. When the last unit of capital using the old inputs is scrapped, the workers are entirely superfluous. The absolute cost of featherbedding through time depends on the length of time it takes to complete the change in technology. If this is perceived, then the featherbed rule should foster the more rapid introduction of a new technology and one that is radically different.[1] While research on this is not complete, it is suggested that this model is fruitful in explaining the history of the dispute concerning crew consist rules in the railroads. The critical factors are thus the character of the new production function and the time period between introduction and total substitution.

A less optimistic result comes about if it is assumed that some skills are still required even under the new technology. In this instance one sees that the problem is not corrected from the demand side and in fact may grow at a

---

[1] This assumes absence of co-operation by other unions. *Supra.*

rate consistent with the increase in some parameter, such as the amount of matrix work in the printing trades.

In the former case, that involving the complete change in technology, the market can resolve the problem of the firm in the long run, but not in the latter case. Given that there are supply and demand conditions which may forestall a resolution of the problem, is there any way out of the feather-bedding dilemma? One might also point out the fact that even though the problem say from the supply side is soluble in the long run, it may be deemed that the period is too long, both from the firm's position as well as in tying up manpower resources.

Private Programs

The threat of technological unemployment can give rise to programs to ease the adjustments. Recent experiments such as the Armour, West Coast, and Kaiser agreements have been proposed as models to be followed in other agreements. The advantages of these plans are that they are arrived at privately and do not countenance redundant labour. It would appear that the market is effective in ending the problem of featherbedding by providing a more attractive alternative to the parties. Are these programs desirable alternatives? If they are desirable, what conditions are necessary for their adoption?

Longshoring has a fragile existence as a separate industry or trade. The rationale for a separate union stems from the historic irregularity of shipping, yielding a fluctuating labour demand and with low integration in the industry, separate and corrupt unions.[2] Whenever the trade is regularized, as in coastwise shipping, or the market decasualized, through restricted entry in the hiring hall, the unions cease to have a separate identity and become submerged into teamster or ocean shipping unions. The restrictive rules have arisen out of the corrupt, casual labour market and have tended to disappear with organization. Faced with technological change, as well as hostility from the Teamsters, the ILWU leadership pressed demands on their membership for a program that allowed management to institute work rules changes. The *quid pro quo* was a management-financed fund of some 29 million dollars to be used for early and regular retirement benefits, death benefits, and the stabilization of workers' income against declines due to changes in technology. The primary burden of disemployment resulting from technological change was to be borne by the workers last to arrive in the industry, many of whom are not members of the union. The union agreed not to object to alterations in rules and new technology, except in the case of speed-up. However, the ILWU have opposed changes quite regularly, as shown by the heavy use of arbitration.

The agreement has been advantageous to the parties. Management has added flexibility. The union has ended the hostile period with management and can concentrate on protecting itself against the Teamsters and resolving international problems.

In the meat industry, the Armour program has devoted considerable energies in studying displacement problems caused by plant shutdowns or

---

[2] The corruption arises from the ease of discriminating pricing.

elimination of divisions, as well as alternative ways of dealing with the workers' problems. The Armour Automation Committee has sponsored useful research that has resulted in some steps that have aided the displaced. For example, an early warning system for plant shutdown and the TAP program. The activities that have received most attention are in the labour market sphere of retaining and placement.

Featherbedding was never an alternative open to the meat industry unions. The structure of the industry precluded such strong union policy. The emergence of new plants and firms in geographic areas that are difficult and costly to organize, as well as lower entry barriers, has made the industry more competitive.

The unions in the meat industry show increasing dissatisfaction with this endeavour. This plan has been in jeopardy because of union frustration that reflects their inability to enforce an employment guarantee solution. It is also important to note that this is the only plan that has actually lived with the problem of structural unemployment.

The Kaiser sharing plan has as one of its activities a program for employment security in addition to productivity sharing. The plan allows the employer to introduce new techniques and alter work rules, but alleviates the insecurity usually associated with this. Workers displaced by technological changes are bumped into the plantwide pool, maintaining their former wages.

There has been no real test of the plan, and the high attrition rate at the Fontana plant makes it unlikely that the pool will be too costly. The high attrition rate, estimated at 8 percent, and the twenty-six week eligibility requirement were originally viewed as being in excess of manpower reductions due to altered operations. The company has bought the freedom to adjust procedures with an employment guarantee of dubious value. The union has acceded to changes in technology elsewhere and in fact is not known either for featherbedding or particular concern about permanently unemployed steelworkers.

The reason for this lack of interest, in addition to the character of the union utility function, is basic to understanding the limited role of private agreements in handling the displaced. These programs are adequate for avoiding conflicts but are not in fact perfect substitutes for featherbedding, as the institution of featherbedding or its continuance in the case of longshoring was not a real alternative.

The cause of featherbedding is employment insecurity. The restrictive rules maintain jobs for the displaced. The alternative for featherbedding is the placement of displaced workers in other jobs and this normally means outside the firm or industry. While the Armour program attempts this, it is at once hampered by the inadequacies of public services and is an alternative to public services. Labour market functions performed by either the former employer or union are likely to be on a crisis basis. To adequately move workers from their old jobs implies careful planning based upon labour market surveys, employment projections, and training techniques in diverse industries. To invest in this activity would require a considerable incentive, and it is on this point that the future of these plans in handling employment insecurity breaks down.

The return to both labour and management of shifting workers smoothly out of their own province is either zero or close to it. What incentive is there for a particular union to invest in preparing workers for membership in another union and, *a fortiori*, management investing for the benefit of other firms. Today the Armour Automation Committee is resorting to public services more and more — for these are best suited for handling the real problems. The main contribution that the programs can make is in mobilizing the public service. However, a really efficient service would hardly need this catalyst.

Conclusion

While the market through substitution can end the problem of redundant labour under specified conditions, it can only offer a superficial answer to the real problem of union insecurity. Both the limited interest of labour and management and the technical requirements of appropriate labour market policy require that a more vigorous program of public labour market activity be adopted. Further, it is to the interest of the economy to broaden the industrial basis of union organizations. The market does not seem to aid, and in fact may retard, broader trade union organization. Without the broadening of their scope, even plans for labour market activity as positive alternatives to featherbedding may collapse against the weight of organizational self-preservation.

H. CURRENT STATE OF MICROECONOMICS

The purpose of this section is twofold. It is intended to provide a contemporary view of what microeconomics is and what is good or bad about microeconomics in its present state. It also seeks to draw attention to some of the most persistent controversies in contemporary economics.

We have now reached that happy state where we can begin to talk meaningfully about the specific market behaviour of individual economic units. Many economists are not convinced by Galbraithian attacks on standard economic theory. Reading 25 questions the validity of the ideas of America's most widely known economists, and goes on to label them more or less unhelpful. Reading 26 is Galbraith's reply, and Reading 27 is Gordon's rejoinder. The reader shall have to decide for himself whether Galbraith or Gordon has the better of the debate. One thing is certain, these three articles can be said to have contributed something to the general advance of economic writing.

25. THE CLOSE OF THE GALBRAITHIAN SYSTEM*

Scott Gordon

The Problem of Evaluation

J. K. Galbraith's new book, *The New Industrial State,* can be regarded as the further elaboration of ideas which first caught wide public attention sixteen years ago with the publication of his *American Capitalism* and subsequently with *The Affluent Society.* Some significant differences can be seen between the first and last of these, but it is apparent to anyone who reads them together that the three are to a considerable extent companion volumes, amplifying themes which run through all. The title of this review article may be premature in the sense that one should not assume that further books on these great themes will not flow from Galbraith's prolific pen, but with *The New Industrial State,* his view of the nature of the modern economy and his identification of its major problems are now clear and can be considered as a potential system of ideas. Ten years ago, in *The Affluent Society,* Galbraith noted that his mind was turning toward matters which now find expression in his new book and, despite the fact that he has been writing other books and doing many other important things these past ten years, *The New Industrial State* may be considered as a work of mature reflection by America's most widely known economist. It is perhaps time, then, to make a general evaluation of Galbraith's economic thought, to try to locate its place in the history of the science, and to appraise the contribution it may make to our understanding of the modern world.

One must begin with a candid recognition that the academic reader of Gailbraith's books is under a strong temptation to react negatively to the author's style and method of discourse. He waives the scholarly conventions in favour of a rhetoric which is designed to appeal to the lay reader. But the stylistic techniques he employs to this end increase the difficulty of grasping the substance and structure of his thought and work against a fair and

---

*Reprinted from Scott Gordon, "The Close of the Galbraithian System," *Journal of Political Economy* (July-August, 1968), pp. 635-44, by permission of the editor and author.
Professor Gordon is Chairman, Department of Economics, Indiana University, Bloomington, Indiana, and Professor of Economics, Queen's University, Kingston, Ontario. Professor Gordon, who is a Canadian, taught for many years at Carleton University, Ottawa.

objective appraisal of it by an orthodox, scholarly mind. Galbraith is satiric, scornful, and flippant. There is often a sneer at his pen point. He makes use of much verbal fretwork and delights in the sudden reversal. He loves paradoxes and aphoristic generalizations so much that he often allows a witty sentence to stand when it really requires retooling in order to carry accurately the content of his thinking. An even greater barrier, especially to the economist, is that Galbraith is *simpliste*. There are innumerable passages in his books which make one ache with vexation at his overgeneralization, exaggeration, and stereotyping. His treatment of the "conventional wisdom" of the older economists, one of his favourite pegs on which to pin a donkey's tail, reflects an occluded memory of some old lectures in the history of economic thought that would have been better if completely forgotten. His treatment of what modern economists think is derived largely from the Arcadian world of the elementary textbook. When he himself deigns to be analytical along the lines of conventional economic theory, he is often sloppy. In addition to all this, he carries on a continuous vendetta against the economists of the academic establishment; his barbs sting and some go close to the vitals, which makes it difficult either to be objective in evaluating his work or to avoid bending over backward in the effort to be so.

Nevertheless, these difficulties must be overcome. Galbraith's ideas have become important elements in the contemporary popular culture of American social thought. If we are to assess their validity, we must not be put off by his disregard for the scholarly conventions or by our own wounded pride. We must go to the substance of his main themes.

The New Industrial State as a Planned Economy

The pivotal point of Galbraith's economic thought is the theme of *American Capitalism* — that the American economy is characterized by a high degree of concentration and that the analysis of economic processes by means of the traditional models of economic theory is therefore meaningless. In *The New Industrial State* he carries this argument further, not in the direction of the "theory of countervailing power," which was the constructive analysis of the earlier book, but toward the conclusion that the American economy is not only no longer a competitive economy but that it is not even a market economy. The independence of consumer preferences and factor offers, the profit incentives of the producing units, and the price mechanism which, in traditional theory, knits the system together, are all swept away, and the "heartland of the economy" (the industrial sector) is represented as "managed" by the giant corporations which dominate its various industries. "The firm controls the prices at which it buys materials, components and talent, and takes steps to insure the necessary supply at these prices. And it controls the prices at which it sells and takes steps to insure that the public, other producers or the state take the planned quantities at these prices. So far from being controlled by the market, the firm, to the best of its ability, has made the market subordinate to the goals of its planning."[1] The qualification in the last sentence quoted would suggest an examination of the constraints which act as exogenous controls over the firm, but Galbraith does not

---

[1] J. K. Galbraith, *The New Industrial State* (Boston, Massachusetts, 1967), p. 110.

proceed in this direction. The qualification disappears utterly, and the picture that emerges of the modern large corporation is that it has unlimited power to reach forward and control its product demands and to reach backward and control its factor supplies. The demand and supply functions of the Galbraithian world all have price elasticities that are either infinite or zero, and often they degenerate to single points. Under such assumptions, it is not surprising that traditional market theory is regarded as yielding little insight into the mechanism of economic organization. In *American Capitalism* the business firm was considered to be constrained by the other major institutions of the economy, labour unions, and government, but in *The New Industrial State* these are viewed not as competing repositories of power but as complementary organisms which have joined with the great corporation to assist it in its "planning."

These developments, in Galbraith's view, have not resulted from fortuitous circumstances; they are inherent in the logic of modern technology. The day of the "entrepreneurial firm" is over. The modern industrial firm is operated by a "technostructure" of talents which manages the various processes of the firm down through its hierarchical levels and whose goals are primarily to maintain the autonomy of the organization itself and to promote its growth. What makes the modern giant corporation effective in the pursuit of its aims is organization. If there is genius at work, it is not to be found in any human frame; the "technostructure" consists of quite ordinary men who are welded into a managerial team. The English language does not contain a voice that is passive enough to express the essential idea. The corporation is simply "doing its thing," as the hippies would say, and its managerial members are doing theirs, governed by the imperatives of modern technology. Moreover, Galbraith asserts, these imperatives are not confined to capitalistic economies. Technological determinism is a law of industry which transcends political ideologies and social systems. He sees, accordingly, a convergence of the economic systems of all mature industrial states not, as some have claimed, because the Soviet-type economies are introducing some markets and capitalistic economies are introducing some macromanagerial elements, but because in both cases the "heartland" of the economy consists, as it *must,* of planning systems.

The Galbraithian view of the modern economy has innumerable antecedents in the sense that the death of the market has often been announced and with it, usually, the impotence of traditional economic analysis. But one need not linger over this. In specific terms, Galbraith's picture most distinctly evokes memories of Thorstein Veblen, who foresaw a kind of revolution by the technocrats who would take over the operation of the economy. Galbraith tells us that this revolution is already complete. Veblen's "Soviet of Engineers" is essentially the same as Galbraith's "technostructure." In both views, these developments are considered to evolve from the inherent nature of modern production technology. There are normative similarities too. Veblen looked forward to the replacement of the price system by "engineers" as an advance in logic, order, and efficiency; yet he could not keep from speaking of it with a tinge of irony and even bitterness. The same is true of Galbraith. When he writes on these matters, his adjectives and adverbs carry reproaches and misgivings, but the substance of the argument is that the new world that is managed by the technostructures of the large corporations is far more efficient, both in the static sense and in the promotion of innovation, than a world of market organization. In the last chapters of *The New Industrial State,* Galbraith pleads for intellectuals to bestir themselves over the problems of political and economic power that these developments have created and asks, rather vaguely, for the use of government as a controlling and directing force. His main difficulty is, however, the same as Veblen's in the end: there is no practical (and perhaps no philosophical) difference between asserting that something is inevitable and considering it to be desirable.

Galbraith's analysis of the American economy is constructed upon his conception of the legal and organizational nature of the modern industrial firm. The essentials of this conception derive from Berle and Means' classic of thirty years ago, *The Modern Corporation and Private Property*. The delineation of the modern firm offered in *The New Industrial State* is, in such terms, largely conventional, but it is expressed vividly and effectively. There are some people left, including some economists, who persist in regarding the corporation as a purely instrumental device, an association of individual venturers of capital, and there are some areas of economic policy where anachronistic conceptions of this sort have been seriously misleading. Because it is likely to be so widely read, *The New Industrial State* may render good service in bringing, once again, to the attention of a wide audience one of the most momentous facts of the modern age, the emergence of the corporation as a primary social institution.

Galbraith's concept of the "technostructure," however, overstresses the monolithic nature of the corporate managerial system, and it is more likely to become a cliché than a useful tool of analysis. The decentralization of modern managerial organization indicated by Peter Drucker's *The Concept of the Corporation* has no reflection in *The New Industrial State,* though this development is, one would think, of the utmost importance in appraising the corporation's role as an economic and social institution. Galbraith also has little to say about other important modern developments, such as the growth of the conglomerate-type corporation and the phenomenal rise of pension funds as actual and potential owners of corporate stocks. In short, *The New Industrial State* does not enter upon an examination of the important recent and current developments in corporate evolution, some of which would seem to this reviewer to be very germane to the central thesis there presented. That the picture of the corporation contained in the book is consequently somewhat old hat and commonplace should not, however, obscure the fact that it is essentially true, and very important. The modern large corporation *is* largely free of stockholder control; it *does* supply internally a large part of its capital requirements; it *is* run by its managers; and the managerial bureaucracy *is* a coherent social-psychological system with motives and preferences of its own.

When we turn from Galbraith's picture of the internal organization of the modern corporation to his view of the external environment in which the corporation operates, however, the picture becomes much less satisfactory. The corporation here appears as a very strange organism indeed. It controls completely all the important elements of its environment. It has no need to accommodate itself to any exogenous circumstances; it is able to mould these to suit itself. Such a corporation would be like no organism, biological or social, that ever was, for it would encounter no constraints upon what it wishes (or is impelled) to do, which is to grow. Theoretically, we should observe all major industrial firms growing infinitely large, each of them, moreover, instantaneously! This is a caricature, but it serves to focus attention on the important question, which is: What are the factors that prevent this from occurring and how do they operate? It is not sufficient simply to say that "of course" rabbits or ants or humans or General Motors cannot overrun the earth, eliminating all other organisms. One must discover the mechanism that prevents this from happening. Scientific explanation is an essay on the constrained maximum; no less so when we examine the growth of firms. But the Galbraithian firm knows no constraints. "The size of General Motors is in the service not of monopoly or the economies of scale but of planning. And for this planning — control of supply, control of demand, provision of capital, minimization of risk — there is no clear upper limit to the desirable size. It could be that the bigger the better."[2]

But it can't be the bigger the better (relative to the total economy) for General Motors, United States Steel, and General Dynamics all at once. The Galbraithian picture is only plausible at all if one considers one firm at a time. It may be plausible to say that there is no market, as economists understand it, for automobiles or for steel, but what happens in the case of automotive steel where two "technostructures" confront one another? It is hardly sufficient to say, as Galbraith does, that they make contracts with one another without describing what governs the terms they arrive at.[3] The "countervailing power" thesis of *American Capitalism* might be invoked here, but Galbraith does not employ it in the analysis of *The New Industrial State,* and nothing else is introduced that might play a similar explanatory role. We are left with a microeconomics *sans* Walras — a particular equilibrium analysis in which the equilibrium is nonsensical.

This points to the main defect of Galbraith's conception. He deals with the organization of the individual firm, but he says nothing about the organization of the *economy.* How is the economy organized into a coherent system? By means of what mechanism or procedure are the activities of the "five or six hundred firms" that constitute "the heartland of the modern (US) economy" made to mesh?[4] Galbraith rejects the market mechanism of traditional economics, but he offers no answer of his own to these fundamental questions. *The New Industrial State* fails to present a coherent picture of what it sets out to describe, the organization of the American economy. It seems to me that Galbraith slips from the propostition that the firm plans to the proposition that the economy is planned, without realizing that such statements possess only a verbal similarity. His view of the forces making for a convergence of Soviet-type and capitalistic economies is marked by similar elisions.

Nevertheless, this does not mean that the traditional conception of American capitalism is a satisfactory one. There is no central planning agency which commands the economy, but there has been an immense proliferation of governmental policies at federal, state, and local levels over the past fifty years, and it is conceivable that the United States today is, in this way, more of a planned economy than is, say, Yugoslavia. On another plane, we have to recognize that fundamental changes have taken place in the control of American industry and that the traditional concept of private property is now inapplicable to this sphere of American life. Perhaps "private enterprise" as a concept for the analysis of the American economy and "socialist enterprise" for the Soviet Union are of little use, and we should regard both economies as essentially bureaucratic systems. Perhaps the "iron law of

---

[2] *Ibid,* p. 76.
[3] *Ibid,* p. 30.
[4] *Ibid,* p. 9.

oligarchy" is necessary to make the "imperatives of modern technology" into a fruitful analytical conception. Galbraith, however, does not explore any of these avenues of investigation, nor does he develop any others to amplify has analysis. The main lines he draws are correct (though not as novel as he consistently implies), but though he writes at length, he puts very little upon his canvas that does more than ink over ever more heavily the first broad intuitive strokes.

Realism or Romanticism?

The consumer enters the Galbraithian picture of the American economy as a puppet of the production system — his function is to purchase whatever the technostructure has decided to produce in the quantities and at the prices set by the technostructure's plans. It is tempting to discuss this view as an exaggeration or to try to dispose of it by demonstrating its analytical or empirical invalidity. It would be easy enough to argue, for example, that if the management of demand costs anything, an efficient technostructure would try to accommodate whatever independent preferences consumers possess rather than try to mould them into exotic shapes. Or, it would be easy to challenge Galbraith to show empirical support for his view that the techniques of demand management he speaks of are effective in altering the allocation of income between savings and aggregate consumption or among broad consumption categories.[5] But this would be a profitless contention. Galbraith himself has noted that "although the truth rarely overtakes false-hood, it has winged feet as compared with a qualification in pursuit of a bold proposition."[6]

The big issue that is really involved here is that human wants are cultural phenomena. Galbraith is not to be faulted on this fundamental point or on his view that great consequences for economic theory spring therefrom. In a society where the production system forms a large part of the culture, and thus helps mould the wants it is created to satisfy, how do we establish any solid footing for the analysis of the economic process and the determination of its efficiency? But here again, the main criticism that must be levelled against Galbraith is that he does not explore the important issues raised by his own viewpoint. On the question of the determinants of consumer wants, he is in fact astoundingly naïve. He seems to believe that it is the affluence of America that has made wants susceptible to manipulation and that in poor societies wants are natural or, as he puts it, "original" with the individual. Every Gothic spire in Europe, every temple in India, certifies the power of dominant social institutions in achieving major manipulations of income allocation, even in very poor societies. Any anthropologist could tell him how far removed from the "original" are the consumption patterns of even the most primitive peoples who live on the edge of existence.

The opposition Galbraith draws, in both *The Affluent Society* and *The New Industrial State,* between the natural wants of the poor and the culturally attenuated wants of the rich cannot be sustained. As a basis for a philosophy of distributional equity, it is the weakest of foundations; as an

---

[5] Note this astonishing statement: "If advertising affects the distribution of demand between sellers of a particular product *it must be supposed that* it affects the distribution as between products" (Galbraith, *The New Industrial State*, p. 305; my italics).
[6] Galbraith, *The Affluent Society* (Boston, Massachusetts, 1958), p. 30.

explanation of "social imbalance" — why we live in a society of clean houses and dirty streets — it is not penetrating. But that does not mean that the underlying issue — the cultural determination of wants — is unimportant. Eighty years ago, Alfred Marshall, who created so much of the modern economics which Galbraith deplores, noted that as civilization advances, wants are more and more the *results* of economic activity rather than the causes of them. The point is fundamental. It is hard enough to view economic theory as an exploration of the logic of allocating given resources to the satisfaction of given wants in a world where neither wants nor resources will stand still. In a world in which the wants change *as a result of* our economic efforts to satisfy them, economic theory is faced with subtle and difficult problems and, moreover, problems which will not remain within the boundaries of "positive" economics.

A great deal of Galbraith's writing may be viewed as hinging on this question. In a sense, there is an economic sociology or, as Marshall would have put it, an "economic biology" contained in his theory of technological determinism. But it does not seem to me that the issue is examined in Galbraith's books with the profundity of thought or scholarship it deserves and requires. In his specifics, Galbraith sticks to the most hackneyed theme of modern social literature — the power of advertising. His general stance is also an old and dusty one — the degradation of man by the economic system. His writing recalls the bitter plaints of the Victorian romantics — Carlyle, Dickens, Ruskin, and others — who looked upon the youthful face of industrialism and found it a monstrous evil. Galbraith looks upon it in its "maturity," and though his reaction is more urbane, it is essentially the same cry. The machine has been installed in the garden; the human birthright is being sold for a mess of GNP; the economic mechanism does not feed man but feeds upon him, and calmly spits out the bones. A century ago Ruskin admonished, "There is no wealth but life," and Galbraith echoes, "What counts is not the quantity of goods, but the quality of life."[7]

It is a great and lyrical theme, one of the most emotive in romantic literature, and it has always enjoyed a good market among the kind of public that, as Harry Johnson once observed, read (or, at least, buy) only one book a month. Who is there philistine enough to care not if he seems to deny the superiority of aesthetic and humane values over mere "goods"? But the argument is essentially wrongheaded. If there is anything that deserves to be called "conventional wisdom" with all the derision that Galbraith has so firmly attached to that phrase, it is the idea that there is an inherent conflict between the satisfaction of material wants and the needs of the cultivated spirit. Material welfare and the "higher" humanism are complementary, not competing, things. The civilized sensibilities flourish where there is economic plenty; and the more the better, even when it is devoted in part to automobiles and television sets. The common man is not a noble primitive who has been spiritually pauperized and morally enslaved by material progress; he has in fact been freed and elevated by it. There is much more distance to go along this road, even in the "affluent society" of the United States.

Not to mince words, there is an unavoidable tinge of dissimulation in the claim that we should not concern ourselves any longer with raising the levels of national output and material welfare. It simply comes too easily to

---

[7] Galbraith, *The New Industrial State,* p. 8.

anyone who resides some two or two and a half sigmas to the right of the nation's average income. My ophthalmologist tells me (at thirty dollars an hour) that he has property in New Mexico and that things were fine until the Braceros began to go into the factories and their wages rose. "But," I demur, "their incomes were very low before." "Ah," he informs me firmly, "but they were happy — happier than you and I." Such a one as that will nod comfortably over numerous passages in *The Affluent Society* and *The New Industrial State,* enjoying a little costless mental anchoritism and a mild flirtation with "progressive" ideas. He might even convince himself that he appreciates and sympathizes with the superior values of those youthful aesthetic ascetics who flock to the asphalt Waldens of Haight-Ashbury and Washington Square.

Even if we regard Galbraith solely as a popular social philosopher whose main aim is to question the values of contemporary American society, there is much in his writing that is, in my opinion, misguided. But an economist must recognize that his argument goes beyond this. To Galbraith, the modern economists are Pharisees and Talmudists — they are to be driven from the Temple altogether and their methods of analysis and investigation banished from the discussion of public affairs. But, one must ask, what is to take their place? If the analysis of the economy as a system of markets is not relevant to the study of current American trends and problems, then what is? On this point Galbraith leaves us with a void. He offers no alternative system of economic analysis or even the sketch lines of one that might be built. (There was a suggested approach in *American Capitalism,* the first and best of Galbraith's major works, but it has not been developed in the subsequent books.)

If we are persuaded, for example, that a gross imbalance exists between social and private consumption, does Galbraith offer us anything as promising for dealing effectively with it as the modern analysis of "public goods" which has been constructed upon the foundations of orthodox economics? If we take the view that corporate giantism is a consequence of industrial technology and the development of planning systems in management, does it help at all to conclude, as Galbraith does, that antitrust policy is obsolete and let it go at that? He offers no system of economic or political analysis that would enable us to construct an alternative line of policy. How would we tackle, by means of Galbraithian economics, such serious current problems as racial discrimination in our systems of production and consumption, the decay of the central cities, the further promotion of equity and security, the maintenance of an open and viable international economy? If we read *The Affluent Society* and *The New Industrial State* with such questions in mind, we emerge empty-handed. We may, I think, claim that orthodox economics has contributed a modest bit to the examination of such questions, and there are certain lines of current investigation that promise a great deal more. Galbraith berates and ridicules contemporary economic theory, but if realism, relevance, and usefulness are to be the criteria, he cannot make his criticisms from the standpoint of an advocate of a superior system. There is no coherent analytical system that meets such tests in his own work of the past decade.

Galbraith's books have not been well received by economists. He has by now grown to expect that and cunningly suggests, with the aid of *ad hominem* argument, that the merit of his views is thereby certified. He writes with wit on the "conventional wisdom" of economists, but there is a sour taste in many of these passages — as of grapes, perhaps. Yet, by any test except the rigorous one of scholarship, he is a highly successful author. His books and articles enjoy a very large audience and have opened to him the doors of prestige, power, and wealth. He has chosen to write *sub specie temporis,* and has done so with consummate skill, but it is clear that he hopes his books will prove to be *sub specie aeternitatis* also. How do they seem to rank in that great contest?

It is always hazardous to declare what the Muses will in time decree; the history of economic and social thought is filled with many surprises. But it seems quite certain to this reviewer that Galbraith's work will not be the foundation of a new school of economics and that its impact on social thought in general is unlikely to outlast the immediate consciousness of the author's contemporaries. But immortality has many circles, and Galbraith's name is now firmly fixed on the high middle ranges where dwell the spirits of the effective gadflies of an age. His books will be of scholarly interest to the library moles of the future who will use them in their attempts to understand the complex intellectual agitation of a society that is powerful beyond measure and yet is cataleptic with doubt and fear.

26. PROFESSOR GORDON ON "THE CLOSE OF THE GALBRAITHIAN SYSTEM"*

John Kenneth Galbraith

I have been puzzled as to whether — and how — to respond to Professor Scott Gordon's recent survey (1968) of my several books. He has read them with attention which any author must take as a compliment. He has also emphasized matters I would like to have emphasized, and on a number of these — the decisive difference to the theory of the firm that is made by the modern corporation, the limitations of "positive" economics in contemporary reality — he comes a certain way in my direction. I sense that he could be persuaded further. But then, as the paper proceeds, he falls into a practice that can perhaps best be called professional scholarly denigration. This involves assuming a posture of superior scholarship or scientific method in order to demolish what the critic in question finds personally repugnant. It is a difficult art form, for its practitioner after taking his stand on a high scholarly plane must, since he is not disinterested, resort to rather low techniques of argument. The contrast has only to be pointed out in order to be patent and perhaps even embarrassing. I do not want to embarrass Professor Gordon, and I can soften my charge only a little by saying that he may be unconscious of the practice into which he has slipped. I have concluded, however, that I should, though as gently as possible, indicate what he has done.

None of this, I must make clear at the outset, implies that the books with which he deals are without fault. I have said many times that I was determined, especially in *The Affluent Society* (1958) and *The New Industrial State* (1967), to enlist an audience larger than that of technically learned economists. These books dealt with matters on which I could be fairly certain to encounter a measure of professional reluctance or even hostility. I could avoid being judged and dismissed by an inherently adverse jury only by involving a larger public. (I am sure that Professor Gordon will agree that my position would be a bit tenuous were he my judge.) Although

*Reprinted from John Kenneth Galbraith, "Professor Gordon on 'The Close of the Galbraithian System'," *Journal of Political Economy*, July-August, 1969, pp. 494-503, by permission of the editor and author.

Dr. Galbraith is Paul M. Warburg Professor of Economics, Harvard University, Cambridge, Massachusetts.

I hold to the view that there are few important ideas in economics that cannot be stated accurately in clear English, I could be open to a charge of imprecision of expression. My only plea is that to write carefully without jargon is a good deal more difficult than to write in the professional vernacular, for I have done both.[1] More important, these books, especially *The New Industrial State,* are of some breadth. This, I would urge, is neither their virtue nor their vice but their nature as given by their purpose. I would not claim that they can be so without some sacrifice of depth of scholarly detail. Indeed, I suspect that I have been more impressed than others by this deficiency. In working on *The New Industrial State,* as I entered upon each new section, I made the usual canvass of the literature to see what I had missed in more casual reading. Immediately after the book was published I began encountering interesting items that I had missed, and this process has continued ever since. And, of course, there have been factual and other mistakes.[2] But as these are not the central concern of Professor Gordon, so they need not be mine here.

I am interested in the box which Professor Gordon has built for himself. First, as required by this effort, he affirms his own commitment to the highest standards of scholarship. It is by this test that he finds me wanting; "by any test *except the rigorous one of scholarship,* [my italics] he is a highly successful author." Then Professor Gordon finds himself promptly seduced to criticism which even the most easygoing scholar would, I believe, find remarkably unscholarly and unmotivated. There are, of course, no absolute tests of deficiency here; but it will be generally agreed that if grave faults are simply asserted but not proven — if not even examples are offered; if there is liberal use of loaded words; if there is argument *ad hominem* that cannot be persuasively supported from knowledge of the particular person; if argument is condemned on the basis of an obviously careless or superficial interpretation, and perhaps most of all if a case is grossly altered in order to make it vulnerable and then, being so made vulnerable, is successfully attacked — there is some lack of scholarly rigour. One finds Professor Gordon, after proclaiming such rigour, employing all these devices. The last two lead him to exceedingly far-fetched conclusions. Let me take up very briefly each of these aberrations.

His charge of scholarly deficiency is breathtaking. My treatment of earlier currents of economic thought, where relevant to my argument, "reflects an occluded memory of some old lectures in the history of economic thought that would have been better completely forgotten."[3] This is indeed pretty bad and would seem to call for some very strong support. Alas, there is none. Nor is there for the equally severe charge that my resort to analysis along conventional lines is "often sloppy." That contention, and its effect on

---

[1] Although critics, including Professor Gordon, regularly charge such imprecision, they rarely come up with examples that alter the argument. In the defensive manner of all authors, I am tempted to conclude that imprecision in economics is naturally associated with the use of clear English.

[2] On a very early page the early printings had an inconceivable error exaggerating the share in GNP of the largest industrial corporations. Professor Meade (1968) has rightly taxed me with failing to make clear the very great difference between planning within the market framework and planning that embraces the market. Professor Meade's criticisms are, I think, a model for temperate scholarly debate.

[3] This charge applies, I imagine, to the introductory chapters of *The Affluent Society,* which summarize the ideas that lie back of our present preoccupation with production. Without wishing to enter a defence of them it might be relevant to point out that, in the nearly eleven years since the book was published, they have almost entirely escaped criticism. That can hardly be said for the rest of the book.

conclusions, would seem to have called especially for evidence.[4] Finally, and more probably wrong, is his charge that I rely excessively on "the Arcadian world of the elementary textbook." For here I carefully stated my method. It was to employ the admirable texts of Paul Samuelson and Robert Dorfman when I had need to summarize the state of current belief and pedagogy. One would be interested in knowing an alternative for this purpose. On growth-maximization models, sources of savings, organizational theory, the cost of automobile-model changes — all the hundred and one other matters where I have cannibalized sources for information or ideas — Professor Gordon will find no resort whatever to textbooks, Arcadian or otherwise. And to establish this would not have required even very strenuous scholarship.

As to loaded expressions — words and phrases that have emotional as distinct from or in addition to their technical effect — one could compile a considerable list from Professor Gordon's brief article. My books are consigned to the "contemporary popular culture," which surely conjures up some rather hideous images in the cultivated mind; my view of the corporation is both "somewhat old hat and commonplace";[5] I am made guilty by association with "Victorian romantics," readers who are enjoying "costless mental anchoritism," "mild flirtation with 'progressive' ideas," and the "youthful aesthetic ascetics who flock to the asphalt Waldens of Haight-Ashbury and Washington Square." It would not be wise for me to forbid such words to every critic. But once again we are back to Professor Gordon's own commitment to rigour, a commitment which allows him to attack my writing as "satiric, scornful, and flippant" and to involve something which I judge much worse which he calls "verbal fretwork." My purpose here, again, is not to plead my innocence but to show in what contradictory position this method puts the man who presumes to judge.

There are two arguments *ad hominem* to which I would advert. I am thought to be blinded to the problems of the poor by personal affluence[6]

Maybe I might also be allowed a footnote on my association with this part of our subject. To Professor Gordon's distress I must confess that lectures were not a part of my intellectual preparation — I had only two sets, one from the late Carl Plehn of the University of California which, to the best of my knowledge, no one ever remembered, and another from the late G. F. Shove at Cambridge University on which, more unfortunately, my memory is very dim. The classroom that winter was extremely cold and that occupied my thoughts. But I was at Cambridge in the days when Piero Sraffa, a great friend, was working on the Ricardo papers on which he was later to be joined by Maurice Dobb, also a friend of those times. This was an invitation, rare in modern times, to steep oneself in Ricardo, Malthus, and James Mill and to go back to Smith and on to John Stuart Mill and, more superficially, his contemporaries. This interest has in some degree remained.

[4] Not that the charge could not be sustained, though I trust in limited degree. I am very dissatisfied, for example, with my model, if such it can be called, of maximization by the technostructure (Robin Marris, "Economic Systems: Planning and Reform: Cooperation," *American Econ. Review,* 58 [March, 1968]). But beyond some hierarchy of the things maximized — growth, security, technological virtuosity, and earnings — I have seen no way of expressing the matter which does not involve sacrifice of what is intuitively plausible for what would be theoretically more elegant.

[5] He is careless, I believe, on this. My views are held to be "old hat and commonplace" because of my neglect of the conglomerate, possible control (or influence) by pension and presumably other investment funds and of techniques of managerial decentralization à la General Motors. The first I do not, in fact, neglect; though I wrote before the recent explosion of conglomerates, firms such as General Dynamics do play a substantial part in my argument. It is not yet at all clear that stock holdings by funds related or unrelated to the firm affect the autonomy of the technostructure, and it would be against my argument that they could do so without damage to its autonomy. I might have made that point. I had no reason to deal with managerial structure beyond the diffusion of power associated with the concept of the technostructure. No one can be held responsible for the book he did not intend to write.

[6] I have always thought it an elementary test of an economist's practical competence that he provide himself — legitimately and without obvious professional compromise — with whatever money he might need. This I have done for thirty or more years with relatively little effort helped by some

and to have allowed a sour taste to enter my books because of personal pique over their reception by economists. Such argument is especially dangerous for one who affirms scholarly rigour, not because the argument is associated with bad taste — that is a subjective not a scientific matter, and we can all survive it — but because no critic will ever be as good a witness on the man he attacks *ad hominem* as the man himself. I naturally regard myself as normally compassionate, and it is my view that must prevail. But here I have some supporting evidence. *The Affluent Society* began as a study of poverty; for a long while the working title was "Why People are Poor." The section on why poverty survives in a rich society, now rather dated, I see regularly credited with a role in getting this subject on the national agenda. I hope this is so. More objectively, it brought me a certain part in writing the original Office of Economic Opportunity legislation and until I was expunged along with Dr. Spock — not, I believe, for lack of sympathy for the poor but for lack of sympathy for the Vietnam policy — a position on the statutory advisory council to that agency. If I have bitterness toward my fellow economists, it is so subjective that I am wholly unaware of it. I had previously been impressed with how well I had got away with books that, as Professor Gordon states, make no major effort at professional ingratiation. It is also perhaps damaging to the rigour of Professor Gordon's case that the last time I defended myself (against Professor Robert Solow, 1967), it was held that I aroused the envy of other economists. The bitterness was not in my soul but theirs. I wonder if this line of speculation is really very rewarding.

Now as to the use of careless or superficial interpretations as the basis for criticism. I argue that the wants of *very* poor people are derived from physical circumstances and are thus inflexible and that with more income and a greater opportunity for choice, psychological determinants become more important. This brings the opportunity for operating on the psyche and so influencing the choice. The higher the level of income, broadly speaking, the greater the opportunity for such management. This is a rather brief statement of a complicated matter, but it will do. And Professor Gordon is right in saying that I attribute much importance to this consequence of increasing affluence.

He counters by pointing to "every Gothic spire in Europe, every temple of India" as showing the "power of dominant social institutions in achieving major manipulations of income allocation, even in poor societies." But does this alter the personal consumption situation of the poor in these societies? Would anyone deny that income can be squeezed from the poor by spiritual

---

luck. But Professor Gordon has exaggerated sadly the returns to be made from writing in our time and society. Others have indicated curiosity, and I see nothing against a full disclosure. In the seventeen years since its publication in 1952, *American Capitalism* in all editions has earned $35,000. *The Affluent Society* since 1958 has earned $138,000 on the American edition and perhaps $20,000 as an absolute maximum (a considerable compilation task would be involved in knowing) on the British edition and the twenty or thirty translations. A common price for a translation was $150. The average over the nine years to the publication of *The New Industrial State* was thus $17,500 a year. But I allotted a substantial portion, perhaps half when I was in Cambridge, to secretarial, research, and other assistance for *The New Industrial State* or academic duties along the way. It is not without interest that in the United States the author of even a very successful book (as I assume I can describe *The Affluent Society*) would not live in very splendid fashion in the absence of other income. A new edition of *The Affluent Society* will appear this year, and because of improved bargaining position the revenues will be substantial. However I no longer receive them. *The New Industrial State*, combining large sales with improved bargaining position, does promise to be substantially more remunerative than the earlier books. It remains that all who want effortless wealth are strongly advised to have invested some years ago in IBM.

or temporal authority or, indeed, that this is (or was) other than a reason why they are poor? Because Shah Jahan, the greatest of builders, could indulge his fancy with the Pearl Mosque or the Taj Mahal (or its adjacent places of worship if Professor Gordon wants to remain strictly with religion), this does not mean that the Hindu villager could do likewise, or could influence that choice or had any options, assuming he wanted to remain alive, but to concentrate his consumption on bread grains.[7]

Additionally, there can be few economic propositions empirically more securely established than that people of lowest income, wherever they are found, spend an overwhelming proportion on food, and on the cheapest of the available foods. Anthropologists may agree, as Professor Gordon avers, that this diet differs from that of "original"[8] or primitive man. But this does not introduce any substantial element of contemporary choice. That choice and therewith the possibility of persuasion are rigidly limited is not only empirically but also mathematically demonstrable.

Having found choice among those who obtain wealth in the poor countries, as distinct from the poor, Professor Gordon goes on to conclude that my view, as just adumbrated, is "astonishingly naïve" and that I "seem to believe that it is the affluence of America that has made wants susceptible to manipulation and that in poor societies wants are natural." That I do believe and I think most reasonable men will believe it. It is also in a sense rather naïve. But rigorous scholarship does not prefer complexity based on misunderstanding to a simple truth. And it recognizes, and this is sometimes very difficult, that reality in economics very often has a naïve aspect by which the learned mind is repelled.

Now I come to the last of the practices into which Professor Gordon has slipped, the use of exaggeration to render careful argument absurd. Here I must put a certain responsibility on the reader. I ask him to consider my final and most careful statement of how extensively the consumer is managed and what power is assumed by the producer in the industrial system — a proposition essential to my argument. Then I ask him to consider Professor Gordon's rendering of that argument. Both call for some attention. Here is my statement:

> The time has come for yet another word of summary. In virtually all economic analysis and instruction, the initiative is assumed to lie with the consumer. In response to wants that originate within himself, or which are given to him by his environment, he buys goods and services in the market. The opportunities that result for making more or less money are the message of the market to producing firms. They respond to this message of the market and thus, ultimately, to the instruction of the consumer. The flow of instruction is in one direction — from the individual to the market to the producer. All this is affirmed not inappropriately, by terminology that implies that all power lies with the consumer. This is called consumer sovereignty. . . . The unidirectional flow of in-

---

[7] Perhaps Professor Gordon is arguing that the rich in these communities — rulers and priests — were part of the society and somehow enjoyed its sanction for their exactions and expenditures. This would be hard to argue in the case of the Moghuls, for they were intruders from abroad and alien in religion. I doubt that it would be more demonstrable, as regards the very poor, in the age of the cathedrals.

[8] This word seems to have been a source of misunderstanding. I use it to characterize wants which begin with the individual (or his stomach) in contrast with those that are given to him by an advertiser or a neighbour. Professor Gordon has also I think a trifle carelessly associated the term with some anthropologically "original" man. However, his point is not improved by this interpretation.

struction from consumer to market to producer may be denoted the Accepted Sequence.

We have seen that this sequence does not hold. And we have now isolated a formidable apparatus of method and motivation causing its reversal. The mature corporation has readily at hand the means for controlling the prices at which it sells as well as those at which it buys. Similarly, it has means for managing what the consumer buys at the prices which it controls. This control and management is required by its planning. The planning proceeds from use of technology and capital, the commitment of time that these require and the diminished effectiveness of the market for specialized technical products and skills.

Supporting this changed sequence is the motivation of the technostructure. . . .

It follows that the accepted sequence is no longer a description of the reality and is becoming ever less so. Instead the producing firm reaches forward to control its markets and on beyond to manage the market behaviour and shape the social attitudes of those, ostensibly, that it serves. For this we also need a name and it may appropriately be called The Revised Sequence.

Those who yearn for the defeat of their enemy are said to wish that he might write a book. Far better that he should resort to overstatement. I do not suggest that the revised sequence has replaced the accepted sequence. Outside the industrial system — beyond the limits of the large corporations — the accepted sequence still rules. Within the industrial system it is of diminished importance in relation to the revised sequence. Here too the consumer can still reject persuasion. And, in consequence, through the market he and his fellows can force accommodation by the producer. But consumers, and the prices at which they buy, can also be managed. And they are. The accepted and revised sequences exist side by side in the manner of a reversible chemical reaction. Doubtless it would be neater were it one way or the other. But, again, the reality is plausible but untidy.[9]

Now here are the sentences in which Professor Gordon summarizes my position.

. . . qualification [that is, that the consumer has market influence] disappears utterly, and the picture that emerges of the modern large corporation is that it has unlimited power to reach forward to control its product demand and to reach backward and control its factor supplies. The demand and supply functions of the Galbraithian world all have price elasticities that are either infinite or zero, and often they degenerate into single points.

The Corporation here appears as a very strange organism indeed. It controls completely all the important elements of its environment. It has no need to accommodate itself to any exogenous circumstances such as the consumer; it is able to mould these to suit itself . . . the Galbraithian firm knows no constraints.

The consumer enters the Galbraithian picture of the American economy as a puppet of the production system — his function is to purchase whatever the technostructure has decided to produce in the quantities and at the prices set by the technostructure's plan.[10]

This restatement of my position will not, I think, be considered a work of scholarly rigour. And having so rearranged matters — using the exaggeration

---

[9] J. K. Galbraith, *The New Industrial State* (Boston, Massachusetts, 1967), pp. 211-13.

[10] Scott Gordon, "The Close of the Galbraithian System," *Journal of Political Econ.*, 76, No. 4 (August, 1968), pp. 635-44.

against which out of some experience I had arranged routine protection — Professor Gordon has no difficulty in getting an absurd result. The firm in my system is subject to no social restraint. It is part of no system. Without the rearrangement the problem Professor Gordon identifies does not arise. Firms can affect the position of their individual demand functions. In so doing they affect and stabilize the market response, my major point, and therewith the distribution of resources and the level of personal saving, the distribution of time between effort and leisure, and the social urgency associated with production. There is no reason, given its cost and ubiquity, to derogate the role of advertising in this process. But these efforts operate against the similar efforts of other firms — a process I have sketched although far from fully described — and against the increasing market resistance of the consumers and the increasing cost (as Professor Gordon rightly observes) of a given increment of sales. These are the constraints. They would not exist with total producer sovereignty,[11] but they do with lesser producer power. And this, in turn, is a very different world from that of consumer sovereignty.

Such is the rather irregular and self-damaging technique of argument which Professor Gordon employs. Its unwisdom will, I think, be evident, and I have no wish to press matters further. On some other questions I think he is in error, but let me confine myself to one. He holds that my conclusions, as compared with those of more orthodox practitioners, are not operative. They offer no guide to racial discrimination in economic activity, "the decay of the central cities, the maintenance of an open and viable international economy," and other urgent matters. I hope this is not so, for my urgent concern has been to make economics relevant to such practical questions. But I wonder if Professor Gordon has tried very hard to apply these ideas. Surely some discrimination is to be explained by the way the modern industrial firm uses and rewards labour in association with the technostructure as compared with the market economy of the rural South. Surely the differences between the educational system brought into existence to serve the industrial system and that sustained by the market economy add to this discrimination. None of this is noticed by the orthodox theory of the firm. Could it not be that the decay of our cities is partly related to the skill with which we are persuaded of the priority of other wants? Is it not possible, as I argue in *The New Industrial State,* that the urban community is also lost in the lacunae of our planning — that were automobile production as unplanned as the provision of urban amenity or even urban housing, we would travel under conditions of considerable dilapidation? Is this planning not one of the difference between air travel and telephonic communication on the one hand and surface travel, local and long distance, on the other? Few things were farther from my mind as I worked out these ideas than the problems of international relations between the developed countries. I have been almost as astonished as others at the way they have been brought to bear on the American corporate presence in Europe and our technological advantages there, and perhaps, purely to impress Professor Gordon, I will one day protest the excessive popularization of my views.

---

[11] Analogy is a tricky and often unfair business, but it is my impression that Professor Gordon would not be on stronger ground had he attacked anyone who asserted the existence of monopoly by first attributing to him an assumption of total monopolization and then inquiring as to the restraints on the monopolist.

Professor Gordon ends his article (after relegating me to the "library moles" of the future, who also have my sympathy) by referring to my appeal to a contemporary "society that is powerful beyond measure and yet is cataleptic with doubt and fear." I would sense that the orthodox avenues of thought have not been helpful to him in understanding this doubt and fear. And if the individual is the sovereign arbiter of his economic fate, and presides by his choices in a market economy over the ultimate productive decisions of the economy, public and private, such doubt and fear will indeed be puzzling. But if the individual has become the instrument — partial, I hasten to affirm — of great bureaucracies, public and private, military and civilian, which now in some measure order, which is to say plan, his life, will these reactions seem so strange? Surely some alarm is to be expected if social decision rests extensively with the Pentagon and the industries supplying it. And that is implicit in my system if I may call it that. It is not revealed in what Professor Gordon defends as "the modern analysis of 'public goods'." And surely there are similar reasons for anxiety as we contemplate producer sovereignty — partial, I hasten to point out — over roads and automobiles and air pollution by the road builders and General Motors. I would be the first, or anyhow one of the many, to agree that my argument leaves much to be decided. But it surely helps if we have learned to look in the right places or in the right direction.

27. THE GALBRAITHIAN SYSTEM: REJOINDER*

Scott Gordon

Professor Galbraith gives me a pretty good drubbing in his response to my appraisal of his major economic works (1969). I doubt that I can make him less displeased with me by what I have to say in rejoinder, but there are a few things that require another word or two.

I think that we may as well leave it to the reader to decide whether my article constituted "professional scholarly denigration" rather than legitimate criticism. I know of no way to confront such an indictment myself, and there seems to be no merit in an exchange of epithets. Similarly, against the charge that I am an interested party, I am powerless, since Professor Galbraith does not say what he conceives my interest to be or how it is relevant to the evaluation of his books. It is like being indicted for "conspiracy."

There are some critical remarks in my article that might have been given documentation or reference. I did not do so because I felt that they were based broadly on Professor Galbraith's writing rather than on professional nit-picking of isolated points here and there. I am sorry that Professor Galbraith feels so keenly my characterization of his treatment of the older economists, but I was attempting to be accurate, rather than witty. To support my judgment I could have pointed to his characterization of Marx as dealing with capitalism as a monopolized, not a competitive, system,[1] or I could have quoted passages like: "Malthus and Ricardo, held that . . . any surplus wealth, above the requirements of bare subsistence, would be promptly absorbed into additional mouths that wealth itself would spawn."[2] But it was indeed, as he suspects, the introductory chapters of *The Affluent Society* which mainly motivated my criticism, because in these pages Professor Galbraith is not merely providing some interesting historical reading; he is trying to establish one of the main themes of the book: the long-standing

*Reprinted from Scott Gordon, "The Galbraithian System," *Journal of Political Economy,* September-October, 1969, pp. 953-56, by permission of the editor and author.
Professor Gordon is Chairman, Department of Economics, Indiana University, Bloomington, Indiana, and Professor of Economics, Queen's University, Kingston, Ontario.
[1] J. K. Galbraith, *American Capitalism: The Concept of Countervailing Power* (Boston, Massachusetts, 1952), p. 174; Galbraith, *The New Industrial State* (Boston, Massachusetts, 1967), p. 48.
[2] Galbraith, *American Capitalism,* p. 108.

foolishness, pessimism, and possible knavery of economists. The
᠎nt of the classical economists that supports this characterization is
erroneous. Obviously I could not literally know that it was written
old lecture notes — I meant only to say that it reads like the
᠎ntional wisdom about classical economies of the generation before last.

If there is one thing I would not want to dispute, it is the usefulness of
elementary textbooks in indicating the main lines of professional opinion of
a period. But Professor Galbraith, it seems to me, has misused them, by
treating propositions that are essentially pedagogical devices as if they were
meant to be literal descriptions of the economy. One could have great sport
by opening a textbook in elementary physics and exclaiming that physicists
are so remote from the real world as to believe that a ball may roll down an
inclined plan without friction. What is there in my article that could
conceivably have given Professor Galbraith the impression that it is my view
that "the individual is the sovereign arbiter of his economic fate, and
presides by his choices in a market economy over the ultimate productive
decisions of the economy"[3] except possibly that he believes that anyone
who regards orthodox economic theory as a useful tool of investigation
holds such stereotypes?

It was not my intention to call into question Professor Galbraith's compassion for the poor or his personal efforts to assist them. *The Affluent
Society* may have begun as an essay on "Why People Are Poor," as Professor
Galbraith avers, but it is clear that it did not end by answering that question.
The message of the book, as I took it, is that there is no longer any need to
expand productivity — the good society for all is attainable without that, for
we are now sufficiently "affluent." "Poverty survives in economic discourse," Professor Galbraith then said, "partly as a buttress to the conventional economic wisdom. Still, in a world of a weekly industrial wage of
eighty dollars and a $3960 median family income, it can no longer be
presented as a universal or massive affliction. It is more nearly an after-
thought."[4] In retrospect, this does not seem to be a clear-eyed perception. If
the advice of the book had been followed literally, the results would have
been very bad. In the decade after 1958 the number of poor in the United
States (according to the Social Security Administration's criterion) was cut
in half, and the evidence seems to be indisputable that high employment and
rapid productivity growth were the agencies mainly responsible for it.
Professor Galbraith would instead have had us sharing our "affluence" of
$3,960 a year. In rereading my review on this point, I see that I did become
rather acerbic. There are those to whom poverty, whether it is much or little,
is a profound social blight, worthy of dedicated and penetrating study and
demanding informed attack; but there are also those to whom it seems to be
a mere political or social titillation. I apologize to Professor Galbraith for
suggesting that he is to be placed among the latter; what I was trying to say
is the *The Affluent Society* provided much food for that type of reader but
little nourishment for the serious student of a serious economic and social
problem.

Professor Galbraith claims that in my review I have misinterpreted the
argument of *The New Industrial State*. For my part I could complain that he
has not been overly scrupulous in his presentation of my interpretation. He

---

[3] Galbraith, "Professor Gordon on 'The Close of the Galbraithian System'," *Journal of Political Econ.*,
77, No. 4 (July-August, 1969), pp. 494-503.
[4] Galbraith, *The Affluent Society* (Boston, Massachusetts, 1958), p. 323.

quotes his own text at length and consecutively, but he selects six sentences or partial sentences here and there from my article, doctors two of them, stitches them together as a summary of my representation of his views, and then remarks that "this restatement of my position will not, I think be considered a work of scholarly rigour." I should hope not. The reader will have to examine Professor Galbraith's book more fully and read my article more fully if he is to decide whether the latter is, as claimed, a distortion of the former.

My rendition of Professor Galbraith's thesis is, however, indeed incorrect, if what he meant to say in *The New Industrial State* is that "firms can affect and stabilize the market response," which he now calls his "major point." My article was built largely around the theme, which I took Professor Galbraith to be advancing, that the American economy is a planned, not a market, economy, which seemed to me to reflect a simple analytical, or perhaps verbal, error: the equation of the internal planning of the firm with the global planning of the economy. If all that Professor Galbraith really meant to claim is that large firms have some market power there is no quarrel, but then why such a flourish of trumpets to announce such a small, and elderly, mouse? Professor Galbraith chides me for "the use of exaggeration to render careful argument absurd," but that shoe surely fits his own foot well. It seems to me that the uncomfortable hole that Professor Galbraith has dug for himself is that in its exaggerated form (his own preference would be for the term "bold") his thesis is absurd, but in its careful and qualified form it is banal.

One should applaud Professor Galbraith's willingness to alter his position when it is shown to be untenable, but he does so largely by making it vague, and the critic is left to wrestle with a wraith. This being so, it is perhaps unwise to argue further on the basis of what one presumes his views to be. However, I have to risk a repetition of the various charges that Professor Galbraith has brought against me on one important point. Part of my criticism of *The New Industrial State* was due to what I took to be its (implicit) political argument. It is an argument that has been put forward with increasing frequency of late years over a broad front — regarding political organization, economic policy, education, the press, etc. This argument is that personal, political, economic, and intellectual freedom in modern industrial society is an illusion. Everyone is enslaved, though few recognize it. That being so, there is no conflict of ideology between the philosophy of freedom and that of repression. Repression is universal, and it is simply a matter of who are to be the masters. *The New Industrial State,* it seems to me, is this type of plea for a repressive oligarchy; a left-liberal oligarchy to be sure — the despots are to be benevolent — but a *dirigiste* society nonetheless. This is a false argument, and potentially a tragic one. It must be rejected by anyone who values freedom and human progress, and who recognizes the necessity to wage a constant struggle against the hardening of social institutions and the entrenchment of élites. The power of big business is an argument for breaking up its structures and for counterpoising them, not an excuse for incorporating them into a comprehensive master political bureaucracy. Is not the latter, in fact, what the concern about "the Pentagon and the industries supplying it" is all about? Professor Galbraith fails to draw the proper pluralist conclusions from his own description of the contemporary American scene because he views "the imperatives of modern technology" as leading inevitably to a society of unified control and "planning." We could, indeed, solve problems such as urban blight by organizing our cities like corporations with firm lines of command (and obedience) and the unlimited use of advertising, or propaganda. The externalities would all be internalized, preference functions would be altered, and the inconsistencies of "the affluent society" would be resolved. But one wonders who is to be cast in the role of Lorenzo il Magnifico, how he is to be chosen, and how constrained? It is a common failing among some modern "progressive" writers that their left hand does not seem to know what their right hand is doing. For this reason, among others, in my review article I placed Professor Galbraith in the lineage of Carlyle and Ruskin and the other Victorian romantics.

In sum then, and to put the matter bluntly, I was arguing in "The Close of the Galbraithian System" that there is, in fact, no technically viable system of economic analysis in Professor Galbraith's books, but there is an implicit normative system of political philosophy in *The New Industrial State*. If the fact that I find the latter system repellent makes me an interested party, "unscholarly and motivated," then so be it. Some of my friends tell me that I have been guilty of irreverence as well.

III. MACROECONOMICS: THE ECONOMY AS A WHOLE

We turn now from the study of the parts of the economy to the study of the economy as a whole, or, from *microeconomics* to *macroeconomics*. Focussing on the overall output of the economic system, macroeconomics examines the adjustment of the economy to changes in the *level* of aggregate demand or total expenditure. The range of issues that surround economic instability are the primary topics of macroeconomics.

In Section A we discuss the specific goals of macroeconomic policy. In Section B we review Canada's recent economic performance, and outline some of the performance challenges for the 1970s. Section C examines the various forms money may take and discusses the authentic revolution in the banking industry. Section D explains how the quantity of money in circulation and interest rates affect aggregate expenditures, and hence, influence prices, production, and employment. Section E brings government spending, taxation, and borrowing into the picture, and Section F discusses the policies which are available to government units to help in stabilizing the economy.

A. FUNDAMENTAL ECONOMIC AND SOCIAL GOALS FOR CANADA

The overall purpose of economic policy at the national level has always been to maximize the welfare of the nation. But within this broad purpose the specific goals of national policy have undergone continuous changes as economic life has changed and as new economic problems have evolved. In the early phases of the development of free-enterprise economies, economic objectives as such were not explicitly articulated. Steady economic growth, full employment, and price stability were more or less taken for granted. As a result, public economic policy concentrated largely on achieving the efficient working of a freely competitive system based on property rights and individual initiative.

The development of conscious and positive national economic goals emerged when many of the postulates of classical economic theory were challenged by events after 1929. The act creating the Bank of Canada in 1934 was perhaps the first manifestation of macroeconomic policy in Canada. In the words of the preamble to the Act, the function of the Bank was

> ". . . to regulate credit and currency in the best interests of the economic life of the nation, to control and protect the external value of the national monetary unit and to mitigate by its influence fluctuations in the general level of production, trade, prices, and employment, so far as may be possible within the scope of monetary action, and generally to promote the economic and financial welfare of the Dominion."

Also, in April, 1945, the Canadian government issued a White Paper in which it declared the achievement of a "high and stable level of employment and income" to be a major aim of government policy. In other words, out of the experiences of the Great Depression and World War II full employment, economic growth, and price stability emerged as positive economic objectives.

The act establishing the Economic Council of Canada (1963) calls upon the Council to study and advise upon the medium- and long-term development of the Canadian economy in relation to the attainment of certain basic economic and social goals. These aims are stated as full employment, a high rate of economic growth, reasonable stability of prices, a viable balance of international payments, and an equitable distribution of rising incomes. The meaning and measurement of these goals are outlined in Reading 28.

In 1962, the Canadian government appointed a Royal Commission "to inquire into and report upon the incidence and effects of taxation imposed by Parliament . . . upon the operation of the national economy, the conduct of business, the organization of industry and the positions of individuals." In its 2,600 page report published in 1966, the Commissioners explained that in order to appraise the existing tax system and suggest improvements they needed to know the central goals of Canadian society. Reading 29 sets out what the Commission considered to be a widely, though not universally, accepted set of national values.

28. ECONOMIC GOALS FOR CANADA TO THE 1970s*

The Economic Council of Canada

Full Employment

We believe that, over the medium-term future, economic policies should be actively directed toward achieving a target of a 97 percent rate of employment (or a rate of unemployment of not more than 3 percent). This objective has important implications for other objectives — such as the maintenance of reasonable price stability and a viable balance of payments position — and an effective combination of policies will be required to achieve these various objectives in a consistent fashion.

Certain features of this employment target deserve special emphasis. First, we do not regard this to be an ultimate or satisfactory goal for all time. We would hope that with sustained improvement in our economic performance it may eventually become realistic to aim for an even better performance in the level of employment. Second, the 97 percent employment objective, whose attainment is to be worked for over the medium-term future, is intended to be an *average annual rate*, which allows for seasonal variations. Third, the target rate is a *national average*, within which there will be some regional variation. Fourth, the rate is intended to reflect a goal for a year of high business activity; short-term movements away from the target could occur at some stages of the business cycle, but persistent deviations would suggest a shortfall from the target. Fifth, the employment target should not encompass any sizable element of either long duration unemployment of individuals or of long duration unemployment in areas where special measures are required to deal with the problems of structural unemployment. Finally, to be realistic, this target necessarily implies favourable international economic conditions — in particular, a high level of employment in the United States.

---

*Reprinted from Economic Council of Canada, Fourth Annual Review, *The Canadian Economy from the 1960s to the 1970s,* 1967, pp. 3–8, by permission of Information Canada.

Economic Growth

Economic growth is usually measured in terms of long-term rates of increase in the volume of a country's total output, or its per capita output (a rough measure of improvements in the standard of living). Another concept is that of output in relation to the manpower required to produce it (a measure of advances in productivity). This is a concept which we emphasize.[1]

Taking all factors together, we conclude that actual physical output of the Canadian economy should grow by an average annual rate of 5 percent per year in 1965-70 to attain potential output by the end of this decade. For 1970-75, when the labour force will grow somewhat more slowly, an average annual rate of growth of 4¾ percent is an appropriate objective.

Reasonable Price Stability

The goal of reasonable price stability was formulated in the following terms in our *First Annual Review:*

> The goal of reasonable price and cost stability is one which is extremely difficult to define. In terms of our preceding discussion of the important role of prices in our economy, and because of the need for flexibility in the pattern of relative prices, we do not believe that a rigid structure of constant prices is a desirable or feasible objective. These flexible price adjustments in response to changes in underlying demand and supply conditions in our market economy should result in some year-to-year variability in overall prices. However, we would regard persistent and rapid price increases as inappropriate and dangerous. After careful consideration, we have assumed that if annual average rates of changes in prices and costs to 1970 can be contained the limits of [1.4 percent and 2.0 percent], this would represent the attainment of a satisfactory degree of price and cost stability . . . .

We still believe that this is an appropriate goal over the medium-term future.

A Viable Balance of Payments

We emphasize that the balance of payments objective should be not merely the maintenance of a flow of total international receipts adequate to cover the country's international payments, but also some strengthening of Canada's international economic position. In line with these requirements, as well as the high potential rates of increase in employment, income, and output, we concluded in our *First Annual Review* that, even under favour-able international conditions for expanding Canadian exports, the current account payments deficit (and accompanying net capital inflow) at potential output in 1970 would be of the order of $1.5 to $2.0 billion. . . . After a careful reappraisal, we have concluded that this goal was appropriately formulated in these terms and is still relevant.

----

[1] Excerpt from *First Annual Review, Economic Goals for Canada to 1970,* 1964, p. 12.

Equitable Distribution of Rising Incomes

The goal of an equitable distribution of rising incomes is another very complex matter, defying simple formulation. Much of our earlier work in this field was concerned with the identification, measurement, and analysis of regional disparities, a long-standing Canadian problem.

[The legislation establishing the Council refers to the broad goals of a high and consistent rate of economic growth and a sharing by all Canadians in rising living standards. Regional participation in rising living standards is obviously an important aspect of this latter goal, and our terms of reference specifically direct us "to study how national economic policies can best foster the balanced economic development of all areas of Canada". . . . The problem of integration and balance, in the sense of assuring an appropriate participation on the part of each region in the overall process of national economic development, has long been an elusive goal and a continuing concern of the people of Canada. . . .

Our concept of regionally balanced economic development can now be outlined. There are, we suggest, two main, interrelated considerations involved in moving toward a better regional balance. The first is the importance of reducing the relative disparities in average levels of income as they presently exist among the regions. . . . The second consideration is the need to assure that each region contributes to total national output, and to the sustained, long-run growth of that output, on the basis of the fullest and most efficient use of the human and material resources available to the region. . . .

The narrowing of income disparities, and the achievement of this result consistently with our other basic economic and social objectives, remains one of the most difficult issues confronting the country as a whole.] [2] However, income distribution has many other important facets which need attention. We need more information about the distribution of income among individuals, families, and various occupational groups. Why do some groups receive little benefit from the general rise in incomes and living standards? What elements lie behind the vicious circle of poverty that still traps far too many of our citizens? Some of the problems here may range far beyond the realm of economic studies. Yet these difficult matters will have to be understood and faced if appropriate policies are to be devised to achieve this goal.

---

[2] From *Second Annual Review, Toward Sustained and Balanced Economic Growth,* (Queen's Printer, Ottawa, 1965).

29. THE CANADIAN ECONOMY AND ITS OBJECTIVES*

The Royal Commission on Taxation

We believe that four fundamental objectives on which the Canadian people agree are:
1. to maximize the current and future output of goods and services desired by Canadians.
2. to ensure that this flow of goods and services is distributed equitably among individuals or groups.
3. to protect the liberties and rights of individuals through the preservation of representative, responsible government and maintenance of the rule of law.
4. to maintain and strengthen the Canadian federation.

To Maximize the Growth of Output

. . . We believe that the tax system should be used, in conjunction with the other instruments, to achieve the following specific goals under this general objective:

> (a) maintenance of full and continuous utilization of Canadian resources through policies designed to maintain an adequate demand for Canadian output.
> (b) maximization of the rate of increase in the productivity of all Canadian resources assuming full employment is achieved. . . .
> (c) prevention of wide or prolonged fluctuations in the general level of prices, and at the same time maintenance of the flexibility of individual prices in the economy.

The Equitable Distribution of Output

The government can change the distribution of the flow of goods and

*Reprinted from the Royal Commission on Taxation, *Report, Vol. II,* "The Use of the Tax System to Achieve Economic and Social Objectives," 1966, pp. 7–18, by permission of Information Canada.

services among individuals and groups of individuals, by imposing higher taxes on some than on others, by making larger transfers of purchasing power to some individuals or groups than to others, and by providing public goods and services that benefit some more than others.

In our opinion there is a consensus among Canadians that the tax expenditure mechanism (including transfers) is equitable when it increases the flow of goods and services to those who, because they have little economic power relative to others, or because they have particularly heavy responsibilities or obligations, would otherwise not be able to maintain a decent standard of living. . . . Our principal concern is that the allocation of taxes, given the existing transfer mechanism and public expenditures, should be such as to achieve an equitable distribution of the flow of goods and services among Canadians.

The Protection of the Liberties and Rights of the Individual

In a democracy such as Canada, restrictions on the liberties of individuals are accepted primarily because those who make the laws are representatives of, and responsible to, the public. The legislative process ensures that the laws serve the public good. Maintaining and strengthening this democratic process is a fundamental general objective.

The Strengthening of Federal-Provincial Relations

Strengthening of the federation requires realization of the following goals:

> (a) the maintenance of the autonomy of the provinces within the agreed division of powers and responsibilities between the federal and provincial governments;
> (b) the development of a flexible tax system that can adjust to the changing needs and aspirations of the people and the provinces in which they live;
> (c) the transfer of resources, through the federal government, from rich to poor provinces, so that the residents of the latter can, if they choose, enjoy minimum standards of public service without undue tax burdens;
> (d) the undivided control of the instruments needed to maintain the stability and growth of the economy if dispersal would reduce control over Canada's collective economic destiny;
> (e) the acceptance of the proposition that the fiscal relationships among all the governments will require continuous reexamination, renegotiation, and adjustment.

Priority of Objectives

The list of objectives that has been compiled is an extremely ambitious one, and we are under no illusion that all of these desirable ends can be easily achieved. We realize that some of the objectives are in conflict, in the sense that movement toward one goal means that others might be achieved less adequately. Simultaneous realization of all the goals in some degree will constitute success if, as we hope, our choices as to the appropriate compromises adequately reflect the consensus of informed Canadians. . . . We assign a higher priority to the objective of equity than to all the others. . . . We are convinced that unless this objective is achieved to a high degree all other achievements are of little account.

B. ECONOMIC PERFORMANCE AND POTENTIAL

We have identified the main objectives of national economic policy as full employment, a high and sustained rate of economic growth, reasonable price stability, a viable balance of payments position, and an equitable distribution of rising incomes. There is also general agreement that these basic goals must be carried out within the framework of a dynamic, free, competitive, predominantly private enterprise system. This means that there should be a minimum of restraint, from both public and private sources on the freedom of entry into competitive business, and on changes in demand and in our productive activity. It also means that there should be substantial equality in economic opportunity.

Recent history has shown that few, if any, of our national objectives can be expected to be realized automatically. A review of the operations of the Canadian economy since World War II indicates that we have encountered at one time or another inflation, unemployment, slow rates of growth, and crises in the balance of payments. One inference to be drawn from this experience is that the real problem lies not in how to pursue some particular objective, but in how to achieve *all* our widely accepted goals simultaneously and consistently. The various objectives are not always compatible with each other. Public and private policies designed to accomplish a particular aim such as full employment or a rapid rate of economic growth may be in conflict with the measures needed to avoid inflation or to maintain a viable balance of international payments. Thus, there is always the need to reconcile conflicting tendencies and to achieve consistency. Otherwise, the central goals are not likely to be attained either simultaneously or separately over the long run. Reading 30 reviews Canada's economic performance from 1950 to 1970. What this analysis shows is that the recent performance of the Canadian economy has clearly been mixed.

Reading 31 focusses on the tasks to be accomplished by the Canadian economy during the 1970s. This analysis assesses the nation's future economic potentials for growth and development.

30. THE PERFORMANCE OF THE CANADIAN ECONOMY DURING THE FIFTIES, SIXTIES AND SEVENTIES*

Bank of Montreal

History, of course, economic or otherwise, does not divide itself conveniently into decennial compartments, and an analysis of economic developments within such artificial constraints cannot hope to be rigorous or definitive. In addition, in this fast-moving age, anyone who tries to use the past as a strict guide to the future is almost sure to be grossly misled. Nevertheless it may be enlightening to sit back and take a broad overview of recent historical patterns in the hope that the basic trends that emerge will help to provide at least some general parameters for assessing the shape of things to come.

In some respects, the transition from the 1960s to the 1970s is not unlike that from the 1950s to the 1960s. As was the case ten years ago, Canadians can look back at a decade in which their economy, on the whole, performed most satisfactorily. In the "Fabulous Fifties" the average annual rate of growth was 5.3 percent in real terms and in the "Soaring Sixties" it was 5.2 percent.[1]

Yet as both decades ended, there were some serious problems. At the end of the fifties, Canadians were faced with a high rate of unemployment and a stagnating economy. At the close of the sixties, the unemployment rate was once again edging upward but the foremost problem confronting our monetary and fiscal authorities at the beginning of the seventies is clearly not one of stimulating the economy but keeping it under restraint until inflationary pressures ease. Despite this tendency for the Canadian economy to end a decade on a somewhat sour note, there was no lack of optimism about the sixties ten years ago and there are very few today who are not looking for bigger and better advances in the seventies, once the obstacles of inflation have been hurdled.

In the modern, complex world, economic growth can no longer be said to result solely from the classic factors of production, land, labour, and capital. Technological innovation, monetary and fiscal policy, psychology, social conflict, and many other factors all have a more or less direct influence on

---

*Reprinted from Bank of Montreal, *Business Review*, January 28, 1970, by permission of the editor.
[1] Based on B of M Estimate as are all 1969 plots on charts.

economic progress. Yet at the risk of oversimplification, it is often useful to go back to some of the basic ingredients, and it is an old adage but a true one that a country's people are its most important asset.

In Canada, the postwar years were characterized by a high birth rate and this generally persisted throughout the fifties. Thus the country moved into the sixties with a relatively large group of young people; in the 1961 census there were 6.2 million in the 0-14 age group, representing 34 percent of the total population, in comparison with 4.3 million, or 30 percent, at the time of the 1951 census. During the sixties, the birth rate fell markedly as, under the influence of "the pill" and other factors, social habits changed in the direction of smaller families.

Looking forward through the seventies, there are indications that the birth rate will level out or even rise somewhat. While many of the social influences of the sixties will continue to prevail, the proportion of the population in the marriageable age group will be larger. With the generally high level of training and education they have received, they should be able to command good incomes and a higher rate of family formation might reasonably be expected.

The changing age composition of the population has other important implications. While pressure on school facilities of the kind that built up during the fifties and sixties will diminish considerably, there is little relief in sight for universities, particularly in view of the trend toward more students continuing their education through university and even into graduate school. On the other hand, those born in the fifties will, in many cases, be making their first productive contributions to the economy and, with their better training and education, they should act as an impetus to the economy's productivity and growth.

Just as there have been notable changes in the age structure of Canadians in the last two decades, there have been similar changes in the age composition of the labour force, in this case, complicated by changing participation rates for men and women. As can be seen from Figure 2, the male participation rate has declined steadily, while the female participation rate has shown an equally persistent tendency to rise, with the result that the

FIGURE 1

BIRTH RATES*

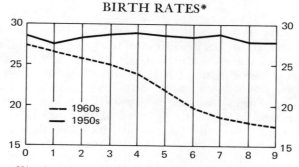

*Number of births per 1,000 of population.

ratio of men to women in the labour force declined from 78 percent in 1950 to 68 percent in 1969.

Generally speaking, the male participation rate fell most rapidly during periods of slow growth or recession, such as the late fifties and early sixties. This pattern is to be expected because when jobs are hard to get and hold, those in the younger age groups will stay in school rather than enter the labour force, while men who have retired will not attempt to get a job. Throughout the whole period, in fact, the trend toward younger men remaining longer in school or college and the increased social security benefits accruing to those over sixty-five have probably been the principal factors in the decline of the male participation rate. While these influences will undoubtedly continue to have some effect into the seventies, it is expected that the male participation rate will begin to level out.

FIGURE 2

PARTICIPATION RATES*

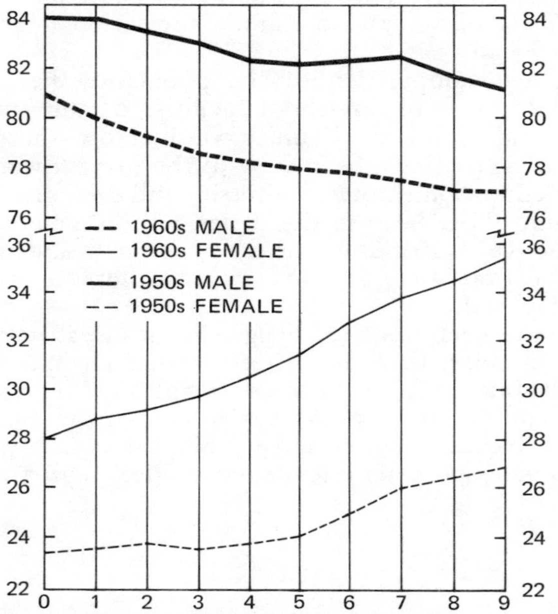

*Number of males or females in the labour force as a percentage of the total male or female population 14 years of age and over.

The rise in female participation rates, which began to manifest itself in the mid-fifties and accelerated in the sixties, resulted from a different set of factors. Better and higher education of women, together with the rise of the service industries, opened up more attractive job opportunities for the female population. The percentage of married females in the labour force rose from 11 percent in 1951 to 34 percent in 1969 and, in many cases, wives were working because they wanted to, and liked their jobs, rather than for pecuniary reasons alone. In addition, labour-saving devices in the home and the practice of not starting a family for several years after marriage added to the influx of females into the labour force. As in the case of the male participation rate, the pace of economic activity had a noticeable effect on the female rate, with the most pronounced increases coming in the years of buoyant economic growth. The trend toward more female participation in the labour force should continue into the seventies, but will probably increase more slowly as family formations increase.

As might be expected, the employment pattern has shown much more variation in response to the pace of economic activity than that exhibited by the labour force. The lowest unemployment rates for the entire period were in the early fifties. After a brief pause in 1954, employment again grew strongly during the natural resource based boom, but with the recession of 1958, the unemployment rate shot up to 7 percent and a serious unemployment problem became one of the legacies of the fifties to the sixties. As the economy picked up steam, the gap between labour force and employment was steadily narrowed until 1966 when the low point of the decade was reached. Thereafter, as inflation and other problems interfered with stable economic growth, and the use of restrictive policies became necessary, the rate of unemployment began to rise again to its present level of about 5 percent, and once more Canadians enter a new decade with a relatively high proportion of the population out of work.

The outlook for the seventies will depend in a large measure, in the early years at least, upon the success achieved in controlling price pressures and defeating inflationary psychology. Canada's population mix assures that the labour force will continue to grow at a relatively rapid pace as those who put off looking for work in the sixties in order to continue their education will enter the job market in the coming decade. Thus the problem of getting the economy back on the path of stable growth assumes increasing importance.

In view of the extreme preoccupation with price increases at the present time, it is interesting to observe from the GNE price deflator chart (Figure 4) that prices in the sixties actually rose less than in the fifties. In fact, the

FIGURE 3

LABOUR FORCE AND EMPLOYMENT*

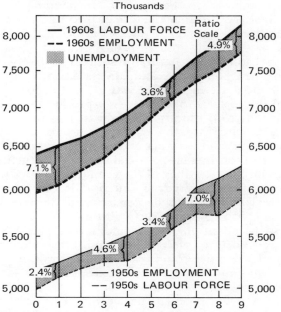

*Percentages shown are unemployment rates for high and low years.

FIGURE 4

PRICES*

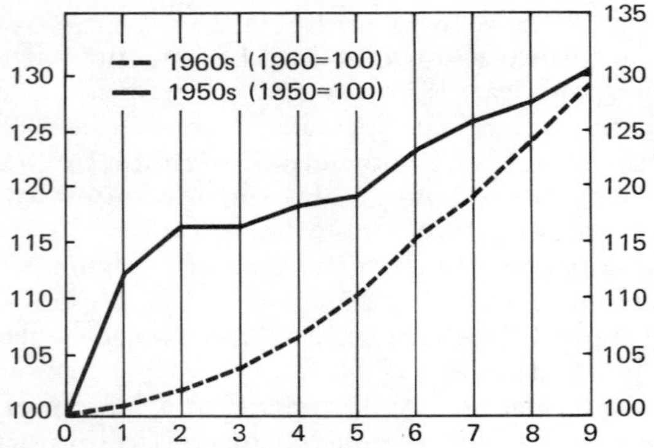

*GNE price deflator

price increases of the last few years have been considerably less severe than
in the early fifties when, after the removal of wartime controls, the pent-up
demand of the forties, the reconstruction needs of Europe, and the exigencies
of the Korean conflict vented their full force on the Canadian economy,
with the result that between 1950 and 1952 prices rose at an average rate of
almost 8 percent per annum. Thereafter, price increases flatten out until
mid-decade and the beginning of the natural resource boom. In the sixties,
the price index line forms almost a perfect geometric curve with the rate of
increase accelerating fairly constantly throughout the decade.

With current emphasis so heavily on the reduction of inflationary
pressures, it is to be expected that the rate of price increases will moderate in
the coming years, but–a number of factors indicate that there will be substantial upward pressure on prices throughout the seventies. Worldwide
demand for both capital and natural resources is likely to become even
stronger over the next ten years and, unless advances in technology and
exploration can contribute in a major way on the supply side, competition
will intensify and the costs of these factors of production will be bid up.

Consumer demand, too, promises to add fuel to the fires. The spending
patterns of those moving into the 23-34 age group are considerably more
liberal than their elders, and with many earning good salaries, their influence
will be felt in the market. Increasing social security and medical benefits also
tend to impart an inflationary bias to the economy as does the fact that only
about 20 percent of our present population is old enough to have experienced the effect of a serious depression and the remaining 80 percent
seem less concerned with saving for difficult times.

Government spending in the fifties and sixties produced an interesting
pattern. At the federal level, defence expenditures in connection with the
Korean War played a decisive role in the early fifties but for the rest of the
decade, increases were moderate with the exception of a slightly sharper rise
in 1958. This moderation was carried through until the mid-sixties after
which the slope of the line steepens noticeably. This acceleration in government spending came mainly in the categories of social welfare and transfers

to other levels of government, with the fastest growing transfer items in the fields of health, education, and welfare.

At the provincial and local level, the rise in government expenditures was considerably more rapid than at the federal level during both decades. In addition to disbursements for health and welfare, major investments had to be made in the school system, in roads (as the number of motor vehicles increased from 2.6 million to 8 million), and in providing services for new housing.

While, as noted earlier, primary and secondary school enrolment has passed its peak, there will continue to be substantial pressure during the seventies on university facilites. In addition, regeneration of cities will constitute a major demand and there will be little let up in the fields of health and welfare, particularly in view of the advent of medicare and the crucial need to combat poverty. The control of pollution in all its varied forms and the transportation boom will also make their claims on the government coffers, so that, all in all, the decade of the seventies is likely to witness continuing demand on the government sector.

In the private sector allusion has already been made to consumer spending which has been rising steadily and may be expected to continue to rise. Business gross fixed capital formation, on the other hand, has followed a more erratic pattern. In the early fifties, strong demand forces and the need to retool after wartime production produced several years of rapid growth in investment. After a brief pause in 1954, the discovery and development of new natural resources again sent investment on a steep upward climb. Then came a longer correctional period that lasted into the early sixties, before, once again, capital formation gathered steam and rose to new heights.

FIGURE 5

GOVERNMENT EXPENDITURES*

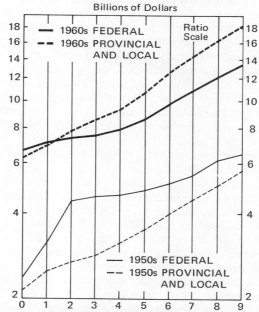

*Including all transfer payments but excluding Canada and Quebec pension plans and hospital expenditures.

FIGURE 6

BUSINESS GROSS FIXED CAPITAL FORMATION

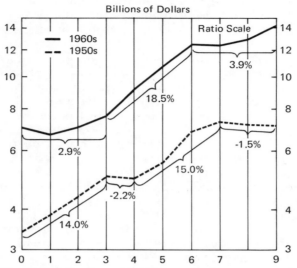

Billions of Dollars

Percentages represent average annual rates of change between years indicated

During the last few years we have been encountering a pause somewhat similar to the one that characterized the end of the fifties and the beginning of the sixties. Is capital investment once more poised for a take-off? There are many indications that it is, and that once anti-inflationary restraints are relaxed, the seventies, like the fifties and sixties, will register a period of strong investment growth. The rate of technological advance in the fifties, and more particularly in the sixties, was extremely rapid, and the coming decade should see the implementation of many of the results, especially in such fields as transportation and communication. The opening of the Arctic and the rising market for British Columbia's natural resources will also involve substantial capital outlays. On the housing side, the expected increase in family formations will assure a high demand for residential capital.

In the field of international trade, Canada's record in the sixties was much better than in the fifties. During the early years of the fifties, postwar reconstruction demands and again the Korean conflict produced a rapid expansion of exports, but at the same time the surge in capital investment in Canada resulted in heavy imports of machinery and equipment. As the decade wore on, other sources of supply were built up around the world and Canada's competitive position deteriorated. In addition, the inflow of foreign investment into Canada created a strong demand for Canadian dollars and, in the circumstances of a floating exchange rate, our currency moved to a premium in world markets and the competitiveness of Canada's exports was further undermined.

In 1962 the Canadian dollar was pegged at US 92½ cents and thereafter the trade deficit in goods and services narrowed. In 1965 the export picture

FIGURE 7

EXPORTS AND IMPORTS OF GOODS
AND SERVICES

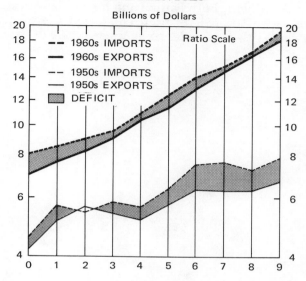

further brightened with the negotiation of the auto pact with the United States, and in the succeeding years motor vehicle shipments to that country provided the main impetus to a strong export growth. Imports, however, continued to increase at a rapid rate in response to the sustained rise in capital spending, and so the deficit remained substantial. In the closing years of the decade, exports were affected by the deterioration of the world wheat market, but imports responded even more to the virtual stagnation of investment, and in 1968 Canada almost registered a surplus for the first time since 1952.

It is difficult to predict the course of Canada's foreign trade in the decade to come. The outlook for wheat, at least for the immediate future, is not bright, and the initial impetus of the auto pact in bringing trade in automobiles into somewhat better balance is certainly nearing its end. On the plus side, arrangements have been made for the sale of vast quantities of raw materials to new buyers, and the content of Canadian exports is trending toward more fully manufactured goods for which demand should not only be steadier but more buoyant. As a corollary to this, Canada's dependence on foreign sources for machinery and equipment should lessen so that even in the face of a new surge of capital expansion, the gap between imports and exports should remain within reasonable bounds.

What does all this add up to for Canada in the seventies? Despite the current array of problems, it is hard not to be optimistic. Canada's population mix and improved levels of training and education point both to a strong sustained level of demand, and also to increases in productivity that will help to improve the supply picture. The Canadian economy will continue to rely heavily on natural resources but the manufacturing sector should become increasingly sophisticated and account for an ever larger share of total activity. The rising emphasis on social problems that appeared in the sixties will be carried into the seventies and social improvements will constitute a major claim on our resources. All in all, the demands on the economy will be heavy but Canada is one of the most richly endowed countries in the world with both natural and human resources, and once the disruptive forces of inflation have been conquered Canadians can, on the whole, look forward with confidence to another decade of new records.

31. THE PERFORMANCE CHALLENGES FOR THE SEVENTIES*

Economic Council of Canada

There are many economic challenges for Canada in the 1970s. A large number of them arise from questions about how Canadians wish to make use of their growing resources to meet the future aspirations of their society — about how to determine priorities among the vast and growing list of competing claims on national productive capabilities, and about how our economic system can serve these ends in the most appropriate and effective ways.

Another group of challenges — those with which we are basically concerned here — are the economic performance challenges. These arise in the context of five basic economic and social goals — full employment, a high and sustained rate of economic growth, reasonable price stability, a viable balance of payments position, and an equitable distribution of rising incomes. During the past quarter-century they have become, both in Canada and elsewhere, more comprehensive, more explicit, and more ambitious. They may also have become more difficult to attain consistently, especially under conditions of increased international economic interdependence, rapid urbanization, the substantial shift toward the service industries, and swift technological and other change. The key requirement for sustained good performance in relation to these goals is that they must be achieved concurrently, even though they are not all complementary and reinforcing. We have viewed the following performance challenges of the 1970s agains the background of these considerations.

Measuring Up to Potentials

In the 1960s, Canada entered a period of accelerated potential growth, arising mainly from the accelerated growth of its labour force, and hence of potential employment. The extended period of exceptionally high birth rates from the late 1940s, through the 1950s means that there will be large

*Reprinted from Economic Council of Canada, *Performance and Potential mid-1950s to mid-1970s,* September, 1970, pp. 65—71, by permission of Information Canada.

numbers of new entrants into the labour force in the 1970s. As a result, Canada's potential growth rate will be high for the 1970s, both in relation to historical experience in Canada and in relation to the potential growth rate of most other industrial countries.

To attain potential output in 1975, Gross National Product (in constant 1969 dollars) will need to rise at an average annual rate of about 5½ percent from 1969 to 1975. This would imply an increase (in terms of 1969 dollars) of over 30 billion to a level of close to 110 billion in 1975. Over the last half of the 1970s, the potential growth rate of the Canadian economy would still be high — over 5 percent. This would imply a further increase in GNP in the latter part of the 1970s of about an equivalent real dollar magnitude, so that potential GNP by 1980 would be roughly of the order of 140 billion (in 1969 dollars).

A very large rise in employment will be needed to reach the full-employment potential of the economy by 1975 — about 1.3 to 1.4 million more jobs than now exist in 1970. Moreover, over the 1975-80 period, about 1.2 million additional jobs will be required. In other words, at least 2½ million net new jobs will be required in Canada over the coming decade.

Along with this, there will be a need for a large rise in new capital investment to provide both equipment and structures for the rapidly rising numbers of employed persons, and housing and other social capital — especially in the country's rapidly growing urban areas. On the basis of the calculations underlying our *Sixth Annual Review*, the volume of total government and private investment is estimated to rise by well over 7 percent per year from 1969 to potential in 1975, or from 17 billion in 1969 to over 26 billion in 1975 (in constant 1969 dollars). This includes, among other things, an allowance for building more than 1¼ million new housing units over these six years.

The maintenance of a strong growth rate in productivity — that is, the efficiency with which labour, capital, and other productive resources are used — will also pose a major challenge. Productivity growth is at the heart of the process of economic growth. It is the essential means, in the longer run, of achieving higher standards of living and an enhanced quality of life for all Canadians. Also, Canada will almost certainly be facing heightened competition in world export markets in the 1970s, from both developed and developing countries, and in both resource and highly manufactured products. In these circumstances, the maintenance of strong and sustained productivity growth is a matter of central importance to the satisfactory performance of the economy as a whole. Moreover, given the highly capital-intensive nature of the Canadian economy, continued access to outside sources of capital will be required throughout the 1970s. Under conditions of well-sustained world growth, the coming decade is likely to be one of heavy competing demands for world supplies of capital. This makes it imperative that available capital be managed with a high degree of competence and efficiency.

There are, of course, some factors that will operate to support improved productivity growth in the 1970s, notably the rising levels of experience, skills, and educational attainments of the labour force. But there are also some other factors that may tend to increase the difficulties of sustaining good productivity growth — for example, the smaller scope for reallocating resources from some sectors in which average *levels* of productivity have been relatively low, such as agriculture and fishing, to other sectors in which they are relatively high.

A new ingredient in the challenges both for adequate job creation and for productivity growth in the 1970s will be the unprecedented flow into the labour markets of high-level manpower from the postsecondary educational systems. This influx of highly educated manpower should provide some of the initial returns from the vast public investment in education that was made during the 1950s and 1960s. This expansion involved, among other things, an attempt to enlarge the availability of high-level manpower. Undergraduate enrolment in universities increased during the 1960s at a rate of over 10 percent per year and graduate enrolment at over 20 percent per year. At the same time a new system of postsecondary institutions in the form of community colleges and institutes of technology was established.

The returns from the expansion in education could be substantial during the 1970s. But greater attention needs to be directed to the possibilities here, and various adjustments are needed in the private and government sectors of the economy in order to employ effectively and productively the rapidly rising volume of high-level manpower. The US economy has demonstrated that effective use can be made of larger proportions of more highly educated manpower than now exist in Canada. But the magnitude of the adjustment problems should not be minimized, if surpluses or underutilization of such people are to be averted in Canada, during this period of very rapid growth in the supply of such manpower flowing from the educational system. Adjustments in the recruiting and manpower utilization policies and practices of employers are needed. Adjustments may also be required in the attitudes and training of some of these highly educated young people whose schooling could prove to have been too highly concentrated on academic matters in the light of the types of jobs that are most likely to become available during the 1970s. The universities must increasingly face the challenge of giving greater attention to preparing students for nonacademic employment and for flexible adaptation to changing patterns of job opportunities which cannot be easily and accurately anticipated.

Behind these tremendous challenges of appropriate new job creation, new capital formation, and sustained productivity growth, lie other major challenges — the challenge of generating a large (but not excessive) growth in demand, the challenge of achieving a high rate of domestic savings and adequate access to external capital, the challenge of facilitating flexible adjustments to fundamental structural changes in patterns of production and consumption, to mention only a few.

Price Stability

No less important in the 1970s will be the challenge of reconciling good performance in price stability with good performance in relation to employment and growth potentials. We have never regarded full employment and price stability as "either/or" objectives. Rather, the essential challenge is to pursue both of these goals together in a balanced way and in a longer-run time perspective.

Reconciliation of the employment and price goals will require the application of more than the "big levers" of monetary and fiscal policy. What is required, in addition to appropriate operation of the demand policies, are other policies that can reach into the economic process to stimulate productivity growth, strengthen competitive forces, and eliminate rigidities that often exist on the supply side leading to inflationary pressures and expectations. These structural rigidities cannot be eliminated by monetary and fiscal restraints.

The maintenance of price stability in our view is a *long-run challenge*. Indeed, only if we approach this goal on this basis, are we likely to achieve a price performance consistently as good as, or better than, that of the United States and other industrial countries. It should therefore be viewed as a continuing task *for the whole decade ahead* – perhaps even one that could become an increasingly difficult challenge. Inflationary forces are highly complex. They emanate from both domestic and external sources, from both demand and supply imbalances, from structural shifts and institutional rigidities, from a wide range of cost and income pressures, and from lack of adequate resistance, for various reasons, to such pressures. International price changes will have a significant influence on Canada's price performance in the 1970s. But so will domestic conditions. In this contest, much attention is generally focussed on demand conditions – and with good reason, for this is a highly important matter. But more attention needs to be devoted to other matters that are no less important – including supply, cost, and competitive conditions; the bases for achieving strong productivity growth to facilitate stability (and, wherever possible, reductions) in unit labour and capital costs; and the instabilities and cost increases in the housing sector, which have made it a major source of inflation.

In this context, there are two special problem areas to which Canadians will need to devote more attention in the 1970s. One is the challenge of finding appropriate conditions under which the construction sector, which has become a major source of instability in the economy, may better serve the public interest and its own interests. The other is the even more important challenge of finding effective means for limiting the broad tide of inflation flowing from the rapidly growing service sectors of the economy – health and education, government administration, public transportation, and even many of the commercial services. As already noted above, in these sectors, measured productivity increases appear to be low, and price increases strong and sustained. As we noted earlier, many of these activities tend to be operating on an essentially "cost-plus" basis.

Maintaining a Strong International Position

The maintenance of a strong international position will also be an important performance challenge for the 1970s. Increased exports and the maintenance of adequate access to external sources of capital are needed in order to finance both the increased imports of goods and services that Canadians will demand, and increased Canadian foreign investment and aid. Fortunately, market prospects are generally bright at the outset of the decade. We have already drawn attention to the large growth of potential markets in the 1970s among our principal trading partners. There may, of course, be significant problems in some fields (such as markets for Canadian agricultural products); these problems imply a continuing need for vigorous export effort, as well as sustained efforts to ease trade restrictions affecting these exports. On the other hand, there are broad elements of strength in the export position in forest and mineral products, as well as in various highly manufactured goods. But Canada's potential in international trade in the 1970s cannot be achieved unless producers and exporters struggle unrelentingly, with appropriate supporting government policies and programs, to enhance their competitiveness in domestic and world markets. Moreover, they may well have to do so under conditions that may not be as favourable as in the 1960s, when the substantial devaluation of the Canadian dollar was an important factor strengthening the international competitive position of many industries.

The maintenance of a strong international position will also not be assured unless international co-operation is energetically pursued by Canada and her trading partners as a mutually beneficial goal. As already noted early in this report, the past decade has been a period of rapidly growing economic interdependence among nations. This has been reflected, among other things, in the huge expansion of world trade; the greatly increased mobility of capital, technology, and manpower; and the rise of the multinational corporation. This trend toward greater economic interdependence will continue to be a prominent feature of international life in the 1970s, perhaps even on an increasing scale, if world economic development is generally strong and well sustained.

Increased international economic interdependence has, on the whole, been a factor contributing powerfully to the historical growth and development of the Canadian economy. Over a century ago, at the time of Confederation, Canada was a largely empty country, with a small and underdeveloped economy. Without inflows of people, capital, knowledge, and technology from abroad, and without the development of growing external markets for Canadian products, Canada's economy would have remained small and relatively underdeveloped. But this country's high degree of international interdependence has not only brought benefits but has also given rise to problems. A general trend toward increased international economic interdependence over the coming decade would not only provide new opportunities for Canadians, but would also raise new questions about how the interests and aspirations of Canadians can best be served in such conditions. One of the major challenges of the 1970s will be that of finding effective means to harness the benefits arising from widening economic interdependence to the development of a more mature and self-confident national economy.

Equitable Distribution of Rising Incomes

The more equitable distribution of rising incomes will undoubtedly come into greater prominence as an economic and social goal in the 1970s. In particular, the challenges of narrowing regional economic disparities and eliminating poverty clearly need, and will claim, increasing emphasis. There are, of course, important human and social reasons for placing more emphasis on these challenges. But there are good economic reasons too. As we have emphasized in our earlier work, poverty — especially poverty of the dimensions and characteristics evident in Canada — places an economic burden on society. It acts as a brake on Canada's economic growth and imposes economic costs that detract from the well-being of *all* Canadians. Similarly, regional disparities, which reflect, in economic terms, unutilized or underutilized resources of human capital and relatively inefficient use of productive resources in low income regions, also detract from good economic performance — not only for the region but for the national economy. Thus, for the 1970s, substantial progress toward the elimination of poverty and the narrowing of regional disparities should be considered not only as challenges that should embody concern for the human and social consequences of the existence of poverty and wide disparities, but also as major *economic performance* challenges.

C. MONEY AND BANKING

Money, by overcoming the difficulties of barter transactions, deserves to be ranked as one of man's greatest inventions, or developments, for it has evolved over the ages. By facilitating the exchange of goods and services through the establishment of a regime of prices, money has played a leading role in making possible the specialization of industry, the organization of production upon the basis of a minute division of labour, and the establishment of nationwide and international markets. Thus Honor Croome, a British economist, contends that splitting exchange into buying and selling is "a discovery of more importance to human material progress than the splitting of the atom is ever likely to be." Perhaps not an altogether too sweeping statement in the face of the widespread technological progress of the past two centuries.

At present there is widespread disagreement as to which financial assets should and should not be included in the term "the money supply." In consequence, the validity of many propositions relating to monetary and banking matters often depends on exactly what is meant by the quantity of money. What may be shown to be the case with a wide definition of the concept may well be untrue of a narrow definition, and vice versa. Reading 32 uses a money supply matrix to suggest certain logical concepts and measures of money supply.

Until recently, the granting of highly liquid loans for short-term commercial purposes was generally looked upon as an essential characteristic of commercial banks. Times have changed, and the banks have greatly expanded their activities to include the purchase of large volumes of securities and the extension of many kinds of loans and services. Indeed, commercial banks are on their way to becoming "department stores of financial services." Reading 33 comments on the forces that have made the banking industry a leader in innovation and diversification today, and indicates some potential drawbacks of diversification.

32. THE CONCEPT AND MEASURE OF MONEY SUPPLY*

J.A. Galbraith

Measures of money supply are usually built up on a piecemeal basis. Individual items are identified or defined as money and added to other such items to obtain something that is referred to as "money supply." Each likely item is examined on its merit and a decision made, with supporting argument where it is felt called for, whether or not to include the item in the money supply. There is no overall uniform plan for selection or rejection. An example of the procedure is provided by government deposits. When the decision is made not to count government deposits in the money supply, the supporting argument often used is that central government behaviour is not motivated by money holdings to the same extent as is the behaviour of other spending units. A similar example is provided by the universal omission of money holdings of banks from the money supply measures. This is justified on the grounds that such money holdings serve as reserves for money issued by the banks and such reserves should not be counted.

In other words, in the usual way in which the concept and measure of money supply is built up, there does not seem to be any overall plan to serve as a guide. The money supply measure is built up piece by piece. As a result it is not easy to assess its logical consistency or to understand the concept that is being measured.

An alternative approach is to set out some overall plan or arrangement with the aid of which money supply concepts and measures can be formulated. A money supply matrix is one such plan or arrangement. What is here called a money supply matrix is simply a row and column arrangement, with a row for each supplier of money, and a column for each major holder of money. Such a matrix is not concerned with settling the question of "what is money," but rather with "what money" or "whose money" is being incorporated into money supply.

The matrix originates with the commonplace observation that all items of

---

*Reprinted from J.A. Galbraith, "The Concept and Measure of Money Supply," *The Canadian Banker*, Winter, 1965, pp. 28—35, by permission of the editor and author.
Dr. Galbraith is director of economic research, Royal Bank of Canada and Professor of Economics, McGill University, Montreal.

money issued and outstanding must be held by someone, and is built up on the common-sense notion that if an item is money it remains money for as long as it is outstanding regardless of who holds it. For example, if coins are money, it does not seem logical to stop classifying them as money when they are transferred from the public to banks.

In a modern economy the items generally classed as money are coins, notes, and deposits.[1] The suppliers of these items are the central government which operates a mint that produces coins, the central bank which may issue notes as well as deposits, domestic banks, and domestic near-banks if they issue transferable deposits similar to those of the banks. In the money supply matrix presented here, these money suppliers are listed in the left-hand column.[2]

Different categories of money holders are listed across the top of the matrix to provide the column headings. The four money suppliers shown in the left-hand column are also shown as holders of money and so provide the headings for the first four columns under "holders of money" in the matrix. Any one supplier of money can be a holder of the money items issued by the other suppliers. Column (5) in the matrix, headed "all others," includes all other holders of the money items issued and represents not only the general public but nondomestic central banks, central governments, banks, and near-banks.

In the boxes formed by the rows and columns are entered the items issued by the supplier listed in the row heading and held by the holder listed in the column heading. Thus, in the box formed by row (2), headed "central government," and column (2), headed "banks," are entered the coins issued by the central government and held by domestic banks.

The coins and notes entered in the various boxes are, of course, domestic currency items and represent amounts issued and outstanding.[3] Only domestic currency deposits are entered in the matrix and only those deposits of a type generally used as a means of payment. This means that deposits must be transferable directly between parties. A deposit that must be converted into currency before the sum it represents can be transferred is not capable of serving directly as a means of payment. In other words, strictly speaking, only deposits capable of being transferred directly to others, either by cheque or by giro, or some other order, should be entered in the money supply matrix.

Deposits are also entered net of supplier's float. This float arises because it takes two entries to transfer a deposit. When the two entries cannot be made on the same day, the first entry to be made alters the amount of deposits issued and outstanding. For example, a cheque drawn on bank B and received for deposit at bank A increases deposits at bank A the moment it is credited to the depositor's account. When the cheque gets back to bank B, say a day or two later, it is debited to a deposit account there, and deposits are reduced. While the cheque is in transit, or float, deposits are larger than

---

[1] These are the main means of payment. No doubt numerous examples can be found of items being used as a means of payment in isolated, local, or specialized transactions and circumstances. If such items are not statistically important in the total of all items used as a means of payment, the items can be ignored.

[2] Only domestically-based banks and near-banks are listed as suppliers. Foreign banks (and near-banks) not located in the country may provide deposits denominated in the currency of that country. Euro-dollar deposits are of this nature. Such deposits are not entered in the money supply matrix.

[3] This includes coins and notes lost and destroyed, and excludes any foreign currency coins and notes that may be in circulation.

TABLE 1

A MONEY SUPPLY MATRIX

Holders of Money

Suppliers of Money	(1) Central Bank	(2) Banks (domestic)	(3) Central Government	(4) Near-banks (domestic)	(5) All Others	Totals
(1) Central Bank	–	notes, deposits	notes*, deposits	notes*, deposits	notes*, deposits	notes, deposits
(2) Central Government	coins*	coins	coins*	coins*	coins*	coins
(3) Banks (domestic)	–	deposits*	deposits**	deposits*	deposits*	deposits
(4) Near-banks (domestic)		–	deposits	deposits	deposits	deposits
Totals	coins*	C.B. deposits, bank deposits*	C.B. deposits, bank deposits**, near-bank deposits	C.B. deposits, bank deposits*, near-bank deposits	C.B. deposits, bank deposits*, near-bank deposits	C.B. deposits, bank deposits, near-bank deposits

Notes

(1) Only includes domestic coins, notes, and deposits, issued and outstanding.

(2) All deposits are net of float—i.e., represent what deposits would be if none in process of being transferred, or if all entries in deposit accounts could be made simultaneously. Only deposits subject to chequing or otherwise transferable should be entered.

(3) A—means none held.

* Items always included in official measures of Canadian money supply.

** Item included in one official measure of Canadian money supply.

they otherwise would be. Hence, by deducting from deposits cheques in the hands of the banks which have not yet been charged against the deposits drawn upon, deposits are shown as they would be if all entries for transferring deposits could be made on the same day. Thus, deposits shown in the matrix are the amounts issued and outstanding adjusted for float.[4]

The entries in the various boxes of the matrix may now be examined. Row (1) records all the domestic money items issued by the central bank. Under the conditions assumed for this matrix, the central bank issues domestic currency notes intended for circulation and deposits. These notes and deposits must be held by someone. Accordingly, in the matrix the notes are shown as being held by domestic banks, the central government, domestic near-banks, and all others. It is assumed that the central bank does not hold any "issued" notes, just unissued notes, so that there is no entry made in row (1), column (1). Deposits with the central bank, also recorded in row (1), are normally held by banks and the central government. But, even in Canada, some near-banks (the Quebec savings banks) hold central bank deposits. And since column (5), headed "all others," includes foreign central banks and official international organizations which may hold central bank deposits provided by the country in question, central bank deposits are also shown in the matrix as being held by all others, in column (5).

The central government frequently runs the mint, as is the case in Canada and the United States. Consequently, the central government in the matrix is shown as a supplier of money. Through the mint it issues coins which will be held by all holders of money shown in the matrix. The central bank will certainly hold some issued coins, as an inventory asset, and various departments (other than the mint) of the central government, as a result of their money transactions with the public, will be found holding issued coins in their tills. Domestic banks provide domestic currency deposits that may be held by other domestic banks (hence the entry in row (3) column (2)),[5] by the central government, by domestic near-banks, and by the public, including foreign banks. A central bank, however, normally does not hold deposit balances with a domestic bank, and hence no entry is made in row (3) column (1). If domestic near-banks issue transferable deposits, these deposits may be held by the central government (the Government of Canada has some deposits with the Quebec savings banks), by other domestic near-banks, and by the public. The central bank and domestic banks normally will not hold near-bank deposits; hence, in row (4) nothing is recorded under columns (1) and (2).

The money supply matrix as constructed and filled in can now be used to suggest certain logical concepts and measures of money supply. One logical measure of money supply never advocated or used, however, would be the total of the row or column totals recorded in the lower right-hand corner of the matrix. This might be called "everybody's money supply." It is the sum total of all domestic money items issued, and outstanding, by domestic-based suppliers, which equals the total amount of all such money items held by all.

---

[4] They include those deposits that have been forgotten by their holders.

[5] On a consolidated basis deposits issued by domestic banks and held by other domestic banks would be netted out. The figures are entered here on a combined basis because domestic deposits held by domestic banks represent money outstanding and so should be shown as such. The same applies for domestic near-bank deposits held by other domestic near-banks.

Smaller and more restricted money supply measures may be extracted from the matrix. All the money items issued by one or more, but not all, of the suppliers of money could be used to give a measure of money supply. Such a measure can be compiled by taking one or more (but not all) of the row totals shown in the last column. This would give a concept of the money supply as the amount of all money items issued by the suppliers selected. For example, the total of the first three rows in the matrix would give as a concept of the money supply all money items issued by the central bank, central government, and domestic banks, regardless of where held.

Other, and different, measures of money supply, corresponding to other concepts of money supply, can be obtained by concentrating on the holders and ignoring the suppliers. These measures are given by the totals of the columns. Thus, the total of column (5) gives a measure of money supply that corresponds to the concept of all money items held by the general public, regardless of who provided the items.[6]

Official measures of money supply combine usually both a holder and a supplier concept. That is, they take the money items issued by certain suppliers that are in the hands of certain holders. For example, the money items issued by the first three suppliers in the matrix and held by the last two holders, in columns (4) and (5), give a logically consistent measure of money supply. This measure is obtained by adding rows (1) through (3) in columns (4) and (5). The resulting figure does not give total money supply, or "the" money supply. It represents money items issued by the central bank, the central government, and domestic banks, and held by domestic near-banks and the general public.[7]

In countries, such as the United States, where near-banks do not provide transferable deposits, row (4) of the matrix would be empty. In Canada, where near-banks do provide transferable deposits, omission of near-bank deposits from official measures of money supply means a narrowing of the concept of what is being measured, namely, money items issued by the central bank, the central government, and domestic banks held by certain holders.

The logical consistency of the two official Canadian measures of money supply may now be assessed with the aid of the money supply matrix.[8] One of the measures is made up of coins and notes outside the chartered banks plus all chartered bank Canadian dollar deposits. This includes all coins

---

[6] Ignoring the money items of other holders here is perfectly logical and consistent with the concept of measuring only the money holdings of the general public and calling the total "money supply." Hence, in this case, the money holdings of banks, the total of column (2), representing the cash reserves of the banks, are excluded for the obvious reason that they are not part of the money holdings of the general public. There is no need for an involved explanation that cash holdings of banks serve as backing for other money items and so bank holdings should be excluded to avoid double counting. Similarly, the exclusion of central government money holdings is equally simple to explain on the grounds that here it is desired to measure only the money holdings of the general public. Again, there is no need for a more tortuous explanation in terms of government money balance behaviour being radically different from that of the general public. In other words, a money supply matrix also offers a simpler means of explaining the exclusion of items from any given restricted money supply measure.

[7] This may also be viewed as a net supply concept since it can be derived by deducting from the total amount of coins, notes, and deposits issued by these three suppliers, the coins, notes, and deposits held by these three suppliers — that is, by deducting the totals for the first three rows in columns (1) to (3) from the totals for rows (1) to (3).

[8] Only the formulation of the analytical framework of the official measures is considered. Imperfections in filling in the framework, such as the inclusion of nontransferable deposits, are not discussed.

issued by the central government (the Royal Canadian Mint) except those coins held by the chartered banks, as can be seen by reference to row (2) in the matrix. It excludes the entries in row (1) under column (2) but includes the entries for notes in row (1) under columns (3), (4), and (5), while excluding central bank deposits under these columns in that row. It appears inconsistent to count central bank notes in the hands of certain holders but not to count their holdings of central bank deposits. In row (3) all entries are counted, even chartered bank deposits held by other chartered banks, as recorded under column (2) for row (3). This inclusion of interbank deposits is not consistent with the omission of coins, notes, and central bank deposits held by banks. The omission of these items is consistent with a money supply measure that aims at showing the amount of money supply items held by nonbanks. The inclusion of interbank deposits is not consistent with this aim.

The official measure would be logically consistent if — in addition to excluding all of row (4), as it does — it also excluded all of column (1), which it apparently does not, all of column (2), and if it included everything in the first three rows of columns (3) to (5). This would give a figure for money supply representing all the money items issued by the central bank, the central government, and banks held outside the banking system and the central bank. This would not be a total money supply figure in any sense because of the omitted items, but it would be a logically consistent measure.

Another official measure of money supply in Canada is obtained by deducting government chartered bank deposits from the official measure just described. This eliminates the entry for deposits under column (3) in row (3) of the matrix but includes the entry for notes and coins in column (3). Again, it is logically inconsistent to remove all government deposits from a money supply measure without also removing government holdings of coins and notes.

A logically consistent measure of money supply, which excludes the central government, would take only the items under columns (4) and (5), for at least the first three rows. This would give a money supply measure representing the concept of all money items provided by the central bank, the central government, and domestic banks, held outside the central bank, the central government, and domestic banks.

Deviations between official measures of money supply and logically consistent measures are not necessarily significant. Many deviations may be justified on the grounds of statistical convenience. The main value of constructing logically consistent money supply measures from a money supply matrix and comparing official measures with them is to help keep clear what the actual measures represent if even only approximately. Use of a money supply matrix in this way should help to improve understanding and interpretation of money supply measures.

33. WHAT SHOULD A BANK DO?*

Paul S. Nadler

In his famous article, "Marketing Myopia"[1] Theodore Levitt indicated that many industries have faced serious trouble simply because they did not define their functions properly. The railroads let the airlines, trucks, and buses take away much of their business because they felt they were in the railroad business and not the transportation business. Similarly the motion picture companies did not recognize that they were in the entertainment industry and not just the movie industry until television had caused considerable financial havoc. Once an industry recognizes what its real function is and starts to compete in its proper sphere, Mr. Levitt concluded, then it can adjust to change and continue to play an important role in the economy.

Mr. Levitt's article is of extreme importance to banking today; for bankers throughout the world are wondering, "What should a bank do?"

In the United States at present, banks not only provide a wide variety of specialized lending services but also collect rent, prepare freight bills for truck lines, send out bills for doctors, own and lease airplanes, and even handicap golf tournaments and race horses on their computers. Is this banking? Or has the industry gone so far in reevaluating what its role should be and taken on such glamorous new functions that it could damage its efficiency and safety in accepting deposits and lending and investing money. This is the key issue today that will determine the posture of commercial banking in the years ahead.

Background

In evaluating what a bank should do, it is impossible to ignore the basic about-face the industry has taken in recent years in evaluating its function.

---

*Reprinted from Paul S. Nadler, "What should a Bank Do?" *The Canadian Banker,* March-April, 1969, pp. 32-34, by permission of the editor and author.

Dr. Nadler is Professor of Business Administration, Rutgers University, New Jersey.

[1] Theodore Levitt, "Marketing Myopia," *Harvard Business Review,* (July-August, 1960).

This is the industry that traditionally accepted only chequing account deposits and made only loans to business firms — and even these were only on a short-term, self-liquidating basis. Thus the mutual savings banks developed in the United States because the commercial banks would not accept savings deposits; the savings and loan associations developed because the commercial banks would not make mortgage loans; the finance companies thrived because banks would not make personal loans; and subsidiary services such as mortgage brokers, factors, and receivables finance companies organized and grew because banks did not take an imaginative look at the needs of the public for financial services.

What brought about the change that has made this banking industry a leader in innovation and diversification today? In the United States there are several basic reasons that can be singled out.

The Slower Rate of Growth of Demand Deposits

With high short-term interest rates developing in the middle and later years of the 1950s and through the 1960s — both for international balance of payments reasons and to fight inflation at home, business firms became far less willing to leave surplus funds sitting in chequing account deposits, on which American banks are not allowed to pay interest. In order to keep this money from leaving the banks and going into open market securities, such as US Treasury Bills, the banks had to start paying attractive interest rates on time deposits — thus keeping the same money but paying interest for it, whereas in the past these funds had been held free.

Similarly, individuals curbed their demand deposit balances, so the banks had to buy even more of their growth through the payment of attractive interest rates on time and savings deposits for individuals too.

This need to buy growth when it previously had been costless put the commercial banks in a serious earnings squeeze. And aggressive bankers realized that they would have to expand the scope of their operations if a serious decline in profitability were to be avoided. This became especially true after the change in the Federal Reserve Board's Regulation Q, at the beginning of 1962, allowing the commercial banks to pay 4 percent for savings deposits when previously they had only been authorized to pay a 3 percent ceiling rate. This in itself was the final straw that motivated many bank managements to broaden their service offerings and in other ways to become more aggressive.

The Advent of the Computer

A second force that helped bring about this radical change in banking's scope was the advent of the computer. At first most banks just utilized their computers to tackle more efficiently the same jobs they had been handling before — notably demand deposit accounting, transit, and consumer, commercial, and mortgage loans. But after a while, more imaginative bankers recognized that if they were to get real profitability out of their expensive data processing equipment, they would have to use it for new services and more efficient management decision making too. Thus banks developed the quantity of new services that have received so much attention. In addition, they have started to develop central files and full management information systems to tell them just how profitable certain customers' total relationships are and specifically what the costs really are of offering various services and maintaining specific bank functions.

James J. Saxon

Finally, with regard to the United States, the advent of Mr. James J. Saxon as Comptroller of the Currency played a major role in changing bank functions in the early 1960s. For Mr. Saxon took the approach that bank flexibility and change was all to the good, and he therefore preferred to disapprove change only when he felt a specific development was harmful. This was in opposition to much traditional thinking in banking that the status quo is best and any change should be accepted only item by item after examination.

Competition

While these three specific forces appear to be the immediate causes of change in banking, behind them is a basic underlying tone of extreme competition that has developed on both sides of the balance sheet — largely because banking's competitors have redefined their own scope of operations and service. Thus in lending, banks now face competition from the captive financing subsidiaries of manufacturing companies that finance the products sold by the manufacturing unit. Banks also compete for loans against finance companies, leasing companies, factors, government lending agencies, and even against the more generous credit terms of suppliers and the greater income tax flexibility that allows companies the equivalent of an interest-free loan from the government through the use of accelerated depreciation of capital facilities.

In solicitation of deposits, they compete against savings banks, savings and loan associations, credit unions, insurance companies that have tried to stress the savings component of insurance purchase, and the attractiveness of open market securities of the federal government, states, provinces, and municipal governments, and private borrowers.

Banking thus recognized that it has no exclusive province except in the handling of demand deposits — and even this is eroded away in the US by the lesser willingness of individuals and business firms to hold noninterest-bearing chequing account balances. Since this competition all developed from other industries broadening the definition of their function, banking in turn has been given added impetus to redefine its own scope of operations. Thus, whereas through the years most banks looked upon themselves simply as banks, now, in line with Mr. Levitt's ideas, it might be said that they are defining themselves as *financial servicers* — involved with every aspect of provision of financial service that is not specifically illegal.

This is why banks now handle mortgage origination and servicing for others, run insurance operations, and have even tried to establish mutual funds — a financial service expansion that has been halted in the US, at least temporarily, by opposition in the courts. It also provides the rationale for the development of the specialized data processing services such as handicapping golf tournaments and determining the power needs of the local utility.

What do banks expect to gain from this diversification? Basically they hope to reverse the inroads that other industries have made on their role in the economy and at the same time improve banking's profitability. But in addition, the banks that have undertaken new services and widened their own self-image have been able to develop within themselves the feeling that they are "going somewhere." This feeling of motion is terribly important for the maintenance of an effective organization with strong morale and the attraction of bright new employees — people whom they would otherwise not be able to get because of the fear that the bank job would not be challenging enough.

Are There Drawbacks?

Are there drawbacks to this expanded image and scope of the commercial banking industry? It is hard to see them. Certainly bank stockholders are not hurt by the revitalization of banking that new services provide. As for the depositors, one can assume that their deposits will be equally safe; for new services do not involve great risk of capital, and bank regulatory agencies will not adopt different standards on new services than they do on traditional services such as trust operations, international divisions, and the traditional receipt and lending of funds.

On the other hand, one can say that the public is provided both with new services and also with more intense competition in some of the areas where nonbanks were operating alone before the banks expanded their scope. In a free market economy, this is all to the good.

As to whether it should be banks that handle freight payments, doctor billing, and the myriad of other services now being provided, the answer appears to be that banks are a natural for these services. Bankers have traditionally been the data handlers for the economy, and the banker is also the person to whom business people are most willing to reveal confidential data. It is hard, then, to find basic objections to bank expansion into full financial service companies from the viewpoint of depositors, stockholders, or the public.

Conclusion

While banks have been widening their own scope to be full financial servicers instead of just commercial banks, in the United States a new trend has developed toward the establishment of one bank holding companies. Through this vehicle, at this writing, banks have become able to expand their scope even further and establish or buy companies in a wide variety of fields, both financial and nonfinancial, to be run as enterprises separate from the bank operation.

A discussion of the one bank holding company trend would be a different matter. For this would involve the question not just of the scope of commercial bank operations but also of what other types of companies the corporation that owns a bank may also control. Here there are enough questions of risk, antitrust violation, and concentration of power to require much further examination than can be developed in the present article.

But with regard to the branching out of the regulated commercial banks to offer more financial and data processing services than in the past, one can only offer applause. The banking industry has finally come out of its narrow shell and redefined itself so that the individual bank can be of much greater service to its customers than ever before.

This is definitely in line with breaking away from "marketing myopia" and recognizing that it is the customers' needs for types of credit and financial services, rather than the tradition of the bank, that should determine the scope of bank operations.

In this regard, the broadened self-image of what a bank is and what a bank should do should bring no adverse consequences; rather it should strengthen the viability and augment the usefulness of the commercial banking industry.

D. MONETARY POLICY

Adam Smith and the economists who came later, particularly those of the "Classical School," fully recognized the importance of money in facilitating exchange, but they did not attribute to money any significance as an economic "prime mover." They regarded money as great "convenience" to economic life, but as of no consequence in determining the level of economic activity. These early economists held that "production creates its own demand." This means, at least in theory, that since human wants are infinite in relation to the scarce means of satisfying them, and since the process of production will always generate purchasing power equal in amount to the value of the goods produced, there can never be any general oversupply of commodities in the market, or alternatively, any general deficiency of demand for goods and services. Closely related to this was the belief that an economy continuously tends toward full employment of all its resources, and toward production at all times of its capacity output.

It took the Great Depression of the 1930s with its mass unemployment, far less than capacity levels of output, and general deficiency of demand for all goods and services, finally to delete these propositions from the articles of faith of economists. Once they were cast aside, it became apparent that among the variables that determine actual levels of production, employment, and income in the economy at any time, monetary factors are among the most important. Changes in the stock of money and the speed or velocity with which money moves from one person to another cause changes in the total demand for goods and services, on which output, employment, and income levels ultimately depend.

Since contemporary theory recognizes that money is an important factor in the operation of our economy, the effects exerted by money are not to be left to chance. Money is to be deliberately managed with a view to assisting in the achievement of those goals for which society expresses a desire. Monetary policy, then, is the management of the expansion and contraction of the volume of money in circulation for the explicit purpose of attaining some desirable combination of the economy's objectives.

There are two major schools of thought regarding the process by which monetary factors influence aggregate spending and income. One emphasizes the role played in the transmission process by changes in the cost and availability of credit. The other emphasizes the role played by changes in the stock of money. According to the latter view it is increases in the stock of money that pushes spending and income upward, while according to the former view it is the lower rate of interest and the greater availability of credit that pushes spending decisions up, and these decisions in turn lead to an upward pull on the money supply via the rising demand for bank loans. Reading 34 presents the arguments for the money-supply approach to monetary policy. It also reviews the reasons for the revival of belief in the potency of monetary policy, suggests what monetary policy can and cannot do, and indicates how monetary policy should be conducted.

Not surprisingly, interest in Canada has been stimulated by the running debate in the United States between the proponents of the money-income (money-supply school) and the money-credit-expenditure (neo-Keynesian) schools of thought. Even more important is the fact that the Bank of Canada now stresses that monetary policy operates chiefly through its effect on credit conditions generally — that is, on the cost and availability of money throughout the economy. Reading 35 describes the historical development of the credit-conditions doctrine, and comments on the apparent disagreement between the Bank of Canada and the Economic Council of Canada regarding the appropriate control variable — the stock of money or interest rates.

In recent years there has been a growing controversy as to whether non-bank financial intermediaries, being exempt from immediate central bank control, are able to thwart the credit policies of the monetary authorities. Reading 36 considers the impact of the so called "near-banks" on monetary policy and concludes that controls on such institutions for purposes of monetary management are unnecessary.

34. THE ROLE OF MONETARY POLICY*

Milton Friedman

There is wide agreement about the major goals of economic policy: high employment, stable prices, and rapid growth. There is less agreement that these goals are mutually compatible or, among those who regard them as incompatible, about the terms at which they can and should be substituted for one another. There is least agreement about the role that various instruments of policy can and should play in achieving the several goals.

My topic for tonight is the role of one such instrument — monetary policy. What can it contribute? And how should it be conducted to contribute the most? Opinion on these questions has fluctuated widely. In the first flush of enthusiasm about the newly created Federal Reserve System, many observers attributed the relative stability of the 1920s to the System's capacity for fine tuning — to apply an apt modern term. It came to be widely believed that a new era had arrived in which business cycles had been rendered obsolete by advances in monetary technology. This opinion was shared by economist and layman alike, though, of course, there were some dissonant voices. The Great Contraction destroyed this naïve attitude. Opinion swung to the other extreme. Monetary policy was a string. You could pull on it to stop inflation but you could not push on it to halt recession. You could lead a horse to water but you could not make him drink. Such theory by aphorism was soon replaced by Keynes' rigorous and sophisticated analysis.

Keynes offered simultaneously an explanation for the presumed impotence of monetary policy to stem the Depression, a nonmonetary interpretation of the Depression, and an alternative to monetary policy for meeting the Depression and his offering was avidly accepted. If liquidity preference is absolute or nearly so — as Keynes believed likely in times of heavy unemployment — interest rates cannot be lowered by monetary measures. If investment and consumption are little affected by interest rates — as Hansen and many of Keynes' other American disciples came to believe — lower interest rates, even if they could be achieved, would do little good.

*Reprinted from Milton Friedman, "The Role of Monetary Policy," *American Economic Review,* March, 1968, pp. 1-17, by permission of the editor and author.
Dr. Friedman is Professor of Economics, University of Chicago.

Monetary policy is twice damned. The contraction, set in train, on this view, by a collapse of investment or by a shortage of investment opportunities or by stubborn thriftiness, could not, it was argued, have been stopped by monetary measures. But there was available an alternative — fiscal policy. Government spending could make up for insufficient private investment. Tax reductions could undermine stubborn thriftiness.

The wide acceptance of these views in the economics profession meant that for some two decades monetary policy was believed by all but a few reactionary souls to have been rendered obsolete by new economic knowledge. Money did not matter. Its only role was the minor one of keeping interest rates low, in order to hold down interest payments in the government budget, contribute to the "euthanasia of the rentier," and maybe, stimulate investment a bit to assist government spending in maintaining a high level of aggregate demand.

These views produced a widespread adoption of cheap money policies after the war. And they received a rude shock when these policies failed in country after country, when central bank after central bank was forced to give up the pretence that it could indefinitely keep "the" rate of interest at a low level. In this country, the public dénouement came with the Federal Reserve-Treasury Accord in 1951, although the policy of pegging government bond prices was not formally abandoned until 1953. Inflation, stimulated by cheap money policies, not the widely heralded postwar depression, turned out to be the order of the day. The result was the beginning of a revival of belief in the potency of monetary policy.

This revival was strongly fostered among economists by the theoretical developments, initiated by Haberler but named for Pigou, that pointed out a channel — namely, changes in wealth — whereby changes in the real quantity of money can affect aggregate demand even if they do not alter interest rates. These theoretical developments did not undermine Keynes' argument against the potency of orthodox monetary measures when liquidity preference is absolute since under such circumstances the usual monetary operations involve simply substituting money for other assets without changing total wealth. But they did show how changes in the quantity of money produced in other ways could affect total spending even under such circumstances. And, more fundamentally, they did undermine Keynes' key theoretical proposition, namely, that even in a world of flexible prices, a position of equilibrium at full employment might not exist. Henceforth, unemployment had again to be explained by rigidities or imperfections, not as the natural outcome of a fully operative market process.

The revival of belief in the potency of monetary policy was fostered also by a reevaluation of the role money played from 1929 to 1933. Keynes and most other economists of the time believed that the Great Contraction in the United States occurred despite aggressive expansionary policies by the monetary authorities — that they did their best but their best was not good enough.[1] Recent studies have demonstrated that the facts are precisely the reverse: the US monetary authorities followed highly deflationary policies. The quantity of money in the United States fell by one-third in the course of the contraction. And it fell not because there were no willing borrowers —

---

[1] In Milton Friedman, "The Monetary Theory and Policy of Henry Simons," *Journal of Law and Economics,* 10 (October, 1967), pp. 1-13, I have argued that Henry Simons shared this view with Keynes, and that it accounts for the policy changes that he recommended.

not because the horse would not drink. It fell because the Federal Reserve System forced or permitted a sharp reduction in the monetary base, because it failed to exercise the responsibilities assigned to it in the Federal Reserve Act to provide liquidity to the banking system. The Great Contraction is tragic testimony to the power of monetary policy — not, as Keynes and so many of his contemporaries believed, evidence of its impotence.

In the United States the revival of belief in the potency of monetary policy was strengthened also by increasing disillusionment with fiscal policy, not so much with its potential to affect aggregate demand as with the practical and political feasibility of so using it. Expenditures turned out to respond sluggishly and with long lags to attempts to adjust them to the course of economic activity, so emphasis shifted to taxes. But here political factors entered with a vengeance to prevent prompt adjustment to presumed need, as has been so graphically illustrated in the months since I wrote the first draft of this talk. "Fine tuning" is a marvelously evocative phrase in this electronic age, but it has little resemblance to what is possible in practice — not, I might add, an unmixed evil.

It is hard to realize how radical has been the change in professional opinion on the role of money. Hardly an economist today accepts views that were the common coin some two decades ago. Let me cite a few examples.

In a talk published in 1945, E. A. Goldenweiser, then Director of the Research Division of the Federal Reserve Board, described the primary objective of monetary policy as being to "maintain the value of Government bonds . . . This country" he wrote, "will have to adjust to a 2½ percent interest rate as the return on safe, long-time money, because the time has come when returns on pioneering capital can no longer be unlimited as they were in the past."[2]

In a book on *Financing American Prosperity*, edited by Paul Homan and Fritz Machlup and published in 1945, Alvin Hansen devotes nine pages of text to the "savings-investment problem" without finding any need to use the words "interest rate" or any close facsimile thereto.[3] In his contribution to this volume, Fritz Machlup wrote: "Questions regarding the rate of interest, in particular regarding its variation or its stability, may not be among the most vital problems of the postwar economy, but they are certainly among the perplexing ones."[4] In his contribution, John H. Williams — not only professor at Harvard but also a long-time adviser to the New York Federal Reserve Bank — wrote: "I can see no prospect of revival of a general monetary control in the postwar period."[5]

Another of the volumes dealing with postwar policy that appeared at this time, *Planning and Paying for Full Employment*, was edited by Abba P. Lerner and Frank D. Graham and had contributors of all shades of professional opinion — from Henry Simons and Frank Graham to Abba Lerner and Hans Neisser. Yet Albert Halasi, in his excellent summary of the papers, was able to say, "Our contributors do not discuss the question of money supply. . . . The contributors make no special mention of credit policy to remedy actual depressions. . . . Inflation . . . might be fought more effectively by raising interest rates. . . . But . . . other anti-inflationary meas-

[2] E. A. Goldenweiser, "Postwar Problems and Policies," *Fed. Res. Bulletin,* 31 (February, 1945), p. 117.
[3] P. T. Homan and Fritz Machlup, eds., *Financing American Prosperity* (New York, 1945), pp. 218-27.
[4] *Ibid.,* p. 466.
[5] *Ibid.,* p. 383.

ures . . . are preferable."[6] *A Survey of Contemporary Economics,* edited by Howard Ellis and published in 1948, was an "official" attempt to codify the state of economic thought of the time. In his contribution, Arthur Smithies wrote: "In the field of compensatory action, I believe fiscal policy must shoulder most of the load. Its chief rival, monetary policy, seems to be disqualified on institutional grounds. This country appears to be committed to something like the present low level of interest rates on a long-term basis."[7]

These quotations suggest the flavour of professional thought some two decades ago. If you wish to go further in this humbling inquiry, I recommend that you compare the sections on money — when you can find them — in the Principles texts of the early postwar years with the lengthy sections in the current crop even, or especially, when the early and recent Principles are different editions of the same work.

The pendulum has swung far since then, if not all the way to the position of the late 1920s, at least much closer to that position than to the position of 1945. There are of course many differences between then and now, less in the potency attributed to monetary policy than in the roles assigned to it and the criteria by which the profession believes monetary policy should be guided. Then, the chief roles assigned monetary policy were to promote price stability and to preserve the gold standard; the chief criteria of monetary policy were the state of the "money market," the extent of "speculation," and the movement of gold. Today, primacy is assigned to the promotion of full employment, with the prevention of inflation a continuing but definitely secondary objective. And there is major disagreement about criteria of policy, varying from emphasis on money market conditions, interest rates, and the quantity of money to the belief that the state of employment itself should be the proximate criterion of policy.

I stress nonetheless the similarity between the views that prevailed in the late twenties and those that prevail today because I fear that, now as then, the pendulum may well have swung too far; that, now as then, we are in danger of assigning to monetary policy a larger role than it can perform, in danger of asking it to accomplish tasks that it cannot achieve, and, as a result, in danger of preventing it from making the contribution that it is capable of making.

Unaccustomed as I am to denigrating the importance of money, I therefore shall, as my first task, stress what monetary policy cannot do. I shall then try to outline what it can do and how it can best make its contribution, in the present state of our knowledge — or ignorance.

What Monetary Policy Cannot Do

From the infinite world of negation, I have selected two limitations of monetary policy to discuss: (1) it cannot peg interest rates for more than very limited periods; (2) it cannot peg the rate of unemployment for more than very limited periods. I select these because the contrary has been or is widely believed, because they correspond to the two main unattainable tasks

---

[6] A. P. Lerner and F. D. Graham, eds., *Planning and Paying for Full Employment* (Princeton, 1946), pp. 23-24.
[7] H. S. Ellis, ed., *A Survey of Contemporary Economics* (Philadelphia, 1948), p. 208.

that are at all likely to be assigned to monetary policy, and because essentially the same theoretical analysis covers both.

Pegging of Interest Rates

History has already persuaded many of you about the first limitation. As noted earlier, the failure of cheap money policies was a major source of the reaction against simple-minded Keynesianism. In the United States, this reaction involved widespread recognition that the wartime and postwar pegging of bond prices was a mistake, that the abandonment of this policy was a desirable and inevitable step, and that it had none of the disturbing and disastrous consequences that were so freely predicted at the time.

The limitation derives from a much misunderstood feature of the relation between money and interest rates. Let the Fed set out to keep interest rates down. How will it try to do so? By buying securities. This raises their prices and lowers their yields. In the process, it also increases the quantity of reserves available to banks, hence the amount of bank credit, and, ultimately the total quantity of money. That is why central bankers in particular, and the financial community more broadly, generally believe that an increase in the quantity of money tends to lower interest rates. Academic economists accept the same conclusion, but for different reasons. They see, in their mind's eye, a negatively sloping liquidity preference schedule. How can people be induced to hold a larger quantity of money? Only by bidding down interest rates.

Both are right, up to a point. The *initial* impact of increasing the quantity of money at a faster rate than it has been increasing is to make interest rates lower for a time than they would otherwise have been. But this is only the beginning of the process not the end. The more rapid rate of monetary growth will stimulate spending, both through the impact on investment of lower market interest rates and through the impact on other spending and thereby relative prices of higher cash balances than are desired. But one man's spending is another man's income. Rising income will raise the liquidity preference schedule and the demand for loans; it may also raise prices, which would reduce the real quantity of money. These three effects will reverse the initial downward pressure on interest rates fairly promptly, say, in something less than a year. Together they will tend, after a somewhat longer interval, say, a year or two, to return interest rates to the level they would otherwise have had. Indeed, given the tendency for the economy to overreact, they are highly likely to raise interest rates temporarily beyond that level, setting in motion a cyclical adjustment process.

A fourth effect, when and if it becomes operative, will go even farther, and definitely mean that a higher rate of monetary expansion will correspond to a higher, not lower, level of interest rates than would otherwise have prevailed. Let the higher rate of monetary growth produce rising prices, and let the public come to expect that prices will continue to rise. Borrowers will then be willing to pay and lenders will then demand higher interest rates — as Irving Fisher pointed out decades ago. This price expectation effect is slow to develop and also slow to disappear. Fisher estimated that it took several decades for a full adjustment and more recent work is consistent with his estimates.

These subsequent effects explain why every attempt to keep interest rates at a low level has forced the monetary authority to engage in successively larger and larger open market purchases. They explain why, historically, high and rising nominal interest rates have been associated with rapid growth in the quantity of money, as in Brazil or Chile or in the United States in recent years, and why low and falling interest rates have been associated with slow growth in the quantity of money, as in Switzerland now or in the United States from 1929 to 1933. As an empirical matter, low interest rates are a sign that monetary policy *has been* tight — in the sense that the quantity of money has grown slowly; high interest rates are a sign that monetary policy *has been* easy — in the sense that the quantity of money has grown rapidly. The broadest facts of experience run in precisely the opposite direction from that which the financial community and academic economists have all generally taken for granted.

Paradoxically, the monetary authority could assure low nominal rates of interest — but to do so it would have to start out in what seems like the opposite direction, by engaging in a deflationary monetary policy. Similarly, it could assure high nominal interest rates by engaging in an inflationary policy and accepting a temporary movement in interest rates in the opposite direction.

These considerations not only explain why monetary policy cannot peg interest rates; they also explain why interest rates are such a misleading indicator of whether monetary policy is "tight" or "easy." For that, it is far better to look at the rate of change of the quantity of money.[8]

Employment as a Criterion of Policy

The second limitation I wish to discuss goes more against the grain of current thinking. Monetary growth, it is widely held, will tend to stimulate employment; monetary contraction, to retard employment. Why, then, cannot the monetary authority adopt a target for employment or unemployment — say, 3 percent unemployment; be tight when unemployment is less than the target; be easy when unemployment is higher than the target; and in this way peg unemployment at, say, 3 percent? The reason it cannot is precisely the same as for interest rates — the difference between the immediate and the delayed consequences of such a policy.

Thanks to Wicksell, we are all acquainted with the concept of a "natural" rate of interest and the possibility of a discrepancy between the "natural" and the "market" rate. The preceding analysis of interest rates can be translated fairly directly into Wicksellian terms. The monetary authority can make the market rate less than the natural rate only by inflation. It can make the market rate higher than the natural rate only by deflation. We have added only one wrinkle to Wicksell — the Irving Fisher distinction between the nominal and the real rate of interest. Let the monetary authority keep the nominal market rate for a time below the natural rate by inflation. That in turn will raise the nominal natural rate itself, once anticipations of inflation become widespread, thus requiring still more rapid inflation to hold down the market rate. Similarly, because of the Fisher effect, it will require not merely deflation but more and more rapid deflation to hold the market rate above the initial "natural" rate.

---

[8] This is partly an empirical not theoretical judgment. In principle, "tightness" or "ease" depends on the rate of change of the quantity of money supplied compared to the rate of change of the quantity demanded excluding effects on demand from monetary policy itself. However, empirically demand is highly stable, if we exclude the effect of monetary policy, so it is generally sufficient to look at supply alone.

This analysis has its close counterpart in the employment market. At any moment of time, there is some level of unemployment which has the property that it is consistent with equilibrium in the structure of *real* wage rates. At that level of unemployment, real wage rates are tending on the average to rise at a "normal" secular rate, that is, at a rate that can be indefinitely maintained so long as capital formation, technological improvements, etc., remain on their long-run trends. A lower level of unemployment is an indication that there is an excess demand for labour that will produce downward pressure on real wage rates. The "natural rate of unemployment," in other words, is the level that would be ground out by the Walrasian system of general equilibrium equations, provided there is embedded in them the actual structural characteristics of the labour and commodity markets, including market imperfections, stochastic variability in demands and supplies, the cost of gathering information about job vacancies and labour availabilities, the costs of mobility, and so on.[9]

You will recognize the close similarity between this statement and the celebrated Phillips Curve. The similarity is not coincidental. Phillips' analysis of the relation between unemployment and wage change is deservedly celebrated as an important and original contribution. But, unfortunately, it contains a basic defect — the failure to distinguish between *nominal* wages and *real* wages — just as Wicksell's analysis failed to distinguish between *nominal* interest rates and *real* interest rates. Implicitly, Phillips wrote his article for a world in which everyone anticipated that nominal prices would be stable and in which that anticipation remained unshaken and immutable whatever happened to actual prices and wages. Suppose, by contrast, that everyone anticipates that prices will rise at a rate of more than 75 percent a year — as, for example, Brazilians did a few years ago. Then wages must rise at that rate simply to keep real wages unchanged. An excess supply of labour will be reflected in a less rapid rise in nominal wages than in anticipated prices,[10] not in an absolute decline in wages. When Brazil embarked on a policy to bring down the rate of price rise, and succeeded in bringing the price rise down to about 45 percent a year, there was a sharp initial rise in unemployment because under the influence of earlier anticipations, wages kept rising at a pace that was higher than the new rate of price rise, though lower than earlier. This is the result experienced, and to be expected, of all attempts to reduce the rate of inflation below that widely anticipated.[11]

To avoid misunderstanding, let me emphasize that by using the term

---

[9] It is perhaps worth noting that this "natural" rate need not correspond to equality between the number unemployed and the number of job vacancies. For any given structure of the labour market, there will be some equilibrium relation between these two magnitudes, but there is no reason why it should be one of equality.

[10] Strictly speaking, the rise in nominal wages will be less rapid than the rise in anticipated nominal wages to make allowance for any secular changes in real wages.

[11] Stated in terms of the rate of change of nominal wages, the Phillips Curve can be expected to be reasonably stable and well defined for any period for which the *average* rate of change of prices, and hence the anticipated rate, has been relatively stable. For such periods, nominal wages and "real" wages move together. Curves computed for different periods or different countries for each of which this condition has been satisfied will differ in level, the level of the curve depending on what the average rate of price change was. The higher the average rate of price change, the higher will tend to be the level of the curve. For periods or countries for which the rate of change of prices varies considerably, the Phillips Curve will not be well defined. My impression is that these statements accord reasonably well with the experience of the economists who have explored empirical Phillips Curves.

Restate Phillips' analysis in terms of the rate of change of real wages — and even more precisely, anticipated real wages — and it all falls into place. That is why students of empirical Phillips Curves have found that it helps to include the rate change of the price level as an independent variable.

"natural" rate of unemployment, I do not mean to suggest that it is immutable and unchangeable. On the contrary, many of the market characteristics that determine its level are man-made and policy-made. In the United States, for example, legal minimum wage rates, the Walsh-Healy and Davis-Bacon Acts, and the strength of labour unions all make the natural rate of unemployment higher than it would otherwise be. Improvements in employment exchanges, in availability of information about job vacancies and labour supply, and so on, would tend to lower the natural rate of unemployment. I use the term "natural" for the same reason Wicksell did — to try to separate the real forces from monetary forces.

Let us assume that the monetary authority tries to peg the "market" rate of unemployment at a level below the "natural" rate. For definiteness, suppose that it takes 3 percent as the target rate and that the "natural" rate is higher than 3 percent. Suppose also that we start out at a time when prices have been stable and when unemployment is higher than 3 percent. Accordingly, the authority increases the rate of monetary growth. This will be expansionary. By making nominal cash balances higher than people desire, it will tend initially to lower interest rates and in this and other ways to stimulate spending. Income and spending will start to rise.

To begin with, much or most of the rise in income will take the form of an increase in output and employment rather than in prices. People have been expecting prices to be stable, and prices and wages have been set for some time in the future on that basis. It takes time for people to adjust to a new state of demand. Producers will tend to react to the initial expansion in aggregate demand by increasing output, employees by working longer hours, and the unemployed, by taking jobs now offered at former nominal wages. This much is pretty standard doctrine.

But it describes only the initial effects. Because selling prices of products typically respond to an unanticipated rise in nominal demand faster than prices of factors of production, real wages received have gone down — though real wages anticipated by employees went up, since employees implicitly evaluated the wages offered at the earlier price level. Indeed, the simultaneous fall *ex post* in real wages to employers and rise *ex ante* in real wages to employees is what enabled employment to increase. But the decline *ex post* in real wages will soon come to affect anticipations. Employees will start to reckon on rising prices of the things they buy and to demand higher nominal wages for the future. "Market" unemployment is below the "natural" level. There is an excess demand for labour so real wages will tend to rise toward their initial level.

Even though the higher rate of monetary growth continues, the rise in real wages will reverse the decline in unemployment, and then lead to a rise, which will tend to return unemployment to its former level. In order to keep unemployment at its target level of 3 percent, the monetary authority would have to raise monetary growth still more. As in the interest rate case, the "market" rate can be kept below the "natural" rate only be inflation. And, as in the interest rate case, too, only by accelerating inflation. Conversely, let the monetary authority choose a target rate of unemployment that is above the natural rate, and they will be led to produce a deflation, and an accelerating deflation at that.

What if the monetary authority chose the "natural" rate — either of interest or unemployment — as its target? One problem is that it cannot know what the "natural" rate is. Unfortunately, we have as yet devised no method to estimate accurately and readily the natural rate of either interest or unemployment. And the "natural" rate will itself change from time to time. But the basic problem is that even if the monetary authority knew the "natural" rate, and attempted to peg the market rate at that level, it would not be led to a determinate policy. The "market" rate will vary from the natural rate for all sorts of reasons other than monetary policy. If the monetary authority responds to these variations, it will set in train long-term effects that will make any monetary growth path it follows ultimately consistent with the rule of policy. The actual course of monetary growth will be analogous to a random walk, buffeted this way and that by the forces that produce temporary departures of the market rate from the natural rate.

To state this conclusion differently, there is always a temporary trade-off between inflation and unemployment; there is no permanent trade-off. The temporary trade-off comes not from inflation *per se*, but from unanticipated inflation, which generally means, from a rising rate of inflation. The widespread belief that there is a permanent trade-off is a sophisticated version of the confusion between "high" and "rising" that we all recognize in simpler forms. A rising rate of inflation may reduce unemployment, a high rate will not.

But how long, you will say, is "temporary"? For interest rates, we have some systematic evidence on how long each of the several effects takes to work itself out. For unemployment, we do not. I can at most venture a personal judgment, based on some examination of the historical evidence, that the initial effects of a higher and unanticipated rate of inflation last for something like two to five years; that this initial effect then begins to be reversed; and that a full adjustment to the new rate of inflation takes about as long for employment as for interest rates, say, a couple of decades. For both interest rates and employment, let me add a qualification. These estimates are for changes in the rate of inflation of the order of magnitude that has been experienced in the United States. For much more sizable changes, such as those experienced in South American countries, the whole adjustment process is greatly speeded up.

To state the general conclusion still differently, the monetary authority controls nominal quantities — directly, the quantity of its own liabilities. In principle, it can use this control to peg a nominal quantity — an exchange rate, the price level, the nominal level of national income, the quantity of money by one or another definition — or to peg the rate of change in a nominal quantity — the rate of inflation or deflation, the rate of growth or decline in nominal national income, the rate of growth of the quantity of money. It cannot use its control over nominal quantities to peg a real quantity — the real rate of interest, the rate of unemployment, the level of real national income, or the rate of growth of the real quantity of money.

What Monetary Policy Can Do

Monetary policy cannot peg these real magnitudes at predetermined levels. But monetary policy can and does have important effects on these real magnitudes. The one is in no way inconsistent with the other.

My own studies of monetary history have made me extremely sympathetic to the oft quoted, much reviled, and as widely misunderstood, comment by John Stuart Mill. "There cannot...," he wrote, "be intrinsically a more insignificant thing, in the economy of society, than money; except in the character of a contrivance for sparing time and labour.

313

It is a machine for doing quickly and commodiously, what would be done, though less quickly and commodiously, without it: and like many other kinds of machinery, it only exerts a distinct and independent influence of its own when it goes out of order."[12]

True, money is only a machine, but it is an extraordinarily efficient machine. Without it, we could not have begun to attain the astounding growth in output and level of living we have experienced in the past two centuries — any more than we could have done so without those other marvelous machines that dot our countryside and enable us, for the most part, simply to do more efficiently what could be done without them at much greater cost in labour.

But money has one feature that these other machines do not share. Because it is so pervasive, when it gets out of order, it throws a monkey wrench into the operation of all the other machines. The Great Contraction is the most dramatic example but not the only one. Every major inflation has been produced by monetary expansion — mostly to meet the overriding demands of war which have forced the creation of money to supplement explicit taxation.

The first and most important lesson that history teaches about what monetary policy can do — and it is a lesson of the most profound importance — is that monetary policy can prevent money itself from being a major source of economic disturbance. This sounds like a negative proposition: avoid major mistakes. In part it is. The Great Contraction might not have occurred at all, and if it had, it would have been far less severe, if the monetary authority had avoided mistakes, or if the monetary arrangements had been those of an earlier time when there was no central authority with the power to make the kinds of mistakes that the Federal Reserve System made. The past few years, to come closer to home, would have been steadier and more productive of economic well-being if the Federal Reserve had avoided drastic and erratic changes of direction, first expanding the money supply at an unduly rapid pace, then, in early 1966, stepping on the brake too hard, then, at the end of 1966, reversing itself and resuming expansion until at least November, 1967, at a more rapid pace than can long be maintained without appreciable inflation.

Even if the proposition that monetary policy can prevent money itself from being a major source of economic disturbance were a wholly negative proposition, it would be nonetheless important for that. As it happens, however, it is not a wholly negative proposition. The monetary machine has gotten out of order even when there has been no central authority with anything like the power now possessed by the Fed. In the United States, the 1907 episode and earlier banking panics are examples of how the monetary machine can get out of order largely on its own. There is therefore a positive and important task for the monetary authority — to suggest improvements in the machine that will reduce the chances that it will get out of order, and to use its own powers so as to keep the machine in good working order.

A second thing monetary policy can do is provide a stable background for the economy — keep the machine well oiled, to continue Mills's analogy. Accomplishing the first task will contribute to this objective, but there is more to it than that. Our economic system will work best when producers and consumers, employers and employees, can proceed with full confidence that the average level of prices will behave in a known way in the future —

---

[12] J. S. Mill, *Principles of Political Economy*, Bk. III, Ashley, ed., (New York, 1929), p. 488.

preferably that it will be highly stable. Under any conceivable institutional arrangements, and certainly under those that now prevail in the United States, there is only a limited amount of flexibility in prices and wages. We need to conserve this flexibility to achieve changes in relative prices and wages that are required to adjust to dynamic changes in tastes and technology. We should not dissipate it simply to achieve changes in the absolute level of prices that serve no economic function.

In an earlier era, the gold standard was relied on to provide confidence in future monetary stability. In its heyday it served that function reasonably well. It clearly no longer does, since there is scarcely a country in the world that is prepared to let the gold standard reign unchecked — and there are persuasive reasons why countries should not do so. The monetary authority could operate as a surrogate for the gold standard, if it pegged exchange rates and did so exclusively by altering the quantity of money in response to balance of payment flows without "sterilizing" surpluses or deficits and without resorting to open or concealed exchange control or to changes in tariffs and quotas. But again, though many central bankers talk this way, few are in fact willing to follow this course — and again there are persuasive reasons why they should not do so. Such a policy would submit each country to the vagaries not of an impersonal and automatic gold standard but of the policies — deliberate or accidental — of other monetary authorities.

In today's world, if monetary policy is to provide a stable background for the economy it must do so by deliberately employing its powers to that end.

Finally, monetary policy can contribute to offsetting major disturbances in the economic system arising from other sources. If there is an independent secular exhilaration — as the postwar expansion was described by the proponents of secular stagnation — monetary policy can in principle help to hold it in check by a slower rate of monetary growth than would otherwise be desirable. If, as now, an explosive federal budget threatens unprecedented deficits, monetary policy can hold any inflationary dangers in check by a slower rate of monetary growth than would otherwise be desirable. This will temporarily mean higher interest rates than would otherwise prevail — to enable the government to borrow the sums needed to finance the deficit — but by preventing the speeding up of inflation, it may well mean both lower prices and lower nominal interest rates for the long pull. If the end of a substantial war offers the country an opportunity to shift resources from wartime to peacetime production, monetary policy can ease the transition by a higher rate of monetary growth than would otherwise be desirable — though experience is not very encouraging that it can do so without going too far.

I have put this point last, and stated it in qualified terms — as referring to major disturbances — because I believe that the potentiality of monetary policy in offsetting other forces making for instability is far more limited than is commonly believed. We simply do not know enough to be able to recognize minor disturbances when they occur or to be able to predict either what their effects will be with any precision or what monetary policy is required to offset their effects. We do not know enough to be able to achieve stated objectives by delicate, or even fairly coarse, changes in the mix of monetary and fiscal policy. In this area particularly, the best is likely to be the enemy of the good. Experience suggests that the path of wisdom is to use monetary policy explicitly to offset other disturbances only when they offer a "clear and present danger."

How should monetary policy be conducted to make the contribution to our goals that it is capable of making? This is clearly not the occasion for presenting a detailed "Program for Monetary Stability" — to use the title of a book in which I tried to do so. I shall restrict myself here to two major requirements for monetary policy that follow fairly directly from the preceding discussion.

The first requirement is that the monetary authority should guide itself by magnitudes that it can control, not by ones that it cannot control. If, as the authority has often done, it takes interest rates or the current unemployment percentage as the immediate criterion of policy, it will be like a space vehicle that has taken a fix on the wrong star. No matter how sensitive and sophisticated its guiding apparatus, the space vehicle will go astray. And so will the monetary authority. Of the various alternative magnitudes that it can control, the most appealing guides for policy are exchange rates, the price level as defined by some index, and the quantity of a monetary total — currency plus adjusted demand deposits, or this total plus commercial bank time deposits, or a still broader total.

For the United States in particular, exchange rates are an undesirable guide. It might be worth requiring the bulk of the economy to adjust to the tiny percentage consisting of foreign trade if that would guarantee freedom from monetary irresponsibility — as it might under a real gold standard. But it is hardly worth doing so simply to adapt to the average of whatever policies monetary authorities in the rest of the world adopt. Far better to let the market, through floating exchange rates, adjust to world conditions the 5 percent or so of our resources devoted to international trade while reserving monetary policy to promote the effective use of the 95 percent.

Of the three guides listed, the price level is clearly the most important in its own right. Other things the same, it would be much the best of the alternatives — as so many distinguished economists have urged in the past. But other things are not the same. The link between the policy actions of the monetary authority and the price level, while unquestionably present, is more indirect than the link between the policy actions of the authority and any of the several monetary totals. Moreover, monetary action takes a longer time to affect the price level than to affect the monetary totals and both the time lag and the magnitude of effect vary with circumstances. As a result, we cannot predict at all accurately just what effect a particular monetary action will have on the price level and, equally important, just when it will have that effect. Attempting to control directly the price level is therefore likely to make monetary policy itself a source of economic disturbance because of false stops and starts. Perhaps, as our understanding of monetary phenomena advances, the situation will change. But at the present stage of our understanding, the long way around seems the surer way to our objective. Accordingly, I believe that a monetary total is the best currently available immediate guide or criterion for monetary policy — and I believe that it matters much less which particular total is chosen than that one be chosen.

A second requirement for monetary policy is that the monetary authority avoid sharp swings in policy. In the past, monetary authorities have on occasion moved in the wrong direction — as in the episode of the Great Contraction that I have stressed. More frequently, they have moved in the right direction, albeit often too late, but have erred by moving too far. Too late and too much has been the general practice. For example, in early 1966, it was the right policy for the Federal Reserve to move in a less expansionary direction — though it should have done so at least a year earlier. But when it moved, it went too far, producing the sharpest change in the rate of monetary growth of the postwar era. Again, having gone too far, it was the right policy for the Fed to reverse course at the end of 1966. But again it went too far, not only restoring but exceeding the earlier excessive rate of monetary growth. And this episode is no exception. Time and again this has been the course followed — as in 1919 and 1920, in 1937 and 1938, in 1953 and 1954, in 1959 and 1960.

The reason for the propensity to overreact seems clear: the failure of monetary authorities to allow for the delay between their actions and the subsequent effects on the economy. They tend to determine their actions by today's conditions — but their actions will affect the economy only six or nine or twelve or fifteen months later. Hence they feel impelled to step on the brake, or the accelerator, as the case may be, too hard.

My own prescription is still that the monetary authority go all the way in avoiding such swings by adopting publicly the policy of achieving a steady rate of growth in a specified monetary total. The precise rate of growth, like the precise monetary total, is less important than the adoption of some stated and known rate. I myself have argued for a rate that would on the average achieve rough stability in the level of prices of final products, which I have estimated would call for something like a 3 to 5 percent per year rate of growth in currency plus all commercial bank deposits or a slightly lower rate of growth in currency plus demand deposits only.[13] But it would be better to have a fixed rate that would on the average produce moderate inflation or moderate deflation, provided it was steady, than to suffer the wide and erratic perturbations we have experienced.

Short of the adoption of such a publicly stated policy of a steady rate of monetary growth, it would constitute a major improvement if the monetary authority followed the self-denying ordinance of avoiding wide swings. It is a matter of record that periods of relative stability in the rate of monetary growth have also been periods of relative stability in economic activity, both in the United States and other countries. Periods of wide swings in the rate of monetary growth have also been periods of wide swings in economic activity.

By setting itself a steady course and keeping to it, the monetary authority could make a major contribution to promoting economic stability. By making that course one of steady but moderate growth in the quantity of money, it would make a major contribution to avoidance of either inflation or deflation of prices. Other forces would still affect the economy, require change and adjustment, and disturb the even tenor of our ways. But steady monetary growth would provide a monetary climate favourable to the effective operation of those basic forces of enterprise, ingenuity, invention, hard work, and thrift that are the true springs of economic growth. That is the most that we can ask from monetary policy at our present stage of knowledge. But that much — and it is a great deal — is clearly within our reach.

---

[13] In an as yet unpublished article on "The Optimum Quantity of Money," I conclude that a still lower rate of growth, something like 2 percent for the broader definition, might be better yet in order to eliminate or reduce the difference between private and total costs of adding to real balances.

35. CREDIT CONDITIONS AND THE BANK OF CANADA*

John H. Young

This article has been written to draw attention to a controversy about the functions and operating methods of the central bank. Ordinarily, there is no need to emphasize the fact that a disagreement exists among those concerned with a particular area of economic policy. In this case, however, the controversy over whether the central bank should be primarily concerned with the state of "credit conditions," or whether it should focus attention on the quantity of "money," has apparently been conducted in such muted tones in Canada that few are aware that it has been taking place. Nevertheless, it is plainly on the record. In almost every speech, report, submission, or comment issuing from the Bank of Canada in the last five years it has been reiterated that the Bank exerts its influence through its impact on credit conditions, that is, the cost and availability of credit. Similarly, in each of its three Annual Reviews, the Economic Council of Canada has indicated that in its view the basic strategy of monetary policy, subject to qualifications, should be to expand the money supply roughly in line with real output or potential output.

The nature of the disagreement can perhaps be best introduced by a brief review of the way in which the discussion of these matters has developed in recent years. While the issue of what they should regard as the proximate objective of their actions has been of concern for central bankers for a long time, the recent discussion was greatly stimulated by the appointment in Great Britain in 1957 of the Committee on the Working of the Monetary System. This Committee, commonly referred to as the Radcliffe Committee (after its Chairman), reported in 1959 and a controversy ensued on its suggestion that the authorities should be concerned with the "whole liquidity position" rather than simply the supply of money.

The inquiry conducted by the Radcliffe Committee was followed by the appointment of the Commission on Money and Credit in the United States and this issue was open for consideration from an American point of view.

---

*Reprinted from John H. Young, "Credit Conditions and the Bank of Canada," *The Canadian Banker*, Spring, 1967, pp. 198-207, by permission of the editor and author.
Dr. Young is Professor of Economics, University of British Columbia, Vancouver, and Chairman of the Prices and Incomes Commission.

The Commission on Money and Credit did not attack the question directly and in general adopted an eclectic position. This eclecticism was in sharp contrast to the firm views expressed by modern American quantity theorists, notably Professor Milton Friedman and his associates, who argued that the central bank should concentrate its attention on the quantity of money and, indeed, should follow a fixed rule of regular additions to the money supply.

There were thus at least two vigorously supported positions on the appropriate functions and operating methods of central banks when the Royal Commission on Banking and Finance commenced its work in 1961-62. One might well have entertained some doubts that the Bank of Canada would be able to provide an answer for the Commission. Neither the Radcliffe Committee nor the Commission on Money and Credit had been entirely satisfied with the positions taken by their respective central banks and it was well known that the Bank of Canada had been widely criticized in the late 1950s both for its performance and the rationale offered for its decisions.

At first reading, the Brief offered by the Bank of Canada did not immediately dispel fears of this kind. In some areas, particularly on the effects of monetary policy on the economy, it was weak. Further it has generally been the case in the last five years that written material from the Bank has been so carefully rounded and qualified that the reader who is not alert can easily slide by a sentence or a paragraph without realizing that something has been said. Two or more readings are usually necessary to detect the nuances and it is to be feared that in this rather hectic age there are few people left who will take the trouble to savour sentences in which every word and phrase has been the subject of the most earnest attention.[1]

It is thus not surprising that the full implications of a few key sentences on "credit conditions" were not recognized immediately by all readers and, indeed, have apparently gone unrecognized by most readers to the present day. Some of the key sentences are the following:

> The operations of the Bank of Canada exert their influence on the level of demand for goods and services through their effects on credit conditions. By credit conditions is meant the whole range of terms and conditions affecting borrowing and lending and the purchase and sale of financial assets: the level and structure of securities prices and yields, institutional lending and deposit rates, and the various requirements (over and above the payment of a certain rate of interest) which lenders require of borrowers as a condition of making funds available, e.g., the specification of standards of credit worthiness, collateral security, repayment periods, etc. (II, par. 11)

> In summary, the job of monetary policy is to assess the nature and impact of all the factors bearing on credit conditions and to decide whether in the circumstances it should allow them to be fully reflected in credit conditions, or whether and to what extent it should try to reinforce or mitigate their effect. (II, par. 75)

These sentences outline the main elements of the credit conditions approach to central banking. Since it is the essence of this approach that central banking must be looked at as part of a wider framework of policy, these sentences need to be supplemented by a comment made by the Governor of the Bank of Canada when giving testimony before the Commission:

---

[1] In view of the troubled times through which the Bank passed not many years ago this concern with balance and moderation is understandable.

> ...in some ways debt management is very similar to monetary management...
> In these circumstances it is obvious that very close co-ordination between debt
> management and monetary management is desirable.[2]

The credit conditions approach is therefore best regarded as referring to both
monetary and debt policies rather than to monetary policy alone. This
approach maintains that it is through credit conditions, that is, the cost,
terms, and availability of credit that the monetary and debt authorities
affect the level of demand, and it is credit conditions which the authorities
should watch rather than the quantities of particular financial assets.
Further, any change in credit conditions must have been initiated, or
acquiesced in, by the authorities and therefore reflect their policy.

This approach was taken over by the Royal Commission on Banking and
Finance and runs like a thread through the chapters of the Report. Oddly
enough most readers of the Commission Report and, as far as one can judge,
most readers of the last five Annual Reports of the Bank of Canada appear
to have ignored it. Perhaps those who ignore it are tacitly in agreement with
the views being expressed and consider them so conventional and well
established as not to be worthy of comment. For example, Mr. Herbert
Stein's review of the Report in the *Journal of Political Economy* (June,
1966), which in general was both penetrating and witty, contained the
following comment:

> The chapters of the Report dealing with the use of fiscal and monetary policy to
> achieve the over-all economic objectives of the society cover ground on which
> there is now an international conventional wisdom. While the subject is treated
> with unusual clarity, there is little here to disturb the conventional wisdom, with
> one possible exception. The possible exception relates to the stability of the
> exchange rate. (p. 272)

Perhaps it is not thought that a difference in approach to monetary and debt
policies is sufficiently fundamental to constitute a breach with the international conventional wisdom but there is certainly a considerable variety in
the descriptions which central bankers of other countries give of what they
do. To go no further than the United States, views have repeatedly been
expressed in recent years by senior officials of the Federal Reserve System
which suggest that monetary policy decisions are "based primarily on
judgment as to the flow of bank credit and money that is appropriate for the
economy and not on judgment as to some level and pattern of interest rates
that is deemed to be appropriate."[3]

It is also noteworthy that the Annual Reports of the previous Governor of
the Bank of Canada for 1959 and 1960 lay stress on a quantity rather than a
price approach, that is, on the supply of money rather than on credit
conditions. In the 1959 Report this view was put as follows:

> The primary function of a central bank is to regulate the total quantity of
> money which is a short phrase rather arbitrarily[4] applied to the combination of
> the amount of currency in circulation outside the banks plus the amount of the

---

[2] *Annual Report*, 1962, p. 73.
[3] *The Federal Reserve System: Purposes and Functions*, 1961, p. 122.
[4] This rather casual acceptance of the arbitrary nature of the definition of "money" is fairly common
among those who favour a quantity of money approach. Professor James Tobin noting a similar
tendency in *The Monetary History of the United States* by Milton Friedman and Anna Jacobson

deposit liabilities of those banking institutions which are required to maintain a reserve of deposits with the central bank expressed as a percentage of their own deposit liabilities. (p. 12.)

This was echoed in the 1960 Report in the following terms:

The primary function of the central bank is to provide the chartered banks with a volume of cash reserves adequate to support an appropriate level of bank credit and deposits. (p. 18.)

There has therefore been an important change in recent years in this country. Yet there are grounds for saying that the credit conditions approach is a rediscovery rather than an innovation. This was brought home to me in a discussion with an economist who had been interested in monetary and debt management matters in the 1940s, had turned his attention to other things in the 1950s and returned to the study of monetary matters in the 1960s. His response to the suggestion that this was a new and better way of looking at monetary policy was that he had never thought of it in any other way.

There are two reasons why this type of reaction should occasion no surprise. One is that the credit conditions approach lies in the mainstream of monetary thinking in the twentieth century. While it could be described as Keynesian it is not Keynesian in any narrow sense of the word. Given the advances made in Sweden by Wicksell and his followers and the contributions of other English economists including Lavington, Hawtrey, Robertson, and Hicks it is not unlikely that things would have gone in this direction even if Keynes had never lived, although the process might well have been a slower one.

There was a time when the economist's first introduction to money was the quantity theory. For the last twenty or thirty years money has usually been first introduced as a way of influencing rates of interest which in turn influence expenditure. Thus the notion that monetary and debt authorities should devote their attention to interest rates and, where there are imperfections, to the availability of credit rather than the quantity of money, comes naturally to almost any economist under the age of fifty-five or sixty.

The second reason why the credit conditions approach appears so conventional is that a similar way of looking at things tended to be the rule during the war and early postwar years. There was complete co-ordination of monetary and debt policies with the central bank taking all the steps required to achieve the credit conditions thought necessary for fighting the war and handling the reconstruction. It is natural therefore, for anyone who followed monetary and debt policies in the 1940s to see nothing novel about the credit conditions approach.

The confusion which arose in Canada on these matters during the 1950s partly derived from a misreading of the lessons of the early postwar years and partly from the unwillingness on the part of the government to be associated with unpopular monetary restraint. When it became evident that the policy of maintaining low and stable interest rates was inappropriate in the face of postwar conditions of excess demand, the central bank came under criticism for having pursued a monetary policy which was destabiliz-

---

Schwartz remarked: "Sometimes Friedman and his followers seem to be saying: 'We don't know what money is, but whatever it is, its stock should grow steadily at 3 to 4 percent per year.'" ("The Monetary Interpretation of History," *American Economic Review,* (June, 1965), p. 465.)

ing. It was not too difficult to infer from this that what was required was a good deal of independence for the central bank in order to prevent a recurrence of such a state of affairs. What perhaps should have been inferred from this experience was that the government had been mistaken in the monetary and debt policies which had been pursued. What was needed was better monetary and debt policies and not that the Bank should be placed in a position, and encouraged, to pursue a form of guerilla warfare if there was disagreement on policy.

Unfortunately, the notion that the Bank should adopt its own line on monetary policy was reinforced by the reluctance of the government to accept responsibility for monetary policy when restraint was the order of the day. First Mr. Harris and then Mr. Fleming explicitly renounced responsibility for monetary policy although no steps were taken to shift responsibility for debt management to the Bank. Thus the very odd situation developed in which the federal government was put in much the same position as other borrowers. It could set the terms on which it would try to borrow but was not in a position to see that the monetary policy being pursued was consistent with these debt decisions.

Under these circumstances the central bank had an incentive to go as far in the direction of a quantity approach to monetary policy as circumstances permitted. A quantity approach has the advantage of tending to hive off the activities of the central bank from those of the government. It enables the central bank to argue that the state of credit conditions is not its responsibility but results from the interplay of all public policies, including monetary policy, and the forces at work in the economy as a whole.

When something approximating the traditional relationship between the government and the Governor was restored at the time of the appointment of the present Governor, there was a certain logic in the explicit adoption of an approach to monetary and debt policies consistent with that relationship. This is not to say that the underlying intellectual content of the new credit conditions approach was not much different than that of the earlier period. The more active use of monetary policy in the 1950s stimulated a good deal of writing on monetary theory and a wider interest in financial institutions. Much of this work stressed the degree of similarity between banks and other institutions not described as banks, and similarly stressed the minor differences between financial assets which fall within the definition of "money," and financial assets generally regarded as lying outside this definition. All of this suggested a continuum both of institutions and assets and argued against any narrow quantity of money approach. In a sense therefore, the new approach was a natural outgrowth of recent developments in economic analysis.

So far we have been concerned with describing the credit conditions approach and attempting to explain why it was necessary to discover, or at least rediscover, a way of looking at monetary and debt policies which fits so well with twentieth-century economic analysis and fully recognizes the need for co-ordination of the actions of the Bank and the government. This is not the place to attempt a thorough examination of the advantages and disadvantages of this approach compared with others. Since reference has been made to the Economic Council, however, some comments are in order on the relative merits of credit conditions as opposed to the supply of money as a proximate objective of monetary policy.

At the outset it should be emphasized that while the differences between the quantity approach and the credit conditions approach are important, there is no implication in the credit conditions view that the level of bank deposits is not important in determining interest rates and the availability of credit, or more generally, that the level of a broader range of assets is not important. Indeed, it is the apparent narrowness of the difference between a quantity approach and the credit conditions way of looking at monetary and debt policies which has led to a failure to recognize that this difference is a significant one.

Thus, in spite of the fact that both the Bank of Canada and the Porter Commission explicitly rejected a quantity approach in favour of credit conditions, the Economic Council put forward a quantitative formula approach without feeling that it was necessary to defend their choice. In the event, the qualifications in the direction of the credit conditions approach which the Council felt impelled to make have meant that very little is left of the formula. Since these qualifications help to indicate the weaknesses of a quantitative approach, we shall look first at the formula proposed by the Council and then at the qualifications. In the *First Annual Review* the formula read as follows:

> The general long-term requirement suggested here is an upward trend in the money supply broadly in step with the rise in real output. (p. 58)

In the *Second Annual Review* this became:

> We believe that the basic strategy of monetary policy should be concerned with expanding the money supply roughly in line with growing potential output, with a view to facilitating stable expansion of final demand. (p. 187)

No change was made in the *Third Annual Review;* the Council merely quoted itself on this topic from the *Second Annual Review.*

The first Council injection on the money supply came in the *First Annual Review* in December, 1964, followed by another in December, 1965, and a third in November, 1966. From the last quarter of 1964 to the third quarter of 1966, the average rise in real output has probably been between 6 and 6½ percent while the rate of growth of potential output has presumably been lower. This suggests that in the period covered, the rate of growth of currency and chartered bank deposits should have been less than 6 percent per year. In fact, between September, 1964, and September, 1966, the average annual increase in currency and chartered bank deposits held by the general public was 9.8 percent, while the annual average increase in currency and chartered bank deposits (including government deposits) was 9.2 percent. There is no doubt that if the monetary authority had followed the Council's advice, credit conditions would have been a good deal tighter than, in fact, they were. Yet in the *Second* and *Third Annual Reviews* it is not suggested that monetary policy has been noticeably too easy.

Indeed, while putting forward a formula to apply over the long run, the Council was aware of the problems which would arise in attempting to follow any formula approach over the short run. As they pointed out in the *First Annual Review:*

> ... the monetary authorities will clearly find it necessary in practice to maintain a highly flexible approach in dealing with the day-to-day requirements of debt management and changing conditions in financial markets. (p. 108)

It would have been difficult not to offer a qualification of this kind in view of recent events in Canada.

The Council was also aware that any formula approach in Canada would have to be qualified by a sensitivity to monetary conditions abroad, particularly in the United States. As the Council put it in the *Second Annual Review:*

> Once again, however, it should be emphasized that the monetary authorities will only have a limited degree of independence to pursue any basic course of policy which does not evolve in relatively close accord with monetary conditions in the United States. (p. 188)

It would have been useful to emphasize here that it is interest rate differentials which are particularly relevant and therefore it is again credit conditions to which the authorities must be sensitive.

Day-to-day management and international considerations militate against a formula approach for Canada and, in these days of closely related financial markets, probably militate against this approach in almost all countries. A further consideration, which has played an important part in leading to a discrepancy between the rate of growth of potential output and the rate of growth of the supply of currency and chartered bank deposits, has been shifts in the preferences of Canadians among relatively liquid claims. This was particularly relevant in 1965 as a result of the failure of Atlantic Acceptance. In that year the rate of growth of the money supply was an average which included a 6.5 percent increase in currency outside banks and demand deposits, a rise of 9 percent in personal savings deposits and a 54.1 percent increase in nonpersonal term and notice deposits. An interesting table 30 in the *Annual Report* of the Bank of Canada for 1965, draws attention to these and other changes which occurred during the year. This was unusual but there have been enough shifts among relatively liquid claims held by the public to suggest the dangers of using as a guide to monetary policy a magnitude as arbitrarily defined as the supply of "money."

Lest these critical comments are interpreted to mean that adherence to the credit conditions approach involves denying the relevance of the supply of "money," or the supply of a wider range of liquid assets to the level of interest rates and the availability of credit, it should be repeated that this is not the case. All that is being asserted is that for those who think that monetary and debt policies affect the economy through their effects on interest rates and the availability of credit, it makes sense to operate with an eye directly on rates and availability and not on the quantity of a particular set of liquid assets. This is particularly so in the case of Canada where the significance of interest rate differentials between this country and the United States make it important that these differentials do not widen or narrow without good reason. The very sharp and inappropriate rise in interest rates in Canada in the fall of 1960 when the Bank of Canada was paying attention to quantities, rather than prices, indicates what can happen. On the other hand, the vigour and success with which the Bank has met serious market situations, such as the Cuban crisis of October, 1962, the British Bank Rate change of November, 1963, and the failure of Atlantic Acceptance in June, 1964, indicate that the adoption of the credit conditions approach has not been without practical consequences.

More important than these considerations is the contribution of the credit conditions approach to a clearer understanding of general economic policy. The "constitutional" problem which plagued the relations between the Bank and the government a few years ago was a serious barrier to a healthy economic policy, but so also was the "money supply" view of its function taken by the Bank of Canada. It is widely recognized that the reassertion of the traditional notion of dual responsibility by the present Governor at the time of his appointment, removed a serious barrier to successful economic policy. What is less widely appreciated is the importance of the credit conditions approach in emphasizing the recognition that general economic policy must be viewed and executed as a co-ordinated whole.

The general tone of this article may suggest that given the credit conditions approach there is little more to be done in clarifying the nature of monetary and debt policies. This is certainly not the case. It might even be argued that the name which has been given to this way of looking at things has some weaknesses. The term "credit conditions" is easily misunderstood to refer only to the availability of credit and not to both interest rates and availability. Indeed, the *Annual Report* of the Bank of Canada for 1965 contained two sentences which talked about credit conditions *and* interest rates. Moreover, the word "credit" is often associated with particular types of lending and thus the term credit conditions given too narrow a meaning. The term "financial conditions" might avoid some of these difficulties.

Going beyond terminological matters, the very fact that the monetary authority has adopted a more direct but more complex guide for its actions increases the need for adequate up-to-date information on the terms and conditions of lending through a variety of channels. Moreover, beyond the question of effects within the financial system lie the central questions in this area which concern the effects monetary and debt policies have on decisions to spend. The more there is a tendency to think of economic policy as a co-ordinated whole, the more important it is to have as accurate a view as possible of the likely effects of the use of each of the instruments of policy. Much remains to be learned here. While it is easy to say that more should be done, there are few things more important in reaching sensible policy decisions than as complete an understranding as possible of the probable effects of these decisions. But that is another subject.

36. NEAR-BANKS AND MONETARY CONTROL*

J. A. Galbraith and Anna L. Guthrie

The Study Committee on Financial Institutions was appointed by the Government of Quebec in December, 1965, with Jacques Parizeau as Chairman, and the following Committee members: Michel Bélanger, Deputy Minister of Industry and Commerce; Robert Després, Deputy Minister of Revenue; Douglas Fullerton, Financial Consultant; and Yves Pratte, QC, who resigned in December, 1968 on his appointment to head Air Canada. The Committee was set up to examine the legislation governing financial institutions under the jurisdiction of Quebec and was specifically directed to consider whether or not these near-banks should be made subject to control by the Bank of Canada (p. ix).**

The analysis of this point is one of the most interesting parts of the Committee's final Report, published in 1969, and particularly important today. For, with the resurgence of near-bank growth in 1969, with near-bank legislation being reviewed, not only in Quebec, but in Ontario and elsewhere, and with the trend toward broadening the scope of near-bank activities, the question of monetary control over near-banks is of immediate concern — as reflected in the House of Commons Standing Committee on Finance, Trade, and Economic Affairs, in its Tenth Report on the study of interest rate levels, asking the Bank of Canada to consider the need for more direct control over near-banks. In view of this concern, it is important that the Report's analysis and recommendation with respect to monetary control be carefully interpreted and analysed. Accordingly, it is on this aspect of the Report that our comment concentrates in an attempt to clarify the issues for public debate and policy decisions.

---

*Reprinted from J. A. Galbraith and Anna L. Guthrie, "Near-Banks and Monetary Control," *The Canadian Banker,* July-August, 1970, pp. 26-28, by permission of the editor and authors.
Dr. Galbraith is Director of Economic Research and Miss Guthrie is Associate Economist — both with the Royal Bank of Canada.
**Originally published in French as *Rapport du Comité d'Etude sur les Institutions Financières* (Quebec: L'Editeur officiel du Québec, 1969), pp. xiv, 310, $3.00. This comment uses the English edition, *Report of the Study Committee on Financial Institutions* (Quebec: Quebec Official Publisher, 1969), pp. xiv, 268, as the basic source, but the French edition has also been read and consulted. Page references, separated by a semicolon, are cited for both editions, those for the English edition first.

The Report first considers whether or not the existence of near-banks "detracts from the effectiveness of monetary policy" (p. 158; 185). Specifically, the analysis postulates a tight money policy and examines what near-banks might do to upset that policy, ignoring that the Bank of Canada can sterilize any upsetting action. Three possibilities are examined: near-bank growth, a reduction in near-bank cash ratios, and a running down of near-bank liquidity.

Near-bank growth is seen as occurring when the public shifts funds from banks to near-banks. Two hypothetical balance-sheets are constructed (pp. 164-65; 192) to demonstrate that such a shift of funds will expand the near-banks at a time when the central bank is contracting the banking system. In other words, the examples show the near-banks growing when the banks are declining, which is an offset to a tight monetary policy.

The Report presents no empirical work of its own to prove if, in fact, near-banks do offset monetary policy in the foregoing fashion. It alludes vaguely to studies by others, finds none completely conclusive, but concurs that the findings support the view "so far, near-banks have not put any serious difficulties in the path of monetary policy" (p. 166, 173, 194; pp. 201-202).

As supporting evidence, the Report cites the argument that near-banks have been no more flexible than banks in reacting to changing monetary conditions (p. 172; 200). Presumably, this is intended to mean that the near-banks have been unable to induce funds to shift to them from the banks in times of tight money. The general proposition here is that if both the banks and near-banks are equally flexible in all aspects of their competition, including rates, neither can gain on the other during periods of easy or tight money. If that is so, near-banks cannot offset monetary policy. Unfortunately, the Report does not limit the freedom of banks to compete with near-banks for the public's funds, near-banks cannot offset monetary policy by inducing a shift of funds to them.

Developments in 1969 and early 1970 have provided a clear example of what can happen if the freedom of the banks to compete is restricted. Since 1968 the larger banks have been constrained by moral suasion to limit the rates paid on their short-term Canadian dollar deposits.[1] In the tight money year of 1969 and on into 1970, this informal ceiling on deposit rates, applied only to the banks, permitted the near-banks once again to grow faster than the banks. The Report indicates no awareness of this situation, but argues that since the 1967 Bank Act gave the banks substantial competitive advantages over the near-banks, near-bank legislation must be liberalized to keep the near-banks competitive (pp. 213-14; 252).

Instead of pursuing the implications for monetary policy of freedom for banks and near-banks to compete, the Report falls back on the argument that the demand for near-bank claims varies directly with that for bank deposits (pp. 170-171; 199), and cites the Porter Report adoption of this view (p. 172; pp. 200-201). Such a relationship between near-bank and bank liabilities means that near-banks must grow (or contract) in step with the banks. This is based on the proposition that the public keeps its holdings of

---

[1] Bank of Canada, *Annual Report,* 1969, p. 12.

near-bank claims in some fixed proportion to its bank deposits. So as bank deposits expand, the public increases its holdings of near-bank claims proportionately, and *vice versa*. There is nothing novel here.[2]

A little more novel is the suggestion that near-banks may offset monetary policy by reducing their cash ratios in times of tight money. But here the discussion is somewhat confused. When the possibility is first introduced (p. 160; p. 187) it is not made clear whether a reduction in near-bank cash ratios has the same effect as a reduction in cash ratios for banks — an expansion in the size of the system. Yet later (p. 167; p. 195), it is implied there is no clear distinction between near-banks running down their liquidity and a reduction in near-bank cash ratios. If that is so, a reduction in cash ratios by near-banks means no more than a change in the composition of an unchanged total of assets, which of course is different from what would happen to banks if they could reduce their cash ratios. (If banks could reduce their cash ratios, total bank deposits would expand.)

A reduction in near-bank cash ratios does not produce an overall expansion of near-banks if the public does not allocate its holdings of intermediary claims between those of near-banks and banks in some constant proportion. In that case, the public merely holds some desired absolute amount of near-bank claims, and any additional funds made available by the near-banks out of their cash balances with the banks, simply end up in the public's holdings of bank deposits. There would be, of course, as the Report is aware, a velocity effect that can be upsetting to a restrictive monetary policy.

In the opposite case, when the public divides its financial intermediary holdings between banks and near-banks in some fixed proportion, a fall in near-bank cash ratios does produce an expansion in near-bank size, as the Porter Report has shown,[3] because some of the cash released by the near-banks from their balances ends up in the public's holdings of near-bank claims.

An expansion of the banking system may also follow, in the absence of counteraction by the Bank of Canada. This is now possible in Canada due to the higher legal cash ratio against demand deposits and the lower ratio against time deposits. The near-banks, in reducing their cash ratios, run down their demand deposits with the banks, which pass into the hands of the public. The public then allocates these deposits between demand and time deposits according to its preference for these types of deposits. As a result, the bank deposits shifted to the public, and held partially as time deposits, require less cash than when they were held entirely as demand deposits by the near-banks, thus freeing some cash from legal requirements.

Having raised the possibility that near-banks might reduce their cash ratios in periods of tight money, the Report proceeds to investigate the behaviour of these ratios (pp. 160-63; pp. 187-90). Unfortunately, the discussion of the observed changes in near-bank cash ratios is not very useful because it does not specify what is being measured.

The observed ratios are necessarily average ratios, but they are obviously being used to measure the preference of near-banks for cash at the margin.

---

[2] An analysis of the literature on this and related points is attempted in J. A. Galbraith, "Monetary Policy and Nonbank Financial Intermediaries," *The National Banking Review*, 4 (September, 1966), pp. 53-60, reprinted in John Lindauer, ed., *Macroeconomic Reading* (1968), pp. 324-29 and in Sid Mittra, ed., *Money and Banking: Theory, Analysis, and Policy* (1970).
[3] Canada, *Report of the Royal Commission on Banking and Finance* (Ottawa, 1964), p. 112.

But suppose that the marginal cash ratios near-banks work to are less than the average ratios. For example, near-banks might work to zero marginal cash ratios, that is, they might hold some fixed minimum amount of cash regardless of the amount of their liabilities to the public. Under this kind of cash behaviour, observed cash ratios will fall as near-banks grow. This fall in observed cash ratios would not be a reflection of a changing preference for cash, as is implied when speaking of a deliberate reduction in cash ratios. Yet it is only a change in preference for cash that should be considered as an independent offset to monetary policy.

Similarly, if near-bank cash, which is not precisely defined in the Report, includes interest-bearing time deposits with banks, a shift out of these into other assets is, for the near-banks, comparable to a shift from one type of earning asset to another and not to a reduction in working cash. Nevertheless, from the point of view of monetary policy, the effect is the same as if working cash balances were reduced, that is, near-banks will have excess cash and be able to expand. However, some of the near-bank funds previously in bank time deposits will likely end up in bank demand deposits and, with a higher reserve ratio against demand than time deposits, the cash requirements of the banks will be raised, which may cause the banks to contract if the Bank of Canada does not intervene.

In analysing a reduction in near-bank liquidity as an offset to a restrictive monetary policy, the discussion of the Report (pp. 167-68; pp. 195-96) is relatively straightforward. As the Report correctly concedes, if near-banks accumulate liquid assets when the demand for credit is weak and dispose of them during a period of monetary restraint, there is an increase in the velocity of money. The Report concludes that on *a priori* grounds the contribution of near-banks to accentuating fluctuations in velocity "is not negligible" (pp. 167-68; p. 196).

Yet, as the Report itself points out, it is not only near-banks but also banks and others that run down liquidity during a credit squeeze. If that is so, near-bank behaviour is no different from bank behaviour. Therefore, it is only proper to single out a reduction in near-bank liquidity as an independent offset to monetary policy if near-banks have greater scope than banks for reducing their liquidity.

Near-Banks and Bank of Canada Control

The analysis in the Report on how near-banks affect monetary policy is background for answering the question about the advisability of Bank of Canada control over near-banks. Control is interpreted to mean imposing a fixed cash ratio on near-banks and making them hold cash balances with the Bank of Canada (p. 158; p. 184).

The Report recommends against a fixed cash ratio because near-bank cash ratios "do not fluctuate widely in practice, hence the effect produced by a statutory minimum requirement would be limited" (p. 168; p. 197). However, there is the contrary recommendation in the Porter Report to contend with. The Report on Financial Institutions realizes Porter does not recommend cash reserve ratios for near-banks for monetary policy reasons (p. 172; p. 201), but does not completely understand why Porter wants them (pp. 172, 174-75; pp. 201, 203-204).

Briefly, Porter's position is that a fixed cash ratio imposed on banks helps monetary policy, making its effects more predictable. That being the case, equity requires imposing similar ratios on near-banks.[4] The counter argument, if one accepts Porter's basic premise that fixed bank cash ratios help monetary policy,[5] is to impose on banks cash ratios no more onerous than they would themselves maintain in a free state. Such legal cash ratios would not make the banks any worse off than near-banks left free to carry whatever cash they needed.

In considering if near-banks should carry cash balances with the Bank of Canada, the Report finds that this would make only one essential difference. Shifts of funds by the public between banks and near-banks would lead automatically to corresponding losses or gains in bank cash (p. 169; pp. 197-98). If the cash shifted funds from the banks to the near-banks, the banks would lose cash and have to contract. Bank of Canada balances (cash) would be shifted to the near-banks from the banks causing bank cash ratios to fall below the legally required levels and forcing the banks to contract deposits until the ratios were restored to required levels.

This, of course, is beneficial when the Bank of Canada is being restrictive and funds shift this way, as the Report shows in a balance-sheet example. But, as the Report is also quick to state (p. 169; p. 198), a shift of funds by the public the other way, from the near-banks to the banks, would cause an automatic expansion in bank cash, that is, the banks would gain Bank of Canada balances from the near-banks, something that does not happen now. In that case, it would be more beneficial for a restrictive monetary policy not to have near-bank balances at the Bank of Canada. In short, it is not necessarily desirable to make near-banks keep balances with the Bank of Canada for the automatic effect this would have on bank cash when funds shift between banks and near-banks.

However, the Report does not rely on this argument to recommend against having near-bank balances at the Bank of Canada. It seems instead to rest its case on the grounds that the proposal would accomplish nothing since near-bank liabilities move in step with those of the banks (pp. 170-71; p. 199). Indeed, it is to be regretted the Report did not make explicit the implicit assumption built into its examples (pp. 169-70; pp. 198-99) that moving near-bank cash balances to the central bank does not make near-banks more sensitive to the impact of monetary policy, at least in the form of open-market operations. Sensitivity to open-market operations depends on the nature of an institution's clientele and not on the location of its cash balances.[6]

Conclusion

From this analysis of the Report's discussion of the basic question of near-banks and monetary control emerges the conclusion that the Report's

---

[4] See Report of the Royal Commission on Banking and Finance, pp. 390-91.

[5] For the case against legal cash requirements and supporting literature, see J. A. Galbraith, The Economics of Banking Operations (Montreal, 1963), p. 433; Donald B. Marsh, "Johnson's Tour of the Northern Dominion," The Canadian Journal of Economics and Political Science, 30, No. 15, (May, 1964), pp. 263-64; idem. "Johnson's Tour: A Rejoinder," The Canadian Journal of Economics and Political Science, 31, No. 11, (February, 1965), p. 127; and W. Earle McLaughlin, Chairman and President, The Royal Bank of Canada, "Submission to the Royal Commission on Banking and Finance," Supplement to The Canadian Banker (Spring, 1963), pp. 153-54.

[6] This point is clearly stated in McLaughlin, op. cit., p. 150, par. 7, and p. 153, par. 21, and developed in Galbraith, "Monetary Policy and Nonbank Financial Intermediaries," p. 54.

recommendation against making near-banks subject to direct Bank of Canada control could have been put more forcefully and definitely. It could have been made on the grounds that near-banks, given stable cash ratios and no more scope than banks for running down liquidity, cannot reduce the effectiveness of monetary policy so long as full and free competition permits the banks at least to preserve their share of the market. Under those conditions, controls on near-banks for purposes of monetary policy are unnecessary.

E. GOVERNMENT REVENUE AND EXPENDITURE

Although there are many ways in which government affects economic welfare, it is through taxation and expenditures that the functions of government are most directly felt. Indeed, changes in the size and composition of government spending and the volume of tax revenues reflect with a fair degree of accuracy any alterations in the scope and character of government's role in the economic system. It is with the public sector's role as a transactor, that is, as a receiver and disposer of "income," that this section is concerned.

Public finance deals with the financing of organized governments of various kinds; under our federal system, government finance, like all government operations, is carried on independently by federal, provincial, and local or municipal governments.

In order to command the services of productive agents, governments must have money. The money to meet government outlays comes primarily from four sources: taxation, borrowing, commercial and administrative revenues, and the issue of noninterest bearing currency (this method is open only to national governments and sometimes only through indirection).

Basically, there are only three different kinds of taxes: those which are levied on income, those which are levied on wealth and transfers of wealth, and those which are levied on consumption expenditures. One of the most important characteristics of a good tax system is that it should be fair. But how is fairness in taxation achieved? There are two possible criteria which may be used. One is known as the benefit principle and the other as the ability-to-pay principle. According to the former principle, people and firms are taxed in proportion to the benefits they receive from the expenditure of the tax monies. According to the latter, each taxpayer is required to contribute to the cost of government in accordance with his financial ability. Reading 37 identifies and describes nine other characteristics of a good tax system.

The tax-paying capacity of a nation depends in an important measure on the final resting place of the tax burden. The person or business upon which a tax is levied may not be the bearer of the final burden. Instead, the tax may be shifted, that is, passed on to someone else. The incidence of a tax is its final resting place. Thus, in appraising the merits of a tax system, the incidence of particular taxes must be given special attention. Otherwise the real impact on certain groups may be underestimated. Reading 38 examines the incidence of taxation in Canada.

37. PRINCIPLES OF TAXATION*

Ontario Committee on Taxation

Equity is the prime, but by no means the sole, characteristic of a good tax system. After due consideration, we have selected no fewer than nine principles which, together with equity, should form the basis of a sound revenue structure. Some of these are derived from considerations of equity, others are prompted by the need for efficiency. We enumerate them here for the sake of convenience and will proceed to discuss them in turn. They are:
1. adequacy,
2. flexibility,
3. elasticity,
4. balance,
5. neutrality,
6. certainty,
7. simplicity,
8. convenience, and
9. economy of collection and compliance.

Adequacy

This principle requires virtually no explanation. It is a self-evident proposition that to be satisfactory, a tax system must be capable of providing the flow of funds that a government deems appropriate in any given period. We note, however, that the principle of adequacy can become highly relevant when the relative merits of grants and taxes are discussed in connection with provincial and municipal revenue systems.

Flexibility

By flexibility is meant that a tax system should be so constituted that

---

*Reprinted from the *Ontario Committee on Taxation, Report,* Toronto, 1967, pp. 16-20, by permission of William Kinmond, Queen's Printer and Publisher.

government, by discretionary action, can readily increase or decrease the flow of tax funds in response to changing circumstances, which can stem either from considerations of expenditure requirements or of economic policy. Obviously, some taxes, such as those on property and on personal income, are more flexible than others, in that rate alterations can be graded so as to accommodate small as well as large changes in revenue requirements. The principle of flexibility can thus be deemed to be satisfied if a revenue system is comprised in part of flexible taxes.

Elasticity

The principle of elasticity is closely related to those of adequacy and flexibility. This principle requires that a revenue system be composed in part of taxes whose yields respond closely to changing economic circumstances without deliberate changes in rates. It is important that the principle be fulfilled for two reasons. First, elasticity enables governments to meet rising service demands occasioned by economic growth without the disturbance of frequent rate changes. Second, elastic tax yields are an important adjunct of fiscal policy in that they can serve as automatic stabilizers, leaving a greater proportion of income in the private sector in times of adversity and dampening inflationary pressures in times of prosperity.

Balance

This principle is to be found in certain textbooks under such names as "multiplicity" or "plurality," but we have chosen the term "balance" in order to emphasize the kind of plurality that a tax system should possess. The need for a balanced plurality of taxes is grounded partly in the requirements of flexibility and elasticity, partly in equity, and partly in administrative considerations. As to flexibility and elasticity, it is readily apparent that some taxes are more flexible, others more elastic. Thus the property tax is relatively unresponsive to economic change but highly flexible, whereas consumption taxes are rather more elastic but relatively inflexible. A tax system should therefore have a sufficient multiplicity of taxes to take account of these characteristics. In the domain of equity, if a tax system is to conform to the basic rule of equal treatment of equals, it must not only be able to take differing individual situations into account but also be virtually foolproof in terms of evasion. If we may quote the Right Honourable Hugh Dalton, a former Chancellor of the Exchequer of the United Kingdom:

> Anomalies as between persons, which are liable to arise under a single tax, are liable to be corrected under a multiplicity of taxes. And evasions, which may be comparatively easy under a single tax, are more readily detected under the check and countercheck which a multiple tax system may provide. Thus valuations for death duties and the previous income tax returns of the deceased may be checked against one another.[1]

---

[1] Hugh Dalton, *Principles of Public Finance,* 4th ed., (London, 1954), p. 31.

Multiplicity, then, is an important key to elasticity, flexibility, and equity. But it is not an end in itself. For one thing, the number of taxes that reflect elasticity, flexibility, and equity is limited. Furthermore, to quote Mr. Dalton again:

> ... though a multiple tax system is generally preferable to a single tax system, too great a multiplicity is not desirable. Advocates of "broadening the basis of taxation" are to be distrusted. Of this fellowship was [one] who said, "if I were to define a good system of taxation, it should be that of bearing lightly on an infinite number of points, heavily on none." But there is not necessarily any less total pressure under such a system for, as mathematicians know, the sum of an infinitely large number of infinitely small weights may be greater than a single moderate weight. Moreover, a large number of taxes, however small, usually involves a large cost and a large amount of vexation in collection.[2]

To this we wish only to add the thought that too great a multiplicity of taxes may dissipate altogether taxpayer consciousness of the cost of government, consciousness that is certainly desirable in a constitutional democracy. Thus we subscribe only to that multiplicity of taxes consistent with flexibility, elasticity, equity, and sound administration — in short, to a principle of balance.

Neutrality

The principle of neutrality is directly related to the objective of efficiency in the use of the human and material resources of society. We do not suggest that, in order to be neutral, a fiscal system must exert no influence on the economic behaviour of persons or businesses. When the fiscal operations of all levels of government in Canada involve, as they do, almost one-third of gross national product, it is clear that no such thing is possible. Our approach to neutrality is rather in terms of applying the rule of least price distortion in the choice of taxes. If one assumes that the pattern of relative prices determined by competitive market forces tends to encourage the most efficient allocation of the nation's resources, then to the extent that a tax system minimizes its distortion of relative prices, it minimizes its interference with productive efficiency. An important implication follows, namely that the more general a tax, the less it will normally interfere with individual choices on the part of producers, resource owners, and consumers. From this point of view, such general taxes as those on income and retail sales are to be preferred to selective excise taxes applied to a narrow range of commodities.

Understood in terms of least price distortion, the principle of neutrality is violated if consumers are taxed on their expenditures for goods but not for services. The principle is likewise violated if governments provide tax concessions in order to induce particular firms or industries to locate in areas where, in terms of the most efficient use of resources, they would not otherwise go. In its broad context, however, the efficient use of resources involves not only the private costs incurred by a firm but also the social costs arising from its operation in a particular location. Again, neutrality will be

---

[2] *Ibid.*, p. 32.

violated where the revenue system imposes heavier taxes on some legal forms of business organization than on others. To be neutral, the tax system should provide similar treatment for individual proprietors, partnerships, co-operatives, and all forms of corporate enterprise. We are, of course, fully aware of the enormous practical difficulties involved in providing such neutral treatment.

We do not wish to argue that neutrality is a principle of taxation that should be followed under any and all circumstances. It is appropriate only when economic efficiency is a prime criterion of policy. On frequent occasions, governments are legitimately more concerned with other goals and will consciously depart from neutrality in order to further these objectives. What should be recognized, however, is that where tax neutrality is abandoned, the efficient allocation of resources, in the short run at least, will be impeded.

Certainty

The principle of certainty as to the time, manner, and amount of payment of tax has been advocated for centuries. Adam Smith regarded a small degree of uncertainty as a much greater evil than "a very considerable degree of inequality,"[3] in that it subjected the taxpayer to the arbitrary decisions of the authorities. A further argument for certainty is the desirability, in an era of high government expenditure, that the citizen be well informed of his tax burden so that he may relate it to the benefits he derives from public services. If the individual is not well informed, he may make decisions about government spending that might have been different had he been aware of the facts. A particular risk is that being only dimly aware of his total tax burden, he will underestimate the cost of the public services with which he is provided. This is particularly likely where many of his taxes are hidden in the prices of the goods and services he purchases, rather than imposed upon him directly.

If the principle of certainty is valid, and we believe that it is, then those direct taxes that cannot be shifted, or that can be shifted only to a limited degree, are superior to any taxes that can be hidden or easily shifted. On this basis, the personal income tax is superior to corporation income tax which sooner or later must be borne by individuals as consumers, shareholders, or employees. Similarly, a visible retail sales tax is superior to a consumption tax levied at the manufacturer's level. Again, as it affects the relative merits of subsidies or tax concessions as forms of government financial assistance, the principle of certainty favours subsidies, for their costs are more readily ascertainable to government and public alike than are the costs of tax concessions or exemptions.

Finally, the principle of certainty should apply with force to the content of tax statutes. At the very least, no tax law should be written in such a way that it contains provisions that the government either cannot or will not enforce effectively. An obvious example of such a provision can be found in the Ontario Retail Sales Tax Act which stipulates that residents of Ontario are liable for sales tax on goods bought outside but transported into the province for their use. To the extent that such a requirement is known to be

---

[3] Adam Smith, *The Wealth of Nations,* Modern Library ed., (New York, 1937), p. 778.

the law but is not enforced, the reputation of the government as a lawmaker, to say nothing of respect for the law itself, is imperceptibly lowered in the public esteem. The principle of certainty demands statutes that are at once enforceable and enforced.

Simplicity

We wish to comment only briefly on the relation between certainty and simplicity. The principle of simplicity will lend strong support to certainty provided it is applied with care. The point is, of course, that indiscriminate striving for simplicity will yield statutes that leave too much unsaid and hence that can only be applied with a wide scope for administrative discretion — discretion that will unduly impinge on certainty. Again, undue simplicity may make it impossible to recognize the varying circumstances of particular taxpayers. Hence the principle of simplicity must be considered as dictating the greatest clarity within the limits set by certainty and equity. It should be understood that after every effort has been made to apply the principle of simplicity in the sense indicated above, certain taxes, notably those on personal and corporate income, will be embodied in statutes that are irreducibly but still appreciably complex.

Convenience

The principle of convenience is highly significant in relation to the time, place, and manner in which a taxpayer is called upon to discharge his obligations. It is in accordance with this principle that municipalities have developed instalment systems for the payment of property taxes and have, in some instances, permitted payment through chartered banks and other specified places of business. The principle of convenience is not simply a matter of good public relations. Observance of this principle redounds to the direct advantage of government by simplifying compliance and by reducing costs. With regard to the latter, there can be no doubt that the deduction of income tax at the source, a practice introduced by the Dominion during World War II, has greatly simplified government fiscal operations by increasing the speed of cash flows and hence reducing the need for short-term borrowing.

Economy of Collection and Compliance.

The principle of economy applies both to the costs incurred by government in collecting taxes and to those incurred by the taxpayer in complying with his tax obligations. The principle of economy, especially in relation to the costs incurred by government, dictates not the lowest possible cost but the lowest cost consistent with equity and effective enforcement. Thus it is blatantly false economy for governments to employ unqualified assessors at rock-bottom rates of remuneration. Such practices can result only in inefficiency, discrimination, and multiplying appeals and hence increasing the cost of taxpayer compliance. Properly understood, the principle of economy requires the employment of competent public servants in sufficient numbers.

38. THE INCIDENCE OF THE TOTAL TAX STRUCTURE*

W. I. Gillespie

The tax revenues that are examined in some detail are shown in Table 1. This table differs somewhat from the usual published statistics of DBS. The taxes are for net general revenue, and the provincial and municipal data are on a comparable basis for the fiscal year 1961. The tax rental payments to the provinces have been treated as provincial tax revenue for the year 1961. In addition, social security contributions have been included in the tax estimates.

TABLE 1

TOTAL TAX PAYMENTS, 1961*

Revenue Source	Total Tax Payments		Total Tax Payments Exclusive of Taxes Exported to Foreigners	
	Millions (1)	% (2)	Millions (3)	% (4)
1. Individual income tax	$2,137	21.4	$2,137	22.9
2. Corporate profits tax	1,610	16.1	1,191	12.8
3. Succession duties	151	1.5	151	1.6
4. General sales taxes	1,400	14.0	1,400	15.0
5. Selective excises	1,482	14.8	1,440	15.4
6. Import duties	535	5.3	535	5.7
7. Property tax	1,399	14.0	1,300	13.9
8. Social Security	600	6.0	600	6.4
9. Other taxes	676	6.8	575	6.2
10. Total Taxes	9,990	100.0	9,329	100.0

*For all levels of government: Intergovernmental transfers are deleted.
Source: DBS, *Financial Statistics of Federal, Provincial and Municipal Governments, 1961.*

---

*Reprinted from W. I. Gillespie, "The Incidence of Taxes and Public Expenditures in the Canadian Economy," *Studies of the Royal Commission on Taxation*, Ottawa, 1966, excerpts from pp. 31-67, by permission of Information Canada.
Dr. Gillespie is Professor of Economics, Carleton University, Ottawa.

Shifting Assumptions

The Individual Income Tax

The individual income tax is assumed to rest with the initial payee, that is, the tax is not shifted. This tacitly assumes that total factor supplies, labour and capital, are fixed. While this is a limiting assumption, if secondary changes are more or less neutral in their distributional implications, it is not so restrictive as it first might seem.

The Corporate Profits Tax

The corporate profits tax is assumed to fall partially (one-half) on profits, while the remainder is shifted forward to consumers. That portion of the tax that falls on profits is allocated by a distribution of dividends received. The part of the tax shifted forward to consumers is allocated by a distribution of total consumption. This treatment of the corporate profit tax arises out of the lack of consensus concerning the incidence of the tax.

General Sales Tax on Consumer Goods

The general sales tax on consumer goods is assumed to be borne by the consumer. The tax is allocated by a distribution of total consumption expenditures. This treatment is based on the general consensus among economists that the sales tax on consumer goods is, in fact, borne in proportion to total outlays on consumption.

Two Canadian taxes fall within the scope of a general sales tax on consumer goods — the general manufacturers' sales tax, and the provincial retail sales tax.

Selective Excise Taxes

Selective excise taxes are assumed to fall on the consumers of the taxed products. The main excise taxes are on sales of liquor, tobacco, and motor fuel; there are many minor excise taxes which range from radios to playing cards and amount in total to no more than 11 percent of all excises. Selective excise taxes are allocated by the distribution of consumption expenditures on the taxed articles, that is, the excise tax on tobacco is allocated to smokers and it is distributed by a percentage distribution of consumption expenditures on tobacco, by income class.

The Property Tax

The property tax is of considerable importance, both because of its importance as a revenue source on the local level, and, due to this, its decisive weight in the allocation of the tax payments among the lower income groups. To the extent that the real property tax is applied to the *value of land* it cannot be shifted, and thus rests on the owner. That part of the property tax yield from business land is borne by business owners and is allocated by the distribution of dividends received. The portion of the property tax yield from farm land is borne by farm operators who own their own farms, and is allocated by the distribution of the estimated value of farm property (exclusive of the farm operator's house). That part of the property tax yield from residential-owner-occupied real estate is borne by the home owner and distributed by the estimated value of owner-occupied homes, while the tax yield from residential-renter-occupied real estate is borne by the landlord and is allocated by the distribution of net rental income. That part of the property tax yield from business and farm improvements is in the nature of an excise tax on the value of buildings and, as such, is capable of being shifted to consumers. Assuming these portions of the property tax are shifted, then the former is allocated by a distribution of total consumption while the latter is allocated by a distribution of expenditures on food products.

That part of the property tax on the assessed improvements of owner-occupied homes is again assumed to remain with the owner; and it is allocated by a distribution of the estimated value of owner-occupied homes. In the case of renter-occupied homes, though, the property tax on improvements is, in effect, an excise tax on the cost of providing rental units. Our assumption is to allocate the entire tax share falling on rental improvements to the tenant.

Selective Factor Taxes

It is assumed that a tax on the earnings of a certain factor (for example, wages) remains with the recipient.

Succession and Estate Taxes

It is assumed that all succession and estate taxes can be allocated to income-recipients in the open-end upper income bracket.

Hospital Insurance Premiums

It is assumed that hospital insurance premiums or taxes remain with the payee; that is, such taxes are not shifted. This tax is allocated by a distribution of hospital insurance tax payments.

Customs Import Duties

It is assumed that customs duties are shifted to the consumers of the taxed commodities. In this manner import duties are similar to a general excise tax on consumption.

"Other" Taxes

The category "*other*" taxes includes: (i) motor vehicle licences, (ii) natural resource revenues, (iii) taxes on the premium income of life insurance companies, and (iv) municipal business taxes. Motor vehicle licences are allocated by a distribution of expenditures on automobiles. Taxes on life insurance premiums and municipal business taxes are allocated by distributions of the value of life insurance paid and total consumption, respectively.

TABLE 2

EFFECTIVE TOTAL TAX INCIDENCE FOR THE TOTAL TAX STRUCTURE, 1961*

Line	Tax Source	Family Money Income Class							
		Under $2,000	$2,000-2,999	$3,000-3,999	$4,000-4,999	$5,000-6,999	$7,000-9,999	$10,000- and over	Total
		Percentages							
1.	Federal Taxes, Total	27.3	16.9	18.0	17.3	19.3	20.7	23.8	20.2
2.	Individual Income Tax	1.1	1.9	3.3	4.5	7.2	8.8	10.4	6.9
3.	Corporation Income Tax	6.5	3.4	2.8	2.3	2.4	2.7	6.1	3.4
4.	Sales Tax	8.0	4.2	4.2	3.7	4.0	4.1	2.7	3.9
5.	Selective Excises	4.3	2.6	2.6	2.3	2.5	2.4	1.5	2.3
6.	Import Duties	4.7	2.3	2.2	1.9	2.0	2.0	1.3	2.0
7.	Estate Duties	—	—	—	—	—	—	1.4	.3
8.	Social Security Contributions	2.7	2.5	2.9	2.6	1.2	.7	.5	1.5
9.	Provincial and Local Taxes, Total	32.7	16.0	14.2	13.1	13.5	13.5	14.6	14.5
10.	Individual Income Tax	.1	.3	.5	.7	1.1	1.4	1.6	1.1
11.	Corporation Income Tax	2.0	1.1	.9	.7	.7	.8	1.9	1.0
12.	Sales and Excises	8.2	4.5	4.6	4.3	4.7	4.5	3.0	4.4
13.	Succession Duties	—	—	—	—	—	—	1.5	.3
14.	Hospital Insurance Premiums	2.6	.9	.7	.5	.4	.3	.1	.5
15.	Property Tax	16.3	6.8	5.4	4.8	4.3	4.0	3.8	4.8
16.	Other Taxes	2.7	1.6	1.4	1.3	1.4	1.5	2.2	1.6
17.	Social Security Contributions	.8	.7	.8	.8	.9	.9	.5	.8
18.	Total Taxes, All Levels	60.0	32.9	32.2	30.5	32.8	34.2	38.4	34.7

*Using the "broad income" base.
Note: Details may not add to totals due to rounding.

Empirical Results: The Standard Pattern of Tax Incidence

With these qualifications in mind, taxes are allocated by the assumptions given above and the results are expressed as a percent of income. The resulting pattern of total tax incidence for the year 1961 is set forth in Table 2. Table 2 contains the effective tax rates for each income class for all taxes. The total tax structure (line 18) is regressive over the first four income classes — up to an income level of $5,000 — and mildly progressive throughout the remainder of the income scale. When the "adjusted broad income" base is used, the regressivity over the lower income brackets extends up to an income level of $3,000 beyond which the total tax incidence is progressive. Due to the uncertain nature of the effective tax rate in the upper income bracket, it is not clear just how progressive the tax system is over the upper income brackets. In general, though, the incidence of the total tax structure is regressive *at least* up to an income level of $3,000 (using the "adjusted broad income" base) and *at most* up to an income level of $5,000 (using the "broad income" base).

The federal tax structure (line 1) is regressive over the first two brackets and progressive beyond. This pattern is the result of several contrasting forces: first, the individual income tax (line 2) is progressive throughout the entire income range. The corporate profits tax (line 3) is regressive up to an income level of $5,000, and progressive beyond; such regressivity over the lower income brackets is explained by the portion of the tax that is shifted forward, and which is distributed by total consumption expenditures. The general sales tax, selective excises, and import duties all exhibit regressivity up to an income level of $5,000, proportionality from $5,000 to $10,000, and regression beyond.

The provincial and municipal tax structure (line 9) is regressive over the first three income brackets, and almost proportional beyond. The proportional pattern beyond an income level of approximately $4,000 is a result of the element of regression being slightly more than offset by an element of progression. The progressivity is inserted by the individual income tax and the corporate profits tax, although these taxes bear nowhere near the weight in the provincial and municipal tax structures that they do in the federal tax structure. Besides the sales and excise taxes, the property tax also lends weight to the regressive nature of the total provincial and municipal tax structure over the lower income brackets. The property tax (line 15) is regressive over the entire income range. Hospital insurance taxes are regressive over the entire income range, but their weight is minor within the provincial and municipal tax structure.

To sum up, given certain assumptions as to the incidence of each tax, the evidence — with due allowance for some unquantifiable margin of error — suggests that the distribution of effective tax rates is regressive up to an income level of *at least* $3,000 and *at most* $5,000, and progressive beyond. It is this element of regressivity of the tax structure that is important when considerations of tax equity are involved. In total, one-third of all families are affected by the regressiveness up to $3,000, while almost two-thirds are affected by the regressiveness if it persists up to an income level of $5,000.

F. FISCAL POLICY

Government spending and revenue collection account for about one-fifth of Canada's gross national product. These fiscal activities encompass a vast array of purposes and projects — national security, health and social welfare, transportation and communications, law enforcement, education, and so on. Inevitably, those actions affect output, employment, income, and prices whether or not there is a conscious and coherent "stabilization and growth" policy. And over the past third of a century, economists and public officials have given more and more attention to the possibilities of *deliberately* using governmental spending, taxing, and borrowing — in short "fiscal policy" — for stabilization and growth. Fiscal policy can, indeed, be a potent instrument for influencing economic activity. The only relevant question is *how* it should be exercised.

Reading 39 examines the historical development of fiscal policy, comments on the limitations of fiscal policies, and describes the relationship between fiscal and monetary policy.

It is widely accepted that an "easy fiscal policy" can permit or stimulate growth of total demand and that "fiscal restraint" can curb it. But, in this context, what is "easy" and what is "tight"? Closely related to this is the question of how shifts from easy to tight policies (or vice versa) influence the economy. Reading 40 explains why discussions of fiscal policy in Canada and appraisals of its impact on the economic system are frequently distorted and sometimes misleading, and discusses three different budget concepts and their limitations.

Is fiscal policy dead? Only a few years ago it seemed that fiscal policy was all that mattered. Monetary considerations were largely ignored. Now the pendulum of economic thinking may be swinging to the opposite extreme. Most economists believe that such a swing is ill-advised. Reading 41 goes to the heart of the issue and tries to explain the monetarist view of fiscal policy.

39. WHAT DOES IT REALLY MEAN?
FISCAL POLICY*

Henry C. Murphy

Until the Great Depression of the 1930s, and the fundamental economic rethinking that it occasioned, the term "fiscal policy," in the rare instances when it was used at all, meant merely a policy (any policy) which affected the "fisc" — that is, the public treasury. Such policies usually related principally to taxation. The term "fiscal policy" could also in those days have been applied, by extension, to policies concerning public expenditure — although it was generally assumed that there would be no policy concerning public expenditure other than to get the necessary work done as cheaply and as efficiently as possible.

Nowadays, the term "fiscal policy" appears much more frequently and has acquired a rather specific meaning. One occasionally reads in newspapers, even those of general circulation, that such and such a country is "tightening its fiscal policy" or is "relaxing its fiscal policy." The term "fiscal policy," used in a rather specific sense, is now very much a commonplace for economists, and even for politicians, and finds its way into articles written for the common man, particularly the type of article often labelled "news analysis." What does it really mean today?

Developed in Industrial Countries

The particular meaning of the term "fiscal policy" which will be described in this article was developed in industrial countries and has primary application to them. For reasons that I shall give later, the main thrust of the particular type of fiscal policy here described — that is, government financial policy for economic stabilization — has only a limited applicability to developing countries. While the term "fiscal policy" is frequently used at the present time in responsible policy prescriptions for developing countries, it is generally used in the wider sense of "government financial policies designed to

*Reprinted from Henry C. Murphy, "What Does it Really Mean? Fiscal Policy," *Finance and Development,* June, 1970, pp. 14-20, reprinted by permission.

Dr. Murphy is Senior Adviser of the Fiscal Affairs Department of the International Monetary Fund, Washington, D.C. He was an economist for the US Treasury Department from 1935 until 1948.

benefit the economy" (largely by diverting resources from lower priority uses to higher priority uses, especially those stimulating economic growth), and as a measure of anti-inflationary policy; for reasons which will be developed later, fiscal policy has very limited usefulness in developing countries as an instrument for the cyclical stimulation of employment.

The Older Orthodoxy

When the author came to the US Treasury as a young economist in the mid-1930s, orthodox opinion held that the only proper criteria for taxation were fairness, public acceptance, and ease of administration. Furthermore, the only proper purpose in levying taxes was to meet government expenditures. The act of taxing or refraining from taxing was not to be used for ulterior purposes — such as, for example, increasing employment or increasing or holding down prices. The only proper purpose of taxation was to raise money to meet government expenditures and the taxes were to be as "neutral" as possible: that is, they were to change the existing flow of income and expenditure as little as possible. (The change in income flow implicit in progressive taxation was justified solely on the basis of the "fairness" criterion of taxation.) Furthermore, the budget, that is, the total of receipts and expenditures, was to be balanced as nearly as feasible in each peacetime year. This had been the orthodox opinion for generations, being based upon the teaching of the so-called classical economists of the eighteenth century and their successors.

This orthodoxy, of course, was never as pure in practice as it was in theory. Protective tariffs had been levied for many years — against the advice of generations of economists — and, as indicated by the name (and also by the effect), their principal motive was one ulterior to that of raising revenue. Furthermore, articles deemed to be of doubtful benefit to society, such as liquor and tobacco — or fine laces and fine linens — as determined by the sometimes shifting views of those in authority, had been taxed at higher rates than those applicable to articles deemed more socially beneficial.

Furthermore, in the United States, the judicial branch of government had long since taken note of the tremendous potential of taxation for non-revenue purposes in the dictum enunciated by Chief Justice Marshall that "the power to tax is the power to destroy."

However, the exceptions to the old orthodoxy just noted were all on what would now be called a *micro*economic scale — that is, they were intended to affect the demand for particular commodities and the profitability (or even the existence) of particular enterprises, not to effect what we would now call *macro*economic adjustments in the economy — that is, adjustments in the aggregate scale of employment, prices, and incomes. Indeed, the desirability — or even the possibility — of making such adjustments was never discussed or even imagined.

Forces of Change

During the 1930s forces were already at work which would overturn the old orthodoxy just described and replace it with a new orthodoxy called *fiscal policy*: that is, the policy that government receipts and expenditures should be consciously planned, particularly in their aggregate amounts, so as to effect beneficial changes in the overall level of incomes, prices, and employment.

Such major changes in the direction of economic theory are usually preceded, accompanied, or spurred on by changes in the external environment. In the present case, the relevant change in the external environment was the Great Depression of the 1930s. Never before, since the development of industrial societies, had there been a depression on such a scale. The spectacle of men unemployed amidst ample technological know-how, well-equipped factories, and plentiful raw materials; of little pigs slaughtered to reduce the "oversupply" of pork while men went hungry, forced on society a rethinking of its basic economic ideas.

Hitherto, unemployment had been explained negatively as due to "frictions" or imperfections in the working of the economic order; there was no *positive* explanation for unemployment in the old economic theory. It became increasingly clear, however, as the 1930s dragged on, that the massive worldwide unemployment and depression which they brought with them could not be explained adequately by negative concepts such as "friction" or "imperfection." A positive explanation was needed.

Monetary Policy

In the last few years prior to the onslaught of the Great Depression in 1929, there had been a basic optimism that depressions were a thing of the past because the discovery of "monetary policy" in the 1920s had made them impossible in the future. Industrial countries, therefore, sought in the 1930s to combat the oncoming depression by means of monetary policy, that is, by lowering the cost and increasing the availability of money for business investment. For reasons which cannot be detailed here (as this article is on fiscal policy), monetary policy proved inadequate to the challenge. Businessmen were not tempted to borrow money when they took a pessimistic view of the profit outlook for business. Money became cheaper and cheaper, but the added cheapness became less and less effective as a means of spurring business. There is still some dispute whether monetary policy might have been successful in combating the depression of the 1930s if it had been used earlier and more energetically. A few economists say it would, but most now believe that it is intrinsically inadequate for dealing with developing depressions except in their early stages, and is especially inadequate for deep depression situations. The basic difficulty is that the newly created funds simply pile up in the banks and will not move out into business. This was expressed in the economic *bon mot* of the 1930s, "you can't push a string."

The Teaching of Keynes

In the meantime, what proved to be a more efficacious instrument for attacking economic depressions was being developed on another sector of the economic scene. The British economist, John Maynard Keynes, in his writings in the 1930s, had pointed out that a decision to save does not necessarily lead to a decision to invest an equal amount, and that the earlier assumption of most economists that it did, had been based on premises less general than they had supposed — premises which, in effect, *assumed* rather than proved that there would be full employment. Keynes, therefore, set out to develop a "general theory" of economics which showed that it was possible for economic equilibrium to be established at low — that is, deep depression — levels of employment as well as at high levels of employment. This new economics knocked out the theoretical underpinnings of the old "Treasury view" (in the United Kingdom and elsewhere) which had held that government expenditures financed by borrowing did not increase employment because they merely diverted what would otherwise have been an equal amount of private (investment) spending to the government. Keynes had shown that, while public borrowing doubtless absorbed private *saving*, in times of deep depression the "counterpart" of the private saving so absorbed would more likely have been unemployment than private investment. This is the heart of the "general theory." Keynes, in his practical, day-to-day activities, consequently advocated increased public spending financed by borrowing in times of depression, as his theory had shown that in such times the deficits of national governments should be viewed, not merely as the amounts by which taxes failed to cover expenditures, but as positive instruments by which the *aggregate* level of incomes and employment could be increased — while, again, under conditions of deep depression, prices would be increased very little.

Keynes' ideas were picked up rather rapidly, particularly in the United Kingdom and the United States, and Keynesian economics, as the "new economics," spread rather quickly in the academic world. Much modified, it now dominates economic teaching in all of the industrial countries of the Western world. The theoretical basis of this new economics will not be further enlarged upon; its leading *policy* prescription is that national governments should plan their revenues and expenditures and the balance between them, not merely with reference to the specific objectives of each tax and each type of expenditure, but also so that aggregate taxation and expenditure will, on the whole, promote desired overall objectives.

Development of the "New Economics"

It should be noted that, in the course of extensive academic discussions, principally in the 1940s, what had originally been conceived as a one-purpose policy for use in fighting depression had become enlarged to become a two-purpose policy, for use either in offsetting inflation or depression, as was appropriate at the time. This development had the corollary of discovering a useful ulterior purpose for fiscal surpluses as well as for fiscal deficits — that is, fiscal surpluses were helpful in controlling inflation. While, as previously stated, the spread of the new economics was rapid throughout the academic world, acceptance of its policy recommendations in the world of politicians and businessmen came much more slowly.

The spread of the new economics had very little effect in ameliorating the hardships of the last years of the Great Depression. The Depression was in fact brought to an end by heavy government expenditures in preparing for and fighting World War II, which were not accompanied by commensurate tax increases. Government finance in World War II, consequently, provided a massive "demonstration effect" of what could be done for depressed economies by large government expenditures financed by borrowing.

In the light of this demonstration effect, and spurred on by the urging of young men coming from the universities, politicians and businessmen asked themselves in the late 1940s and early 1950s whether the good economic side effects which had come about incidentally as the result of the war could not be recreated in peacetime by conscious fiscal policy. In addition, the transition of the ideas of the new economics to the realm of practical politics was helped by the fact that "peace," as it had been understood earlier, never really came after World War II; military expenditures remained very high and so provided a continuation on a smaller scale of the "demonstration effect" of the war. In many cases such military expenditures, combined with other large expenditures and lax tax policies, overshot the mark of high employment, and so provided a "demonstration effect" in the opposite direction — namely, one concerning the effect of undue government deficits in stimulating inflation in overextended economies.

Limitations of Fiscal Policy

In the early days of the development of fiscal policy it was assumed, particularly by young graduates of Western universities returning to their homes in developing countries, that the new gospel of fiscal policy was as applicable in their own countries as in the industrial countries in which they had studied. In those days, it will be remembered, fiscal policy was still rather one-sided, directed more against depression than against inflation. It was assumed that it could be applied with as much success in reducing chronic unemployment in, say, India, as in reducing cyclical unemploymernt in the United States or the United Kingdom. This assumption proved to be incorrect. In times of depression industrial countries have large pools of unemployed productive resources of skilled and unskilled labour, of unused or underutilized (but efficient) capital equipment, and of managerial skills which, given increased demand, can be rapidly put to use for increasing production. This situation is not duplicated in the developing countries which suffer from chronic unemployment. In these countries the unemployed factors are unbalanced; the "pools" are especially lacking in labour of the necessary skills, in managerial techniques, and in unused (but efficient) capital equipment. In these circumstances, therefore, the injection of increased purchasing power by fiscal policy tends to work itself out, not primarily in increased production, as it does in industrial countries in time of depression, but principally in increases in prices and imports.

Chronic unemployment, not susceptible to successful treatment by fiscal policy, is the commonest in developing countries, and cyclical employment, which is subject to successful treatment by fiscal policy, is the commonest in industrial countries. Chronic unemployment, however, exists in industrial countries — for example, note the inability of the United States to reduce its unemployment rate much below 4 percent even with substantial inflation — while some cyclical unemployment exists in the developing countries. As the proportion of cyclical unemployment to total unemployment is low in the developing countries, and fiscal policy is a blunt instrument which cannot be pinpointed by sector or industry, it cannot be much used for relieving cyclical unemployment in the developing countries without important adverse effects in the form of domestic inflation and balance of payments difficulty. Consequently, responsible prescriptions of unemployment-oriented fiscal policy for developing countries are now generally concentrated on ways of using the power of government finance to divert resources from lower priority uses to higher priority uses (particularly investment in productive capital) and to providing, through taxation or otherwise, incentives for productive investment.

Fiscal policy is as effective in counteracting inflation in developing countries as it is in industrial countries, and it can, to a limited extent, mitigate the hardships arising in developing countries from external causes (for example, declining export prices) inasmuch as reserves are available or can be borrowed to offset the external drain inevitably incident to expansive fiscal policy.

The basic idea of stabilizing the economies of industrial countries by using government surpluses and deficits as counterweights is so simple that it may seem surprising that it had not occurred earlier to the many acute economic thinkers of the nineteenth and early twentieth centuries, who were also spurred on by what appeared to them to be rather severe depressions in their own time. It may seem strange that the idea of fiscal policy had to wait until the mid-twentieth century to be born.

Perhaps the principal reason for the late development of the idea of "fiscal policy" is that fiscal policy can be really meaningful only when the expenditures of national governments have come to comprise a substantial proportion of their respective gross national products (GNP). This was not so in most industrial countries until well on into the twentieth century, and, consequently, the development of the macroeconomic concept of the use of government finance as a counterweight to fluctuations in the rest of the economy had to wait until the size of government expenditures relative to total private expenditures in the respective economies had grown to somewhat near its present magnitude. The causes of the growth in the relative magnitude of the expenditures of national governments were primarily social and political, rather than economic, in character. An inquiry into the nature of these causes is outside the scope of this article. It should be noted, however, that the forces bringing about this change have been pervasive throughout the world — operating in the industrial and the developing countries alike. Indeed, the proportion of the expenditure of a government to total expenditure in its economy, while higher for the industrial countries than for the developing countries, is related more to the time of the observation than to the phase of the economic development of the country. When the United States was a young, struggling, developing country, its government expenditures were so small as a proportion of its GNP that even an energetic fiscal policy, as that is now understood, could have provided no important counterweight to unemployment or inflation in the private sector of the economy. The same thing can be said, to a somewhat lesser degree, of the other principal industrial countries of today. On the other hand, the expenditures of the governments of the poor developing countries of today are, in general, many times greater as proportions of the total size of their respective economies than were the expenditures of the governments of the principal industrial countries of today at the same stage in their economic development.

It should be added that, as fiscal policy depends heavily on planning, in addition to the development of sufficiently large underlying aggregates "in the real world," it was also necessary, in order to make fiscal policy practical, that these magnitudes should be *perceived* by planners and politicians. When the magnitudes of the underlying aggregates are approximately —

and contemporarily — known to economic planners, an entirely new type of thinking arises in which the aggregates, instead of being taken in isolation, are understood and operated upon as affecting one another. This "new type of thinking" is the heart of the modern science of macroeconomics. It is difficult for anyone familiar with the subject today to realize how little was known before the Great Depression of the underlying magnitudes of current developments — at least in time to be of practical policy assistance. The development of modern techniques for data gathering and data organization — and especially the development of national income accounting — may, therefore, be put down as a secondary "necessary condition" for the development of fiscal policy as we know it today.

Relationship with Monetary Policy

In discussing the events leading to the advent of fiscal policy, it has been necessary to touch glancingly on "monetary policy," as the first (and unsuccessful) refuge of the public authorities in combating the Great Depression. Both types of policy — fiscal and monetary — are now very much alive and there is a growing academic literature, and even public discussion, of the proper "mix" of fiscal and monetary policies to be applied on different occasions. Before considering the matter of such a mix, however, it is necessary to distinguish further between fiscal and monetary policy, as they are easily confused.

Monetary policy, as already noted, is the policy of increasing or decreasing the cost and availability of money for business purposes as a means of influencing the general level of prices, incomes, and employment. Fiscal policy is the policy of changing the total amount and kinds of government receipts and expenditures and the overall surplus or deficit for the same purposes. While the kinds as well as the total amounts of government receipts and expenditures are important, fiscal policy might be said, as a first approximation, to be the policy of planning government surpluses and deficits for the purpose of effecting changes in desired directions in the general level of prices and incomes in the economy. Under present conditions in the principal industrial countries, a "strong" fiscal policy or a "strong" monetary policy means one which is strongly oriented in the contractionary direction.

It is very difficult to separate the two kinds of policy. Suppose, for example, that a government runs a surplus and "saves" the same amount by holding the surplus in idle bank balances — even more effectively, in idle central bank balances. As a *fiscal* policy instrument, the surplus will have a restrictive effect on the economy because the government will be subtracting more from incomes in the private sector by taxation than it will be adding to them by expenditure. But, the act of saving the surplus will have the side effect of reducing the money supply available to the private sector and so making credit less available and more expensive. This added side effect may have an even more contractionary influence on the economy than the "direct" effect of the fiscal policy "proper"; and this added side effect will be an instance of *monetary*, not fiscal, policy.

To take the matter the other way around, suppose a government incurs a deficit. As a fiscal policy measure, this will have an expansionary effect on the economy because the government will be adding more to the incomes of the private sector by expenditure than it will be taking away from them by taxation. But, by analogy with the earlier discussion of a surplus, if the government finances the deficit by increasing the money supply, this will have the added side effect of increasing the availability and decreasing the cost of money to the private sector. This additional expansionary force, which may or may not be more powerful than the "primary" effect of the net addition to private incomes, will be an instance of *monetary*, not fiscal, policy.

The general principle that may be derived from the two preceding paragraphs is that a governmental action can be said to be "pure" fiscal policy only if it is taken in such a way as to be neutral in its effect on the availability of money to the private sector, that is, if the government forthwith pays any surpluses back to the private sector (as by the retirement of debt not held by banks) and finances any deficits without adding to the money supply or otherwise making money more available to the private sector. Monetary policy, likewise, can be said to be pure only when it is conducted in such a way as to have no effect on the amounts which government receipts and expenditures add to or subtract from private incomes.

Examples of pure monetary policy are fairly common in the real world. Examples of pure fiscal policy, however, are much harder to come by, as any policy involving a change in government receipts and/or expenditures almost inevitably involves a corresponding policy with respect to financing the associated surplus or deficit. It follows that the fiscal policies that are actually discussed by journalists are almost always mixed with monetary policy. A pure fiscal policy is almost as rare as a pure metallic element occurring in nature. Just as it is the task of metallurgists to reduce metallic ores to pure metals (so that they will be more useful), so it is the task of economists to reduce actual policies to their pure fiscal and monetary elements so that their effects can be better understood.

Determining the most appropriate mix of fiscal and monetary policies in the present circumstances of any particular country is a complex task and beyond our present scope. There are, however, some generally agreed elements that should be considered in determining the correct mix of fiscal and monetary policy on any particular occasion. They might be listed as follows:

1. Fiscal policy, although it affects business investment, has its greatest impact on consumer incomes, adding to them by public expenditure and reducing them by taxation. This, in turn, increases or decreases consumer demand and so has an important impact on prices and employment.

2. Monetary policy, although it has some effect on current consumer expenditure, has its greatest impact on business investment (including private investment in housing).

3. Fiscal policy, although it affects the balance of payments to an important extent, has its greatest impact on domestic incomes, prices, and employment.

4. Monetary policy, although it affects domestic activity importantly, has an especially great impact on the balance of payments, as it directly influences international capital flows by changing the interest rate differentials among the several countries.

5. Fiscal policy has a particularly strong impact when the need is to *expand* the economy — as it creates income *directly* — rather than merely creating a potential for increased income if businessmen feel inclined to invest.

6. Monetary policy is apt to be ineffective in a deep depression, as the funds which it creates may merely pile up in banks if, as is then apt to be the case, businessmen take a dim view of profit prospects. Monetary policy can be particularly effective, however, in *braking* an inflationary boom, as there is no veto on business expansion more absolute and effective than the lack of funds.

40. THREE BUDGET CONCEPTS AND THEIR LIMITATIONS*

Economic Council of Canada

The Budget as an Indicator

There is a wide variety of ways in which changing government expenditures, tax rates, tax structures, and debt management operations may affect demand that cannot all be readily encompassed in simple total measures. Also there are many ways in which government budgetary items may affect private spending (sometimes very significantly, and without major shifts in government budgets themselves). Perhaps in due course more comprehensive and sophisticated measures of fiscal policy may come into more general use. But in the present "state of the art" of fiscal policy appraisal, attention is usually focussed, at least initially, on the fiscal balance — the deficit or surplus in government accounts (that is, the margin by which revenues fall short of, or exceed, expenditures). On this basis, it has become a part of the conventional wisdom that deficits tend to have expansionary effects on total demand and that surpluses tend to constrain total demand.

Yet discussions of fiscal policy in Canada and appraisals of its impact on the economy are frequently distorted, and sometimes misleading, owing to the use of partial and incomplete information, and to difficulties in interpreting the available information. Among the considerations frequently limiting assessments of fiscal policy are:

— the use of the federal government accounts only, leaving out of account the fiscal position of the provinces and the municipalities (a particularly important matter in Canada, since the combined budgets of provincial and municipal governments are now considerably larger than the budget of the federal government; the former also now have considerably greater access to growth-related tax sources than in earlier years);

— the use of the administrative accounts of government (the accounts which are the focus of attention in the budget speeches of Ministers of Finance and Treasurers), which were designed for budgetary control purposes and not for the broad assessment of economic effects;

*Reprinted from Economic Council of Canada, *Performance and Potential mid-1950s to mid-1970s*, September, 1970, pp. 44-50, by permission of Information Canada.

— the failure to take into account the transactions of the Canada and Quebec Pension Plans, which are now generating revenues well in excess of pension outlays; and

— the use of "actual" deficits or surpluses as measures of fiscal stimulus or restraint, without regard to the prevailing level of economic activity (fiscal policy both affects and is affected by demand; for example, when slack exists, government revenues are depressed, and budgetary deficits may simply reflect low levels of economic activity rather than a fundamentally expansionary fiscal policy).

In brief, if budgetary deficits and surpluses are to be used as measures of fiscal "ease" or fiscal "restraint," the central question is: *What deficits or surpluses?* We believe that the most useful presentation for assessing fiscal impact in the national accounts budget and, more specifically, what can be called the *high-employment budget position* on a national accounts basis. The catch is that several different accounting presentations can be (and are) used to describe government operations. Each is designed for a particular purpose and can, in fact, be misleading if used for some other purpose.

Three Budget Concepts and Their Limitations

By way of illustrating some of the options available, let us consider for a moment the federal government position alone. Chart 1 shows the budgetary balance of the federal government on three different accounting bases — the administrative, cash, and national accounts presentations. We will return to the high-employment version of the latter shortly.

CHART 1

THREE ALTERNATIVE PRESENTATIONS OF THE FEDERAL BUDGET POSITION, FISCAL YEARS ENDING MARCH 31

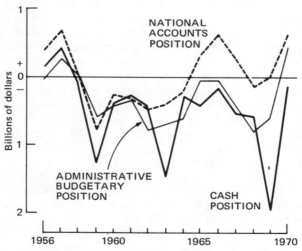

Source: Based on data from Department of Finance and Dominion Bureau of Statistics.

Each of these budgetary concepts suggests quite different readings of fiscal ease or restraint for different years. For example, in most years in the middle or late 1960s, the administrative and cash budgets were in deficit when there was a surplus balance on the national accounts basis.

What is perhaps most frequently referred to as the "budgetary position" is the balance in the administrative budget. This presentation, which is the central feature of the annual Budget Speech of the Minister of Finance, is designed essentially for administrative and control purposes. But it does not cover the transactions of some very important government funds, notably those for old age security, unemployment insurance, and government trust and pension funds; nor does it include the very substantial loans and advances to the private sector. On the other hand, it does include a number of internal bookkeeping transactions, such as appropriations to special funds, which do not represent flows between the government and the private sector.

The statement of government cash transactions is more comprehensive than the administrative budget since it includes the net effects of government borrowing and lending operations as well as changes in the trust and pension accounts that affect the government's cash position. It is useful for the government's own cash management and is of considerable relevance for financial analysis.

The national accounts presentation of the budget is, however, more explicitly designed to meet the needs of economic analysis. It takes a wider range of transactions into account than the administrative budget, and it excludes transactions of a purely internal bookkeeping nature. It does not, unfortunately, in its present form, cover the government's borrowing and lending operations (which largely explains the difference in levels of the cash and national accounts balances in Chart 1).[1] These can also have important indirect economic effects. But it does have another major advantage. For reasons outlined above, the position of all governments should be taken into account in appraising fiscal policy. The national accounts presentation has in fact been developed to encompass, on a comparable basis, the accounts of all governments in Canada within a broad accounting framework employing consistent definitions throughout. In other words, not only can the federal position be consolidated with that of provincial and municipal governments but the impact of government transactions can be tied in directly with other sectors of the economy. Neither of these things can be done with the administrative budget or the cash statement.

The High-Employment Budget

The high recording of government transactions on a national accounts basis — something that has been done in federal Budget Speeches since 1964 — is an essential and considerable step toward facilitating economic analysis of the budget. But there is still a problem. The actual budget surplus or deficit, even on a national accounts basis is the result of two sets of forces: the budget program (taxes and expenditures), and the strength of total demand in the economy. What we are interested in is how to attain full employment growth, and whether policy actions will move the economy toward, or away

---

[1] What is required for the future is a still more comprehensive presentation linking *both* revenue-expenditure and financial transactions within a framework suitable for economic analysis.

from its potential growth path. In other words, we would like to distinguish the "direct" effect of policy actions from the "feedback" effects of other forces on the budgetary balance in the economy. To assist in this, and to provide a better basis for policy advice and decision making, it is useful to have an estimate of what the fiscal balance would look like when the economy is operating at potential output, given *existing* tax rates and *existing* government expenditure programs.

Chart 2 illustrates the *actual* national accounts budget position (for all levels of government and including the Canada and Quebec Pension Plans) and the estimated high-employment budget position on a similar basis. The gap between these is a measure of the difference between what the fiscal balance actually *was*, and an estimate of what it *would have been* at potential output (given the existing tax rates and structure, and existing expenditure programs). Thus, when the economy was operating close to potential output, as in 1956-57 and 1965-67, there was little, if any, gap. On the other hand, in the early 1960s, when there was substantial slack in the economy, the gap was fairly large. This simply implies that, under these conditions, government revenues were considerably depressed by the relatively low levels of economic activity.

The implication of this chart is that the setting of fiscal policy cannot be judged with reference to the actual deficit or surplus position. The substan-

CHART 2

HIGH-EMPLOYMENT FISCAL POSITION
AND ACTUAL FISCAL POSITION

National Accounts Basis — All Levels of Government

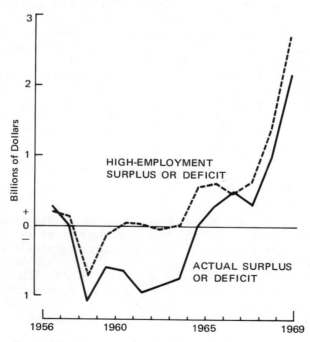

Source: Based on data from Dominion Bureau of Statistics and estimates by Economic Council of Canada.

tial actual deficits of the early 1960s essentially reflected the impact on the fiscal position of the large degree of economic slack, rather than an expansionary fiscal policy. A far more illuminating approach to the assessment of fiscal policy is to look at the fiscal position that would exist at high employment. On this basis, any significant surplus would represent a restraining posture — a posture tending to hold the economy below potential. Conversely, any significant deficit on this basis would represent an expansionary posture — a posture tending to push the economy above potential. Thus, as indicated by the high-employment budget position shown in Chart 2, fiscal policy was expansionary in 1958 and highly restrictive in 1968-69.

Performance and Potential

We do not wish to oversimplify these matters. There are, of course, some imperfections in the use of high-employment budget measures as an indicator of policy settings. In this context, Dr. Arthur Okun, a former Chairman of the US Council of Economic Advisers, has recently stated:

> As fiscal experts will recognize, the full employment surplus is an imperfect measure of budgetary impact. Three of its flaws are: (1) It sums and nets all types of expenditures and revenues as though they had equal bang-for-a-buck, which they don't; (2) it lags behind to the extent that government orders and contracts may influence private inventory investment (and employment demand) before they show up in the federal account; (3) it may show misleadingly large surpluses in a time of inflation if revenues respond more — and more promptly — to rising prices than do expenditures. We can adjust the full employment surplus for these to a degree, but we need better quantifications of fiscal impact. Still, for all its flaws, the full employment surplus is a shining jewel compared to the actual surplus (or deficit), which makes it appear that fiscal policy has shifted whenever a swing in private demand alters federal revenues.[2]

But, in spite of these, this approach provides, in our judgment, the most useful basis for discussions of such settings.[3]

---

[2] *The Political Economy of Prosperity,* The Brookings Institution, Washington, D.C., 1970, p. 121.

[3] In any such discussions, two further important points need to be kept in mind. The first is that there are various important ways in which Canadian demand-management policies, particularly monetary policy, are influenced by general economic conditions and demand policy settings in the United States. The second is that there are important interconnections between monetary and fiscal policies, as well as between these and debt-management policy, exchange policy, and other policies.

41. THE MYTH OF FISCAL POLICY: THE MONETARIST VIEW*

Ira Kaminow

Times are changing. What is obvious today was obviously wrong yesterday; this is as true of questions involving economic issues as any others. Many of us, for example, believe in the efficacy of fiscal policy — in the government's power to influence the level of national income by its own spending and taxing policies. Indeed, the expenditure-income chain explanation of the operation of fiscal policy is part of today's conventional wisdom. The government spends more or spurs private spending by taxing less, and so creates more jobs and higher profits. The new income so created generates additional demand and private spending, creating even more income.

All this is Keynesian economics — the so-called New Economics. But it wasn't long ago that the Keynesian Revolution was rejected by most laymen, and not long before that, that it was rejected by most economists. Today, with victory in hand, the New Economics is facing a counter-revolution which may again change the economic thinking of the nation. There is a small but highly vocal group of economists who are suspicious of Keynesian economics in general and of fiscal policy in particular. The members of the group are sometimes called the Monetarists.[1]

Monetarists view the controversy over economic theories as being like a law suit. As judges, they rule that the New Economists have presented no acceptable historical evidence in support of the income-expenditure theory. As litigants, they present the following case: (1) over the years, the major movements in national income have been associated with major movements in the money supply and *vice versa*; (2) no equally strong or systematic relation can be found to support the Keynesian view of the operation of fiscal policy; (3) therefore, monetary forces have played a much more

*Reprinted from Ira Kaminow, "The Myth of Fiscal Policy: The Monetarist View," *Business Review,* Federal Reserve Bank of Philadelphia, December, 1970, pp. 10-18, by permission of the editor.

Dr. Kaminow is Economist, Federal Reserve Bank of Philadelphia: formerly he was Assistant Professor of Economics, Ohio University, from 1967 to 1969.
[1] Strictly speaking, the Monetarist view involves more than mere suspicion of the efficacy of fiscal policy. Indeed, one can be a Monetarist and still agree that fiscal policy has a powerful and systematic influence on the economy. Nevertheless, the popular press identifies Monetarists with those who believe that monetary policy is much more important than fiscal policy, and this usage of the term is adopted here.

important and/or more stable role in determining national income than fiscal forces. Monetarists do not claim that the income-expenditure chain is erroneous in principle — merely that history tells us it is too weak or unpredictable to be of much use for economic policy.

A Simple Explanation of the Monetarist View

How do the Monetarists reconcile their view of history with the apparently powerful logic of the income-expenditure chain?[2] The heart of the Monetarist view is the supply of and demand for money — a dramatic shift from the usual emphasis. Because of the near total victory of the New Economics (at least in introductory textbooks on economics) in the fifties and sixties, the spotlight of popular policy discussions has been firmly set on the pivot point of Keynesian economics — the demand for goods.

A look at the economy from the perspective of the money side of things (or the goods side, for that matter) will reveal only a partial and perhaps slightly distorted picture of the economy. Nevertheless, anyone who has been to the circus knows how difficult it is to look at all three rings at once and that there is something to be gained from looking at only one at a time.

Although not all economists agree on the definition of money, we will not break too much with tradition if we use the term to mean all assets that are generally accepted as a means of payment. More concretely, we can define money as the sum of coins, paper currency, and chequing account deposits.

An easy way to illustrate the Monetarist view is to suppose that a certain quantity of money is required to support any particular level of income. When national economic activity (as measured by income) rises, more money is required to carry on conveniently day-to-day transactions; when economic activity declines, households and businesses find that they engage in fewer transactions, and hence, need less money. More specifically, we can assume that the demand for money balances *relative* to the level of income (what economists call desired *relative* money balances) is fixed. By way of illustration, we can imagine that institutional arrangements — like the availability of credit cards and the length of the average pay period — lead the public to desire money balances equal in value to 10 percent of national income. If annual national income is $800 billion, then desired balances would be $80 billion.

What happens if the economy has more money than it requires? Say, for the sake of argument, that the actual stock of money in the previous example is $90 billion, or $10 billion more than is required. Since money yields no pecuniary return, households and businesses will attempt to exchange money for other assets — assets that yield satisfaction directly (like television sets) and assets that yield a pecuniary return (like stocks and bonds). The increased demand for goods and services will stimulate greater output and perhaps will boost prices as markets respond to the new demand. At the same time, the increased demand for financial assets like stocks and bonds will drive interest rates down. The decline in interest rates will further

---

[2] A completely accurate answer to this question is extremely complex. There is no reason, however, why the complexities and nuances should keep us from the essence of the Monetarist argument. A look at the simplest version of the theory (a version not seriously proposed by anyone) will reveal more than an investigation of one which requires endless digressions and footnotes and which reflects the particular views of only one or two Monetarists.

encourage the demand for goods by making credit cheaper. This will induce still higher prices and output. The pace of economic activity will quicken. Economic activity will continue to increase until income is pushed up to a level consistent with the $90 billion money stock — that is, to $900 billion.

The rigid relationship between the demand for money and national income makes this environment inhospitable to fiscal policy. If the national goal is to raise income, it can be achieved only by raising the money stock. An increase in government expenditures won't work except for a very short time. As soon as income rises a bit, the money stock will be inadequate. There will be a general scramble for money, and the private demand for goods will decline as businesses and households try to increase their holdings of money. Consequently, income and output will be pulled back down by the limited money stock.

Stated somewhat differently, any increase in government expenditures (not accompanied by an appropriate increase in the money stock) will be matched by an equal decline in private expenditures; any decrease in government expenditures (not accompanied by an appropriate decline in the money stock) will be matched by an equal increase in private expenditures.

The key that allowed monetary policy to work in the simple world just described is the constancy of desired *relative* money balances. In order to achieve an equilibrium, annual national income will always adjust so that it is ten times the stock of money. If we can control the money supply, we can control national income. The key that locked fiscal policy out is that government taxing and spending policies have no effect on desired relative money balances. No matter what fiscal policies are followed, annual national income will always tend to be ten times higher than the stock of money. In these two keys are the germs of the Monetarist position: (1) although demand for relative money balances is not fixed, it is the most stable and predictable variable on which we can count for economic policy; and (2) although fiscal policies may have some influence on desired relative money balances, they do not have a strong, predictable influence. Therefore, fiscal policies are of relatively little or no use.

A Look at the New Economics from the Money Side

Advocates of the New Economics do not agree that income is the only variable that exerts a strong, predictable influence on the demand for money. They argue that a typical family might find it very convenient at some given level of income to go about its daily business with an average chequing account balance of $100. But convenience must be balanced against cost. One hundred dollars in the chequing account is not earning interest. When the interest rate on savings accounts is very low, the household may indeed hold a $100 chequing account balance. But let the interest rate rise substantially and the household may decide that it can get by with only $75 or $50 worth of money. The lower money balance might mean more bother — more accurate balancing of the chequebook, more trips to the bank — but the bother is compensated by the greater interest income. In short, the New Economists argue that both the level of income and the interest rate determine the desired stock of money. By adding this additional ingredient — interest rates — the New Economist can salvage the argument for the expenditure-income chain.

Keynesians expect roughly the same kind of initial response to fiscal policy as do the Monetarists. An increase in government expenditures drives income up, and the existing stock of money becomes inadequate to handle the additional income. In an effort to acquire more money, people try to sell nonmonetary financial assets such as bonds. As the supply of these assets rises relative to demand, interest rates begin to rise to make them more attractive to buyers. This hike in interest rates is the key that is supposed to let fiscal policy back in. Higher interest rates mean that the economy will be able to support a higher level of income with the given stock of money. With higher interest rates, households and businesses find it advantageous to economize on the use of money — to make the existing stock "go farther." The economy will, after the initial shock of added government expenditures, come to rest at a higher level of national income — and higher interest rates. The higher interest rates are necessary; otherwise, the public could not be induced to hold the same quantity of money at the higher level of activity. Put in slightly different terms, the ratio of desired money balances to income will decline because interest rates have risen.

An extreme version of the Keynesian view gives rise to the so-called liquidity trap. Imagine what would happen if the public were willing to hold whatever money balances were offered at the prevailing interest rate. The public would make no attempt to convert new money balances into other assets, regardless of how much money the authorities pumped into the economy. Any new money that was placed in the economy would be willingly held at the existing interest rate and income. Monetary policy is completely frustrated if and when we get into the trap because then the public's actions are unaffected by changes in the money supply.

In contrast, recall that in the simple Monetarist case the demand for *relative* money balances doesn't change. Individual members of the public never will be willing to hold unlimited quantities of money. If new money is added to the economy, the public will have "too much" money and will try to get rid of the excess. This process will drive income up to a new equilibrium.

Does it Matter if the Interest Rate Matters?

The single most revealing element in the encounter between Monetarists and New Economists is that they cannot agree on the relevance of the relevance of the interest rate. The Monetarist Milton Friedman wrote:

> ... in my opinion no "fundamental issues" in either monetary theory or monetary policy hinge on whether [the demand for money depends on interest rates].[3]

The Keynesian Paul Samuelson wrote:

> ... the minute you believe that [the demand for money depends on interest rates], you have moved to ... the post-Keynesian position.[4]

---

[3] Milton Friedman, "Interest Rates and the Demand for Money," *Journal of Law and Economics*, (October, 1966), p. 85. For some technical reasons, not all Monetarists would agree 100 percent with this quotation. For our purposes, however, it seems to reflect adequately the Monetarist view.
[4] Paul Samuelson, "The Role of Money in National Economic Policy," *Controlling Monetary Aggregates*, (Boston: The Federal Reserve Bank of Boston, 1969), p. 12.

Keynesians insist that the interest rate is the added gear in the mechanism that allows fiscal policy to work. For them, fiscal policy (viewed from the money side of the economy) gives authorities control over the interest rate and, through the interest rate, control over desired *relative* money balances. The Monetarists insist that this control must be inconsequential because they see no evidence that it has worked in the past. (New Economists, of course, dispute the charge of lack of evidence.) For the Monetarists there are two possibilities: (1) fiscal policy has had an erratic, unsystematic effect on the interest rate and, hence, an unobservable effect on national income, or (2) fiscal policies have been so mild as to have only a small effect on interest rates.

The issue (regarding the demand for money) that is of primary importance to the Monetarist is the stability and predictability of desired relative money balances. Evidence of a highly unstable and unpredictable ratio of money balances to national income would directly contradict the efficacy of monetary policy. In terms of the Keynesian theory, the instability would arise if we fell into a liquidity trap. The Monetarists are therefore considerably more interested in whether a trap exists than in whether the demand for money is sensitive to the interest rate.

Historical Evidence I: The Demand for Money

It is time to fish or cut bait. A number of issues have been raised and questions asked about the demand for money. What kinds of answers does history provide? To make things manageable, we can concentrate on three key questions: (1) Does the demand for money depend on income? (2) Is the demand for money sensitive to interest rates? (3) Have we ever been caught in a liquidity trap?

Question One: What Role for Income?

Virtually every empirical study undertaken has shown that the demand for money depends on the level of income. Sometimes the relationship is based on a linkage between current income and money demand through the level of transactions of the sort we discussed earlier. Sometimes the relationship is based on more subtle arguments.

These more subtle discussions generally presume that economic well-being is a more important determinant of the demand for money than is the volume of transactions. The discussions take as their point of departure the notion that improved economic status for a nation (or an individual) means a greater demand for most assets, including money. In fact, at least one economist believes that money is a luxury in the sense that the demand for it rises very rapidly as a nation (or individual) moves up the economic ladder.

The two measures of economic well-being that have been used to explain the demand for money are wealth and permanent income. Everyone is familiar with the notion of wealth, and there should be no dispute that it is one measure of economic well-being. The meaning of permanent income, however, is not widely known.

Permanent income is most simply described as expected average lifetime income. It is a good measure of economic well-being because it is adjusted for temporary ups and downs. A day labourer who happens to be working his way through medical school has a higher *permanent* income than his coworker whose actual or *measured* income is the same but whose ambitions and income expectations are more modest.

Economists who take the permanent income approach do not deny the importance of measured income. They argue that current and past levels of measured income are the most important influences on permanent income. They claim that expectations are largely formulated on the basis of past experience.

Question Two: How Important is the Interest Rate?

Historically, the interest rate has influenced the demand for money.[5] This much we know with virtual certainty — that is, if unanimity of opinion implies certainty of knowledge. There is some disagreement, however, on just how important the interest rate has been. Some economists, like Milton Friedman and Maurice Allais, take the view that the interest rate is so unimportant in determining the demand for money that little is lost if it is ignored. Other investigators, however, have presented evidence that the demand for money is highly sensitive to changes in the rate of interest. Perhaps the most sensitive relationship was found by Allan Meltzer who estimated on one occasion that any given percentage change in long-term interest rates would be matched by an equal percentage change (in the opposite direction) in the demand for money.

The disagreement over the importance of the interest does not follow "party lines." As it turns out, all three of the economists mentioned in the last paragraph are Monetarists. Estimates of the interest sensitivity by Keynesians are greater than zero but less than Meltzer's.

A major reason for all this disagreement about the importance of the interest rate is that it is often difficult to untangle the influence of interest rates from other influences on the demand for money. Interest rates vary in a more or less systematic way over the business cycle — they generally go up during expansions and down during economic contractions.

Other variables that are likely to influence the demand for money also behave more or less predictably over the cycle. This raises the possibility that an investigator will wrongly attribute the influence of some other variable to interest rates, or the influence of interest rates to other variables.

Milton Friedman and Anna J. Schwartz, in particular, argue that an uncritical reading of history has led to an overemphasis on the role of the interest rate in determining the demand for money.

It is well known that relative money balances (the ratio of money balances to income) fall during expansions and rise during contractions. Generally speaking, therefore, relative money balances are high when interest rates are low (during slumps), and are low when interest rates are high (during booms). The interest rate seems to do a good job in explaining movements in the demand for relative money balances.

Friedman and Schwartz argue that there is another factor to explain movements in relative money balances over the cycle. It is based on the idea of permanent income (expected average lifetime income) mentioned earlier.

---

[5] There are, of course, many interest rates. We shall ignore here the important question of selecting the appropriate one.

During economic downturns, people anticipate that things will get better; so permanent income is higher than measured income. During periods of prosperity, people guess that incomes are unusually high; so permanent income is lower than measured income. Over the cycle, permanent income fluctuates much less than measured income because people recognize that a good deal of income fluctuations are transitory. If the demand for money depends on permanent income, it will fluctuate relatively little over the business cycle because permanent income is relatively stable over the cycle. Therefore, during periods of recovery, the demand for money will rise more slowly than measured income, so relative money balances (the ratio of money balances to measured national income) will fall. During periods of contraction, the demand for money will fall more slowly than measured income, and relative money balances will rise.

Friedman and Schwartz offer some evidence in support of their views in their famous study *A Monetary History of the United States*. For example, they point to the period, 1932-1937, during which both interest rates and relative money balances fell. This pattern is clearly inconsistent with the interest-rate explanation of movements in the demand for money. The 1932-1937 experience is very easily explained by the permanent income concept. In the mid-1930s, the economy started to climb out of the depths of the Great Depression. Income was rising. Nevertheless, vivid memories of 1929, 1930, and 1931 lingered. People were not so sure that the recovery was going to be sustained. Permanent income rose, but not so fast as measured income. Desired money balances, which respond to permanent income, grew more slowly than measured income. So, the ratio of money balances to measured income fell.

Not all economists agree that the Friedman and Schwartz evidence is convincing. A number of studies have shown that the interest rate has had a strong influence even if one accepts the permanent income hypothesis. In fact, Friedman and Schwartz seem to have retreated slightly on this point. In 1966, Friedman wrote "most estimates [of the interest rate sensitivity], including some we have obtained in our own subsequent work are higher . . . than the estimate Anna J. Schwartz and I used in *A Monetary History*."[6]

Question Three: Have We Ever Been Trapped?

The answer to this question can be stated very succinctly: the great weight of historical evidence indicates that we have never been in a liquidity trap. A number of studies have attempted to find periods in American history when the public was willing to hold whatever quantity of money balances made available. Over the periods investigated, the public has always made attempts to unload excess money balances in exchange for other assets.

A Summary

Studies of the demand for money can be thought of as the first round in the debate over the efficacy of monetary and fiscal policy. The nice thing about the first round is that each side can go back to its corner confident that it took the round on points. Monetarists smell victory because of the absence

---

[6] Milton Friedman, *op. cit.*, pp. 72 and 73.

of any evidence of the existence of a trap. To them this is the crucial issue. Keynesians are delighted with the outcome because of the overwhelming evidence of the interest sensitivity of the demand for money.

Historical Evidence II: The Monetarists' Grand Experiments

The second round in the debate brings us back to the beginning — to the Monetarist claim that (1) the major movements in national income have been associated with major movements in the money supply and *vice versa,* and (2) no equally strong or systematic relationship can be found to support the Keynesian theories. For the Monetarist, none of the evidence on interest rates and the demand for money can change these facts. For Keynesians, these "facts" are highly debatable.

Without getting involved in the technical arguments, we can briefly indicate the debate on this evidence.

Keynesian Objection 1: Mere association does not imply causation. The close relationship between money and national income could reflect a causal influence running from money to income; from income to money (if, for example, the monetary authorities tried to provide enough money to meet the needs of trade); a dependence of both money and income on some third variable; or, as is most likely, a little bit of all three. There is, in short, no way to determine the strength or predictability of the causal link from money to national income using the Monetarist's tools.

Monetarist Response: We agree that mere association does not imply causation. Indeed, we even agree that there has been some influence running from income to money. Our point is that a major cause of the observed coincidence of movement is the effect of monetary forces on national income. There is no need to debate this on a conjectural level, however, because history is not totally silent on this point. There is some opportunity to examine situations in which it is unlikely that the direction of causation went from income to money. One illustration includes those times in history when the money supply has increased because of gold inflows or for other reasons unrelated to income. During these periods, income has risen after the rise in the money supply.

Keynesian Objection 2: The Monetarist's tools may be too crude to pick up the strong influences of fiscal policies. It is a mistake to presume such influences do not exist simply because the impact of fiscal policies cannot be measured by the somewhat naïve techniques of the Monetarist. The workings of fiscal and monetary policies on the economy are very complex. There is no shortcut to the very hard work of learning about complex and subtle interrelations in the economy.

Monetarist Response: We could not agree more. The economy is certainly complex, and we know very little about it. In fact, this is what we have been saying right along. We conclude that on the grounds of our ignorance, we ought to go with what we've got, and what we've got is this relationship between the supply of money and national income. If more complicated tests show how fiscal policy works, then it will be time to use them. Right now we cannot unlock the code.

Keynesian Objection 3: Your tests are not as conclusive as you think. The definition of monetary and fiscal variables is open to question. We have come up with definitions different from yours that show a strong correlation between fiscal policy and national income.

Monetarist Response: We believe that our measures of fiscal and monetary forces are superior to the Keynesians' measures. We frequently get the impression that the Keynesians choose their measures more because they give good results than because they seem reasonable from an economic standpoint.

A Summing Up

It is easy to be pessimistic over the state of the art of economic policy. One can find competent economists at every point on the spectrum between "only money matters" and "money doesn't matter at all." To be sure, the great majority take more moderate positions, but even the moderate range is wide and offers rather diverse policy prescriptions. It would be safe to say that the economics profession could under no conceivable set of circumstances offer anything like a "standard" policy prescription. The point is frequently made that the only thing on which most economists will agree is that policy was wrong. But there is rarely any agreement on what correct policy would have been or even what the actual policy was.

The gloominess of the state of affairs, however, is broken by occasional rays of hope. We are currently devoting more resources than ever before toward finding out how the economy works. Millions of dollars have been spent on large-scale econometric models of the United States. Builders of these models claim that they have made long strides in the past decades. It is in these models and in other attempts to interpret economic history that the real hope lies.

There has been a marked shift in the great economic debate since the initial victories of the New Economics. In the late 1940s and early 1950s, it was generally believed by Keynesians that money didn't matter at all. By the early and mid 1960s, the Monetarists had made sufficient headway to shift the question from "does money matter?" to "does fiscal policy matter?" The New Economists have largely recognized the importance of money, but not its dominance. The Monetarists, however, continue to question the empirical relevance of fiscal policy.

IV. THE WORLD ECONOMY

The countries of the world are bound together in a network of economic, political, social, and cultural relationships. The links are strong at some points, weak at others. But in the aggregate they are pervasive and compelling, for each region of the universe is in some degree dependent on all the others. Possibly the future of mankind depends as much on recognition of this increasing and general interdependence as it does on any other single maxim in economics or political science.

History demonstrates that when the mutual dependence of nations is disregarded, the inevitable result is frustration and conflict. When international relationships are extended and strengthened, the outcome is advanced efficiency and progress. The first approach may provide the conditions for nationalism, autarchy, and war. The second may lay the basis for a world economy.

Our first concern in Part IV will be with the benefits from international trade. Then to gain a better understanding of trade problems, we shall examine Canada's balance of international payments. Next, we shall explain various foreign exchange systems, and the mechanisms for restoring international equilibrium. After that, the perennial problem of protectionism versus free trade is discussed. Finally, the current problems of international development are presented, and Canada's response is examined. This set of readings is intended to provide a basis for understanding the economic relationships among nations. It is especially timely because, according to the Right Honourable Lester B. Pearson, former Prime Minister of Canada (1963-1968), "A growing and prosperous world economy, with all sharing the growth, will be in everyone's interest and to everyone's advantage. Wretchedness and poverty in one part of the world, with the conflict and desperate hopelessness it creates, is bound to affect stability and progress in all other parts."

A. BASIS OF INTERNATIONAL TRADE AND CANADA'S TRADE PATTERN

Among the nations of the world Canada takes sixth place in terms of total merchandise trade. Only the United States, West Germany, the United Kingdom, France, and Japan trade more. Our trade per capita exceeds that of any of the major traders named and, although not the world's highest (Belgium and Luxembourg, Singapore, the Netherlands, Switzerland, Sweden, and Denmark surpass Canada) it is more than three times the American. To a much greater extent than most countries, Canada lives by trade.

The benefits from international trade are direct and simple: a more efficient allocation of the world's resources through specialization and exchange, and therefore higher living standards for all people than would be possible were each country to strive for self-sufficiency. Reading 42 describes the fundamental principles underlying international trade and the gains therefrom.

Periods of sustained economic growth and prosperity in Canada have historically and almost invariably been associated with dynamically expanding exports and imports, and the last half of the 1960s was no exception. Reading 43 discusses the factors behind the recent strength in Canada's external trading position, and comments on the long-term prospects for Canadian trade.

42. INTERNATIONAL TRADE BENEFITS AND ECONOMIC POLICY*

John W. Knudsen

International trade is at a crossroad this year. On the one hand, there is the continuing postwar effort to remove the barriers to trade erected in the 1930s which has culminated in the Kennedy Round of trade negotiations. When the tariff reductions agreed upon are fully implemented in 1972, tariffs will be lower than at any other point in modern history. Negotiations to reduce nontariff barriers are now taking place. On the other hand, there are currently several developments which point to a possible move away from freer trade. Rapid rises in imports, due partly to tariff reductions and balance of payments problems in some countries, have led to a resurgence of protectionist sentiment. In the United States, many bills have been introduced into Congress calling for increased tariffs, quotas, and other government measures to protect domestic industries from import competition. There is some danger that if one country increases its protection others will retaliate and there will be a return to the trade wars of the 1930s.

In view of these conflicting developments and the widespread interest in trade policy, this article points out some of the benefits of trade and discusses what is required to obtain them.

The Gain from Trade

An immediate cause of international trade is differences in prices of home-produced goods and imported goods. A commodity will be imported when an entrepreneur discovers that the foreign price converted to domestic currency units (including the transportation cost and duty) is less than the domestic price at which he hopes to sell it. Importing seems clearly beneficial when the imported commodity is one that would be very difficult to produce at home. But the gain from bringing in cheaper foreign goods that

*Reprinted from John W. Knudsen "International Trade Policy," *Monthly Review of the Federal Reserve Bank of Kansas City,* September-October, 1970, pp. 11-16, by permission.
Mr. Knudsen is an economist with the Research Department of the Federal Reserve Bank of Kansas City, Missouri.

can be produced reasonably well at home requires more discussion. It is the import of such goods that competes with domestic production and leads to requests for protection.

Suppose that an importer determines that he can bring in a widget from abroad for $3 just like one produced and sold at home for $5. Clearly there is a potential for private profit in importing such widgets. The more significant question, however, is whether the nation as a whole gains by such a transaction. If imports and exports pay for each other, foreigners will have to be persuaded to purchase $3 worth of exports for each widget imported. In order to produce these additional exports, resources will have to be transferred from the production of widgets to the production of commodities that can be exported. The nation does gain if more resources are required to produce the widget at home than to produce the additional exports to pay for importing it, because resources saved by importing goods can be used to produce other desired goods. In a competitive economy, prices tend to reflect opportunity costs; that is, the price of a commodity indicates the cost of producing it in terms of the opportunity foregone by not producing something else. Thus, if a widget's domestic price is $5, its production at home would use resources that could be used instead to produce $5 worth of other goods. By giving up the domestic production of a widget, enough resources are released to pay for an imported one with $3 worth of exports and still have resources left over to produce $2 worth of additional goods. Trading for goods instead of producing them at home enables us to have more goods; that is, trade enables us to make more efficient use of our resources.

As long as opportunity costs are different at home and abroad, the home country will be able to export goods to pay for its imports. Differing opportunity costs imply that some goods in each country can be produced relatively cheaper than in other countries. A country is said to have a comparative advantage in such goods. Under competitive conditions, the exchange rate will translate the differing opportunity costs into the differing money costs to which profit-maximizing businessmen respond. Trade will then take place with the home country importing goods and services which are relatively cheap abroad and specializing in the production and export of goods that are relatively cheap at home. Each country gains by this specialization because the goods are imported at less cost in terms of resources than if they were produced at home. Both the pattern of trade and specialization and the gains from trade are determined by differing opportunity costs.

Trade does not leave local commodity prices unchanged. As imports of a commodity increase, there is a tendency for the difference in price at home and abroad to disappear, eliminating the incentive for businessmen to further increase imports. The home price and the level of home production at this point depend on how costs change as production falls at home and increases abroad. If the cost does not increase as the foreign country increases its output, the domestic industry will be forced out of business and all its resources will be reallocated to the production of other goods. This result will be even more likely if increasing production and sales make it possible for the foreign country to exploit economies of scale and reduce the price. On the other hand, if increasing costs prevail in the industry, costs may increase abroad and decrease at home as adjustments are made. If equality of costs is reached before the domestic industry disappears, the industry will continue to prevail at home but on a reduced scale.

To summarize, the main benefit of trade is the opportunity to buy some of the goods we consume at cheaper foreign prices. This allows consumers more choice in the spending of their incomes and allows more efficient use of productive resources. Trade offers this opportunity, regardless of why the foreign prices are lower. It should be pointed out, however, that the price system does not work perfectly and that prices do not always accurately reflect opportunity costs and comparative advantages. Within a given country, prices tend to be distorted by monopoly power, by taxes, and by such things as pollution which are not always counted in the cost of producing a product. Externally, prices are distorted by various factors which tend to hinder trade by making foreign prices higher. These hindrances include transport costs, marketing costs, and various types of trade barriers imposed by governments. The relative costs of transportation and marketing have tended to fall over time. Governments, of course, are in a position to reduce their interference in trade. The next section will discuss some of the reasons why countries have comparative advantages in certain goods.

The Pattern of Trade

The traditional explanation of comparative advantage emphasizes various differences between countries. The one most often mentioned is unequal relative endowments of productive resources among countries of the world. The most abundant resource in each country will tend to be cheaper than that resource in other countries. Each country will tend to have a comparative advantage in those goods that use more of the abundant factor because they can be produced at a relatively lower cost. A country with an abundant labour supply should have a comparative advantage in goods that require relatively more labour in their production. A country well endowed with a certain natural resource tends to export this natural resource, or goods which embody it. Since resource endowments can change over time, countries do not always have a comparative advantage in the same commodities. Changes in endowments may arise from changes in the labour force as populations grow, from the accumulation of capital via saving, and from the discovery of new supplies of natural resources. Differences between countries in population and income growth, in the saving rate, and in the discovery of natural resources lead to differences in changes in resource endowments. Thus, the pattern of comparative advantage and trade tends to shift over time.

The emphasis on differences in resource endowments as a cause of trade implies that trade flows will be greatest between countries that are the most different. This proposition may explain trade in natural resources and foodstuffs, but it does not satisfactorily explain trade in manufactures which accounts for almost two-thirds of world trade. Most manufactures move between the highly industrialized countries which are most alike in their relative endowments of labour and capital and in their demand structures. One reason for this is that the increased specialization which accompanies industrialization widens opportunities for profitable trade. Another reason is that, in addition to the hindrances to trade arising from transport costs and protection, there are also special marketing problems associated with exporting.[1] It is costly to develop a market for a manufactured item such as a piece of capital equipment or a consumer good. It is natural that the costs of

---

[1] Staffan Burenstam Linder, *An Essay on Trade and Transformation,* (New York, 1961).

marketing a new good would be less at home simply because the producer would be more familiar with the mechanics of the market and consumer tastes in his own country. Once established at home, the commodity will most likely be exported first to other industrial countries where living standards and tastes are similar to those at home. In addition, the industrial countries grow more rapidly and, therefore, offer more promising market opportunities than do the nonindustrial countries.

How the pattern of comparative advantage and specialization in manufactures evolves among the industrial countries over time appears to be greatly influenced by the location of product innovation and the presence of economies of scale, including the specialization of resources. The country in which the innovation of a product takes place has at least a temporary monopoly in world markets. The presence of economies of scale could enable the country to continue its domination of world markets. Differences between countries in demand structures and resource endowments are important, but any explanation of trade in manufactures must take into account the role of innovation, economies of scale, and marketing problems.

The product cycle explanation of how trade patterns develop over time emphasizes changes that industries and products undergo over time, such as changes in the methods of production, in the requirements for labour and capital, and in product marketing.[2] In the new product phase of the cycle, skilled labour is required, both for the initial low volume of production and for research and development, which makes production costs high. Marketing costs are also high because of the difficulty of introducing a new product. In the growth phase of the cycle, capital is invested in the development of mass production techniques which create economies of scale. The innovating firm is now likely to encounter competition as other firms acquire the production techniques and develop slightly different versions of the original product. Finally, in the mature phase, production techniques become more standardized through the use of sophisticated capital equipment. Capital requirements are high but this enables the industry to use unskilled instead of skilled labour and reduces costs. The product itself also becomes more standardized, which tends to reduce marketing costs. Because of these changes, a country which has a comparative advantage in a product in one phase of its development may lose it to other countries in later phases.

Various studies have shown that the United States has had a comparative advantage in the introductory phase of the product cycle for many commodities because of commercial and productive innovations. Relatively high expenditures by many industries on research and development have enabled the United States to be innovative. The industries that spend the most on research and development tend to have the best export performance.[3] The incentives for all this research and development come from several sources. US Government policy has encouraged spending on research and development and many commercial innovations are the result of fallout from government research. In addition, there are two national characteristics that encourage research and development. One is that we have high labour costs and, therefore, an incentive to develop labour-saving techniques and capital

---

[2] Seev Hirsh, *Location of Industry and International Competitiveness,* (Oxford, England, 1967).
[3] William Gruber, Dileep Mehta, and Raymond Vernon, "The Research and Development Factor in International Trade and International Investment of United States Industries," *Journal of Political Economy,* 75 (February, 1967).

equipment. The other is that our per capita incomes are high and so, therefore, is the demand for sophisticated consumer goods. In both of these respects, this nation is generally ahead of other countries and, therefore, is able to export labour-saving machinery and expensive consumer goods as wages and incomes increase abroad.

The product cycle approach implies that, while a nation such as the United States may have a comparative advantage in innovation, the monopoly it enjoys in the export of any new product tends to be temporary. Eventually, production abroad will begin to compete with US exports. How soon production abroad actually begins depends on how high trade barriers and transport and export marketing costs are, because the higher these are the more will be saved by producing abroad for the foreign market. Exports from the United States, of course, serve to demonstrate the size of the foreign market and the possibility of starting local production on an economical scale. As foreign production increases, the United States may find itself competing with the foreign-produced goods in third markets and even at home. In recent years, the large international corporations, especially US-owned corporations, have been very important in the transfer of production among countries. These corporations are in a position to weigh the alternatives of producing a particular commodity in one country and shipping it to the market in another country or transferring the production technology to this latter country and manufacturing the product there. The transfer can take place either through direct investment in foreign production facilities or by licensing the use of its process and production of its products to foreign enterprises.

The United States is most likely to lose its comparative advantage in industries that enter a mature phase because these industries use a relatively large proportion of unskilled labour. Because technology in mature industries is standardized and easily transferred, there is a tendency for these industries to locate in countries where this type of labour is cheaper than in the United States. Because of their low wage labour and because of economies of scale in mature industries, these countries would be able to sell the product relatively cheaply in world markets. Wages of unskilled labour in the United States are relatively high because of the higher average productivity and wages of all workers. The United States has invested large quantities of capital in better machinery and technology and in acquiring labour skills, all of which increase worker productivity. In most growth-phase industries, where the United States frequently has been a leader in developing better equipment and technology and where higher skills are important, high productivity tends to offset high wages. But it is true that, in mature industries, high US wages may not be offset by high productivity. Foreign unskilled workers in these industries frequently have the same equipment and technology to work with as unskilled workers in the United States and thus are likely to be just as productive. The difference is that the unskilled workers in most foreign countries have lower wages because they, on the average, are less well trained and have less capital to work with. Thus, the average productivity of all workers is lower and so are the wages of unskilled labour.

Because many less developed countries have an abundance of unskilled labour, it would appear they would have a comparative advantage in mature industries. There are, however, some factors which tend to hinder the transfer of mature industries to these countries. Probably most important is the fact that the high wage countries have traditionally protected their maturing industries from low wage competition. Another factor hindering the transfer of mature industries to the developing countries is the fact that such industries are characterized by the use of not only unskilled labour but very sophisticated capital equipment. In most cases, the technology and equipment of mature industries are available for purchase in the developed countries. The developing countries, however, have low savings and, therefore, lack sufficient funds to transfer mature industries without outside assistance. Finally, there are marketing problems that hinder the transfer of mature industries. Even though the products of such industries are highly standardized, it may be difficult for developing countries to penetrate the markets of the advanced countries where they have a comparative advantage. Because large international corporations are in a position to provide the production processes and to oversee the marketing of the final product, they are very important, and will be more so in the future, in facilitating the transfer of mature industries to the developing countires. This, of course, means that the developed countries may be confronted more often with the painful task of transferring resources from their mature industries.

The Role of Policy

It is evident that the essence of international trade is constant change and that the benefits of trade require both the initiation of change and adjustment to it. The basic benefit of trade is that countries are able to obtain goods cheaper in terms of resources by importing than by producing them at home. That is, the opportunity to trade allows a more efficient utilization of the world's resources. The second benefit of trade is that, through it, countries can take advantage of the economies of large-scale production and distribution present in the growth and mature phases of the product cycle. The third benefit of trade is the tendency for trade to increase the scope of competition in the countries of the world. Not only must large firms face competitors at home but in the whole world, and increased competition helps to restrain inflation. Finally, trade encourages the dissemination of new technology and new products throughout the world. The constant changes in international trade, however, produce uncertainty and the adjustment to the changes often forces firms to develop new techniques and products, or to go out of business, and in workers having to find new skills and jobs. Governments, in appraising trade policy, must balance the benefits that trade offers against the desire to protect domestic firms and workers from uncertainty and painful adjustment. This appraisal involves value judgments — personal opinions about how desirable the benefits are and how undesirable the uncertainty and adjustments are.

In many respects, the trade changes are little different from other economic changes such as technological developments and domestic demand change that can also lead to the obsolescence of industries and categories of resources. But, because of uncertainty about foreign developments and the ever-present possibility of change in the trade policies of both the home country and foreign countries, business and labour have more fear of change in the international trade area. Since, historically, governments have interfered to a large extent in international economic affairs, they frequently are called upon to ameliorate the uncertainties and adjustments caused by trade changes. The use of tariffs and quotas for this purpose tends to reduce international trade and its benefits. In addition, the imposition of tariffs and quotas tends to invite retaliation by foreign countries which would further reduce trade. The result would be inefficient use of the world's resources.

Adjusting to increasing imports is especially difficult when they are the products of mature industries. The equipment used in these industries is frequently highly specialized and not easy to convert to the production of other products. Workers are mostly unskilled and not in demand in other less mature industries. Both business and labour leaders in these industries are acutely aware of the relative ease with which the technology of these industries is transferred to low wage countries and of the role the large international corporations play in this transfer. It is said that import competition is unfair because the wages of unskilled workers in the United States are kept high by government regulations and that labour will be impoverished by imports. As pointed out above, however, unskilled workers in this country have a high wage because of the higher average productivity of workers generally. In fact, many of the industries that have good export performance in the United States are ones that pay high wages. The competitive position of such industries is not likely to be harmed by cheap foreign labour but is very likely to be harmed by foreign retaliation against protectionist moves by the United States.

43. CANADIAN TRADE: RECENT STRENGTHS AND GROWING MATURITY*

The Bank of Nova Scotia

Sudden transformations in Canada's external trading position have occurred in the past, but seldom with the speed with which a huge trade surplus was accumulated in the first six months of this year. In this short space of time the trade balance — and in particular the extended growth of export receipts — emerged as virtually the only vigorous element of expansion in a slowing Canadian business situation. It was also, of course, a major consideration in the decision to allow the Canadian dollar to float on the 1st of June after several months of upward market pressures.

The factors behind the recent unexpected strength in the trade sector (see Chart 1) are complex. Among the more obvious special influences were the catching up of mineral exports after major strike disruptions last year and the unusual extension of Canadian benefit arising out of Canada-US automotive trade. Along with these, a mixture of underlying factors have to be disentangled, some short-run and cyclical, and others arising from the lingering presence of inflation and high defence outlays which have characterized the US economy since 1965. Still other considerations, of a longer-term and more lasting nature, have played a part in reshaping Canada's trading position.

Cyclical swings have been apparent recently in both the inward and outward flows of Canadian trade, particularly in connection with the contraction in US housebuilding (affecting lumber) and with the decline in both US and Canadian markets for cars and other consumer durable goods. Yet in relation to the general business slowdown in the two countries, Canada's total exports have remained much stronger than would normally be the case (even after the special factors noted above). At the same time Canada's imports from all foreign sources have been relatively restrained.

A fair part of the explanation for these developments undoubtedly lies in considerations of a broader and longer-term character. For several years, the overall world trading environment has been unusually favourable for an exporting country like Canada. Spurred on by the inflationary conditions of the US economy, and by sustained expansion in continental Western Europe

---

*Reprinted from the Bank of Nova Scotia, *Monthly Review,* Toronto, July, 1970, by permission.

and Japan, the value of world exports rose by over 27 percent between 1967 and 1969; and despite the slowdown in the US economy over the past twelve months, the growth in world trade up to mid-1970 has remained almost as strong. One factor in this growth obviously has been the strength in the major overseas economies, which has had the effect, until fairly recently, of continuing an upward momentum in export prices, both of industrial materials and of manufactured goods. But a further, less obvious, influence has been the severe pressure on the productive capacity of many US industries that was maintained up to late last year at least; because of lags between orders and deliveries, this has continued to influence trade flows in the first half of this year. This situation has almost certainly been to the advantage of Canadian producers — opening up additional export opportunities and also limiting the pressures of import competition in the Canadian market.

CHART 1
CANADA'S TRADE GROWTH

MERCHANDISE TRADE

Quarterly Totals, Seasonally Adjusted at Annual Rates

$ Billions Ratio Scale

2nd. Q. 1970 BNS Est.

EXPORTS

IMPORTS

The Bank of Nova Scotia

Along with these favourable external developments, Canadian industries have been reaping the advantages of a growing domestic economy and of major trading policy initiatives which have recognized the importance of larger-scale and more efficient production. Most notable in the policy area, of course, have been the introduction of the Canada-US Automotive Trade Agreement in 1965 and the Kennedy Round of reciprocal tariff reductions (the latter also including some special new provisions for many types of machinery). Reflecting all these influences, the structure of Canadian trade has been undergoing a major shift — with an increasing proportion of exports being made up of manufactured goods, and import flows also adjusting to the development of more specialized and more competitive lines of domestic production. Because this shift has been going on while manufactured goods have remained the fastest growing element of world trade, the advantages to Canada have been all the more pronounced. It has to be remembered, though, that the greatest single stimulus, to manufacturing and to exports as a whole, has come from the massive increase in automotive trade under the Canada-US Auto Pact. So large has been the imprint of this special arrangement on export and import totals that the underlying trends of Canada's trade are often missed.

Canada-US Trade

The benefits which the Auto Pact brought to Canada's net trading position with the United States were not generally expected to continue much beyond 1968, but by 1969 (according to Canadian figures) an approximate balance had developed, compared with deficits running over $700 millions in the mid-1960s. In the past six months, moreover, there has been a noticeable improvement beyond this. A good deal of the recent outcome reflects the weakness of new car markets (in line with the general fall-off in consumer sentiment and, probably, a poor stock market performance). Because the model-mix in North America has been leaning toward the production in Canada of smaller cars which have been less prone to a downswing in sales, Canadian production in general has remained fairly immune.

The further improvement this year in Canada's automotive trade with the United States appears to reflect current economic conditions, in the sense that Canadian productive capacity was already adapted to a demand for smaller North American models. Under different economic circumstances, there could well be a fall-back from the present very favourable balance in automotive trade, but the basic improvement which had already occurred is undoubtedly a lasting one. In the current discussions regarding the future of the Auto Pact, the two governments will be trying to sort out what is temporary from what is an irreversible structural change.

CHART 2

MAIN MARKETS FOR CANADIAN EXPORTS

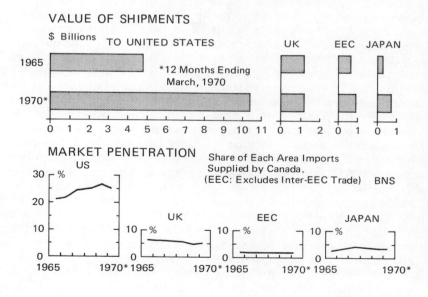

Apart from automobiles, other Canadian products have expanded their sales in the United States. Staples such as wood pulp, newsprint, petroleum, and nonferrous metals have met with an increasing demand and there has also been some interesting progress by manufactured goods. The exchange rate depreciation in 1962 was no doubt one favourable influence on the latter, and the long expansion of the North American economy through the 1960s gave Canadian industries an opportunity to expand the scale of their operations and improve their competitive ability. More recently, the take-off in US labour costs after a long period of stability has encouraged competition from the rest of the world, and Canadian goods have been in an advantageous position to ease particular bottlenecks in US resources. Partly because of such pressures, various kinds of specialized machinery exports have been in strong demand right into this year. Recently, too, other items such as furniture, clothing, toys, and sporting goods have made good progress.

All in all, materials and goods other than automotive products have contributed about half of the increased value of Canada's exports to the United States in the last five years (see Chart 2). With this growing strength on one hand, and a slightly slower growth of imports over the past three years on the other, Canada's balance of nonautomotive trade with the United States has moved into a surplus since 1968 after deficits through most of the earlier 1960s. Placed alongside the gains made in the automotive trade, this has provided a welcome counterweight to the burgeoning deficit that Canada runs in nonmerchandise transactions with the US.

New Markets Overseas

Canada's exports to countries other than the United States used to turn largely on the fortunes of wheat. In the bumper years of the mid-1960s, for example, wheat sales of around $1 billion a year accounted for a quarter of overseas shipments and about 16 percent of all exports. But by 1969 the subsequent slump in the world wheat market had cut Canada's sales in half, and wheat took up only 12 percent of overseas sales (5 percent of total exports). It is doubtful whether the particular set of favourable world market conditions prevalent a few years ago will ever recur; already, with the first adjustments being brought about under the federal government's "Operation LIFT" program, a sizable shift of farm resources out of wheat into other land-uses has been set in motion.

Fortunately from the point of view of export sales, other markets overseas have successfully filled the breach left in recent years by wheat. As Chart 2 shows, Canada has seen its exports multiply by maintaining or increasing its share of two of the world's fastest growing areas — the European Economic Community (EEC) and Japan. Over the long run, Canada's share of the UK's imports has been declining slowly, and in the subdued conditions of 1968 and 1969 shipments actually declined. Since last December, however, exports to Britain have been breaking all records and in the first six months of this year had risen some 29 percent over the same period of last year. This was largely a consequence of a very strong recovery in shipments of lumber and nickel after the holdups during Canadian labour disputes last year. Further disruptions to normal trade flows — this time a strike by Britain's own longshoremen — may well have led to anticipatory buying of Canadian raw materials in the last month or two.

Japan and the West European countries have been taking much larger quantities of basic materials such as wood products and minerals, while manufactured goods have been making inroads in Latin America and some other parts of the world. In Japan's case, major increases in shipments of copper ore, wood pulp and aluminum have more than made up for a drop in wheat sales, and further expansion in mineral exports seems certain as a result of Japan's participation in several major resource development projects — especially in British Columbia. This year, for example, coal is beginning to be shipped in much larger quantities as the massive new mines and transportation facilities in BC come into operation. On the basis of existing Japanese contracts, coal shipments will very soon reach $100 millions a year, so that coal should become a major export commodity within a very short time.

Export and Import Highlights

Exports have continued to diversify in recent years, while import patterns have on the whole held in line with trends in domestic economic activity. These overall characteristics are shown up in Chart 3, which illustrates the evolving composition of Canadian trade. On the export side, *farm and fish products* have obviously lost ground, reflecting the fall-off in wheat sales. Some of this loss has been made up for by other agricultural products — last year, for instance, there were large meat exports, and this year barley has recovered strongly.

The *forest products* industries, whose export earnings last year reached

CHART 3

CHANGING TRADE COMPOSITION

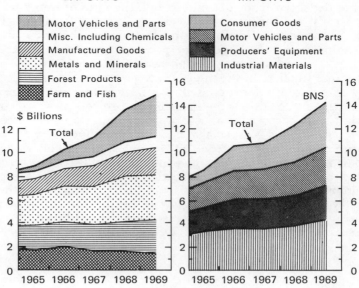

$2.9 billions, broke out of a long period of sluggish growth when new pulp and paper capacity became available around 1968. Much of the new output of wood pulp has been exported to the United States, but overseas sales have experienced a marked expansion, too. Higher lumber production, resulting from the new sawmills which came into operation at the same time, initially found ready markets south of the border; more recently, however, the US construction industry has been experiencing a decline, and even though some of the slack has been made up for by increased sales to the United Kingdom and Japan, total lumber exports have been on a downswing for the best part of a year. Newsprint shipments to the United States also began to weaken this year in line with the business slowdown.

The *metals and minerals* group, by contrast, has continued to enjoy buoyant markets through the first half of this year. These commodities, which accounted for $3.8 billions in 1969, are not so heavily dependent on US market conditions as forest products, though in the case of petroleum and natural gas, of course, Canadian exports go exclusively to the south. These latter two items have almost doubled in the past five years, and it now remains to be seen to what extent the unquestionably strong US demand for energy will eventually bring about a further enlargement of the permitted quantities. In view of the developing shortage of US natural gas it seems almost certain that Canadian gas exports will rise substantially more.

The new growth in exports of *manufactured goods* stands out clearly from the chart. Automotive products, of course, now take the lion's share and accounted for nearly a quarter of all exports last year. Other manufactured goods took up a further 14 percent, to bring the share of manufactured goods close to 40 percent of the total. Among machinery items, there has been a steady expansion of foreign sales of materials-handling equipment and machinery for specialized industrial purposes. This momentum has carried on through to the present, whereas the earlier fast growth in aircraft and communications equipment faded last year.

On the import side, too, manufactured goods have been accounting for much of the recent change in pattern. Most of this, in turn, has been related to larger shipments of automobiles and parts into Canada. If automotive products are deducted from the import bill, the ratio of imports to GNP has held very steady for the past five years, at about 13 percent. During the mid-sixties, when domestic expansion was supported by a major wave of business capital spending, imports of producers' equipment accelerated in step. Similarly, when business spending eased off in 1967-68, the increases in imports became smaller. In the modest recovery of capital spending in 1969, however, the apparent import content was heavier than usual, partly perhaps because of the interruptions in investment projects due to construction disputes, but also because of a large wave of imports of advanced business equipment and controls — especially electronic computers.

In consumer goods apart from automobiles, the trend of imports has shown a fair resemblance to consumer spending. Industrial materials imports also show a broad reflection of domestic swings, but again the movements were not in unison last year; in this instance, labour disputes in the Canadian steel industry led to an abnormal inflow of iron and steel, while imports of fabrics and textiles reflected the increased amount of low-cost competition from overseas. Chemicals and plastics were also imported in larger quantities in 1969.

Although some of the special forces at work in this year's trade performance — such as the rebound after strike interruptions and the rapid rise of world metal prices — had by June about run their course, others had not. Overseas markets continued to draw in large amounts of Canadian raw materials, and automotive exports apparently have avoided the worst of the slump in North American car sales. Yet for the remainder of this year it is most unlikely that the export performance will maintain anything like its recent momentum. In some individual markets (petroleum, following the cutback in permitted export quotas to the United States; and pulp and paper, especially with the price disadvantage introduced by the floating of the dollar) there are signs of a slackening in export shipments. Meanwhile the general trade background remains heavily coloured by the awkward adjustment of the US economy through a period of slowdown, not to mention the complications posed by difficult labour negotiations in both countries.

If the US economy successfully navigates the transition to a less inflationary, less defence-oriented environment, the overall setting of world trade and Canadian exports in the next few years could alter a great deal. On the demand side, the United States might not be so compelled to draw in extra quantities of goods from outside, since its domestic resources ought to fall into better balance. On the price side, in turn, one would expect a greater degree of cost competition to develop, internally in the US and elsewhere.

Another related question affecting Canada's position over the long run has to do with the so-called "terms of trade." Over the past five years there has been a favourable movement in its export prices compared with its import prices — amounting to five percentage points. With an easing of inflationary US demands, this advantage could begin to unwind, giving greater urgency to the objective of preventing manufacturing costs from straying out of line.

Looked at from the point of view of Canada's own international position,

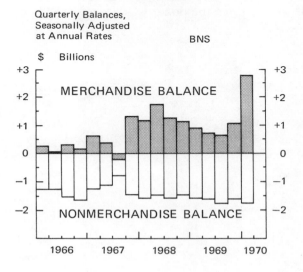

TRADE BALANCES

the recent strengthening and broadening of exports together with a contained growth of imports have to some extent been well-timed, for as Chart 4 suggests, the gap which has to be covered on nonmerchandise transactions has been steadily growing. With the anticipated expansion of spending by Canadians on foreign travel, and a further growth of interest and dividend payments, the balance could deteriorate substantially more over the next few years. If Canada is to retain a reasonably healthy current account balance, a continued strong performance in merchandise trade will be very necessary.

The long-term prospects for Canadian trade will as always depend on the existence of a generally favourable international climate. Through the 1960s there were doubts about the adequacy of world foreign exchange reserves for financing trade. Looking back, these doubts seem exaggerated, for the value of the world's trade managed to grow far more quickly than the world's production. With the successful creation early this year of additional reserves — the Special Drawing Rights in the International Monetary Fund — and with some needed adjustments over the past year in several exchange rates, this problem has become less urgent. What is becoming much more of a concern is the course of trading policies in different parts of the world. The Kennedy Round of tariff cuts, now substantially achieved by most participants (and already fully implemented by Canada) has certainly been giving stimulus to industrial exporting nations. But no new initiatives toward liberalization have yet been taken as a follow-up, and indeed the international mood has seemed to turn the other way. For Canada there are the added uncertainties surrounding Britain's new attempt to join the EEC, as well as concern over the growing protectionist sentiment in the US Congress. In view of the nontariff barriers to trade still being ingeniously applied and the increasing dissatisfaction over the protective shields which the world's large trading groups appear to be setting up around themselves, there is a clear need for a major co-operative effort in the period ahead.

If some of these uncertainties are successfully resolved, Canada will be in a good position to try to maintain the position of strength it has built up in trade over the past few years. This strength has been partly based on some temporary advantages, which may soon pass. But short-run factors should not obscure the fact that there have been some far-reaching improvements of a more durable nature since the dollar was pegged at 92½ cents US.

B. FINANCING OF INTERNATIONAL TRADE AND FOREIGN EXCHANGE RATE SYSTEMS

Foreign trade is only half the story of a country's external economic transactions. The other half consists of such things as the international movement of capital, dealings in gold and foreign exchange, and variations in the international credit position resulting from operations with the International Monetary Fund. A statement that summarizes *all* the economic transactions that occur in a given period between one country and the rest of the world is called a "balance of international payments" — or, simply, "balance of payments."

The balance of payments is based on a double entry system, which provides for each debit to be matched by a credit. This accounts for the truism that the balance of payments always balances. Yet the expression "a deficit in the balance of payments" along with its reciprocal, "a surplus in the balance of payments," is constantly used in public discussion. Is it a contradiction in terms? In economic usage, it is not, and the reason is quite straightforward. A so-called overall surplus or deficit does not — according to this usage — represent the balance of *all* items in the balance of payments, but only the balance of a certain selection of transactions. Hence what is called surplus or deficit is a matter of definition.

Reading 44 is a clear explanation of what is meant by the balance of payments. It examines four broad classes of balance of payments deficits, and discusses Canada's postwar balance of payments position on these bases. Finally, it reviews the role of Canada's monetary, fiscal, and exchange rate policy in causing and correcting Canada's balance of payments problems in the interval between 1950 and 1962. The general analysis makes clear that the determination of balance of payments deficit or surplus is far from being a fully objective exercise. It has the clearly normative aspect of providing a guide for national economic policy. This suggests that we should define a deficit or surplus in terms of the need for action.

The term foreign exchange means simply the money of another country. Also, the foreign exchange rate is simply the price paid for the currency of another country. More specifically, the rate of exchange in Toronto on London is the price in dollars and cents of the right to claim a pound sterling in London. Like any other price the exchange rate is determined by the forces of supply and demand. But governments very seldom allow these underlying forces to work by themselves, with the result that in actual practice the rate may be drastically influenced or even precisely determined by the way in which the government interferes in the exchange markets. Exchange rates are important because they are an integral part of the total prices of foreign goods and services as well as all other types of transactions included in the balance of payments. Though a balance of payments statement always balances, nations are not always in equilibrium in achieving that balance.

Canada has had considerable experience with both fixed and flexible exchange rates. From 1940 to 1950 Canada followed the policy of fixed exchange rates. In 1950 the government abandoned this policy and established a floating rate system. For the next twelve years the Canadian authorities allowed the exchange rate to respond to the normal play of economic forces. On May 2, 1962, following a sharp decline in the official exchange reserves, the government announced that henceforth the Canadian dollar would be "pegged" at 92.5 US cents. There was no need to reconsider the exchange rate adopted in 1962 until the second quarter of 1970 when severe upward pressure developed on the Canadian dollar. Accordingly, on May 31, 1970, Canada moved to a floating rate, and up to the time of writing the Canadian dollar has fluctuated in the range of 95.5 to 99.5 US cents.

Reading 45 reviews the reasons for Canada's latest resort to floating exchange rates, and comments on its implications for the international monetary system and for domestic credit conditions.

44. CANADA'S INTERNATIONAL TRADE AND PAYMENTS: AN EXAMINATION OF RECENT TRENDS*

David W. Slater

Before President Kennedy proposed the interest equalization tax, a particular interpretation of Canada's recent international trade and payments position had received a widespread acceptance. This was: that Canada experienced rather large persistent deficits in her international payments during (roughly) the last half-dozen years; that these deficits have been partly corrected since 1960, by devaluation, by some domestic belt-tightening and by some reorientations of private and public policy in Canada; but that fiscal and monetary restraint and caution are important continuing requirements in Canadian governmental and private economic policy. The proposed new US tax on foreign investment has reinforced this interpretation.

The object of these notes is to explore trends in and interpretations of Canada's recent experience in international trade and payments. What have been the trends? In what senses, if any, has Canada experienced balance of payments deficits in recent years? When? Why? How and to what degree were such deficits corrected? Is the widely accepted interpretation of Canada's balance of payments experience entirely consistent with the evidence? May other factors bearing on the trends have been neglected? May policies of austerity and fiscal and monetary caution have been inappropriate, or at least substantially so? What was the role of Canada's monetary, fiscal, and exchange rate policy in causing and correcting Canada's balance of payments problems?

Because of the sensitive nature and the analytical difficulties of some of these issues, the notes that follow will be to some degree an exercise in two-handed economics. My personal view is that much of the discussion of deficits in Canada's balance of payments has been too glib, that such questions as in the preceding paragraph should be asked, and asked, and asked again. From those who cry deficit we should demand evidence as to the existence and nature of such deficits. It is also my personal view that Canadian economic policies have been too cautious in recent years — and

*Reprinted from David W. Slater, "Canada's International Trade and Payments," *The Canadian Banker*, Autumn, 1963, pp. 5-25, by permission of the editor and author.
Dr. Slater is President of York University, Toronto. Formerly he was Professor of Economics, Queen's University, Kingston, Ontario.

that exaggerated notions about the size, persistence, and troublesome nature of deficits in the country's balance of payments are responsible for some of this excessive caution.

Concepts of Balance of Payments Deficits

Balance of Payments

A country's balance of international payments is a statement on the internation level which is very much like a statement of sources and uses of funds of a business corporation. In principle a country's balance of international payments records all economic transactions across its borders during a period of time. Exports and imports of goods, of transportation, tourist, and business services; of claims to securities, bank balances, and real property; of gifts, of gold, and of interest and dividend transactions — all are recorded in a country's balance of payments. The transactions are between individuals, institutions, and governments resident in a country and like parties resident outside the country. Usually all transactions are recorded in the currency of the country for which the balance of payments statement is being constructed.

These balance of payments transactions may be arrayed in various ways; one such arrangement is summarized in Table 1 with estimated figures for Canada for 1962. The current account and the long-term capital transactions together may be thought of as giving rise to a net "source" or "use" of foreign exchange during a period of time; for example, in 1962 these items together provided a net "use" of foreign exchange for Canada of $130 million (see Accounts A and B of Table 1). The short-term capital transactions may be a provider or user of foreign exchange also; for 1962 as a whole, they "provided" $336 million of foreign exchange (see Account C of Table 1). Thus, for 1962 as a whole, the current, long-term capital and short-term capital accounts taken together were a net provider of about $206 million of foreign exchange to Canada. Under a fixed exchange rate system, the government's gold and foreign exchange accounts and special international financial assistance act as the monetary balance wheel, filling the net gap between sources and uses on the other accounts. Considering 1962 as a whole the Canadian monetary authorities were net recipients of special financial international assistance of $330 million of foreign exchange (measured in Canadian dollars). This assistance, together with the net provision of $206 million noted above, permitted the exchange reserves to be increased by about $537 million (also measured in Canadian dollars).

Accounting Exercises or Indicators of Economic Problems

Having indicated the nature of a country's balance of payments, as a kind of internation source and use of funds statement, what are balance of payments deficits? The term is used in various senses; let us first indicate common uses which are not our concern. The term balance of payments deficit (and the parallel term surplus) is often used to refer to various particular accounting balances in elements within a country's balance of payments position, such as a country being a net user of foreign exchange on tourist account or shipping account. Accounting deficits occur on some transactions and sur-

TABLE 1

A SUMMARY OF CANADA'S BALANCE OF INTERNATIONAL PAYMENTS
FOR THE CALENDAR YEAR 1962
(millions of Canadian dollars)

	Sources and Uses of Foreign Exchange		
Item	Credits Sources +	Debits Uses −	Net Source (+) or Use (−)
A. Current Account Transactions			
1. Merchandise Exports (adjusted)	6,364		+ 155
2. Merchandise Imports (adjusted)		6,209	
3. Transactions in transportation, tourist and business services; interest and dividend receipts and payments; other current transactions	1,984	2,987	−1,003
4. Total Current Account Transactions	8,348	9,196	− 848
B. Long-term Capital Transactions			
5. Direct Investment	525	100	+ 425
6. Outstanding Canadian Securities (net)		52	− 52
7. New Issues and Retirements of Canadian Securities	708	295	+ 413
8. Foreign Securities (net)		79	− 79
9. Loans by Government of Canada	129	7	+ 122
10. Other (net)		110	− 110
11. Total—Long-term Capital Transactions	1,362	643	+ 718
12. Cumulative Total of above	9,710	9,839	− 130
C. Short-term Capital Transactions (excluding monetary, gold, and government foreign exchange transactions)			
13. (net)	336		+ 336
14. Cumulative Total of above	10,046	9,839	+ 206
D. Monetary, Gold, and Government Foreign Exchange Transactions			
15. Special international financial assistance	330		+ 330
16. Change in official holdings of gold and foreign exchange (−equals increase)			− 537

pluses on others. Sometimes such accounting exercises are extended to measures of deficits or surpluses on particular transactions with particular countries or groups of countries. By themselves, such accounting deficits or surpluses do not generally provide an indication of a satisfactory or unsatisfactory state of a country's international position; just as partial accounting balances on a corporation's source and use of funds statement do not generally indicate the financial health of the business. For a country just as for a company, a balancing of the inflow and outflow of funds on each detailed element of the accounts (or on each account with each customer) provides no guidance to appropriate policy at all.

The balance of payments deficits with which we are concerned are economic situations which are inconsistent or unviable, actual or potential international economic situations for a country which may have to be changed so as to alter inflows of foreign exchange in relation to outflows. The changes required may be large or small, temporary or persistent, and they may be brought about by the processes of adjustment inherent in economic systems or they may require changes in government policy. Thus, not every balance of payments deficit constitutes a major problem, but it is the problem cases that command the most of our attention. (Balance of payments surpluses may demand serious attention too, but it is the deficit cases that concern us mainly in these notes.) As not all the problems of payments deficits are equal, some distinction and specification of the nature of such deficits is required.

Kinds of Deficits

Discussions of deficit problems in a country's balance of international payments conventionally take place at four levels. They concern: (1) monetary and working capital problems; (2) problems of reconciling internal and external economic conditions and interests in a business cycle context; (3) structural or fundamental balance of payments deficits in an economic sense; and (4) political and social problems. The indicators of the deficit situation, the causes of the difficulties, the nature of the problems, and the policies that are appropriate depend on the kind, degree, and duration of the deficit. To say only that a country has a balance of payments deficit is no more helpful than to say that a company has financial problems. For the company as for the country, the essence of the analysis is to indicate the nature, cause, degree, and duration of the problems, and the alternative policies that may be used to solve the problems.

The nature and indicators of the four broad classes of balance of payments deficit will be indicated more fully later; here we only indicate the general nature of each level of discourse on such deficits. The first level, unviable external monetary conditions, is indicated mainly by the behaviour of foreign exchange reserves, short-term international indebtedness, and foreign exchange rates. The concern is with short-run external monetary conditions. The second level of economic discourse regarding balance of payments deficits concerns the relationships between internal and external circumstances and policies of a country, particularly with respect to actual or potential monetary conditions in the balance of payments on the one hand and the level of income and employment within a country on the other. The third category of balance of payments deficits refers to difficulties in economic efficiency and growth and in attaining satisfactory levels of living because of problems of adapting to changes in the position of a country in the world economy (including the attainment of satisfactory relations between the external and internal value of a country's currency). All three of these levels of analysis and discussion are primarily economic.

The term, "balance of payments deficit," has been used to refer to a situation that is considered by some to be politically or socially undesirable. In my view, such use of the term is inappropriate because a country may not have a deficit in any of the senses set out above. It may, however, have a continuous excess of current international payments over receipts associated with a continuous net inflow of capital from abroad. The latter may be objectionable on political and social grounds; much fuel can be added to political fires by, for example, discussions of increased foreign ownership and control of a nation's industry and resources. Such situations are commonly referred to as balance of payments deficits, the amount of deficit being measured by the net capital inflow, or, what amounts to the same thing, by the excess of payments over receipts in current international trade in goods and services. In my view, the term "deficit" should not be used in this context, because confusion results from applying the same term to several different phenomena. This writer prefers the phrase "inappropriate use of foreign financing" for the above situation. This phrase focusses much more directly on the problem than does the term deficit. A net capital inflow is not a clear indicator of an inappropriate or unsatisfactory international situation.

Some Allegations About Canada's Deficits

The "conventional wisdom" concerning Canada's balance of payments in recent years is that the country has experienced balance of payments deficits in all of these senses; that is, (1) an external monetary deficit; (2) a conflict between external monetary conditions and internal stabilization goals; (3) conflicts between Canada's opportunities in the world economy and internal economic efficiency and growth; and (4) an "inappropriate use of foreign financing." Some writers have emphasized one aspect of deficit and others another aspect. The concept of deficit used by various people has not always been clear, and analysis has slipped back and forth rather sloppily from one realm to another. Some people indicate deficits by reference to exchange reserves and rates; others point to short-term indebtedness; still others point to a net excess of payments on current account transactions; and still others point to various partial accounting deficits. There appears to be a general consensus that Canada had a balance of payments deficit but, because the elements in the deficit were unclear and confused, the consensus was more misleading than helpful. It is this writer's contention that: (1) Canada did not have any significant clear-cut external monetary deficit; (2) that the conflicts between internal and external balance with respect to stabilization problems and policy were and still are grossly exaggerated, and many of these conflicts are due to our own follies; (3) that there were some elements of structural difficulty in Canada's position in the world economy during the last half-dozen years, but that these problems were never as severe as the conventional wisdom now holds, and much of the difficulty arising from these situations was due to errors in Canadian government policy; and (4) that it is by no means self-evident that a reduction in net capital inflows is in Canada's interest in a social or political sense.

"Monetary Deficit" in Canada's Balance of International Payments?

In this writer's judgment Canada has not experienced any significant monetary deficit in her balance of payments during the last dozen years. But some ambiguous signs of such a deficit did appear in 1960 and 1961; and the exchange crisis of 1962 must be reconciled with the general contention.

A monetary deficit in a country's balance of international payments is mainly indicated by one or some combination of the following criteria: (1) a substantial net reduction in a country's holdings of gold and foreign exchange reserves (indicated by Section D of the accounts in Table 1); (2) a substantial increase in a country's net short-term indebtedness on private and governmental account (indicated by Section C of the accounts in Table 1); (3) under a fixed exchange rate system, the price of foreign exchange at the upper limit of the agreed range for much of the time, or devaluation required to avoid a monetary deficit; (4) under a floating exchange rate system, a trend of substantial and persistent increase in the prices of foreign exchange.[1]

Until nearly the end of 1960 Canada was on a floating exchange rate system, without sustained interventions directly in the market by the exchange authorities. In these circumstances, criterion (4) and perhaps private transactions under criterion (2) are the principal relevant indicators of the monetary disequilibrium in the country's balance of payments. The Canadian price of US dollars moved only within a narrow range from about 94½ to 98 (usually in a narrower range) in the years 1957 to 1960, with no clear trend; the rate was not more than 2 percent higher toward the end of the period than at the beginning.[2] These exchange rate changes do not indicate an external monetary disequilibrium between 1957 and 1960.

A slight and somewhat ambiguous indication of an external monetary disequilibrium is provided, however, by the substantial increase — about $550 million — in Canada's short-term indebtedness in 1959 and 1960 (see Table 2). The excess of payments on current account transactions over receipts on long-term capital account amounted to over $700 million for the two years. On balance Canadians drew down their short-term claims on foreigners; and on balance foreigners increased their short-term claims on Canadians. But how should such changes be interpreted? They might be a sign of external monetary weakness of the Canadian dollar, of the using up of Canada's line of external short-term credit, that is, of a monetary balance of payments deficit. However, other interpretations are more plausible. A flow of funds into Canada was attracted by the relatively high returns to short-term lending in Canada during this period. Also expectations of continued strength of the Canadian dollar in foreign exchange markets may have led to some speculative short-term capital inflow, or at least, to limited coverage of exchange risks of short-term capital inflows coming into Canada on other accounts. Or, short-term capital inflows may have followed as a by-product of some other changes in the structure of trade.

In 1961 Canada was on an informal fixed exchange rate system, the rate being influenced somewhat by official interventions prior to June, 1961, and more openly and systematically by such interventions after June, 1961. In the circumstances criteria (1), (2), (3), and (4) all become relevant indicators of monetary balance of payments deficits. In three of the four quarters of 1961 the current account deficit exceeded the net capital inflows, but for the year as a whole the excess was less than $200 million. The capital inflows

---

[1] If a country has a special trade or exchange controls, additional criteria are relevant. Also forward foreign exchange transactions may indicate deficits.
[2] The estimates are based on data found in the Bank of Canada: *Statistical Summary,* various issues.

in short-term forms were exceptionally large, about $420 million for the year. The country's exchange reserves were increased by over $200 million and the monetary authorities apparently had no problem maintaining the exchange rate in the range which they considered desirable. This evidence suggests that a case could be made that Canada experienced an external monetary balance of payments deficit in 1961, but the case is not strong; and such deficit as may have occurred was quite small. The case rests on two indicators. The first is the excess of the current account deficit over the capital inflow in long-term forms, despite devaluation of the Canadian dollar, of cumulatively increasing magnitude from the fourth quarter of 1960 to the third quarter of 1961. The other indicator is the significant increase in the country's net short-term indebtedness, aside from the country's exchange reserves. The argument is an extension of that advanced for 1960, except that the former rests almost completely on the build-up of the country's net short-term indebtedness.

While these signs may be taken as indicators of a small monetary balance of payments deficit for Canada, other factors suggest that this interpretation should be somewhat discounted. The uncertainties over Canadian monetary, exchange rate, fiscal, and foreign borrowing policies in 1961 limited the actual and planned long-term capital inflows. The inflows were exceptionally small in comparison with those indicated by underlying economic circumstances and given the general structure of the then-existing capital market policies and arrangements. Exchange speculation, interest arbitrage, and other factors appear to have contributed to making the short-term capital inflows exceptionally large. Finally, the effects of devaluation and other changes in reducing the current account deficit were only beginning to be felt. Thus the excess of the current account deficit over the long-term capital inflows, and the rather large short-term capital inflows both tend to exaggerate the degree of monetary disequilibrium in Canada's balance of payments in 1961.

The development of and relief from Canada's exchange crisis in 1962 has been suggested as the clearest indication of a monetary deficit in Canada's balance of payments. There is no doubt about the existence of a short-run emergency deficit in Canada's exchange position. But this deficit had almost no connection with the underlying balance of payments situation of Canada. In this writer's judgment the exchange crisis was almost completely a crisis of confidence, much of which could have been avoided by a different set of Canadian policies. The anatomy of the crisis is by now quite well known. In the first quarter of 1962 a (not unusually large) net use of foreign exchange on current account transactions took place. Long-term capital inflows were unusually small, and some net short-term capital outflow took place. Thus the net use of foreign exchange on the current account had to be met out of Canada's exchange reserves, under the informal pegged exchange rate system then in vogue. Early in the second quarter of 1962, these trends worsened, and the government shifted to a formally pegged exchange rate system (under the IMF arrangements) and devalued the Canadian dollar in the process. The monetary authorities did not bolster the exchange reserves at the time of pegging the dollar, nor did they take other measures to support adequately the newly pegged exchange rate. The crisis worsened through the election campaign. After the election in June, 1962, special international financial assistance was sought and emergency measures taken to alleviate the crisis.

The crisis rather quickly subsided thereafter, giving rise to the appearance of a monetary surplus in Canada's balance of payments; and this despite the extended period of intense political uncertainty in the nine months following the election of June, 1962. The statistics for the year as a whole are set out in Table 1. The excess of the current account use of foreign exchange over the long-term capital inflow was only $130 million. Aside from the official exchange transactions, a net short-term capital inflow of $336 million took place. For the year as a whole, it is rather hard to defend the contention that the country experienced a monetary deficit in the balance of payments. The development of and the alleviation of the exchange crisis can be considered as a short-term emergency phenomenon, related almost completely to the development and resolution of a crisis of confidence.

Balance of Payments "Deficits": Conflicts Between Prosperity Within a Country and Net International Current Account Payments

Some Possibilities

In his annual report for the year 1962, the Governor of the Bank of Canada referred to the consensus that Canada had too large a deficit in the current account of her balance of payments in the conditions of substantial unemployment and unused productive capacity at home in recent years.[3] The main idea was that policies to reduce the current account deficit would increase the internal level of employment and output. Some other crude and some other sophisticated ideas have also been included within the consensus. At the crude level some people have treated the current account deficit as a major cause of economic stagnation and excessive unemployment in Canada. And, on a much more sophisticated plane, the problem has been viewed, not as that of reducing the current account deficit absolutely, but of keeping the deficit under control while prosperity is increased by domestic measures so that expansionary policies at home are not inhibited unduly by current external payments developments.

What are the connections between the net use of foreign exchange on current account transactions in the balance of payments and internal prosperity and depression? Could reductions in the current account deficit be treated as a policy variable to increase internal prosperity? How? Under what circumstances? With what consequences? Are the answers different for a country on a flexible exchange rate system, as Canada was for more than a decade up to late 1960, than the answers for one on a pegged exchange rate system? Did the current account position inhibit domestic policies to promote prosperity for Canada in recent years? Did Canada experience rather large and persistent conflicts between its current account position and internal prosperity in recent years? How? When? How might these conflicts have been resolved? What attempts at resolution were made? Did they work? If not, why not? We will concede that under some circumstances and policies, significant conflicts may arise between net payments on current account and domestic prosperity. These possibilities are somewhat different on a fixed exchange rate and on a floating rate system.

---

[3] Bank of Canada, *Annual Report of the Governor of the Bank to the Minister of Finance,* for the year 1962, p. 7.

However, the conflicts may be due primarily to the policies that are pursued by the country. They may be (at least partly) resolved by changes in policies. More important, however, in this writer's opinion the actual conflicts have been somewhat exaggerated for Canada.

Formal Connections Between Net Current Account Payments and Internal Income Flows

In a situation of substantial unemployment and unused productive capacity at home the central economic problem is to obtain an increase in the quantity demanded of the productive inputs located within a country (manpower, plant and equipment, and resources). The lessons of Keynesian economics indicate that this is most likely to be achieved in the short run by increasing the total demand for inputs located in a country, and this in turn is most likely to be achieved by increasing the total spending on the goods and services produced in a country. Of the flow of goods and services which comes available within a country, some are derived from imports of goods and services (including both final and intermediate goods and services) and some are derived from the use of inputs located within the country (see Figure 1). (Thus, the flow of goods which comes available within a country during a period of time is larger than the current output from the productive inputs located within a country.) Of the flow of goods and services which comes available within a country, some are sold to foreigners; thus both foreign and domestic demand for goods coming available in Canada determine the rate of sale.

FIGURE 1

SIMPLIFIED SPENDING AND INCOME FLOWS

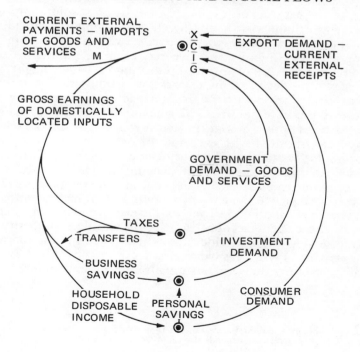

The relations between an excess of payments (demand for imported goods and services) over receipts (export demand) in the current account of a country's balance of payments and the level of internal employment may now be examined. Other things being equal, the direct effect of a reduction in the excess of current payments over current receipts will always increase the demand for domestic inputs, no matter what the absolute behaviour of the exports and imports may be. An increase in export demand relative to the associated increase in demand for imported goods and services (see Figure 1) will work in this direction; but so will a decrease in the demand for imported goods and services which was more than an associated decrease in export demand. About these technical relations there is no doubt, but it is one matter to accept these relations and quite another to accept the current account position as a cause of unemployment, or as an instrument to reduce unemployment within a country. Will other things be equal? How may the current account deficit be reduced and with what other short-run and long-run consequences? If the current account position is a potential source of difficulty, given a vigorous domestic expansionary policy, how may these difficulties be met?

Reducing the Current Account Deficit as a Policy Instrument to Improve a Nation's Prosperity

Under a given set of economic arrangements and policies, a nation can be thought of as having a schedule of imports of goods and services in which the rate of importation depends on the level of internal prosperity. Similarly, a nation faces a set of export opportunities which depend in part on the economic policies pursued by the country. The principal idea in using a reduction in the current account deficit as a policy instrument to improve national prosperity is to reduce the schedule of imports of goods and services in relation to the set of export opportunities by an absolute improvement in the export opportunities with no change in the import schedule, or by an absolute reduction in the import schedule, with no change in the set of export opportunities, or by a relative reduction in the import schedule in comparison with the set of export opportunities which might occur with either increases or decreases in export opportunities. The most common mechanisms to reduce a current account deficit include depreciation or devaluation of the external value of a country's currency, changes in expenditure patterns within a country which reduce the import schedule, that is, the imports associated with each rate of overall expenditure, and intensified use of import restraints and export encouragements. It is always possible for a nation to reduce the current account deficit by means of policy, though the combination of techniques that may be required to accomplish a given degree of change in the current account deficit may be different in one circumstance than another.[4] The real issues are whether such a policy reduction in the current account deficit will improve prosperity or not, in what degree, and with what side effects; and, what is the merit of such a policy in comparison with feasible alternatives?

Generally speaking, the serious students of economic policy have rejected

---

[4] The mixture of policies required to accomplish these ends differs substantially under fixed and flexible exchange rate systems and depends also on other circumstances.

the idea that the reduction of current account deficits in balance of payments by means of policy is an effective way to increase a nation's prosperity. Whatever one country accomplishes by this means is at the expense of other countries; thus such policies are generally dubbed "beggar-thy-neighbour." Moreover, the degree of short-run improvement in the prosperity of a country which might be accomplished by such policies is thought to be small when the indirect implications are considered too. Finally, the long-term side effects of such policies are generally regarded by economists as almost always bad.

It is one thing to argue for or against beggar-thy-neighbour policies. It is quite another to argue for policies which provide excessive help to the prosperity of neighbours; or about policies which limit the benefits that neighbours receive from the internal expansionary policies of a country. It is quite possible that a nation might follow policies which in effect export employment rather than unemployment to neighbours, and such policies may be quite inappropriate. Nothing that is worth having in the short run or long run may be gained by such a policy. Or, to take the more subtle case, even if it would be "nice" to allow a substantial spill-over from a nation's domestic expansion policy to the prosperity of one's neighbour, a nation may not be able to afford such a spill-over. Thus a case may arise, not for a beggar-thy-neighbour policy, with respect to reducing the current account deficit, but for a not-benefit-thy-neighbour or a charity-begins-at-home policy in which the size of the current account deficit associated with increasing internal levels of prosperity would be reduced. This is a tricky exercise, for if all countries pursue such a policy the effect is much like a beggar-thy-neighbour policy. Also the degree of restraint that can be justified on these grounds is difficult to ascertain.

Another complicating feature of policy is that the problem may not be a pure case of business-cycle-current-account-balance interrelationship. Rather there may be a mixture of cyclical and structural or fundamental deficits in a country's balance of payments, in which case, policy issues may become very complex. A devaluation might be a beggar-thy-neighbour policy in the cyclical context, but not in the structural deficit context.

If a country devalues in a situation of mixed deficits, how can one tell whether the degree is appropriate to the structural aspects of the problem without adding a measure of a beggar-thy-neighbour policy. Another danger is in making too small a devaluation for fear of being charged with beggar-thy-neighbour tactics.

Canadian Policy Regarding These Conflicts

Let us now turn from theoretical possibilities to the record of policy realities in Canada. Could Canada have defended an active policy to reduce the current account deficit in the light of what might reasonably have been expected in the circumstances of persistent unemployment? How might Canada have followed a policy of reducing the current account deficit? How efficient could such a policy have been? Did Canada, by permitting unduly large current account deficits, inhibit the exercise of domestic expansionary policies?

Before tackling the business and growth cycle aspects of these questions, a digression regarding depreciation and devaluation must be made. For several years, it has been the opinion of this author that Canada experienced structural disturbances to its foreign trade and balance of payments position after the mid-1950s, and that a depreciation of the exchange rate under a flexible exchange system, or a devaluation of the Canadian dollar under a pegged rate system were appropriate changes in these circumstances. The implication of this position is that the monetary authorities should have intervened in a number of ways to encourage a depreciation of the external value of the Canadian dollar, as they could have done. (This writer has been critical of the devaluation of the Canadian dollar in 1962, but because of the way in which the exchange rates and funds were managed by the government.) The effect of such intervention (or of the pegging of a devalued Canadian dollar) would have been to reduce the current account deficit, a change that was appropriate in terms of the structural disturbances to which the economy had to adjust. The effect would, incidentally, have tended to increase levels of income and employment within Canada, and appropriately so, for some of the unemployment and underemployment was due to structural causes. But none of this argument implies that Canada should have and could have used a policy reduction in the current account of the balance of payments as corrective to business cycle aspects of Canadian economic problems.

Quite a reasonable argument can be made that, throughout much of the last half-dozen years, the net foreign trade effect of Canadian policy was to beggar Canada rather than Canada's neighbours. The policy was intermittently being shifted in the right direction prior to the exchange crisis. The policies then adopted tipped the balance toward a beggar-thy-neighbour result, though one that could have been made tolerable if more vigorous expansionary policies had been pursued in Canada. These are tentative judgments but let us explore the argument and the evidence.

The normal pattern is for the foreign capital inflow into Canada and the size of the country's current account deficit to become exceptionally large during periods of exceptionally rapid growth and business cycle booms, such as occurred in the mid-1950s. The capital inflows and the size of the net payments on current account ordinarily decrease rapidly and in large measure as business cycle recessions and periods of slower growth emerge (for example, in periods such as those after mid-1957 though the beginnings of these developments arose prior to 1957). The exceptional feature of Canada's experience between mid-1957 and late 1960 was the sustained high level of the capital inflows into Canada and the current account deficits and the maintenance of a substantial premium on the Canadian dollar. Several factors seem to have accounted for this experience. First, the structural adjustments tended to sustain the current account deficit. These will be discussed below. Second, as Professors Johnson and Barber have (separately) pointed out, Canada pursued a surprisingly tight monetary policy, which tended to sustain the net capital inflows at high levels, the premium on the Canadian dollar and the current account deficit. Government debt management policy also contributed to this trend. Third, just as there was a lag in the development of capital inflows into Canada when the big boom developed, so there was a lag in the decline of such capital inflows after the big boom passed. Thus, even in the absence of the tight money policy in Canada, there probably would have been a somewhat exceptionally large (for the circumstances) long-term capital inflow. Fourth, for quite some time, the Canadian authorities did nothing to reorient their export promotion, their expenditure patterns, and their encouragement to home consumption so as to reduce the current account deficit.

Beginning in 1960, and particularly in 1961 (after the Coyne controversy drew to a close), Canadian policy began to change. The baby budget, the suasion against foreign borrowing, the interventions in the exchange market, the export promotion, the Bladen Committee, the buy-at-home campaigns and programs — all of these started nudging the current account balance into a situation that was more consistent with our real economic opportunities and our employment objectives. This does not mean that all the policies were appropriate. The policies often worked haltingly and at cross-purposes. The mixture of structural, growth, and business cycle problems was not particularly well sorted out, and the confusion slowed up in the mixture of policies. The intervention in the exchange market was not well timed, nor accompanied by the bolstering of exchange reserves and vigorous internal policies in such a way as to make the policy efficient and defensible. The undue tightness in monetary policy persisted.

This writer has already said most of his piece on the exchange crisis of 1962. The rudderless policies and the procrastination of the government made the crisis much worse than it might have been; indeed the crisis had little or no relation to the underlying balance of payments situation. But the extent of the crisis led (at least temporarily) to an undervaluation of the Canadian dollar in exchange markets, to surcharges for a considerable period of time, to an excessive dose of buy-Canada campaigns, and to some continued abnormal restraints on imports.

Structural or Fundamental Disequilibrium in Canada's Balance of Payments

The third element in the consensus about Canadian balance of payments deficits in recent years is that the country experienced a structural or fundamental disequilibrium. This is a most important issue, partly because the depreciation or devaluation of a country's currency is likely to be a more appropriate policy for dealing with such problems than with cyclical ones. Limitations of space rule out extended comments on the existence, nature, and appropriate policy for structural disequilibrium; some ideas are advanced tentatively below but they will have to be developed in later articles.

By a structural or fundamental deficit in a country's balance of payments is meant a situation in which it is apparently not possible to attain simultaneously a monetary balance of payments equilibrium, relatively full employment of the available manpower, productive facilities, and resources, and the real level of living that had been expected or forecast from the kinds of skills and facilities previously developed. Structural or fundamental problems in a country's position in the world economy may arise from a persistent decrease in external demand for the products that have been produced and exported; or from the loss of some comparative cost advantages; or from a shift in tastes within a country toward imports; or from the drying up of external sources of capital; or from the reduction in investment opportunities within a country; or from shifts in expectations. To correct the problems substantial changes in the production structure within a country are required, and perhaps quite large changes in the country's real international economic arrangments and expectations regarding income and wealth.

Of course, not all structural or fundamental disturbances give rise to structural or fundamental deficits of a worrisome sort. Such deficits arise when the disturbances which are adverse to an economy are large relative to the capacity of a nation's productive structure to change, or when comparatively large and rapid revisions have to be made in the expectations of owners of skills and productive facilities concerning the levels of living they may attain. Such structural problems are distinct from business cycle and growth problems, but they may occur in conjunction with the latter in which case each class of problem makes the other more difficult to cope with.

Has Canada experienced substantial structural disturbances in its trade and finance position in the world economy during the last six or seven years? What disturbances? When? Bearing in mind the nature of Canada's exchange rate system up until late 1960, did such disturbances result in a structural or fundamental deficit in Canada's balance of payments? Were cyclical changes and the economic policies which Canada pursued of the sort to worsen or correct a structural deficit? Have the structural deficits been corrected? How?

In this writer's judgment a number of significant structural or fundamental disturbances adverse to Canada's world economic position did take place during the last half-dozen or so years. First, the export markets for food and industrial materials of the sort Canada has been equipped to export have been generally soft during the last half-dozen years. These trends have been well documented in successive annual commodity surveys by the United Nations. Canada's terms of trade deteriorated. Second, Canadian tastes appear to have shifted somewhat toward imported goods between 1955 and 1960. Third, for some time during and following the mid-1950s, the world competitive position of Canada's industries deteriorated somewhat. The delayed effects of the postwar inflation together with the huge Canadian investment boom in the mid-1950s increased Canadian costs. The undervaluation of the European currencies and the strength of the European recovery in the mid-1950s held down their export costs for a time, despite rapid increases in wage rates in Europe. Fourth, the relaxation in the cold war made Canada a less attractive source of supply for the United States and Western Europe, because the potential strategic disadvantage of other sources of supply was reduced.

Should such adverse structural disturbances have given rise to a structural or fundamental disequilibrium in the Canadian payments? According to the theory of the subject, they should not have because the country was on a flexible exchange rate system. Such adverse circumstances should result in enlarged current payments, reduced current receipts, and reduced capital inflows into a country; but all of these should be reflected in a depreciation of the flexible exchange rate which in turn corrects the balance of payments, and provides the proper signals for the structural adjustment in production within the country. With depreciation, export sales are encouraged, as are the substitutions of domestic goods and services for imports. According to this argument, one might still refer formally to a structural deficit in the Canadian balance of payments, but the reference would be to an interim situation which is in the process of being corrected.

How could Canada have experienced a period of serious structural deficit in her balance of payments prior to December, 1960, when the country was on a flexible exchange rate system? We know that, despite the structural disturbances, Canada's exchange rate did not depreciate significantly before the end of 1960, in line with the expectations set out in the previous paragraph. We know that many people have argued that the Canadian dollar was overvalued in the circumstances (though the actual short-term capital flows did not reflect such judgments). How could such an overvaluation come about? Part of the explanation is Canada's tight money and debt management policies which helped to sustain the capital inflows at high rates and thus tended to maintain a high external value for the Canadian dollar. Another part of the explanation may be the lags in adjusting patterns of external borrowing behind the changes in underlying capital conditions in Canada. Still another part of the explanation may be a delay in the appearance in exchange market transactions of underlying changes in Canada's external economic conditions. Still another possibility is that the cyclical changes in Canada's balance of payments position may have masked somewhat the structural changes so that the degree of structural disequilibrium was underestimated. All of these are possibilities that require careful exploration; but one other possibility must also be explored. This is that the structural disturbances have been exaggerated, and the capacity of the Canadian economy to deal with these disturbances has been grossly underestimated, given sensible Canadian monetary, exchange rate, and fiscal policies.

What about the correction of the deficit — structural, or cyclical, or "what have you"? Between late 1960 and May, 1962, the external value of the Canadian dollar was reduced by about 10 percent; temporary import surcharges were imposed from late June, 1962 until March, 1963 (on a somewhat decreasing scale over the period); export promotion and import limitation crusades were accentuated during the same period; and some increases in the restrictions on imports remain. It is also well known that the tightness of Canadian monetary policy of last summer has been relaxed somewhat, but that relatively high differentials between Canadian and United States interest rates have been maintained. Also Canadian (and United States) levels of money costs of production have been held down in comparison with those of most Western European countries in recent years.

Have all these changes corrected the deficits? — corrected the overvaluation of the Canadian dollar that persisted for several years up to and including 1960? How? In what degree? Regarding the questions only a few tentative judgments may be advanced here. First, the balance of payments numbers suggest correction. The current account deficit was reduced to low levels in the fourth quarter of 1962 and the first quarter of 1963. Private capital inflows were in excess of the current account deficits. The exchange reserve position of the country improved. And the full impact of devaluation and some of the other policies had not been felt. Secondly, on purely economic grounds and prior to the June budget in Canada and the Kennedy interest equalization tax proposal of July, this writer had reached the conclusion that the Canadian dollar was undervalued. Or, to put the same point another way, Canada had reached the position of having a balance of payments surplus rather than a deficit in the monetary sense, in relation to internal prosperity (given the limited vigour to expansionary policies in Canada) or in relation to the real prospects in Canada's position in the world economy.

Prior to the June budget and the Kennedy proposal, in this writer's opinion, there were only two possible arguments in support of an interpretation of Canada's balance of payments position as one of deficit. The first is of the political and social necesssity of Canada ceasing to have a capital inflow in a balance of payments sense, or, to set an even more severe test, of ceasing to rely on net foreign financing for current transactions. The latter is

TABLE 2

THE CANADIAN BALANCE OF INTERNATIONAL PAYMENTS

SELECTED DATA, 1953-1962

(all figures in millions of Canadian dollars)

Year and Quarter	Merchandise Transactions (adjusted) Exports	Imports	Total Current Account Transactions: Items giving rise to Receipts	Payments	Net Source (+) or Use (−) of Funds on Merchandise Account	Current Account	Capital Transactions Net Source (+) or Use (−) of Funds Long-term Forms[3]	Short-term Forms[1]	Total of (8) and (9)	Special International Financial Assistance	Government Transactions Monetary, Gold, and Foreign Exchange	Balance Current Plus Long-term Capital (7) + (8)[2]
(1)	(2)	(3)	(4)	(5)	(6)	(7)	(8)	(9)	(10)	(11)	(12)	(13)
1953	4152	4210	5737	6180	−58	−443	+708	−213	+495	—	+38	+265
1954	3929	3916	5520	5952	+13	−432	+579	−23	+556	—	−124	+147
1955	4332	4543	6072	6770	−211	−698	+410	+44	+654	—	+44	−288
1956	4837	5565	6621	7987	−728	−1366	+1423	−24	+1399	—	−33	+57
1957	4894	5488	6622	8077	−594	−1455	+1301	+49	+1350	—	+105	−154
1958	4887	5066	6579	7710	−179	−1131	+1112	+128	+1240	—	−109	−19
1959 I	1060	1218	1364	1792	−158	−428	+280[4]	+99	+379	—	+49	−138
II	1355	1551	1765	2216	−196	−451	+253[4]	+241	+494	—	−43	−198
III	1286	1380	1816	2138	−94	−322	+273[4]	+52	+325	—	−3	−49
IV	1449	1423	1847	2150	+26	−303	+283[4]	−47	+236	—	+67	−20
Total, Year	5150	5572	6792	8296	−422	−1504	+1089	+345	+1444	—	+70	−415
1960 I	1281	1324	1615	1941	−43	−326	+397	−71	+326	—	+11	+71
II	1321	1508	1737	2214	−187	−477	+283	+194	+477	—	+82	−194
III	1398	1316	1956	2083	+82	−127	+86	−23	+63	—	−40	−41
IV	1392	1392	1802	2115	—	−313	+74	+239	+313	—	−14	−239
Total, Year	5392	5540	7110	8353	−148	−1243	+840	+339	+1179	—	+39	−403

1961	I	1266	1260	1606	1943	+6	−337	+186	+256	+442	—	−105	−151
	II	1477	1478	1902	2213	−31	−311	+270	+92	+362	—	−51	−41
	III	1557	1419	2158	2220	+138	−62	+199	−199	—	—	+62	+137
	IV	1619	1559	2068	2340	+60	−272	+135	+272	+407	—	−135	−137
Total, Year		5589	5716	7734	8716	+173	−982	+790	+421	+1211	—	−229	−192
1962	I	1395	1402	1748	2081	−7	−333	+25	−56	−31	—	−364	−308
	II	1620	1665	2103	2465	−45	−362	−14	−217	−231	+707	−114	−376
	III	1628	1559	2288	2322	+69	−34	+267	+460	+727	—	−686	+223
	IV	1721	1583	2209	2328	+138	−119	+448	+149	+597	−377	−101	+229
Total, Year		6364	6209	8348	9196	+155	−848	+718	+337	+1055	+330	−537	−130

[1] Excluding monetary, gold, and government foreign exchange reserve transactions.

[2] + = net source; − = net use of funds.

[3] The long-term forms and short-term forms are according to the concepts used in the DBS publication cited below.

[4] For 1959, the quarterly details re long-term capital movements included in "Other Capital Movements" are not available. The annual total of a $28 million inflow was allocated equally among the quarters.

Source: DBS: *The Canadian Balance of International Payments*, various annual and quarterly reports. The latest data were from the publication 67-001, Vol. 10, No. 4, March, 1963.

the more severe requirement, because to attain it, Canada would have to achieve a substantial net capital outflow position in a balance of payments sense as we now measure the latter. This is a political and social argument, not an economic one. The second ground for arguing that Canada had a deficit in her balance of payments is quite different. It might be argued that Canada was going to pursue a very much more vigorous domestic full-employment policy, and that if she did her imports of goods and services would be increased substantially relative to her exports; and that it would be impossible or undesirable to arrange things so that the potential increment to the deficit on current transactions would be financed by an enlarged capital inflow. Thus it might be argued that, even if Canada did not now have a deficit on her balance of payments, she would have a deficit if she pursues the vigorous domestic full-employment policy. Estimations of this sort are difficult to make. In any case this writer tends to reject such a line because it should be possible to deal with such a potential problem by adjustment of the mixture of policies that are pursued by a country like Canada.

Does the June budget and the Kennedy proposal regarding increased taxation on United States foreign investment alter the interpretation of deficit or surplus in Canada's balance of payments? Let us deal with the budget first, because it was more clearly on the record at the time of writing of these notes (in late July). It is by no means clear that the net effects of the budget will be expansionary with respect to internal prosperity in Canada. The tax changes are, on balance, contractionary in effect, while some elements of expenditure and debt management changes may be expansionary. Thus the budget itself may have little direct bearing on the current account position in the Canadian balance of payments. The effect of the budget on the net capital inflow into Canada is by no means clear as yet. If the Kennedy proposals go through, they will clearly tend to reduce the rate of capital inflow into Canada, requiring a reduction in the country's net payments balance on current account transactions. But the legislation was not available at the time of writing, nor the details regarding Canadian exemptions from the new United States tax. It was thus quite impossible for this writer to evaluate the degree of change that the proposed new legislation and practices would have on Canada's position.

45. FLOATING THE CANADIAN DOLLAR*

The Bank of Nova Scotia

The attention of the Canadian financial community, which had been preoccupied for some months with the performance of the stock market, was suddenly diverted in May to the situation surrounding the Canadian dollar. For several months, there had been large increases in foreign exchange reserves and strong upward pressure on the value of the dollar. These pressures finally culminated on May 31st in the freeing of the dollar from its fixed parity of 92.5 cents US, and up to the time of writing it has fluctuated in the range of 95.5 cents to 97.1 cents.

The recent strength of the Canadian dollar has taken many people by surprise, especially in the light of the country's varied economic problems and of the continuing slowdown in the United States. Yet for over six months now this country has been turning in a remarkably strong trade performance, while at the same time the firmness of its official anti-inflationary policies has stood out in contrast not only to the United States but also to most major overseas countries. Considerations such as these are the basic makings of any exchange rate appreciation.

Through the early months of this year, however, assessment of the Canadian position was greatly complicated, first by the fact that the favourable trade performance quite obviously owed much to a happy conjuncture of several temporary influences, and secondly by the difficulty until quite recently of seeing any convincing price results from the firmer Canadian policies. In addition, there were growing signs of protracted sluggishness in the US market that gave further reason for doubting whether the strength in the trade picture would be a lasting phenomenon. Such considerations clearly bulked large in the views of the Canadian authorities. As events turned out, however, it was the unsettlement of US financial markets set off by the sudden movement of US troops into Cambodia that finally pushed the foreign exchange situation beyond the bounds that the authorities felt could be any longer sensibly resisted. During May, indeed, the flow of funds had clearly moved into what could be called a speculative stage, with

---

*Reprinted from The Bank of Nova Scotia, *Monthly Review,* May-June, 1970, Toronto, by permission.

FIGURE 1

THE CANADIAN DOLLAR FROM 1940 TO THE PRESENT

United States Cents Quarterly Averages of Noon Spot Rates

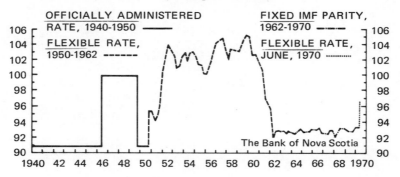

transfers motivated both by concern about the US situation and by the prospects of a Canadian appreciation. And publication of the end-of-May reserves was due in early June. It was at this stage that the authorities decided to float the Canadian dollar.

Sources of Strength

From even this brief outline of the events leading up to the decision to once again permit the Canadian dollar to float, it will be clear that there has been a mixture of both long-term and short-term influences at work. Among the longer-term considerations affecting Canada's trading position, the relationship vis-à-vis the United States has, of course, been to the fore. The volume of Canadian exports to the United States has received considerable stimulus over the past five years, especially from the far-reaching changes brought about by the Auto Pact. Over the past two or three years, moreover, the general price performance of the Canadian economy, while far from satisfactory, has slightly bettered that of the United States and, more recently, it has become appreciably better than that of the US and of most other industrial countries. More important, perhaps, from the point of view of market expectations about future prices, the firm hand which the Canadian authorities have managed to exert over domestic economic activity has tended to show up in sharp contrast with the wavering which still besets US monetary and fiscal policies in the long struggle to bring inflationary pressures under control.

Meanwhile, over the past six months a number of shorter-run factors have combined both to improve Canada's trade position with the United States and to enlarge its trading surplus with overseas countries. Most notable, undoubtedly, has been the catching up on exports of copper, nickel, and iron ore, following extended labour disputes last year, at the same time as overseas markets for industrial materials and world prices for such products have been in a strong boom phase. In the January-March quarter, in fact, average prices of Canada's raw material exports were nearly 10 percent higher than a year earlier. Meanwhile, exports of wheat were showing a slight but encouraging recovery; oil shipments surged strongly for a few months; and, in the face of declining North American car markets, Canadian exports of autos and parts remained well above year-ago levels while imports dropped appreciably — a result in part of greater Canadian concentration on smaller models whose sales have held up better than those of larger models.

Apart from the reduced inward movement of autos and parts, Canadian imports in general have been more subdued than suggested by most forecasts of Canadian business and investment conditions (the year-over-year increase for the January-May period being on the order of 5 to 6 percent). All told, then, for the five-month period exports have been up 15 percent (with those to the US up 8 percent and those overseas up 33 percent) while imports in total have risen less than 2 percent.

With such a pattern, Canada's trade surplus through this period has swelled to an annual rate of over $2½ billions — or roughly double any previous Canadian experience. This has easily exceeded the usual large deficit on service transactions (such as interest and dividend payments, tourist transactions, and so on) with the result that the overall current account balance has been registering a *surplus* at an annual rate around $900 millions compared with a much more normal *deficit* of about $700 millions during 1969. Even if this rate of surplus cannot be sustained for any length of time, and it probably cannot, the fundamental Canadian balance of payments position seems to be distinctly stronger than in the mid-sixties.

Apart from this favourable trend in the current account, Canada has continued to obtain sizable long-term capital inflows both through direct foreign investment in Canadian subsidiaries and through Canadian borrowing abroad. Up till late March or early April, new issues were being placed in New York in large volume, especially by provincial governments who find it desirable to meet part of their needs there even though there may be no great advantage from an interest rate point of view.

Another major influence in this period has been the swing in international transactions in outstanding securities. For several years prior to 1969, such transactions had involved substantial net outflows of funds, notably in the form of Canadian purchases of US equities. During 1969 and the early part of 1970, however, the balance swung increasingly into Canada's favour. In part this has probably reflected the general decline in US equity prices, but the enlarged Canadian sales of US stocks since last November also no doubt owe something to the White Paper tax proposals published at that time.

When the April statistics were published showing that Canada's exchange reserves had reached the record high of $3,822 millions (with a rise of nearly $600 millions in only four months), the financial community for the first time in several years began to ponder the implications of such strength. At this stage, moreover, US financial markets began to react both to President Nixon's decision to move troops into Cambodia and to concern about a weakening budgetary position. Signs of growing transfers of funds to Canada were underlined by the rapid drop in the domestic cash balances of the Canadian government, which implied that large amounts of Canadian dollars were being used to acquire the influx of foreign exchange and to keep the rate on the Canadian dollar from rising above the upper limit of its fixed range (roughly 1 percent above the official parity of 92.5 cents US).

As always, this sort of environment feeds on itself, as those who conduct normal transactions in foreign exchange take precautionary measures to avoid unnecessary risks. Exporters speed up the repatriation of earnings while importers delay payment as long as possible. Pressures develop in the short-term capital market to acquire Canadian dollars just in case. The very rapid escalation of such understandable business manoeuvres has been a principal feature of the international money market in the last decade, and this was once again clearly in evidence during the month of May. In fact, the scale of buying of US dollars by the Bank of Canada was somewhat greater than the market realized, since a large volume consisted of "forward" purchases of US dollars which did not require immediate payment in Canadian cash by the government. After the dollar was floated, the Minister of Finance announced that the authorities had made forward purchases of US $360 millions in May over and above the "spot" or cash additions to reserves during the month amounting to US $262 millions.

The first and natural reaction of the Canadian government to the strength of the foreign exchange inflow and the rapid decline in government balances was to arrange a fresh supply of domestic cash and to seek means of checking the influx of foreign funds. With these objectives in mind, the government on May 11th announced an unusual combination of measures, the first portion of which was the borrowing of $250 millions through a special issue of Treasury bills to the chartered banks. In order to prevent this transaction becoming a source of unwanted monetary expansion, the central bank simultaneously raised the secondary reserve requirements of the chartered banks from 8 percent to 9 percent, effective in July. This action froze the additional holdings of Treasury bills in the banks, thus preventing the banks from liquidating them in order to make loans or acquire other assets. At the same time, it was not the intention of the central bank at that moment to convey any particular signal of a change in domestic monetary policy, though there was clearly a hope that the somewhat reduced level of Canadian short-term interest rates would be maintained in the face of a renewed uptrend in the United States, so helping to discourage inward capital movements. The Bank Rate was reduced from 8 percent to 7½ percent as a symbol to show that the increase in secondary reserves was not to be interpreted as a domestic tightening action but was aimed at external capital movements.

In ordinary circumstances, these steps might have been expected to meet the problem and enable the government to hold the Canadian dollar within its permissible limits of fluctuation around the 92.5 cents parity. However, US market conditions became increasingly unsettled and the inward flood of exchange continued after only a brief abatement. A further tranche of Treasury bill borrowings could have been arranged, but the real problem was to find some effective way of checking the inflow of funds under existing market conditions. A formal raising of the official parity might have been a way to achieve this objective, but with the clear risk that the choice of a new parity might not be sustainable, having in mind the unsettled situation in the United States and the difficulty of assessing all the factors at work.

In the background there was also a recognition that the embarrassment of riches in exchange reserves was bound to be a source of potential friction with the United States, keeping in mind Canada's exemption from the restrictions which the United States has imposed on capital outflows to most other countries. Moreover, with important and controversial negotiations over energy policy and the automotive agreement in the offing, a very high and rising level of exchange reserves was far from an attractive proposition.

Thus it was that over the weekend of May 30-31, the government decided to let the dollar float and find a new level.

Exchange Policy Choices

In announcing the decision to float the dollar, the government was making a significant departure from the policy followed since the spring of 1962 — that is, of maintaining a fixed official parity according to the rules agreed upon in the International Monetary Fund. For nearly twelve years prior to 1962, the Canadian dollar had also floated relative to the US dollar; and the original move in this direction in September, 1950 had been undertaken in circumstances not greatly unlike those in May, 1970. After the outbreak of the Korean War, and with heavy demands on Canadian natural resources from a hard-pressed US economy, a flood of money came into the country, giving rise to the same sort of pressure on Canadian government cash balances as we have seen recently. In the three months from July through September, 1950, about US $550 millions were added to the exchange reserves; in March, April, and May, 1970, the figure was US $660 millions, not counting the US $360 millions of "forward" dollars.

Despite the large measure of success of the floating rate policy over a decade or more, it fell into disfavour in 1962, in part because of an immediate payments crisis but more broadly because of the controversial character of internal financial policies in the second half of the fifties and early sixties. In the background, too, there was a growing feeling that, if at all possible, Canada should strive to adhere to the rules of the game as agreed to under the IMF and that such rules were sound ones for a country with a heavy dependence on international transactions.

As it turned out, the return to a fixed exchange rate in 1962 had some distinct advantages in the turbulent financial conditions of subsequent years. The loosening of exchange control in Britain and Europe, and the rapidly rising flow of international capital movements, meant that various currencies were subjected to frequent and powerful external influences. Successive efforts of the US government to control outward capital flows by taxes and guidelines were also a new factor to be reckoned with, as was the broad general effort to secure agreement on a new form of international liquidity (the now-established Special Drawing Rights). At the same time, many Canadian businessmen felt that a fixed exchange rate was a positive advantage in providing stable conditions for foreign business. In such circumstances there has until very recently been no pressing need to reconsider the exchange rate adopted in 1962, and probably no intention on the part of the authorities to revert to a floating rate even for a temporary period. The change in thinking was forced by circumstances, as had been the case in both 1950 and 1962.

As a member of the International Monetary Fund, Canada is committed to observe the rules of the international financial system until such time as the rules are changed or broadened for everyone. This does not mean that the Canadian decision to float the dollar was a deliberate contravention of the IMF rules, though there may well be some debate as to the degree of prior consultation that was carried out. In fact, the IMF would appear to be well aware of Canada's special situation, and it has welcomed the indicated intention of the Canadian authoritis to remain in close consultation with the

Fund and to resume an effective par value "as soon as circumstances permit."

Moreover, there is the precedent set by West Germany which last October under quite different conditions allowed the Deutschemark to float for about a month. Against a background of extended international debate about the desirability of an appreciation of the mark, this brief period of floating helped push the rate upward by about 6 percent after which the German central bank interceded and repegged the mark at about 9 percent above its previous value. At the time, there was very little criticism of the German action, and indeed the eventual result was widely considered to be a step in the right direction of effecting needed periodic adjustments in major currencies.

Implications for the International Monetary System

In essence, the floating of the Canadian dollar reflects the special Canadian problems of trying to cope with the exceptional payments pressures which conditions of US financial instability can create in a structure of very widespread cross-border relationships. At times, in other words, Canada has little choice but to use a floating rate as an emergency buffer against external pressures which cannot be adequately dealt with through normal monetary or fiscal measures. Nor in Canada's special situation could it resort very effectively to the temporary import and exchange controls which other countries from time to time have used. At the same time, there can be no doubt that Canadian exchange rate action does have implications for the broader world exchange situation, and in the current period one effect of the Canadian decision to float has been to shift the movement of volatile funds toward other strong currencies, most notably the German mark, the Swiss franc, and the Dutch guilder, so adding appreciably to their particular problems of financial management.

Recent developments thus have brought a distinct sharpening of interest in the investigations which for some time have been underway of possible methods for liberalizing the world exchange rate system. The IMF itself asked its Executive Directors in 1969 to examine various alternatives which have been suggested, such as the widening of the range within which currencies may fluctuate around a given fixed parity rate (the "wider band"), and the proposal for periodic fractional adjustments in exchange rates in response to market influences (the "crawling peg"). Their report will be presented to the members of the IMF at its annual meeting next September.

It is of some interest that this reexamination has been going on while specific positive moves were being made to broaden the supply of international liquidity through Special Drawing Rights, or SDRs. The first allotment of SDRs, amounting to US $3.4 billions, was distributed to the members of the IMF in January, 1970. Recently suggestions have been made at gatherings where central bankers meet together that SDRs might eventually assume a key-currency role which is currently enjoyed primarily by the US dollar and, to a lesser extent, by the pound sterling.

The case for a general system of floating rates, while not without its respected proponents, seems less likely to attract broad support than some less radical departure from the present system of fixed rates. While the machinery of the IMF provides for revaluations of currencies in either direction, the fact is that the machinery has, with only a few exceptions, been used to bring about devaluations. One lesson to be learned from the German and Canadian experiences is that the present relatively rigid system allows pressures to build up which lead to convulsive changes. A system which would introduce a greater degree of gradualism into the machinery of international adjustment would perhaps help to avoid the sharp adjustments which occur from time to time. A more flexible system might pose new problems, but the fact is that the highly developed market in forward exchange transactions should prevent the development of unstable conditions which make the business decisions of importers and exporters unduly difficult.

Implications for Credit Conditions

The floating of the Canadian dollar was accompanied by a reduction in Bank Rate from 7½ percent to 7 percent and an announcement on June 1st that the planned restrictions on consumer credit would not be proceeded with. The following week, the three-month Treasury bill rate dropped abruptly from 6.34 percent to 5.91 percent. This quickly influenced other short-term money market rates, such as the chartered banks' ceritificate of deposit rates, finance company and commercial paper rates, and the competitive instruments of trust and loan companies. The general reduction in short-term rates was clearly an immediate policy objective, in order to discourage the inflow of funds and to offset the profitability of buying Canadian dollars spot and selling them forward.

The decline in short-term rates has spread less rapidly to medium-term and longer-term securities. With a large volume of unfunded debts still remaining to be financed in the bond market, and a continuing shortage of funds in the mortgage market, a pronounced drop in long-term rates was not to be expected. Even so, with recent increases in US rates, some medium and long Canadian rates have actually dipped below US levels, a phenomenon which does not occur often or last long. This has discouraged the raising of substantial new capital issues in the New York market, and has induced US holders of Canadian bonds to liquidate them and repatriate the funds for investment in US obligations which carry record high yields. In addition, it is believed that for some time there has been moral suasion by the federal government on the provinces to refrain from aggravating the problem by borrowing in the US market.

The decline in money market rates has now spread to the prime lending rate and the nonchequing savings rate of the chartered banks, which have been reduced by ½ percent in most cases. This brings the prime rate well below open market rates for debenture financing by corporations and governments, and might tend to discourage the proper funding of long-term capital programs. A similar development has occurred in the United States in recent months, causing continued pressure on commercial bank liquidity and tying up funds which could be used for other purposes.

The inducing of a capital outflow by the easing of credit will assist the government in containing the level of the exchange reserves and perhaps in bringing them down to a more appropriate level. At the same time, a greater degree of credit ease will help to offset the impact of a higher rate of exchange on a broad range of export industries and on manufacturing business in Canada which competes with imports. Nevertheless the shift to a moderately easier credit position does not signal the complete abandonment of restraint on the Canadian economy. A heavier foot on the accelerator will have to await concrete evidence that the rate of inflation has been brought under effective control.

How long the Canadian dollar will be allowed to float will more than anything else turn upon a clearing up of recent uncertainties in US economic and financial conditions. To choose a fixed rate before then would run the risk of once again encouraging unmanageable pressures in the exchange market with consequent disruption to domestic financial policies. Over the next few months, some of the recent special factors in Canada's trading position will undoubtedly be disappearing, and exports in general may show a clearer reflection of the persisting US slowdown and the recent softening of world commodity markets, quite apart from whatever deterrent effects there are from a higher priced dollar. In such circumstances, the authorities will clearly be wary of choosing an exchange rate which proves to be so high that it weighs unduly on Canadian output. Yet there also will be reluctance to set a rate so low that it fails to take adequate account of the stronger elements that have come into the Canadian payments position. To the extent that the authorities recognize Canada's interests in co-operating under the rules of the international monetary system, they will probably also be conscious of the desirability of reestablishing a fixed parity with the IMF as soon as possible. To balance off all these considerations, and to choose a viable rate, will call for a high order of official analysis and judgment.

C. THE PROTECTIVE TARIFF

The gains from international trade are incontrovertible yet the history of world economics is replete with efforts to impede it. Traditionally, the most important form of impediment thrown up in the path of free international trade has been the protective tariff. Under a protective tariff, certain commodities produced in foreign lands are made dutiable at rates designed to exclude these products or greatly reduce imports of them, thus leaving the home market wholly or largely free for exploitation by domestic producers turning out the same kinds of goods.

The long history of tariff legislation has been accompanied by the development of a large number of arguments in favour of protective tariffs. These arguments include the following: a protective tariff increases employment; only reciprocal reductions of tariffs confer any economic benefits on a country; protective tariffs are needed for the purpose of allowing new domestic industries to establish themselves; a tariff promotes a higher rate of population growth. While there is undoubtedly some truth in these propositions, there are also serious qualifications and shortcomings. Reading 46 analyses these four lines of argument in a Canadian context and presents an excellent discussion of commercial policy in Canada.

Ever since Confederation, the notion of "balanced regional development" has been an implicit, if not explicit, objective of Canada's economic policy. Reading 47 examines the regional effects of the Canadian tariff structure, and indicates how the problem of regional balance might be affected by freer trade.

Following World War II there was a powerful commitment by the major trading countries of the world to change the restrictive trade policies that had been so costly during the 1930s. In 1947, the General Agreement on Tariffs and Trade (GATT) was signed by Canada, the United States, and twenty-one other nations. The Agreement provides for unconditional most-favoured-nation treatment for all parties and pledges all signers (by 1970, there were seventy-seven full menbers in the GATT) to do all in their power to limit interferences with trade. So far there have been six rounds of multilateral trade negotiations held under GATT arrangements. The first, in 1947, constituted a major step in the reduction of tariffs on a worldwide basis. This was followed by four further tariff conferences of more modest scope — in 1949, in 1951, in 1956, and in 1960-62. The sixth round of negotiations (the so-called Kennedy Round) was concluded at the end of June, 1967, after four years of negotiations. It was heralded as the greatest bout of multilateral tariff slashing ever undertaken. Reading 48 summarizes the main features of the Kennedy Round agreements, and discusses the implications of the Kennedy Round for Canada. It emphasizes that the benefits offered to Canadian exporters by the Kennedy Round are substantial but by no means automatic.

46. CANADIAN COMMERCIAL POLICY: THE TARIFF QUESTION*

J. H. Young

Over the course of the years, a host of arguments have been put forward which purport to show economic benefits deriving from tariffs. Many of these arguments in effect deny propositions which when once understood are generally accepted. As a result, a considerable part of the literature on tariff policy is devoted to the analysis and refutation of arguments which are erroneous, and can be recognized as erroneous by reference to basic economic principles. Considerable care is necessary, however, in analysing propositions of this kind. They are frequently quite wrong in the form in which they are put forward, but it is often found that there are conditions under which they may have some merit. For example, consider the proposition that a tariff adds to employment. It is easy to see how this idea developed. A tariff clearly promotes the employment of resources in a protected industry, and it is easy to slide from this obvious fact to the proposition that this employment constitutes a net addition to employment in the economy as a whole. There is an element of this kind of thinking in the reports of the Tariff Board on the automobile industry in the 1930s. In its 1936 report, the Board calculated the "cost" of the automobile tariff in terms of the enhanced prices paid by consumers, and also estimated the amount spent by the industry on labour, materials, and other purchases. Summarizing the position it took in its 1936 report, the Board wrote as follows in 1939:

> The Board found in the 1936 report that the industry contributed from $40,000,000 to $47,000,000 in expenditures in Canada and had "cost" the Canadian consuming public about $14,000,000. The Board at that time came to the conclusion that it was "good business" for Canada reasonably to encourage the maintenance and expansion of the Canadian automotive industry.

---

*Reprinted from J. H. Young, *Canadian Commercial Policy*, a study prepared for the Royal Commission on Canada's Economic Prospects, Ottawa, 1957, pp. 75-80, 87-93, by permission of Information Canada.
Dr. Young is Professor of Economics, University of British Columbia, and Chairman, Prices and Incomes Commission, Ottawa.

Here it seems to be assumed that in the absence of the automobile tariff the resources employed in this industry would be unemployed. This is the extreme opposite of the assumption frequently made in international trade analysis. There it is often assumed that full employment exists both before and after the imposition of a tariff, and that the tariff therefore merely leads to a reallocation of employed resources rather than to an increase in employment. Under conditions such as those of the last fifteen or twenty years the latter assumption is clearly the one more closely in accord with the facts. Full employment has been the rule, interspersed with short periods of cyclical unemployment. These were not the conditions which ruled in the decade in which the Tariff Board reports on the automobile industry were written, and it is easy to see why it was felt that the full-employment assumption was inappropriate. Indeed, in view of the difficulties being encountered at that time it is not difficult to understand the tendency to associate protection with employment. Even Lord Keynes, who later became a leading advocate of a freely trading world, was prepared to advocate a general tariff for the United Kingdom as a short-term emergency measure in the catastrophic days of the early 1930s. Such a policy, if confined to one country, will in fact yield a favourable result on the level of employment in that country. What in effect happens is that the country which raises barriers against imports may for a time be able to export some of its unemployment to its neighbours.

Knowledge of this possibility is not, however, restricted to any one country. Policies of this kind, which have been appropriately christened beggar-my-neighbour policies, are almost certain to call forth retaliation from other countries. Once other countries move to protect their own employment level by raising barriers against the initiating country, then the favourable effect on employment in the initiating country tends to be lost. If, as often happens, the retaliation goes further than the original change, the initiating country may find itself worse off than in the original position and may as a result decide to retaliate against the retaliators. It is not difficult to foresee the consequences if a chain reaction of this kind develops. If anything was learned from the depression of the 1930s, it was that it was desirable to develop a framework of international agreements which would prevent the initiation and cumulation of beggar-my-neighbour policies of this kind.

To sum up, the proposition that protection increases employment has a certain popular appeal because it is assumed that any increase in employment in protected industries represents an increase in total employment. It is obvious that under full-employment conditions such as those of the last fifteen or twenty years this cannot be the case. It is much less obvious, but also true, that even under conditions of general unemployment it is unlikely that tariffs can be used effectively to increase employment. A reduction in unemployment can be secured, but since this is at the expense of other countries, and since they will in general take steps to protect their own level of employment, any gain through the use of measures of this kind is likely to be very short-lived.

Examples could be given of a variety of other arguments which purport to show economic benefits deriving from tariffs which offset or more than offset the higher costs of protected commodities. Historically, most of the propositions of this kind have appeared at some time in discussions of commercial policy in Canada, but in general the level of debate on the tariff is a good deal higher in Canada than in many other countries. The Canadian economy is so obviously dependent on trade that resort to some of the more superficial arguments for protection would be regarded as absurd. Those who favour either a retention or an increase in existing Canadian trade barriers usually begin by granting the truth of the general proposition that free or freer trade confers an economic benefit. They go on to argue that in the case of present-day Canada there are special reasons why trade barriers confer economic or quasi-economic benefits.

There are three lines of argument in support of this view which crop up again and again. It is argued, first, that freer trade would be desirable if other countries were prepared to accept a policy of this kind. Because other countries are unwilling to lower trade barriers, it is suggested that it is in Canada's interest to retain or increase existing Canadian barriers. A second line of argument which frequently appears is the so-called infant industry argument for protection. It is accepted that tariff protection involves some economic cost at present, but it is suggested that some of the industries being protected will at a future date be able to operate in Canada without tariff protection. It is therefore concluded that it may be worthwhile to forego some income now in order to enjoy a higher income in the future. Finally, frequent reference is made to the effect of the Canadian tariff on population growth. It is suggested that in the absence of special encouragement to secondary industry there will be a lack of employment opportunities in Canada, immigration will be discouraged and emigration encouraged and, as a result, Canada's population growth will be retarded. All of these lines of argument have received a good deal of attention in the general literature of the subject, and all three merit careful consideration.

The view that the continued existence of other countries' tariffs (particularly the United States tariff) is a conclusive argument for the retention or increase of the Canadian tariff has always figured prominently in Canadian tariff history. It was used with effect at a time when the preferred alternative of both political parties was a wide measure of reciprocity with the United States. It was argued at that time that it was clearly unfair that large and well-established American manufacturers should be able to compete quite freely in the Canadian market while Canadian producers were excluded from the United States market. "Reciprocity of trade or reciprocity of tariffs" was the battle cry, and when the United States showed an unwillingness to accept the former, the National Policy tariff was introduced to provide a measure of the latter. As pointed out above in the outline of Canadian tariff history, even when opportunities have arisen for reciprocity of trade they have not always been accepted by Canada. It is certainly clear, however, that a measure of reciprocity has been a *sine qua non* of substantial Canadian tariff reductions.

The general notion that only reciprocal reductions of trade barriers confer any economic benefits has probably been reinforced in recent years by the procedures followed in international tariff negotiations. Negotiators who have represented their governments at these conferences have in general attempted to secure the largest possible reductions in the tariffs of other countries, while granting the smallest possible reductions in their own country's tariff. Given this example, it is easy to adopt a pattern of thought which regards a reduction in a country's tariff as simply a concession to other countries and a cost to the reducing country.

This kind of thinking is not quite as irrational as it looks, but it must be admitted that there is something paradoxical in the spectacle of a country being bribed to adopt a course of action which is in its own long-term economic interest. In general, a country will gain by reducing its own trade barriers regardless of the actions of other countries, although this need not always be the case. Under some circumstances, the increase in imports brought about by the reduction of trade barriers will lead to a higher price for the imports purchased, and the increased exports required to pay for the higher level of imports may have to be sold at a somewhat lower price. If either or both of these price movements should occur, this would mean a worsening of the terms on which the country exchanges goods, and this would significantly offset any gain resulting from the change. If a single small country is involved the effect of its policies on world prices is likely to be small, and it is therefore unlikely that there will be a significant adverse movement of this kind. For a country in this position the general principle applies that it will benefit over the long run from a reduction in its own tariff, even if the reduction is a unilateral one. Similarly, it is in its long-run economic interest to retain low barriers even if other countries choose to raise theirs.

What makes little sense in terms of long-term economic interests may make more sense in terms of short-run economic and political considerations. The reduction of a subsidy or tariff may pose considerable political problems, and a government which agrees to such a reduction may indeed feel that certain political costs are involved. It therefore may be anxious to minimize such concessions, or at least try to gain enough concessions from other governments to obtain the support of producer interests which have benefited from the tariff concession received. Moreover, the possible short-run consequences are not simply political in nature. The gains from tariff reductions are not likely to materialize immediately, and if the reductions are sufficiently widespread and substantial, some short-run, adverse economic effects are to be expected. If the depressing effect of such reductions on some protected industries can be offset by the expansionary effect following upon tariff reductions in other countries, the adjustment process will be eased.

In addition, a unilateral reduction of a country's tariff may have some effect on the terms on which it exchanges exports and imports. If the reduction in trade barriers is reciprocal rather than unilateral, it will lead to an increase in the demand for exports. Thus, even if the initial reduction in trade barriers leads to an increase in the demand for imports, and if this in turn leads to an increase in their price, this may be counterbalanced by an increase in the price of exports arising from the increase in the foreign demand. If this is the case, the terms of trade may be unaffected or even move in a favourable direction. Insofar, therefore, as the terms of trade are sensitive to changes in commercial policy, a reciprocal reduction enjoys a considerable advantage over a unilateral one. It can also be argued that two tariff cuts are better than one, and if a tariff reduction can be made to yield a double fruit, this is certainly to be preferred to a unilateral one. The negotiator understandably feels that it is wasteful to dissipate bargaining power which could be used to obtain a two-way reduction, in order to garner the smaller yield of a unilateral one. Indeed, negotiating considerations may often suggest courses of action directly contrary to a country's immediate economic interest. For example, a decision may be made to retaliate for some action taken by another country in the full recognition that the retaliation will add to, rather than subtract from the adverse effect of the action. It may be felt that if it becomes generally known that a particular country will not retaliate against those who injure it, this may remove some of the inhibitions of other countries and over time lead to a series of injuries. In view of all these possibilities, it is not surprising that the actions of other countries, particularly the United States, can have a crucial effect on Canadian tariff policy.

A second line of argument which has frequently appeared in Canadian tariff discussions and has been widely discussed in the literature on commercial policy is the infant industry argument. In its simplest form this argument runs as follows. A country may be well suited to the production of a particular commodity which is currently being imported, but because foreign producers are experienced and well-established there may be a reluctance on the part of businessmen to start or expand the domestic production of the commodity. It is argued that under these circumstances the government should be prepared to grant the domestic industry temporary protection; the protection to be withdrawn when it is evident that the domestic industry can stand on its own feet and meet foreign competition without assistance.

Consider a situation in which a particular industry has been accorded protection, has made use of the protection for a period of years and either has finally achieved an export status or has at least been able to compete successfully with foreign producers in its domestic market without a tariff. Even here where it would appear that a successful application has been made, some questions remain unanswered. There is, for example, no way of being sure that a similar result would not have been obtained in the absence of protection. It costs businessmen very little to ask for a tariff, and the extra profits resulting from a successful application for protection are always welcome. If such requests are refused the investment is often still forthcoming. Suppose, however, that for this industry a good case can be made that in fact the investment would not have been forthcoming. The industry being considered may be characterized by decreasing costs. Perhaps it can be shown that the first few firms in the industry necessarily laboured under a considerable disadvantage in competition with well-established firms abroad, but with the multiplication of firms the availability of trained personnel and widespread knowledge of the processes involved made the task of later firms much easier. The early firms in effect provide a service to other firms for which they receive no payment. Under these circumstances it could be held that an industry which otherwise would not have existed within the country has been brought into existence by temporary government assistance and achieved viability.

But this assistance has involved a cost. During the interval in which the industry was being established, consumers of the industry's product have in effect been subsidizing it. If a bounty rather than a tariff had been used, the government would have a record of all the payments made to the industry over the interval, and this would provide a first approximation of the community's investment in the industry. As in the case of other investments, this one would be expected to yield a rate of return; unless it could be shown that the community was benefiting, and could be expected to benefit in the future, to an extent equal to or greater than the benefit which would have been secured by an alternative use of the funds, then doubts would remain on the wisdom of the policy. Such benefits are extremely difficult to measure. If it could be shown that because of the saving in transportation costs the domestic price of the industry's output was, and could be expected to be, lower than the landed price of foreign goods, this would provide an offset. Similarly, if it could be shown that the existence of the industry conferred a benefit on other industries for which no payment was received, this would also constitute an offset to the cost. The latter point, referring to the external economies arising from particular industries, has generally been regarded as the principal *raison d'être* of infant industry assistance. There are some who have argued that the creation of a cadre of technicians and entrepreneurs is of such importance as a catalyst in economic growth that a policy of this kind may prove successful in underdeveloped countries. Whether or not this is so for economically backward countries, it would be generally agreed that conditions in advanced countries, including Canada, differ fundamentally from those encountered in less developed economies.

Canada has a considerable number of entrepreneurs with accessible capital, and whenever the scale of intricacy of any particular development prevents domestic exploitation of a favourable opportunity, American companies and investors are often eager to assume the risks of the experiment. If some initial losses have to be accepted, to be counterbalanced later by gains on a substantial scale, then in general there are investors available with sufficiently long purses who will not be frightened away by teething difficulties. Thus with respect to availability of technical know-how, capital, and entrepreneurial talent, Canadian industry is in a position not differing greatly from that of American industry. Where the Canadian situation differs, it is with respect to unrestricted access to the large United States market. A particular manufacturing process may be regarded as uneconomic in Canada, not because of difficulties in getting started, but rather because the scale of the market is insufficient to permit competitive production. This is a disability which is not temporary. Thus many Canadian manufacturers are quite frank in pointing out that the protection they require is permanent rather than temporary, or at least as permanent as American trade barriers.

This does not mean that there are no situations in which some temporary assistance would be worthwhile. For example, there are some regions of Canada which have lagged behind the rest of the country in terms of economic development, and because of population immobility, income differences have developed and been perpetuated. It has sometimes been suggested that some temporary aid to particular industries locating in these regions might form part of a general scheme of regional assistance. As indicated above, it has often been urged that direct subsidies would be preferable to tariff protection in such cases. A subsidy keeps down the price of the final product and therefore assists the industry in obtaining a larger market for its output. Moreover, a more accurate record can be kept of the costs involved if a subsidy is used; and if the purpose were to influence location, a flexible instrument such as a subsidy might prove more effective.

It is perhaps worth pointing out that governments at all levels already provide a number of services to private firms including, in particular cases, the provision of capital at preferred rates. It might be argued that there is little justification in setting up rigid tests for the subsidization of promising industries when much looser criteria prevail in other types of government expenditure. There is little doubt that if any reasonably careful screening is applied, the amount of waste involved in mistaken infant industry assistance might be quite small. If the extent of government activities is large, and the time of ministers and capable officials very limited, it can be argued that their time could be better employed in applying more stringent tests to other types of government expenditure. Applying sound economic principles, there is little point in devoting excessive time and effort to achieve perfection in one area, if rough rules of thumb are applied elsewhere. It seems unlikely, however — unless other aims than those of economic development are to be served — that many significant opportunities will arise in an advanced country such as Canada, in which it will prove worthwhile to subsidize types of production which do not meet the normal tests of the market.

A third line of argument given prominence concerns the connection between the tariff and the population sustaining capacity of the Canadian economy. This is a subject which has been accorded a good deal of attention in discussions of the Canadian tariff, and the argument supporting the view that the tariff has promoted and will promote a higher rate of population growth has appeared in several versions. In its simplest form it merely asserts that the tariff creates job opportunities; greater employment in turn encourages immigration and discourages emigration, and this in turn promotes a higher rate of population growth. This type of reasoning is based on an oversimplified view of the economic process, and most proponents of the argument prefer to present their case in a more complex form. In one of the versions of this argument it is pointed out that secondary manufacturing industries are more labour-intensive than alternative types of employment, and that the encouragement given to their expansion by the tariff has been (and will be) necessary to provide employment opportunities for a rapidly growing population. It is difficult to know precisely what assumptions are being made in this form of the argument, but in some presentations it appears that certain rigidities are being assumed in the structure of the economy. For purposes of identification it will therefore be referred to as the "structural" version of the population sustaining argument. An example of the structural argument is to be found in Dr. Mackintosh's study for the Royal Commission on Dominion-Provincial Relations. Discussing the general effect of a tariff, he said:

> If the country concerned is economically immature and its most effective industries are of the exploitation type in which the ratio of population to resources is low, the diversion of labour and capital occasioned by the protective tariff will be to industries employing more labour relative to resources. If this diversion can be achieved with moderate protection, the result is likely to be that, though the numbers engaged in export exploitation industries will be reduced, the total population will be increased while the national real income per head will be reduced. In the degree that there are broad economies, industrial, social and governmental in a large population, aggregate real income may be increased.

Another version of the population sustaining argument which does not rely on rigidities but rather stresses the redistributive effect of the tariff has been put forward by Professor Barber. Barber argued that, in the absence of both the Canadian and American tariffs, total Canadian income and the portion of it accruing to labour would undoubtedly be higher. He further argues, however, that the American tariff, by imposing high rates on manufactured commodities, distorts the Canadian economy in the direction of less labour-intensive goods. A Canadian tariff on manufactured commodities tends to offset this distortion although, as Barber points out, the imposition of an additional set of trade restrictions has lowered Canadian per capita income. He considers that it is possible that labour's share of the diminished income might be so increased by the redistributive effect of the tariff that the absolute level of labour income is higher than it would have been in the absence of the Canadian tariff.

The structural and redistributive arguments will be considered in reverse order, beginning with the redistributive effect of the Canadian tariff. It has long been known that changes in commercial policy can have an effect on the distribution of income. For example, the abolition of the Corn Laws in Great Britain in the middle of the nineteenth century opened the way for the free entry of grain from the outside world, and thus introduced additional competition for British agriculture. Over the long period adjustments took place, but those who owned land throughout the period found themselves with a resource which was highly specific to agriculture. It is true that they could dispose of their land, but under the new circumstances in which land-intensive commodities were being imported from abroad, the capital value of their land was lower than it would have been in the absence of the change. It could be argued, therefore, that the abolition of the Corn Laws had an adverse effect on landowners; their situation being more favourable with restrictions on the entry of grain than in the absence of these restrictions. Since it can be shown that the gain to the economy as a whole was greater than the loss to the landowners, it is clear that those losing by the change could have been compensated by those gaining, and as a result all groups in the economy could have benefited from the change. Since in fact the landowners were not compensated for their losses, it is not surprising that they resisted the change and were never fully reconciled to it.

A similar argument on somewhat less secure foundations has been put forward for Australia and Canada. Here the conditions of the United Kingdom apply in reverse. In the case of the new countries, land — by which is meant not only agricultural land but also timber, water, and mineral resources — is the abundant factor of production, and labour has been treated as the scarce factor. Under these circumstances it has been argued that a tariff which excludes or reduces the import of labour-intensive commodities, will lead to a redistribution of income in favour of the scarce factor, labour. It is further argued that while the existence of the tariff will lower total income, it is possible that labour's share of the smaller income will increase sufficiently to leave the return to labour higher than it would have been in the absence of the tariff. Thus it is concluded that the Canadian tariff may have encouraged immigration and discouraged emigration and thus promoted a larger population.

There has been a good deal of theorizing on this topic in recent years, much of it restricted to highly simplified assumptions. In the case of Canada it is argued that the burden of the decrease in income has fallen upon the owners of land and national resources. Since the proportion of national income accruing to the private owners of natural resources from ownership alone cannot be very large, it seems highly unlikely that in fact the main burden of the tariff has been borne by these owners. Given the magnitudes involved, there seems to be more reason to suppose that the tariff has lowered rather than raised the return to labour in Canada. Whatever the answer may be, there is general agreement that if a transfer of income to labour is desired it can be carried out at less economic cost by taxes and subsidies of an appropriate kind. The only merit (if it is a merit) possessed by a proposal that a tariff should be used for this purpose is that it is a less painful method of extraction. Its economic cost is not as apparent to the public as an equivalent set of explicit taxes and subsidies.

The structural version of the population sustaining argument may be subject to the same type of criticism as the redistributive argument. When it is suggested that income per head will be lower but population higher, the implicit assumption which may be made is that labour's share of income is so increased that, while per capita income is lower, wages are higher because of the redistributive effect of the tariff. If this is the case, the structural argument is simply a variant of the redistributive argument and nothing more need be added to what has already been written. It may be, however, that a somewhat different argument is being put forward which admits that the tariff will lead to lower wages but suggests that employment opportunities will be so much more abundant because of the tariff that immigration will be encouraged and emigration discouraged.

The issue here involves the degree of flexibility which prevails in an economy such as that of Canada. This line of argument assumes that a form of structural unemployment can persist in Canada which will not yield to changes in wage rates. If there are widespread rigidities of this kind, a situation could exist in which wages are fairly high, but unemployment significant and continuous. Given a lack of jobs, immigration will be discouraged and emigration encouraged. A tariff, it is suggested, will lead to a fall in real wages; but by promoting the production of more labour-intensive commodities it will lead to an increase in job opportunities and, through a rise in employment possibilities, to an increase in population. Those who believe that widespread rigidities of this kind are likely to exist in Canada will find this line of reasoning convincing. On the other hand, those who are impressed with the remarkable capacity of the economy to adjust to changing circumstances, as so vividly exemplified by the rapid and complete absorption of the armed forces and war workers following World War II, will find this approach much less convincing. They would be inclined to argue that if appropriate steps are taken through monetary and fiscal policy to maintain a high level of employment, the lower income resulting from the introduction of additional trade barriers will constitute a discouragement rather than an encouragement to population growth.

While a great deal of emphasis is placed on the population sustaining argument at present, a reference to the recent history of Canada's population growth would suggest that this emphasis is misplaced. Canada's population growth depends on three elements: natural increase, immigration, and emigration. Presumably few would argue that the tariff has any significant effect on birth or death rates and no more need be said about it. This leaves immigration and emigration.

A careful study of Canadian immigration would throw some light on what have been limiting factors in recent years, but even in the absence of such a study it is clear that apart from cyclical disturbances no significant difficulties have arisen in the last ten years in absorbing immigrants into the labour force. This would suggest that the so-called absorptive capacity of the Canadian economy has not been a bar to higher immigration. It is true that certain administrative provisions regarding the nature and extent of job opportunities in Canada have played some part in reducing immigration, but these are probably best regarded as protective devices for minimizing adjustments among immigrants and domestic employees. No one demands that Canadian high school students should be forced to remain in school unless openings are available for them, yet similar reasoning is sometimes applied to immigrants. If the objective is an increase in immigration, it would seem that the appropriate method is through an alteration in immigration policy. There seems to be no reason to suppose that the absorptive capacity of the Canadian economy would limit immigration if governmental barriers were removed. Changes in tariff policy can have little effect on the real determinants of immigration, that is, immigration policy and the availability of immigrants.

Turning now to emigration, it is well known that over the whole period since Confederation, Canada has lost by emigration almost as many people as have been gained by immigration. What is perhaps not so well known is that the absolute level of emigration to the United States since the end of World War II has been lower than in any other comparable peacetime period since Confederation, while relative to total population the flow is insignificant when compared with the latter portion of the nineteenth century or even the 1920s. If emigration to the United States had been zero during the whole postwar period the effect on total Canadian population would have been very small. In view of the substantial and long-lasting disparity in real wages in the two countries it is unlikely that the flow could in fact be reduced to zero or reversed, so that no significant gain in population can be expected from any effect of tariff policy on emigration regardless of the direction of the influence. Perhaps conditions will change in the future, but thus far there has been no indication of this.

Since any curtailment of emigration could have little effect on the rate of population growth, and since the level of immigration is in large measure determined by considerations other than those likely to be influenced by commercial policy, it is by no means easy to see the connection between population growth and tariff levels. In the past, with unrestricted immigration and large-scale emigration, the influence of the tariff on size of population — whether positive or negative — raised a significant question. In the light of what has been said about the present determinants of Canadian population growth, this connection can have little practical importance today.

47. NATIONAL TARIFF POLICY AND BALANCED DEVELOPMENT*

Economic Council of Canada

Of all the major instruments of national economic development, perhaps none has proved to be a more potent source of interregional tension than the system of protective tariffs and related commercial policy devices. It is a time-honoured and enduring ritual at federal-provincial conferences on fiscal and economic problems for Ontario to remind the country that it provides about 45 percent of the total direct tax revenues flowing into the national treasury, and for the Atlantic and western provinces to rejoin that, among the various burdens they carry, the tariff provides Ontario with its sheltered market while most of their own producers must sell abroad at competitive world prices. Over the years regional unevenness of the cost of the protective tariff has been regularly used to support arguments for providing an elaborate structure of regional and national transportation subsidies, special assistance to primary producers in agriculture, fisheries, and mining, tax concessions of particular regional interest, and revenue equalization payments to the lower-income provinces.

As we have already indicated, the initial purpose and effect of the protective tariff, together with a national transportation system, was to establish an east-west trading relationship, involving a considerable degree of regional economic specialization. The manufacturing and industrial core of the country developed in Ontario and Quebec, with a strong primary resource orientation in the other regions. The expectations of the Atlantic provinces that they would also perform an important national manufacturing and service function were frustrated both by changing technology and by the westward shift of North American population and activity. How much this broad historical picture of regional patterns might have been altered by a basically different commercial policy cannot be known. But it is relevant for our purposes to look at the regional effects of the tariff in the present day, and to suggest how the problem of regional balance might be affected by freer trade.

In broad terms, we can distinguish two major influences upon the various

*Reprinted from Economic Council of Canada, *Fifth Annual Review,* September, 1968, pp. 154-56, by permission of Information Canada.

regions resulting from the imposition of a tariff on imported goods — one from the side of consumption and the other from the side of production.

The broad structure of the tariff and the traditional view of its national and regional impact are generally familiar. One of the main effects of tariffs is that purchasers of goods pay higher prices for certain commodities than they would pay for the same goods at duty-free import prices. The amount involved is what has been called the "cash cost" of the tariff. Earlier studies have suggested that this "cash cost" of the Canadian tariff is substantial. Not only do Canadian consumers pay substantially more for many finished products as a result of the tariff, but most Canadian producers pay more for a wide variety of materials, machinery, and components as a result of the tariffs on these items; and these higher costs of production are reflected in the prices of goods produced in Canada. All Canadian consumers and producers share in the cash cost of the tariff to the extent that tariffs affect the price of the goods they buy. But the impediments that tariffs impose to access to some cheaper sources of supply in adjacent areas of the United States tend to result in a somewhat larger cash cost in the Atlantic region and the western provinces than in central Canada.

But a far more important effect of tariffs is that they tend to depress the levels of output per employed person in Canada. In particular, tariffs shelter or cause inefficiency in contemporary Canadian industry by encouraging product diversity over a wide range of protected products, limiting efficiencies that could otherwise be gained from scale and specialization. This was one of the major conclusions in Chapter 6 of our *Fourth Annual Review*, in which we indicated that the effects of Canadian and foreign tariffs combined are reflected in higher prices for machinery and other material inputs, and in the basic structural pattern of large net imports of manufactured products.[1] Recent studies have concluded that this "production effect" of the tariff (both Canadian and US) may be very substantial — indeed that the economic costs to Canada may be significantly higher than the "cash cost" of the Canadian tariff — and that these combined economic costs may constitute a very significant element in the large and persistent gap in productivity levels and in the average levels of real standards of living between Canada and the United States. In fact, this element could well be even larger than that arising from the educational disparities between the two countries discussed in the *Second Annual Review*.

In summary, the consumption aspect of the national tariff suggests important relative gains in real income for the Atlantic, Prairie, and British Columbia regions if the tariff were reduced or eliminated. There would be little net change in Quebec, and some relative decline in Ontario. But if the production aspects of the tariff are even more important than the consumption aspects, large, new, and difficult questions arise about tariffs — questions which cut across many traditional views. For example, is it perhaps the main manufacturing regions of central Canada, rather than the Atlantic region or the western provinces, that are now bearing the main economic costs of tariffs? Also, is it possible that substantial tariff reductions, even though they would benefit Canadians in all parts of the country, may have the effect of *widening* rather than *narrowing* regional income disparities — particularly between Ontario and the Atlantic region? And have the tariff

---

[1] See also D. J. Daly, B. A. Keys, and E. J. Spence, *Scale and Specialization in Canadian Manufacturing,* Staff Study No. 21, Economic Council of Canada (Ottawa, 1968).

reductions over the past two decades in fact been tending to offset other forces working towards the narrowing of interregional disparities (thus helping to explain the stubborn persistence of the wide disparities in Canada)? The Council does not have answers to such questions at this time, but these and related questions raise important issues requiring further examination.

48. ADJUSTING TO THE KENNEDY ROUND*

H. A. Hampson

The Kennedy Round has rightly been called "the biggest step toward freer trade in the century," even though its impact on Canada's export prospects is not measurable in specific terms. Perhaps the situation presented to Canada by the Kennedy Round can best be described as like that in which a previously rather restrained young lady suddenly appears at a cocktail party in a very low-cut dress which reveals qualities hitherto more to be guessed at than proven: the goal is now somewhat more clearly in sight and a number of uncertainties about its desirability have been removed, but the really significant barriers to its realization have yet to fall. Those experienced in such matters would immediately take heart, however, for it would seem to them that the most important aspect of this development was that significant new opportunities were being signalled in an area hitherto untapped by them, which — though offering a real challenge — might yield highly interesting returns.

The opportunities offered to Canadian exporters by the Kennedy Round are real enough, not least because the agreement does in fact signal a willingness on the part of those countries accounting for 80 percent of world trade to accept more open, multilateral trading patterns. In 1968, even a relatively weak American administration was able to contain the inevitable protectionist reaction by successfully bottling up in committee some 700 bill proposing quotas or other restrictions on twenty major trading products.

Tariff Reductions

Some 70 percent of the world's dutiable industrial exports were affected by Kennedy — the sixth and most important postwar round of general tariff reductions — with about two-thirds of the cuts being 50 percent or more,

---

*Reprinted from H. A. Hampson, "Adjusting to the Kennedy Round," *The Canadian Banker*, January-February, 1969, pp. 7-10, by permission of the editor and author.
Mr. Hampson is President, Capital Management Limited, Montreal, and Chairman, General Adjustment Assistance Board. He served on the Royal Commission on Canada's Economic Prospects and was Secretary to the Royal Commission on Banking and Finance.

and the average reduction on tariffs being approximately one-third. When the phased reductions have been completed, the tariffs faced by Canadian exporters of industrial products will in most cases be reduced to 10 percent or less; in the US market — the most significant for us — most tariffs will be cut by half. These are significant amounts, particularly for high technology industries like radio and aircraft equipment in which a 5 percent tariff barrier can be surmounted but a 10 percent or higher level is prohibitive. In general, the American cuts are taking place over a five-year period at 20 percent per annum (the second took place on January 1, 1969), while the Common Market countries and certain other industrial nations made a 40 percent cut on July 1st last year and will make three further cuts of 20 percent at the beginning of each of the years 1970, 1971, and 1972.

Canada is now one of the world's high tariff countries and will still have protection ranging from 15 percent to 20 percent — and sometimes higher — on many items.

Among the other aspects of the Kennedy Round negotiations — although not formally tied to them — were the International Grains Agreement and a convention on antidumping procedures which — while removing arbitrary national practices — will enable quick action to be taken in cases of injury. In the context of the Kennedy Round package also — a single Canadian tariff item and common rate of duty was established for the broad range of machinery used by most Canadian manufacturing and service industries; the rate is 15 percent compared to about 22½ percent formerly. This duty may be remitted by the Governor-in-Council on the recommendation of the Minister of Industry, Trade and Commerce, when the machinery is not available from production in Canada and the remission is in the public interest.

Challenge and Opportunity

All these Kennedy Round developments will be helpful to previously established Canadian exporters, and should be significant enough in many cases to permit a large number of Canadian firms, who have served only the domestic market, to enter export markets for the first time. This will not be true for some higher-cost producers who must still hurdle barriers of 10 percent or more, particularly when they manufacture a standardized product which can be more economically produced closer to the final consumer of the goods. But with these exceptions, the Kennedy Round has created a new climate of opportunity for Canadian exporters.

Yet our export prospects will continue to depend primarily on the world economic and financial environment; on Canadian government policies, since these can seriously affect the competitive position and incentives of Canadian exporters; and on the attitudes and resourcefulness of Canadian manufacturers themselves.

With an economy particularly oriented toward world trade and closely connected to other capital markets, Canada has a special interest in ensuring that the international financial system works smoothly and that world production and employment expand in an atmosphere of reasonably stable prices. Canada is the world's fifth largest trading nation, behind the US, Germany, the UK, and France — with Japan catching up fast. Moreover 23 percent of our income comes from exports, compared to 5 percent for the US, 12 percent for Japan, and 21 percent for Germany.

Whether measured from a century ago or from just a few years back, Canadian exports have grown more rapidly than national production and have provided much of the stimulus to our economic and population growth, to our industrialization, and to the high per capita incomes we enjoy. This growth has been due in part to the fact that world trade has been growing faster than world production. 1968 again saw a continuation of this trend — despite the slowdown occasioned by the problems of the two major reserve-currency countries and the franc and the mark, by some moderation in the growth of the Japanese economy and the uncertainties associated with international liquidity arrangements.

International Reserves

Surprisingly good progress has been made in recent years in creating supplementary international reserves. However, we are still a long way from having an international monetary system able to generate the growth of international reserve assets needed to prevent reserve shortages which could restrict international trade — and thus national production and employment. The various expedients and *ad hoc* arrangements of the past few years have worked reasonably well — and are probably, indeed, to be regarded as a permanent and desirable feature of a landscape in which currency speculators are bound to appear from time to time — but a stronger basic framework, of which the newly created special drawing rights, or SDRs, form an integral part, is needed. International money will not manage itself any more than domestic money does, and a dependable international monetary system is needed to ensure that adjustments in individual countries are consistent with economic growth and maximum stability of currency values — rather than forcing resort to beggar-thy-neighbour policies which interfere with the free movement of money, capital, and goods and services among nations.

While solutions to these problems are, at one level, necessarily largely in the somewhat esoteric preserve of academic economists and central bankers, and, at another level, dependent on the economic soundness of policies pursued by individual countries, the Canadian business and banking community could well show more interest in this subject and put more pressure on the Canadian government to take the lead in arriving at satisfactory solutions. Weakness in the international monetary system may not be a limiting factor on Canadian exports in the short term but positive steps must be taken if the progress made in 1968 is to lead to further measures to improve the world's capacity to finance a growing level of trade and capital movements.

Government Policy

Canadian export prospects are most likely to be affected, both in the short and longer term, by various policies of the Canadian government. First among these, of course, are broad monetary and fiscal policies since failure to restrain excessive demand quickly leads to inflationary pressures and rises in unit costs of production which affect the competitive position of our exporters. The burden on fiscal policy was particularly pronounced when

Canada's exchange reserves — as well as its exchange rate — were to all intents and purposes fixed. This resulted in a number of instances when Canadian monetary policy had to permit easier credit conditions than domestic economic considerations warranted — and thus added fuel to the inflationary fires — because it had to be primarily concerned with preventing the accumulation of excessive reserves under our agreement with the United States. The recent removal of the ceiling on our reserves will allow somewhat more scope for restrictive monetary policies when they are needed — scope that the Bank of Canada was quick to take advantage of by raising Bank Rate on December 17th.

It is ironic that the central bankers' obsession with fixed exchange rates is undermining the very virtues always claimed for fixed rates; the free flow of capital and trade is being impeded by guidelines necessary to maintain these rates, and world policy makers are having to tolerate inflation — indeed even encourage it — in order to restore balance between those countries with strong international positions and those with weak ones. In any event, as long as more flexible exchange rates, or ranges of rates, are ruled out, Canadian exporters must rely heavily on fiscal policy to ensure that they are not priced out of world markets by inflationary cost increases at home.

No one can assert that the course of Canadian fiscal policy in recent years has been particularly reassuring; indeed it is probably fair to say that if an undervalued exchange rate had not been established in 1962, the course of fiscal events since 1965 in particular would have had far more serious repercussions on our exports than it has.

All levels of government have shown unwillingness to adopt temporarily unpopular measures, particularly when those really cut into spending programs, as opposed to widely publicized window-dressing. As a result, expenditures have at times got completely out of control and we now have a very high level of taxation and spending in Canada — equal to about 36 percent of gross national product or 42 percent of national income. The percentage for the US is about five points lower despite a much higher defence burden.

One can only hope that henceforth more attention will be paid to such matters as the priorities in government spending, improved efficiency in the use of public funds, better co-ordination among policies, and a willingness to restrain expenditures in boom times. It is not unreasonable to demand that Canada's performance in this area should be at least as good as that of our principal trading competitors.

Our export prospects will be importantly affected by more specific government policies like those relating to manpower, education, and research and development. One hears a great deal about our alleged "technology gap" with other countries although we do not spend very much less on research and development than do the Japanese, who are outstandingly good at taking technology and turning it into improved products and vigorous economic growth. Part of Canada's problem may be that government spends too much, and industry too little of the money that is now available; but perhaps the main difficulty is that there is not sufficient incentive for Canadian manufacturers to develop and apply technology. A reduction and restructuring of taxes may well, therefore, produce more fruitful results in the area of technology than a comparable increase in government spending on R & D.

Improved technology and improved export markets go hand in hand, since it is only through longer, less costly, and more specialized production runs that many of the benefits of modern technology can be fully exploited. The

Kennedy Round's potential benefits for Canadian industry will thus be fully realized only if other measures are taken to improve the structure of our industry. For instance, a rethinking of Combines policy to allow whole industries to rationalize their production by having each firm specialize in one or two lines, rather than attempt to produce twenty or thirty, is certainly long overdue. The use of special tariff reductions, where needed, in concert with such a program would ensure that effective competition was maintained.

International industry agreements, like the automotive pact, can also play a very useful role in bringing about more efficient industry structures; the automobile parts industry was initially very sceptical about this program, but it has led to an impressive increase in Canadian production, great gains in productivity and efficiency, and enhanced profitability of the independent Canadian companies relative to the subsidiaries of US companies. More important, it has shown the industry that it can be competitive, and it has now become far more aggressive in foreign markets generally. There are many other industries, including aluminum and fine paper, where such an approach to industry rationalization could lead to higher Canadian exports.

General Adjustment Assistance Board

Any approach to improving the structure of Canadian industry will, however, fail if resources are devoted to propping up declining or inefficient industry, a practice that is successfully avoided in Sweden, whose standard of living is now higher than ours. The idea of backing success rather than prolonging failure is the basic idea at the General Adjustment Assistance Board. It is encouraging, on the basis of our so-far limited experience, to see how many Canadian manufacturers are demonstrating resourcefulness and enterprise in cracking into export markets or in significantly expanding sales abroad as a result of the Kennedy Round. The technology, design, and sales efforts needed to achieve this creates an expanded market which in turn makes it possible to finance these activities on a more economic basis. Canadian companies producing winter apparel, frozen foods, prefabricated houses, skidoos, and pleasure boats are but some examples of real export success.

These companies follow a certain common pattern: they have reassessed their product lines; worked on research and development; modernized production facilities; improved their market research and sales efforts; and, most important of all, resolved to sell something in the export markets.

Those determined to export can use the facilities of the Export Credit Insurance Corporation, which have recently been broadened, and the Trade Commissioner's Service. In addition, there is aid available for those who produce defence goods for foreign markets. Finally, the General Adjustment Assistance Board offers insurance of up to 90 percent of the risk of loss on industrial loans by private lenders to those who are restructuring their operations as a result of a significant opportunity offered by the Kennedy Round. Financial assistance is only made available when adequate financing cannot be obtained on reasonable terms and conditions. Some applicants for assistance may not have the resources within their own organizations to develop adequate plans for reorganization of their operations; in these cases the Board can share up to half the cost of needed consulting services.

While such government programs are helpful, private industry could play a more active role in finding, exploiting, and financing export trade. There are opportunities for an entire industry, or two industries jointly, or a consortia of varying enterprises, to set up specialized trading companies which would maintain the necessary representation abroad, carry needed inventories, and provide the marketing and financial services needed to compete vigorously on a worldwide market basis. Private financial institutions, both in Canada and abroad, could play a constructive role in these developments. The Canadian banks, as a result of recent legislative changes, are now freer to innovate and compete, and it is to be hoped that legislation will soon remove the restrictions from smaller — and often more innovating and enterprising — financial institutions which could also play a constructive role in financing and promoting Canada's foreign trade.

Canadians have the market position and knowledge; the skills; the technology; the power and other natural resources; and — most importantly — the enterprise and ability, to compete successfully in world markets. Much remains to be done in reducing tariffs — on a general basis as well as industry by industry — and in lowering nontariff barriers, like licences, taxes, product standards, customs administration, and government buying program. Moreover, ways have to be found of promoting East-West trade on a sound basis and of bringing the developing countries and agriculture more into the pattern of free and unhampered multilateral trade. Further progress may be slow for a while, but the nature of economic developments and the necessity of international specialization of labour and production make it inexorable that the move towards freer trade will continue. The only force likely to reverse this would be a collapse of the international monetary system, and I do not believe that is likely to happen: people usually adopt the sensible course — but only after they have first explored all the alternatives.

Canada's manufactured exports have more than quadrupled since 1963 to a rate approximating $4½ billion per annum, and are twice the size of the exports of the forest products industry, three times those of agriculture, and bigger than all metals and mineral products combined. Automobiles and parts account for over half this gain, but there has been a generalized improvement in the manufacturing sector.

Canadian industry, and particularly manufacturers in Canada, have the willingness and capacity to capture an increasing share of a growing world market, given reasonable fiscal and other policies on the part of the Canadian Government. In the process, Canada will become a more technical and industrialized economy, more specialized in its production, and more efficient in its output. Indeed, it may not be too outrageous to assume that in a few years Canada will have a very sizable annual surplus on its overall current account (it has had one on its merchandise account since 1961) and become one of the world's leading exporters of capital to the less developed nations whose attainment of decent standards of living must be a concern of us all.

D. UNDERDEVELOPED ECONOMIES

On the periphery of the world economy, living in a marginal existence, are some hundred countries with about two-thirds of the world's population. These are the economically underdeveloped nations of Asia, Africa, and Latin America. They are at the bottom of the welfare scale when judged by any of the important economic criteria. Their annual incomes average about $150 per person, not even one-twentieth of that in Canada. The life expectancy of their citizens averages about twenty or thirty years, or roughly half that in the more advanced nations. At least three-fourths are illiterate. When measured by the daily per capita calorie intake, a very significant proportion of their population is persistently on the brink of starvation. Clearly, the underdeveloped economies present one of the major challenges facing the world today.

Reading 49 summarizes and evaluates the economic performance of the underdeveloped countries during the 1950s and early 1960s. It discusses the role of capital, entrepreneurship, skill, and foreign trade in the process of economic development, and comments on the high levels of unemployment in the underdeveloped regions of the world. This analysis shows that historical experience can be a valuable guide for both development theory and policy.

In his *Protestant Ethic and the Spirit of Capitalism* (1905), Max Weber, a German sociologist, developed a thesis concerning the intimate connection between the ascetic character which Calvinism fostered and the rise of capitalist institutions. Ever since there has been controversy about the impact of religious belief on the economic actions of mankind. Does religion impel men to economic achievement, or is it a hindrance? Reading 50 argues that criticism of Weber's thesis is founded upon misunderstanding or exaggeration of what Weber said, and that its implications for economic motivation and development problems are more important than has been generally acknowledged. From this analysis it is apparent that religious or ideological inspiration is one of the essential conditions for economic expansion within any given economy.

Experience suggests that the task of economic development must be done by those on the spot. In virtually every case of significant and sustained economic growth most of the initiative and means of development have been provided by that nation's domestic economy. Yet external aid can serve as a vital supplement to any nation's development process and very frequently may be the deciding factor in the success or failure of its endeavour to break through the barriers to sustained economic progress.

Since World War II the economically advanced countries have provided economic assistance to most of the underdeveloped economies. This aid was prompted primarily by humanitarian considerations and by the requirements of the cold war. Government-to-government aid may be of three types: loans, grants, or technical assistance. Reading 51 reviews the Canadian external aid program, indicates some of the problems that are faced in its application, and offers some frank opinions concerning the role of foreign aid. It also argues that more is required than economic growth to produce a truly just and equitable world society.

49. REVIEW OF ECONOMIC DEVELOPMENT*

W. Arthur Lewis

The underdeveloped countries did reasonably well during the 1950s. According to the United Nations' statisticians,[1] gross domestic product increased at an annual rate of 4.6 percent in Latin America, 4.2 percent in the Far East (excluding Japan and mainland China), 5.2 percent in southern Asia, and 4.1 percent in Africa. At the beginning of the decade economists were concerned about whether these countries could make the minimum critical effort needed to exceed population growth, then thought to be 2 percent, now accelerating disquietingly to 2½ and 3 percent. Growth rates exceeding 4 percent have shown that capital, entrepreneurship, skill, and foreign trade are not such formidable obstacles as they were thought to be. In reviewing each of these categories, I shall use the occasion to consider some of the concepts which economists have been using to analyse the problems of economic growth.

Capital

Capital has not been as scarce as expected, first because the capital-output ratio turned out to be unusually low, second, because more foreign aid became available, and third, because some of these countries are managing to save more.

In 1950, economists thought that the capital-output ratio was around 4 (net); actually in the 1950s it has often been even between 2 and 3, both in developed and in underdeveloped countries. We do not yet know why, or

*Reprinted from W. A. Lewis, "A Review of Economic Development," *American Economic Review*, May, 1965, pp. 1-16, by permission of the editor and author.
Sir Arthur is Governor, Caribbean Development Bank, Bridgetown, Barbados. Formerly, Dr. Lewis taught at the London School of Economics, Manchester University, University of the West Indies, and Princeton University.
[1] *World Economic Survey*, 1963, p. 19. The figure for Africa is probably too high. On the other hand, an earlier estimate by the Economic Commission for Africa (*Industrial Growth in Africa*, p. 3) that commodity output grew by 2.1 percent per annum is too low, since it assumes that the growth rate of agriculture was only 1.4.

whether the change is permanent. Let us note four possible explanations. First, Western Europe has been exploiting a backlog of technological progress, accumulated during the interwar stagnation. The underdeveloped countries may be reaping a similar harvest — will certainly do so as soon as they tackle their agriculture properly. Second, expenditure on infrastructure may be abnormally low; underdeveloped countries are putting a lot of money into transportation and power, but they are still starving housing and the public services. Third, the high growth rates of industrial production (ranging between 6 and 10 percent) and of services have effected considerable transfers from less to more productive sectors of the economy. And, finally, high rates of growth of population, in countries where land is abundant, produce a proportionate growth of agricultural output, using little capital. The question whether in some other countries, such as India or Egypt, the marginal productivity of labour in agriculture is zero seems to arouse fierce passions, though the answer does not seem to be relevant to any particular problem.

When we turn to the transfer of capital from the developed to the underdeveloped world, we are on firmer ground. The United Nations[2] estimates that the net flow increased from about two billion dollars in 1950 to about six billion dollars in 1960. Six billion dollars was about 3½ percent of the national incomes of the underdeveloped world and was therefore associated with about a quarter of their rate of growth at the end of the decade. This is a very considerable achievement for those of us who have made ceaseless propaganda for foreign aid.

It would be pleasant to be able to report a universal increase in domestic ratios of saving, resulting from these high rates of growth and of aid, but alas only a minority of countries have risen to their opportunity. The best documentation is for Latin America, where if the Economic Commission for Latin America[3] is right, the ratio of gross domestic savings to gross domestic product fell, for the continent as a whole, from 16.8 percent in 1950-54 to 15.6 percent in 1955-61, or 15.2 percent in 1960. Fragmentary evidence suggests that the rest of the underdeveloped world did not do much more than maintain domestic savings ratios (for example, Philippines from 9.0 percent in 1950 to 9.5 percent in 1960; Nigeria from 8.3 in 1951 to 8.6 in 1957) but there were also spectacular exceptions, such as India, from about 6 percent (net) in 1950 to about 8 percent in 1960, and Jamaica, from 12.2 (gross) in 1950 to 16.1 percent in 1960.

Some of the countries which failed to improve their savings ratios nevertheless increased the take of public expenditure, which can be just as important for growth. The 1950s were a good decade for education, for public health, and for roads. Since both savings and public expenditure come out of the surplus of output over private consumption and improve future productive capacity, they should be considered together when measuring achievement. Availability of foreign capital enabled some governments to put improvement of the public services ahead of improvements in the savings ratio during the 1950s.

We do not have enough evidence to test theories of how income distribution and the propensity to save change as per capita income increases. The

[2] *The International Flow of Long-Term Capital and Official Donations, 1959-1961,* and earlier publications in this series.
[3] *The Development of Latin America in the Postwar Period,* p. 10. Domestic saving equals investment minus the surplus on current account in the balance of payments.

fall in export prices relative to domestic costs was important, since the export sector saves more and is more highly taxed than the rest of the economy. ECLA estimates that adverse terms of trade cost Latin America 3.6 percent of national income, comparing 1960 with 1950, but one would still have expected the savings ratio at least to be maintained, since per capita real output increased by 19 percent. Presumably significant changes in private saving require longer periods and bigger per capita changes.

The slow rate of change of private savings is one reason why more importance is now attached to increasing public saving. This, however, is not easy. First, the marginal rate of taxation is lower than the average in most of these countries; so the percentage share of public revenue falls as national income increases. Radical reforms are required in tax structure if public revenue is even to keep up with public expenditure. Second, where public services are rudimentary, rapidly increasing expenditures on these services are just as important as increased savings and will for some time absorb most of the increase in revenues. Third, the rate of change must inevitably be slow. Attaining self-sustaining growth means reducing the ratio of private consumption to gross domestic product from around 80 to say around 70 percent. Any attempt to reduce the ratio of consumption faster than by about one-half of one percent of gross domestic product per year will defeat itself, and also create political unrest. It defeats itself because output cannot be increased without increasing consumption, since growth reproduces social turbulence, which can be contained only by devoting increased resources to welfare and consumption. My limit of one-half of one percent assumes that per capita consumption must grow at least 60 percent as fast as per capita output, in the relevant ranges. Attempts to move faster than this, whether through taxation, inflation, or rationing, are likely to end in riots.

International economic aid is supported by different people for many different reasons. Insofar as its object is to give the big push which creates the opportunity for self-sustaining growth, its success must be measured by the extent to which countries do indeed increase their investment in men and resources faster than current consumption. And if this is the test, then there is something to be said for tying the distribution of foreign aid to actual performance. In another place[4] I have produced a formula for this, making the amount of aid a country receives a multiple of

$$\frac{S_{-1}}{GDP_{-1}} - \frac{S_{-4}}{GDP_{-4}}$$

where S = expenditure on gross investment (minus foreign aid) plus current government expenditure (minus defence and welfare transfers), and subscripts refer to years.

Nobody wants to be governed by a rigid formula, but if we want foreign aid to show results in promoting progress toward economic dependence, it should be more closely linked to performance. These issues can no longer be evaded, because the future of foreign aid is now critically in doubt, not only in the United States, but even in France, where aid has hitherto been sacrosanct. Most aid is given for political reasons, and much of the current

---

[4] "Allocating Foreign Aid to Promote Self-Sustaining Economic Growth," in *Motivations and Methods in Development and Foreign Aid,* Proceedings of the Sixth World Conference of the Society for International Development, 1964.

disillusionment springs only from belated discovery that political aid cannot achieve all that is expected of it. Nevertheless, it has to be admitted that the nonpolitical aid is also distributed haphazardly, whether by bilateral or multilateral agencies; better criteria and better results might win wider support.

Entrepreneurship

Growth rates exceeding 4 percent suggest that the shortage of entrepreneurship cannot have been the major obstacle it is normally thought to be. It is well known that these countries have no shortage of small-scale entrepreneurship; the desire to make money and the willingness to gamble are endemic. What lacks is the experience of organizing large-scale businesses. Assuming that this lack of experience springs from lack of desire, or from institutional inhibitions, historians have devoted much paper to considering what social and ideological climate spawns successful large-scale enterprise; and the social psychologists have now joined them. The last fifteen years have thrown little light on their theories, except, perhaps, to question the quantitative importance of their problem. Perhaps, too, those politicians were right who said that the end of imperialism and racial subjugation would spark a surprising release of energy.

Meanwhile the shortage of large-scale domestic entrepreneurship has been met to some extent by foreign enterprise. Here the 1950s saw a marked change in the attitudes of governments. During the 1930s and 1940s the air resounded with diatribes against foreign investors, but in the 1960s newspapers in Europe and North America are full of advertisements in which the governments of newly independent states offer foreign investors innumerable incentives, including exemption from taxes. Foreign entrepreneurs have not been allowed to do much for agriculture or for trade, but their contribution in mining and manufacturing is a major explanation of the high rates of growth of industrial production.

The shortage has also stimulated governments to assume some of the attributes of entrepreneurship themselves. The governments of underdeveloped countries do not command either the capital or the administrative skills necessary to play any significant role as managers of industrial or agricultural enterprises, though some have tried, often for ideological reasons. They can play a more important role in creating a favourable climate for private entrepreneurship, helping with improved infrastructure, market research, feasibility studies, technical advice, and financial aid. Development theory makes a great deal out of external economies, whether in explaining the low level of investment, or assessing the advantages of geographical concentration, or tracing the history of growth through linkages, or arguing the case for the government as a promoter of interdependent investments. The analysis has been influential, though factual evidence remains scarce.

Governments have done better at stimulating the private sector than at controlling it, not surprisingly, since both the statistics and the personnel for efficient control are lacking. Many controls have hindered more than helped, especially by restricting the smaller businessmen, some of whom are the hope for the future. Also, the new states often begin with hostility between politicians and administrators, and need to find a new equilibrium which will reduce corruption and arbitrary decisions. The record is spotty even in the public sector. Most governments have made development plans, but few take their own plans seriously, although planning could undoubtedly help to bring more order into public sector programs. Governments have first to learn to control the public sector before they can hope usefully to control the private sector.

The sector to which government initiatives could contribute most is agriculture, which has, alas, been the most neglected. Everybody talks about the necessary framework for agriculture — the agricultural research stations, the extension agents, farm institutes, animation, water supplies, fertilizers, land reform, and so on — but little gets done. Prime ministers have had their minds on other things: on political questions such as neutralism, Pan Africanism, Afro-Asian unity, and the like, or in the economic realm mainly on industrialization; and since most great men can achieve no more than one or two things at a time, agriculture has had to content itself with occasional lip service. Agriculture will have to be seen to be important before any considerable progress will be made.

This change is beginning in countries where agricultural stagnation is the obvious cause of the shortage of foreign exchange. But the crucial role of agriculture is also obvious in the elementary arithmetic of economic growth. For it is easy to show that national income cannot attain a rate of growth of 5 percent in Asian and African conditions. At present none of these countries is able to increase agricultural output faster than 3 percent per annum. Assume optimistically that industrial output increases by 10 percent per annum. Then, if agriculture contributes 50 percent of gross national product and industry 12 percent, the growth of commodity output averages out, initially, at 4.4 percent. Output of services grows slightly faster than output of commodities; so that gross domestic product as a whole would grow at a maximum rate of 4.6 percent. Given the failure to reform agriculture, the rates of growth actually achieved in the 1950s are a matter for congratulation. One must assume that the United Nations call for 5 percent in the 1960s is mainly a call for a massive assault on agricultural stagnation, without which such a target is impracticable. Also, the call should not be mixed in with the discussion of foreign aid, since it is with the governments of the underdeveloped countries that the initiative lies in agriculture.

Skill

Shortage of skills has been even less of a bottleneck than shortage of entrepreneurs. In part this has been due to the large international flow of technical assistance. Despite the breakup of the colonial empires, there are now more European and American technicians in Asia and in Africa than there were in 1950, and the numerous channels through which this movement is organized are an achievement in which the world can take some pride.

Nevertheless, technical assistance is marginal. Leaving aside for the moment the agricultural sector, the amount of skill which these countries can currently absorb is relatively small, mainly because their nonagricultural sectors are relatively small. Where half the population is in agriculture, the number of jobs requiring a secondary education does not exceed 10 percent of the occupied population, nor do the jobs requiring university education exceed 2 percent.[5] The majority of countries in Asia and Latin America (but not all) have as many secondary educated people as they need for strictly economic purposes, and many of them have many more such people than they can absorb in current market conditions. There are shortages of particular types. In general there is too much literary education and not enough technological, but this defect is easily remedied. The number of technical institutes and special training institutions has multiplied quite rapidly in underdeveloped countries. What most of the Asian and Latin-American countries need is better quality rather than more quantity.

Africa's situation is quite different. There, in 1960, less than 1 percent of the population had received a secondary education and less than 10 percent primary education. This situation is now changing rapidly since these countries have become independent and have made education a first priority.

There is no evidence to suggest that economic development is accelerated by supplying more educated people than the market can absorb. India is one of the best educated underdeveloped countries, but not conspicuously the most successful in economic development. An oversupply of educated people creates great frustrations, stimulates excessive migrations to the towns, and results in political turbulence. All this makes the political situation more exciting; but though the long-run effects of political excitement on development may be positive, the short-term effects seem to be zero, or even negative.

The biggest problem in education is the relation of schooling to agricultural improvement. The problem does not arise in plantation agriculture, since the planters, who are the decision makers, can adopt the latest techniques whether their workers are literate or not. We cannot doubt that literate farmers are likely to absorb new technology more rapidly than illiterate farmers. Illiterate farmers can be taught the most obvious things and have made important decisions, such as changing from subsistence to commercial crops. But it must be a goal to have as soon as feasible an agricultural system in which every farmer is literate.

The problem is the transition. Putting the children into school, which costs a great deal of money (as much as 3 or 4 percent of national income) does not guarantee that one will have literate farmers. Much depends on the speed with which one moves from 10 percent of rural children in school toward 100 percent, for when the figure is only 10 percent, that 10 percent knows that it will get jobs off the farms, at wages from two to three times as high as the average farmer's income. If one raises the proportion to 60 percent within ten years, as some West African countries have done, the 60 percent also expect to get jobs off the farms at high incomes. They cannot be attracted by three acres and a hoe; only a modernized agriculture capable of high yields per man could hope to hold them. Hence the only way to effect a smooth transition is to keep the rate of modernization of agriculture and the rate of expansion of rural schooling in step with each other. This is not a case for less schooling so much as a case for faster modernization of agriculture — for greater expenditure on research, agricultural credit, water supplies, and so on.

Given the time it takes to organize the right kind of agricultural framework for small farming, expenditure on adult education in the countryside,

[5] For amplification of this statement see my articles, "Education and Economic Development," *Social and Economic Studies,* (June, 1961), and "Secondary Education and Economic Structure," *ibid.,* (June, 1964).

including short courses for farmers at residential centres and other forms of community development, will probably at this stage prove more productive in Africa than money spent on getting all rural children into primary schools, desirable as that is for innumerable reasons, political and social no less than economic.

Foreign Trade

Foreign trade has played its customary role as the engine of growth in most of these countries but not in all. Both the terms of trade and the rate of growth of trade have been high by comparison with prewar statistics.

The terms of trade for primary as against manufactured products averaged higher in the 1950s than at any time in the preceding eighty years. The first half of the 1950s was especially good because of the Korean War and heavy stockpiling in the United States and elsewhere. The terms of trade deteriorated in the second half of the decade and on till 1962, since when they have moved upward. However, even in 1962 they were 5 percent above 1929, which preceded the Great Depression.

The volume of exports from underdeveloped countries increased at an annual rate of 3.6 percent, which is also much higher than before. But this rate is lower than the growth of national income because of the important part played by import substitution, especially in Latin America.

We are being deluged with literature arguing that the underdeveloped countries cannot grow at an adequate rate if the developed countries increase their demands for the exports of underdeveloped countries at an annual rate as low as 3½ percent. Such literature ignores the important part played by import substitution in economic development. Most of the calculations assume rates of growth of national income, consumption, industrial production, and imports which are not mutually consistent. A little arithmetic shows that if one assumes continuance of the current rate of growth of industrial production, the underdeveloped countries must soon be supplying themselves with nearly all the manufactures they need.[6] They have the necessary minerals and fuels, and the skills are not hard to learn. It is better that they should not be forced into autarchy since comparative advantage demands that, even if net imports be low, this is only because large imports of some manufactures are matched by large exports of others. Recent international discussion has focussed rightly on the market for the manufactures of underdeveloped in developed countries; this is likely to be much more important in future than the never-ending talks on primary products. Some of us believe even that the time is not far off when the underdeveloped will be net importers of primary products and net exporters of manufactures. This is not only because of high population growth, which the new techniques of family limitation will soon begin to control. More fundamentally, it is arguable that the real competitive advantage of temperate

---

[6] Currently these countries use manufactures equal to about 30 percent (including raw materials) of national income, of which about one-third are imported. If national income grew at 5 percent per annum, use at 6 percent, and production of manufactures at 8 percent, net imports of manufactures would fall to zero in twenty-two years. If the growth rate of production of manufactures is assumed to be lower, so must the growth rate of national income, and therefore of use of manufactures. Considering how slowly agriculture is growing, national income cannot grow by 5 percent if manufacturing is growing by less than 8 percent.

countries is in agriculture, since their temperate climates are more favourable to the retention of soil fertility than the harsher climates of the tropics.

To the individual underdeveloped country, import substitution offers less opportunity for growth with diminishing trade than it does to the group taken as a whole. Only the largest countries (possibly China, India, the USSR, and the United States) have that wide variety of climates and minerals which is a necessary condition for development as a closed economy. Everywhere else a rise in real income must increase the imports of some commodities. These imports have to be paid for either by expanding exports or by releasing foreign exchange through import substitution. In the nineteenth century, growth was sparked by exports, which generated incomes and so also stimulated production for the home market. In the second half of the twentieth century, import substitution has offered some countries an easy path to growth, without dependence on increasing exports. However, once the limits to import substitution are reached, the rate of increase of exports sets a ceiling to the rate of growth of output, since natural resource limitations make it impossible to have balanced growth for the home market only.

Economists have produced a turgid literature on balanced growth. Most writers do not make clear whether they are concerned with the balance between production for the home market and production for export or are concerned only with production for the home market.

If one assumes a closed economy, the pattern of production must obviously be related to the pattern of domestic demand. The original Rosenstein-Rodan proposition was to the effect that in a closed economy with unemployment, an entrepreneur could employ some of the unemployed with greater confidence if he knew that other employers were simultaneously offering employment in other industries; for his workers would spend some of his outlays on buying their goods, but their workers would spend some of their incomes on buying his. A parallel proposition in the two-sector model says that if the two sectors trade with each other, the expansion of the one can be brought to an end by the stagnation of the other. These propositions have not been upset by any of the subsequent writing, most of which has merely demonstrated that, while demand and supply are linked, the link is not absolutely rigid. Some production can take place in advance of demand; innovating suppliers create demands which did not previously exist; in other sectors it is safe for capacity to lag behind demand; the availability of entrepreneurial talents will decide where demand may lag, and where it may go in advance; inventions usually bunch in a few industries, in response to shortages, rather than spread all over the economy; and so on. Much controversy has raged around such propositions, not because they are controversial, but because economists like to be controversial.

Maintaining a proper balance between production for the home market and production for export is a much more important subject, because failure to do this has serious consequences for the balance of payments, for prices, and for the growth rate of the economy. Attempts to increase output faster than the growth rate of exports will give rise to what the Latin Americans now call "structural inflation." This literature, too, is much obscured by irrelevancies. Structural inflation is not due to being underdeveloped, to having a high rate of population growth, to exporting mainly primary products, or to having difficulty in raising taxes; the British economy is the clearest contemporary example of structural inflation, and it has none of these characteristics. Neither is structural inflation due to investing more than is saved, or to running a budget deficit; these cause demand-pull inflations, whereas structural inflation is a cost-push phenomenon.

A simple example illustrates the species. Suppose that a country produces only two commodities, motor cars and wheat, and consumes only these two commodities. Suppose also that through technological progress the output of cars is increased, but structural barriers hold down the output of wheat. The increase in real income increases the demand for wheat. This is met by importing wheat. Thus, income generated in the production of cars is used to buy imports; there is a deficit in the balance of payments, and deflation in the home market, represented by a surplus of cars. This structural deflation is turned into structural inflation by the measures taken to right the balance of payments. Devaluation or tariffs or import controls will raise the price of wheat and therefore the cost of living, and so a cost-push inflation spiral will start. Four solutions are possible. One solution would be to reduce the output of cars to the level of home demand. This reduces employment and damps the rate of growth of national income. We can call this the British solution, since this is what Britain has done regularly over the past fifteen years; it is also what Latin-American economists accuse the International Monetary Fund, rightly or wrongly, of wanting them to do. The second solution would be to go out into the world market and sell more motor cars. This is the Japanese solution. The rate of growth of the economy is then set by the degree of success in exporting. The third solution would be to break the agricultural bottleneck and have balanced growth in the narrow sense of patterning domestic production on domestic demand. This is the Mexican solution. The fourth solution would be to force the public to consume what is being produced; namely, more cars rather than more wheat, whether by subsidizing cars, or by taxing wheat, or by some system of rationing. This was the old Russian solution.

Only two of these solutions appeal to economists; namely either to sell more exports or to break the bottleneck. Nothing in economic science can tell us *a priori* which is preferable, but great passions have been aroused by our prejudices. Economists reared in the free-trade tradition tend to look first for the opportunities for increasing trade; whereas a later generation, which learnt in the interwar years to be wary of dependence on exports, prefers to explore first the opportunities for increasing the productivity of home supplies. Inefficient governments chose neither of these solutions. They either damp down growth or try to push ahead despite imbalances. The latter policy has produced its full crop of foreign exchange shortages, devaluations, and inflations. The process is cumulative; persistent cost-inflation discourages both exports and import substitution, so aggravating the foreign exchange shortage, and giving the spiral another push. Whatever merits a policy of persistent inflation may or may not have in a closed economy, in an open economy it can work havoc with employment and growth, by causing a country to price itself persistently out of world markets. A perpetually overvalued currency can be the chief cause of economic stagnation.

One of the advantages of input-output analysis is that it puts these problems into their proper framework. A projected increase in national income results in projected increases in final demands. In balancing demand and supply for each commodity separately, the law of comparative costs is invoked (perhaps in the form of linear or preferably nonlinear programming) to decide the appropriate balance between imports, exports, and production for the home market. Economists are asking whether the new "indicative planning" has really contributed anything to the rate of growth of the French economy. In less developed countries the making of such projections could not but improve existing planning procedures, so long as good statistics are available and so long as projection is not confused with prophecy. I suspect that if such exercises were done correctly, most of the countries which have been concentrating on the home market would find that a shift to exports would pay, and most of those now concentrating on exports could do better by giving more attention to import substitution.

Unemployment

One disturbing factor must be set against the high rates of growth of output and investment on which we have been congratulating ourselves; namely, the rising levels of unemployment in the underdeveloped countries.[7] This cannot be documented because there are no reliable statistics of unemployment, but it is everywhere a cause of concern. The phenomenon is unexpected, since rapid growth and high investment ought not to increase unemployment but to reduce it.

This unemployment is not due in the first instance to rising populations. In a well-organized society, surplus population shows itself in disguised unemployment on family farms and in other traditional places, whereas what we are now talking about is unemployment of people working for wages and living in big towns.

The simplest approach to understanding the causes of unemployment is through the model which divides the economy into a growing modern capitalist sector and a traditional subsistence sector which feeds labour to it as required. Unemployment is growing rapidly for two reasons: first, because the traditional sector is expelling labour too rapidly; and, second, because the modern sector is taking in too few because it is too highly capital intensive.

One reason why the traditional sector is discharging labour too rapidly is the unusually large differential between wages in the modern sector and earnings in the traditional sector. We are used to assuming a differential of about 50 percent, and to assuming that the modern sector can grow at a constant wage level. This seems to have happened in the nineteenth century, but in the twentieth century trade-union pressure, nationalistic governmental pressure on foreign enterprises, and the new social conscience of big entrepreneurs are combining to raise wages very sharply in the modern sectors of the developing economies, and it is now not unusual to find some unskilled workers in the modern sector earning three or four times as much as the average small farmer. This causes a sympathetic increase in wages in traditional occupations, and since productivity is very low in these occupations, employers get rid of domestic servants and of the surplus clerks and messengers whom their businesses have traditionally sheltered. The high wages in the modern sector also attract people out of the countryside into the towns, where they manage to live by doing a few hours occasional work per week.

---

[7] I have treated this subject more fully in "Unemployment in the Developing Areas," in *Proceedings of the Third Biennial Midwest Research Conference on Underdeveloped Areas* (Chicago, 1965).

Imbalance between the modern and the traditional sectors is not confined to wages. An important factor in Africa is the rapid acceleration in the output of rural schools, which are now producing more primary school graduates than the rural economy is able to absorb at the wages they expect. So young people are flooding into African towns. The excessive rate of growth of a few towns is a problem throughout the underdeveloped world. This is compounded by errors of policy in industrial location and by concentrating development expenditures on these few large towns, making them much more attractive than the villages and the small country towns in terms of water supplies, transportation, schools, hospitals, electric light, and opportunities for unemployment relief. Holding the surplus in the country-side until required has always been a problem in developing economies. The British poor relief authorities gave it much attention at the end of the eighteenth century and the beginning of the nineteenth, and tried to prevent people from coming into the towns if work was not available.

The other aspect of this problem is the high capital intensity of the new investment, not in the sense of the ratio of capital to output, which we have seen is low, but in the sense of the proportion of the national income invested which is required to provide additional employment for one more man. Most of these countries are surprised at how few people have found employment in the growing sectors of the economy, especially manufacturing, mining, and transportation, despite the high investment which has been taking place.

High capital intensity is appropriate when it embodies greatly superior technology, without demanding very high skills. The Ohlin approach to comparative costs puts us against high capital intensities, but Ohlin's model assumes that countries have the same technology and differ only in the relative scarcity of resources. In comparing developing with underdeveloped countries, it is more appropriate to use the Ricardian version of the law of comparative costs, which stresses instead relative differences in productive efficiency. Now there is no *a priori* reason for developed countries to have a comparative efficiency advantage in capital intensive industries, and one can easily construct cases where the comparative advantage remains with the underdeveloped country, even when the relatively higher cost of capital is taken into account. Since this result is unfamiliar, I am attaching an arithmetical example as an appendix to this paper.

Economic theory offers no reason why development must increase rather than reduce employment. Capital investment as such must increase employment in a system with an infinitely elastic supply of labour, since it cannot pay in such a system to increase the ratio of capital to labour. Just as important as capital investment, however, is the introduction of new technology. This may operate in either direction, but on balance tends to be labour-saving. Karl Marx asserted that the employment-destroying effects of new technology must more than offset the employment-creating effects of capital investment, but he produced no arguments in favour of this proposition, and proved to be wrong in the nineteenth century. It does not follow that he must be wrong in the twentieth century. The underdeveloped economies lag so far behind in technology, that the opportunities for introducing labour-saving methods are immense, and it could well happen that the new employment created in the factories, in modern forms of transportation, and in modern services could be more than offset by the employment destroyed in handicrafts, traditional forms of transportation, and old-fashioned types of personal service.

This possibility is heightened by the tendency of wages to rise sharply in the modern sector. The higher wages are, the more it pays to import cheap machinery from the developed countries, and therefore the less employment investment creates. Not only are the newest industries highly capital intensive, but some of the well-established, older export industries, such as mines and plantations, are finding themselves squeezed by their inability to pay the wages that are being demanded and offered by more profitable enterprises; and the opportunities for import substitution are also diminished. Professors Liebenstein and Galenson have urged upon us the desirability of high capital intensity in underdeveloped countries as a source of profits and therefore of savings and investment. Unfortunately, that policy would be feasible only if the labour surplus remained disguised and could therefore be ignored; it is not practicable when the unemployed are roaming the streets and burglarizing your houses. Most developing countries have to give the highest priority to providing employment now rather than to maximizing consumption or income or employment in ten years time.

Economists have also developed a theory of the desirability of assessing the real social value of a project by calculating with shadow factor prices differing from the actual factor prices. In the situation described, they would recommend calculations in which the existence of unemployment is recognized by attributing a low wage to labour, below the actual wage. This is arguable on paper, but how does one translate it into practice? Investment decisions are made, not by economists making calculations in government offices, but by private decision makers and by civil servants, all of whom are under pressure to produce at minimum costs in money terms, and the government does not possess the resources with which to subsidize labour so as to bring the wage down to the shadow price, or the administrative capacity to substitute an effective licensing system for the price system of the market. The only way to achieve decision making on the basis of a low shadow wage is to have a low actual wage.

Recognition of the connection between wages and employment has opened up a gulf between trade-union leaders and political leaders in new states, especially where the government is the chief employer of labour, or is concerned about the adverse effects of high wages on exports, import substitution, and employment, or even prefers high profits to high wages because it can tax profits more easily than wages. Governments have therefore begun to think in terms of an incomes policy. Minimization of unemployment requires that wages should be tied to average agricultural incomes at a level sufficiently high to produce the labour required by the expanding nonagricultural sector, but not so high as to produce a great outflow which the towns cannot yet absorb. If at the same time vigorous measures are raising agricultural productivity, mass consumption will rise sharply, not merely because people are transferring from the lower level of the traditional sector to the higher level of the modern sector, but also because both levels are rising. Without some such policy, development must result in sharply increasing unemployment.

We are back in the political sphere. Trade unions are not likely to accept an incomes policy from governments in which they have no confidence, whether because the politicians are corrupt, indifferent, reactionary, or inefficient. Economists in the twentieth century usually call upon governments to redress the imperfections of the market, just as their forebears in the nineteenth century looked to the market to replace the imperfections of the government. The last fifteen years have lengthened the list of things which governments can usefully do and improved the statistical and theoretical tools for making decisions, but only a handful of governments show promise of rising to their opportunities. Here the economist must hand the development problem over to his colleagues in the other social sciences.

Appendix

1. Assume that before "Libya" adopts new technologies, the position is that one man produces:
in "Germany" 20 steel or 3 baskets
in "Libya"   1 steel or 1 basket
Therefore, "Libya" specializes in baskets.
2. Now introduce new technology to Libya. Assume that the factor proportions are the same in both countries, in physical terms, namely:
in steel   1 man + 1   capital
in baskets 1 man + 0.25 capital
3. Suppose, however, that capital makes much more contribution to steel-making than to basketmaking. The former is a simple operation, which Libyans can do as well as Germans, given the capital; but the latter (basketmaking) is a skilled occupation, in which the Libyan output is still far short of the German, even with capital. The position is now that one man, with the appropriate capital produces:
in Germany 20 steel or 3 baskets
in Libya   16 steel or 1.75 baskets
4. The difference is now smaller in steel than in baskets, but we cannot tell which should specialize in which without the relative prices of labour and capital. Suppose that labour costs one mark in Germany, one franc in Libya. Suppose that a unit of capital costs, on a rental basis, 2 marks in Germany and 3 francs in Libya. The relative cost of capital is higher in Libya because (*a*) it takes more labour to make a unit of capital, (*b*) capital maintenance is more expensive, (*c*) capital has a shorter life, and (*d*) the rate of interest is higher.
5. Costs per unit can now be calculated. They are:
Germany, steel 0.15 marks; baskets 0.50 marks
Libya,   steel 0.25 francs; baskets 1.00 francs
Hence, steel is relatively cheaper in Libya than in Germany.
6. The moral is that the Hecksher-Ohlin test (relative scarcity of factors) gives the answer by itself only if the production functions are the same (that is, if Ricardian differences are absent). In normal cases one must combine Ricardo and Ohlin to get the right answer.
7. The right answer will favour capital intensity in the countries which are short of capital if capital can be used without skill. As Leontief says, the real superiority of developed countries is not in capital-intensive but in skill-intensive industries, and though these two categories overlap, they are not identical.

50. THE PROTESTANT ETHIC AS A GENERAL PRECONDITION FOR ECONOMIC DEVELOPMENT*

Niles M. Hansen

Problems of economic development have inevitably stimulated interest in human motivation as it pertains to economic action. In this regard, frequent allusion has been made to Max Weber's *The Protestant Ethic and the Spirit of Capitalism.* This paper argues that understanding of Weber's thesis concerning both the Protestant ethic and capitalism has been frequently erroneous or incomplete, and that when his thought concerning the metaphysical foundations of economic rationality is seen in an adequate context its implications for economic motivation[1] and development problems are more important than has been generally acknowledged. More specifically, the present analysis holds that Weber's basic ideas concerning the practical economic effects of the economic actor's value orientation are valid within the framework of any given economic system.

The first two sections attempt to clarify Weber's thought concerning the nature of the Protestant ethic and its relation to capitalism. The remainder of the article deals with the contemporary significance of Weber's insight for economic development in Soviet Russia and in the newly developing countries.

The Protestant Ethic

One of the principal barriers to an understanding of this concept has been

*Reprinted from Niles M. Hansen, "The Protestant Ethic as a General Precondition for Economic Development," *Canadian Journal of Economics and Political Science,* November, 1963, pp. 462-473, by permission of the editor and author.

Dr. Hansen is Professor of Economics, University of Texas at Austin, and Director, Centre for Economic Development.

The author wishes to acknowledge the helpful comments and suggestions of Professor Arthur Schweitzer.

[1] Economic motivation was generally related to the social psychology of religion in Weber's thought. The section "Motives of Economic Activity," in *The Theory of Social and Economic Organization* is misleading, as Parsons points out, because it only deals with the "structural basis of an interest in income, without attempting to analyze the underlying motivation any further. Important contributions to various phases of this problem are to be found in other parts of Weber's work," notably his comparative studies of religion (Max Weber, *The Theory of Social and Economic Organization,* A. M. Henderson and Talcott Parsons, trans., Talcott Parsons, ed. (Illinois, 1947), p. 319).

the tendency of critics to link the ethic to a particular dogma. Professor Hagen, for example, claims that the Weber thesis holds "that industry and hence innovation are directly associated with religious dogma rather than the two being co-results of a third factor."[2] This conclusion is based on a study of denominational backgrounds of Scottish entrepreneurs during the Industrial Revolution (1760-1830). By linking Weber's thesis to Calvinist dogma and by taking the Presbyterians as the chief holders of Calvinist dogma, Professor Hagen is led to conclude that

> Weber's thesis refers not to conformity but to dogma, and if that thesis is correct, the Scottish Presbyterians even more than the English Nonconformists should be the innovators. But of the twelve Scottish entrepreneurs for whom we have information only three were members of the established Presbyterian Church. Another three were of dissenting Calvinist sects, two were Nonconformists, and four were Anglicans.
>
> It is clear, I think, that the common denominator is not dogma but independence — in psychological terms, need autonomy. . . . This conclusion countering the Weberian thesis is perhaps the most exciting addition to previous analysis suggested by the statistical study.[3]

Thus, according to Hagen, independence of judgment is the cause of entrepreneurial ability and religious nonconformity. But what of the fact that one-third of the entrepreneurs were Anglicans? "There is no inconsistency," states Hagen, because "Church membership is after all a formal matter which to some deviant individuals is not of central concern and with respect to which they may follow a conventional course." Thus, one of the Anglicans was attracted by the Quakers and another believed that Scripture rather than dogma was the sole guide to religious conduct. In other words, they were not typical Anglicans but were more interested in the ideals of the nonconforming sects.[4]

Professor Rostow has also limited the importance of the Protestant ethic to situations influenced by Calvinist dogma. He argues against proponents of the motivating significance of the Protestant ethic: "In a world where Samurai, Parsees, Jews, North Italians, Turkish, Russian, and Chinese civil servants (as well as Huguenots, Scotsmen, and British north-countrymen) have played the role of a leading élite in economic growth, John Calvin should not be made to bear quite this weight."[5] Here again Weber's concept is bound to a specific dogma.

Rostow further contends that "allusion to a positive scale of religious or other values" is not a sufficient condition for the emergence of a dynamic élite to spur economic growth. Two additional conditions must obtain: first, the élite "must feel itself denied the conventional routes to prestige and power by the traditional less acquisitive society of which it is a part," and, secondly, "the traditional society must be sufficiently flexible (or weak) to permit its members to seek material advance (or political power) as a route upwards, alternative to conformity."[6]

The above arguments raise three fundamental issues with respect to Weber's thought. First, did Weber argue for a monocausal theory, in psycho-

---

[2] Everett E. Hagen, *On the Theory of Social Change* (Illinois, 1962), p. 298.
[3] *Ibid.*
[4] *Ibid.*, pp. 298-99.
[5] W. W. Rostow, *The Stages of Economic Growth* (Cambridge, 1960), p. 51.
[6] *Ibid.*

logical terms, of the development of capitalism? Second, to what extent is Weber's concept of the Protestant ethic bound to Calvinist dogma? And third, in what degree is this concept held to be a sufficient condition for the appearance of modern capitalism?

It must be emphasized that *The Protestant Ethic* is only a fragment of Weber's work on world religions and economic history. A great deal of misunderstanding has resulted from failure to evaluate *The Protestant Ethic* in the larger context of his writings. Weber was always concerned with the motivational forces behind the appearance of modern rational capitalism in the Occident and its failure to emerge in other cultural contexts.[7] *The Protestant Ethic,* as one part of a larger system, attempts to

> explain genetically the special peculiarity of Occidental rationalism, and within this field that of the modern Occidental form. Every such attempt at explanation must, recognizing the fundamental importance of the economic factor, above all take account of the economic conditions. But at the same time the opposite correlation must not be left out of consideration. For though the development of economic rationalism is partly dependent on rational technique and law, it is at the same time determined by the ability and disposition of men to adopt certain types of practical rational conduct. When these types have been obstructed by spiritual obstacles, the development of rational economic conduct has also met serious inner resistance. . . . In this case we are dealing with the connection of the spirit of modern economic life with the rational ethics of ascetic Protestantism. Thus we treat here only one side of the causal chain.[8]

In view of Weber's intentions it is incorrect to argue, as H. M. Robertson has done, that "Weber attempted to establish a reverse chain of causation from that advanced by Marx in the economic interpretation of history. He sought a psychological determination of economic events."[9] There can be no doubt that Weber rejected economic determinism as found in Marx, but he also makes no claim to have found Marx standing on his head and turned him right side up with the help of Calvin. Weber does not speak of psychological determinism, but rather of "affinity" and "connection" between a psychological phenomenon and socio-economic conditions. He was clear that it was "not my aim to substitute for a one-sided materialistic an equally one-sided spiritualistic causal interpretation of culture and of history."[10]

Weber admitted that the data for his thesis were selected with a bias since his view is "by no means the only possible one from which the historical phenomena we are investigating can be analyzed."[11] This is in keeping with Weber's methodology, in which scientific concepts do not exhaust reality but involve selection, and are in this sense unreal. The relativity involved in the valuation and selection prevents their being considered as final concepts even within the logically possible limits of science. The "Protestant ethic" is an ideal type, a generalizing construct which attempts to explain what would happen under certain hypothetical conditions which are objectively possible in the world of concrete events. The ideal type is sufficiently abstract to be

---

[7] The nature of modern capitalism is discussed below.

[8] Max Weber, *The Protestant Ethic and the Spirit of Capitalism,* Talcott Parsons, trans. (New York, 1958), pp. 26-7.

[9] H. M. Robertson, *Aspects of the Rise of Economic Individualism* (Cambridge, 1935), p. xii.

[10] Weber, *Protestant Ethic,* p. 183.

[11] *Ibid.,* p. 47.

widely applicable and, in addition, is an exaggeration of empirical reality so that it may go beyond a merely common trait or a statistical average.[12]

Weber's ideal-typical method inevitably involved a certain neglect of the evolving historical character of Calvinist theology and its role in economic motivation. Tawney and Fischoff,[13] among others, have criticized Weber on this point. Such valid objections, however, easily lapse into an implicit assumption that Weber identified the Protestant ethic with certain dogmas of Calvin or Calvinism, an assumption made explicit by Hagen and Rostow. This obscures what is probably the basic contribution of Weber's thesis, namely, that the metaphysical orientation (be it Calvinist or otherwise) of the economic actor has a crucial (though not monocausal) influence on economic behaviour.

There should be no doubt that the power of the practical ethic to rationalize the organization of capital and labour is more important than the *particular* irrational dogmas which fostered the ethic. Weber was not concerned with dogma as such but with social and economic actions. In *The Protestant Ethic* he specifically stated that his purpose was to deal "with the connection of the spirit of modern economic life with the rational ethics of ascetic Protestantism."[14] The rational ethic is strictly a practical matter since Weber always maintained that the dogma behind the "rational ethics" was irrational. He was not concerned with theological compendia but "rather in something entirely different: the influence of those psychological sanctions which, originating in religious belief and the practice of religion, gave a direction to practical conduct and held the individual to it."[15] In a later study Weber again took up the relationship of the Protestant ethic to rational capitalism. His position was quite explicit: "The author has always underscored those features in the total picture of a religion which have been decisive for the fashioning of the *practical* way of life, as well as those which distinguish one religion from another."[16]

In view of the above it is difficult to see how Hagen can maintain "that industry and hence innovation are directly associated with religious dogma" in Weber's thought. Hagen's "refutation" of Weber's thesis is most curious. Although Weber explicitly used the term Puritan "always in the sense which it took on in the popular speech of the seventeenth century, to mean the ascetically inclined religious movements in Holland and England without distinction of Church organization or dogma, thus including Independents, Congregationalists, Baptists, Mennonites, and Quakers,"[17] Hagen limits the thesis to Scottish Presbyterians. In fact, the evidence which Hagen puts forth, including that which shows that the Anglican entrepreneurs were oriented toward the tenets of the ascetic sects, directly supports Weber's thesis. Moreover, Hagen's explanation of entrepreneurial motivation in terms of need autonomy is inadequate. Why should feelings of "need autonomy"

---

[12] For a more elaborate discussion of the ideal type see Talcott Parsons, *The Structure of Social Action* (New York, 1937), pp. 601-6.

[13] R. H. Tawney, *Religion and the Rise of Capitalism* (London, 1926), pp. 211-13; Ephriam Fischoff, "The Protestant Ethic and the Spirit of Capitalism: The History of a Controversy," *Social Research*, 11 (1944), pp. 61-77.

[14] Weber, *Protestant Ethic*, p. 27.

[15] *Ibid.*, p. 97.

[16] Max Weber, "The Social Psychology of the World Religions," in *From Max Weber: Essays in Sociology*, H. H. Gerth and C. Wright Mills, trans. and eds., (New York, 1958), p. 194. The italics are Weber's.

[17] Weber, *Protestant Ethic*, p. 217.

appear and result in increased industrial and innovational activity in Great Britain and not in Italy, Spain, or India? We are not told. As a more ultimate (though not exclusive) explanation, that of Weber is, by the principle of parsimony, more convincing.

Rostow's equation of the Protestant ethic with the thought of Calvin is similarly misleading. However, the basic part of his argument is that value orientation is not a sufficient explanation for the appearance of an entrepreneurial élite. Rostow's contention that "the new élite must feel itself denied the conventional routes to prestige and power by the traditional less acquisitive society of which it is a part" is erroneous because it implies that the acquisitive instinct is somehow the fundamental element in the development of modern capitalism. As Weber saw, the acquisitive impulse has always existed and is not to be confused with capitalism or economic rationality. The financial aristocracy of north Italy was certainly no less acquisitive than the northern Protestant bourgeoisie, but this did not produce the kind of rationalized entrepreneurship and labour in Italy that characterized the Protestant north. However, if the words "less acquisitive" are deleted from Rostow's condition, the resulting proposition is quite in harmony with Weber's own thought:[18]

> The development of a rational religious ethic has had positive and primary roots in the inner conditions of those social strata which were less socially valued.
>
> Strata in solid possession of social honor and power usually tend to fashion their status-legend in such a way [that] ... their sense of dignity feeds on their actual or alleged being. The sense of dignity of socially repressed strata or of strata whose status is negatively (or at least not positively) valued is nourished most easily on the belief that a special "mission" is entrusted to them; their worth is guaranteed or constituted by an *ethical imperative,* or by their own functional *achievement.* Their value is thus moved into something beyond themselves, into a "task".... Resentment has not been required as a leverage; the rational interest in material and ideal compensations as such has been perfectly sufficient.[19]

Weber is assuming, of course, that Rostow's second subcondition obtains, namely, that the traditional society is so constituted as to allow the minority an opportunity for spiritual and material compensation.

In general, then, Rostow's conditions for the emergence of an entrepreneurial élite do not add to what is already found in Weber, and even tend to obscure analysis of underlying motivation by the introduction of the "acquisitive" issue. In fact, his discussion of the "sources of entrepreneurship" does not throw any light on the question of motivation. Though he acknowledges that "constructive entrepreneurial acts of the take-off period" have rarely been guided by "motives of an unmixed material character,"[20] he does not show, as Weber does, how a metaphysical ethic may affect economic actions. By identifying the Protestant ethic with a particular dogma, Rostow, like Hagen, is led to undervalue the effects of the ascetic ethic in

---

[18] As Hoselitz has pointed out, Italian economic development was held back because the financial aristocracy would not allow sufficient flexibility for the Reformation to take roots in Italy (Bert Hoselitz, *Sociological Aspects of Economic Growth* (Glencoe, Illinois, 1960), p. 109). The issue here is not a matter of relative acquisitiveness but of a conflict between an entrenched traditional society and a repressed minority (see Rostow's second condition above).
[19] Weber, "Social Psychology of the World Religions," pp. 176-7. The emphasis is Weber's.
[20] Rostow, *The Stages of Economic Growth,* p. 52.

practical affairs.[21] Only Weber's analysis gives an adequate understanding of motivation and the conditions constraining or favouring nascent entrepreneurial activity.

The Protestant Ethic and Capitalism

It has been alleged that Weber attributed the rise of capitalism to the Protestant ethic. This has been most forcefully argued by H. M. Robertson: "If it is true that modern capitalism is the product of a new spirit of capitalism introduced with the Reformation, it must necessarily follow that there was no capitalism before that time."[22]

Such an argument has no justification from either *The Protestant Ethic* or Weber's work as a whole. In *The Protestant Ethic* he clearly stated that he had "no intention whatever of maintaining such a foolish and doctrinaire thesis as that the spirit of capitalism . . . could only have arisen as the result of certain effects of the Reformation, or even that capitalism as an economic system is a creation of the Reformation."[23]

The contention that Weber held that Protestantism gave birth to capitalism is refuted by numerous other works of Weber and Weber scholars, and the interested reader is referred to them.[24] Nevertheless, he believed that the development of modern capitalism was strongly reinforced and conditioned by the Protestant ethic and that capitalism took on unique attributes under its impetus.[25]

The effect of the Protestant ethic on saving and investment (not to be confused with the "acquisitive instinct") has generally been emphasized to such an extent that two other effects, no less important for modern capitalism, have tended to be disregarded: the capitalistic organization of labour and the technical utilization of scientific knowledge.

To Weber the dominant characteristic of precapitalistic labour is a desire

---

[21] The relevance of the ascetic ethic "beyond the orbit of Protestantism" is taken up below.
[22] Robertson, *Aspects of the Rise of Economic Individualism*, p. 33.
[23] Weber, *Protestant Ethic*, p. 91.
[24] See, for example, Weber, *General Economic History* (New York, 1961), pp. 207-13; *Protestant Ethic*, pp. 19-24; *Theory of Social and Economic Organization*, pp. 278-80; *From Max Weber*, Gerth and Mills, eds., pp. 168-9, 227. Excellent secondary sources are *From Max Weber*, pp. 65-9; Reinhard Bendix, *Max Weber: An Intellectual Portrait* (Garden City, 1960), pp. 71-99; and Fischoff, "Protestant Ethic and the Spirit of Capitalism."
It should be emphasized that Fischoff's widely known history of the Weber thesis controversy is deficient in at least two respects. He underrates Weber's emphasis on the causal importance of the Protestant ethic for modern capitalism by failing to distinguish clearly between the latter and the various types of political capitalism which have always existed in one form or another (p. 76). Secondly, he concludes that Weber's essay is more important in sharpening "our appreciation of . . . doctrinal history" and in paving "the way for the formulation of an adequate social theory of religion" than in promoting "our knowledge of past economic life" (p. 77). Such a conclusion is completely untenable both in view of Weber's stated aims in *The Protestant Ethic* and in the light of Weber's whole work on religion and economic behaviour.
[25] Although there was no simple mechanical relationship between the Protestant ethic and capitalism, the former evidenced a strong "elective affinity" with a capitalism that was already strongly emerging in many respects. "The term 'elective affinity' was taken from the title of a novel by Goethe. Weber used it frequently to express the dual aspect of ideas, i.e., that they were created or chosen by the individual ('elective') and that they fit in with his material interests ('affinity')." (Bendix, Max Weber, p. 85.)
In addition to the motivating force of the Protestant ethic, Weber held that six presuppositions were necessary for the emergence of modern capitalism: (1) rational capital accounting, (2) freedom of the market for labour and commodities, (3) rational technology, (4) calculable law, (5) free labour, and (6) commercialization of economic life (Weber, *General Economic History*, pp. 207-9).

to live according to custom, earning only enough to support traditional needs. The attitude that labour should be performed as if it were an end in itself is not a product of nature and cannot simply be evoked by more pay. The Protestant ethic was "bound to affect the productivity of labour in the capitalistic sense of the word. The treatment of labour as a calling became as characteristic of the modern worker as the corresponding attitude toward acquisition of the business man."[26]

Weber realized that the scientific progress initiated by the Renaissance, which did so much to lay the groundwork for modern capitalism, was not related to Protestantism in any important degree. Luther, for example, repudiated Copernicus, a Catholic. Even though Catholicism was frequently hostile to the new science, scientific progress and Protestantism must not be identified. Nevertheless, if the ascetic Protestant sects were not interested in pure science, they did foster important contributions to applied science, that is, to technology. Where the material needs of daily life were involved, the same rationalization which characterized entrepreneurship and labour was also applied to putting science in the service of technology and capitalist production.[27]

It is now necessary to consider the relevance of the Protestant ethic in the modern world.

The Contemporary Perspective

At the time of Weber's death the world of nineteenth-century Europe was in shambles. We are only now beginning to attain an adequate perspective of the changes wrought by the upheaval of the two world wars which marked the transition to the contemporary world. Nevertheless, it has already become clear that we live in "one world," where the liberal-democratic tradition of the West is in fundamental competition with communism (which was hardly a going concern at the time of Weber's death) for the allegiance of the newly developing countries. It is therefore pertinent to inquire whether or not the Protestant ethic has any relevance within this contemporary world setting.

There is no evidence that Weber attributed anything beyond purely historical significance to the concept. He had stated that "the religious root of modern economic humanity is dead; today the concept of the calling is a *caput mortuum* in the world."[28] To Weber the dominance of ascetic Protestantism was replaced by the optimism of the Enlightenment in economic thought. The invisible hand now came to guide economic behaviour in a "harmony of interests" within a new mechanical system which could, and did, dispense with transcendental motivation. In the end, then, Weber left capitalism in a completely secularized, but stable, state. Yet at the conclusion of his last work there is a certain tone of foreboding:

> Economic ethics arose against the background of the ascetic ideal; now it has

---

[26] Weber, *Protestant Ethic*, pp. 58-67, 178-79. Hannah Arendt notes that Weber's analysis of modern capitalism, including man's estimate of labour, is the only approach which has "raised the question of the modern age with the depth and relevance corresponding to its importance." (*The Human Condition* (Garden City, 1959), p. 369.)

[27] Weber, *General Economic History*, p. 270; *Protestant Ethic*, p. 249.

[28] Weber, *General Economic History*, p. 270.

been stripped of its religious import. It was possible for the working class to accept its lot as long as the promise of eternal happiness could be held out to it. When this consolation fell away it was inevitable that those strains and stresses should appear in economic society which since then have grown so rapidly.[29]

The "Protestant" Ethic and Soviet Russia

The "strains and stresses" which had already been evidenced in such events as the revolutions of 1848, the Paris Commune uprising, and the 1905 Revolution in Russia resulted in the final rupture, during World War I, of the emerging capitalism of Russia.

Despite the economic progress which had been made during the latter half of the nineteenth century, Russia lagged far behind the industrial West on the eve of the Revolution. By 1912 over three-fourths of the adult population were still peasants. Nobles, government officials, merchants, and burghers together accounted for little more than one-eighth of the population. In his classic on pre-Revolutionary Russia, Sir Donald Wallace noted that in 1912 "the scarcity of large towns in Russia is not less remarkable than their rustic appearance." Despite various reforms "the progress of the peasantry was not so rapid as could be wished." Furthermore, "many years" would still be required before "that wealthy enlightened *bourgeoisie* which Catherine endeavored to create by legislation . . . acquires sufficient social and political significance to deserve the title of *tiers-état.* "[30]

One of the major drawbacks to material progress in Tsarist Russia was lack of a practical rationalizing force in economic affairs equivalent to the world-oriented ascetic ethic of the Protestant West. As Weber emphasized, in all cultures other than that in which modern capitalism developed, practical rational economic motivation had been largely precluded by religious attitudes which emphasized magic, sacerdotalism, or other-worldliness in one form or another. These factors certainly characterized pre-Revolutionary Russia.[31]

Wallace noted "the strong tendency both in the clergy and in the laity to attribute an inordinate importance to the ceremonial element of religion." Religion in the Russian Church was "simply a mass of mysterious rites, which have a secret magical power of averting evil in this world and securing felicity in the next." He remarked that the Protestant concept of an "inner religious life" was completely foreign; in its place "the ceremonial part of religion suffices." The Russian peasant had "the most unbounded, childlike confidence in the saving efficacy of the rites which he practices."[32] It is, therefore, not surprising that the revolutionaries attempted to eradicate the old religious basis of Russian culture. In its place they introduced the religion of Marxism, with its surrogate Protestant ethic.

---

[29] *Ibid.*

[30] Sir Donald Mackenzie Wallace, *Russia on the Eve of War and Revolution* (New York, 1961), pp. 93, 176, 193, 367.

[31] It is pertinent to note that in the Russian steppes a religious sect called the Molokánye possessed doctrines similar to those of Presbyterianism, though the sect had no apparent contact with the West. In contrast to their fellow Russians the Molokánye were characterized "by their sobriety, uprightness, and material prosperity." Since the Molokánye did not appear to be different from the surrounding population in any respect but religion, this factor must be given its due as a determinant of their material progress. See *ibid.*, pp. 392-401.

[32] *Ibid.*, pp. 371-91.

It was emphasized above that the particular dogma giving rise to the Protestant ethic is of secondary importance. There is no necessity that it even be "Protestant" in the theological sense, though its irrational metaphysics must foster a worldly oriented rationality in economic life. Textbook discussions of the operations of the Soviet economy rarely give more than lip service, if that, to the power of Communist ideology to provide the type of metaphysical conviction necessary to overcome traditionalist attitudes in favour of methodically rational economic behaviour. The denunciations of cruelty and repression which characterizes our public discourse on communism are not without applicability to Calvin's Geneva.

> But such denunciations, far from . . . clarifying our understanding of socialism and communism, only serve to muddy our minds. They obscure the fact that the literature of socialist protest is one of the most moving and morally searching of all chronicles of human hope and despair. . . . It is very doubtful if the Church . . . would come off much worse than communism from the point of view of betrayal of original ideas. . . . Certainly history should teach us that it is only by penetrating to the inspirational fervor which they evoke . . . that we can begin to understand the full force behind these secular religions of our time.[33]

Crane Brinton's historical perspective on Marxism is particularly relevant:

> It stands toward the central democratic form of the Enlightenment in some ways as Calvinism stands toward traditional Christianity of the Roman Catholics . . . Marxism is a rigorous, dogmatic, puritanical, determinist, firmly disciplined sect. . . .
>
> Marxism, especially as it has been worked out in Russia, is one of the most active forms of religion in the world today. . . .
>
> Indeed, there is, in almost the common acceptance of the term, a *puritanical* aspect of Marxism; the Marxist is as scornful as any Calvinist of the merely Epicurean side of life, of vulgar, gross pleasures and even more of their aristocratic refinements.[34]

There are two principal ways by which Marxist ideology has affected economic change in Russia. First, it has been a direct motivating force in the lives of the "devout," those who feel a duty to forward the industrialization process and thus usher in the heavenly city of the classless society (in both Puritanism and Communism a determinist philosophy paradoxically results in active effort to implement the state of salvation), and, secondly, it has provided a "legitimate"[35] basis for the social and political order within which economic development has taken place.[36]

---

[33] Robert L. Heilbroner, *The Future as History* (New York, 1959), pp. 113-14.

[34] Crane Brinton, *Ideas and Men* (New York, 1950), pp. 478-79, 485. The emphasis is Brinton's.

[35] Weber discusses the basis of the legitimacy of an order in *Theory of Social and Economic Organization*, pp. 130-32. He notes that "Submission to an order is almost always determined by a variety of motives. . . . In a very large proportion of cases, the actors subject to the order are of course not even aware how far it is a matter of custom, of convention, or of law."

[36] The effect of religion on Japanese economic development was primarily felt through its influence on the structure in which economic change took place. The *samurai* class of aristocratic officials was motivated by an ideology which fundamentally contributed to Japan's industrialization, a process which took place primarily under government auspices. *Samurai* ethics encouraged business enterprise, hard work, and frugality, as contrasted with purely speculative or acquisitive behaviour. See Robert N. Bellah, *Tokugawa Religion: The Values of Pre-Industrial Japan* (Illinois, 1957), pp. 187-93.

The practical consequences of Marxist ideology in the Soviet Union are illustrated by the following:

> Persistence, industriousness, all-out effort, the constant striving for perfectionist goals, the refusal to be satisfied with what one has attained — such qualities were of course related to the "building of Communism," that is, the tasks enunciated by the party leaders. Virtuous conduct in personal life was inseparable from political life.[37]
>
> The "New Man" in Soviet psychology is he who overcomes his anarchic spontaniety in favor of leaderlike abstinence from immediate impulse gratification; he who suppresses sentiment and private feeling through systematic thought and planned purposeful activity in wholehearted pursuit of the party line. Virtue and charisma are attached by the culture to those who show this rational mastery over impulse and greed as against mere passive capacity to endure deprivation.[38]

Thus, although the Communist and capitalist systems are externally different, each has required a religious (or ideological) component to motivate methodical, rational application of human means toward economic ends; and the effects of the metaphysical orientation have been quite similar.[39] Of course New Soviet Man is not simply a twentieth-century ascetic Protestant.[40] Emulation of Western technology, patriotism, education,[41] and coercion have all contributed to shaping Soviet economic development; yet there is no reason to believe that any of these factors could, in itself, provide the intensity of motivation necessary for sustained industrial expansion.

Finally, if the Soviet pattern follows that of the West, it may be expected that the fervour of the motivating ideology will subside once the economic system becomes a "going concern." There are already clear indications that ideological intensity is subsiding in favour of a kind of Victorian conformity and bureaucratic efficiency. Of this we shall have more to say below.

The Protestant Ethic and the Economically Underdeveloped Countries

It has been argued that historically the "Protestant" ethic has been necessary for the achievement of relatively high sustained growth within both capitalist and communist frameworks. It may be expected, therefore, that a similar

---

[37] Ralph T. Fisher, Jr., "The Soviet Model of the Ideal Youth," in *The Transformation of Russian Society* Cyril E. Black, ed., (Cambridge, Mass., 1960), p. 628.

[38] Henry V. Dicks, "Some Notes on the Russian National Character," *ibid.,* p. 640.

[39] The feeling of a "calling" in Soviet life is quite akin to that of the Puritans. See Gabriel Jaray, *Tableau de la Russie jusqu'à la mort de Staline* (Paris, 1954), pp. 55-58.

[40] In keeping with Lenin's expectations the psychology and customs of the peasants have been very slow to change. Consequently the agricultural sector has been notoriously lagging.
Rostow contrasts the problems created by the "easy-going psychology" of the peasants with the Soviet proletariat, which "is a new class . . . without long tradition or collective memory." (W. W. Rostow, *The Dynamics of Soviet Society* (New York, 1952), p. 222.)

[41] Puritan and Marxist ideologies have each lent themselves to fostering literacy and learning; in each case education has been regarded not so much as an end in itself as a tool for the furtherance of sectarian goals.
The general effects of nationalism on economic development have not yet received the attention they deserve. Nationalist sentiments may be useful in promoting a feeling of obligation conducive to the rational application of labour and capital accumulation. But this is by no means necessarily the case, for, as Lewis has pointed out, "the 'new men' in politics and the 'new men' in economic activity are not the same, do not necessarily spring from the same class, and are not always in sympathy with each other." For a more general discussion of these issues see W. Arthur Lewis, *The Theory of Economic Growth* (Homewood, Illinois, 1955), pp. 26-29, 153-54, 423-24.

phenomenon will be required for growth in the present underdeveloped countries, where, with varying degress of intensity,

> there has been no bridge between religion and the practical action of the workaday world. In such cases, the economy and all other actions in the world has [*sic*] been considered religiously inferior, and no psychological motives for worldly action could be derived from the attitude cherished as the supreme value. In their innermost beings, contemplative and ecstatic religions have been rather specifically hostile to economic life.[42]

Religious influences will not rationalize daily life where the supreme values are contemplative in nature or where the means of grace are purely magical or sacramental in character. For example, Professor Hsu has stated that "Weber came closer to the truth than any other scholar" in attributing lack of economic development in China to Confucian ethics.[43]

Granting development aid funds to an underdeveloped country will not in itself foster the emergence of an entrepreneurial class or an economically practical labour force of sufficient importance to provide a foundation for self-sustained growth. In this respect, the efforts of the United States are at a distinct disadvantage compared to those of the Soviet Union, which exports not only funds and technical advice, but also a rationalizing ideology with the power to capture and dominate the minds of men. While the specific metaphysical foundations of capitalist motivation have largely lost their significance in the modern world, those of Communism have not.[44]

The present perspective indicates that rationalizing forces already present within most underdeveloped societies might be exploited to help secure economic development. Ideological and religious values which have been dismissed as irrational and of only negative significance to economic growth can be used in many cases as motivational bases for rational economic action.

In India, for example, groves of acacia trees were better tended when they were designated Krishnaban (Krishna grove); a similar situation obtained in Greece when plantings were accompanied by the ritual blessing of the Orthodox priest. Citations from the Koran have been effectively used in numerous instances to reinforce health and developmental measures.[45] Of even greater interest are the activities of the more ascetic and reform-minded elements within major non-Christian religions. Geertz, in his study of social and economic change in Indonesia, has noted that

---

[42] Weber, "Social Psychology of the World Religions," p. 289.

[43] Francis L. K. Hsu, "Cultural Factors," in *Economic Development: Principles and Patterns,* H. F. Williamson and John A. Buttrick, eds., (Englewood Cliffs, New Jersey, 1954), pp. 332-33, Hsu mistakenly accuses Weber of ethnocentrism because he called the Confucian ethic irrational. Weber in fact attributed a high degree of rationality to Confucianism as such; it was irrational only in its effects on practical economic life. See Weber, "Social Psychology of the World Religions," p. 293-4.

[44] The thousands of persons in underdeveloped countries who are willing to risk their lives on behalf of Marxist ideology are as conspicuous by their presence as those willing to do likewise for capitalism (much less Protestantism) are by their absence. From the liberal-democratic viewpoint this may be deplorable, but this philosophy is largely meaningless to those lacking at least a satisfactory minimum of material goods.

Were it not for the East-West struggle for the allegiance of the underdeveloped areas the ideological fervour of the Soviets would probably have abated more into bureaucratic conformity than it has already. This is, of course, not applicable to China, whose economy is not yet a really "going concern."

[45] George M. Foster, *Traditional Cultures: and the Impact of Technological Change* (New York, 1962), pp. 160-62.

In the light of the theories of Max Weber concerning the role of Protestantism in stimulating the growth of a business community in the West, it is perhaps not surprising that the leaders in the creation of such a community in Modjokuto are for the most part intensely Reformist Moslems, for the intellectual role of Reform in Islam has, at least in some ways, approached that of Protestantism in Christianity.

Thus despite marked cultural differences, economic development in Modjokuto is tending to take the classic form we have known in the West. An at least in part religiously motivated, generally disesteemed group . . . arising out of a tradition-alized trading class . . . [is] attempting to secure an improved status in a changed society through the rational, systematic pursuit of wealth.[46]

Similarly, McClelland has found that Weber's concept of the Protestant ethic is by no means limited to the history of the West. In India, for example, it also appears to be the ascetic religious sects like the Jains and the Parsees who have been most successful in business. "In neither the East nor the West has it been the secular-minded materialists, primarily interested in money and what it will buy for them personally who have been successful in business."[47]

Thus there is diverse evidence indicating that already existing values can be used to motivate economic growth. Nevertheless, there is a marked tendency in economic thought to neglect the importance of religious values in underdeveloped countries, or to underestimate the difficulties involved in attempting to alter existing institutions radically. Wolf, for example, has suggested that values and motives be altered by changing existing institutions.[48] In the light of existing evidence this would, if pushed to its logical conclusion, favour the methods adopted in China. Perhaps this path will ultimately prove to be the most feasible from an economic point of view, but a liberal-democratic philosophy of development precludes such a choice. Moreover, in attempting to impose our own values we may only foster resentment.

Since Tönnies, and especially since Max Weber, it has become a commonplace of social science that the world of the illiterate is of necessity a world peopled by sacred beings and given richness and meaning primarily by sacred values. To him, his government, his social order and his political decisions are like to appear as religious institutions, while our . . . efforts appear to be lacking in religious significance, or even to be grossly anti-religious. We often forget this, or we badly under-estimate its importance.[49]

In general, then, it has been argued that Weber's concept of the Protestant ethic has much broader applicability than even he could realize, and that this fact has been obscured by criticism based on inaccurate or misleading premises. Religious or ideological motivation is one of the fundamental prerequisites for economic development within any given system. Development along democratic lines cannot overturn existing values and institutions

---

[46] Clifford Geertz, "Social Change and Economic Modernization in Two Indonesian Towns: A Case in Point," in Hagen, *On the Theory of Social Change*, p. 394.
[47] Quoted in Benjamin Higgins, *Economic Development* (New York, 1959), p. 300.
[48] Charles Wolf, Jr., "Institutions and Economic Development," *American Economic Review* (December, 1955), pp. 867-83.
[49] Bruce L. Smith, "Communications Research on Non-Industrial Countries," *Public Opinion Quarterly*, 16 (Winter, 1952), p. 535.

nor can our own be imposed on societies in which they have no meaning. However, practical economic motivation can be implemented within existing institutions, perhaps by education which emphasizes those aspects of a given religion which favour rational economic application in this world. The precise way in which this may be done on a large scale is beyond the scope of the economist's tools, but the pressures of Marxist ideology leave little time for inaction.

51. CANADIAN INTERNATIONAL ASSISTANCE*

Maurice F. Strong

There has been, throughout the 1960s, a steady increase in the importance and priority which the Canadian Government has given to international assistance. At the time of greatest government austerity, in this year's budget, when many other departments were having expenditures cut back or frozen, the authorization for CIDA was increased by $28 million to a total of $364 million. And in the foreign policy review, the firm commitment is made to increase it by a further $60 million next year and, in future years, to try to increase the percentage of the national income allocated to development assistance; this means, in effect, a minimum increase each year of about $40 million. The aim, as the Paper says, is to move Canada "towards the internationally accepted targets." These are themselves "moving targets": they have been changed during the sixties, and we are again confronted with a new set of targets as we face the second Development Decade. They are useful as a means of providing impetus toward an improved performance, but they are not adequate as a measure of the real value and effectiveness — or even the relative performance — of the rich countries' contributions to the LDCs. When you consider that Portugal is at the top of the tables compiled by the Development Assistance Committee (DAC) which are based on presently accepted targets, and when you consider the DAC figures can include aid to present as well as former colonies, I think you'll see the weakness of the targets as a basis for comparison. Certainly, Canada's performance would be considerably enhanced if these tables included development aid to our own less developed regions.

Nevertheless, by any standard — the DAC tables or a broader comparison — there is on Canada's part a quickening of the assistance effort; the importance of that, at a time when the effort of some major donors seems to be slackening, needs to be stressed.

Volume of aid, of course, is one index. Quality is quite as important. The

---

*Remarks by Maurice F. Strong on September 19, 1970, during the International Teach-In at the University of Toronto. Reproduced by permission of the speaker.
Dr. Strong left the Presidency of the Canadian International Development Agency at the end of 1970 to become Secretary General of the 1972 UN Conference on Human Environment. Formerly he was President of Power Corporation, Montreal.

reorganization which has taken place inside CIDA in recent years, the recruitment of professionals to the CIDA staff, the posting to embassies and high commissions abroad of CIDA field personnel, these are among the many measures which have improved the quality of our operations. The spreading of the Canadian program through Africa during the sixties, with the Franco-phone section as large now as that in Commonwealth Africa, has meant we have tapped a good deal of Canadian talent to serve in those countries which was not attracted to the earlier program in Asia. And this year we are launching a selective bilateral program in Latin America which will utilize more varied talent. These changes, coupled with the comparatively generous terms of development finance which Canada now offers, give us a fair claim to saying that we have today one of the most enlightened programs among the seventeen donor countries that are grouped in the Development Assistance Committee (or DAC). I would dare to say that, if you were to canvass professionals from other countries working in the development field, they would tell you the Canadian program is among the best of the bilateral operations.

Only Sixteen Months of our Defence Budget

But none of this means that we are saints. Canada spent a lot more money on waging war between 1939 and 1945 than it has on helping the poorer countries since. Even today our twenty years of aid authorizations, amounting to $2,500,000,000 are only equivalent to sixteen months of this country's present defence budget. And for several years our actual disbursements have lagged considerably below authorizations, although this gap is now being closed. Last year we disbursed $308,000,000, a leap from the $186,000,000 of the year before.

There is one reservation I have to make here. Many of us would like to see much more done. But no government can be that far ahead of what the general public is prepared to support. Having said that, I should add that I am cheered by the way in which the governments of Lester Pearson and Pierre Trudeau have set the priorities of international assistance up against the immediate and visible demands they face at home, and given an increasingly significant priority to international assistance. "The world must be our constituency," Mr. Trudeau said in Edmonton in 1968. Since then, his government has acted in that spirit.

Another encouraging move has been the initiative taken by Canada to help spread more fairly between the rich and poor nations the benefits derived from modern science and technology. It is one of the sadder ironies of twentieth-century development that the inventions of science and technology have on the whole only served to widen the gap between rich and poor.

While the northern states grew strong and rich through these inventions and their thriving markets stimulated further research for new materials, almost the opposite has happened to the south. Modern medicine has dramatically cut the death rate of populations in the LDCs, but modern technology has only just begun to help them produce the food and the other materials which they need if they are to be assured of a decent life on even basic terms. In some areas research has clearly worked against the interests of the LDCs: not only is 98 percent of the world's expenditure on research and development still made in the industrialized countries, according to a recent study, but there is almost as much money spent in those countries on developing synthetics as is spent on all forms of research and development in the poorer countries; and synthetics, of course, can cut away at the very foundations of a poorer country's export economy, as Tanzanians well know from the problems that now beset their sisal industry.

The imbalance can probably only be corrected by deliberate acts of policy on the part of the industrialized nations. It was at any rate in this belief that the Canadian Government launched the International Development Research Centre, and provisionally committed $30,000,000 toward its budget for the first five years. Much of the Centre's research will take place in developing countries; all its work will be aimed at easing those countries' problems. When the twenty-one member board of directors, including ten from other countries, holds its first meeting in October, the Centre will be on its way to tackling a most significant task.

Tied Aid, and How to Untie It

Now let me turn to some of the criticisms of the Canadian and other programs. I have talked about the volume of aid; the real value of it is undoubtedly reduced by the conditions surrounding procurement which are tied to many offers of assistance. Tied aid can reduce the real value to the recipient by as much as 40 percent in some extreme cases. By requiring that a recipient country shop for its capital equipment in your own market, it restricts the range of choice, reduces competition, and can load the recipient country with considerably higher costs. The Pearson and Peterson reports came down strongly on the side of untying aid as widely and quickly as possible; and there is no compelling economic justification for tied aid, since the reduced value to the recipients cannot be justified by any corresponding benefits that it brings to the economy of the donor.

The obvious question that follows is: why do we persist in tying any of our aid? In facing that question, I should first make some specific points about the nature of Canadian tied aid. First, although I have quoted a figure of 40 percent reduction in the face value with some cases of tied aid, this is the extreme figure. The Canadian tying provisions have resulted in an average reduction of more like 5 to 8 percent; the reduction in value is that much smaller on average because many of the tying arrangements involve Canadian goods that are of a competitive price in the world market, most notably food products. Capital equipment, on which tying restrictions have the heaviest effect, is a smaller item in Canada's list when compared to other donor countries.

Secondly, the amount of our assistance that is now to be subject to any tying requirements is now only about 50 percent of the total. This is one of the major advances achieved this year, and consolidated in the policy review. Before this year the requirement that there should be an 80 percent Canadian content in any particular tied project was relaxed to 66 $^2/_3$ percent. Then this year a number of other changes have been authorized which substantially reduce the tied aid element in the Canadian program: (1) the decision that 20 percent of our bilateral assistance can be offered on a completely untied basis; (2) the increase in the multilateral proportion of our aid total to about 25 percent; (3) the decision that Canada should absorb the shipping costs which the recipient countries have up to now borne on Canadian goods; (4) the increase in our support of the program of private agencies; and (5) the launching of the International Development Research Centre, for which financing will be provided on an untied basis.

These changes have the effect of reducing the proportion of Canadian aid that is tied to less than 50 percent. There are problems in moving further — at least, in moving further on a unilateral basis. A good deal of public support for the development aid program, particularly in the business community, has been based on the fact that it is used largely to finance the provision of Canadian goods and services to the LDCs, thus providing an important source of financing for Canadian exports and of jobs for Canadians. It would be difficult to sustain this support if Canadian aid funds were seen as being used, to too great an extent to finance purchase of materials and equipment in other countries which denied similar opportunities to Canadian suppliers. Other countries, of course, have similar problems and this is why the question of untying must ultimately be resolved by internationally agreed action that involves all the major donors. I am pleased to say that important progress is now being made in this direction under the auspices of DAC, and as a direct result of the Pearson Commission recommendations on the subject.

Breaking the Multilateral Logjam

Another significant issue has been the proportion of assistance Canada and others should offer through multilateral channels. Our proportion, ranging between 15 and 20 percent, has in the past been much higher than the average for the DAC countries, which is under 11 percent. Now, as a result of the policy review, we have set our aim at 25 percent.

In principle, I am convinced that development assistance must be made more and more multilateral. But here again, there are important practical constraints on the rate at which we can move in this direction. Many donor countries attach great importance to the direct relationships they maintain with the developing countries receiving their assistance under bilateral programs; and indeed a great deal of their aid has its basis in the special ties between particular donors and recipients which have resulted from their colonial past. Also the capacity of the multilateral development organizations to utilize aid funds effectively is in itself a constraint on the rate of growth of multilateralization although the capacity of these institutions is growing steadily. The recent report by Sir Robert Jackson on the development capacity of the United Nations system documents very candidly the limitations in its capacity to use more funds effectively, following a period of impressive growth. Also, it should be said that despite the advantages and principles of multilateral aid there are still many kinds of aid, particularly in the technical assistance area, that can be more effectively administered on a bilateral basis. And the distinctions between bilateral and multilateral aid are themselves becoming, in many instances, much less sharp and important. For bilateral aid is being provided to a growing extent within a multilateral framework, in which donors' programs are more closely co-ordinated and subjected to the application of much more rigorous development criteria.

Canada is playing a very positive role both in increasing the resources available to the multilateral agencies and increasing the degree of multilateral co-ordination and influence on bilateral programs. It is a solid supporter of the UN Development Program which combines preinvestment surveys with technical assistance; and it took a leading part, at the end of 1968, in the moves to replenish the funds of the World Bank affiliate, the International Development Association. The IDA, because it offers fifty-year interest-free loans (as Canada also does), was the most hopeful source of finance for projects of many of the poorest countries, and the drying up of its funds in 1967-68 produced a major logjam.

Canada not only led the way in helping to break this logjam but also agreed to increase its contributions in order to make up the shortfall in the contributions of some other members. Canada also took an important initiative in the agreement reached recently for replenishment of the International Development Association for the next three years at a level of $800,000,000 per year — double the previous level. Again, we agreed to make a contribution in excess of our normal pro rata share to make this possible.

Political Strings and Trade Versus Aid

Bilateral programs involve political strings — that is inherent in any relationship between governments. The strings, of course, may never be tugged or even tweaked. In Canada's case political considerations undoubtedly have counted in the selection of countries receiving Canadian aid during this past decade, in a new concentration on the Commonwealth Caribbean states, in Francophone and in Commonwealth Africa. But they don't count in the same way in the choice of projects undertaken in those countries. For example, political or ideological strings have not been a factor in Canada's relations with two African states which are following a distinctively socialist path, Tanzania and Algeria. Conversely, political considerations played what I assume most of this audience would call a proper part in determining that Canada offer Botswana this year the largest single loan yet made to any African state — $18,000,000 to provide power generating equipment for the country's new mining industry — and a loan that will help reduce Botswana's economic dependence upon neighbouring South Africa.

Another subject at issue is the question of trade. It is sometimes posed as the slogan "Trade rather than aid." At this stage, though, they can't be thought of as alternatives to each other. We need to aid, and help build up, their capacity to earn from trade. At the same time, we shouldn't be using aid as a substitute for not making more fundamental changes in our trading arrangements. Aid is in one sense the easy stage, the stage of buying time to do the more difficult job of changing the world trading patterns which are dictated today by the developed countries. This is an awkward area even for Canada in prosperous days, and made more difficult by higher levels of unemployment in areas where trade changes could have most effect.

Again, I should inject a reservation on this subject. Some people have suggested that if Canada dropped all its tariff barriers to the developing countries it would do them far more good than our present or future assistance programs. That is carrying possible effects into wild exaggeration. A study of this point done for the CIDA review by M. Pierre Frechette suggested that a total elimination of tariffs would provide the developing countries with a maximum additional $50 million of trade; and that $50 million would be worth much less than that amount, as an equivalent of direct aid. (His study was based on 1964 figures, and although the base is broader today the proportional increase would be roughly similar, due to the limits of what economists call "demand elasticity." The developing countries could, for instance, expect to increase the sale of their primary products here by only about 7 percent. The increase of manufactured and semimanufactured goods would be greater, certainly, but they start from a smaller base of sales.)

Having said that, I should add that there has been some hard work done by the DAC countries in efforts to agree on arrangements for giving preferential rates to products from developing countries. The UN Conference on Trade and Development, with delegations from 121 countries, agreed unanimously in New Delhi two years ago to plan what is called a "generalized system of preferences" for the developing countries, which could increase their export earnings and promote their industrialization. The general hope then was to have the system in operation by 1970. That hasn't happened; but in the course of many subsequent meetings, some important steps have been taken toward agreement. The problems that remain are not all due to hesitation by industrialized countries to lower tariffs far enough, or open their markets to enough products, or to their insistence on safeguards and escape clauses to protect some of their own industries if they look like becoming the victims of these new cheaper imports. Certainly there are stumbling blocks here. But another controversial issue — the question of existing preferences — has tended to divide both the LDCs and the industrialized countries among themselves. For example, the African states which have a preferential association with the European Economic Community are reluctant to see such regional preferences eliminated, while Latin American states line up with the United States in wanting that to happen. The Canadian hope is that these regional preferences can be harmonized and fitted into a general system of preferences, while on the issue of tariff cuts, the Canadian offer has been seen by most LDCs as wide enough in scope — although criticized by some as not yet being deep enough. The negotiations during the next few months, while likely to be difficult, may also be decisive.

There are nontariff barriers for these countries also to cross to get access to our markets, and one of them is obviously the knowledge barrier. We need to help them improve their marketing. One of Canada's first bilateral programs in Latin America is a pioneering scheme to advise Brazilian exporters on prospects for marketing their products in Canada.

The building up of the LDCs' trading ability involves the transfer of technological and management techniques. I think Gunnar Myrdal, in his latest book *The Challenge of World Poverty,* makes an important point when he puts his weight behind proposals to speed this transfer through "management contracts." These proposals involve a developing country making a contract with a foreign concern, not to come in as a fully-fledged entity that could in the end prompt resentment and nationalization but as a management unit that might also provide some initial capital but which is paid off on a strict fee basis. It would be paid for the job it does in building up an industry and in training local replacements for themselves. This sort of arrangement could avoid some of the suspicion that surrounds repatriation of profits by foreign firms.

Now, having plunged you into the depths of a lot of figures and facts about the Canadian program, let me soar for a while in the clearer air — or is it the clouds? — and open up the wider question behind all aid programs. What is the role of aid? Does it really help the developing countries? Does it represent or support a new form of "colonialism"? Are the donor countries hurting the chances of these countries to find their own best way to a more worthwhile life?

Speaking personally, I have a great deal of respect for some of the views of those who think aid can do (and has on occasions done) harm in encouraging people of the developing countries in the wrong kinds of activity, and in loading them with economic and social costs quite out of line with what they ultimately see as their best long-term interests, and in supporting existing power structures and institutional arrangements which are admittedly inadequate. Ivan Illich has put this thought often very vividly. In an article last November in *The New York Review of Books* he began by saying: "We recognize at once that the importation of Cadillacs should be heavily taxed in Peru, that an organ transplant clinic is a scandalous plaything to justify the concentration of more doctors in Bogota"; and he then went further to argue against the value system that fills the roads with private cars rather than buses, and that puts such emphasis on impressive school buildings for the young and neglects adult education. Gunnar Myrdal has also begun to criticize the way in which a small upper class dominates (and in practice distorts) the basis of a developing country's educational efforts. "Status and degrees are given undue importance, reflecting the system of valuations in an élite society," he says and also observes that "Adult education is played down everywhere in the non-Communist world." We in the richer countries must take a good deal of blame for this situation, for material belongings, status, and degrees have been the values respected here and we have had few qualms in transplanting these attitudes to other countries.

Does this, though, mean that because some aspects of aid programs can distort values, or consolidate a distortion of them, we should withdraw entirely lest any touch from us taints or twists their growth? I do not think so. Western influences would still permeate those countries, through television and magazines and many other sources, long after every CIDA expert and CUSO worker had been pulled home. Rather, the experience gained by those Canadians working abroad should — if they are sensitive — lead them to question profoundly the values which they mostly accepted uncritically when at home. I know that this has happened in the case of many CUSO returned volunteers, and I welcome it.

Again, to concentrate predominantly upon the harm which aid programs may do makes it very easy for those who say, "Don't do anything." We cannot make perfection in the existing arrangements and institutional mechanisms a precondition for action. It could all too easily provide an excuse for us to fall back to the laissez-faire days of unconcern and irresponsibility. No doubt, there are people who argue that this would be a preferable situation, that there would be less exploitation than exists today. I cannot agree. With all its deficiencies, direct aid, even when it has been motivated by dubious political and economic considerations, has made an important contribution to improving the lot and the prospects in life for millions of the world's poor people. True, it hasn't solved the fundamental problems of world poverty and, at present levels at least, cannot be relied upon alone to do this. But aid programs have done, and can do, much to help. And there has been, I believe, a strong underlying element of internationalism in the aid programs of the last two decades, despite narrower considerations that are sometimes visible on top.

If this were not so, why have nearly all developing countries — except China — continued to want some help from the outside? It is one thing for some of us, at this luxurious distance, to be theoretically against aid; but we have to assume that the governments of these countries really know what they want. That is not to deny that much of what we offer may turn out to by less valuable to them than they hoped, because of the conditions we have been in the habit of attaching to it.

Profound Changes in our Time

It is clear by now that some of the present institutional and structural arrangements in developing countries must be changed — in some cases, radically. Indeed, some significant changes are under way. I have been impressed how in several countries — and Tanzania and Algeria are examples — the political leaders have been able to make profound changes, and at the same time had the confidence and ability to accept foreign assistance and use it to their own clear advantage. And the Chinese achievement of the last twenty years is impressive for the way that they have managed to reach a respectable level of development without much foreign assistance, and indeed none in recent years.

There is no question that in many countries, radical — even revolutionary — changes must be made within the societies before economic and social development can hope to effect a real improvement in the lot of the masses of their people. In some such cases foreign aid can in fact help postpone such changes by creating the illusion of growth and sustaining regimes that are resistant to real change. But this does not mean that revolution is the answer everywhere, and I am equally convinced that there are many instances in which the people of developing societies would benefit most from changes which can be carried out in a more peaceful and evolutionary manner. Canada is surely an example of my point. The poor in Canada today are far less imprisoned in poverty than their fathers and grandfathers were; and our society has not had to be completely overturned for the great majority of Canadians to enjoy a better way of life.

A little time back, I touched on the benefit to Canadians who work abroad, that their eyes are opened to issues at home which they may have brushed past before. Only the supremely arrogant would suggest we are the purveyors of all wisdom about development. (In parenthesis, the distinction made in jargon between "developing" and "developed" countries unfortunately feeds this arrogance.) Many, and I hope most, of the Canadians who are working abroad discover that developing countries provide lessons that have relevance to Canadian problems. The plain truth is that we have not dealt with many social and economic problems as well as some of the new nations are now doing. I can cite the disruption of families during the process of urbanization, the wreckage that is sometimes left of a rural community and the loneliness of new urban workers. The problems of development, the many side effects of change, are most acutely seen in the alternatives facing Canadian Indians today.

It is important to stress, as the Pearson Report does in greater detail, that the developing countries have overcome enormous difficulties to achieve results in these last ten or twenty years which compare well with what countries in the Western world achieved at their stage. And that phrase itself is misleading; for our stages of development have been strung out over generations, while the new countries of Africa and Asia have had to face tasks telescoped very dauntingly into a short time frame. The tasks they face of welding national unity, building up a competent civil service, planning for an equitable distribution of wealth and opportunities among their peoples, these and other tasks come thick upon them in the first years of independence; we in contrast have been allowed generations of time to tackle these issues.

Not by GNP Alone

But now comes a sober note. We should be very realistic in seeing that, even if these countries reach the highest targets of economic growth and we for our part meet the top targets for transfer of resources, the net result will still be a widening of the absolute gap between the rich and the poor countries. The Pearson Report makes this point clearly, even when it optimistically calculates the years it will take Chile or Gabon to reach the standard of living which the French enjoy today. The world of 1990 or 2000 A.D. is still going to be divided between a rich minority and the poor and the very poor who will represent the majority of mankind. If we confine our attempts to build a better world within these targets, the best we can hope to do is to improve, if only by a little, the lot of the very poor. Implicit in the exhortations of targeteers is the suggestion that we are going to solve all problems by achieving their targets. I think it is dangerous to suggest that this could be so.

Is this, then, the sort of society we should want for the world? Success, in the terms of the aid targeteers, is not going to produce a truly just and equitable world society. To rely upon the growth of the Gross National Product as a prime index of progress is a practice already being discredited in the rich countries; to apply the same standards for the poorer countries is to condemn them always to being regarded as second-class world citizens. Growth by itself is clearly not enough. Alongside it must go a restructuring of institutions, and a reordering of value systems — and the establishment on a world basis of a true sense of community, in which there is a greater acceptance of mutual responsibility. This shared responsibility should transcend national, international, and ideological divisions, and must involve a more equitable sharing of resources and opportunities, as well as a common commitment to maintaining the balance between man and nature on which the future of all human life depends.

Toward a World of Fair Shares

Even at their best, present foreign aid programs represent just a first primitive step toward the evolution of an international system which will have built into it more continuing and impersonal mechanisms for the transference of resources in order to remove poverty and equalize opportunity on a global basis. The present system of direct aid in the form of conditional giveaways is a no more durable basis for the relationship between nations and societies than were the soup kitchen and the dole as a relationship between rich and poor within our national societies. But it has provided us with the beginning of such an international system and the basis for broadening and extending it.

There are other areas in which progress is being made in the direction of creating a more ordered world society. The creation of special drawing rights was an historic act that vested in an international body, the International Monetary Fund, a right which traditionally has been the closely guarded prerogative of nation states — the right to create currency — or its equivalent. Agreement now seems near, following lengthy discussions in Geneva, on a treaty to ban weapons of mass destruction from the ocean floor and there are encouraging signs of possible international agreements for the setting up of a supernational regime to regulate the exploration and exploitation of the sea beds "as the heritage of all mankind."

But the way will not be easy. Power continues to reside primarily in the individual nation state whose reluctance to part with it provides one of the principal barriers to effective international action. Nevertheless, there are a growing number of fields which simply cannot be dealt with effectively within the jurisdiction of individual nation states; and the recognition of this is providing the political basis for agreement on selective international action on such urgent problems as the protection of the environment on which the common fate of the entire human community depends.

The United Nations, which this year is celebrating its twenty-fifth anniversary, provides us with the essential foundation on which we must build this kind of world order. Its weaknesses and deficiencies reflect our own collective shortcomings, but it remains the principal repository of our common aspirations and hopes for the future.

And so it is in this larger perspective of the overriding necessity of constructing the framework of a more ordered and more equitable world society that I see the importance of international development assistance. For, in the long run, development assistance will not succeed unless it contributes to the creation of a more equitable and just life for all mankind. And effective world community cannot be achieved unless it is based on a substantial measure of equity in the sharing of the world's resources.

V. CURRENT ECONOMIC ISSUES

So pervasive are the problems with which modern economics deals that it is not mere rhetoric to say that achievable solutions are vital to the welfare, if not the survival, of our society. But economic issues, like most social questions, seldom can be settled once and for all. Today's answers may apply for a time; yet as possibilities and aspirations change, old problems reappear or new ones materialize. Clearly we live in a changing milieu, which is disturbing to those who prefer to abide strictly according to procedures devised in the past. Too often they prefer to ignore change rather than adapt to the realities of new circumstances. But probably never again can we afford to scorn innovation. We must be not only aware of its existence but must be fully prepared to cope with problems as they arise.

We start this section with a question: do corporate officials have a "social responsibility" that goes beyond serving the interests of their stockholders and their customers? Section B examines new developments in corporate structure and discusses the questions surrounding foreign direct investment in Canada. In Section C we consider the problem of inflation: its causes and cures. In Section D we discuss one of the critical challenges facing contemporary society, namely, environmental pollution. We close with an attempt to predict the important economic issues of the future.

A. ECONOMICS AS A MORAL SCIENCE

The chief production unit in a private enterprise economy, as we have already pointed out, is the business firm. It is within this unit that the basic economic decisions are made. These decisions have wide impacts — on workers, on consumers, on the community at large. To be sure, there is a wide variety of possible repercussions of their actions which business firms, and their managers, take into account in making their choices; decisions are taken in a certain political, economic, social environment, not in a vacuum. But the decisions are nonetheless the businessman's to make.

There has been much apprehension recently concerning the social and economic responsibility of the business community. In this connection, Reading 52 argues cogently that businessmen must take a hard second look at the philosophy and the practices of free enterprise. The competitive market system as an ethical-moral system is examined and found inadequate, and proposals to supplement or replace the market ethic are indicated.

Have businessmen a higher duty than profits? Reading 53 says yes, and supports its answer with several arguments. It is quick to remark that in the past, business was not sufficiently concerned with the needs of youth, the unskilled, the unemployed, and the poor, and asserts that businessmen of today must become more involved in the resolution of such problems. In other words, businessmen must establish by their conduct the proposition that free enterprise not only *receives* from society, but gives full value in return. The inference is clear; if businessmen do not rise to the challenge of the development of the community as a whole, they will become increasingly subject to social control.

52. WHAT'S WRONG WITH THE OLD BUSINESS ETHIC*

James Kuhn

Businessmen today are instructed in their ethical responsibilities by codes of conduct prepared by government committees, industrial advisory groups, labour union councils, and churchmen. Though they may not like all the proffered advice, they recognize that business ethics are not easily formulated or simply applied. With the best of intentions to do good and not injury, businessmen often fail. In trying to avoid the injustices of inflation bankers provoke the misery of long-continued unemployment; textile manufacturers invest in new communities, creating jobs and opportunities there, only to destroy jobs and blight lives in the old communities; responsible corporate managers provide welfare benefits for employees and discover that they have made their beneficiaries into captive wards; automobile manufacturers offer liberating means of transportation to the nation only to find their product killing and injuring people by the tens of thousands, and contaminating the air of city dwellers.

A century ago, businessmen did not find ethics so difficult a problem; certainly ethics were not the concern of committees or a matter for government pronouncements. The free competitive market of the nineteenth century took care of business ethics, while it allowed pursuit of self-interest; it restrained selfishness, as if with an "invisible hand," bending each person to serve the common good. Competition penalized those who abused consumers and rewarded those who dealt justly. The businessman had to concern himself only with personal deportment. If he was a God-fearing, upright pillar of the community, little else was asked of him. If he made profits, he was ethical; he served consumers by offering them what they wanted, and his profits were his reward for serving people as they wished to be served and as God desired that they be served. God favoured the elect with His blessings of profits. "God gave me my money," old John D. Rockefeller maintained, and many agreed with him.

---

*Reprinted from the *Columbia Forum,* 7, No. 3 (Summer, 1964). Copyright 1964 by the Trustees of Columbia University in the City of New York.
Dr. James Kuhn is Professor of Industrial Relations, Graduate School of Business, Columbia University.

The competitive market system was for businessmen of a century ago, as it was for Adam Smith, an ethical, moral system. It rewarded and penalized, nourished and starved, enriched and impoverished, according to a standard that was not always understood, but that, like the judgment of God, was righteous and just. Men were caught up in the powerful forces of the market, acting as they had to act. Subsistence wages for meatpackers, dawn-to-dusk hours for garment workers, and damp, dirty, and dangerous conditions in coal mines were the requirements of the market, not the ethical responsibility of the businessmen.

Those who suffered under the system did not always appreciate its ethic and attempted to limit and restrict the market. Some workers organized unions and the unorganized sought legislative help. Businessmen fought back, denouncing unions and higher wages, and their judicial friends struck down minimum-wage and child-labour legislation; but they were not motivated simply by greed or prejudice. They were attempting to preserve the free market, a system that was ethical as they saw it. However grave the ills of the market might be, the consequences of interfering with its working would be infinitely worse, they believed. With ethical fervour and moral indignation, they sought to protect the market — its autonomous competitive restraint upon selfish and greedy men — for the greater well-being of mankind.

Today we may think them wrong, but they were not fools. They understood the selfish side of man. With Alexander Hamilton, they agreed that "every man ought to be supposed a knave, and to have no other end, in all his actions, but private interests. By ... means of [these interests] make him cooperate to public good, notwithstanding his insatiable avarice and ambition." The market allowed each to seek his selfish pursuit but guided him, whether he would or no, into the paths of righteousness — into the service of his fellow man. Businessmen of a century ago understood what we easily forget: that men will be as good as they have to be — and only sometimes as good as they can be. The coercive pressures of competition and the fierce play of the market held men in check, pronouncing ethical judgments as long as men left those judgments alone, submitted to them, and concerned themselves solely with their own self-interests. The market itself provided an elegant ethical system, reducing the concern of the businessman to the making of profits. Where in an earlier age kings and princes had borne the responsibility for judging the ethical merit of prices and wages with the commonweal in mind, now the market, sanctified by the thesis of Adam Smith, became the judge — sublime, impersonal, and automatic.

The impressiveness of the market system and the relief it provided for harried consciences make it still attractive. Many businessmen harken to its call and some economists today continue to preach its doctrines. Advocacy of the market ethic is understandable, and insofar as it contributes to the continuous debate of public interest, it is desirable; but apotheosis of the market is dangerous and idolatrous. In suggesting that the competitive market was an institution of nature, guided by an invisible hand, Adam Smith provided his later disciples with the rationalization that it was the direct creation of God — a holy instrument for fulfilling His purposes. They forgot that men had created the market and in raising it high had fashioned a golden calf. They alienated themselves from the fulfillment of Smith's hope, which was that the free market would bring a gain in individual liberty for all and an increase in the wealth of the nation; and in turn the market alienated them from each other and their fellow men who bore the market's injustices.

Both the alienation and the anger of those who suffered under the market have led businessmen of the last generation to reconsider their claims for the market and their own responsibilities to their fellow men. They know that they often talk about, more than they seek, the competition that they publicly extol, and in too many cases they actually thwart competition. The cynic may conclude that the businessman's shock at denunciation of competition is matched only by his shock at finding anyone actually practising it. Many uneasy businessmen no longer feel justified by profits, and the advertisements of some of them suggest that only the indiscreet would boast of profits. Instead they stress service, research, productivity, and patriotism. "Progress is our most important product," says one of their slogans. They transform what once were profits into the less obvious depreciation allowances, stock bonuses, and reinvestment funds.

The uneasiness over profits has not been induced by socialist critics, accusing unionists, or left-wing liberals so much as by the size and impact of the modern corporation. Do the managers of our giant corporations reap the rewards of profits for responding to the opportunities of free competition, or do they mould the market to their design? Alfred Sloan, long-time head of General Motors, suggests in his recent autobiography that the latter is often the case. He and his fellow managers plotted their price strategy so that they would "earn" handsome profits (20 percent return on invested capital) even if consumers wanted no more than 55 percent of all the cars that General Motors could produce. They could flout a great part of the market and still garner the rewards reserved for those who serve the market. Further, they could evade the market's whiplash of losses even if they produced only about one-third of their productive capacity.

Protected from the market by their assured profits, the company managers were free, to a remarkable degree, to conduct their business as they saw fit. During the late fifties, officials of General Motors, along with those of the other automobile oligarchs, were in effect free to tax the consuming public some $5 billion annually for styling, or, as one manager called it, for "jazzing up new models." Are annual model changes worth $5 billion to this nation? Do they take precedence over adequate schooling, improved housing, and medical care? Mr. Sloan denies any moral or ethical responsibility for the choice he helped make to use national resources to produce bigger fenders and shinier grilles. He asserts, as do the other business leaders of the automobile industry, that he and his colleagues are but passive agents of the market, divining or responding to consumer demand. The assertion is bold indeed in the face of the promotion, advertising, administered pricing, allocating, and rationing they engage in.

Managers of large firms like to suppose that they are inconspicuous actors in the drama of industrial life, that they merely play the parts assigned to them. Roger Blough, for example, would have us believe that United States Steel, the largest employer in Birmingham, Alabama, and the largest buyer of goods and services in the city, has no influence upon the politics of the community. If the Birmingham city council were to double property taxes, however, one cannot help but wonder if the managers of United States Steel would have no influential advice to offer.

In 1960, when the Ford Motor Company bought out the British stockholders of English Ford for $300,000,000, the company officials assured the public that the matter was merely one of tidying up internal administration. In fact, the transaction involved much more. The Secretary of the Treasury publicly but vainly appealed to the Ford officials to consider the effects of the transaction upon the American gold reserve and the stability of the dollar. The Treasury expected a deficit of about $4.5 billion for the year, and the drain of an additional third of a billion dollars — or an increase of more than 7 percent in the deficit — as a result of Ford's move was a serious blow. Government officials, fearing that the already precarious situation would grow worse, took various measures to halt the flow of gold by reducing government purchases abroad. One of them was to order home from Europe the wives and children of servicemen abroad. The order was not wholly put into effect, but in later months the number of dependents abroad had dropped considerably — 40 percent fewer families were able to move overseas and those who did had to pay their own way. In answer to criticism, the Secretary of Defence simply said: "Our people are accustomed to sacrifice." Apparently the government officials believed that the long-run benefits of foreign investments by American business abroad outweighed the costs to human morale sustained by the families of servicemen.

Firms so large that they can tilt the national economy and shake the lives of thousands to whom they owe no legal responsibility raise serious problems for us and for their managers. They have become great polities, more influential in our lives and fortunes than many of the states. In 1958, a year of recession, eight corporations enjoyed revenues greater than the tax revenues of the state of California ($3 billion), and forty-six had revenues of more than $1 billion each (which only seven states could equal). Officials who administer state funds for education, transportation, agriculture, welfare, police, and legal services — which are as productive as any services provided by business — are regularly and directly accountable to all their citizens. They must account to the urban residents for money spent to aid agriculture, and to the rural population for money spent on police protection in the cities. Corporation officials, on the other hand, are accountable only to their stockholders, and not to those otherwise affected by their decisions. One big firm, General Electric, has pointed out that 45,000 suppliers and nearly half a million small companies are directly dependent upon it for all or part of their income from selling and servicing General Electric products; indirectly dependent upon the company is a still greater number of stores, businesses, and livelihoods. But General Electric does not account to any of its dependents as the officials of a state government do. The great price conspiracy trial of 1960 proved that General Electric and companies like it can and do control the market; their officials control the very device we have traditionally relied upon to force businessmen to serve the public good.

Surely businessmen know, as do all who hold offices in great bureaucracies, that they exercise great power and influence over the lives of others. Their dilemma is that they often feel compelled to act in their impersonal official capacities in ways that contradict their personal ethic and civil laws. No wonder they seek to escape personal responsibility by asserting that the market determines their decisions and makes their ethical code. How else are they to resolve their problem? How much more comfortable to claim that the boss, the market, or the system forces them to act as they do, than to seek ways of meeting their responsibility.

If businessmen are to meet their ethical responsibilities, where will they find explicit guides? The admonitions of government committees and industrial advisory groups to "tell the truth," or at least not to "mislead the public," are worthless, and so are the cries of union councils and the pious appeals from churchmen for individual goodness. If the market no longer exerts the restraint it once was expected to do, self-interest continues to incite every businessman, and fierce rivalries for position in industrial bureaucracies drive him to produce "good" records and higher profits. The difficulties of the businessman's ethical position are compounded by the multiplication of large organizations under his command and thus of the power he wields.

To be sure, some businessmen have proclaimed standards of their own making for themselves and their organizations. But when they have resolved to act in the "unified best interests of all" and vowed to "do right voluntarily," they have often done no more than provide grist for the public relations staff and cover for price-rigging. General Electric, for example, has already had to return $75 million wrongfully taken from its customers — hard-pressed school districts, the armed services, government agencies, and utility companies — but the total sum mulcted by all of the electrical equipment firms involved in the price conspiracy is far greater than that amount. We can conclude that to depend upon the voluntary good will of men of great power or of "soulful" corporations is to depend in vain. Adam Smith warned long ago that "people of the same trade seldom meet together, even for merriment and diversion, but the conversation ends in a conspiracy against the public or in some contrivance to raise prices."

A. A. Berle, Jr. has suggested that we might create a corporate conscience by developing keepers of it. We need, he says, men who will advise managers and question their corporate decisions as did the lords spiritual for the kings of olden times, and he fearlessly nominates professors and journalists for the task. But what would be the gain for the other citizens in entrusting the safekeeping of business ethics to professors instead of to businessmen themselves? Would this not merely substitute one élite for another — and perhaps a more pretentious, self-righteous élite at that? We ought to be as wary of an élite as of the invisible hand of the market.

Who then can — how then can we — foresee, sort out, comprehend, and evaluate the multitudinous, complex contingencies of modern industrial life? How is the rightness of a higher price for steel to be judged, or of a lower wage for automobile workers, or of a change in railroad work rules, or of moving a plant from Detroit to Lebanon, Tennessee? In each case some people are hurt and others helped; some groups profit and others are taxed. The public loses even as it gains. Short-run benefits may be long-term burdens, and vice versa. Those who must decide the issues face a bewildering mixture of necessity and freedom, coercion and initiative. The moral man in such a world is one who foresees the hidden consequences of his actions. He may not know specifically what the consequences will be, but he knows that they will surely follow, and that they will be both good and bad. He will therefore be willing to work through and be bound by procedures that confront him with the considerations of those who will be affected.

The American people have traditionally approached matters of ethics procedurally, not proscriptively or prescriptively. We have not attempted to determine the "just" price for labour, for example. At first we allowed the demand and supply of the market to fix it, and we accepted whatever price or wage resulted — and we accepted it not because it was "just" as measured against some arbitrary standard, but rather because it was the outcome of a "just" or ethical market. When dissatisfaction with the working of the labour market grew strong and unmistakable thirty years ago, we encouraged a new procedure, collective bargaining, through which wages could be determined.

Though we rejected the free market as a determinant of wages, we did not reject the idea of procedurally determined wages. We did not hope to find the "just" wage, but rather a better method for setting wages.

At first we protected unions, fostering their growth to offset the power of corporations. At the same time we encouraged collective bargaining, by which managers and workers would confront each other with reason, persuasion, and finally economic strength to fix wages and working conditions palatable to both sides of the table. If the market could no longer restrain corporate power, we hoped that the unions would. The nation accepted collective bargaining generally, as an improvement over the free market. More recently the public has learned to fear collusive bargaining between unions and employers, and it has demanded new rules to preclude it. Congress has established guarantees of democracy in unions, hoping thereby to ensure bargaining and wage determination responsive to the workers' interests. We are now finding that neither employers nor unions are sufficiently concerned with the needs of youth, the unskilled, and the unemployed. We have also found the bargainers heedless at times of the public's need for continued service and production, as for example in the transit strikes and the newspaper shutdown, so new procedures for maintaining service while setting wages have been suggested: compulsory arbitration, third-party neutrals, union-management study groups, continuous bargaining without deadlines, and consumer representation at the bargaining table.

In areas other than wage setting — such as pricing, investment, product design, method of sales, quality control, and advertising — business may be yet unrestricted by the market, and free to pursue ends not at all harmonious with the common good. As in the case of labour, should we not try to devise procedures that will require managers of large corporations to respond to the interests of others whose lives and opportunities their decisions affect? Unless competitive restrictions can be strengthened and revitalized, we need new restraints on selfish pursuit, that production may be bent to serve the consumers' community. If we are concerned, for example, with the shabby treatment often meted out by corporations to their dependent dealers or with the abusive tactics sometimes used by large companies to keep small suppliers in line, could we not encourage the dealers and suppliers to organize, granting them protection and bargaining rights similar to those that the unions have? We need not determine the substance of their relationship with the large corporations, any more than we do in labour-management relations; in the organizing, a new procedure would develop that would supplement or replace the market of Adam Smith, now weakened and inadequate. We would not admonish corporate managers to forsake their own interests, nor would we depend upon paternalistic charity to protect the dealers and suppliers. The latter would enjoy a measure of strength to protect themselves, and out of the clash of interests might come benefits to the public as each side restrained the other.

There are further procedural checks we can devise. Just as we favour our giant industrial corporations with subsidies, depreciation allowances, tariffs, grants, and favourable tax deductions, so we might encourage other groups to seek and to demand new protections and a voice in corporate decisions that affect their members — and all of us. We might encourage professional employees, such as engineers, to establish and enforce standards to protect their profession and their individual members in the vast corporation. Just as we passed the Pure Food and Drug Act, so we might give real support to private groups devoted to product testing, aiming further to inform the consumer and to restrain misleading advertising. Or we might, through greater subsidies and tax allowances, nurture consumer co-operatives as we do the oil, aircraft, and maritime industries, and thus provide more sources of competition. Or we might urge redistricting to lessen the rural domination of state and county government, so that we might legislatively provide what our large corporations seem unable or unwilling to produce — efficient urban transportation and restored cities fit to live in.

From the clash of interests arising out of the new procedures we can expect no magically final answers, of course, any more than the collective bargaining of unions solved our wage problems once and for all. New and altered procedures may help solve pressing problems now, only to raise new ones for the future. But such is the nature of man's ethical efforts. Our widom and understanding allow us to seek no more than proximate, tentative solutions that must be continually subject to reexamination.

53. THE SOCIAL AND ECONOMIC RESPONSIBILITY OF THE BUSINESS COMMUNITY *

G. Arnold Hart

On October 1, 1969, G. Arnold Hart, Chairman and Chief Executive Officer, Bank of Montreal, addressed the fortieth Annual Meeting of the Canadian Chamber of commerce held at Halifax, N.S. After indicating that he intended to confine his remarks to areas of concern for which the business community could legitimately be said to have some responsibility in the sense of accountability for action or inaction, Mr. Hart noted that "self-interest alone demands that business play its full role in ensuring that the healthy development of the community as a whole is not inhibited by failure or decay in any of its parts." He then went on to say:

Looking at the subject matter of my address in this broad context, I think a useful starting point is the phenomenon of poverty — the apparent anomaly of chronic poverty in the midst of a remarkably affluent society where most people are not only very well off, both by historical standards and by comparison with the vast majority of mankind today, but are also firmly convinced that they may look forward with confidence to a still better material standard of living in the future. It is easy enough to produce statistics to demonstrate the extent of the gains that have been made, to show how a larger and larger proportion of our people are enjoying a higher and higher standard of living. It is also easy to be led to believe, as many do, that we now have within our grasp for the first time in history the technical and economic possibility of eradicating poverty from our midst.

This may be. But for some reason this wonderful prospect has so far eluded us, and is not very much closer to realization now than it was a generation ago when we all stepped forth into the brave new world we were going to create out of the ruin of the Great Depression and the ashes of the Second World War. It is, of course, a fact that for those who have shared fully in the rise in living standards in the intervening years the gains have been tremendous. And it is also no doubt true that there are relatively fewer people today in Canada who are really poverty stricken in the sense of living in destitution without access to the basic necessities of existence. However,

*Reprinted from Bank of Montreal, *Business Review,* October 29, 1969, by permission.
Mr. Hart is Chairman and Chief Executive Officer, Bank of Montreal.

the poor, and indeed the poverty stricken, are still with us in very large numbers.

Precisely how large those numbers are is a matter of definition but there is really no questioning the orders of magnitude . . . . We still have to count in millions the number of Canadians who live in conditions of poverty that imply educational privation, inadequate housing, poor nutrition, bad health, and other physical and psychological handicaps which, for many of our people, spell out a vicious circle of unemployment and frustration leading to unemployability and hopelessness. Cause and effect are admittedly difficult to sort out when you get onto this sort of treadmill but it seems evident to me beyond any shadow of a doubt that the breaking of the circle must be a top priority in any civilized society.

But what, you may ask, has all this got to do with the social and economic responsibility of the business community? Is it not enough for business, in the pursuit of profits, to produce, and to sell at prices determined by market forces, the goods and services the public wants — and to do this as efficiently as possible, thus contributing to economic growth and the expansion of general prosperity that is supposed to cause poverty to wither away? If anyone ever really held this simplistic view, the experience during the postwar period, when there has been an almost uninterrupted rise in total output and a dramatic rise in average standards of living, must surely have dispelled the idea that economic growth alone will cure the problem of poverty and its attendant social ills.

In fact I doubt that there are many people, among those who have thought about these matters at all, who ever really believed that economic growth would by itself do the trick. But they have tended to think, at least until recently, that the social problems inherent in a maldistribution of earning power and incomes were primarily the responsibility of governments and of nonprofit organizations. Business involvement therefore has by and large been confined to the payment of taxes and to making donations to charities, without direct corporate participation in community affairs apart from the efforts of individual businessmen in their personal capacities.

However, I think it has become increasingly apparent that new approaches are needed. Certainly the welfare approach to the solution of social problems and economic disparities has not proved particularly effective, except as a palliative to relieve acute distress, and this is becoming increasingly recognized by governments as well.

The curious thing about all this is the ambivalence which many of us in the business community have shown toward government. On the one hand, we have tended to leave the welfare baby on the government doorstep and on the other have consistently inveighed against government spending, the stultifying effects of our welfare system, and the disincentives to initiative and progress throughout the economy that are inherent in that approach. I admit that I have been as prone as anyone to express this view and, in fact, I remain convinced that it is a valid one. However, I think that where some businessmen, including myself, have gone off the track in the past in criticizing the traditional governmental approach to some aspects of social policy, was in doing this without really suggesting anything constructive to take its place aside from the well-known virtues of hard work, thrift, and charity, and the undoubted benefits of private enterprise and individual initiative.

I believe in these qualities today just as strongly as I ever did but the real problem is how to convince the less fortunate members of our society that such virtues can in fact be rewarded. It certainly won't be done by hand-outs, even though income maintenance is a necessary component of any program to relieve poverty, nor in my view can effective self-help programs be successfully mounted by government alone. I am coming more and more to the view that, if the problems of chronic poverty are to be met and the numbers afflicted by this disease significantly reduced, there must be a more direct involvement by the business community in the provision of training programs to upgrade skills and generally to help poor families, especially the young people in poor families, to develop their income-earning potentials.

Having said this I hasten to add that I think we would be misleading ourselves if we thought the business community could make a major impact on these problems on our own. I have two reasons for saying this. In the first place the phenomenon of poverty is so deep-rooted and pervasive that it will take a very long time for any program to show appreciable and lasting results. In the second place the kinds of things that need doing cannot be done profitably by business on a large enough scale to be really effective. And let us face it, if something cannot be done profitably, or at least without loss, it won't be done at all on a continuing basis by private enterprise no matter what the calculation may be of long-term indirect gains to be derived from the prevention of further social decay. Enlightened self-interest is a strong motivating factor but it is not self-interest, and certainly not enlightened, to drive yourself into bankruptcy in the process.

This is why I believe there must be direct inducements, through tax incentives or in other ways, if the resources of private enterprise are to be enlisted to mount the sort of attack on poverty that is required. And this is why I also believe that some of us in the business community must revise our

FIGURE 1

UNEMPLOYMENT

As a Percentage of the Labour Force

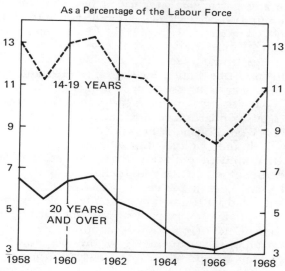

attitude toward government and be less reluctant to enter into partnership with government to achieve our common goals.

So far I have discussed broad and apparently intractable problems that require for their solution responsbile participation by business, with a responsible attitude toward partnership with government. Another group of problems of this sort has to do with the despoiling of our physical environment by pollution — specifically, water pollution, air pollution, and noise pollution. To be sure none of these can be effectively attacked on a broad front without government involvement — either by regulation, or by financial inducements to offset the costs of pollution abatement, or by financial disincentives for the continuation of socially undesirable practices, or by some combination of these three. It is true that legislation to these ends does exist in some jurisdictions and that an aroused public opinion has caused a recent spate of announcements of new programs. It is true, as well, that some industries have already, without the immediate threat of government sanction, done a great deal — and a great deal that has been expensive — to control the amount of undesirable material that is being poured out into our environment. However, these efforts must be considered marginal in relation to the size of the total problem, which can only be attacked effectively by co-ordinated programs under the aegis of government.

Whatever reservations one may have about the program to deal with water pollution recently announced by the federal government, I think we should be grateful that they have at last taken a credible initiative in proposing the Canada Water Act. And I say this even though the program is going to cost a great deal of money, so much, in fact, that there is reason to question the basic philosophy of the federal proposal to the effect that it is the polluters who must pay — meaning essentially the industries concerned and the municipalites. Since the costs will be so high they must surely be spread, directly or indirectly, over a wider group than these two, and it is perhaps best to recognize this at the outset.

Nevertheless, this is a commendable initiative which I believe should enjoy the support of the business community as a whole. Indeed, if it is to be pushed through the tangle of political jurisdictions into a workable law that will not penalize any particular category of industry, the overt support of the business community may well be required. Given the long-run stakes, in which we all have an interest, I think that for the business community to take such a positive attitude would be to behave responsibly. Business should also adopt a positive attitude toward the growing problem of air pollution by encouraging and supporting similar legislation to set standards of air quality.

Noise pollution is a growing problem as well, and one for which it may be very difficult, in view of the many local jurisdictions involved, to define enforceable national standards for maximum noise levels. However, it is certainly worth a try, and business in general, as well as the industries more directly concerned, should give their full support.

There is another kind of pollution that is of great concern to me but which is by far the most difficult to handle. I am referring to "people pollution," if I may coin a phrase to describe the processes by which people's minds get filled with unwholesome ideas of one kind or another. I know I would be treading on very dangerous ground if I were to suggest that there should be any kind of control, by administrative or other means, of what people can read, or see at the movies or on television or on the stage, or hear in the classrooms of our schools of higher education. Freedom of the press and all the other mass media, as well as academic freedom, are hard-won rights that are jealously guarded in a democracy, and properly so if democracy itself is to survive and flourish.

But this very freedom is prone to abuse in a society that is at once affluent, permissive, and highly advanced in its communications technology. It is all too easy for the unsavoury to be made to appear commonplace and therefore acceptable; for the occasional human mistakes of people in high office, in the conduct of their private and public affairs, to be given wide currency; for a socially undesirable act or attitude on the part of a business-man or an industry to be played up out of all proportion to its importance in the total scheme of things; and for any of these to provide the raw material of half-truth that some lecturers use quite cynically to undermine the beliefs of our youth in the values of our society. In the circumstances is it not all the more important for us in business to set a proper example, both in the conduct of our own affairs and by demonstrating by our actions that our approach toward the social and economic problems of our day is unquestion-ably positive and responsible?

This leads me, by a rather circuitous route, to the last major area of concern I wish to touch upon tonight but one which perhaps transcends all others in both importance and difficulty. A great deal has been written about the rebellion of youth, the idealism of youth, the generation gap, the dropout, the hippie movement, student power, nonviolent student activism, violent student radicalism, and all the other phenomena associated with youth.

I do not pretend to understand all these phenomena — nor do I think it is possible to understand them completely — but I think it is important to try, because the nature of our whole society and culture in future will depend,

FIGURE 2

STUDENTS REMAINING IN SCHOOL
As a Percentage of Grade 2 Enrolment

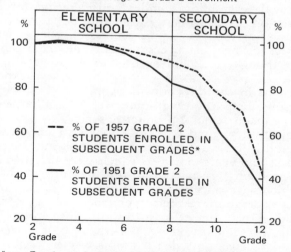

*e.g., Enrolment in Grade 12 (in 1967) amounted to 42% of the number of students who had enrolled in Grade 2 (in 1957).
Source: Economic Council of Canada.

perhaps more than at any previous period in history, on the way in which the youth of today resolves his inner conflicts in his search for an identity. And the way in which he resolves these conflicts and the attitudes he develops toward society will depend to a very large extent on the kind of image that is projected by significant sectors of the so-called "establishment" . . . .

It may be that the reason we (the business community) are not getting through to our young people is that they simply do not believe what we are trying to say and therefore do not listen. I would not discount the fundamental idealism of many of our youth, and if what we in business are doing does not appear to them to be relevant to, or consistent with, their concept of a progressive and just society in which human values are more important than material ones — the material things they now take for granted — then communication with them may be impossible. If there is a credibility gap of this sort, and I believe there is, then it must be closed if we are to reach them, and this can best be done by the force of example, not rhetoric — by action, not words . . .

There is no end to the number and variety of initiatives that could be taken by business to get itself meaningfully and productively involved in the attack on problems of the sort I have touched upon. A glance at any of the publications of the National Industrial Conference Board relative to their conferences on corporate urban programs in the United States will give an indication of the range. Moreover, a random sample of annual reports of American companies suggests a degree of awareness about the responsibility of the corporation to participate in the attack on critical national and local problems — as well as a willingness to make the effort — that is almost totally absent from the published reports of Canadian companies. This does not necessarily mean that nothing is being done here, and many of you may know, as I do, of very commendable corporate initiatives at the local level, but whatever is being done is certainly not very visible nationally.

It is, of course, a matter for each firm to decide in what direction it is likely to be able to make the greatest contribution. We in the Bank of Montreal have had several ideas under consideration for some time but before embarking on any program we wanted to be reasonably sure, not that whatever initiative we took would be successful, but rather that it would have the greatest chance of success among the many choices available. Accordingly we thought it would be best to do something in a field that would enable us to draw in some way upon our own experience and this seemed to point us in the direction of people, that is, in the direction of trying to do something to bring some wasted and undeveloped human resources into the mainstream of productive society.

With this objective in mind we had a look at some of the training and placement programs that employers in the United States have been engaged in during the past few years, many of which were designed initially to deal urgently with problems arising out of the mounting urban crisis in that country but which have since acquired a life and momentum of their own. After careful consideration of their experience we came to the conclusion that we should direct our efforts toward those young people in our community who, for one reason or another, have never acquired the basic skills and attitudes that are needed if they are to be regularly participating members of the labour force. What we are looking at is a spectrum of society that is sometimes described as disadvantaged — not just economically but physically, emotionally, and socially. Some of the people are described as "dropouts" although this can be a misnomer for someone who may well have dropped out from school but never really had an opportunity to "drop in" to the meaningful and constructive part of our society. Words such as "hard-core unemployed" are also used, but we are hoping to help some young people avoid sliding into the trap that will, in fact, make them another statistic in the impersonal phrase "the hard-core unemployed."

Specifically, what we have in mind at this stage is a rather small-scale pilot project in one or more major urban areas of Canada. The objective will be to seek out young people who have never, either because of the lack of appropriate skills or because of an unsatisfactory environmental background, been able to establish a good employment record. We will be looking for young people who are no longer in school but who did not go far enough with their formal education to acquire the basic reading and computational skills that they need to aspire to office jobs even at the lowest entry level. We will be looking in particular for people with this sort of background who are nevertheless willing to let us try to convince them that they can reach a level of achievement that will enable them to hold down a steady job and who are willing, moreover, to be convinced that the effort is worth their while.

Details of our program have not yet been worked out but it must obviously be a blend of remedial education, counselling, and on-the-job training, with financial support during the process, and with the promise of a job at the end of the training period if they come up to the required standards.

We know that the problems in mounting a program of this nature are immense but, as I have already indicated, we hope to benefit from the experience of major banks and other employers in the United States, which is by now rather extensive. We will not hesitate to take appropriate advantage of whatever help may be available from government agencies such as the Manpower Division of the Department of Manpower and Immigration in Ottawa. We will welcome the advice and counsel of anyone with relevant experience in this field. And we will make the results of our experience freely available to any other employers who wish to embark on a program with similar objectives.

I regret that our planning is not yet far enough advanced for me to give you more details. All I can add to what I have already said is that we have made a corporate commitment to proceed with a pilot project just as soon as administrative arrangements can be worked out. We do not know what the results will be. We may fall flat on our faces or we may find, as many employers in the United States have found, that we have uncovered a hitherto untapped and undeveloped source of productive workers capable of playing a useful role as employees and as members of the community.

But let there be no mistake about our motives. Compassion is certainly a factor but it is only a part of the mix. Our motives are firmly rooted in concern for the healthy development of the total society in which we operate and the knowledge that our own long-run corporate interest will be best served if we participate fully in the search for solutions to some of the more difficult problems facing society in our time.

During my remarks tonight I have touched upon a wide range of social and economic issues. I have done so in the conviction that the responsibility of business transcends its own immediate interests and that the corporation of today must become more involved in the resolution of problems of the sort that have been discussed here during the past few days. In short, if business is to play its full part as a constructive force in the development of our society, it must concern itself directly with the goal of improving the quality of life in Canada for all Canadians.

B. BUSINESS CORPORATIONS, THE ECONOMY AND SOCIETY

The dominant form of business organization in Canada, judged by output and employment, is the corporation: most of the largest firms are organized in this way. The corporation's chief advantage over other forms of organization is its efficiency in mobilizing money capital in large quantities. Because of their strategic position in acquiring funds, corporations are typically in a better position to realize "mass production economies" than are proprietorships or partnerships. However, this is not the whole story. Many Canadians are worried about the implications of big business and business concentration for the operation of the market system. Does bigness imply, for example, the existence of significant monopoly power? Will a few large corporations come to dominate the entire economic life of the country? Can we have the efficiency we desire without at the same time generating adverse monopoly and economic power? These are some of the questions for which we will be seeking answers in the selections that follow.

Among the new features of business organization is the emergence of more and larger firms that have manufacturing operations, frequently on a specialized and integrated basis, in several countries. In general, it would appear that such firms have significant competitive advantages arising from the ability to combine large quantities of capital goods, competent management, skilled professionals, and advanced technology, and to move these to economic locations for production. Reading 54 reviews the growth of so-called multinational corporations, their importance for the development of economic resources and the difficulties they face in the world today. It should be added that the rising importance of the international firm poses two important problems for our economy, according to the Economic Council of Canada: "how to foster more effective Canadian-based participation in the rapid growth and development of multinational corporations, and how to make the capabilities and potentials of such firms best serve Canadian economic goals when their future development and even their present activities can perhaps be readily shifted elsewhere." *(Seventh Annual Review,* 1970, p. 89.)

Closely related to this is the question "whether a country can have a meaningful independent existence in a situation where nonresidents own an important part of that country's basic resources and industry, and are therefore in a position to make important decisions affecting the operations and development of the country's resources." (Irving Brecher and S. S. Reisman, *Canada-United States Economic Relations,* Ottawa: July, 1957, p. 116.) This, of course, raises the whole issue of the extent to which Canadian business is externally owned and controlled. Reading 55 reviews the evolution of the debate over foreign ownership of Canadian industry and commerce, and the performance of foreign-owned enterprises in Canada. It concludes that the record of foreign-owned firms in relation to exports, imports, and the transfer of knowledge has clearly been mixed. Even so, it asserts that most *generalized* criticism of such companies are at odds with the available facts on performance. Reading 56 focusses on the assumed threat of foreign direct investment to the political independence of Canada, and analyses the areas of possible public concern. It also lists the pros and cons of the policy proposals of the government's Task Force on the Structure of Canadian Industry (The Watkins Report).

54. THE MULTINATIONAL CORPORATION*

First National City Bank of New York

Multinational corporations deserve study. There is no agreement about what "multinational" means precisely, as interest and involvements across national boundaries vary from case to case. Some purists prefer to use the term "transnational" to designate companies that operate in several countries, and reserve "multinational" for those that are truly multinational in operations, management, and philosophy — a stage only few corporations have reached thus far.

Hard to define, multinational corporations are also hard to measure. The scope of productive facilities established by world companies ouside of their home countries is obviously related to the magnitude and composition of direct investment in plant and equipment. For the United States, such direct investments abroad total, at book value, something like $65 billion today. Much less is known about direct foreign investments of other countries; but since quite a few large firms of British or Continental nationality rank as multinational companies, foreign investments by non-American corporations are obviously important.

A report prepared by Dr. Sidney E. Rolfe cites a few figures developed by the statisticians of the Organization for Economic Cooperation and Development that throw, for the first time, some light on this little-explored corner of the international economy. For 1966, when US direct foreign investments amounted to $55 billion, direct foreign investments of other industrial countries were estimated at $45 billion. The world total thus worked out to $90 billion. These are book values; at market rates, these investments were much higher. Since much of American foreign investment, especially in manufacturing in Canada and Europe, has been built up only since the late fifties, but European investments date back to well before 1914, the market values of European investments are probably larger relative to book values than in the case of US investments.

Britain's direct investments abroad were recently valued at the equivalent of $18 billion. No data are available for the Netherlands, a major investing

---

*Reprinted from First National City Bank of New York, *Monthly Economic Letter*, June, 1969, pp. 69-71, by permission.

country, or for Italy and Belgium; estimates for these countries are, however, included in the OECD aggregate. Switzerland has sizable investments abroad. France has expanded overseas investment in recent years. German direct investments abroad, checked by two world wars, are now developing substantially. Japan, too, has begun to rebuild its foreign investments.

Of the estimated $90 billion world total of international direct investments in 1966, about two-thirds was located in developed countries. Foreign direct investments in the United States totalled some $9 billion (by the end of 1968, they rose to about $11 billion). The remaining third was situated in the less developed parts of the world. The greatest single component was manufacturing, with over $36 billion, of which three-quarters was in developed countries. Oil, with $26 billion, nearly half of which was in the less developed countries, was next.

How Much Foreign-Based Output?

How much the multinational corporations produce in their foreign-based facilities is nowhere recorded in official statistics. But, judging from the work done by Mr. Judd Polk of the US Council of the International Chamber of Commerce, $1 of direct international investment at book value generates each year $2 of foreign-based output. If so, the value of output associated with foreign-based facilities of American corporations would seem to be of the order of $130 billion a year. While inferences like these may contain fairly large margins of error, there is no doubt that foreign-based output is substantial.

Thus, US enterprise abroad is, to use Mr. Polk's image, something like the third biggest economy in the world — comparable in size to the gross national product of Japan or Germany, the largest national economies after those of the United States and the Soviet Union. M. Jean-Jacques Servan-Schreiber has characterized this state of affairs as an American challenge. But, in fact, the challenge is multinational, for industrial nations other than the United States also generate, through their own direct international investments, something like $80 billion of foreign-based output. Approximately one-fourth of this output is produced in the United States, but the bulk is spread throughout the rest of the world. Even Russia and certain other Eastern European countries participate in the internationalization of output, as evidenced by Italo-Russian arrangements to produce cars in Russia.

Two US Examples

In this setting, attention is naturally focussed on the United States. From an inquiry into the scope of operations of foreign manufacturing subsidiaries of US corporations in 1965 — the lastest data available — it appears that their sales of machinery almost doubled during the first half of the sixties, reaching $9.2 billion. During the same period, the exports of these categories of goods from the United States increased by only one half to $6.7 billion. For automobiles and other transportation equipment, sales of US foreign subsidiaries were already in 1960 almost three times as large as US exports; but while the latter increased by two-fifths between 1960 and 1965, sales of US subsidiaries expanded by three-fourths to $10.8 billion.

These two examples show that US exports, while continuing to expand, have become relatively less important than the foreign-based output of American corporations. For US exports as a whole, the average rate of expansion over the past decade works out at 7.5 percent a year; but, judging from the growth of direct investments, the foreign-based output has increased at the rate of 9 percent. The output has grown in the most strategic, the most profitable, and the most rapidly growing segments of foreign economies, particularly in Canada and in Europe.

The reasons leading US corporations to establish foreign subsidiaries are complex. A corporation that has already expanded its exports is naturally drawn into direct investment — at first, in marketing facilities, and then, as necessary, in plants — to participate in growth potentials and, hence, profits abroad. Often, the corporation has no choice but to establish manufacturing facilities abroad in order to overcome trade barriers (tariffs, quantitative restrictions, etc.) and, in particular, the discrimination arising from the establishment of integrated markets like the European Economic Community. Often, too, it must move into markets to which it may be unable to continue exporting from its home base — particularly if labour costs are also relatively attractive there. To secure economies of scale, the multinational corporation builds overseas plants big enough to provide for market expansion; and, as a result, its involvement in international operations tends to grow by leaps and bounds — so long at least as future profitability looks promising.

These trends and developments must, or course, be seen within the framework of the US balance of payments as a whole. The foreign subsidiaries of US corporations are buyers of US exports. While they may to some extent compete with their parent companies in export markets in third countries, they do not necessarily displace exports that would otherwise be made from the United States. Most importantly, what is referred to as the "foreign-based" output of US corporations is a combination of foreign factors of production with US research-intensive engineering, management, and finance (although local financing has become increasingly important). But the US balance of payments benefits from receipts of income, royalties, and fees — receipts that last year were, at $6 billion, twice as large as the total of new funds flowing into direct investment abroad. In the meantime, the strain on the US balance of payments is also being relieved by the fact that a considerable part of the funds used by US corporations for direct investment abroad is now being raised in markets outside the United States.

In brief, so long as US technology preserves its lead in industry as well as in agriculture and services and so long as the US economy does not become addicted to inflation, there will be a flow of exports. But, given the US propensity to import, a substantial merchandise trade surplus may well have become a matter of the past. Interestingly, Britain had a trade surplus in only three years during the century before World War I when it was the world's banker. England's offset was its large income from overseas investment. American enterprise has now reached a stage of involvement abroad where earnings from foreign investment, issuance of equities in foreign capital markets, and borrowings abroad provide an entirely new scope and dimension for the US balance of payments.

A Touch of Realism

Multinational corporations — scanning the world as they do for investment opportunities to maximize the results obtainable from their research facilites, technical skills, patents, equipment, capital, and experience — have a vital role in raising world output and living standards. In host countries, multinational corporations are a growing source of economic progress, create employment, pay good wages, provide tax revenues to the government, and help to build up exports. Shareholders of corporations do, of course, expect a reasonable return on their investment — given the entrepreneurial risk involved, which is actually held down by the process of geographical diversification. As to the home countries of multinational corporations, they hopefully anticipate that, in a world in which the political boundaries of nation states are too narrow and constrictive to provide the best scope for modern business, their prosperity will be enhanced by the prosperity of others.

Yet, despite their undeniable accomplishments and the promise of the future, multinational corporations encounter many difficulties. They are, of course, part of the economy of the countries in which they operate. But, not too surprisingly, national interests of host countries sometimes diverge from those of the home countries of multinational corporations in such matters as taxation, antitrust questions, and balance of payments controls. Thus, while US corporations have been urged to step up repatriation of profits, their host countries may favour smaller remittances and greater reinvestment of profits. In the process, it is overlooked that investment income helps balance the accounts of nations that are prosperous enough to export capital.

Governments are validly concerned about the goals and policies of multinational corporations and about their involvement in business and employment conditions in their countries. Not infrequently, host countries also fear that foreigners — even friendly and efficient foreigners — may acquire undue control over large segments of their basic industries. They want their nationals to participate in the ownership, management, and technology of the multinational corporations that operate in their countries.

Last but not least, along with aspirations for rapid economic development, there has been in much of the world a resurgence of economic nationalism — a blend of old-fashioned protectionism with sensitive political overtones. Excessive nationalism has given rise to manifold and delicate problems which sometimes erupt into frictions and conflicts.

To strengthen the world's economic interdependence and cohesion, much thought has been given to removing obstacles that hamper international direct investment, elaborating an agreed-upon code of good behaviour for both home and host countries and providing for a uniform treatment of multinational corporations throughout the world. A multilateral convention on the settlement of international investment disputes has been sponsored by the World Bank. The emphasis placed in this context on international investment must not, of course, be allowed to distract attention from tariff and nontariff trade barriers, exchange rate problems, double taxation of corporate income, and other related matters.

Much will depend upon acceptance of multinational corporations as desirable and, indeed, indispensable catalysts in the process of economic development, and on their success in overcoming misunderstandings and misapprehensions about threats to economic independence. But time is of the essence. For nations can ill afford to neglect *any* opportunity for improving economic efficiency.

55. FOREIGN OWNERSHIP REVIEWED*

H. E. English

Foreign investment in Canada has been essentially a textbook case of long-term international flow of capital to an area of unexploited opportunity for higher profit.

The Historical Perspective

Immediately after the war, the Americans had a great deal of liquid capital and an increasing concern about declining sources of raw materials. They were afraid to risk much in most parts of the "developing" world; and since Europe was not in the running to export raw materials, Canada was a logical investment choice.

During and after the war, vast iron and petroleum deposits were discovered in Canada. The Korean War and rocketing prices stimulated frenzied exploration and the capital required could only be found by the great US mining and petroleum companies. European companies could not possibly command foreign exchange for dollar investments of these magnitudes. In Canada, only the government could have invested on the same scale, and the politicians and electorate would have taken a distinctly negative view of sinking tens of millions of dollars in dry holes.

At the same time, a booming Canada had become a substantial market for industrial equipment and consumer durables products. The population had doubled since the late 1920s and the GNP stood at three times its level at that time. It made a lot of sense to establish or expand branch plants in Canada to produce finished goods.

After the Fact

By the mid 1950s the resource investment boom was over. By the late 1950s

*Reprinted from H. E. English, "Foreign Ownership Reviewed," *The Canadian Banker*, January-February, 1970, pp. 13-17, by permission of the editor and author.
Dr. English is Director of the School of International Affairs and Professor of Economics, Carleton University, Ottawa.

the European economies were established on the road to economic integration with the European Common Market and the European Free Trade Association. This led to a marked shift in the foreign investment activity of US firms away from Canada toward Europe. There has since been growing US investment interest in parts of the developing world as politics have stabilized somewhat and conditions of investment become more clearly specified.

Since 1958, therefore, there has been little if any increase in the relative importance of US investment in Canada. There has been somewhat more European investment activity, but since the early 1960s European and American investment together have barely kept pace with domestic investment. The percentage of foreign ownership of Canadian mining and manufacturing industries has changed little during the past decade.

The Evolution of the Controversy

The debate over foreign ownership dates from the time of the Royal Commission on Canada's Economic Prospects. Although that Commission was chaired by Walter Gordon, the man who later became one of the chief spokesmen on this issue, the report contained a moderate review of the facts and called attention to the need for more data if the full implications of the situation were to be understood.

During the Diefenbaker regime there were many political pronouncements about the degree of US influence, but the only specific policy development was the passing of the Corporations and Labour Unions Returns Act. This required fuller reporting of activities of large private corporations and international unions. However, by the time it was passed, the Act was so watered down that it promised much less disclosure than had been anticipated. A lively controversy was generated during those years by the Governor of the Bank of Canada, James Coyne, replete with clarion calls about the effect that foreign capital inflow was having on the then depressed Canadian economy. The irony of that particular phase of the debate was that the Governor's own tight money policy was contributing to an inflow largely motivated by the higher Canadian interest rates on public borrowing. This inflow was sustaining the high value of the Canadian dollar with the consequent stimulus to imports and constraint on exports.

The 1960s saw the focus shift away from the balance of payments effects which understandably dominated the Coyne controversy. Prosperity returned gradually to Canada, and the propensity to look for an outside scapegoat to explain Canada's unemployment problem declined. The debate on foreign ownership was kept alive mainly by efforts of a few individuals, of which Walter Gordon is best known. As Minister of Finance, he dramatized the issue with his remarkable budget of June, 1963.

During the following years the emphasis shifted to three other issues:
1. The importance of Canada retaining control over the so-called "commanding heights" of the economy — the financial and publication industries are the main examples usually cited. Specific controversies in this area centred on the Mercantile Bank case and on the limitation of Canadian editions of foreign magazines.
2. The Canada Development Corporation — to enable Canadians to compete more effectively in financing new resource development. This is not yet off the ground.

3. The main argument, however, turned on the efficiency of foreign firms and their contribution to Canadian growth. Disquieting evidence indicated that foreign investment had not led to efficient Canadian manufacturing establishments, or even earned the high rates of return which ostensibly justify the international flow of capital.

The Watkins Report

In 1967, four years after the Liberal government came to power and ten years after the publication of the Report of the Gordon Commission, the government established a task force on foreign ownership and the structure of Canadian Industry, headed by Professor Melville H. Watkins at the University of Toronto.

The report of the Task Force appeared in January, 1968. There can be no doubt that it was strongly influenced by Professor A. E. Safarian, one of the economists on the force. His publication, *Foreign Ownership of Canadian Industry,* which appeared in 1966, focussed on the structure and performance of foreign-owned companies in Canada on the basis of data collected in the fifties and early sixties.

The Task Force gave Professor Safarian the opportunity to evaluate new data and a recent book develops that evaluation. The balance of this article deals mainly with the findings and conclusions it sets forth.

Performance of Foreign-Owned Firms in Canada

Safarian focusses mainly on five aspects of the structure and performance of industry. The first two are structural and the next three "performance" characteristics. They are: (1) participation of foreign citizens in the management and on the boards of Canadian companies; (2) the autonomy of the subsidiary; (3) foreign trade of subsidiaries; (4) import performance of subsidiary firms; (5) research and development activities.

Management. He confirms, not too surprisingly, that companies that are more than 50 percent foreign owned are likely to have foreign presidents. The foreign companies may afford promising Canadian managerial talent the opportunity to work for a time in the parent firm's managerial group in the United States. An overall judgment is required as to the contribution of foreign ownership to the quality of management, and whether this contribution more than compensates for any cost to Canada arising out of the unwillingness or inability of foreign nationals to manage the Canadian subsidiary in accordance with Canada's interests. These are difficult dimensions to measure, particularly the latter factor, since Canadian governments control taxation and regulatory powers that define Canadian interests and provide the incentive to management to act in accordance with these interests.

Autonomy of the Subsidiary. What degree of autonomy on the part of the subsidiary is desirable from Canada's viewpoint? Although Canadian authorities stress "the desirability of as much autonomy as possible," some economic factors create a tendency to centralization, while other considerations promote decentralization. Evidence that 80 percent of 185 reporting firms enjoyed substantial decentralization of decision making suggests that decentralization forces are stronger. Less autonomy is seen in those more recently established subsidiaries, which are the only foreign branches of foreign companies, and which maintain close technical integration between parent and subsidiary.

Autonomy and centralization are fundamentally related to the functions of industrial management and ownership. Complete managerial autonomy does not necessarily mean that a firm will go for maximum profits, since so long as a firm is reasonably profitable, management may prefer to stimulate sales in the expectation that its own prestige will be enhanced by this policy. On the other hand, if decisions are dominated by the parent firm in the interest of maximizing the rate of return to the parent, this may not necessarily mean as rapid a rate of growth or as high a profit for the subsidiary. Decisions may, for example, be based on tax considerations. It is impossible to generalize about the net economic advantage or disadvantage of different degrees of autonomy, so that one must conclude that only on noneconomic grounds is autonomy a clear advantage. The economist must try to assess the economic cost in individual cases, so that policy makers can decide whether it is worthwhile.

Foreign Trade of Subsidiaries. Any comparison of the trading activity of foreign-controlled firms with that of Canadian-owned firms must be interpreted with care. In many of the natural resource industries, Canada has such large reserves and such an advantage over other countries that a high percentage of the output of such industries is exported. As foreign-controlled firms predominate in this sector, it is not surprising that their export performance is good.

In manufacturing industries, efficient operation may in some cases require or make possible specialized export activity. In other cases, however, a firm may be able to operate sufficiently by supplying the Canadian market only. In still other cases, it may be impossible to reach internationally competitive cost levels because trade barriers prevent the required large-scale production and export of specialized products.

Safarian compares the relative importance of exports of American-owned firms in the manufacturing sector with the relative share of the same firms in total capital invested in manufacturing. He makes the same comparison for petroleum and mining industries. In both cases he finds the export performance of the US-owned firms better than other firms. Particularly in the heterogeneous manufacturing sector Safarian is unable to demonstrate that the foreign-controlled firms are doing as well as they could. What he *is* able to demonstrate is that they are not pursuing an effective policy of restricting exports by their Canadian subsidiaries. His destination figures on exports show that Canadian subsidiaries export more to the United States market — 60 percent of the exports of manufacturing subsidiaries go to the US market — than subsidiaries in other countries.

Import Performance of Subsidiary Firms. Subsidiary firms import more than domestic Canadian firms. Most of these imports are for resale without further manufacture, and only a minority are for processing and assembling. This reflects the much wider range of US manufactured goods and the advantages of importing the more specialized products rather than producing them here.

Research and Development Activities. The study includes valuable information on the flow of technology know-how from parent to subsidiary and of the payments made for this flow. Since these payments are usually far less than the cost of independent development of the technology in Canada, it is not difficult to explain our much lower level of industrial research and development expenditure. A more difficult question to assess is the extent of the disadvantage to Canadian industry. Some claim that the possibility of developing distinctive Canadian products is seriously reduced. Others suggest that if a subsidiary participates in a distinctive fashion in the research and development program of the international company, it is likely to be in a much better bargaining position in seeking access to markets in the United States and overseas where the parent company does business.

Safarian finds that the Canadian subsidiaries that are largest relative to the foreign parent are engaged in more research; that the subsidiaries with product mixes that differ from those of the parent are doing more research.

His main conclusion is that some industries are much more heavily involved than others, and that differences on this account are much more important than differences associated with residence of the owners or other considerations. Like resource exploration and various kinds of selling activity (advertising, style change, etc.), R and D activity is a reason for firms to build and operate many plants, and thus spread overhead burden of product development and differentiation.

Therefore international companies are more likely to be found in this type of industry than in those where multiplant economies are not available. These circumstances would appear to be of such general importance that it seems better for a country with many subsidiaries to devote its policy efforts to assuring its industry access both to the world's technology and to markets for technology and intensive goods, on terms as equal as possible to those enjoyed by the parent firm, rather than to attempt to give priority to supporting the R and D activities of purely domestically-based firms.

Profitability and Efficiency

In explaining the inadequacy of his data on profitability, Safarian calls attention to the number of foreign subsidiaries in Canada that are operated as private companies and are not required to disclose financial data. It is interesting that the recent government decision to require more disclosure has not been greeted with alarm. The main concern of industry representatives who have commented has been to the effect that the general application of disclosure rules makes them much more palatable.

When Safarian comes to actual rates of return of nonresident and resident owned firms, he finds that the data is in a form which makes meaningful comparison almost impossible, thanks to the difference in mix of companies in the group he identifies. There is no evidence that foreign-owned firms make higher rates of return.

The author relies more on data on unit cost which he collected in connection with his earlier study. He found the unit cost of production of the subsidiary to be substantially higher than that of the parent firm in a majority of cases. This symptomizes the real problem in the structure and efficiency of the Canadian manufacturing industry. It leads Safarian, as it led the Task Force, to conclude that the Canadian policy environment in which foreign-owned firms operate has resulted in excessively diversified and often undersized production units that are not able and willing to exploit even those economies of scale that would be possible within the Canadian market without assuming access to foreign markets. This is the consequence of the kind of competition or rivalry that occurs under tariff protection when there are few large firms dominating an industry's productive activity.

It is possible for each firm to cover cost and make a modest profit while pricing at just below that price which would induce imports (that is, approximating the foreign plus the Canadian tariff). This does not itself explain why such firms would not attempt to push one another out through vigorous price competition in order that the survivor might have a larger share of the Canadian market and thus be able to achieve more economies of scale. The main reason why such a competitive struggle does not usually emerge is that the risk of recurrent price war and of possible elimination from the market is greater than the attraction of the higher level of profits. So long as some profits can be made, the status quo is more appealing. These attitudes are strengthened by the fact that the dominant firms have all been in business for some time, are quite well acquainted with each other's corporate practices, and can reasonably confidently carry on with certain kinds of selling competition (advertising, packaging, style changing), each hoping that it might improve its share of market by these means. The fact of foreign ownership further strengthens these attitudes because subsidiary firms are well aware that the financial strength of the parent would make it difficult for anyone to win a competitive struggle. The problem is particularly severe in industries that are engaged in selling activity, since brand names give established firms a secure position with respect to at least some of their customers. Foreign subsidiaries are concentrated in manufacturing industries in which brand names and other forms of product differentiation are common, because exploitation of the large and relatively fixed outlays on selling and design, research and development, supplies a motive for foreign investment, especially by American firms in Canada where the same sort of products can be readily marketed.

Thus the historic policy of Canadian governments, designed originally to protect infant industries while they developed, has failed to have that effect. Instead it has become the basis of a pattern of industrial practice that is tied closely to tariff and other trade barriers. The chief accomplishment of the Task Force has been to detail, for the first time in a government sponsored document, the inefficiencies caused by Canada's commercial policy combined with the characteristic conduct of industries with five or ten dominant sellers (oligopoly).

Safarian's contribution to this exercise in public education calls attention to the nature and limits of the relevance of foreign ownership and puts the stress on other factors that have given rise to the structural problem.

The controversy about foreign companies has largely shifted to two other issues, neither of which is strictly relevant to an assessment of the performance of foreign subsidiaries in Canada:

1. the general impact of the multinational corporation on the state — the controversy that has been dramatized by the writing of Kenneth Galbraith and J. J. Servan-Schreiber;
2. certain political implications of foreign control, in particular the issues associated with the extraterritorial application to the subsidiary of the laws of the state in which the parent firm resides, especially, of course, the impact of US law on Canada through the corporate affiliations.

Only when these issues have been evaluated will it be possible to determine whether Canadian policy can cope with the problem and to review the merits of various policy proposals that have been advanced.

56. THE LARGER ISSUES OF FOREIGN OWNERSHIP*

H. E. English

When the government's Task Force on the Structure of Canadian Industry reported, it seemed that at last the key issues relating to foreign ownership had been explored. The main weight of the Report stressed that foreign investment had been substantially beneficial to Canada; that the greater problems in the Canadian industrial structure could be remedied by publicity and competition, and without serious challenge to the continued operation of subsidiaries in Canada.

But there were other threads in the Report to suggest a greater disquiet over foreign ownership. This concern emerges from the sections of the Report dealing with the multinational corporation and extraterritoriality. The arguments on these sections of the Report have never been backed by the empirical support which appears in A. E. Safarian's writings on the performance of subsidiary firms operating in Canada. It is therefore surprising that much of the recent discussion has centred on these issues. One is tempted to suggest that those who are preoccupied with the foreign ownership issue have moved from a battlefield where Safarian's evidence has dealt them a defeat to another field where there is still sufficient shortage of evidence to enable them to make a stand.

Let us look again at the sections of the Task Force Report dealing with the multinational corporation and the extraterritoriality issues and then turn to its reappraisal of the policy proposals.

Multinational Corporations and the Nation State

At the outset, the Watkins Report raises the issue of the multinational corporation and the extent to which its interests diverge from those of the nation state. Interest of the large companies may diverge for at least three

*Reprinted from H. E. English, "The Larger Issues of Foreign Ownership," *The Canadian Banker*, March-April, 1970, pp. 18-22, by permission of the editor and author.
Dr. English is Director of the School of International Affairs and Professor of Economics, Carleton University, Ottawa.

reasons: (1) the presence of noncompetitive elements in the market situation; (2) the nationality of the management; (3) the varied efforts of each state to attract business investment away from others.

Such departures apply not only to the corporation, but to the individual state, particularly the one where the head office is.

Many of the departures of multinational corporations from what is commercially or politically desirable behaviour are not really the result of the corporation itself but of conditions under which it is obliged or enabled to operate. For example, noncompetitive conditions in a national market would cause any industry operating in such a market to adopt patterns of behaviour which would be inappropriate if there were more active competition in that market. Reactions may have little or nothing at all to do with the nature of the foreign-owned firm or the existence of foreign ownership. The Watkins Report itself includes extensive argument on this point. If the multinational corporation is to be identified as the source of any problem, it must be demonstrated that in the absence of the multinational nature of the corporation the situation would be different.

The conclusions of the Report leave the very strong impression that the factors causing faulty structure and performance in Canadian industry are largely independent of the existence of foreign ownership. If the appropriate conditions existed, it would be difficult to identify unique problems arising primarily out of the operations of multinational corporations in this country.

The second general point is that under internationally competitive conditions, there are important built-in constraints to noneconomic performance. First, the restraints on competition associated with the restricted national market are *ipso facto* limited by the removal of trade barriers. Second, the effects of various forms of government subsidy designed to attract industry to a particular country become more apparent, and the competition of national governments becomes more obviously self-defeating. Because governments operate in most industries in these circumstances as a kind of oligopolistic interdependence, it may still be necessary to reach explicit agreements among governments if rival industrial incentive policies are to be kept within reason, but this is true whether or not international corporations are involved.

The basic argument about the response of the multinational corporation to national preference patterns in a host country is that the size of the multinational corporation has grown to the point that one can no longer rely on the forces of competition to ensure that consumers in any national market will get what they want. This assessment has not yet been adequately tested by evidence.

Other evidence, however, can be cited. If the large international companies have significant cost advantages over smaller firms, then clearly the international company should come to enjoy a dominant position in North Atlantic or even world markets. Oddly enough the available evidence does not support this contention. The scale of operations required for research and development and selling activities varies widely from industry to industry. Apart from a very few industries associated with defence and aerospace products, the size of firms required to support effective research and development is not large relative to the size of the US market, and therefore relatively small in the context of North Atlantic or world markets. If international companies are to dominate the international market, it will be through effective measures to limit the "diseconomies" of large-scale and bureaucratic structures. Governments nationally and internationally may have to give increasing attention to the limitation of those expensive selling and distribution activities that make it possible for large firms to sell at higher prices, since these practices are most likely to cause concentration of markets in the absence of substantial real economies of large-scale production or research and development.

Direct evidence on concentration must also be examined. The postwar years have seen the expansion of the international companies in North America and elsewhere. It has happened in a dramatic fashion because the fifties and sixties provided the first opportunity for a peacetime boom since the twenties.

The growth and diversification of industrial activity and the parallel growth of the largest of the companies have been matched by growth and integration of the market. Even in the United States itself, the concentration of industry has not changed perceptibly, and both in North America and Europe the large concerns based in the United States and Canada have had to contend with new competition from European companies and the Japanese. The European response to branches of US firms has been an attempt to advance the size of their own enterprises, although it is difficult to be sure whether it is economies of scale or larger market shares that they seek. In any case, given the integration of European national markets, it is most likely that concentration of market power is not as great in most European countries as it was ten and twenty years ago.

The growth of international activity of US firms was mainly an adaptation to the new opportunities offered by expansion of Canada's national market, and by the founding of the European trading groups. Since the first decade of postwar development in Canada, and more recently in Europe, following the estabishment of the EEC and EFTA, there has been little if any growth in the relative importance of external direct investment activity. The absence of real economies of scale continues to be an important deterrent to further concentration of world markets. This does not mean that governments may not need to take co-ordinated action to prevent collusion among international companies, but it does mean that domination of the North American or North Atlantic market is less easily achieved than domination of the Canadian market.

It is also important that government should pay particular attention to one practice for which they are more directly responsible. National governments could well be increasingly vulnerable to efforts to acquire initial financial advantages, in exchange for favourable local decisions, as trade barriers are eliminated. The Task Force's discussion on the question of collaborative government action respecting international companies gave inadequate attention to the importance of avoiding the wasteful matching of incentives.

Extraterritoriality

The basic position of the Task Force on the issue of extraterritoriality is that when foreign laws affect the operations of the international company, the company becomes the tool of a foreign government, and because of this, whatever the net benefit or cost to the host country, defence of its own sovereignty becomes paramount.

The Task Force seems rather naïve about the meaning of sovereignty in the modern world. While it is reasonable for the Canadian government to insist that foreign laws should not, through corporate ownership arrangements, have a contradictory impact upon the Canadian economy, it does not follow that it is rational for Canada to take action against the extraterritorial effects of other countries' policies when these are in *line* with Canada's interest. The report generalizes too much when there is a need for hard thinking and more factual evidence as a basis for social policy.

The Balance of Payments Guidelines

The most important kind of extraterritorial result is that effected through the US balance of payments guidelines. They threatened to have an overriding effect on operating and investment decisions of US subsidiaries in Canada, and this kind of threat could well change the emphasis in decisions which should be based primarily on the usual commercial and economic criteria. The fundamental rationale in policy to control the balance of payments has been lost over the years. Under the international agreements which permit a country to take defensive action it is assumed that interference with trade and capital flows, on balance of payments grounds, should be for the purpose of correcting *temporary* disequilibrium. If the problem is truly chronic, it is assumed that more fundamental adjustment is required and will take place either through exchange rate adjustment or appropriate monetary and fiscal action. The objection to interference with normal trade and capital flows in these circumstances is much more fundamental than a question of extraterritoriality.

The fact that Canada requested and was given relief through an exemption is readily understandable politically. Furthermore since the continuing US balance of payments difficulties are partly the result of noneconomic considerations, one might justify the guidelines approach rather than more fundamental adjustment. But to a student of international economics, the case is a good illustration of the tough problems created by departure from the intent of international commitments regarding balance of payments policies.

If the US guidelines, like Canada's 1962 surcharges and similar British action, had been really temporary, it is doubtful whether Canada would have asked for an exemption. In the first place, it would not have been in keeping with the spirit of international agreements which assume that other countries expect to share the burden of adjustment in temporary balance of payments difficulties. In the second palce, short-term interventions are not likely to have lasting effects on commercial practices.

Antitrust Law

Among the three cases of extraterritoriality discussed in the Watkins Report, the second in importance, judged by its possible impact on Canada, is antitrust law. Here the situation is even more difficult to analyse. In the first place, the philosophies underlying Canadian and American antitrust legislation are almost identical, but this does not mean that the administration of the US law would necessarily serve Canadian interests. In certain aspects of the legislation, for example, the control of mergers and the dissolution of monopolies — approriate policy for the United States — might not suit the Canadian market situation at all.

Economies of scale in production, research, and development might be achieved by larger units in Canada, whereas the scale of operation of the parent firms in the United States would not often require a merger on any economic grounds. On the other hand, agreements affecting prices, or division of market and patent pools in the United States, could have spillover effects in Canada. This would be much easier to control through US legislation and its application than through any Canadian counterpart.

Trading with the Enemy Act

The most clear cut cases of extraterritorial effects to which there might be general objection in Canada are those associated with the US Trading with the Enemy Act. Here the US law may well have effects which run counter to Canada's foreign policy. Whether the extent of the probable effects is great is another matter. The effort to identify empirical evidence has foundered on the famous "Ford cars to China" case. Whether or not there was a firm intent to order in this instance is not known, but it is difficult to imagine that Canada's export of automobiles to China had much promise.

Flour and potash are another matter. Here the basic Canadian competitive position and supply potential are such that trade with the Communist world could achieve considerable significance. Thus on grounds both of general prerogative and of trading interest, Canada has every reason to resist the application, to Canada, of the Trading with the Enemy Act. The question which remains is how to effect Canada's independence in this matter. The present arrangement by which US-owned firms turn over Communist country enquiries to other Canadian-owned corporations is not very realistic. But the direct involvement of the Canadian government, as proposed by the Watkins Report, appears to give rise to other difficulties. It assumes the competence of a government body to deal in a wide variety of export activity without sacrifice of the usual commercial standards. It also assumes that the Communist world would not seek to embarrass both Canada and the United States by placing orders designed to further irritate Canadian-US disputes over this issue. Except for the limited range of military hardware, where it may be worth maintaining the technological gap vis-à-vis a potential enemy, a general exemption for products of foreign subsidiaries of US firms should surely be sought before a new government body is seriously considered.

All in all, extraterritoriality becomes, like other foreign-ownership problems, a question of measuring net benefits or costs. While the impact of foreign government policies introduces an element of special importance and potentially major interference in Canadian national interests, the authors of the Watkins Report have been led into a much too simplified conclusion on the appropriate public policy in these circumstances. Applying their principles, it follows that any change by the US government in its tariffs should be matched by countervailing Canadian action, whether the US action is in the direction of liberalization or further restriction of trade.

The Policy Question

What can and should Canada do about the issues posed by the foregoing discussion? The conclusion of the Task Force, that, on balance, foreign investment continues to bring substantial net benefits to this country, does not preclude the possibility that the net benefits can be enlarged. Many of the main policy proposals that the Task Force made were both acceptable in principle and in keeping with the traditions of Canadian political life. They included:

1. measures to expand the disclosure requirements affecting foreign subsidiaries, so that Canadian policy makers can better identify the impact of such firms;

2. measures to stimulate competition in the Canadian economy — including a stronger Canadian anticombines policy and a reduction of trade barriers.

Perhaps the main reservation one should mention about the Task Force's formulation of the latter policy is its imprecision in defining the nature or type of trade policy changes which would be most likely to succeed. The kind of industrial rationalization it seeks will not be readily achieved unless the trade barriers, affecting both Canadian exports and imports, are removed over a foreseeable period and with appropriate transitional arrangements.

A shift to more specialized products and enlarged export activity would require assurance of access to the United States, and hopefully other external markets, on terms equal to those of domestic producers supplying these markets. These conditions are more likely to be filled in a regional free-trade arrangement than in the traditional kind of multilateral tariff-paring to which the Task Force appears to refer.

In going on to deal with the larger political issues — the implications of the multinational corporation and of the extraterritorial impact of foreign government policies — the Task Force proposals take on a less realistic aspect.

The problems associated with a public institution for trading with China and other Communist countries have been mentioned.

The proposal that Canada should attempt to counteract the effect of the US balance of payments guidelines seems to miss the point. Either the balance of payments situation in the United States is genuine and requires the co-operation of other countries to avoid serious international monetary repercussions, or the US problem is insubstantial. If the latter is the case, the best policy would be to take joint action to persuade the United States to abandon its restrictive guidelines. But to propose unilateral Canadian action must be the least desirable of alternatives.

The antitrust question clearly calls for policy consultation between Canadian and American governments, but the Task Force Report fails to identify the main problem, and takes refuge in a rather dogmatic position.

As indicated, it appears unwilling to accept the desirable consequences for Canada, which might be achieved through the indirect effects of such foreign laws. On the other hand, it also fails to identify the genuinely undesirable extraterritorial effects of US antitrust law that have been cited more recently — the problem of achieving co-operation between foreign subsidiaries and Canadian firms in the development of specialized production and export to the United States and overseas markets. The question here is how best to achieve rationalization of Canadian production. To what extent are collusive agreements necessary to achieve the desired rationalization? If they are necessary, surely the best approach would be to seek solution through a Canadian-US government agreement rather than an effort at general exclusion of US antitrust impact on Canada, which might be much more difficult to achieve and of questionable desirability. This approach has been adopted in the Basford-Mitchell statement in which the US indicated that its antitrust policy will not be used to frustrate rationalization agreements by Canadian firms.

Recent Developments

In recent months it has become apparent that the Chairman of the Task Force has changed his view about appropriate public policy for international companies, and some of the other members appear also to have somewhat altered their positions, though not as much as Melville Watkins.

Much of the explanation for these second thoughts can be traced to growing cynicism about the interest of the present Canadian government in adopting the policies recommended by the Task Force, and the belief that the proposal of more radical remedies to the New Democratic Party would either increase the political strength of that party, or at least exert leverage on the Liberal government to act on the earlier more modest proposals.

The charge that government has failed to act on the Task Force proposals is only in part justified. In general, governments seldom act very quickly on Royal Commission or Task Force recommendations unless they relate closely to already established legislative priorities. Furthermore some action is underway. In the first place, legislation covering disclosure has been brought forward. In the second place, the government was obliged to wait until the Economic Council had reported on the earlier request for a review of competition policy, before it could be expected to act on the Task Force recommendations relating to this subject. The Economic Council's Report on Competition Policy was published only in the summer of 1969 and legislation is currently being prepared that may well take into account some of the Task Force's recommendations.

The only area in which there is no apparent government activity respecting an important Task Force recommendation relates to its proposal for tariff reduction. In this area the government can argue that it prefers to make important trade policy changes when there is an opportunity for agreements on a reciprocal basis with our chief trading partners.

I would have to agree with the critics, however, that the government continues to shy away from the implications of all recent studies of Canadian industrial structure, namely, that substantial liberalization of trade barriers is the cornerstone of any really effective rationalization program for improving the structure and efficiency of the Canadian economy, including the efficient performance of internationl companies. The commitment to trade liberalization measures may also be the essential basis for the kind of co-ordinated international action required to control these aspects of international oligopoly that lead to an uneconomic concentration of industrial power.

C. INFLATION AND CONTROL MEASURES

One of the more disturbing and persistent problems in Canada since World War II has been a rising general level of prices. The apparent inflationary trend in our economy has been a constant challenge to economists, business-men, financiers, political leaders, and all other citizens concerned with the economic development of our country.

Virtually all economists condemn "galloping" inflation — the sharp, unrestrained advance in prices capable of disrupting economies and crushing their fundamental institutions. Economists are divided, however, on the merits and demerits of "creeping" inflation — small, gradual increases in the price level. Yet such an upward drift in prices is not without its dangers, for small increases, year by year have cumulative effects. For example, a price increase of 2.2 percent per annum compounds to 24 percent in a decade.

A variety of economic and social problems have been attributed to creeping inflation. For instance, some people point out that it arbitrarily and regressively changes the distribution of income and real wealth among individuals and groups in society. In this context creeping inflation has been referred to as "the most unjust and capricious form of taxation." Inflation has also been blamed for lowering economic efficiency. It is said that economic growth is retarded because inflationary pressures reduce the pro-pensity to save. Some economists argue that creeping inflation discourages business efficiency because rising costs are easily passed on to buyers through price increases; the efficiency of labour is reduced, the argument continues, because gains in productivity are no longer a necessary condition of higher wages. Furthermore, it is alleged that inflation causes uncertainty and thus discourages business expansion. Another argument advanced against the toleration of creeping inflation is that rising prices will bring about a deterioration in the Canadian balance of payments position since domestic prices rise relative to prices in other nations, thereby adversely affecting the ability of Canada to export and import. It is not surprising, therefore, that price stability has come to the fore as a major goal of public policy.

In Canada and other advanced economies a rate of price increase of more than 2 percent annually elicits concern or discussion about "inflation." For developing countries, a much higher price rise is required before inflation is considered a problem. Reading 57 indicates that the decade 1959-69 was one of fairly general inflationary tendencies throughout the world, although such tendencies appear weaker and less universal in the underdeveloped countries as the 1970s begin than they did in the 1960s and 1950s. Probably the most striking thing about this selection is that it shows the great range and variability of price experience among nations. Apparently, there is no mechanism in the modern world to keep price movements even roughly the same across countries.

What causes inflation? Unfortunately, no clear-cut answer to this question has been provided. Some say aggregate demand rising faster than aggregate supply "pulls up" prices and wages. Others say prices are being "pushed up" by wage increases forced upon the economy by labour unions, or costs may be raised by business monopolies. Reading 58 distinguishes between the demand factors and cost factors as contributors to inflation, and discusses the nature of creeping inflation to which the Canadian economy has been subject since 1965.

Can inflation of the creeping type be prevented without causing a recession, with its attendant high unemployment and loss of production? Again, no one really knows the answer. Reading 59 focusses on the role and rationale of the Canadian Prices and Incomes Commission as an anti-inflationary body, and examines the various "trade-offs" between inflation and unemployment with reference to a so-called "Phillips Curve" analysis. This selection also considers the United States experience with a voluntary wage-price guidepost.

There is no question but that inflationary expectations have become a central feature in all modern economic systems. As a consequence, some economists suggest going beyond the conventional measures of monetary and fiscal policy. Reading 60 focusses on incomes policies. More specifically, it indicates some reasons for the development of incomes policies in some countries; describes three varieties of an incomes policy that have been used in the Netherlands, the Scandinavian nations, and the United States; and draws some conclusions about the effectiveness of these policies. Note its reasons for arguing that the experience with incomes policies has not been an unqualified success.

57. DEPRECIATION OF MONEY AROUND THE WORLD*

First National City Bank of New York

The complaint that there is too much "month" left over at the end of the "money" is a common cry of wage earners all around the world. Indeed, as the seventies begin, consumer prices are rising in many countries at more than twice the pace of the early sixties. Rapid rates of price increases prompt wage demands that seek to compensate for both past and future losses of purchasing power.

The accompanying tables present our annual survey of comparative rates of the shrinkage of value of money here and abroad. As in the past, we measure the depreciation of money by the rates of decline in the domestic purchasing power of national currencies (computed from the reciprocals of official "cost-of-living" or consumer price indexes), not by rates of inflation. For example, a 100 percent increase in a consumer price index is equivalent to a 50 percent rate of depreciation in the buying power of money.

Calculations of comparative trends in the value of money based on consumer price indexes are, at best, only approximate. The quality of consumer price compilations varies considerably from country to country. Major distortions may be caused by the coverage of only a limited number of goods and services or by heavy weighting of items with government controlled prices. Other deficiencies in consumer price indexes include failure to reflect changes in tastes, quality of goods, and consumption patterns over time.

This year, we are presenting separate listings of industrialized and less-developed countries. In addition, we have estimated the overall rates of depreciation of money in 1970 based on average increases in monthly consumer price indexes for the year to date versus the corresponding period of 1969. Therefore, to the extent that changes in the consumer price movements within a country can be calibrated into a yardstick for measuring changes in the buying power of money, the two tables present a general guide to the erosion in the value of money.

---

*Reprinted from First National City Bank of New York, *Monthly Economic Letter*, September, 1970, pp. 103-104, by permission.

TABLE 1

DEPRECIATION OF MONEY IN INDUSTRIALIZED COUNTRIES

	Indexes of Value of Money (1959=100)		Annual Rates of Depreciation		
	1964	1969	'59-'69*	'68-'69	'69-'70†
Greece	93	83	1.9%	2.3%	2.3%
Finland	79	61	4.8	2.2	2.5
Switzerland	87	74	3.0	2.5	2.5
Australia	92	78	2.4	2.8	3.1
Germany (F.R.)	89	78	2.4	2.6	3.6
Italy	80	70	3.6	2.5	3.7
Austria	85	72	3.2	3.0	3.8
Spain	79	58	5.3	2.2	3.9
Belgium	91	77	2.6	3.6	4.0
Canada	93	78	2.4	4.3	4.0
Luxembourg	93	81	2.1	2.2	4.1
Netherlands	86	67	3.8	6.9	4.1
South Africa	92	79	2.3	2.8	4.4
New Zealand	90	73	3.1	4.7	4.9
Denmark	81	59	5.1	3.2	5.2
United Kingdom	87	71	3.4	5.1	5.3
France	82	69	3.7	5.7	5.4
United States	94	79	2.2	5.1	5.7
Sweden	84	69	3.7	2.6	5.8
Turkey	82	57	5.5	4.8	6.3
Portugal	88	67	3.9	8.1	6.4
Ireland	85	68	3.8	6.9	6.6
Japan	77	60	5.0	4.9	7.5
Norway	85	71	3.3	3.0	8.6
Iceland	63	37	9.5	16.2	11.8

*Compounded annually.
†Based on average of monthly data available for 1970 compared with corresponding period of 1969.

The embers of inflation that smouldered in many industrial countries in the early sixties had ignited by the end of the decade into a blaze. The median rate of depreciation of money in the industrialized countries in 1969 was 3.2 percent as against 1.6 percent in 1960. However, the height of interest rates and the upsurge in wages and export prices in the industrial countries also evidenced the pervasiveness of the inflationary atmosphere. Therefore, in 1969 many countries took steps to cool the inflationary climate.

Signs of lessening price pressures, however, are appearing only with a lag. In the United States, the purchasing power of the dollar has been shrinking over the past two months at less than a 4 percent annual rate, a considerable improvement from the pace that prevailed earlier in the year. For the first seven months of 1970, the average rate of depreciation of the dollar works out to 5.7 percent compared with a 5.1 percent rate for all of 1969.

The average rate of depreciation of money as computed for 1970 diminished compared with last year in only six of the twenty-five industrialized countries listed in the first table. Of these six countries, the moderation of wage and price pressures in Canada and France has been accompanied by increases in unemployment. In many European countries, wage settlements

TABLE 2

DEPRECIATION OF MONEY IN LESS-DEVELOPED COUNTRIES

	Indexes of Value of Money (1959=100)		Annual Rates of Depreciation		
	1961	1969	'59-'69*	'68-'69	'69-'70†
Honduras	92	81	2.1%	2.6%	-0.4%
Thailand	94	83	1.9	2.1	1.5
Morocco	80	77	2.6	2.8	1.5
Venezuela	98	90	1.1	2.3	1.7
Dominican Rep.	86	85	1.6	1.0	1.9
El Salvador	100	96	0.4	-0.3	2.9
Guatemala	100	96	0.5	2.2	3.1
Israel	75	60	4.9	2.4	3.3
Iran	84	78	2.4	3.0	3.3
Bolivia	72	55	5.8	3.1	3.4
Ecuador	83	67	3.8	6.0	3.9
Peru	69	39	9.0	5.9	4.0
Mexico	90	77	2.5	2.8	4.0
Pakistan	87	70	3.6	3.1	4.5
China (Taiwan)	75	63	4.6	4.8	4.6
India	80	56	5.6	0.8	4.8
Colombia	56	36	9.8	9.2	8.1
Argentina	36	13	18.4	7.1	8.8
Jamacia	86	71	3.4	5.8	9.3
Philippines	67	56	5.7	2.8	10.7
Indonesia	5	‡	58.2	5.8	12.0
Korea	51	29	11.5	11.0	14.5
Brazil	11	2	31.4	18.8	17.9
Chile	35	11	19.7	23.4	23.8
Vietnam	84	20	14.9	18.0	27.2

*Compounded annually.
†Based on average of monthly data available for 1970 compared with corresponding period of 1969.
‡Less than one.

of 20 percent or more have given an upward push to the wage-price spiral. Increases in indirect taxes added impetus to price pressures in Norway and Sweden in 1970 and in the Netherlands in 1969.

In two fifths of the less-developed countries shown in the second table, the domestic value of the national currency fell less in 1970 than in 1969. Among the South American countries, whose currencies in the past have suffered serious losses in purchasing power, official stabilization policies in Argentina, Brazil, and Peru over the past two years have begun to show positive results. Stabilization is also a major policy concern in Indonesia, which reduced the annual rate of depreciation of the rupiah from 91 percent in 1966 to 5.8 percent last year. Countries in all stages of development have come to realize that reasonable financial stability is crucial to steady economic progress.

58. WHY ARE PRICES RISING?*

N. D. Modak

Up until the mid-thirties, inflation was regarded as a situation in which there was too much money chasing after too few goods and services. The remedy for inflation was, therefore, the adoption of a tight money policy to bring the supply of purchasing power back into line with the quantity of available goods and services. Conversely, the remedy for slumps and depressions was to increase the supply of money, and with it the general level of prices and prosperity. However, with the publication in 1936 of Lord Keynes' monumental *General Theory,* the whole approach to inflation changed.

The New Economics

Keynes disputed the contention that there is a direct causal relationship between the supply of money and the level of economic activity. He directed attention to the total capacity of the economy as a whole to produce goods and services. If total "effective demand" comprising consumer spending, plus business investment expenditures, plus governmental expenditures is in excess of the output that the economy is capable of producing at its full capacity, prices are "pulled up" by the excess demand and will continue to rise if the pressure continues. According to Keynes, therefore, a state of inflation cannot arise until "after" the full-capacity point of the economy is reached.

At the same time, Keynes suggested that an increase in the supply of money will not, by itself, increase effective demand. He suggested that the supply of money affects economic activity through the interest rate structure. The increased availability of money reduces its cost, boosting investment expenditures, increasing employment, and thus pushing the economy toward its full-capacity potential. However, when interest rates reach very low levels, the cost and trouble of buying and selling securities are weighed

*Reprinted from N. D. Modak, "Why are Prices Rising? " *ICB Bulletin,* 3, No. 2, Spring, 1970, pp. 3-5, by permission of the editor and author. This publication is issued regularly by the Institute of Canadian Bankers, Montreal.

Mr. Modak is Corporate Economist for Cominco Ltd., Vancouver. He is an Honours M.A. from Cambridge University and a Fellow of the Royal Economic Society, London.

against the expected yield, and speculators begin to hold their money in cash, in the hope of better prospects later. This "Liquidity Trap" prevents the economy from achieving its full potential if the critical level of interest rates is inconsistent with it. He concluded, therefore, that monetary policy is not a foolproof instrument for stimulating economic activity.

He felt, however, that if the economy is working beyond its capacity and a state of inflation exists, a cut-back in money supply will increase interest rates, curb business investment and consumption expenditures, and thus cool the situation. However, he argued that the government has a much more direct and efficacious instrument for dealing with the problem. All it has to do is to reduce its own expenditure and/or increase taxes. The first reduces the government's direct contribution to overall demand; the second reduces the consumer expenditure content of overall demand. In either case, the result is a cooling of inflationary pressures. Conversely, an increase in government expenditures and/or a reduction in taxes have a stimulating effect on economic activity. Thus, under Keynes, fiscal policy replaced monetary policy as the principal instrument for controlling economic activity.

Newer Economics

In recent times, extensive historical studies conducted by Milton Friedman of Chicago University show that there has never been a period of severe inflation in any country, or at any time, which was not accompanied by a sharp increase in money supply, and vice versa. He, therefore, discredits fiscal policy and re-enthrones monetary policy as the only effective instrument for controlling economic activity. But Milton Friedman's historical studies also show that there is an indeterminable time lag between the implementation of policy and its effects. Consequently, any attempt to use monetary policy to offset short-term economic fluctuations is likely to increase rather than decrease economic fluctuations. He, therefore, prefers to allow the supply of money to increase at a steady rate of around 4 percent per year, or roughly in tune with the economy's potential for growth, regardless of short-term considerations.

In the meanwhile, recent experience throws considerable doubt on Keynes' proposition that a state of inflation cannot arise unless overall demand is in excess of what the economy is capable of producing.

During the recessions of 1953-54 and 1957-58 when, by definition, demand was below the economy's full-capacity operation level, prices not only did not decline, but actually continued to rise in the face of substantial unemployment. There was no excess demand to pull prices up; yet prices continued to creep upward! An analysis of this peculiar phenomenon has led to the suggestion that even in the absence of excess demand (which "pulls" prices up, according to Keynes), prices can be "pushed up" by rising costs.

The Cost-Push Dilemma

The cost-push explanation of inflation places emphasis on the "supply" side of the problem. It is based on the recognition that in the modern economy, wage rates are not determined by free market forces. They are "administered" rates, arrived at through the collective bargaining process. Consequently, although wages rise in response to excess demand, they do not necessarily fall when there is unemployment. In fact, aggressive collective bargaining can produce rising wages even when the overall demand for labour is falling! Similarly, the current business practice of marking-up prices by a fixed percentage at the wholesale as well as at the retail levels, magnifies the basic cost increases, pushing prices up even higher than they would have been otherwise. Thus, administered prices feed upon administered wages, and the latter upon the former, setting into motion a spiral of cost-push inflation.

Another factor which assists this process is the rapid growth in recent years of the service sector. Productivity improvements here are slower than in industry because of the limited scope for utilizing advanced technology and automation. However, wages in this sector tend to rise along with earnings in other sectors. The rapid and continuing growth of the service sector, therefore, represents a built-in factor pushing costs up, regardless of the presence or absence of demand-pull inflationary pressures.

We are thus squarely impaled on the horns of a dilemma. If we accept the demand-pull diagnosis for our current problem of rising prices, the correct remedy is to dampen demand through tight monetary and/or fiscal measures. But if, in fact, current rising prices are not attributable to excess demand but to cost-push causes, such measures would shrink demand further, increasing unemployment without halting inflation!

The Government and the Economic Council

The federal government's approach to our present problem of inflation is based essentially on the Keynesian analysis, which calls for restrictive fiscal and monetary measures to cut down excess demand. In practice, this is a short-term approach which implies rapid and flexible policy changes to fine-tune the economy in response to emerging conditions. The government feels, however, that in view of the "inflationary psychology" that has developed through the great economic expansion of the sixties, a display of determination (albeit tempered with gradualism) to eradicate it through the continued maintenance of restrictive policies, is essential.

The Economic Council, on the other hand, does not dispute the "ultimate power and effectiveness" of fiscal and monetary measures, but argues that the continuation of tight restraint at the present time is inappropriate. The Council's reasoning can be paraphrased as follows: over the past two years or so, unemployment rates have been running at between 4 and 5 percent. This indicates clearly that the economy is not working at full capacity. Therefore, recent price escalations cannot be attributed to excessive demand. But tight fiscal and monetary policies operate by reducing demand. Consequently, the continuation of current government policies, by reducing demand further, will create more unemployment without halting inflation.

The Council has two further points to make on this subject: first, (following Milton Friedman), that since fiscal and monetary policies operate with an indeterminable time lag, the continuation of current economic restraint could produce a recession in Canada later this year. Second, if, as expected, inflation in the United States is brought under control in the coming months, the recession in Canada could become really serious, because of the consequent reduction in the United States' demand for our goods and services.

The statement that is implicit in the Council's analysis is that current escalating prices are attributable to cost-push rather than to demand-pull causes. Accordingly, the Council reiterates the recommendations it has made in its previous Reviews, concerning "supply policies" to reduce cost-push pressures on the economy. It recommends further that since these supply policies take long to become effective, attention must be paid to them immediately if a repetition of serious inflation in the early 1970s is to be avoided.

An Assessment

Perhaps the weakest link in the Economic Council's argument lies in its definition of the full-capacity operation of the Canadian economy. This requires that the unemployment level must fall to 3 percent of the labour force. Initially, this postulate was meant to be a target toward which we should strive in order to get the best out of the economy. In its present analysis, however, the Council seems to assume inadvertently that this is an immutable law. It proceeds to suggest that because the current unemployment level is considerably over 3 percent, *therefore*, the economy is working below capacity and *therefore*, (following Keynes) current inflationary price rises cannot be attributed to excess demand. The conclusion that continuing restraint will increase unemployment without halting inflation follows automatically from this argument.

Notwithstanding this apparent logical lacuna, the Council's warning that the effects of undue economic restraint now will be felt later is, as indicated above, based on extensive empirical evidence assembled by Milton Friedman and others. Similarly, in the longer term, the recommendation that more attention must be paid to neutralizing cost-push inflationary pressures is obviously sound.

Can Inflation be Prevented?

This brings up to the basic question of whether or not inflationary price rises can be prevented. There cannot be the smallest doubt that stringent monetary and fiscal policies can not only bring the economy to a grinding halt, but can actually cause prices to fall in a regressive spiral of deflation. However, what concerns us now is a different question altogether. The problem now is to prevent prices from rising excessively without causing a recession, with its attendant high unemployment and loss of production.

Put in another way, it can be said that we have already succeeded in reducing the boom-slump amplitude of the prewar business cycle to a smoother expansion-recession rhythm. What we are now trying to do is to tune the economy to a contented purr of rapid and continuous expansion.

This is a new and difficult problem which requires a contemporary solution. No one really knows the answer. In the circumstances, the important thing is to ensure that we do not shut our minds against seemingly revolutionary suggestions which militate against our conventional wisdom. As the great English political philosopher and economist, John Stuart Mill, said: "We can never be sure that the opinion we are endeavouring to stifle is a false opinion; and if we were sure, stifling it would be an evil still."

59. THE NEW PRICES AND INCOMES COMMISSION: SOME THOUGHTS ABOUT ITS TASKS*

The Bank of Nova Scotia

Since the mid-1960s there has been serious concern about persistently high and rising prices in Canada. During this period the impact of surging demands for goods and services has resulted in increasing strains on available resources and shifted the North American economy onto an unsustainable inflationary growth path. In an effort to counter these strong inflationary pressures, the monetary and fiscal authorities in both the United States and Canada have since late last year pursued policies of determined restraint, which in combination with heavy demands for loanable funds to finance the boom, have resulted in record high interest rates.

Unfortunately the inflationary atmosphere has to some extent worked against the normally restraining impact of high interest rates on spending decisions, and expectations have not accordingly been dampened very seriously. Thus, we presently appear to be on the tail end of a five-year period during which first price increases, and more recently the expectation of further price increases, have dominated economic behaviour. Indeed, even in the face of the currently restrictive fiscal and monetary posture there is much evidence to suggest that the problems of curbing rising prices, and the social costs involved in doing so, are substantially greater now than in the past.

The current problems of coping with inflation have renewed public debate about the impact that a gradual slowing in the rate of real economic growth is likely to have on prices and employment. Unfortunately the long-term record suggests that the restraining impact on prices is far from immediate in the North American economy, and also that the same degree of economic restraint in both countries appears to bring higher unemployment rates in Canada than in the United States. At the present time, in addition, prices in both countries have been rising at comparable rates, and yet Canada is experiencing an unemployment rate close to 5 percent compared with a 3½ percent rate in the United States. Clearly, the very tight labour market situation in the United States allows more room for policy manoeuvre than is true of Canada.

---

*Reprinted from the Bank of Nova Scotia, *Monthly Review*, Toronto, September, 1969, by permission.

In the past when economic growth has become too exuberant and strong measures have been required to steer the economy back to a noninflationary growth path, there has been a high cost in terms of idle resources and unemployment. Unfortunately, restraining measures — in their very nature — work first on real output and employment, and only with a lag upon prices. Recent studies also suggest that the time lag involved before such policies begin to slow inflation has lengthened in the 1960s.

It was to minimize the dislocations inherent in such corrective measures that the federal government in a White Paper[1] of last December, proposed the establishment of a Prices and Incomes Commission, which would hopefully assist in constraining price and wage rises.

The Commission, as described in the White Paper, was set up to inquire into the causes and nature of inflation, and to provide leadership for public opinion in this area. The White Paper suggested that the Commission's terms of reference be decidedly short run, and that its primary focus be on costs, prices, incomes, and productivity. Thus it was not intended that the Commission duplicate the work of the Economic Council of Canada — which is essentially concerned with medium- and longer-term problems. This review will focus on the role and rationale of the Prices and Incomes Commission as an anti-inflationary body, and in this context will also examine the various "trade-offs" between wage-price inflation and unemployment with reference to a so-called "Phillips Curve" analysis.

The Commission's Role

Although the terms of reference of the Commission were a bit vague, the original plan was that it carry out studies into the problem of inflation and also undertake a program of public education and moral suasion — sometimes referred to as "jawbone policy." At the same time the White Paper made clear that the Commission was not to "interfere with established and recognized processes of collective bargaining" nor was it intended to "play the role of the policeman."

Since early August the Commission has been pursuing a novel course of action which appears to be aimed essentially at shortening the period of transition back to a noninflationary growth path as well as minimizing the economic pain and disruption of the transition. In the main, the Prices and Incomes Commission has been striving to secure a consensus on a comprehensive package of private and public measures designed to achieve a general scaling-down of price and wage rises in Canada in the next year. Thus it hopes to attain approval for joint action by business, labour, and governments to place effective limits on increases in all forms of incomes in Canada. Should such a consensus be attainable — and at this time it is too early to judge — then the plan is to draft an agreement on objectives for formal consideration at a conference on price stability expected to be convened toward the end of this year. In the words of the Commission "if such an agreement is ratified, a formula will be sought on methods and procedures for dealing with instances of price and income increases which are contrary to the spirit of the agreement."

The emphasis on a formula for wage and price behaviour seems to link the

---

[1] Government of Canada, *Policies for Price Stability*, (Ottawa, 1968).

present Commission's proposal to existing West European programs. But the emphasis on voluntary compliance means that it has more in common with the recent US experiment with wage-price guideposts and a jawbone policy than with the practices adopted in these other countries. Because of this it is worth noting that the US efforts have aroused a good deal of controversy since their formalization in the United States seven years ago. And in recent months, in particular, some members of the Nixon Adminstration have been arguing that reimplementation of guideposts or wage restraints would be unsuccessful since it would lead the public to believe that they are a substitute for broader fiscal and monetary measures, and thus might worsen the inflationary pressures. In a similar vein, the Economic Council of Canada has also been a consistent critic of incomes policy approaches, its doubts appearing to hinge on the efficacy of voluntary wage and price constraints and on political and constitutional considerations.

The new Prices and Incomes Commission has strongly emphasized that it sees its role as supplementing existing monetary and fiscal measures — not replacing them. Thus it argues that its establishment does not imply that existing kinds of economic policies are inherently ineffective, but rather suggests that a successful policy of dampening price pressures using only fiscal and monetary measures may lead to an unacceptable disruption of domestic production and employment as well as hardships in particular regions which are already functioning well below their economic potential. Indeed the Federal Department of Regional Economic Expansion is committed to a policy of stimulating economic activity in those regions which in the past did not share equally in the benefits of economic growth. While the Commission has not yet publicly stated its price and wage level objectives, it is quite clear that to scale prices back down from the recent 5 percent rate of advance to a 2 to 2½ percent annual rate of advance — which is regarded as a reasonably stable price pattern — would require a roughly comparable 2½ to 3 percent reduction in the high rate of average wage advances of the past year.

A Phillips Curve Analysis

The rationale behind the Commission's search for an agreed-upon formula resides in the dilemma facing our policy makers — the near impossibility of reconciling the national twin goals of wage-price stability and full realization of the country's growing productive potential. In fact this policy dilemma has already been dramatically illustrated by a popular economist's tool called the "Phillips Curve." This analytic device, which is named after Professor A. W. Phillips of the London School of Economics, statistically measures alternative potential "trade-offs" between wage inflation and unemployment that a market economy may experience. In this framework a "trade-off" refers to the acceptance of a greater degree of unemployment for some lessening in the rate of wage inflation.

Thus our experience since the early 1960s suggests that a one percentage point dampening in wage pressures is accompanied by approximately a one percentage point rise in the total unemployment rate. Moreover, since there is such a close correspondence between price and wage movements in the economy, the Phillips Curve roughly expresses the linkage — and hence also the trade-off — between price changes and unemployment. The linking factor between price and wage movements in a market economy such as ours is labour productivity. Thus, as a rough approximation, the Canadian econo-

524

my would be able to afford high and rising wages concurrent with relatively stable prices if average gains in labour productivity approximately matched wage increase. Unfortunately, the stimulation of gains in labour productivity in order to dampen rising prices is almost impossible to achieve in the short run, although programs now in effect to upgrade the educational and skill levels of the labour force may afford some long-run advantages in this direction.

The Phillips Curve relating potential trade-offs between wage inflation and unemployment, while an interesting concept in theory, is somewhat difficult to identify in practice. Part of the problem is that the existence of a Phillips Curve suggests that a trade-off can be calculated without taking into account a number of other economic factors — for example, expectations of the public about prices, wages, and profits; longer-run structural changes in the economy; and international economic influences. Thus what we have to consider is not one Phillips Curve, but a family of them, relating wages and employment trade-offs to various levels of expectations about the future and to a variety of influences which may be temporary or accidental.

The chart brings into perspective the magnitude of the dilemma now facing our policy makers and also indicates how inflationary expectations have jolted our economy into a more disagreeable choice between wage-price stability and unemployment. The vertical axis of the chart measures annual rates of increase in average hourly earnings in manufacturing, while the horizontal axis measures total unemployment rates. The points scattered on the chart represent the relationship between wage changes and unemployment in each quarter from 1962 through the present; superimposed on these observed values are two Phillips Curves — the lower one respresenting the time path which we have tended to slide along between 1962 and mid-1968, while the upper Phillips Curve represents our subsequent inflationary experience. Both Phillips Curves are downward sloping, which suggests that a moderation in wage increases — and consequently price rises — can only be accompanied by higher rates of unemployment. These curves describe as nearly as possible the average location of all the individual items plotted on the chart. While it appears fairly easy to draw such a curve through the "scatter" of dots, this has been done more exactly through the use of statistical techniques. The most recent four quarterly periods, highlighted in the upper dashed curve, suggest that inflationary psychology has driven us off our traditional Phillips Curve and into a situation in which the trade-off between wage gains and unemployment is even more intolerable.

If a similar scatter diagram and similar Phillips Curves were plotted for the United States we should probably discover that their curves are lower down than ours, since they historically enjoy a more favourable trade-off between wage-price stability and unemployment. The evidence presented in the chart suggests that for our economy to regain relative price stability — that is, prices rising about 2 percent annually, and wages advancing around 4½ percent — it would require an unemployment rate of 4½ to 5 percent on our first curve, and possibly an unemployment rate in the vicinity of 7 to 8 percent on our higher curve.

Thus, inflationary expectations have not only made the task of curbing excessive demands more difficult, they have also forced us into a position of having to accept a much higher rate of unemployment to curb these inflationary pressures than would have been required in the recent past. Traditional policy measures, should they succeed in curbing the anticipation of further rising prices, could presumably shift us back on to a lower Phillips

FIGURE 1

SHIFTING PHILLIPS CURVES

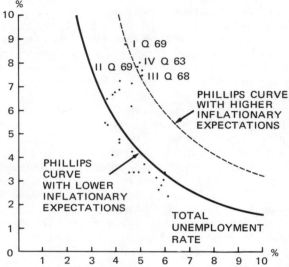

ANNUAL RATES
OF CHANGE IN
MANUFACTURING
HOURLY EARNINGS*

*Percentage increases in manufacturing wages may be approximately translated into consumer price increases by subtracting three percentage points from the wage rises. However, this method is intended to be used only as a very rough form of translating wage increases into price increases — since the Phillips Curve analysis appears to have more meaning in the Canadian setting when it is expressed directly in terms of wages.

Curve — but there is a distinct difference between restraining inflationary pressures and curbing inflationary expectations.

Hopefully, the Prices and Incomes Commission will assist in this complex task — both through the "jawbone approach" of dampening inflationary expectations and through a more direct restraining impact on labour, management, and government price and wage decisions. Indeed there is no reason why we should be satisfied with either the present inflationary Phillips Curve or the earlier trade-off curve. At any period of time a downward shift in the Phillips Curve is a desirable objective, since this makes more feasible the reconciliation of optimum economic growth with wage-price stability.

If economic restraint is unsuccessful in the battle against inflationary expectations, but is successful in slowing the real growth rate of the economy, then we would get the worst of all possible worlds — slow growth, high unemployment, and rapidly rising prices. Assuming the positive — that inflationary expectations will be dampened — then the likelihood is that the earlier Phillips Curve will once again be the relevant one. In other words, it is not sufficient for economic policy to slow our rate of growth and dampen prices temporarily if the public expects prices to start moving up once again with the first relaxation of restraint.

Guidepost Experience in the United States

The US experience with voluntary guideposts has already been briefly touched on but deserves fuller attention since in many respects we may possibly anticipate some of our difficulties from their experience. Government attempts to influence particular wage and price rises had been fairly common prior to the formalization of guideposts. The April, 1962 confrontation between President Kennedy and the US steel producers who wanted to raise their prices was one notable example of such selective pressures. The guidepost principle was first formally raised by the Council of Economic Advisers in their 1962 annual report to the President. In that report the Council proposed the setting up of guideposts for noninflationary economic growth, which were refined in later reports to suggest that, as a benchmark, an industry's wage increases should not exceed the trend growth rate of labour productivity. Their price guideposts called for an appropriate increase in prices if the opposite relationship prevailed. In theory, therefore, an industry's price level should remain stable if wage advances and productivity gains were equal. By 1964 the Council was recommending that the average increase in industrial wages should not exceed 3.2 percent — which was at that time the average annual percentage change in output per man-hour over the previous five-year period.

Apart from various technical differences between the Council's guidepost role and our Prices and Incomes Commission's initiative, there is a distinction which is of overriding importance. In 1962 when guidelines were first being debated in the United States, the North American economy was advancing only sluggishly, but a concern for the country's "balance of payments" position prompted a hard look at the price scene. The debate over voluntary guidelines in the United States took place prior to the income tax cut of 1964 and the major expansion of defence activities which stimulated the US economy and served to accelerate its rate of economic growth.

In contrast, the Canadian Prices and Incomes Commission is arriving on the scene after the economy has been overheated for a considerable time, and after the inflationary psychology has become deeply established in spending decisions. Hence the direction of economic policy in 1962, and the limited inflationary elements then in existence made for a very different environment than we are now facing. In the light of the growing inflationary pressures from 1966 on, the US guidepost program gradually withered away as labour and management resistance hardened. The wage-price constraints gave way because of inadequate support from conventional fiscal and monetary policy, which made it impossible to contain the high wage and price rises. Since taking office, the Nixon Administration has indicated little interest in reviving these guideposts and seems willing to rely on the traditional effects of tight economic policy slowing economic growth and eventually easing price pressures as well. However, the withering away of the guidepost principle in the United States should not imply that this policy was completely ineffective as a tool for containing wage and price pressures. In fact there is considerable technical evidence which suggests that wages and prices during the guideline period actually performed better than one would otherwise have expected. Hence the evidence indicates that the guidepost approach, with all of its drawbacks, was able to shift the US economy onto a more favourable Phillips Curve — the same difficult goal that our Prices and Incomes Commission hopes to attain in the presently more inflationary atmosphere.

Aside from the traditional emphasis on monetary and fiscal restraint, and the more recent attention focussed on incomes policies, there remain other important anti-inflationary weapons, such as policies which spur international price competition or which pursue anticombines regulations more vigorously. These latter two policies have the advantage that they do not involve direct or indirect intervention into actual price and wage decisions.

Both of these approaches deserve support, since it is well known that vigorous price and wage competition has benefits which tend to spread out generally through an economy. The first of these policies has already been tacitly accepted in the Canadian budget of last June which accelerated the implementation of the remaining tariff reductions from the Kennedy Round negotiations. The second has received support from the Economic Council of Canada in its recent studies on restrictive trade practices among the professions and service industries. However, the merit of these proposals should also be judged by their effects other than the direct anti-inflationary impact. At best both policies, if effective, would lead to some lowering of prices, but unfortunately they would not attack the core of the problem of persistently rising prices.

It is clear that the trade-off between unemployment and wage-price stability has worsened recently in Canada because of a deeply rooted belief that price inflation will continue into the future. Looking to the US experience for guidance, we find that contributing to the breakdown of their program was a political backlash against this very technique. Indeed the careful role carved out by our own Prices and Incomes Commission to effect voluntary compliance of labour, management, and governments is intended to avoid exactly such a reaction. If the US experience with a formula for noninflationary growth has any relevance to us, it is likely that the Prices and Incomes Commission will propose a linkage between wage increases, price increases, and productivity as part of their deflationary package. This program will be a complex one to implement, and the success of its approach may prove difficult to measure.

The Phillips Curve analysis of the trade-offs between unemployment and wage-price inflation supports this central theme and suggests that the recent unbroken pattern of rising prices has forced us off our earlier Phillips Curve and onto one which represents harsher alternatives for our economy. The current policies of fiscal and monetary restraint present some risks, but these are risks which are unavoidable at this time. The deeply rooted belief that rapidly rising prices are built into our economic system must be shaken. The need is to jolt the economy out of its highly inflationary state and into a more sustainable growth pattern, while at the same time minimizing the economic dislocation involved in such a transition. This is the challenge now posed to our policy makers. Should the Prices and Incomes Commission succeed in helping to curb the present inflationary psychology, then not only would this have a direct restraining impact on high prices, but it would also hasten the movement back to a reasonable balance between wages, prices, and employment. We wish them well!

60. INCOMES POLICIES: A QUICK CRITIQUE*

Robert H. Floyd

A high and growing level of employment, low unemployment, a stable price level, a high rate of economic growth, and a reasonable balance of international payments are five economic objectives that have top priority in almost all countries. There are numerous economic policies or tools available to any government for use in achieving these goals. Indeed, they comprise a broad spectrum of policy measures, ranging from direct intervention in the economy to very broad and general measures that affect the economy in a primarily indirect manner. Some relatively new measures that have recently received increasing attention in this country are the incomes policies.

This article focusses on incomes policies. To provide background, however, it begins with a brief discussion of more conventional policies and notes some of their alleged deficiencies. These problems have led to development of incomes policies in some nations and, more recently, to calls for such a policy in the United States. The article points out in general terms what actions might comprise an incomes policy and asks how well incomes policies have worked in actual experience, especially with regard to their generally accepted purposes.

More Conventional Policies

On one end of the spectrum of economic policies are two general or aggregate tools — monetary and fiscal policies. Essentially, both monetary and fiscal policy actions indirectly affect the economy. They are designed to *influence* the economic decisions of individuals, rather than actually dictate the decisions. These policies do not determine directly the incomes most of us earn or the prices we pay for our purchases. There are exceptions, of course. Certainly, the income of a person who entirely depends upon Social Security would vary directly with government action. Nevertheless, these

*Reprinted from Robert H. Floyd, "Incomes Policies: A Quick Critique," Federal Reserve Bank of Atlanta, *Monthly Review*, December, 1970, pp. 174-81, by permission.
Mr. Floyd is Economist, Federal Reserve Bank of Atlanta, Georgia.

policies usually operate indirectly, rather than directly, on our economic decision making.

Monetary policy in the United States is determined and carried out by the Federal Reserve System. By adjusting the supply of reserves available to banks, the Federal Reserve can affect the supply of money and available credit in the economy. This, in turn, affects the price of credit, the investment decisions of investors, and the purchasing power of consumers. Thus, total spending in the economy can be spurred either to absorb unused capacity or can be restrained to relieve the pressure on an inflationary economy.

Fiscal policy operates primarily through the budgetary activities of the federal government. By increasing or decreasing its own expenditures, the government directly adds to or detracts from total spending. By lowering or raising taxes, the spending power of the private sector of the economy is increased or decreased.

Calls for Controls

Until recently, general monetary and fiscal policies have carried the burden of the fight against inflation in the United States. They have not been without opposition, however. Some critics contend that, because of the complex and indirect channels through which monetary policy operates, it is effective in cooling an overheated economy only after a long delay. Many observe that, for various reasons, monetary policy discriminates between various sectors of the economy. For example, in a period of scarce credit, housing and state and local governments are usually placed under greater strain than are other sectors.

Fiscal policy is assailed because of the time required to make policy adjustments. Even if changes in expenditures and taxation are effective policy instruments, they usually require Congressional action, which is not always rapid and may be influenced by political considerations.

Worse still, many critics argue that *even if* restrictive monetary and fiscal policies were effective in curtailing excess demand, they would still not be sufficient to stop the spiral of price increases. Thus, we are told that the nation will end up with the worst of all possible worlds — inflation and high unemployment. The current pressures on prices, according to critics, come from the cost or supply side of markets, and monetary and fiscal policies are not effective in fighting this "cost-push" aspect of inflation. How can this be?

There are several reasons why prices may not respond immediately to reduced demand. First, much of the economy is not characterized by numerous, highly competitive small firms, a necessary condition for what economists call "perfect competition." Instead, the economy contains many firms which may have considerable influence over the prices they charge. Once these firms have set a price, they are reluctant to reduce it. Cuts in production are preferred to price cuts when output cannot be sold at existing prices. Also, demand slowdowns are often accompanied by rising costs. Despite production cuts, some companies may be initially reluctant to lay off trained personnel for fear of losing them to other companies. As output falls, output per man-hour, or productivity, tends to fall. At the same time, workers attempt to catch up with past inflation by demanding wage increases. With productivity declining and wage rates rising, unit labour costs of output rise. Thus, even in the face of declining demand, there remain pressures to keep prices from falling.

Eventually the decline in output and rising costs lead to layoffs. Unemployment rises. Unit labour costs begin to fall or rise more slowly. Productivity increases. Companies undertake other cost-cutting procedures. But with continued pressure on wages, the results of these efforts come slowly. Prices may continue to rise for a time. Also, unemployment may continue to rise until workers locate existing job vacancies or until growth in the economy is sufficient to provide new jobs for the unemployed.

Critics of restrictive policies found support for their views in the economic development of the past six or nine months. For a painfully long time, prices seemed to have continued a relentless rise; unemployment has increased; and the economy has behaved sluggishly. Despite recent indications of better price performance, cries are still heard for different policies, either to obtain or to speed the necessary economic adjustments. But what other policies are available?

Recall that monetary and fiscal policies lie at one end of the spectrum of economic policies. At the other end lie direct or compulsory controls. These policies *directly* affect many of the economic decisions of individuals. In general, they are designed to fix specific prices, wages, profits, credit, or perhaps even types of production, especially during periods of inflation. The individual businessman would be prohibited from charging more than a certain ceiling price for his product. The individual worker could not receive more than a ceiling wage for his labour services. The individual consumer also might be prohibited from purchasing any item for which he does not have sufficient rationing points.

Clearly, such policies greatly interfere with freedom of choice. In addition, they substantially distort the workings of a free enterprise economy. Usually, these policies require a large bureaucracy merely to implement the controls. Because they are fixed, prices cannot perform their vital role as signals to producers and consumers, and cannot direct productive resources into areas of greatest demand. Consequently, compulsory controls not only hinder individual freedom but also undermine efficient production processes. As a substitute for well-conceived, responsible monetary and fiscal policies, direct controls are not particularly attractive. Even worse, historical experience has shown that they do not eliminate, but only temporarily suppress, the basic causes of inflation. For example, direct controls could not offset ill-conceived, irresponsible monetary or fiscal policies.

Incomes Policies

The undesirability of compulsory controls has led most critics to seek milder measures. Most often, they have urged that wage-price guidelines be established for the United States economy. This measure has been sought *as a supplement to, not a replacement for,* corrective monetary and fiscal policies. Critics maintain that guidelines would assist the more general measures by shortening the time required for them to slow the rise in prices and thus prevent at least some of the rise in unemployment. Guidelines would assist in offsetting cost-push pressures.

Wage-price guidelines are one variation of another type of economic policy, *incomes policies*. During the 1960s, incomes policies of various sorts were employed to help achieve the goals of stabilization policy in numerous countries. These policies vary from country to country in both objectives and methods, and there is no generally accepted definition of an incomes policy. In the spectrum of economic policies, they fall somewhere between the general or indirect monetary and fiscal policies and direct, compulsory controls. Incomes policies seldom involve actual direct controls but often restrain the more or less free reins allowed by general monetary and fiscal policies.

Most incomes policies are designed to reconcile the economic goals of individuals (such as higher profits by managers and businessmen) with the economic goals of the nation as a whole (such as stable prices). Usually an incomes policy is primarily concerned with the advance of the *general* price and wage levels, rather than with wages and prices in particular industries.

In some countries, the government not only defines acceptable limits for overall increases in wages, prices, and profits but also sets a more or less exact criterion for the distribution of incomes among the various categories of income recipients. For example, the government might decide that, in the aggregate, wage earners should receive 65 percent of the national income.

One reason for the difficulty in defining an incomes policy is the different emphasis given to the various objectives of these measures in several nations. Rather than attempt a general definition, let us look at three varieties of an incomes policy that have been used in the Netherlands, the Scandinavian nations, and the United States. This will highlight the variations in the approaches and also permit us to draw some conclusions about the effectiveness of these policies.

Incomes Policy in the Netherlands

Among the Western nations, the Netherlands has had one of the strongest incomes policies. The dependence of the nation's economy on foreign trade has resulted in extraordinary co-operation between trade unions, business, and the government. All have realized the importance of maintaining the country's international competitive position; all have been willing to accept an incomes policy.

After World War II, the Netherlands faced the task of rebuilding its economy. To assist in accomplishing the reconstruction without sacrificing its international competitive position, a strong incomes policy was adopted. Wage- and price-fixing machinery was established. Although controls were compulsory, they were greeted by an exceptional spirit of co-operation between all sectors of the economy. In 1945, the Labour Foundation was established to formalize co-operation between labour and management. In the same year, an Extraordinary Decree on labour relations set up a Board of Mediators with the power to fix wages and determine rules governing wage changes. The Board was also given the power to administer penalties and sanctions. However, the Board was required to seek the advice of the Labour Foundation and, in practice, generally followed its recommendations.

In 1950, another organization was established — the Social and Economic Council. The Council is comprised of equal representation from government, business, and labour. Whereas the Labour Foundation is concerned primarily with wage policy on the industry level, the Council focusses on broader, national objectives (including the distribution of income).

Between 1945 and 1954, wages were controlled in the Netherlands. No increases were allowed without permission of the Board, and wage boosts were allowed only for cost-of-living increases. Some differences were allowed, however, where job skills differed, in order to induce workers to advance. Since economic recovery was under way, wages as a share of Gross National Product fell during this period.

In 1954, the Council developed a new policy. Rather than merely maintaining the purchasing power of wage earners, real wages would be allowed to increase. Wages as a share of GNP would remain constant. Overall wage increases were negotiated on this basis, largely through collective bargaining. Wage differentials between jobs, however, were permitted to increase.

A new government in 1959 instituted yet another new policy. Emphasis was shifted from economy-wide wage adjustments to changes by particular industries. Wage increases in each industry were tied to productivity advances in that industry, as estimated by the Board of Mediators. Industries with higher than average productivity advances had to pass on some of the advances in the form of both lower prices and higher wages. Falling prices in high productivity industries meant that wage increases could be granted in industries with slow productivity growth and reflected in higher prices without affecting overall prices.

The task proved too difficult for the Board of Mediators, and dissatisfaction with the estimates grew. Accurate estimates of productivity increases by industry are difficult to estimate. Also, rapidly rising wages in other nations put pressure on the Board's standards. Labour demand in the Netherlands was high and wages actually paid often exceeded approved levels.

By 1963, the program had to be changed again. Responsibility for individual negotiations was shifted to the individual firms and unions. Settlements were submitted for approval to the Labour Foundation, which in turn was influenced by the Economic and Social Council's assessment of the economic climate and acceptable wage increases. The Board of Mediators entered the process only if the Foundation disapproved specific settlements, but the Board did retain formal powers to control wages.

These new arrangements did not last; the same demand pressures developed again. In 1967, the entire system was dropped and free negotiations were permitted. The government, however, still retains the power to invalidate individual agreements.

But what about prices? Throughout the postwar period, the government also had extensive legal control over prices. However, the threat of control was sufficient in itself, and actual pricing policies were based almost entirely on voluntary co-operation between the government and business.

Price policy was actually carried out by the Ministry of Economic Affairs. The Ministry received advance notice of price increases for all goods and services, along with the justification for these price hikes. If the Ministry did not approve, it usually requested that they be rescinded. If this failed, legal powers were available to force a rollback.

Throughout the postwar period, price and wage policies were closely co-ordinated. For example, in 1951, prices were raised by 10 percent, but wages by only 5 percent, in order to restore external balance. A 5 percent wage increase in 1964 was passed on into a 5 percent price increase. These close policy links provided the Netherlands' government with considerable influence over wage and profit incomes and the uses to which income was put. Investment expenditures were stimulated, while consumption was minimized.

In summary, the Netherlands moved from a policy of virtually direct controls to progressively less restriction until 1969.[1] There is reason to believe that the policy greatly aided the nation to achieve a stable reconstruction without seriously eroding its international competitive position. As the recovery proceeded, the vital co-operation between economic sectors began to diminish, and the government's ability to rely on voluntary restraint dissipated. Free market forces finally dominated.

The Scandinavian Experience

Among the Scandinavian nations, Norway's incomes policy most closely resembles that of the Netherlands. Both nations faced similar problems. Direct government regulation was relied on to speed postwar recovery without damaging the international competitive position. Price and profits controls were extensively utilized in Norway, but since then have been progressively relaxed. Compulsory arbitration of labour disputes was employed until 1952. However, the various economic policies have not been so closely co-ordinated as in the Netherlands. Wage negotiations, conducted on a national level between union and management groups, usually set patterns for industry- and firm-level negotiations. The government does not enter directly into the negotiations but, rather, merely announces what it considers acceptable settlement limits. Throughout most of the 1950s, government influence was used sparingly. But in 1968, compulsory arbitration was reinstated to settle stalled negotiations. On the whole, government intervention in the economy was not quite as detailed as in the Netherlands; however, it has remained somewhat stronger.

Sweden presents a slightly different picture. The government's policy manoeuvers in that country have been intermittent. The manual labour force and the white-collar labour force are organized into two separate unions, and consequently, it has been more difficult for nationwide bargaining to achieve settlements consistent with national economic objectives. As in Norway, Sweden's formal administrative framework is not as elaborate as in the Netherlands.

Beginning in 1948, the Swedish Government urged unions and management to use a policy of wage restraint in order to achieve price stability. Dividend limitations and higher profits taxes were coupled with the request. The policy worked fairly well from 1949 to the Korean War boom, but in 1952, both wages and prices rose more than 29 percent, and the wage restraint policy was dropped by the government and by the unions. In 1953 and in 1954, the policy was reinstituted, but under the pressure of stronger demand again failed in 1955. Moderate national settlements characterized the second half of the 1950s. The reason was probably reduced demands for labour and goods, rather than union restraint. Prices remained reasonably stable.

The 1960s policy saw little change in Sweden. Central negotiations still set

---

[1] Recently, this trend has been reversed. In 1969 and 1970, the Netherlands' government used price controls with varying degrees of effectiveness. These have now been extended in the form of guidelines until March, 1971. Also the budget proposal for 1971 provides for a temporary wage freeze.

the national pattern for wage settlements. However, strong demand for labour and other factors resulted in local wage payments which have exceeded centrally negotiated settlements. In the latter part of the decade, the government appointed an arbitration committee to aid in settling stalled central wage negotiations.

In general, Sweden's incomes policy has been much milder and more intermittent than those of the Netherlands and Norway. Legal fixing of prices, profits, or wages was not used. Price stability was sought by efforts to hold down wage increases, but compulsory arbitration was not employed. However, this policy has probably been less effective. Substantial wage and price increases have occurred, and during periods of strong demand the policy has been dropped. However, in the face of excess demand, a general price freeze is now being employed.

The United States: Wage-Price Guidelines

The problems and the policy in the United States have been different. Postwar reconstruction was not necessary, and the balance of payments, although a matter of concern, is less important to the total economy. There were, however, two other problems. The 1950s were characterized by slow growth and persistently high unemployment, with the unemployment rate averaging a staggering 6.8 percent in 1958 and 6.7 percent in 1961. Prices during the period remained relatively stable, however.

The task in the early 1960s was to stimulate growth and employment without inducing inflation. Expansionary fiscal and monetary policies were used to spur the growth. To accompany these policies, the 1962 Economic Report of the President announced a set of wage-price guideposts. The statement noted the inflationary bias built into the institutions of the economy, such as the ability of large corporations to offset union-negotiated wage increases by raising prices. Many prices were not determined by competitive market forces, but were "administered." A vigorous application of wage-price guideposts might overcome this bias.

The Report noted that the change in productivity is the basic guide as to whether or not an increase in wages or prices is inflationary. Money wages can increase at the same rate as the overall rate of increase in productivity in the economy without raising the labour cost per unit of output. Thus, the wage increases would not be inflationary. If the rate of productivity in a particular industry is greater (less) than the overall rate, and if its money wages increase equalled the overall rate, the unit labour cost would fall (rise) in that industry. In this case its prices should be lowered (raised). There could be exceptions. For example, rapidly expanding industries might need to bid wages up in order to attract workers, while contracting industries would pay relatively less.

This policy was entirely voluntary. Direct government control of prices and wages was never threatened. However, the persuasive power of the government can still be great. Unjustifiably large wage settlements and price increases were called to the public's attention in order to mobilize public opinion. Shifts in government contracts, the possible freeing of government stockpiles, and the ever-present possibility of antitrust action were powerful incentives for business and labour to accept the guideposts.

The policy worked reasonably well as long as there was unemployment and excess capacity. As demand increased, however, so did pressure on wages and prices. By 1966, transportation and automobile wage settlements, among others, exceeded the guideposts. In 1967, average hourly compensation in the private sector of the economy rose by 6 percent and consumer prices by about 3 percent. The guideposts began to crumble under the weight of excess demand. The 1967 and 1968 Economic Reports of the President recognized the collapse of the policy. Without the threat of compulsory controls, the guideposts could not be enforced. With the guideposts ineffective, the government fell back on conventional monetary and fiscal policies to combat the inflation which resulted from the overheated economy.[2]

Success or Failure?

A review of the experience with incomes policies suggests that they have not been an unqualified success. Nevertheless, there have been instances when inflation probably would have been more severe if some form of incomes policy had not been in effect. These experiences suggest the such a policy is more likely to succeed if certain conditions are present.

An incomes policy seems more likely to hold down wage and price advances in an economy that is less than fully employed than in an economy in which there are few unused resources. Although there is an absence of general demand pressures in an underemployed economy, there may be cost-push pressures in some sectors. This type of policy could be useful in discouraging wage and price increases resulting from the concentration of economic power by either big labour or big business in certain industries. In this case, the incomes policy may hold down excessive administered price and wage increases while monetary and fiscal policies are adopted to help bring the economy to full employment. This seems to have been the case in the United States during the early 1960s.

On the other hand, experience suggests that if the economy were more than fully employed, an incomes policy would collapse. Such was the situation in Sweden in 1952 and 1955. In the United States, wage and price guidelines apparently had some marginal success until 1965 when, with the economy almost fully employed, the policy became ineffective.

Another essential requirement is that the policy must be accompanied by appropriate monetary and fiscal policies. It cannot be used as a substitute for limiting excessive demand. This is especially true when the policy relies wholly on voluntary co-operation. If the government is stimulating purchasing power through deficit financing during a period of full employment and the monetary authorities are adding to purchasing power by expanding the monetary base, no amount of exhortation would prevent businessmen and wage earners from giving in to the temptation to seek higher prices and wages.

An incomes policy would be more effective when there is a well-designed, organizational framework of labour and business and when there is a strong

---

[2] Recently, the President established a National Committee on Productivity, with representatives from labour, business, the public, and the government. The Council of Economic Advisers now prepares reports that spotlight significant areas of inflation. Government purchases and regulations are under review for possible inflationary impact. It remains to be seen whether or not these actions will reduce inflation.

consensus by these organizations in support of the policy. In the European countries where it was apparently effective during certain periods, there were strong labour and business organizations. The Netherlands is an outstanding example. Lacking such a well-designed and well-defined framework, the wage-price guidelines in the United States had to depend a great deal upon rallying the support of the American public on essentially moral grounds. For example, certain price increases in the early 1960s were said to be unjustified or contrary to the public interest. The huge power and influence of the Presidency was brought to bear on those seeking to exceed the guidelines.

As a practical matter, an incomes policy is more likely to be effective when productivity is increasing than when it is not. Conditions of rising productivity make possible an increase in real wages over time without pinching the profits of businesses. Under these circumstances, the policy is more likely to receive support than when productivity, real wages, and profits are declining.

Moreover, it is more likely to succeed if it applies to all sectors of the economy. The application of the policy to wages but not to prices would be ineffective. It must apply to both. For example, in the Netherlands, wage and price policies were closely co-ordinated.

An incomes policy is more likely to be successful when there is a strong threat of foreign competition than when a greater part of the economy is insulated from economic developments in other countries. This was important to the success of such a policy in the Netherlands. Foreign competition mobilized strong public support for it and provided an environment in which prices and wages were under external pressures not to increase too rapidly. On the other hand, if a country — at the same time it adopted an incomes policy — set up barriers to imports, the likelihood of success would be diminished. But it might also increase the need for an incomes policy.

Another implication to be drawn from experience is that success of this type of policy is closely tied to its timing. It might be appropriate at one time and not at another. For example, it could be worthless if applied before other restrictive measures begin to bite. If excessive demand pressures have been eliminated and price increases are stemming mostly from cost-push pressures, the policy stands a better chance of success.

An Incomes Policy Now?

Would an incomes policy be appropriate and effective in the current American economic setting? It is contended by many persons that excess demand has now been largely eliminated in the American economy. The slowdown in the rate of economic growth, the large amount of unused capacity, and the higher unemployment rates are cited as evidence that total demand has been brought under control. At the same time, the continuing rise in prices in some sectors of the economy suggests to these persons that most current increases in prices stem from cost-push factors. This seems, then, to be an appropriate time for applying some kind of an incomes policy.

On the other hand, there are persons who cite the diminishing strength of inflationary forces as evidence that, given time for the economy to adjust, monetary and fiscal policies will turn out effective. These persons argue that, even if the results are not completely satisfactory, one could not expect an incomes policy to do much better. In rebuttal, proponents of an incomes policy, however, argue that it would reduce the time required for monetary and fiscal policies to work, and, at the same time, hold down the rise in unemployment.

Just as it is extremely difficult — if not impossible — to determine how much influence incomes policies have had in the past, it is an open question as to how effective such a policy would be under present conditions in the United States. In any case, too much should not be expected from an incomes policy, should one be put into effect. It would not be a panacea, and it would not work without sacrifice. At best, it would be marginally helpful and would not be harmful to other well-chosen policies.

D. ECOLOGICAL ECONOMICS

The problems of mankind change constantly, especially in the economic sphere. Thus, until very recently, economists ignored the natural environment: it was just taken for granted as one of the "given" elements of the economic problem. It is true, of course, that the physical environment was always implicitly in the background when economists talked of the celebrated law of diminishing returns or when they discussed the impact on unit costs when an industry experienced a depletion of its nonhuman sources of energy and raw materials. But on the whole, very little consideration was given to the effect of the consumption and production process on the quality of the surrounding habitat.

Now that state of indifference is rapidly coming to an end. More and more economists have begun to recognize that as a by-product of its normal, daily operation, the economic process is speedily, and in many cases, unfavourably, altering the environment. The experience of the United States in this respect is particularly illuminating. Americans beget an average of seven pounds each of waste every day; 200 million tons of contaminants from automobiles, planes, and industries are emitted into the atmosphere every year; two million gallons of sewage and other fluid waste pour into US waterways every second; the Ohio River water is used about four times before it gets to the Mississippi; the nation discards every year 48 billion cans, 26 billion bottles, 20 million tons of waste paper, 7 million car bodies; and 3 million tons of waste rock and mill tailings. In addition, noise (or ear pollution) costs Americans $4 billion a year, more than the GNP of many countries.

These examples are sufficient to suggest that the overall debasement of the environment is *itself* a cost, borne by society in terms of less pleasant surroundings, more expensive living costs, bigger medical bills, and higher death rates. From these considerations it emerges that we must prepare ourselves for a new kind of economic problem.

One of the challenges that this problem offers is how to find ways of making the costs of environmental pollution part of the costs of production itself. As Reading 61 points out, one of the "externalities" inextricably associated with the act of production, is the universal tendency for industries to jettison residues and wastes into an ecological system or "ecosystem" that is increasingly cramped for space to absorb them. What was once a "free good" — the sheer absorptive capacity of the air and the land and the water — is now a common property resource of great and increasing value. Thus, what we need are means that will enable us to include the costs that *someone* must bear in the profit-and-loss considerations of the industry that is, however innocently, the source of these costs. This selection goes to the heart of the issue and tries to explain why the automatic market exchange process fails in connection with the many forms of environmental damage.

Sometimes satire is as effective as serious argument — and far more fun. Reading 62 is an example directed at the general problem of pollution control. Note that what is at stake here is not always a question of social cost, but sometimes of who is to bear the cost.

61. ECONOMICS AND ECOSYSTEMS*

Jon Breslaw

Wastes in the Economy

The American economy can be best represented by the concept of a competitive market.[1] If one regards the market as a black box, then there are two processes which do not come within the market's sphere of influence — inputs and outputs. The inputs are raw materials, or resources, used in the economy — air, water, metals, minerals, and wood. The outputs are the residuals — sewage, trash, carbon dioxide and other gases released to the atmosphere, radioactive waste, and so on. We shall consider the residuals first.

The environment has a certain limited capability to absorb wastes without harmful effects. Once the ambient residuals rise above a certain level, however, they become unwanted inputs to other production processes or to final consumers. The size of this residual in fact is massive. In an economy which is closed,[2] the weight of residuals ejected into the environment is about equal to the weight of input materials, plus oxygen taken from the atmosphere. This result, while obvious upon reflection, leads to the surprising and even shocking corollary that the disposal of residuals is as large an operation, in sheer tonnage, as basic materials production. This incredible volume has to be disposed of. It is at this stage that the market process breaks down.

---

*Reprinted from Jon Breslaw, "Economics and Ecosystems," *The Environmental Handbook,* Garrett de Bell, ed., Copyright 1970, pp. 411-19, by permission of Ballantine/Friends of the Earth Book Company.

Mr. Breslaw is a graduate student, Department of Economics, University of California, Berkeley.
[1] The assumption is that while there is some public production and regulation, the choices concerning the use of resources are made in a decentralized, decision-making system, where markets are competitive, and the individual decision makers — industries and individuals — maximize their individual private benefits. If the assumptions that the overall distribution of income is justified on ethical grounds, and that individual preference should be satisfied to the maximum extent possible, given income constraints, are accepted, and that there is open competition, then this decentralized system will produce the maximum welfare and allow the organization of production to produce what each consumer wants within the limits of his income.
[2] A closed economy is one with no imports or exports, and within which there is no net accumulation of stocks (plants, equipment, inventories, consumer durables, or residential buildings).

If the functioning of the economy gave rise to incentives, such as prices, which fully reflected the costs of disposing of residuals, such incentives would be very much in point. This would be especially true if the incentives fully reflected costs to the overall society associated with the discharge of the residuals to the environment. But it is clear that, whatever other normative properties the functioning of a market economy may have, it does not reflect these costs adequately.

Market economies are effective instruments for organizing production and allocating resources, insofar as the utility functions are associated with two-party transactions. But in connection with waste disposal, the utility functions involve third parties, and the automatic market exchange process fails.

Thus, the need to see man's activities as part of an ecosystem becomes clear. The outputs from the black box go through other black boxes and become inputs again. If our black box is putting out too much and overloading the system, one can only expect trouble — and that is what one gets.

If we look at a particular production process, we find that there is a flow of goods or services that consumers or businesses get whether they want it or not. An upstream river may be polluted by an industry, and the downstream user cannot usually control the quality of the water that he gets. If the polluted water wipes out a fishing industry, then there is some cost (the profit that used to be made by the fishing industry) that does not appear on the balance sheet of the upstream user. Similarly, there may be benefits involved — the upstream user may use the stream for cooling, and the hot water may support an oyster farm downstream.

The activities of an economic unit thus generate real effects that are external to it. These are called externalities. A society that relies completely on a decentralized, decision-making system in which significant externalities occur, as they do in any society which contains significant concentrations of population and industrial activities, will find that certain resources are not used optimally.

The tool used by economists, and others, in determining a course of action in making social decisions is the technique of cost-benefit analysis. The basis is to list all the consequences arising from a course of action, such as building a new freeway, and to make estimates of the benefits or costs to the community of all these consequences. This is done in terms of money values and a balance is drawn up, which is compared with similar estimates of the consequences of alternative decisions, such as building a rapid transit network or doing nothing. The sensible decision is to go ahead with those projects where the benefits come out best, relative to the costs. The art of cost-benefit analysis lies in using the scanty information available to assign money values to these costs and benefits. Differences in house prices are a way of getting at noise valuation. Time is obviously worth money: how much can be estimated by looking at what people do when they have a choice between a faster and more expensive way of going from A to B and a slower but cheaper way?

Going back to our slaughtered fish, if the cost of reducing pollution by 50 percent were less than the profit that could be realized from fishing at this level of pollution, then it makes sense to spend that amount. In fact, the level of pollution should be reduced until the marginal cost of reducing pollution (the cost of reducing pollution by a very small amount) is just equal to the marginal revenue from fishing (the extra revenue that is received as a result of that amount less pollution). The question is, where there is no market, how does one get to this state of affairs?

Method One is to internalize the problem so that a single economic unit will take account of all of the costs and benefits associated with the external effects. To do this, the size of the economic unit has to be increased. A good example of this is where one has several fisheries for one limited species of fish, for example, whales. If the fisheries operate separately, each concern takes as many as it can, regardless of the effect on the total catch. If the fisheries were to act in unison, then the maximum catch compatible with a stable population of whales would be taken, and no more — the externalities would have been internalized. Unfortunately, waste products are often so widely propagated in nature and affect so many diverse interests that the merger route is not feasible.

Method Two is the one mostly used at the moment: the use of regulations set up by government and enforceable by law. There are many examples of these: minimum net-hole size in fishing, parking regulations on busy streets, limited number of flights at airports during the night, zoning regulations as applied to land use, and certain water quality laws for industrial and municipal river users. Ideally, these regulations would take into account the different nature of the environmental difficulty, varying both over place and time, for example, high and low flows in streams, windy days for smoke control, etc. There are two main objections to such regulations. In the first place, they are often difficult to enforce, especially if there are high monetary returns involved and the likelihood of being caught is small — flushing oil tanks in the English Channel. The other objection is more sophisticated: in a competitive market the imposition of regulations does not normally lead to the best use of resources. It is better to do this by means of pricing, since this method makes it possible to balance incremental costs and gains in a relatively precise manner. Also, regulations do not provide the funds for the construction and operation of measures of regional scope, should these prove economical.

Method Three involves the legal system and the law of nuisance. Thus when there is an oil spill on your shore and you and your property get covered in goo, then in such an obvious and easy case one would expect prompt damages — but ask the residents of Santa Barbara what they think of courts and oil companies. Thus, though in theory the courts provide a solution, in practice, they are slow and inefficient.

Method Four involves the paying of some monetary rent in order to get the practice of pollution stopped. One way is to pay a producer to stop polluting. Although such payments would be received favourably by the industries involved, the sheer size of the total payments necessary as a means of preventing pollution would put an impossible strain on any budget, and such a solution is only feasible for "special case" industrial operations. Moreover, if a steel mill is discharging its waste into a river, without charge, it is producing steel that is artificially cheap. Paying the mill to stop pollution does nothing to get the steel price back to its rightful value (that is, when all costs are met) in the short run. In the long run, this remains true only if the assumption of a competitive market is weakened.

Another way to implement Method Four would be to charge a polluter for the pollution that he causes. Examples of such charges or taxes would be a tax on sewage effluents which is related to the quality and quantity of the discharge; or a surcharge on the price of fuels with a high sulphur content which is meant to take account of the broader cost to society external to the fuel-using enterprise. This procedure is one usually favoured by economists, since it uses economic incentives to allocate the resources (the waste assimilative capacity of the environment) similar to those generated where market mechanisms can balance costs and returns. The revenue from these charges can be used to finance other antipollution facilities.

The use of charges for the waste assimilative capacity of the environment implies that you have to pay in order to put things out of the black box. Before the environment's waste assimilative capacity was overloaded, it was not used to its full capacity. A resource which is not fully utilized has a zero price; once it is utilized it receives a positive price — which is why charges now have to be imposed. From an ecological point of view this is very good, since now that one has to pay to get rid of a product, it means that this product has a value attached to it, albeit negative. The effect is to restructure industrial processes to take this into account. A society that allows waste dischargers to neglect the offsite costs of waste disposal will not only devote too few resources to the treatment of waste, but will also produce too much waste in view of the damage it causes. Or more simply, if you charge for waste disposal, industries will produce less waste, and the wastes produced will often find use in some other process — recycling. A paper-producing company using the sulphite method will find it advantageous to change to the sulphate method through increased effluent charges. In England, many firms have found profitable uses for waste products when forced to stop polluting. In a few instances, mostly in already depressed areas, plants may be capable of continuing operation only because they are able to shift all or most of that portion of production costs associated with waste disposal to other economic units. When this situation is coupled with one in which the plant is a major part of the employment base of a community, society may have an interest in assisting the plant to stay in business, while at the same time controlling the external costs it is imposing. However these would be special cases which are used to help the adjustment to the new position of equilibrium rather than change the position of the new equilibrium.

Just such an operation has been used in the Ruhr Valley in Germany, starting in 1913. The political power of the Ruhrverband lies in the governing board made up of owners of business and other facilities in the Ruhrverband area, communities in the area, and representatives of the waterworks and other water facilities. It has built over one hundred waste-treatment plants, oxidation lakes, and waterworks facilities. Capital came from the bond market, and operating expenses from a series of charges contingent on the amount and quality of the effluent discharged by the industries and municipalities in the region. This scheme is so successful that, though the Ruhr River flows through one of the most heavily industrialized regions of Germany, one can find ducks living on it. Shed tears for the Potomac.

Nonrenewable Resources

The inputs to our black box consist of renewable resources, such as food and water, and nonrenewable ones such as minerals and land. In considering free resources, it was stated that in a decentralized competitive market economy such resources are not used optimally. In fact, they are overutilized — rivers are overutilized as disposal units, hence pollution; roads are utilized above their intended capacity with resultant traffic snarl-ups. The same holds true for nonrenewable resources: they are not used optimally.

Given a fixed technology, at any time in the past we would have run into a critical condition with respect to our supplies of minerals and metals. It is only changing technology, which makes for the profitable extraction of pretechnical-change unprofitable deposits, that has enabled us to manage without really bad shortages. Hence the present rate of extraction is only justifiable in the belief of future technical progress. Yet this is just the assumption that is now undergoing examination. In the past, man's technical progress was a function of man's incentive and ingenuity; now, however, he has to take into account another factor — the ability of the environment to accept his ravages.

As any child will comment on observing the empty beer cans and discarded packets lying on the roadside and around "beauty spots," this is wrong. It is wrong because we do not put sufficient value on the natural resource — the countryside — to keep it clean. It is wrong for the same reason a second time: we do not put sufficient value on the natural resources — aluminum, plastic, paper, or whatever — so that when we have used them for their original purposes, they are disposed of, as rapidly as possible. The conclusion is clear: both our renewable and nonrenewable resources are not being used optimally.

Take a specific example — oil. What are the factors that determine its price? As usual, demand is a decreasing function of price, and supply an increasing function. The point of intersection dictates the price and quantity sold. When the optimal use of oil is considered, there are two points of view that have to be taken into account. One is the value of the oil to future generations, and the other is the social cost of the use of the oil.

In considering future generations, optimal behaviour will take place in a competitive economy (with private ownership) if the private rate of return is the same as the social rate of return. In noneconomic terms, all this means is that the rate at which the future is discounted by individuals is the same as the rate at which it is discounted by society. There is dispute on this point — that is, whether the two rates are equal or not. However, even if they are, because the individual companies seek to maximize their private benefit, like in the fisheries example, the total exploration of the resources is likely not to be optimal.

At this stage, government comes into the picture. On the conservation side, a scientifically determined MER — maximum efficient rate (of oil flow) — is determined for a particular site. The main effect of this is to stop large fluctuations in the price of oil. Since half the total revenue of oil companies goes into the discovery and development of new deposits, this produces a high overhead cost. In the US, the aim is to produce as large a growth in the GNP as possible, subject to constraints (inflation, full employment, balance of payments, etc.). Hence the tradition of allowing industries to write off the cost of capital equipment against tax, since new capital stimulates the economy (investment) and makes for more efficient production. The oil industry felt that the same principle should apply to its capital costs — the rent it pays on oil deposits. Hence the oil depletion allowance, which allows the costs of rents to be partially offset against profits. The effect of this is to move the supply curve to the right — which results in more oil being sold at a lower price. Thus it encourages oil companies to extract more oil and find new deposits. This is great from a military point of view, but disastrous when the effect of such exploitation of the environment is considered: oil spills at sea, the probable permanent scarring of the tundra in Alaska, and smog in our cities. Yet this is exactly what is meant by social costs, the externalities which do not get considered in the market price.

If the oil depletion allowances were removed or sharply reduced,[3] the oil producing industry could not continue to function at its accustomed level of operation and maintain its accustomed price structure. Similar considerations apply to minerals (mineral depletion allowance). Yet this is only the first step. Another method that would produce the same desired results would be to make the extractor pay for the quantity of mineral or metal that he mines, just as he should pay for the right to discard his waste. This solves a whole lot of problems — by making the original substance more expensive, the demand is reduced, be it for power-using dishwashers, oil-eating automobiles, or resource-demanding economies. Moreover, these products, being more expensive, will not be discarded, but recycled, thus solving in part a pollution problem, as well as a litter problem (if they can be separated). By recycling, there will be less demand for the minerals or metals from the mining companies, since there is this new source of these materials.

To a certain extent, this view of things is recognized. In England, one of the proposals considered for solving the problem of scrapped cars around the countryside was to charge an extra twenty-five pounds on the price of each new car. This would be refundable when the vehicle was brought in for scrapping — a bit like returnable bottles. In the US, the use of natural gas as boiler fuel was recognized as an inferior use of an exhaustible resource. "One apparent method of preventing waste of gas is to limit the uses to which it may be put, uses for which another more abundant fuel may serve equally well" (Supreme Court, 1961). This same result could have been achieved by charging the gas producer for the quantity of gas that he took (as well as rent to the owner of the gas deposit for the right to extract gas from his property). The price that should be charged, like the prices charged for sewage disposal, vary from location to location and depend upon the characteristics of the environment. The price should be high enough to make recycling, if physically possible, both a feasible and desirable process. If the use of the resources causes some social cost — like air pollution — then this should be reflected in the price. So too should the relative scarcity of the resource, compared to substitutable alternatives, be a consideration.

If the socio-economic system fails to change quickly enough to meet changing conditions, then it is incumbent on the people to facilitate such change.

The Future

A prerequisite to any lasting solution to environmental pollution is a zero growth rate — the birth rate equaling the death rate. However, a stable population produces a difficult economic problem in an economy like that of the United States. To remain healthy (to stay the same size or grow), the

---

[3] This departs from the original assumption of a perfect competitive market, and from the point of view of strict economic theory there is some objection to the charge procedure described — it violates the principle of marginal cost pricing. However, methods that are less than theoretically ideal may be optimal in practice, since an important element in determining the best method for actual use is the cost of making marginal refinements. A comparatively crude method that is generally correct in principle will often realize the major share of the gains that could be achieved by more complex and conceptually more satisfying techniques.

economy needs a growing market, since only in a growing market can the capital goods sector remain efficient, given present technology. At first sight, then, the achievement of a stable population is linked to a recession. One might make the assumption that a growing market could still be achieved by allowing per capita consumption to increase at the same rate as the growth of the GNP. However, with restrictions on extraction industries, this will probably not provide a total solution. The slack is more likely to be made up by producing a different type of service — education at regular periods throughout one's life, the move from cities to smaller communities and the investment involved in such a move, the rebuilding (or destruction) of old cities compatible with their new uses. Put another way, the economic slack that will have to be taken up to avoid a depression gives us the opportunity to plan for the future, without worrying about providing for an expanding population.

The essential cause of environmental pollution is overpopulation, combined with an excessive population growth rate; other antipollution measures can be used temporarily, but so long as the central problem is not solved, one can expect no lasting success.

62. IN DEFENCE OF POLLUTION*

J. G. Raycroft

We who support pollution have very little to worry about. All the power and good sense is on our side. As well, conditions in a few years will reach the point of no return, and then we can relax. In the meantime, however, we should answer these unthankful trouble makers who oppose pollution and who have been writing a disturbing number of articles and columns lately. How can they be so narrow? To be against pollution is to be against the public interest. Show me clear sparkling water and I will show you an economically depressed area. How can they ignore these things?

The Maritime provinces, which still have some areas with unprofitably clean rivers and air, are begging for industry to help their people. On the other hand, the rivers of booming southwestern Ontario — the Grand, the Thames, and so on — are exactly what they should be: the sewers of progress. Look what Highland Creek and Don River do for the miracle of Toronto.

A friend of mine in Paris, Ontario once told me that the foam from the Grand River occasionally tumbled onto his lawn. He failed to appreciate that this detergent foam stood for a lot of clean shirts and underwear on thousands of good Canadian labourers and businessmen upstream who are contributing to the gross national product. Surely this is worth all the suds that the river can carry.

In June, 1968, Doyle Klyn of *Weekend* wrote about the charm of "the old swimming hole." She included a picture of one, with children leaping in and seemingly having a good time. One can see from the clean rocks and the lush foliage around clear water that the spot is not polluted. Now comes the clincher: the scene is on the Tangier River in Nova Scotia — part of a backward, unprogressive area that some overly polite people call an "un-spoiled" area of the province. Ironically the very opposite is true; the area is spoiled, because it is subdued by nature. How the people in the town of

---

*Reprinted from J. G. Raycroft, "In Defence of Pollution," *Weekend Magazine,* April 25, 1970, pp. 24-25, by permission of the author.
Mr. Raycroft, who spent ten years teaching history and English at the high school level, is now librarian at South Grenville High School, Prescott, Ontario.

Tangier must long for a pulp mill like the one on the St. John River in New Brunswick, which discharges 40 million gallons of waste a day. How they must ache for the smell of money that rolls from the tall chimneys.

The children in that old swimming hole would be so much better off in a tenement building play area with swings and a high fence for safety and a chlorinated swimming pool a few blocks away. You can rest assured that not one of those boys or girls in the picture has a father who is a company executive or who owns more than one new car.

For ten years now I have watched my native St. Lawrence River become gradually more useful. It is the great intestine of Canada. Back in the thirties when we played hockey on it, we would poke a hole in the ice and drink heartily. But those were the Depression years, and there is your answer. Today, when I tell my children to stay out of its oil and slime, I remind them that my pay cheque and their allowance owe much to this feculence. The river's communities, too, are moving ahead. The new hospital in Cornwall has sealed windows; the air is often unfit for the sick to breathe directly. It has to be purified.

The US has 114 polluted rivers, flowing brown and useful, and the number is increasing as the country becomes greater. Pollution, all forms of it, is synonymous with greatness. In a particular area in Tokyo, Japan, the children in the schoolyards now play with filtering masks on, which is a small price to pay for their parents' having good jobs. As well, their country's wealth can buy Canadian wheat; and there is a whole new industry in mask manufacturing.

Automobiles put lead, among other things, into the atmosphere. Some scientists are trying to scare us by saying that the average citizen is almost halfway to classic lead poisoning. Certainly we are absorbing some lead, and we know that it affects the nerves. So does mercury used in fungicides. But surely that is what tranquilizers are for. And there are new chemicals developed each year to help us.

The population of North America is expected to double in the next thirty years, but if we are lucky it will do better. Toronto needs thousands of people to fill its apartments so that we can build more apartments and sell more refrigerators and so on. This applies to every city and town. Then we must create new cities, and cities must join to form bigger ones. Our government supports this policy, our economy demands it, and the silent majority, bless them, are eager for it. In the light of such tremendous plans in Canada (and in Japan, Germany, US, Russia, and so on around the world) surely the anitpollutionists must feel a bit silly talking about a few sludge worms in Hamilton Bay. As well, they must have read, for example, that if Lake Michigan could be isolated from the effects of civilization, it would take five hundred years for it to cleanse itself. And we are only now getting down to some serious polluting.

Antipolluters are not a new phenomenon. Over twenty years ago a group of them along the Spanish River complained about the KVP Company, a pulp mill. They were brazen enough to take legal action, and got an injunction against the company to stop poisoning the water, which was upheld in courts even after the company's appeals. Fortunately in 1950 Ontario Premier Leslie Frost and his government stepped in to introduce and pass the "KVP Act" in the Ontario Legislature. The act overruled three courts and lifted the injunction.

In 1966, in Buffalo, New York, people of the same ilk had the gall to present a bucket of river sludge to President Lyndon Johnson when he visited their city. Out of politeness to these radicals he said, referring to Lake Erie, "This great inland sea will sparkle again." He knew how to handle agitators, and he must have had a sense of humour. Probably the sparkle he had in mind was the sun reflecting off the oil slicks. The lake is one of North America's most useful waste basins.

Yes, our politicians serve us well, but we should not leave it all to them. Here are five things you can do each day for civilization.

1. If you live in a depressed area, you are probably eligible for special assistance to aid development, such as Industrial Incentive Loans. To shut up antipollutionists warn them that such special favours could be taken away, resulting in the loss of that big industry you are all looking forward to.

2. Remind the carrot-juice, Tiny Tim types that everything cannot be pure. The citizen who was reported to have torn down the "Unsafe For Swimming" signs to save the tourist trade in his district deserves a medal. You don't see "Unsafe For Working" signs at, for instance, the lung-destroying fluorspar mines at St. Lawrence in Newfoundland, in which one hundred miners have died with destroyed lungs in twenty years. How can the purists justify this discrimination in sign posting? What have they got against tourist resorts that they have not got against mining companies?

3. Support the commercial world more fervently. Another medal candidate is Reverend Barry Day who, in Peterborough, on the altar of his church for Thanksgiving, placed an electric motor, a boat, and other locally manufactured objects. Incidentally, I saw in the November 19, 1969, *Telegram,* that Premier Robarts put a couple of smart aleck Trent University students in their place when they sent him a report showing that the raw sewage of Lakefield College School is polluting one of the Kawartha Lakes. If you doubt that your government is working for you, read the whole article; it will lift your spirits. Students like that should be forbidden to use the school bathrooms. That would smarten them up.

4. Fight birth control. Every day on the face of the earth there are around 190,000 more people than there were the day before, but Canada is not getting its share. Everybody benefits with the birth of a baby: diaper makers, nurses, undertakers, schoolteachers, etc. If we do not stop this sinful tampering with nature, where will we get the people to bring to heel the yet unsubdued areas of our country?

5. When common citizens are justified in their complaints, acknowledge them and correct the condition. For instance, the Cuyahoga River in Ohio is so polluted with oils and chemicals that it caught on fire in 1968, burning two bridges and some shoreline. Obviously, this is a hazard, and can be prevented by adding still more pollutants in the form of extinguishing chemicals. Another justified complaint concerns the unfair concentration of sulphur dioxide from a coal-burning generating station in Toronto. Higher stacks (700 feet) are proposed, which will give a wider dispersal. It is certainly not fair that a person on Sheppard Avenue should breathe less sulphur dioxide than a person on Queen Street.

The antipollutionists had success with their agitation against DDT. You would wonder how they could put rodents and car-splattering birds ahead of wormless apples and bigger dividend cheques. But remember, our government must give a little to gain a little. The radicals are appeased, and they are less likely to notice how ineffectual those other antipollution bills are going to be. A token fine imposed on a company will not take the oil off the dead seals and polar bears and put it back in the broken super tanker. The North must be polluted if we are going to progress. For industrial advancement and their own good (which is the same thing) the Eskimos must be brought into our culture and taught a trade. Only blind stubbornness can cause a man to choose a dog team and musk ox meat ahead of a Cadillac and a bowl of Chex.

As I say, there is not much to fear from the antipollutionists, and I believe that their small number will decrease as we make further astounding advances even beyond electric tooth brushes, reducing equipment, snow-mobiles, instant breakfasts, super-jets, defoliation chemicals, and high-rise apartments. It is amazing how organizations like Pollution Probe and SPEC could even be formed and have the nerve to do anything that might hinder in any way such majestically spiralling progress, for which we plan, legislate, educate, and even enforce (for example, Spanish River).

It may not be worth the effort, except for the sake of justice, but perhaps the ringleaders of such groups should be brought into court, or before a government hearing.

We have the law on our side. Like Mr. Spiro Agnew, I believe that the silent majority respects the law, not the placards of rabble-rousers.

E. BEYOND THE PALE

Predicting the future is a dicey business. An understanding of history helps somewhat; yet the future lacks the solid basis in fact available to the careful chronicler of past patterns. Nor can the prognosticator afford merely to advance his hopes and fears as the likely prospect. Rather he must consolidate his interpretations of the lessons of history with an intelligent understanding of the complex forces at work in the "present"; then he should evaluate future *possibilities* in the light of reasonable *probabilities*.

In the following selection, a prominent and eminent American economist classifies future problems into four main groups: (1) the problem of abundance — the growth of affluence itself poses a subtle threat to the functional efficacy of the market machanism; (2) the problem of technology — the cumulative impact of technology is radically altering the basic relation of man and nature; (3) the problem of economic development — despite their considerable achievements, the countries of Latin America, Asia, and Africa have still not crossed the complex threshold of modernization; and (4) the problem of "trained incapacity" — the formal study of economics may box itself in so much that real economic problems will have to be studied outside it.

This selection concludes with the hope that economists will play their full part as a profession in the management of the great transition which lies ahead of us. Needless to say, I share this view.

63. ECONOMICS AND THE FUTURE OF MAN*

Kenneth E. Boulding

A question which is constantly asked of economists these days is whether the development of a technologically created abundance has not destroyed economics altogether and made it obsolete. One finds this view particularly on the vaguely anarchistic left, but it is also present in the writings of men like Robert Theobald.[1] Even in the general field of discussion of liberal church people, this view has received wide currency. There is widespread fear, for instance, that the development of automation will create enormous unemployment, and a great deal of popular literature propounds the view that the onset of universal abundance is going to force us to make drastic changes in an economic system which everybody knows was designed to deal with the problem of scarcity.

Not even economists themselves have been altogether immune to the beatific vision of the abolition of economics. J. M. Keynes envisioned a future in which affluence would become so general that economics would become relatively unimportant:

> I draw the conclusion that, assuming no important wars and no important increase in population, the *economic* problem may be solved, or be at least within sight of solution, within a hundred years. This means that the economic problem is not — if we look into the future — *the permanent problem of the human race.*[2]

Karl Marx envisioned a world

---

*Reprinted from Kenneth E. Boulding, *Economics as a Science*, pp. 141-57. Copyright © 1970, by McGraw-Hill, Inc. Used by permission of McGraw-Hill Book Company.

Dr. Boulding is Professor of Economics, Institute of Behavioral Science, University of Colorado. He taught previously at Michigan, Colgate, Fisk, and McGill Universities, Iowa State College, University College of the West Indies, Kingston, Jamaica, and at International Christian University, Tokyo. He was awarded the John Bates Clark Medal by the American Economic Association in 1949, and the American Council of Learned Societies Prize for Distinguished Scholarship in the Humanities in 1962. He is a past president of the American Economic Association and of the Society for General Systems Research. His books and articles are world-renowned.

[1] Robert Theobald, *The Rich and the Poor: A Study of the Economics of Rising Expectations* (New York, 1960); and *Free Men and Free Markets* (Garden City, New York, 1965).

[2] J. M. Keynes, *Essays in Persuasion* (New York, 1963), pp. 365-66.

where each one does not have a circumscribed sphere of activity but can train himself in any branch he chooses; society by regulating the common production makes it possible for me to do this today and that tomorrow, to hunt in the morning, to fish in the afternoon, to carry on cattle-breeding in the evening, also to criticize the food — just as I please — without becoming either hunter, fisherman, shepherd, or critic.[3]

The classical economists of course were not so sanguine. They did visualize development toward a stationary state, but at its best, it would be, as Adam Smith said, "dull" and at its worst, in the Malthusian vision, it would be horrible, with starvation and misery limiting a hopelessly overcrowded population and a small class of luxurious landlords consuming whatever surplus there might be. The apostles of abundance, of course, may dismiss this as appropriate merely to the early stages of technological development, which science has now made wholly obsolete.

It is my considered view that these projections of the developmental process into a society of effortless abundance in which economics, like the state, has withered away are fantasies arising from a rather naïve extrapolation of what may eventually be seen historically as a rather brief period in the history of man. It is true, of course, that for the last two hundred years man, especially in the temperate zones of the world, has been getting very much richer than he was before, as measured by per capita real income. His provisions have increased in quantity and variety to the point where the scale of human life by comparison with anything that has gone before has become reasonably ample in regard to such provisions as food, clothing, shelter, information inputs, and travel. This is true for about a third of mankind; two-thirds of the human race remain in the condition of severely limiting poverty in which man has lived for most of his history.

There is little doubt that short of catastrophe this process of development will continue and expand to more and more people. Nevertheless, it is a process which will not go on indefinitely. One nonexistence theorem, as the mathematicians say, about the universe is that growth at a constant rate cannot go on forever, or even for very long. Otherwise, there would soon be only one thing in the universe. Every growth curve exhibits a declining rate of growth as the thing that is growing increases in size. We see this in all living organisms; they have a high rate of growth in youth which falls to zero in adulthood and becomes negative in old age. Social organizations and structures eventually follow the same pattern, even though their growth curves are usually not simple but consist of successive periods of rising or falling rates of growth. Eventually, however, the growth of any particular growing structure must come to an end. The economic growth which has been characteristic of the last two hundred years is no exception to this rule. It is not a process which will proceed indefinitely into the future at existing rates. There is a great deal of evidence that it is already slowing down; indeed there is evidence that the growth of the per capita gross national product in those countries which are following the course of successful development is declining as the per capita gross national product itself increases.

Figure 1, in which the rate of growth of per capita gross national product is plotted against the per capita gross national product itself for as many countries as figures are available, tells us a great deal about the present state

---

[3] Karl Marx, *Capital and Other Writings* (New York, 1932), p. 1.

FIGURE 1

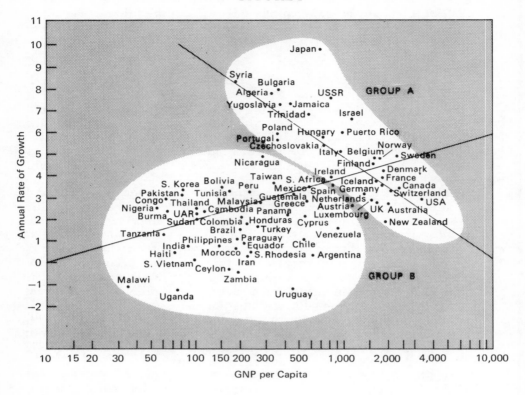

of the world. We see, for instance, that the countries of the world divide themselves pretty sharply into two groups. One group which may be called Group A, consists mostly of countries in the temperate zone. It represents what I would call the "main line" of development. We see clearly that for this group of countries the rate of growth is correlated inversely with the gross national product per capita, which is a measure of how rich they are already. These countries, therefore, follow the principle of the richer, the slower. The second group of countries, which I have called Group B, exhibits virtually no correlation at all between the rate of growth and per capita GNP, suggesting that growth here is a fairly random process and there is no main line of development as yet. These countries are mostly in the tropics, though Chile, Argentina, and Uruguay are depressing examples of countries which unquestionably were on the main line of development at one time, but fell off it as a result of political mismanagement. This shows, indeed, that development is by no means an automatic process and that it is perfectly possible for countries to "take off" and then fall back on the launching pad.

The "main line" which shows the relationship between the rate of growth and the GNP per capita for the Group A countries cuts the zero rate of growth line at about $10,000 per capita. If, therefore, we project the per capita GNP of the successful countries for the next two hundred years we

FIGURE 2

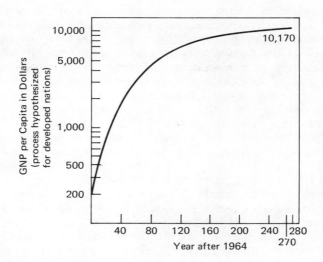

get a figure very much like Figure 2, which shows that if the parameters which are characteristic of the system in the 1960s persist, the rate of growth will slow down very appreciably in another hundred years and virtually come to an end in two hundred. We should not, of course, take these projections too seriously for they can always be falsified by changes in the growth process itself. There is some evidence, indeed, that the growth process is changing. If we repeat this analysis for the 1950s, for instance, we find that the gross national product per capita at which the rate of growth becomes zero is about $5,000 rather than $10,000, which suggests that the growth process itself has been somewhat different in the 1960s from what it was in the 1950s.

Figure 1, incidentally, shows how dangerous correlation analysis can be if it is applied mechanically, as it is all too often. If we do a correlation for all the countries we find that growth actually increases with an increase in per capita GNP. This, however, is pure statistical illusion arising out of the fact that we are aggregating two essentially different systems. It is one of the dangers of the enormous expansion of computing power which has come with the development of the electronic computer that it has reduced the contact of the investigator with the data and hence has increased his power to produce nonsense as well as his power to discover more intricate relationships.

There are considerations more fundamental than the rather mechanical ones outlined above which suggest that the process of human expansion will not go on indefinitely and that we face indeed a major crisis ahead which we may not be able to surmount. The nature of the crisis is summed up in the expression which was coined, I think independently, by both Barbara Ward and myself — the "Spaceship Earth."[4] In the last few thousand years the

[4] B. Ward Johnson, *Spaceship Earth* (New York, 1966); K. E. Boulding, "The Economics of the Coming Space-Ship Earth," *Environmental Quality in a Growing Economy, Essays from the Sixth RFF Forum,* Henry Jarrett, ed., (Baltimore, 1966), pp. 3-14.

human race has been expanding almost continuously in its total population and in what might be called its rate of utilization of the earth's resources. This process has accelerated enormously in the last hundred years. Up to the present time man has lived in the "era of the great plane" in which his image of the world has been essentially that of a flat earth on which he could expand indefinitely with new lands and new resources always somewhere over the horizon. Today the era of geographical expansion has come to an end — there are no empty lands, and the view of earth from space dramatizes the image of man as inhabiting a small, closed spaceship, destination unknown and resources limited.

For the last two hundred years the discovery of new resources and improved means of utilization of old resources through the advance of knowledge has proceeded faster than the expansion of population, at least in the successfully developing parts of the world. We are beginning to face the fact, however, that the kind of "linear economy," which is peculiarly characteristic of modern technology, which extracts fossil fuels and ores at one end and transforms them into commodities and ultimately into waste products which are spewed out the other end into pollutable reservoirs is a process which is inherently suicidal and must eventually come to an end, either through the exhaustion of the resources in the mines and wells at the one end or through the exhaustion of the "sinks," that is, pollutable reservoirs, at the other end. The end of this spectacular process of development through which we are going indeed could easily be a virtually dead earth with all its concentration of ores and energy sources depleted and all its pollutable reservoirs filled up.

Therefore, if the society toward which we are developing is not to be a nightmare of exhaustion, we must use the interlude of the present era to develop a new technology which is based on a circular flow of materials such that the only source of man's provisions will be his own waste products. In a spaceship there are neither mines nor sewers, and man has to find a place for himself provisioned by a circular flow of materials which happens to take a form unusually favourable to him in the place that he happens to occupy. There is no way, of course, thanks to the dismal second law of thermodynamics, that a circular system of this kind can be achieved without inputs of energy. From the human point of view, fortunately, the energy input from the sun can be regarded as virtually inexhaustible, as when that goes the evolutionary process, in this part of the universe at least, is presumably over. All known earthly sources of energy, even uranium, will be exhausted quite rapidly if development continues to accelerate. The possible exception to this is the use of nuclear fusion as an earthly source of energy. The problems which this presents, however, are almost as great as those presented to the man who was looking for the universal solvent when somebody asked him what he would keep it in.

Whatever the technology of the spaceship earth it is clear that economics will not disappear. Indeed scarcity may be more omnipresent than it is in our wildly extravagant and expansive world of today. One could certainly visualize a technology that would provide the basic necessities for physical health and comfort for all. There is, however, an ineradicable scarcity of land, especially of agreeable environments. We already seem to be within sight of an era when the main condition differentiating the rich and the poor will be access to sheer physical space. In matters of food, clothing, warmth, medical care, and so on, one would expect that in the next fifty years in the developed countries the poor will not fare very much worse than the rich.

What the poor will not have, however, is space around them. The labour theory of value originated at a time when the principal source of the scarcity of commodities was the fact that each man only had twenty-four hours a day to spend, of which usually not much more than twelve could be spent in producing commodities. Where the productivity of labour is low, the amount of labour embodied in a commodity may be the principal factor limiting its output and thereby creating value. As labour becomes more productive it may well be that relative prices will depend more on land input than on labour input, despite land-saving improvements, such as the increased yield of crops or the building of skyscrapers. However we look at it, it is virtually impossible to visualize a world in which scarcity has really come to an end, that is, a world in which everybody is satiated with provisions of all kinds.

This is not to say, of course, that the economic system of spaceship earth may not look very different from the economic systems of today, whether capitalist or communist. Oddly enough, the traditional village economy, especially of Asia, may be more a prototype of the world to come than the economies of the great age of expansion in which we are now living, for to a considerable extent the village was cyclical, did return all waste products to the earth, and did not depend very much on imports from outside. It, of course, was a low-level cyclical economy from which we have gratefully escaped. Nevertheless, what we are looking for in the spaceship is a high-level cyclical economy, some of the features of which may have been fore-shadowed in the traditional village.

A very interesting question to which I do not know the answer is what will be the nature of social and economic organization in the spaceship earth. Will it have to be, for instance, a tightly, centrally planned society organized along authoritarian lines, such as we have in the communist states, or will it be a looser, free-market type of economy, using the price system as a motivator for change, where change is necessary, within a sufficient frame-work of generally accepted principles and authority to ensure long-run stability? It is quite possible that both patterns will be feasible. To my own way of thinking, the second would be much to be preferred. A system with private property, a wide freedom of choice of location and occupation, a variety of subcultures and the possibility of moving from one to the other, the kind of things in short that we think of today as characterizing a free society is by no means necessarily incompatible with a spaceship, providing that certain overall, main variables of the system are under social, even automatic control.

There must, for instance, be stability of population or at least a rate of increase which is commensurate with any increase in the carrying capacity of the spaceship. This could be achieved, as I have suggested earlier,[5] through a market mechanism which I have sometimes called my Green Stamp Plan for population control, according to which each human being would receive in adolescence, say, 110 green stamps, 100 of which would entitle the owner to have one legal child. A market would then be set up in these instruments so that those who had a strong desire for children could buy stamps from those who did not want to have children. Individual preferences in this matter could thus be expressed, while at the same time society could maintain overall social control of the rate of growth of population. There would presumably have to be mild sanctions for having illegal children which might

---

[5] K. E. Boulding, *The Meaning of the Twentieth Century*, (New York, 1965).

entail temporary sterilization until the illegal children are paid for in green stamps. This scheme has met with a good deal of disapproval. The alternative, however, would surely be authoritarian control with a set number of children allowed per family and severe sanctions for violating the allotted number.

I use the above plan merely as an illustration of how overall social control of the kind which will be required in the spaceship may be achieved through a market mechanism with the least interference with individual liberty and differentiation of personality and culture. We might well be able to work out similar institutions for the resolution of conflicts, which will be another acute problem in the spaceship. War may be tolerable on the great plane, but it simply will not do in the close confines of the spaceship, and we must devise better methods of conflict resolution than we now have or we will simply not survive as a developed society. I have some hope, therefore, that while the spaceship earth may feel tight and uncomfortable by comparison with the wild freedom of the age of expansion in which we now live, human ingenuity can make it tolerable. It may be indeed that our descendants will regard us as the lucky occupants of a time of exciting transition and look back on our time with much the same nostalgia as we look back on the time of cowboys and Indians. One hopes, however, that it will be a mild nostalgia and that the overall quality of human life will be much higher in the developed society to come than it is now. I have sometimes characterized the whole age of civilization in which we have been living and which is now passing away as a rather deplorable interlude in the state of man characterized by exploitation, war, poverty, large-scale misery, and slavery, as well as by occasional peaks of artistic achievement, a period which lies between the "Eden" of the neolithic, when the lot of the average man apparently was better than it has been under civilization, and hopefully the "Zion" to come in the developed society, when war and exploitation will vanish from the earth.

In the light of this kind of image of the future one might return to economics as it is practised by economists today, and ask what kind of contribution are we making toward the successful handling of the enormous and precarious transition through which mankind is passing. The answer is fairly clear that we are making some contribution, enough indeed to have established us as the most successful of the scientists, at least as judged by our political influence through such things as the Council of Economic Advisers and the Joint Economic Committee in Congress and the mundane fact that our salaries are the highest of all the academic professions, exceeding even those of physicists. Our success has come in two fields: one in macroeconomics and employment policy, and the other in the field of the analysis of economic behaviour and the improvement of the information systems of powerful decision makers by such things as linear programming, program budgeting, and even game theory. Our success in the first field can be visualized very easily if we simply contrast the twenty years after the First World War, in which we had the Great Depression and an international situation which ended in Hitler and the disaster of the Second World War, with the twenty years after the Second World War, in which we had no Great Depression, merely a few little ones, and the United States had the longest period of sustained high employment and growth in its history. In spite of Vietnam, we are certainly further from World War III in 1969 than we were from World War II in the corresponding year of the first period, which would be 1945! Not all of this is due to economics, but some of it is, and even if only a small part of it is, the rate of return on the investment in economics must be enormous. The investment has really been very small and the returns, if we measure them by the cost of the depressions which we have not had, could easily run into a trillion dollars. On quite reasonable assumptions, therefore, the rate of return on economics has been on the order of tens of thousands of percent in the period since the end of World War II. It is no wonder that we find economists at the top of the salary scale!

Our achievements in the improvement of economic decision making are perhaps harder to evaluate. One could argue indeed that economics has had certain negative effects in that it has improved efficiency in the doing of things that probably should not be done at all. This is the problem of "suboptimization," which I have been arguing is one of the real names of the devil, as it is a source of so much human misery. An increase in the efficiency with which we produce what from our point of view of society are negative goods is by no means to be desired. Oddly enough, it is only economics out of all the social sciences that has thought much about this problem or has come up with any solution to it. This, indeed, is the classical problem of the "invisible hand," that is, what are the circumstances under which everybody doing what is best for himself also produces what is best for society. The economists' solution of perfect markets for everything, unfortunately, is impractical in practice, for two reasons. First, there is a strong consumer demand for heterogeneity in commodities. We do not like standardized items, and we do like a great variety of choice. Under these circumstances the number of different commodities offered for sale tends to multiply with the result that the market for each particular commodity is restricted and becomes imperfect. The other reason why perfect competition is impossible is that in a number of areas of economic life there are economies of scale that accrue to very large-scale organizations such as we see in telephones, automobiles, and all the so-called public utilities. Nevertheless, the problem of how to simulate something like perfect markets remains as an unsolved problem of political and social organization, and the economic solution, unacceptable as it may be, is at least a place to start.

In spite of the successes of economics, it has also had two rather conspicuous failures. I would suggest that its first major failure, in the last generation, has been its failure to develop an adequate theory of economic development and to come up with an adequate set of policy recommendations for the poor countries who are not on the "main line" of development, in spite of the large amount of attention paid to this subject. Figure 1 shows very clearly the division of the world into the successfully developing countries of Group A and the unsuccessful ones of Group B. The figures themselves should not be taken too literally, especially in the case of the poor countries, as national income statistics leave a great deal to be desired, but improvement of the data, while it will change the status of a few particular countries, is not likely to change the overall pattern. The failure to provide poor countries with helpful advice is, I suspect, the result of the fact that economists have worked too narrowly within the confines of their own abstractions and their own discipline and have not recognized that a development process is something which involves the total society and that hence purely economic models have a very limited value. The study of development as a total dynamic pattern of social life is one that requires full co-operation between different social scientists and this has not really been forthcoming.

The second failure of economics is in the field of urban poverty and deterioration and the whole matter of the provision of a decent physical environment. The defect here I suspect is more a failure to allocate intellectual resources properly within the economics profession than it is a failure to integrate with other social scientists, although in such matters as the self-perpetuation of poverty subcultures economists have a great deal to learn from social anthropologists. The plain fact is that even when it comes to urban economics, within the narrow framework of such problems as real estate, land speculation, transportation, and tax systems, which are clearly within the general purview of the discipline of economics, we find a serious lack not only of theory but, more importantly, of data. What might be called the economic dynamics or the economic ecology of the city is something that has been given shockingly little attention. Partly this is a result of the accident of the organization of the educational system. Because of the Morrill Act of 1862 and the setting up of land-grant colleges, the agricultural industry quite early developed excellent contacts with all the sciences. As a result of this institutional arrangement, agricultural economics has been blessed with a great deal of money and has developed to the point where the effort which goes into it is far out of proportion to the quantitative importance of the agricultural sector of the economy. We did not develop similar universities for architecture and the building trades. As a result, architecture has remained in a "fine arts" environment with poor contacts with the social sciences. The building trades have remained a bastion of folk technology and small-scale organization, putting virtually nothing into research and keeping isolated from the onrush of science-based technology. Given the combination of weak municipal governments, municipal tax systems which discourage improvements, transportation systems which are destructive of amenity, architects who cater almost entirely to the foibles of the rich, and a building industry which has just barely emerged from the middle ages, it is hardly surprising that our cities are in decay. A major intellectual effort to plot their revival, in which economists should play an important role, is clearly indicated.

A related area which economists have neglected, again perhaps because there has been no real social organization which has provided a niche for these kinds of studies, is the study of the economics of threats, violence, crime, police, and the armed forces. This is an area which has been of increasing importance unfortunately in the last generation. For instance the proportion of the gross national product going into national defence has risen from about 1 percent in 1930 to nearly 10 percent today. This is a very major structural change, yet it has been surprisingly little studied by economists. The economics of police and crime is practically an unknown field. It is about as little developed as the economics of the building industry.

An area where there has been a great deal of effort on the part of economists, with I suspect inadequate productivity, is in the field of money, banking, and finance, which is traditionally the most "economic" of all fields in the social sciences. Perhaps, however, its economic status is just what is the matter with it. Economists have studied the behaviour of innumerable time series and the patterns of revealed data; hardly anybody has studied the actual decision-making processes of financial organizations and especially the processes by which these organizations determine the flow of information and information inputs which determines their decisions. There is a whole area here which might be called the economic sociology of the market. It hardly exists as a field of study, yet I suspect it contains most of the answers to the questions about the financial system which still seem to be unresolved after thirty or more years of hard empirical study of purely financial data on the part of economists.

I would not wish to disparage the great achievements of mathematical economics and econometrics in the last generation in the matter of the development of techniques for the analysis of strictly economic data. Nevertheless, I cannot help wondering whether this is not an effort that is now running into diminishing returns in the sense that it has exploited pretty fully the kind of data which is readily available and is now producing more and more analyses and less and less information. This judgment does not necessarily apply to the quantitative analysis of historical data from the past, especially the more remote past, which has produced some extremely interesting results and is certainly revising our image of human history. Nevertheless, just as no stream can rise above its source, no science can rise above its original data collection, and one would like to see a revival of interest in economics in the improved collection of raw data, especially at the levels of individual and organizational behaviour.

Here again one does not want to disparage the very important work which has been done by such organizations as the Survey Research Centre at the University of Michigan and similar organizations elsewhere in improving the collection of original data. On the whole, however, the quick returns in economics in the last thirty years have been through bright young mathematically inclined economists who have devoted themselves to the analysis of existing data rather than to the collection of new data at the source. Our training methods in graduate schools have accentuated this tendency to the point where we now perhaps have actually retrogressed in the training of people who are skilled in finding out what the real world is like.

It is a sad commentary on the American scene in economics that the only really indigenous American school of economists, the institutionalists, represented for instance by John R. Commons at Wisconsin, left only a handful of descendants. I would not be surprised if the majority of graduate students studying economics in American universities do not even know the names of the great American empiricists and institutionalists of the past. It is fashionable indeed to decry the history of thought as a luxury in these days of econometrics, to proclaim that it is of no greater significance than, shall we say, the history of mathematics. This attitude it seems to me is disastrous, for it limits the graduate student to the fashions of the present and easily leads him into a tight little intellectual box from which there is no escape. The successes of economics should not blind us to the fact that its subject matter is a system far more complex than the systems which are studied by the natural scientists, for instance, and we must recognize that our most elegant models can be no more than the crudest of first approximations of the complex reality of the systems which they purport to represent. If we educate out of our students that almost bodily sense of what the real world is like even though we may see it through a glass darkly, a trait which was so characteristic of the great economists of the past, something of supreme value will be lost. Our graduate schools may easily be producing a good deal of the "trained incapacity" which Veblen saw being produced in his day, and this is a negative commodity unfortunately with a very high price.

Nevertheless, whatever happens to economics the problems will remain and as long as the problems remain, men will be impelled to study them. If the formal study of economics boxes itself in so much that real economics problems will have to be studied outside it, this will be worse for economics than it is for mankind. One hopes, however, that economists will perceive the trap that may lie ahead of them and will play their full part as a profession in the management of the great transition which lies ahead of us.

READINGS
LISTED BY AUTHOR